W9-AUP-211

Exam 70-648: TS: Upgrading Your MCSA on Windows Server® 2003 to Windows Server 2008, Technology Specialist

OBJECTIVE	CHAPTER	LESSON
CONFIGURING ADDITIONAL ACTIVE DIRECTORY SERVER ROLES		
Configure Active Directory Lightweight Directory Service (AD LDS).	5	1
Configure Active Directory Rights Management Service (AD RMS).	6	2
Configure the read-only domain controller (RODC).	5	2
Configure Active Directory Federation Services (AD FS).	6	1
MAINTAINING THE ACTIVE DIRECTORY ENVIRONMENT		
Configure backup and recovery.	8	1
Perform offline maintenance.	8	2
Monitor Active Directory.	8	3
CONFIGURING ACTIVE DIRECTORY CERTIFICATE SERVICES		
Install Active Directory Certificate Services.	7	1
Configure CA server settings.	7	1
Manage certificate templates.	7	2
Manage enrollments.	7	2
Manage certificate revocations.	7	2
CONFIGURING IP ADDRESSING AND SERVICES		
Configure IPv4 and IPv6 addressing.	1	1
Configure Dynamic Host Configuration Protocol (DHCP).	1	2
Configure routing.	2	1
Configure IPsec.	2	2
CONFIGURING NETWORK ACCESS		
Configure remote access.	3	1
Configure Network Access Protection (NAP).	4	3
Configure network authentication.	3	2
Configure wireless access.	4	1
Configure firewall settings.	4	2
MONITORING AND MANAGING A NETWORK INFRASTRUCTURE		
Configure Windows Server Update Services (WSUS) server settings.	9	1
Capture performance data.	10	1
Monitor event logs.	10	2
Gather network data.	9	2

Exam Objectives The exam objectives listed here are current as of this book's publication date. Exam objectives are subject to change at any time without prior notice and at Microsoft's sole discretion. Please visit the Microsoft Learning Web site for the most current listing of exam objectives: http://www.microsoft.com/learning/en/us/exams /70-648.mspx and http://www.microsoft.com/learning/en/us/exams/70-649.mspx.

Exam 70-649: TS: Upgrading Your MCSE on Windows Server® 2003 to Windows Server 2008, Technology Specialist

OBJECTIVE	CHAPTER	LESSON
CONFIGURING ADDITIONAL ACTIVE DIRECTORY SERVER ROLES		
Configure Active Directory Lightweight Directory Service (AD LDS)	5	1
Configure Active Directory Rights Management Service (AD RMS)	6	2
Configure the read-only domain controller (RODC)	5	2
Configure Active Directory Federation Services (AD FS)	6	1
CONFIGURING IP ADDRESSING AND SERVICES		
Configure IPv4 and IPv6 addressing	1	1
Configure Dynamic Host Configuration Protocol (DHCP)	1	2
Configure routing	2	1
Configure IPsec	2	2
MONITORING AND MANAGING A NETWORK INFRASTRUCTURE		
Configure Windows Server Update Services (WSUS) server settings	9	1
Capture performance data	10	1
Monitor event logs	10	2
Gather network data	9	2
DEPLOYING SERVERS		
Deploy images by using Windows Deployment Services	11	1
Configure Microsoft Windows activation	11	1
Configure Windows Server Hyper-V and virtual machines	15	1, 2
Configure high availability	16	1
Configure storage	16	2
CONFIGURING TERMINAL SERVICES		
Configure Windows Server 2008 Terminal Services RemoteApp (TS RemoteApp)	12	2
Configure Terminal Services Gateway	12	2
Configure Terminal Services load balancing	12	2
Configure and monitor Terminal Services resources	12	1
Configure Terminal Services licensing	12	1
Configure Terminal Services client connections	12	1
Configure Terminal Services server options	12	1
CONFIGURING A WEB SERVICES INFRASTRUCTURE		
Configure Web applications	13	1
Manage Web sites	13	2
Configure a File Transfer Protocol (FTP) server	14	1
Configure Simple Mail Transfer Protocol Services (SMTP)	14	2
Manage Internet Information Services (IIS)	13	3
Configure SSL security	13	4
Configure Web site authentication and permissions	13	5

Microsoft®

MCTS Self-Paced Training Kit (Exams 70-648 & 70-649): Transitioning Your MCSA/MCSE to Windows Server® 2008

Orin Thomas
Ian McLean

PUBLISHED BY
Microsoft Press
A Division of Microsoft Corporation
One Microsoft Way
Redmond, Washington 98052-6399

Copyright © 2009 by Ian McLean and Microsoft Corporation
All rights reserved. No part of the contents of this book may be reproduced or transmitted in any form or by any means without the written permission of the publisher.

Library of Congress Control Number: 2009920788

Printed and bound in the United States of America.

1 2 3 4 5 6 7 8 9 QWT 4 3 2 1 0 9

Distributed in Canada by H.B. Fenn and Company Ltd.

A CIP catalogue record for this book is available from the British Library.

Microsoft Press books are available through booksellers and distributors worldwide. For further information about international editions, contact your local Microsoft Corporation office or contact Microsoft Press International directly at fax (425) 936-7329. Visit our Web site at www.microsoft.com/mspress. Send comments to tkinput@microsoft.com.

Microsoft, Microsoft Press, Active Directory, ActiveX, BitLocker, Direct3D, ESP, Excel, Hyper-V, Internet Explorer, MS, MSDN, Outlook, SharePoint, SQL Server, Visio, Windows, Windows CardSpace, Windows Live, Windows Media, Windows NT, Windows Server, and Windows Vista are either registered trademarks or trademarks of Microsoft Corporation in the United States and/or other countries. Other product and company names mentioned herein may be the trademarks of their respective owners.

The example companies, organizations, products, domain names, e-mail addresses, logos, people, places, and events depicted herein are fictitious. No association with any real company, organization, product, domain name, e-mail address, logo, person, place, or event is intended or should be inferred.

This book expresses the author's views and opinions. The information contained in this book is provided without any express, statutory, or implied warranties. Neither the authors, Microsoft Corporation, nor its resellers, or distributors will be held liable for any damages caused or alleged to be caused either directly or indirectly by this book.

Acquisitions Editor: Ken Jones
Developmental Editor: Laura Sackerman
Project Editor: Rosemary Caperton
Editorial Production: nSight, Inc.
Technical Reviewer: Rozanne Whalen
Cover: Tom Draper Design

Body Part No. X15-41549

This book is dedicated to my lovely, loving, and long-suffering wife, Anne. I have dedicated books to her before, but not as many as she deserves.

—IAN MCLEAN

For my good mates Michael Herold (Microworld, Denmark), Rocky Heckman, Jeff Alexander, Jamie Sharp, and Michael Kleef (Microsoft, Australia).

—ORIN THOMAS

Contents at a Glance

Contents

What do you think of this book? We want to hear from you!

Microsoft is interested in hearing your feedback so we can continually improve our
books and learning resources for you. To participate in a brief online survey, please visit:

www.microsoft.com/learning/booksurvey/

Chapter 3   Network Access Configuration   119

Chapter 11 Server Deployment and Activation   561

Chapter 16 High Availability and Storage 807

What do you think of this book? We want to hear from you!

Microsoft is interested in hearing your feedback so we can continually improve our
books and learning resources for you. To participate in a brief online survey, please visit:

www.microsoft.com/learning/booksurvey/

Introduction

This training kit is designed for Windows Server 2003 MCSEs and MCSAs who want to update their current certification credentials to reflect their experience with the Windows Server 2008 operating system. As an MCSE or an MCSA, you are a server administrator who has at least three years of experience managing Windows servers and infrastructure in an environment with between 250 and 5,000 or more users in three or more physical locations. You are likely responsible for supporting network services and resources such as messaging, database servers, file and print servers, a proxy server, a firewall, Internet connectivity, an intranet, remote access, and client computers. You will also be responsible for implementing connectivity requirements such as connecting branch offices and individual users in remote locations to the corporate network and connecting corporate networks to the Internet.

By using this training kit, you will learn how to do the following:

- Configure additional Active Directory server roles
- Maintain an Active Directory environment
- Configure Active Directory certificate services
- Configure IP addressing and services
- Configure network access
- Monitor and manage a network infrastructure
- Deploy servers
- Configure Terminal Services
- Configure a Web services infrastructure

> **MORE INFO** **FIND ADDITIONAL CONTENT ONLINE**
>
> As new or updated material that complements your book becomes available, it will be posted on the Microsoft Press Online Windows Server and Client Web site. The type of material you might find includes articles, links to companion content, errata, sample chapters, updates to book content, and more. This Web site is available at *www.microsoft.com /learning/books/online/serverclient* and will be updated periodically.

Practice Setup Instructions

The exercises in this training kit require a minimum of three computers or virtual machines:

- One Windows Server 2008 Enterprise server configured as a domain controller
- One Windows Server 2008 Enterprise server configured as a member server
- One computer running Windows Vista (Enterprise, Business, or Ultimate)

An evaluation version of both the x86 and x64 versions of Windows Server 2008 Enterprise are included with this textbook. You can also download an evaluation version of Windows Server 2008 from the Microsoft download center at *http://www.microsoft.com/Downloads /Search.aspx*. If you want to carry out the optional exercises in Chapter 16, you need two additional Windows Server 2008 member servers. These servers can be virtual machines. The practices in Chapter 15 require you to install an x64 evaluation version of Windows Server 2008 on physical hardware because Hyper-V cannot be deployed within a virtual machine.

All computers must be physically connected to the same network. We recommend that you use an isolated network that is not part of your production network to perform the practices in this book. To minimize the time and expense of configuring physical computers, we recommend that you use virtual machines. To run computers as virtual machines within Windows, you can use Hyper-V, Virtual PC 2007, Virtual Server 2005 R2, or third-party virtual machine software. To download Virtual PC 2007, visit *http://www.microsoft.com/windows /downloads/virtualpc/default.mspx*. To download an evaluation version of Virtual Server 2005 R2, visit *http://www.microsoft.com/technet/virtualserver/evaluation/default.mspx*. Some virtual machine software does not support x64 editions of Windows Server 2008.

Hardware Requirements

You can complete almost all practices in this book other than those in Chapter 16, using virtual machines rather than server hardware. The minimum and recommended hardware requirements for Windows Server 2008 are listed in Table 1.

TABLE 1 Windows Server 2008 Minimum Hardware Requirements

HARDWARE COMPONENT	MINIMUM REQUIREMENTS	RECOMMENDED
Processor	1GHz (x86), 1.4GHz (x64)	2 GHz or faster
RAM	512 MB	2 GB or greater
Disk Space	15 GB	40 GB or greater

If you intend to implement several virtual machines on the same computer (recommended), a higher specification will enhance your user experience. In particular, a computer with 4 GB RAM and 60 GB free disk space can host all the virtual machines specified for all the practices in this book.

Preparing the Computer Running Windows Server 2008 Enterprise

To install the computer running Windows Server 2008 Enterprise that you use for the practices in this book, perform the following steps:

1. Boot the computer or virtual machine on which you will install the operating system from the Windows Server 2008 Enterprise installation media.

2. On the Install Windows page, select your language, time, currency format, and keyboard or input method and click Next.

3. Click Install Now.

4. On the Type Your Product Key For Activation page, enter the Windows Server 2008 Enterprise product key.

> **NOTE AUTOMATIC ACTIVATION**
>
> Because the practice exercises in this book assume that the computer you are installing is not connected either directly or indirectly to the Internet, clear the Automatic Activation check box during installation and then perform activation at a convenient time later.

5. Click Next. On the Select The Operating System You Want To Install page, click Windows Server 2008 Enterprise (Full Installation) and then click Next.

6. On the Please Read The License Terms page, review the license and then select the I Accept The License Terms check box. Click Next.

7. On the Which Type of Installation Do You Want page, click Custom (Advanced).

8. On the Where Do You Want To Install Windows page, select the partition on which you want to install Windows Server 2008 and then click Next.

   The installation process will commence. This process can take up to 20 minutes, depending on the speed of the hardware upon which you are installing the operating system. The computer will automatically reboot twice during this period.

   You will be asked to change the password prior to logging on for the first time. This is where you set the password for the Administrator account.

9. Click OK and then enter **P@ssw0rd** twice in the dialog box shown. Press Enter. Click OK when you are informed that your password has been changed and you will be logged on.

10. On the Initial Configuration Tasks page, click Set Time Zone and configure the server to use your local time zone.

11. Click Configure Networking. Right-click Local Area Connection and click Properties.

12. Click Internet Protocol Version 4 (TCP/IPv4) and then click Properties.

13. Configure the Internet Protocol Version 4 (TCP/IPv4) properties so that the computer has an IP address of **10.0.0.11** with a subnet mask of **255.255.255.0** and then click OK. Click Close to close the Local Area Connection Properties. Close the Network Connections window to return to the Initial Configuration Tasks page.

14. On the Initial Configuration Tasks page, click Provide Computer Name And Domain. This opens the System Properties dialog box.

15. On the Computer Name tab, click Change.

16. In the Computer Name/Domain Changes dialog box, set the computer name to **Glasgow** and click OK. Click OK when informed that it will be necessary to restart the computer and click Close to close the System Properties dialog box. Click Restart Now to restart the computer.

17. After the computer has rebooted, log on using the Administrator account and the password configured in step 9.

18. Click Start and then click Run. In the Run dialog box, type **dcpromo** and then click OK.

19. On the Welcome To The Active Directory Domain Services Installation Wizard page, click Next.

20. On the Choose A Deployment Configuration page, select Create A New Domain In A New Forest and then click Next.

21. On the Name The Forest Root Domain page, enter **contoso.internal** and click Next.

22. On the Set Forest Functional Level page, leave the default Forest Functional level in place and then click Next.

23. On the Additional Domain Controller Options page, click Next.

24. In the Static IP Assignment warning dialog box, click Yes, The Computer Will Use A Dynamically Assigned IP Address (Not Recommended).

25. When presented with the delegation warning, click Yes.

26. On the Location For Database, Log Files, And SYSVOL page, accept the default settings and then click Next.

27. Click OK to dismiss the blank password warning dialog box and enter **P@ssw0rd** twice for the Directory Services Restore Mode Administrator account. Click Next.

28. On the Summary page, review the selections and then click Next.

    Active Directory Domain Services (AD DS) will now be configured on the computer.

29. When this process is complete, click Finish and then click Restart Now.

30. When the computer reboots, open Active Directory Users And Computers from the Administrative Tools menu and make a copy of the built-in Administrator account with the name **Kim_Akers**. Set the password to **P@ssw0rd**.

Instructions for installing and configuring the Windows Server 2008 Enterprise member server are given in Chapter 2, "Configuring IP Services." The required server roles are added in the practices in subsequent chapters.

Preparing the Computer Running Windows Vista

Perform the following actions to prepare the computer running Windows Vista for the exercises in this training kit.

- **Check operating system version requirements** In System Control Panel (found in the System And Maintenance category), verify that the operating system version is Windows Vista Enterprise, Windows Vista Business, or Windows Vista Ultimate. If necessary, choose the option to upgrade to one of these versions.

- **Name the computer** In System Control Panel, specify the computer name as **Melbourne**.

- **Configure networking** To configure networking, carry out the following tasks:

  - In Control Panel, click Set Up File Sharing. In Network And Sharing Center, verify that the network is configured as a private network and that File Sharing is enabled.

  - In Network And Sharing Center, click Manage Network Connections. In Network Connections, open the properties of the Local Area Connection. Specify a static IPv4 address that is on the same subnet as the domain controller. For example, the setup instructions for the domain controller specify an IPv4 address of 10.0.0.11. If you use this address, you can configure the client computer with an IP address of **10.0.0.21**. The subnet mask is **225.225.225.0**, and the DNS address is the IPv4 address of the domain controller. You do not require a default gateway. You can choose other network addresses if you want to, provided that the client and server are on the same subnet.

Using the DVD

The companion DVD included with this training kit contains the following:

- **Practice tests** You can reinforce your understanding of how to configure Windows Vista by using electronic practice tests you customize to meet your needs from the pool of Lesson Review questions in this book, or you can practice for the 70-648/9 certification exam by using tests created from a pool of approximately 400 realistic exam questions, which give you many practice exams to ensure that you are prepared.

- **An eBook** An electronic version (eBook) of this book is included for when you do not want to carry the printed book with you. The eBook is in Portable Document Format (PDF), and you can view it by using Adobe Acrobat or Adobe Reader.

- **Sample chapters** This DVD includes sample chapters from other Microsoft Press titles on Windows Server 2008. These chapters are in PDF format.

> **DIGITAL CONTENT FOR DIGITAL BOOK READERS**
>
> If you bought a digital-only edition of this book, you can enjoy select content from the print edition's companion DVD. Visit *http://go.microsoft.com/fwlink/?LinkId=142001* to get your downloadable content. This content is always up-to-date and available to all readers.

How to Install the Practice Tests

To install the practice test software from the companion DVD to your hard disk, perform the following steps:

1. Insert the companion DVD into your DVD drive and accept the license agreement. A DVD menu appears.

> **NOTE IF THE DVD MENU DOES NOT APPEAR**
>
> If the DVD menu or the license agreement does not appear, AutoRun might be disabled on your computer. Refer to the Readme.txt file on the DVD for alternate installation instructions.

2. Click Practice Tests and follow the instructions on the screen.

How to Use the Practice Tests

To start the practice test software, follow these steps:

1. Click Start, click All Programs, and then select Microsoft Press Training Kit Exam Prep.

   A window appears that shows all the Microsoft Press training kit exam prep suites installed on your computer.

2. Double-click the lesson review or practice test you want to use.

> **NOTE   LESSON REVIEWS VERSUS PRACTICE TESTS**
>
> Select (70-648 or 70-649) Windows Server 2008, Server Administration Lesson Review to use the questions from the "Lesson Review" sections of this book. Select (70-648 or 70-649) Windows Server 2008, Server Administration Practice Test to use a pool of 200 questions (per exam) similar to those that appear on the 70-648 and 70-649 certification exams.

Lesson Review Options

When you start a lesson review, the Custom Mode dialog box appears so that you can configure your test. You can click OK to accept the defaults, or you can customize the number of questions you want, how the practice test software works, which exam objectives you want the questions to relate to, and whether you want your lesson review to be timed. If you are retaking a test, you can select whether you want to see all the questions again or only the questions you missed or did not answer.

   After you click OK, your lesson review starts.

- To take the test, answer the questions and use the Next and Previous buttons to move from question to question.

- After you answer an individual question, if you want to see which answers are correct—along with an explanation of each correct answer—click Explanation.

- If you prefer to wait until the end of the test to see how you did, answer all the questions and then click Score Test. You will see a summary of the exam objectives you chose and the percentage of questions you got right overall and per objective. You can print a copy of your test, review your answers, or retake the test.

Practice Test Options

When you start a practice test, you choose whether to take the test in Certification Mode, Study Mode, or Custom Mode:

- **Certification Mode**   Closely resembles the experience of taking a certification exam. The test has a set number of questions. It is timed, and you cannot pause and restart the timer.
- **Study Mode**   Creates an untimed test during which you can review the correct answers and the explanations after you answer each question.
- **Custom Mode**   Gives you full control over the test options so that you can customize them as you like.

In all modes, the user interface when you are taking the test is basically the same but with different options enabled or disabled depending on the mode. The main options are discussed in the previous section, "Lesson Review Options."

When you review your answer to an individual practice test question, a "References" section is provided that lists where in the training kit you can find the information that relates to that question and provides links to other sources of information. After you click Test Results to score your entire practice test, you can click the Learning Plan tab to see a list of references for every objective.

How to Uninstall the Practice Tests

To uninstall the practice test software for a training kit, use the Program And Features option in Windows Control Panel.

Microsoft Certified Professional Program

The Microsoft certifications provide the best method to prove your command of current Microsoft products and technologies. The exams and corresponding certifications are developed to validate your mastery of critical competencies as you design and develop, or implement and support, solutions with Microsoft products and technologies. Computer professionals who become Microsoft-certified are recognized as experts and are sought after industry-wide. Certification brings a variety of benefits to the individual and to employers and organizations.

> **MORE INFO   ALL THE MICROSOFT CERTIFICATIONS**
>
> For a full list of Microsoft certifications, go to *www.microsoft.com/learning/mcp /default.asp*.

Technical Support

Every effort has been made to ensure the accuracy of this book and the contents of the companion DVD. If you have comments, questions, or ideas regarding this book or the companion DVD, please send them to Microsoft Press by using either of the following methods:

E-mail

• tkinput@microsoft.com

Postal Mail:

• *Microsoft Press*

  Attn: MCTS Self-Paced Training Kit (Exams 70-648 and 70-649): Transitioning your MCSA /MCSE to Windows Server 2008 Technology Specialist, *Editor*

  One Microsoft Way

  Redmond, WA 98052–6399

For additional support information regarding this book and the DVD (including answers to commonly asked questions about installation and use), visit the Microsoft Press Technical Support Web site at *www.microsoft.com/learning/support/books/.* To connect directly to the Microsoft Knowledge Base and enter a query, visit *http://support.microsoft.com/search/.* For support information regarding Microsoft software, connect to *http://support.microsoft.com.*

CHAPTER 1

Configuring Internet Protocol Addressing

As an experienced administrator with professional qualifications in Microsoft Windows Server 2003, you should already be familiar with Internet Protocol version 4 (IPv4) addressing. You should know how to configure IPv4 settings manually and how to configure a Dynamic Host Configuration Protocol version 4 (DHCPv4) scope and DHCPv4 options to configure IPv4 settings for hosts on your network automatically. In addition, you should know how automatic IP addressing (APIPA) is used to provide alternate configuration when manual configuration is not used and DHCP is not available.

You almost certainly know about Class A, Class B, Class C, and Class D (multicast) IPv4 addresses and default subnet masks, and you probably studied classless interdomain routing (CIDR) and variable length subnet masks (VLSMs) for your Windows Server 2003 examinations, but unless you regularly carry out subnetting and supernetting on your network, you might need some review of these topics.

IPv6 was available for Windows Server 2003 but was not widely used and did not feature significantly in the Windows Server 2003 examinations. However, IPv6 is enabled by default in Windows Server 2008 and is widely regarded as the IP of the future. It is likely to be tested in the Windows Server 2008 examinations.

The Windows Server 2008 70-648 and 70-649 upgrade examinations are not for beginners and neither is this training kit. This chapter is not written to cover old ground, although some review of the more advanced topics is included. It will indicate what you should already know and guide you to resources that enable you to review this knowledge. You are also strongly advised to review the materials you used to study IPv4 and DHCPv4 configuration for the Windows Server 2003 examinations. The chapter concentrates on topics you might not previously have studied—IPv6 addressing and DHCPv6 configuration.

> **NOTE DHCP**
>
> DHCPv4 is often simply referred to as DHCP, with DHCPv6 distinguished only by its version number. However, it is probably a good idea to get used to talking about DHCPv4 and DHCPv6.

Exam objectives in this chapter

- Configure IPv4 and IPv6 addressing.
- Configure Dynamic Host Configuration Protocol (DHCP).

Lessons in this chapter:

Before You Begin

To complete the lessons in this chapter, you must have done the following:

- Installed a Windows Server 2008 Enterprise server configured as a domain controller in the *contoso.internal* domain. Active Directory–integrated Domain Name System (DNS) is installed by default on the first domain controller in a domain. The computer name is Glasgow. You should configure a static IPv4 address of 10.0.0.11 with a subnet mask 255.255.255.0. The IPv4 address of the DNS server is 10.0.0.11. Other than IPv4 configuration and the computer name, accept all the default installation settings.

- Joined a client computer running Windows Vista Business, Enterprise, or Ultimate to the *contoso.internal* domain. The computer name is Melbourne. Initially, this computer should have a static IPv4 address of 10.0.0.21 with a 255.255.255.0 subnet mask. The IPv4 address of the DNS server is 10.0.0.11. You can obtain evaluation software that enables you to implement a Windows Vista Enterprise 30-day evaluation virtual hard disk (VHD) at the following address: *http://www.microsoft.com/downloads /details.aspx?FamilyID=c2c27337-d4d1-4b9b-926d-86493c7da1aa&DisplayLang=en# Instructions*.

- Created a user account with the username Kim_Akers and password P@ssw0rd. Add this account to the Domain Admins, Enterprise Admins, and Schema Admins groups.

- It is recommended that you use an isolated network that is not part of your production network to do the practice exercises in this book. Internet access is not required for the exercises, and you do not need to configure a default gateway. To minimize the time and expense of configuring physical computers, it is recommended that you use virtual machines. To run computers as virtual machines within Windows, you can use Virtual PC 2007, Virtual Server 2005 R2, or third-party virtual machine software. To download Virtual PC 2007, visit *http://www.microsoft.com/windows/downloads/virtualpc/default. mspx*. To download an evaluation of Virtual Server 2005 R2, visit *http://www.microsoft. com/technet/virtualserver/evaluation/default.mspx*.

Lesson 1: Configuring IPv4 and IPv6 Addressing

As an experienced network professional, you should be familiar with IPv4 addresses. You should know that the private IP address ranges are 10.0.0.0/8, 172.16.0.0/12, and 192.168.0.0/16 and that the APIPA range is 169.254.0.0/16. You should be aware that network address translation (NAT) typically allows you to use relatively few public IP addresses to enable Internet access to many internal clients with private IP addresses. You should be able to identify Class A, B, and C networks, but be aware that modern network design uses CIDR. You should know that Class D addresses (224.0.0.0/4) are used for multicasting.

> **NOTE   CLASS A, B, AND C ADDRESSES**
>
> The concept of Class A, B, and C addresses is now considered obsolete and is unlikely to be tested in the upgrade examinations. Nevertheless, in the course of your profession, you will come across administrators who will tell you their organization was allocated two Class C networks ten years ago. You need to know what they are talking about.

You might be less familiar with the IPv6 infrastructure and the types of IPv6 addressing. As IPv6 usage increases, you need to be aware of IPv4-to-IPv6 transition strategy and IPv4 and IPv6 interoperability, particularly the use of Teredo addresses. IPv6 addressing is the main topic in this lesson.

> **After this lesson, you will be able to:**
> - Configure IPv4 settings.
> - Subnet and supernet IPv4 networks.
> - Identify the various types of IPv6 addresses and explain their uses.
> - Identify IPv6 addresses that can be routed on the IPv4 Internet.
> - Implement IPv4 and IPv6 interoperability.
> - Use IPv6 tools.
>
> **Estimated lesson time: 45 minutes**

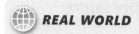

REAL WORLD

Ian McLean

'm probably very fortunate. I'm as comfortable in binary as I am in decimal.

It started a long time ago, when I was about eleven (1011) years old. A schoolmaster took a particular interest in the brighter children (believe it or not, I was one of them) who took a real interest and joy in mathematics. One of the things we played with was number systems. Not merely binary and hexadecimal—we also had fun with duodecimal and nonary.

When I first met a computer at the same tender age, the beast spoke binary and so did I. Computers have been part of my life ever since. When I became an electronics engineer in 1966, binary was my friend and digital logic circuits my specialty.

So when I came to subnet and supernet, I found it easy. Yet all around me, some very clever people were scratching their heads and looking thoroughly confused. I knew almost by instinct that if I wrote 255.255.255.0 and 255.255.254.0, the next in sequence was 255.255.252.0 (obvious, isn't it?) and could immediately translate these numbers into /24, /23, and /22. I've made a fair bit of money from something that's easy for me but difficult for some who are normally much brighter than I am.

IPv6 is the Internet protocol of the future, and you don't supernet or subnet IPv6 networks. However, you still need to know binary to understand hexadecimal fully, and you need to know about the binary *Exclusive OR* function to work with Teredo addresses. I've been saying this for years, and I'll still say it—learn binary.

Configuring IPv4 Addressing

You should already know that an IPv4 address is 32 bits in length and is split into four eight-bit octets. You could write this number in binary, but that would be long and cumbersome. You could also express it in decimal (or any other numbering system), but that would be uninformative. So the usual representation of an IPv4 address is in dotted-decimal notation, for example, 192.168.56.1. A subnet mask is a 32-bit number that consists of a series of ones followed by a series of zeros, for example, 255.255.255.0. This can also be expressed by a slash followed by the number of ones in the mask, for example, /24.

An IP address (IPv4 or IPv6) can be split into two sections, one of which identifies a host and the other the network the host is on. The subnet mask defines which bits in an IP address identify the host and which the network. For example, if you write 192.168.56.0 /24, the /24 represents the /24 subnet mask and indicates that the first 24 of the 32 bits in the IPv4 address is the network identity (ID). The lower the number after the slash in the subnet mask, the greater the number of host addresses available on the subnet.

If a computer on a subnet sends an IPv4 datagram to a computer on another network, the datagram first goes to the default gateway on the subnet. The default gateway address is the address of a multihomed device (for example, a router or a layer-3 switch) that exists on the subnet.

Subnetting logically subdivides a network address space by increasing the number of ones in the network's subnet mask. This enables you to create multiple subnets or broadcast domains within the original network address space. For example, suppose your organization has been allocated the IPv4 network 131.107.0.0 /22 (131.107.0.1 through 131.107.3.254). You could then split this into four subnets: 131.107.0.0/24, 131.107.1.0/24, 131.107.2.0/24, and 131.107.3.0/24. This assumes that your routers or switches support the zero subnet, which all modern layer-3 devices do.

Supernetting logically combines a number of contiguous address spaces to form a single network that can be advertised on the Internet. For example, if you had been allocated the networks 131.107.64.0/24, 131.107.65.0/24, 131.107.66.0/24, and 131.107.67.0/24, you could combine them so your organization advertises the subnet 131.107.64.0/22. In practice, you would use this network only for advertisements and subnet it internally. A well-populated subnet with 1,022 hosts would be impractical due to broadcast collisions, especially if the subnet included clients and servers with earlier operating systems such as Windows XP and Windows Server 2003 that generate a considerable amount of broadcast traffic.

> **MORE INFO   HOW TO SUBNET**
>
> The Quick Check element in this section is unusual in that it contains answers that cannot be found in the chapter text. Its purpose is to check your existing knowledge of IPv4 addressing and subnetting. If you have difficulty answering any of the questions directly, review the material you used to study IPv4 addressing for the Windows Server 2003 examinations or access *http://www.learntosubnet.com*. Although this is not a Microsoft site, it is one that I have recommended to my students for years, and it provides excellent coverage of both binary arithmetic and IPv6 subnetting.

 Quick Check

1. What is the slash notation for the subnet mask 255.252.0.0?
2. What is the maximum number of host addresses available on a subnet with a /23 subnet mask?
3. What is the APIPA address range? Express this as a network address and slash notation subnet mask.
4. Other than the APIPA address range, what networks are used for private IPv4 addresses?

5. What is the hexadecimal number AFFE6409 when converted to dotted decimal notation?

6. What is the binary number 10011101 00110111 10010110 01001001 when converted to dotted decimal notation?

7. Two computers in the *tailspintoys.com* domain have IPv4 addresses 10.0.0.23 and 10.0.1.126. All subnets in the domain have a /23 subnet mask. Are the computers on the same subnet?

8. What is the address range supported by the 172.16.10.128/25 subnet?

Quick Check Answers

1. /14.

2. 510.

3. 169.254.0.0/16.

4. 10.0.0.0/8, 172.16.0.0/12, 192.168.0.0/16.

5. 175.254.100.9.

6. 157.55.150.73.

7. Yes, both computers are on the 10.0.0.0/23 subnet, which supports an address range of 10.0.0.1 through 10.0.1.254.

8. 172.16.10.129 through 172.16.10.254.

Variable Length Subnet Masks

You can configure subnet masks so that one subnet mask is used externally and multiple subnet masks are used internally. This practice enables you to use your network address space more efficiently. Typically, you subnet a network and then further subnet one or more of the subnets you created to provide more subnets, each with fewer hosts.

Suppose, for example, you have been allocated the 131.107.100.0/24 network and you require five networks with 30 hosts per network. However, to implement a wide area network (WAN) connection, you also need a subnet with two hosts. You could simply subnet your /24 network into eight /27 subnets, each with 30 host addresses, and use one of these for your WAN connection. This would give you two spare /27 subnets.

However, this is inefficient. If you need more WAN links, you would need to use a spare /27 subnet for each one. It is more efficient to create eight /27 subnets and then further subnet one of these subnets.

If, for example, you subnetted 131.107.100.0/24 into the eight subnets:

131.107.100.0/27; 131.107.100.32/27; 131.107.100.64/27; 131.107.100.96/27; 131.107.100.128/27; 131.107.160.32/27; 131.107.100.192/27; 131.107.100.224/27

you could then take the final subnet and further subnet it into up to sixteen subnets, each with two host addresses, that is:

131.107.100.224/30; 131.107.100.228/30; and so on.

You can be even more clever and subnet the 131.107.100.224/27 subnet into (for example) four /29 subnets with six host addresses each and then subnet the final /29 subnet into two /30 subnets. The possibilities are endless, but take care not to be too clever and make your subnetting too complex to understand.

> **MORE INFO** **VARIABLE LENGTH SUBNET MASKS**
>
> For more information about VLSMs, visit *http://technet2.microsoft.com/windowsserver/en /library/c4a4bcaf-4c12-4c20-a346-34cef0113a801033.mspx?mfr=true*. This is a Windows Server 2003 link but is also relevant to VLSMs on Windows Server 2008.

The Longest Match Algorithm

In the VLSM example previously described, an IPv4 datagram sent, for example, to the IPv4 address 131.107.100.24 locates the relevant host on the 131.107.100.224/30 subnet, not on the 131.107.100.224/27 subnet. The layer-3 devices that control routing are configured to use the longest match algorithm to route the datagram to the appropriate subnet.

> **MORE INFO** **THE LONGEST MATCH ALGORITHM**
>
> It is unlikely that the upgrade examinations will ask any detailed questions about the longest match algorithm. However, if you want to learn more from a professional point of view, see *http://www.ietf.org/proceedings/03jul/I-D/draft-grow-bounded-longest -match-00.txt*.

Alternate IPv4 Configuration

You can configure IPv4 (and IPv6) by using *netsh* commands, described later in this lesson, or through the TCP/IPv4 Properties graphical user interface (GUI). You access this dialog box from the Network and Sharing Center in Control Panel by clicking Manage Network Connections, right-clicking the appropriate interface, and selecting Properties, selecting Internet Protocol Version 4 (TCP/IPv4), and clicking Properties. This procedure is different from that used in Windows Server 2003 to access the GUI tool for configuring IPv4 settings, and you should become familiar with it.

On the General tab of the Internet Protocol Version 4 (TCP/IPv4) Properties dialog box, you can specify an IPv4 address, a subnet mask, and (optionally) a default gateway (static configuration), or you can configure the interface to obtain these settings automatically. You also have the choice of specifying a static IPv4 address for a DNS server or obtaining this automatically. If you configure a static interface address, you also need to specify a static DNS server address. Automatic configuration is typically through DHCP, but if no DHCP leases are available on the network, an alternate configuration is applied.

You can specify the alternate configuration on the Alternate Configuration tab, shown in Figure 1-1. By default, alternate configuration is through APIPA, but you can specify a static address that can be applied if a DHCP lease cannot be obtained. The Alternate Configuration functionality is useful when you use the computer on more than one network, where one of those networks does not have a DHCP server and you do not want to use an APIPA configuration.

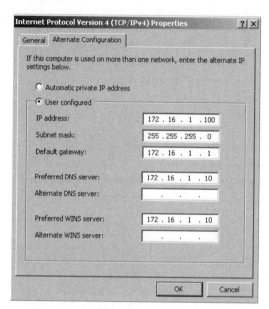

FIGURE 1-1 The Alternate Configuration tab.

Typically, you can use the alternate configuration functionality if you use a mobile computer at your office and at your home. When you are in the office, the computer uses a DHCP-allocated TCP/IP configuration. When you are at home (where you do not have access to a DHCP server), the computer automatically uses the alternate configuration. It is less common to set up an alternate configuration on a server, but you have the option of doing so if you want to.

Configuring IPv6 Addressing

IPv4 and IPv6 addresses can be readily distinguished. An IPv4 address uses 32 bits, resulting in an address space of just over 4 billion. An IPv6 address uses 128 bits, resulting in an address space of 2^{128}, or 340,282,366,920,938,463,463,374,607,431,768,211,456—a number too large to comprehend. This represents $6.5*2^{23}$ or 54,525,952 addresses for every square meter of the earth's surface. In practice, the IPv6 address space allows for multiple levels of subnetting and address allocation between the Internet backbone and individual subnets within an organization. The vastly increased address space available enables allocation of not one but several unique IPv6 addresses to a network entity, with each address being used for a different purpose.

IPv6 provides addresses that are equivalent to IPv4 address types and others that are unique to IPv6. A node can have several IPv6 addresses, each of which has its own unique purpose. This section describes the IPv6 address syntax and the various classes of IPv6 addressing.

IPv6 Address Syntax

The IPv6 128-bit address is divided at 16-bit boundaries, and each 16-bit block is converted to a four-digit hexadecimal number. Colons are used as separators. This representation is called *colon-hexadecimal*.

Global unicast IPv6 addresses are equivalent to IPv4 public unicast addresses. To illustrate IPv6 address syntax, consider the following IPv6 global unicast address:

21cd:0053:0000:0000:03ad:003f:af37:8d62

IPv6 representation can be simplified by removing the leading zeros within each 16-bit block. However, each block must have at least a single digit. With leading zero suppression, the address representation becomes:

21cd:53:0:0:3ad:3f:af37:8d62

A contiguous sequence of 16-bit blocks set to 0 in the colon-hexadecimal format can be compressed to ::. Thus, the previous example address could be written:

21cd:53::3ad:3f:af37:8d62

Some types of addresses contain long sequences of zeros and thus provide good examples of when to use this notation. For example, the multicast address ff05:0:0:0:0:0:0:2 can be compressed to ff05::2.

IPv6 Address Prefixes

The prefix is the part of the address that indicates either the bits that have fixed values or the network identifier bits. IPv6 prefixes are expressed in the same way as CIDR IPv4 (slash) notation. For example, 21cd:53::/64 is the subnet on which the address 21cd:53::23ad:3f:af37:8d62 is located. In this case, the first 64 bits of the address are the network prefix. An IPv6 subnet prefix (or subnet ID) is assigned to a single link. Multiple subnet IDs can be assigned to the same link. This technique is called *multinetting*.

> **NOTE** **IPV6 DOES NOT USE DOTTED DECIMAL NOTATION IN SUBNET MASKS**
>
> Only prefix length notation is supported in IPv6. IPv4 dotted decimal subnet mask representation (such as 255.255.255.0) has no direct equivalent.

IPv6 Address Types

The three types of IPv6 addresses are unicast, multicast, and anycast.

- **Unicast** Identifies a single interface within the scope of the unicast address type. Packets addressed to a unicast address are delivered to a single interface. RFC 2373 allows multiple interfaces to use the same address, provided that these interfaces appear as a single interface to the IPv6 implementation on the host. This accommodates load-balancing systems.

- **Multicast** Identifies multiple interfaces. Packets addressed to a multicast address are delivered to all interfaces identified by the address.

- **Anycast** Identifies multiple interfaces. Packets addressed to an anycast address are delivered to the nearest interface identified by the address. The nearest interface is the closest in terms of routing distance, or number of hops. An anycast address is used for one-to-one-of-many communication, with delivery to a single interface.

> **MORE INFO** IPV6 ADDRESSING ARCHITECTURE
>
> For more information about IPv6 address structure and architecture, see *http://www.ietf.org/rfc/rfc2373.txt*.

> **NOTE** INTERFACES AND NODES
>
> IPv6 addresses identify interfaces rather than nodes. A node is identified by any unicast address that is assigned to one of its interfaces.

IPv6 Unicast Addresses

IPv6 supports the following types of unicast addresses:

- Global
- Link-local
- Site-local
- Special
- Network Service Access Point (NSAP) and Internetwork Packet Exchange (IPX) mapped addresses
- Global unicast addresses

Global unicast addresses are the IPv6 equivalent of IPv4 public addresses and are globally routable and reachable on the IPv6 portion of the Internet. These addresses can be aggregated to produce an efficient routing infrastructure and are therefore sometimes known as aggregatable global unicast addresses. An aggregatable global unicast address is unique across the entire IPv6 portion of the Internet. (The region over which an IP address is unique is called the *scope* of the address.)

The format prefix (FP) of a global unicast address is held in the three most significant bits, which are always 001. The next 13 bits are allocated by the Internet Assigned Numbers Authority (IANA) and are known as the top-level aggregator (TLA). IANA allocates TLAs to local Internet registries that, in turn, allocate individual TLAs to large Internet service providers (ISPs). The next 8 bits of the address are reserved for future expansion.

The next 24 bits of the address contain the next-level aggregator (NLA). This identifies a specific customer site. The NLA enables an ISP to create multiple levels of addressing hierarchy within a network. The next 16 bits contain the site-level aggregator (SLA), which organizes addressing and routing for downstream ISPs and identifies sites or subnets within a site.

The next 64 bits identify the interface within a subnet. This is the 64-bit Extended Unique Identifier (EUI-64) address, as defined by the Institute of Electrical and Electronics Engineers (IEEE). EUI-64 addresses are either assigned directly to network adapter cards or derived from the 48-bit media access control (MAC) address of a network adapter as defined by the IEEE 802 standard. Put simply, the interface identity is provided by the network adapter hardware.

> **MORE INFO** **GLOBAL UNICAST ADDRESS ALLOCATION**
>
> It is unlikely that the upgrade examinations will ask detailed questions about how global unicast address ranges are allocated. However, if you want to know more about this from a professional viewpoint, see *http://tools.ietf.org/html/rfc1887*.

Privacy Extensions for Stateless Address Autoconfiguration in IPv6

Concerns have been expressed that deriving an interface ID directly from computer hardware could enable the itinerary of a laptop and, hence, that of its owner to be tracked. This raises privacy issues, and future systems might allocate interface IDs differently.

> **MORE INFO** **RFC 3041 AND RFC 4941 ADDRESS THIS PROBLEM**
>
> For more information, see *http://www.ietf.org/rfc/rfc3041.txt* and *http://www.ietf.org/rfc/rfc4191.txt*.

To summarize, the FP, TLA, reserved bits, and NLA identify the public topology; the SLA identifies the site topology; and the interface ID identifies the interface. Figure 1-2 illustrates the structure of an aggregatable global unicast address.

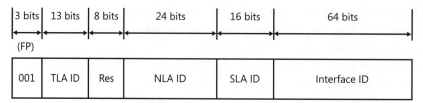

3 bits	13 bits	8 bits	24 bits	16 bits	64 bits
(FP)					
001	TLA ID	Res	NLA ID	SLA ID	Interface ID

FIGURE 1-2 Global unicast address structure.

> **MORE INFO   GLOBAL UNICAST ADDRESS FORMAT**
>
> For more information about aggregatable global unicast addresses, see *http://www.ietf.org /rfc/rfc2374.txt*.

EXAM TIP

You need to know that an aggregatable global unicast address is the IPv6 equivalent of an IPv4 public unicast address. You should be able to identify a global unicast address from the value of its three most significant bits. Knowing the various components of the address helps you understand how IPv6 addressing works, but the upgrade examinations are unlikely to test this knowledge in the depth of detail provided by the RFCs.

LINK-LOCAL ADDRESSES

Link-local IPv6 addresses are equivalent to IPv4 addresses that are autoconfigured through APIPA and use the 169.254.0.0/16 prefix. You can identify a link-local address by an FP of 1111 1110 10, which is followed by 54 zeros (link-local addresses always begin with fe8). Nodes use link-local addresses when communicating with neighboring nodes on the same link. The scope of a link-local address is the local link. A link-local address is required for neighbor discovery (ND) and is always automatically configured, even if no other unicast address is allocated.

SITE-LOCAL ADDRESSES

Site-local IPv6 addresses are equivalent to the IPv4 private address space (10.0.0.0/8, 172.16.0.0/12, and 192.168.0.0/16). Private intranets that do not have a direct, routed connection to the IPv6 portion of the Internet can use site-local addresses without conflicting with aggregatable global unicast addresses. The scope of a site-local address is the site (or organization internetwork).

Site-local addresses can be allocated by using stateful address configuration, such as from a DHCPv6 scope. A host uses stateful address configuration when it receives router advertisement messages that do not include address prefixes. A host will also use a stateful address configuration protocol when no routers are present on the local link.

Site-local addresses can also be configured through stateless address configuration. This is based on router advertisement messages that include stateless address prefixes and require that hosts not use a stateful address configuration protocol.

Alternatively, address configuration can use a combination of stateless and stateful configuration. This occurs when router advertisement messages include stateless address prefixes but require that hosts use a stateful address configuration protocol.

IPv6 Address States

Typically, hosts configure IPv6 addresses by interacting with an IPv6-enabled router and performing IPv6 address autoconfiguration. An address is said to be in a *tentative* state for the short time between its first assignment and verification that it is unique. Hosts use duplicate-address detection to identify other computers that have the same IPv6 address by transmitting a Neighbor Solicitation message that contains the tentative address. If another host responds, the address is considered invalid. If no other host responds, the address is considered unique and valid. A valid address is called *preferred* within its valid lifetime assigned by the router. A valid address is called *deprecated* when it exceeds its lifetime. Existing communication sessions can still use a deprecated address.

> **MORE INFO** **IPV6 ADDRESS AUTOCONFIGURATION**
>
> For more information about how IPv6 addresses are configured, see *http://www.microsoft.com/technet/technetmag/issues/2007/08/CableGuy/*. Although the article is titled "IPv6 Autoconfiguration in Windows Vista," it also covers Windows Server 2008 autoconfiguration and describes the differences between autoconfiguration on a client and on a server operating system.

Site-local addresses begin with fec0, followed by 32 zeros, and then by a 16-bit subnet identifier that you can use to create subnets within your organization. The 64-bit Interface ID field identifies a specific interface on a subnet.

Figure 1-3 shows link-local and site-local addresses (for DNS servers) configured on interfaces on the Windows Server 2008 domain controller Glasgow. No global addresses exist in the configuration because domain controllers are never exposed directly to the Internet. The IPv6 addresses on your test computer will probably be different. Note that in this figure, the Glasgow domain controller has a virtual interface to the virtual machine that hosts the Melbourne client. You configured both computers following the instructions in the "Before You Begin" section at the start of this chapter.

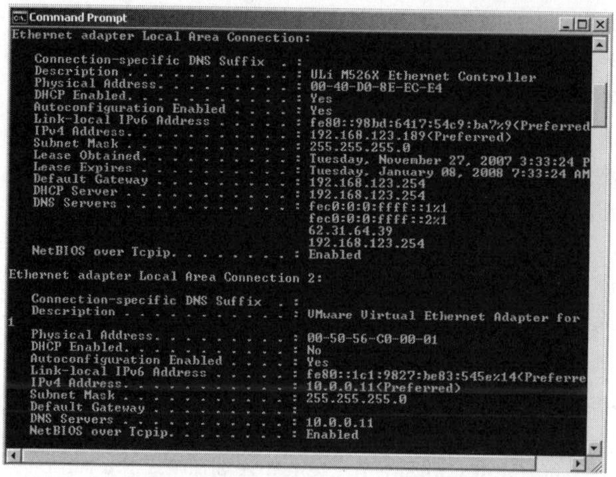

FIGURE 1-3 IPv6 addresses on computer interfaces.

Link-Local and Site-Local Addresses

You can implement IPv6 connectivity between hosts on an isolated subnet by using link-local addresses. However, you cannot assign link-local addresses to router interfaces (default gateways), and you cannot route from one subnet to another if only link-local addresses are used. DNS servers cannot use only link-local addresses. If you use link-local addresses, you must specify their interface IDs—that is, the number after the % symbol at the end of the address, as shown previously in Figure 1-3. Link-local addresses are not dynamically registered in Windows Server 2008 DNS.

For these reasons, site-local addresses are typically used on the subnets of a private network to implement IPv6 connectivity over the network. If every device on the network has its own global address (a stated aim of IPv6 implementation), global addresses can route between internal subnets, to peripheral zones, and to the Internet.

SPECIAL ADDRESSES

Two special IPv6 addresses exist—the unspecified address and the loopback address. The unspecified 0:0:0:0:0:0:0:0 (or ::) address is used to indicate the absence of an address and is equivalent to the IPv4 unspecified 0.0.0.0 address. It is typically used as a source address for packets attempting to verify whether a tentative address is unique. It is never assigned to an interface or used as a destination address. The 0:0:0:0:0:0:0:1 (or ::1) loopback address identifies a loopback interface and is equivalent to the IPv4 127.0.0.1 loopback address.

NSAP AND IPX ADDRESSES

NSAP addresses are identifying labels for network endpoints used in Open Systems Interconnection (OSI) networking. They specify a piece of equipment connected to an Asynchronous Transfer Mode (ATM) network. IPX is no longer widely used because modern Novell Netware networks support TCP/IP. IPv6 addresses with an FP of 0000001 map to NSAP addresses. IPv6 addresses with an FP of 0000010 map to IPX addresses.

EXAM TIP

The upgrade examinations are unlikely to include questions about NSAP or IPX mapping.

IPv6 Multicast Addresses

IPv6 multicast addresses enable an IPv6 packet to be sent to a number of hosts, all of which have the same multicast address. They have an FP of 11111111. (Multicast addresses always start with ff.) Subsequent fields specify flags, scope, and group ID, as shown in Figure 1-4.

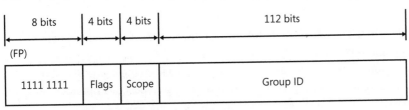

FIGURE 1-4 Multicast address structure.

The flags field holds the flag settings. Currently the only flag defined is the Transient (T) flag that uses the low-order field bit. If this flag is set to 0, the multicast address is well known—in other words, it is permanently assigned and has been allocated by IANA. If the flag is set to 1, the multicast address is transient.

Quick Check

■ What type of address is fec0:0:0:eadf::1ff?

Quick Check Answer

■ Unicast site-local

The scope field indicates the scope of the IPv6 internetwork for which the multicast traffic is intended. Routers use the multicast scope, together with information provided by multicast routing protocols, to determine whether multicast traffic can be forwarded. For example, traffic with the multicast address ff02::2 has a link-local scope and is never forwarded beyond the local link. Table 1-1 lists the assigned scope field values.

TABLE 1-1 Scope Field Values

VALUE	SCOPE
0	Reserved
1	Node-local scope
2	Link-local scope
5	Site-local scope
8	Organization-local scope
e	Global scope
f	Reserved

The group ID represents the multicast group and is unique within the scope. Permanently assigned group IDs are independent of the scope. Transient group IDs are relevant only to a specific scope. Multicast addresses from ff01:: through ff0f:: are reserved, well-known addresses.

In theory, 2^{112} group IDs are available. In practice, because of the way IPv6 multicast addresses are mapped to Ethernet multicast MAC addresses, RFC 2373, "IP Version 6 Addressing Architecture" recommends assigning the group ID from the low-order 32 bits of the IPv6 multicast address and setting the remaining original group ID bits to zero. In this way, each group ID maps to a unique Ethernet multicast MAC address.

> **MORE INFO** **ASSIGNING GROUP IDS**
>
> For more information about assigning group IDs, see *http://www.ietf.org/rfc/rfc2373.txt*.

THE SOLICITED-NODE MULTICAST ADDRESS

The solicited-node multicast address facilitates the querying of network nodes during address resolution. IPv6 uses the ND message to resolve a link-local IPv6 address to a node MAC address. Rather than use the local-link scope all-nodes multicast address (which would be processed by all nodes on the local link) as the neighbor solicitation message destination, IPv6 uses the solicited-node multicast address. This address comprises the prefix ff02::1:ff00:0/104 and the last 24 bits of the IPv6 address that is being resolved.

For example, if a node has the link-local address fe80::6b:28c:16d2:c97, the corresponding solicited-node address is ff02::1:ffd2:c97.

The result of using the solicited-node multicast address is that address resolution uses a mechanism that is not processed by all network nodes. Because of the relationship between the MAC address, the Interface ID, and the solicited-node address, the solicited-node address acts as a pseudo-unicast address for efficient address resolution.

IPv6 Anycast Addresses

An anycast address is assigned to multiple interfaces. Packets sent to an anycast address are forwarded by the routing infrastructure to the nearest of these interfaces. The routing infrastructure must be aware of the interfaces that are assigned anycast addresses and their distance in terms of routing metrics. Currently, anycast addresses are used only as destination addresses and are assigned only to routers. Anycast addresses are assigned from the unicast address space, and the scope of an anycast address is the scope of the unicast address type from which the anycast address is assigned.

THE SUBNET-ROUTER ANYCAST ADDRESS

The subnet-router anycast address is created from the subnet prefix for a given interface. In a subnet-router anycast address, the bits in the subnet prefix retain their current values, and the remaining bits are set to zero.

All router interfaces attached to a subnet are assigned the subnet-router anycast address for that subnet. The subnet-router anycast address is used for communication with one of multiple routers that are attached to a remote subnet.

 Quick Check

- A node has the link-local fe80::aa:cdfe:aaa4:cab7 address. What is its corresponding solicited-node address?

Quick Check Answer

- ff02::1:ffa4:cab7 (the prefix ff02::1:ff00:0/104 and the last 24 bits of the link-local address, which are a4:cab7)

Implementing IPv4-to-IPv6 Compatibility

In addition to the various types of addresses described earlier in this lesson, IPv6 provides the following types of compatibility addresses to aid migration from IPv4 to IPv6 and to implement transition technologies.

IPv4-Compatible Address

The 0:0:0:0:0:0:w.x.y.z (or ::w.x.y.z) IPV4-compatible address is used by dual stack nodes that are communicating with IPv6 over an IPv4 infrastructure. The last four octets (w.x.y.z) represent the dotted decimal representation of an IPv4 address. Dual stack nodes are nodes with both IPv4 and IPv6 protocols. When the IPV4-compatible address is used as an IPv6 destination, the IPv6 traffic is automatically encapsulated with an IPv4 header and sent to the destination, using the IPv4 infrastructure.

IPv4-Mapped Address

The IPv4-mapped 0:0:0:0:0:ffff:w.x.y.z (or ::ffff:w.x.y.z) address represents an IPv4-only node to an IPv6 node to map IPv4 devices that are not compatible with IPv6 into the IPv6 address space. The IPv4-mapped address is never the source or destination address of an IPv6 packet.

Teredo Address

A Teredo address consists of a 32-bit Teredo prefix. In Windows Server 2008 (and Windows Vista) this is 2001::/32. The prefix is followed by the IPv4 (32-bit) public address of the Teredo server that assisted in the configuration of the address. The next 16 bits are reserved for Teredo flags. Currently, only the highest ordered flag bit is defined. This is the cone flag and is set when the NAT connected to the Internet is a cone NAT.

> **NOTE   WINDOWS XP AND WINDOWS SERVER 2003**
>
> In Windows XP and Windows Server 2003, the Teredo prefix was originally 3ffe:831f::/32. Computers running Windows XP and Windows Server 2003 use the 2001::/32 Teredo prefix when updated with Microsoft Security Bulletin MS06-064.

The next 16 bits store an obscured version of the external User Datagram Protocol (UDP) port that corresponds to all Teredo traffic for the Teredo client interface. When a Teredo client sends its initial packet to a Teredo server, NAT maps the source UDP port of the packet to a different, external UDP port. All Teredo traffic for the host interface uses the same external, mapped UDP port. The value representing this external port is masked or obscured by Exclusive ORing (XORing) it with 0xffff. Obscuring the external port prevents NATs from translating it within the payload of packets that are being forwarded.

The final 32 bits store an obscured version of the external IPv4 address that corresponds to all Teredo traffic for the Teredo client interface. The external address is obscured by XORing it with 0xffffffff. As with the UDP port, this prevents NATs from translating the external IPv4 address within the payload of packets that are being forwarded.

The external address is obscured by XORing the external address with 0xffffffff. For example, the obscured version of the public IPv4 131.107.0.1 address in colon-hexadecimal format is 7c94:fffe. (131.107.0.1 equals 0x836b0001, and 0x836b0001 XOR 0xffffffff equals 0x7c94fffe.) Obscuring the external address prevents NATs from translating it within the payload of the packets that are being forwarded.

Exclusive Or

Exclusive Or (XOR) is a binary operation. 0 XOR 0=0; 0 XOR 1=1; 0 XOR 1=1; 1 XOR 1=0. For example, set the scientific calculator on your computer to **Hex** and enter **0A000001**. (The first zero will not be displayed.) This is the Hex equivalent of 10.0.0.1. Click Xor, and then enter **FFFFFFFF**. Click the = symbol. The result, F5FFFFFE, is the obscured 10.0.0.1 address.

Test this by entering **F5FFFFFE** and XORing it with **FFFFFFFF**. You will get 0A000001. (The first zero is not shown.) This is the hexadecimal value of 10.0.0.1.

For example, Northwind Traders currently implements the following IPv4 private networks at its headquarters and branch offices:

- Headquarters: 10.0.100.0 /24
- Branch1: 10.0.0.0 /24
- Branch2: 10.0.10.0 /24
- Branch3: 10.0.20.0 /24

The company wants to establish IPv6 communication between Teredo clients and between Teredo clients and IPv6-only hosts. The presence of Teredo servers on the IPv4 Internet enables this communication to take place. A Teredo server is an IPv6/IPv4 node, connected to both the IPv4 Internet and the IPv6 Internet, which supports a Teredo tunneling interface. The Teredo addresses of the Northwind Traders networks depend on a number of factors such as the port and type of NAT server used, but they could, for example, be the following:

- Headquarters: 2001::ce49:7601:e866:efff:f5ff:9bfe through 2001::0a0a:64fe:e866:efff:f5ff:9b01
- Branch 1: 2001:: ce49:7601:e866:efff:f5ff:fffe through 2001::0a0a:0afe:e866:efff: f5ff:ff01
- Branch 2: 2001:: ce49:7601:e866:efff:f5ff:f5fe through 2001::0a0a:14fe:e866:efff:f5ff:f501
- Branch 3: 2001:: ce49:7601:e866:efff:f5ff:ebfe through 2001::0a0a:1efe:e866:efff:f5ff:ebfe

Note that, for example, 10.0.100.1 is the equivalent of 0a00:6401, and 0a00:6401 XORed with ffff:ffff is f5ff:9bfe.

EXAM TIP

Microsoft supports Teredo addresses. However, the upgrade examinations are unlikely to ask you to generate a Teredo address. You might, however, be asked to identify such an address and work out its included IPv4 address. Fortunately, you have access to a scientific calculator during the examination.

Cone NATs

Cone NATs can be full cone, restricted cone, or port restricted cone. In a full cone NAT, all requests from the same internal IP address and port are mapped to the same external IP address and port, and any external host can send a packet to the internal host by sending a packet to the mapped external address.

In a restricted cone NAT, all requests from the same internal IP address and port are mapped to the same external IP address and port, but an external host can send a packet to the internal host if the internal host had previously sent a packet to the external host.

In a port restricted cone NAT, the restriction includes port numbers. An external host with a specified IP address and source port can send a packet to an internal host only if the internal host had previously sent a packet to that IP address and port.

Intra-Site Automatic Tunnel Addressing Protocol Addresses

IPv6 can use an Intra-Site Automatic Tunnel Addressing Protocol (ISATAP) address to communicate between two nodes over an IPv4 intranet. An ISATAP address starts with a 64-bit unicast link-local, site-local, global, or 6to4 global prefix. The next 32 bits are the 0:5efe ISATAP identifier. The final 32 bits hold the IPv4 address in either dotted decimal or hexadecimal notation. An ISATAP address can incorporate either a public or a private IPv4 address.

> **MORE INFO** **6TO4 GLOBAL PREFIX**
>
> For more information about the 6to4 global prefix and general information about how IPv6 works, see *http://technet2.microsoft.com/windowsserver/en/library/9bcf5d01-a1df -4053-939b-904e207535531033.mspx?mfr=true.*

For example, the ISATAP fe80::5efe:w.x.y.z address has a link-local prefix; the fec0::1111:0:5efe:w.x.y.z address has a site-local prefix; the 3ffe:1a05:510:1111:0:5efe:w.x.y. z address has a global prefix; and the 2002:9d36:1:2:0:5efe:w.x.y.z address has a 6to4 global prefix. In all cases, w.x.y.z represents an IPv4 address.

By default, Windows Server 2008 automatically configures the ISATAP fe80::5efe:w.x.y.z address for each IPv4 address assigned to a node. This link-local ISATAP address allows two hosts to communicate over an IPv4 network by using each other's ISATAP address.

You can implement IPv6-to-IPv4 configuration by using the *netsh interface ipv6 6to4, netsh interface ipv6 isatap*, and *netsh interface ipv6 add v6v4tunnel* IPv6 tools. For example, to create an IPv6-in-IPv4 tunnel between the local 10.0.0.11 address and the 192.168.123

remote address.116 on an interface named *Remote*, you would enter **netsh interface ipv6 add v6v4tunnel "Remote" 10.0.0.11 192.168.123.116**.

You can also configure the appropriate compatibility addresses manually by using the *netsh interface ipv6 set address* command or the TCP/IPv6 GUI, as described in the next section of this lesson.

NOTE 6TO4CFG

Windows Server 2008 does not support the 6to4cfg tool.

Using IPv6 Tools

Windows Server 2008 tools enable you to configure IPv6 interfaces and check IPv6 connectivity and routing. Tools also exist that implement and check IPv4-to-IPv6 compatibility.

In Windows 2008, the standard command-line tools such as *ping*, *ipconfig*, *pathping*, *tracert*, *netstat*, and *route* have full IPv6 functionality. For example, Figure 1-5 shows the *ping* command used to check connectivity with a link-local IPv6 address on a test network. The IPv6 addresses on your test network will be different. Note that if you were pinging from one host to another, you would also need to include the interface ID, for example, *ping fe80::fd64:b38b:cac6:cdd4%15*. Interface IDs are discussed later in this lesson.

FIGURE 1-5 Pinging an IPv6 address.

NOTE PING6

The *ping6* command-line tool is not supported in Windows Server 2008.

Tools specific to IPv6 are provided in the *netsh* (network shell) command structure. For example, the *netsh interface ipv6 show neighbors* command shows the IPv6 interfaces of all hosts on the local subnet. You use this command in the practice session later in this lesson, after you have configured IPv6 connectivity on a subnet.

Verifying IPv6 Configuration and Connectivity

If you are troubleshooting connectivity problems or merely want to check your configuration, arguably the most useful tool—and certainly one of the most used—is *ipconfig*. The *ipconfig /all* tool displays both IPv4 and IPv6 configuration. The output from this tool was shown in Figure 1-3, earlier in this lesson.

If you want to display the configuration of only the IPv6 interfaces on the local computer, you can use the *netsh interface ipv6 show address* command. Figure 1-6 shows the output of this command run on the Glasgow computer. Note the % character followed by a number after each IPv6 address. This is the interface ID, which identifies the interface configured with the IPv6 address.

FIGURE 1-6 Displaying IPv6 addresses and interface IDs.

If you are administering an enterprise network with a number of sites, you also need to know site IDs. You can obtain a site ID by using the *netsh interface ipv6 show address level=verbose* command. Part of the output from this command is shown in Figure 1-7.

```
Command Prompt                                          _ □ ×
Interface Luid     : Local Area Connection* 2
Scope Id           : 0.10
Valid Lifetime     : infinite
Preferred Lifetime : infinite
DAD State          : Deprecated
Address Type       : Other

Address fe80::1c1:9827:be83:545e%14 Parameters

Interface Luid     : Local Area Connection 2
Scope Id           : 0.14
Valid Lifetime     : infinite
Preferred Lifetime : infinite
DAD State          : Preferred
Address Type       : Other

Address fe80::5efe:192.168.123.116%12 Parameters
```

FIGURE 1-7 Displaying IPv6 addresses and site IDs.

Configuring IPv6 Interfaces

Typically, most IPv6 addresses are configured through autoconfiguration, or DHCPv6. However, if you need to configure an IPv6 address manually, you can use the *netsh interface ipv6 set address* command, as in this example: *netsh interface ipv6 set address "local area connection 2" fec0:0:0:fffe::2.* You need to run the command console (also known as the command prompt) as an administrator to use this command. In Windows Server 2008 (and in Windows Vista), you can also manually configure IPv6 addresses from the properties of the TCP/IPv6 GUI. Figure 1-8 shows this configuration.

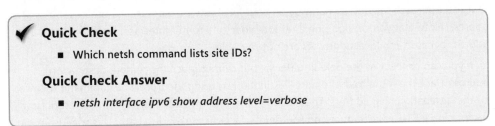

FIGURE 1-8 Configuring an IPv6 address through a GUI.

The advantage of using the TCP/IPv6 GUI is that you can specify the IPv6 addresses of one or more DNS servers in addition to specifying the interface address. If, however, you choose to use command line interface (CLI) commands, the command to add IPv6 addresses of DNS servers is *netsh interface ipv6 add dnsserver*, as in this example: *netsh interface ipv6 add dnsserver "local area connection 2" fec0:0:0:fffe::1.* To change the properties of IPv6 interfaces (but not their configuration), use the *netsh interface ipv6 set interface* command, as in this example: *netsh interface ipv6 set interface "local area connection 2" forwarding=enabled.* You need to run the command console (command prompt) as an administrator to use the *netsh interface ipv6 add* and *netsh interface ipv6 set* commands.

✔ **Quick Check**

- **Which netsh command lists site IDs?**

Quick Check Answer

- *netsh interface ipv6 show address level=verbose*

Verifying IPv6 Connectivity

To verify connectivity on a local network, your first step should be to flush the neighbor cache, which stores recently resolved link-layer addresses and might give a false result if you are checking changes that involve address resolution. You can check the contents of the neighbor cache by using the *netsh interface ipv6 show neighbors* command. The *netsh interface ipv6 delete neighbors* command flushes the cache. You need to run the command console as an administrator to use the *netsh* tool.

You can test connectivity to a local host on your subnet and to your default gateway by using the *ping* command. You can add the interface ID to the IPv6 interface address to ensure that the address is configured on the correct interface. Figure 1-9 shows a *ping* command using an IPv6 address and an interface ID.

FIGURE 1-9 Pinging an IPv6 address with an interface ID.

To check connectivity to a host on a remote network, your first task should be to check and clear the destination cache, which stores next-hop IPv6 addresses for destinations. You can display the current contents of the destination cache by using the *netsh interface ipv6 show destinationcache* command. To flush the destination cache, use the *netsh interface ipv6 delete destinationcache* command. You must run the command console as an administrator to use this command.

Your next step is to check connectivity to the default router interface on your local subnet. This is your default gateway. You can identify the IPv6 address of your default router interface by using the *ipconfig, netsh interface ipv6 show routes*, or *route print* command. You can also specify the zone ID, which is the interface ID for the default gateway on the interface on which you want the ICMPv6 Echo Request messages to be sent. When you have ensured that you can reach the default gateway on your local subnet, ping the remote host by its IPv6 address. Note that you cannot ping a remote host (or a router interface) by its link-local IPv6 address because link-local addresses are not routable.

If you can connect to the default gateway but cannot reach the remote destination address, trace the route to the remote destination by using the *tracert –d* command followed by the destination IPv6 address. The *–d* command-line switch prevents the *tracert* tool from performing a DNS reverse query on router interfaces in the routing path. This speeds up the display of the routing path. If you want more information about the routers in the path, and particularly if you want to verify router reliability, use the *pathping -d* command, again followed by the destination IPv6 address.

 Quick Check

- Which *netsh* command could you use to identify the IPv6 address of your default router interface?

Quick Check Answer

- *netsh interface ipv6 show route*

Troubleshooting Connectivity

As an experienced administrator, you know that if you cannot connect to a remote host, you (or, more probably, a more junior member of your team) first should check the various hardware connections (wired and wireless) in your organization and ensure that all network devices are up and running. If these basic checks do not find the problem, the Internet Protocol Security (IPsec) configuration might not be properly configured, or firewall problems (such as incorrectly configured packet filters) might exist.

You can use the IP Security Policies Management Microsoft Management Console (MMC) snap-in to check and configure IPsec policies and the Windows Firewall with Advanced Security snap-in to check and configure IPv6-based packet filters. Figures 1-10 and 1-11 show these tools.

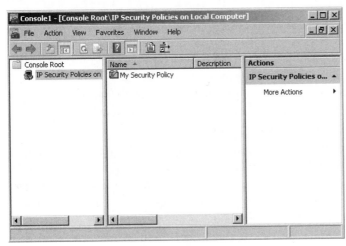

FIGURE 1-10 The IP Security Policies Management snap-in.

MORE INFO   USING NETSH

As with most settings, you can use the *netsh* command instead of the GUI. For example, commands based on *netsh advfirewall* configure the new IPsec features introduced in Windows Server 2008. For more information, see *http://technet2.microsoft.com/windows-server2008/en/library/29933987-90dc-471c-98aa-04e5fa245bb11033.mspx?mfr=true.* Chapter 4, "Network Access Security" discusses this functionality in detail.

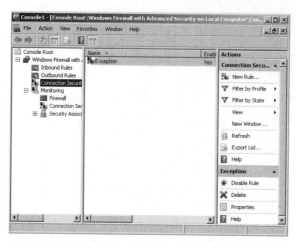

FIGURE 1-11 The Windows Firewall with Advanced Security snap-in.

NOTE   IPSEC6

The IPsec6 tool is not implemented in Windows Server 2008.

You might be unable to reach a local or remote destination because of incorrect or missing routes in the local IPv6 routing table. You can use the *route print, netstat –r* or *netsh interface ipv6 show route* command to view the local IPv6 routing table and verify that you have a route corresponding to your local subnet and to your default gateway. Note that the *netstat –r* command displays both IPv4 and IPv6 routing tables.

If you have multiple default routes with the same metric, you might need to modify your IPv6 router configurations so that the default route with the lowest metric uses the interface that connects to the network with the largest number of subnets. You can use the *netsh inter-face ipv6 set route* command to modify an existing route. To add a route to the IPv6 routing table, use the *netsh interface ipv6 add route* command. The *netsh interface ipv6 delete route* command removes an existing route. You need to run the command console as an administrator to use these commands.

Verifying IPv6-Based TCP Connections

If the telnet client tool is installed, you can verify that a TCP connection can be established to a TCP port by entering the *telnet* command followed by the destination IPv6 address and the TCP port number, as in this example: *telnet fec0:0:0:fffe::1 80*. If telnet successfully creates a TCP connection, the telnet> prompt appears, and you can type telnet commands. If the tool cannot create a connection, it will return an error message.

> **MORE INFO** **INSTALLING TELNET CLIENT**
>
> For more information about telnet, including how to install the telnet client, search Windows Server 2008 Help for "Telnet: frequently asked questions."

Configuring IP Settings

You can configure IPv4 and IPv6 settings through the network interface GUI, and you do this in the practice session at the end of this lesson. However, many professional administrators prefer to use the *command prompt* interface for this purpose. Using commands is often quicker and easier, and commands can be placed in batch files to automate procedures.

EXAM TIP

The upgrade examinations are designed for professional administrators, and configuration through the command prompt is at least as likely to be tested as configuration through a GUI.

The *netsh.exe* command is a very powerful and versatile tool. You can use it to configure IPv4 and IPv6 settings on network interfaces. You can also use the tool to configure DHCP settings (as described in Lesson 2, "Configuring IPsec," of this chapter) and routers, routing protocols, and the Routing and Remote Access Service (RRAS). The main tool to configure Server Core is *netsh*.

You can use *netsh* to show the current settings on your network interfaces, for example:

```
netsh interface ipv4 show config
```

```
netsh interface ipv6 show addresses
```

> **NOTE** **FIGURES SHOWING NETSH COMMANDS**
>
> I have decided not to include figures showing the output of *netsh* commands in this section. Command prompt captures do not come out very well in a book and are difficult to read. However, the main reason is that I hope you will try out the commands yourself and view the real output.

With *netsh*, you configure your computer's IP address and other TCP/IP-related settings. For example, the following command configures the interface named Local Area Connection with the static 172.16.1.100 IP address, the 255.255.255.0 subnet mask, and a 172.16.1.1 default gateway:

```
netsh interface ipv4 set address name="Local Area Connection" static 172.16.1.100
255.255.255.0 172.16.1.1
```

You can also configure an interface to receive its settings automatically, for example:

```
netsh interface ipv4 set address name="Local Area Connection" dhcp
```

If you do not have a DHCP server on your network (you configure this in Lesson 2) and your network is isolated from the Internet, your interface will be configured through APIPA. Test this with the *netsh interface ipv4 show config* command.

If the Local Area Connection interface is the one you set up with a 10.0.0.11 IPv4 address based on the instructions in the "Before You Begin" section, it is a very good idea to restore your settings by using this command:

```
netsh interface ipv4 set address name="Local Area Connection" static 10.0.0.11
255.255.255.0
```

Because you have not specified a default gateway, this setting will be blank. Again, you can test your settings with *netsh interface ipv4 show config*.

You can also configure DNS and (if relevant) WINS settings though the command line, for example:

```
netsh interface ip set dns "Local Area Connection" static 10.0.0.11
```

and:

```
netsh interface ip set wins "Local Area Connection" static 10.0.0.11
```

If you want the address of your DNS server to be configured through DHCP, you can enter this command:

```
netsh interface ip set dns "Local Area Connection" dhcp
```

Similarly, to specify automatic WINS settings, you can use this command:

```
netsh interface ip set wins "Local Area Connection" dhcp
```

You can use the same technique to configure IPv6 settings, for example:

```
netsh interface ipv6 set address "Local Area Connection" fec0:0:0:fffe::11
```

Other IPv6 netsh commands were given earlier in this lesson in the section, "Using IPv6 Tools."

If you are experimenting with IP settings, you can export your current settings to a text file and import them later. In this example, the file is saved on the root of the C drive. In practice, you would create a subfolder to store your configurations. The following command exports your current IP settings to a text file:

```
netsh –c interface dump > c:\configuration1.txt
```

You can import your saved configuration from the text file you created with the following command:

```
netsh –f c:\configuration1.txt
```

These commands export and import all IP settings, not merely IP addresses, and you might get more output than you expect from the import command. You can create and export a number of configurations that you want to use in different locations or for different purposes and import them as required.

> **MORE INFO   NETSH COMMANDS FOR INTERFACE (IPV4 AND IPV6)**
>
> It is possible to describe only a small selection of the available *netsh* commands in this section. For more commands and more information, see *http://technet2.microsoft .com/windowsserver2008/en/library/29933987-90dc-471c-98aa-04e5fa245bb11033 .mspx?mfr=true*.

PRACTICE: Configuring IPv6 Connectivity

In this practice session, you configure a site-local IPv6 address on your domain controller and client computer interfaces that connect to your private subnet (the IPv4 10.0.0.0/24 subnet). You test IPv6 connectivity between your client and domain controller.

> **NOTE   LOGGING ON TO THE DOMAIN CONTROLLER**
>
> You perform the server configurations in this practice session by logging on interactively to the domain controller with an administrative-level account. However, in a production network, this would be bad practice. If you want to make the exercises more realistic, you can log on to your client PC and connect to your server through Remote Desktop or run Administrative Tools on a client and specify the server within the tool.

EXERCISE   Configure IPv6

In this exercise, you configure IPv6 site-local addresses on your domain controller and client computers and test connectivity.

1. Log on to your domain controller on the *contoso.internal* domain by using the Kim_Akers account.

2. In Control Panel, double-click Network And Sharing Center. If you are not using Classic View, first click Network And Internet, and then click Network And Sharing Center. Click Manage Network Connections.

3. Right-click the interface that connects to your private network and choose Properties.

4. If a UAC dialog box appears, click Continue.

5. Select Internet Protocol Version 6 (TCP/IPv6) and click Properties.

6. Configure an fec0:0:0:fffe::1 static site-local IPv6 address.

7. Configure an fec0:0:0:fffe::1 DNS server address.

8. Click OK. Close the Local Area Connections Properties dialog box.

9. Close the Network And Connections dialog box.

10. Close Network And Sharing Center. Log off from the domain controller.

11. Log on to your client PC on the *contoso.internal* domain by using the Kim_Akers account.

12. In Control Panel, double-click Network And Sharing Center. If you are not using Classic View, first click Network And Internet, and then click Network And Sharing Center. Click Manage Network Connections.

13. Right-click the interface that connects to your private network and click Properties.

14. If a UAC dialog box appears, click Continue.

15. Select Internet Protocol Version 6 (TCP/IPv6) and click Properties.

16. Configure an fec0:0:0:fffe::a static site-local IPv6 address.

17. Configure an fec0:0:0:fffe::1 DNS server address.

    The Properties dialog box should look similar to Figure 1-12.

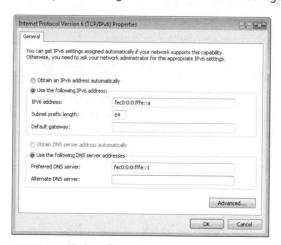

FIGURE 1-12 IPv6 configuration on the client.

18. Click OK. Close the Local Area Connections Properties dialog box.

19. Close the Network And Connections dialog box.

20. Close Network And Sharing Center.

> **NOTE VIRTUAL MACHINES**
>
> If you are using a virtual machine to implement your server and client on the same PC, it is a good idea to close your virtual machine and restart your computer after configuring interfaces.

21. Open the command console on the client computer. Enter **ping fec0:0:0:fffe::1**.

    You should get the response, shown in Figure 1-13, from the domain controller.

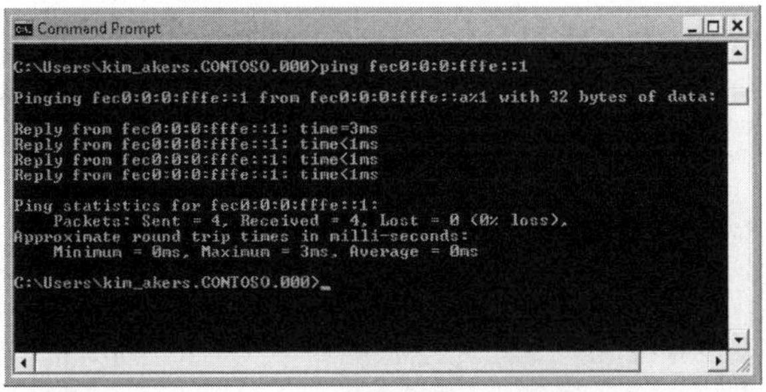

FIGURE 1-13 Pinging the domain controller from the client.

> **NOTE FIREWALL CONFIGURATION**
>
> If the firewall on either your Glasgow domain controller or your Melbourne client blocks ICMP traffic, you must reconfigure this setting (or settings) before this command will work. As a quick fix, you could disable one or both firewalls, but remember to enable them again at the end of the exercise.

22. Enter **ping glasgow**. Note that the domain controller host name resolves to the IPv6 address.

23. Log off from the client computer.

24. Log on to your domain controller, using the Kim_Akers account.

25. Open the command console on your domain controller.

26. Enter **ping fec0:0:0:fffe::a**.

    You should get the response shown in Figure 1-14.

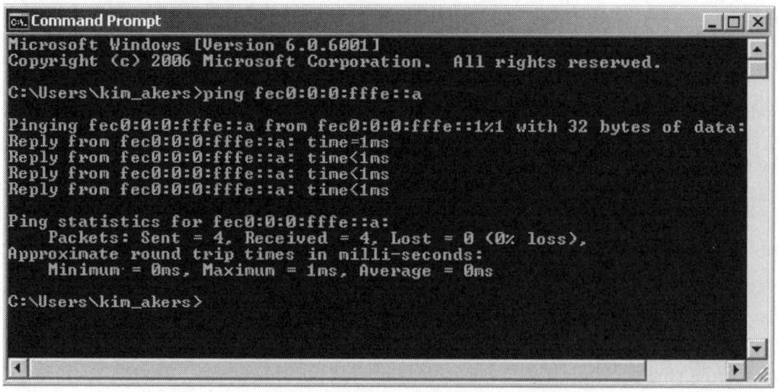

FIGURE 1-14 Pinging the client from the domain controller.

27. Enter **netsh interface ipv6 show neighbors**.

   Figure 1-15 shows the fec0:0:0:fffe::a interface as a neighbor on the same subnet as the domain controller.

FIGURE 1-15 Showing the domain controller neighbors.

Lesson Summary

- IPv4 addressing, subnetting, supernetting, CIDR, VLSM, and NAT are implemented in Windows Server 2008 in exactly the same way as in Windows Server 2003.

- IPv6 supports unicast, multicast, and anycast addresses. Unicast addresses can be global, site-local, link-local, or special. IPX and NSAP mapped addresses are also supported.

- IPv6 is fully supported in Windows Server 2008 and addresses problems, such as lack of address space, that are associated with IPv4.

- IPv6 is designed to be backward-compatible, and IPV4-compatible addresses can be specified.

- Tools to configure and troubleshoot IPv6 include *ping*, *ipconfig*, *tracert*, *pathping*, and *netsh*. You can also configure IPv6 by using the TCP/IPv6 Properties GUI.

- You can use *netsh* commands to configure IPv4 and IPv6 settings.

Lesson Review

Use the following questions to test your knowledge of the information in Lesson 1, "Configuring IPv4 and IPv6 Addressing." The questions are also available on the companion DVD if you prefer to review them in electronic form.

> **NOTE ANSWERS**
>
> Answers to these questions and explanations of why each answer choice is right or wrong are located in the "Answers" section at the end of the book.

1. Which type of IPv6 address is equivalent to a public unicast IPv4 address?

   A. Site-local

   B. Global

   C. Link-local

   D. Special

2. A node has an fe80::6b:28c:16a7:d43a link-local IPv6 address. What is its corresponding solicited-node address?

   A. ff02::1:ffa7:d43a

   B. ff02::1:ff00:0:16a7:d43a

   C. fec0::1:ff a7:d43a

   D. fec0::1:ff00:0:16a7:d43a

3. Which protocol uses ICMPv6 messages to manage the interaction of neighboring nodes?

   A. ARP

   B. EUI-64

   C. DHCPv6

   D. ND

4. Which type of compatibility address obscures its corresponding IPv4 external address by XORing it with 0xffffffff?

   A. Teredo

   B. ISATAP

   C. IPV4-compatible

   D. IPv4-mapped

5. Which command enables you to configure an IPv6 address manually on a specified interface?

   A. *netsh interface ipv6 show address*

   B. *netsh interface ipv6 add address*

   C. *netsh interface ipv6 set interface*

   D. *netsh interface ipv6 set address*

6. You want to configure the network interface Local Area Connection on your computer with the 192.168.10.10 static IPv4 address. The subnet mask is 255.255.255.0, and the default gateway is 192.168.10.1. Which command do you use?

   A. *netsh interface ipv4 set address name="Local Area Connection" static 192.168.10.10 255.255.255.0 192.168.10.1*

   B. *netsh interface ipv4 set address name="Local Area Connection" 192.168.10.10 255.255.255.0 192.168.10.1*

   C. *netsh interface ipv4 set address name="Local Area Connection" static 192.168.10.1 255.255.255.0 192.168.10.10*

   D. *netsh interface ipv4 set address name="Local Area Connection" static 192.168.10,10 255.255.255,0 192.168.10.1*

Lesson 2: Configuring DHCP

As a Windows Server 2003 professional, you should know that DHCPv4 can allocate IPv4 addresses, subnet masks, default gateway addresses, DNS and WINS server addresses, and many other settings and that APIPA can automatically configure IPv4 addresses for use in an isolated private network. This lesson summarizes the DHCPv4 topics that you studied for your Windows Server 2003 examinations and then goes on to examine DHCPv6 scopes. Much of what you already know about DHCPv4 also applies to DHCPv6 (for example, the 80:20 rule). Where this is the case, the lesson talks about DHCP rather than about DHCPv4 and DHCPv6.

> **After this lesson, you will be able to:**
> - Install the DHCP server role.
> - Configure a DHCPv6 scope.
> - Configure DHCP options.
> - Describe how DHCP interacts with other server components.
>
> **Estimated lesson time: 40 minutes**

 REAL WORLD

Ian McLean

A long time ago, when I was an electronics engineer, I worked on the design of one of the first automatic teller machines (ATMs). The device was manufactured and sold to several major banking corporations. Suddenly, banking became a 24-hour service. Customers could withdraw cash from their accounts anytime, morning, noon, and night.

Except that in many bank branches, it didn't happen. Local managers insisted that the ATMs were switched off when the bank was closed, rather defeating the purpose of the service. The problem was perceived loss of control. "There's no way," one manager told me, "that anyone is taking money from my bank when I'm not there!"

The same problem bedeviled DHCP when it was introduced and, in some cases, bedevils it still. Some network managers want to decide exactly what IP address is allocated to what machine. The PC nearest the door is 10.0.0.1, the next one is 10.0.0.2, and so on. They argue that if they know exactly which IP address is allocated to which computer, they can tell where a troublemaker or hacker is located (but not necessarily who it is). They claim that DHCP is a security threat (in spite of its ability to track an IP address to a computer's hardware address). The real reason is, of course, lack of control. The manager is no longer allocating addresses as he or she thinks fit.

The worst case I know of is a network of just under 10,000 hosts, all of them still configured manually. Every other technical person in the organization is desperate for automatic configuration, but the man at the top prohibits it. Needless to say, he does not, himself, configure hosts or debug the resulting network problems.

Most, if not all, ATMs are now switched on 24/7, but it's taken 40 years to get there. Let's hope it's a bit quicker with DHCP.

Summarizing DHCP Features

This section provides a brief review of the DHCP features you studied for your Windows 2003 examinations. If you come across a feature that you have forgotten about or are not sure of, please review it.

MORE INFO   **WINDOWS SERVER 2003 DHCP**

All of the DHCPv4 features in Windows Server 2003 are also implemented in Windows Server 2008, and many of them also apply to DHCPv6. For more information that will help your review, access *http://technet2.microsoft.com/windowsserver/en/library/e24cbe2a-b9f4-412d-9a4a-1c085b2866f11033.mspx?mfr=true* and follow the links.

When you studied for your Windows Server 2003 qualifications, you learned that DHCPv4 enables you to assign IPv4 addresses to network clients automatically and dynamically and to automate IPv4 address and option configuration and distribution across a network. You saw that DHCPv4 options enable you to configure a DHCPv4 server to supply configuration values when assigning a DHCPv4 lease so that you can configure a large number of computers at one time and change configuration as necessary.

Infrastructure Models

You should be aware that three DHCP infrastructure models exist, the centralized DHCP infrastructure model, the decentralized DHCP infrastructure model, and the combined DHCP infrastructure model, and that the optimum locations for your DHCP servers depend upon the model your organization employs. You should know that DHCP works with DNS so that host and (if appropriate) pointer (PTR) records are added to DNS zones when DHCP allocates IP addresses.

DHCP Relay Agents

You should already know that a centralized DHCP (DHCPv4 or DHCPv6) topology requires the deployment of DHCP/bootstrap protocol (BOOTP) relay agents. Additional hardware resources are not generally required for DHCP relay agents; in most cases, the routers positioned between each subnet can assume this role. You learned that where routers cannot relay DHCP messages, you could configure a server to act as a DHCP/BOOTP relay agent. You discovered that DHCP servers are not required for every subnet if the connecting routers support DHCP/BOOTP relay agents.

Optimizing Performance

When you studied for your Windows Server 2003 examinations, you learned that you can optimize the performance of your DHCP servers (in Windows 2008, servers with the DHCP Server role installed) by extending the duration of the IP address lease. You saw that you could enable DHCP support for multiple subnets by using DHCP relay agents, and you could implement DHCP fail-over protection over multiple subnets by using split scope configuration and the 80:20 rule. Other high-availability solutions are clustered DHCP servers and standby servers.

Lease Duration

In the days before private addressing and NAT, there was a sound argument for keeping lease durations short. If you had only a limited number of IP addresses to lease and you had a long duration, then a faulty computer taken out of service would retain its lease for a long time, until the lease expired. As a result, DHCP could run out of IP addresses to lease. Private IP ranges have no shortage of IP addresses. The 10.0.0.0/8 range has over 17 million. Therefore, this problem no longer exists on most networks, and lease durations can be increased. Infinite leases are not recommended because they can cause problems if a computer for which you have set up a reservation is replaced. You cannot simply change the MAC address of the reservation to that of the replacement computer because the replaced computer has that IP address forever, and you need to delete the lease explicitly. However, long lease times have performance advantages because you use the resources required to renew a lease less frequently.

Dynamic and Secure Dynamic Updates

`You should be aware that DHCP provides support for DNS dynamic updates and that DHCP and DNS work with Active Directory to perform secure DNS dynamic updates. DHCP also works with Active Directory Domain Services (AD DS) to prevent unauthorized DHCP servers from running on the network. For example, if a DHCP server is configured with an address scope that overlaps a scope already configured on another DHCP server on the network, the DHCP server will be designated as a rogue server and will not distribute configurations. The first DHCP server on a network running Windows Server 2003 or Windows Server 2008 is automatically authorized in the domain, but you must authorize additional servers manually.

Authorizing Multihomed DHCP Servers

You can sometimes have problems if you authorize a multihomed DHCP server when you install the DHCP Server role by using Server Manager. In this case, when you start the DHCP MMC snap-in, you might find that the multihomed DHCP server is not authorized.

This occurs when Server Manager uses an incorrect IP address for the multihomed DHCP server that is being authorized in AD DS. When a DHCP server contains multiple network adapters and is attached to multiple networks, the IP address Server Manager uses might be invalid for the domain controller that authorizes the DHCP server. In this case, AD DS does not recognize the DHCP server when the DHCP Server role is installed. Server Manager does not prompt you when AD DS does not recognize the DHCP server. The solution in this case is to authorize the DHCP server in the DHCP MMC snap-in manually.

In general, restrict the DHCP server to using only one adapter if the computer has multiple adapters. Also, you cannot have a DHCP server adapter with a dynamic address.

DHCP Scopes and Options

You learned that before DHCP clients can use a DHCP server for dynamic TCP/IP configuration, you must define and activate scopes to manage IP address allocation and distribute options (for example, the default gateway IP address, the DNS server IP address, and the DNS domain name). You saw that scope options inherit server option settings but that any specifically configured scope option overrides the corresponding server option. The same set of options is available for scope and server.

To prevent address conflicts, you must define scopes that exclude the IP addresses of statically configured hosts. You can set exclusion ranges to exclude a static IP address range within a scope. You can also create reservations so that specific hosts, identified by their MAC addresses, are always configured with the same IP address. You can specify DHCP options for reservations. Reservation option settings are inherited from scope option settings, but a specifically configured reservation option overrides the corresponding scope option for that reservation. The same set of options is available for server, scope, and reservation.

EXAM TIP

Remember that scope options inherit the server option settings, and reservation options inherit the scope option settings. A specifically configured scope option overrides the setting inherited from the corresponding server option, and a specifically configured reservation option overrides the setting inherited from the corresponding scope option.

Configuring Reservations

When you are configuring reservations, you need to know the MAC address of the host for which you are reserving an IP address. The Windows Server 2008 *getmac* command-line tool enables you to obtain the MAC addresses of remote computers easily. If you want to avoid typing computer names for every reservation, ensure that your DNS server hosts a remote lookup zone with dynamic updates enabled. When a client reboots, its PTR record is registered in this reverse lookup zone.

When PTR records are available, you can use the *getmac* command with the */s* switch to specify a remote computer and then pipe the output into the clipboard to avoid having to type out the MAC address manually. For example, to create a DHCP reservation for a computer whose IPv4 address is currently 10.0.0.21, open the New Reservation dialog box from the DHCP console, and then type the following command at a command prompt:

```
getmac /s 10.0.0.21 | clip
```

Open Notepad and paste the clipboard contents into the blank text file. You can then copy the MAC address that the *getmac* command has generated from Notepad into the MAC Address text box of the New Reservation dialog box. In the same dialog box, type the IP address you want to assign and a name for the reservation and click Add.

This technique significantly reduces the time for creating DHCP reservations and prevents the inevitable errors that occur when you type in MAC addresses manually.

Using *netsh* Commands

You can configure scopes and reservations through the DHCP console, but many administrators prefer to use the command prompt. This is the only method available to configure settings on Server Core, which does not implement GUIs. As with most configuration settings, you use *netsh* commands. For example, to add the server Glasgow to a list of authorized DHCP servers, you would enter the command:

```
netsh dhcp add server glasgow
```

To add a scope named GlasgowScope with a 10.0.0.0/24 IPv4 network address, you would enter this command:

```
netsh dhcp server add scope 10.0.0.0 255.255.255.0 GlasgowScope
```

When you have created the scope, you can, for example, add a reservation, add an excluded range, add a range of IP addresses to the scope, delete a reservation, delete an excluded range, delete a range of IP addresses, delete a lease, set an option value, and carry out many more configurations.

For example, to add a range of IP addresses, 10.0.0.1 through 10.0.0.254, to the scope, you would enter the command:

```
netsh dhcp server scope 10.0.0.0 add iprange 10.0.0.1 10.0.0.254
```

To reserve the 10.0.0.101 IPv4 address for a computer with the 0040D08EECE4 MAC address, you would enter this command:

```
netsh dhcp server scope 10.0.0.0 add reservedip 10.0.0.101 0040d08eece4
```

To exclude the 10.0.0.1 through 10.0.0.49 range, you would enter this command:

```
netsh dhcp server scope 10.0.0.0 add excluderange 10.0.0.1 10.0.0.49
```

> **MORE INFO   NETSH DHCP COMMANDS**
>
> Only a very small subset of the *netsh* DHCP commands are described here. For more information and a comprehensive list, access *http://technet.microsoft.com/en-us/library /cc772372.aspx* and select **Netsh Commands for Dynamic Host Configuration Server** in the left pane.

DHCP Option Classes

Windows Server 2003 and Windows Server 2008 DHCP include vendor-defined and user-defined option classes that enable you to configure the parameters necessary for network clients to meet the requirements of custom applications. Equipment from different vendors can use different option numbers. You can use the vendor class identifier and the vendor-specific option to add and configure vendor-defined classes. You can also add and configure user-defined classes that are assigned to clients identified by a common need for a similar DHCP option configuration. You can configure scopes to assign the option classes to clients.

> **MORE INFO   VENDOR CLASS IDENTIFIER AND THE VENDOR-SPECIFIC OPTION**
>
> For more information about the vendor class identifier and the vendor-specific option, see *http://rfc.net/rfc2132.txt*.

> **MORE INFO   DEFINING NEW DHCP OPTIONS**
>
> Defining new DHCP option codes and message types is not within the normal remit of the network or domain administrator and is unlikely to feature in your examination. Nevertheless, if you want to learn more about this out of professional interest, see *http://www .rfc-editor.org/rfc/rfc2939.txt*.

An *options class* is a client category that enables the DHCP server to assign options only to particular clients within a scope. When an options class is added to the server, clients of that class can be offered options specific to that class. As stated earlier in this section, option classes can be vendor-defined or user-defined. These are commonly known as vendor and user classes.

You can use vendor classes to assign vendor-specific options to DHCP clients identified as a vendor type. Typically, you cannot configure a vendor class because the class identification is built into the client software of the client and you do not need to populate the class by enabling a client setting.

You can use user classes to assign options to sets of clients identified as sharing a common need for similar DHCP options configuration. User classes are configurable, and you can create new user classes and populate them by configuring a setting on the clients you select.

> **NOTE** **THE DEFAULT USER CLASS**
>
> All DHCP clients belong to the default user class. This is the class in which all options are created by default. When you want an option to apply to all DHCP clients, regardless of their class identification, you should leave the option configured for the default user class.

To implement a user class, you must define the class at the DHCP server by assigning an ID and a set of options. You then assign selected client computers to the class by using the *ipconfig /setclassid* command. When these clients communicate with DHCP servers, they announce their class ID and inherit the options of that class along with the options of the default user class. If a class ID is not manually configured, the client inherits only the options of the default user class.

Superscopes

Windows Server 2003 DHCP introduced superscopes, and you probably studied this topic extensively for your Windows Server 2003 examinations. Superscopes are administrative groupings of scopes that can support multiple logical IP subnets on the same physical subnet. They contain a list of member scopes that can be activated simultaneously. You cannot configure scope-level properties on superscopes but must instead configure these on the member scopes. Superscopes allow a DHCP server to provide leases from more than one scope to clients on a single physical network.

Multicast Support

Both the Windows Server 2003 DHCP service and the Windows Server 2008 DHCP service support Multicast Address Dynamic Client Allocation Protocol (MADCAP) with multicast scopes. MADCAP enables the dynamic assignment and configuration of IP multicast addresses on TCP/IP-based networks. These scopes provide ranges of multicast IP addresses. Multicast scopes do not support DHCP-assigned options, but otherwise, you can configure a multicast scope in the same way that you configure a regular DHCP scope.

MORE INFO   MADCAP

For more information about MADCAP, see *http://tools.ietf.org/rfc/rfc2730.txt.*

Configuring Clients through DHCPv6

You can choose stateless or stateful configuration when configuring hosts by using DHCPv6. Stateless configuration does not generate a host address—which is instead autoconfigured—but it can, for example, specify the address of a DNS server. Stateful configuration specifies host addresses.

Whether you choose stateful or stateless configuration, you can assign the IPv6 addresses of DNS servers through the DNS Recursive Name Server DHCPv6 option (option 0023). If you choose stateful configuration, the IPv6 addresses of DNS servers can be configured as a scope option, so different scopes could have different DNS servers. Scope options override server options for that scope. This is the preferred method of configuring DNS server IPv6 addresses, which are not configured through router discovery.

With DHCPv6, an IPv6 host can receive subnet prefixes and other configuration parameters. A common use of DHCPv6 for Windows-based IPv6 hosts is to configure the IPv6 addresses of DNS servers automatically.

Currently, when you configure an IPv6 scope, you specify the 64-bit prefix. By default, DHCPv6 can allocate host addresses from the entire 64-bit range for that prefix. This allows for IPv6 host addresses that are configured through adapter hardware. You can specify exclusion ranges, so if you wanted to allocate only host addresses in the fec0::0:0:0:1 through fec0::0:0:0:fffe range, you would exclude fec0::0:0:1:1 through fec0::ffff:ffff:ffff:fffe addresses.

 Quick Check

- Which protocol enables the dynamic assignment and configuration of IP multicast addresses on TCP/IP-based networks?

Quick Check Answer

- MADCAP

Several DHCPv6 options exist. Arguably, the most useful option specifies the DNS server. Other options are concerned with compatibility with other systems that support IPv6, such as the UNIX Network Integration Service (NIS).

DHCPv6 is similar to DHCPv4 in many respects. For example, scope options override server options, and DHCPv6 requests and acknowledgements can pass through BOOTP-enabled routers and layer-3 switches (almost all modern routers and switches act as DHCP relay agents) so that a DHCPv6 server can configure clients on a remote subnet.

EXAM TIP

If you want to configure a Windows Server 2008 server as a DHCP relay agent, you must install the Routing and Remote Access Services (RRAS) role service.

As with DHCPv4, you can implement the 80:20 rule so that a DHCPv6 server is configured with a scope for its own subnet that contains 80 percent of the available addresses for that subnet and a second scope for a remote subnet that contains 20 percent of the available addresses for that subnet. A similarly configured DHCPv6 server on the remote subnet provides failover. If either server fails, the hosts on both subnets still receive their configurations.

For example, Tailspin Toys' Melbourne office network has two private VLANs that have been allocated the following site-local networks:

- VLAN1: fec0:0:0:aaaa::1 through fec0:0:0:aaaa::fffe
- VLAN2: fec0:0:0:aaab::1 through fec0:0:0:aaab::fffe

Exceptions are defined so that IPv6 addresses on the VLANS can be statically allocated to servers. In this case, you could implement the 80:20 rule by configuring the following DHCPv6 scopes on the DHCP server on VLAN1:

- fec0:0:0:aaaa::1 through fec0:0:0:aaaa::cccb
- fec0:0:0:aaab::cccc through fec0:0:0:aaab::fffe

You would then configure the following DHCPv6 scopes on the DHCP server on VLAN2:

- fec0:0:0:aaab::1 through fec0:0:0:aaab::cccb
- fec0:0:0:aaaa::cccc through fec0:0:0:aaaa::fffe

DHCP servers, and especially DHCP servers that host 20-percent scopes, are excellent candidates for virtualization because they experience only limited input/output (I/O) activity.

NOTE **VIRTUAL DNS SERVERS**

Like DHCP servers, DNS servers—particularly secondary DNS servers— experience only limited I/O activity and are good candidates for virtualization.

For example, Trey Research is a single-site organization but has five buildings within its site, connected by fiber-optic links to a layer-3 switch configured to allocate a VLAN to each building. VLAN1, allocated to the main office, supports the majority of the company's computers. VLAN3 supports most of the remainder. VLAN2, VLAN4, and VLAN5 each support only a few computers.

In this case, you can configure the DHCP server on VLAN1 to host 80 percent of the VLAN1 address range. You can configure a virtual DHCP server on the same VLAN to host 20 percent of the VLAN2 through VLAN5 address ranges. On VLAN3, you can configure a DHCP server to host the 80-percent ranges for VLAN2 through VLAN5 and a virtual server to host the 20-percent range for VLAN1. If either server fails, hosts on all the VLANs can continue to receive their configurations through DHCP.

NOTE   THE 80:20 RULE

The 80:20 rule is typically implemented within a site because a WAN link (with routers over which you have no control) might not pass DHCP traffic. In general, if you implement DHCP failover by using the 80:20 rule, you need at least two DHCP servers per site.

Installing the DHCP server role and configuring a DHCPv6 scope are practical procedures and are therefore covered in detail in the practice session later in this lesson.

Integrating DHCP with Network Access Protection

You can further increase security on your network by integrating DHCPv4 and DHCPv6 with Network Access Protection (NAP). NAP provides policy enforcement components that help ensure that computers connecting to or communicating on a network comply with administrator-defined requirements for system health and limit the access of computers that do not meet these requirements to a restricted network. The restricted network contains the resources needed to update computers so that they meet the health requirements. When you integrate DHCP with NAP, a computer must be compliant to obtain an unlimited access IP address configuration from a DHCP server. Network access for noncompliant computers is limited through an IP address configuration that allows access only to a restricted network. DHCP enforcement ensures health policy requirements every time a DHCP client attempts to lease or renew an IP address configuration. DHCP enforcement also actively monitors the health status of the NAP client and renews the IP address configuration for access only to the restricted network if the client becomes noncompliant.

When planning DHCP integration with NAP, you must decide whether DHCP NAP enforcement will be enabled on all DHCP scopes, selected DHCP scopes, or no DHCP scopes at all. In addition, you must configure which NAP profile to use for DHCP NAP enforcement. Finally, you must determine how a DHCP server will behave when the Network Policy Server (NPS) is unreachable. A DHCP server can be configured to allow full access, allow restricted access, or drop client packets when the NPS server is unreachable.

MORE INFO   NAP

To learn more about NAP, see *http://technet.microsoft.com/en-us/network/bb545879.aspx*. Also, Chapter 4 gives a more detailed discussion of NAP with DHCP enforcement.

Installing the DHCP Server Role on Server Core

You can deploy the DHCP server role on Server Core by entering the *start /w ocsetup DHCPServerCore* command. This technique is particularly applicable to more complex networks. On Server Core, you configure and administer the DHCP server role by using commands such as *netsh* and *net start* because GUI facilities are not available. By default, the DHCP service does not start automatically on Server Core. You can start the service manually on both Server Core and a full installation by entering the *net start DHCPServer* command. You can configure the service to start automatically on Server Core when Windows starts by entering the *sc config dhcpserver start= auto* command.

> **MORE INFO**   **THE WINDOWS OPTIONAL COMPONENT SETUP TOOL**
>
> For more information about the Ocsetup.exe tool, see *http://support.microsoft.com /kb/936209.*

> **MORE INFO**   **SERVER CORE INSTALLATION**
>
> For more information about installing server roles on Server Core, see *http://technet2 .microsoft.com/windowsserver2008/en/library/47a23a74-e13c-46de-8d30 -ad0afb1eaffc1033.mspx?mfr=true.*

EXAM TIP

Take care to distinguish the command that enables you to install the DHCP server role on Server Core, *start /w ocsetup DHCPServerCore*, and the command that installs the role on a full server installation, *servermanagercmd -install dhcp*.

Using Hyper-V with DHCP

Hyper-V provides a software infrastructure and basic management tools that you can use to create and manage a virtualized server computing environment in Windows Server 2008. A virtualized server environment helps you reduce the costs of operating and maintaining physical servers and reduce the amount of hardware needed to run your server workloads. It can also reduce development cost by reducing the amount of time it takes to set up hardware and software and reproduce test environments.

One of the main advantages of a virtual environment is the ability to create virtual clusters that improve server availability and provide fail-over protection without using as many physical computers as you would need in a failover configuration that does not use virtualization. However, problems can occur when you use DHCP to configure virtual computers in a Hyper-V cluster. It is possible to create a rogue DHCP server on a virtual network and for that rogue server to issue configurations within the cluster. If the Hyper-V host is configured to use DHCP and the rogue DHCP server virtual machine answers first, the Hyper-V host can be configured with an invalid DHCP lease.

You must be very careful if you attempt to implement a DHCP server on a computer running Hyper-V. If a virtual network is linked to your network interface card (NIC), DHCP will not work on the local area network (LAN). The LAN NIC is effectively disabled in the parent partition, which is linked to the virtual network, not the physical network. Microsoft recommends that you run nothing except the Hyper-V role in the parent partition. If you do not use DHCP to configure a Hyper-V virtual cluster, the Failover Cluster Management wizard asks you to supply any IP address information manually.

> **MORE INFO**   **HYPER-V**
>
> For more information about Hyper-V, see *http://technet2.microsoft.com/windowsserver2008 /en/library/5341cb70-0508-4201-a6da-dcac1a65fd351033.mspx?mfr=true.*

DHCP in the Preboot Execution Environment

The Preboot Execution Environment (PXE) enables you to boot computers by using a network interface that is independent of available data storage devices or installed operating systems. It uses network protocols such as DHCP and Trivial File Transfer Protocol (TFTP) and extends the firmware of the PXE client with a set of predefined application programming interfaces (APIs).

> **NOTE**   **PXE CLIENT**
>
> The term *PXE client* refers to the role that a computer takes in the PXE boot process. A PXE client can be a server, desktop, laptop, or any other computer equipped with a PXE boot code.

The firmware on a PXE client tries to locate a PXE redirection service on the network through the PXE redirection service (Proxy DHCP) to receive information about available PXE boot servers. The firmware then asks the boot server for the file path of a network bootstrap program (NBP), downloads it into the computer's random access memory (RAM) using TFTP, optionally verifies it, and then executes it.

The PXE protocol can be viewed as a combination of DHCP and TFTP. DHCP locates the appropriate boot server or servers; TFTP downloads the initial bootstrap program and additional files.

When a PXE boot is initiated, the PXE read-only memory (ROM) requests an IP address from a DHCP server. As part of this process, the client computer identifies itself as being PXE-enabled. When the client obtains a valid IP address from a DHCP server, it attempts to locate and establish a connection with the PXE server to download NBP.

If you use Windows Deployment Services, the PXE server does not need to be authorized. Authorization checks occur only if you choose to enable authorization checking and the PXE server is configured to listen on port 67. In this case, authorization checks take place only in scenarios in which Windows Deployment Services is running on a computer that does not have the DHCP server role installed. If Windows Deployment Services and DHCP are running on the same physical computer, the DHCP server is listening on port 67 and is responsible for ensuring authorization.

Windows Deployment Services

You will typically use Windows Deployment Services (WDS) if you deploy new computers in a medium or large organization. WDS enables you to manage images and unattended installation scripts and provides attended and unattended installation options. It facilitates the partitioning and formatting of physical media, the installation of the client operating system, and post-configuration tasks. WDS simplifies installation and provides consistency across your network environment.

WDS provides server components, client components, and management components. Server components include a PXE server, a TFTP server, and a shared folder and image repository that contain boot images, install images, and files needed for the network boot. They also provide a networking layer, a multicast component, and a diagnostics component.

Client components include a GUI. When a user selects an operating system image, the client components communicate with the server components to install the image. Management components consist of a set of tools to manage the server, operating system images, and client computer accounts.

WDS reduces the complexity of deployments and the cost associated with inefficient manual installation processes; facilitates network-based installation of Windows operating systems, including Windows Vista and Windows Server 2008; and deploys Windows images to computers without operating systems. It supports mixed environments that include Windows Vista, Windows Server 2008, Windows XP, and Windows Server 2003 and provides an end-to-end solution for the deployment of Windows operating systems to client computers and servers.

You can configure WDS by using the WDS MMC snap-in or by using the *wdsutil* command. If you choose to use the *wdsutil* command, you must run the command prompt as an administrator.

MORE INFO PXE SERVER

For more information about how PXE Server works, see *http://technet2.microsoft.com*
/windowsserver2008/en/library/c960fc87-8fe3-4691-8242-7ea0968487741033.
mspx?mfr=true. For more information about the components that make up the PXE Server,
see *http://technet2.microsoft.com/windowsserver2008/en/library/7fcc190d-3e21-481b*
-ba54-f0c20a67f60f1033.mspx?mfr=true.

MORE INFO WINDOWS DEPLOYMENT SERVICES

For more information about WDS, access *http://msdn.microsoft.com/en-us/library*
/aa967394(VS.85).aspx and follow the links.

MORE INFO DEPLOYING WINDOWS VISTA

For more information about deploying Windows Vista on client computers, particularly in a
small organization that does not use Windows Deployment Services, see *http://technet2*
.microsoft.com/WindowsVista/en/library/88f80cb7-d44f-47f7-a10d-e23dd53bc3fa1033
.mspx?mfr=true.

PRACTICE: Installing the DHCP Server Role and Configuring a DHCPv6 Scope

In this practice, you install the DHCP server role on your domain controller and configure a
DHCPv6 scope.

NOTE INSTALLING THE DHCP SERVER ROLE ON A DOMAIN CONTROLLER

For convenience, this practice asks you to install the DHCP server role on your domain
controller. In a production network, in which DHCP performs DNS dynamic updates, you
should install the role on a member server rather than on a domain controller. If DHCP is
installed on a domain controller and is configured to perform dynamic updates on behalf
of clients in DNS zones that are configured to allow only secure dynamic update, you
should specify a user account to update the DNS records.

EXERCISE 1 Install the DHCP Server Role

In this exercise, you install the DHCP server role and specify that DHCPv6 can provide stateful
IPv6 configuration.

1. If necessary, log on to the domain controller with the Kim_Akers account.

2. If the Initial Configuration Tasks window opens when you log on, click Add Roles. Otherwise, open Server Manager from Administrative Tools, right-click Roles in the left pane, and click Add Roles.

   The Add Roles Wizard starts.

3. If the Before You Begin page appears, click Next.

4. Select the DHCP Server check box, as shown in Figure 1-16, and click Next.

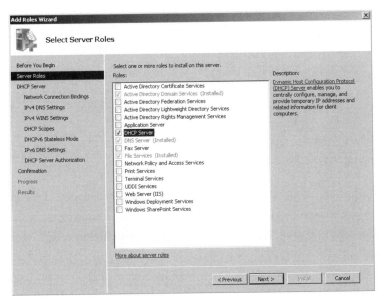

FIGURE 1-16 Selecting to install the DHCP server role.

5. On the DHCP Server page, select Network Connection Bindings. Ensure that only the 10.0.0.11 IPv4 interface is selected for DHCP.

6. Select IPv4 DNS Settings. Verify that the domain is contoso.internal and the Preferred DNS Server IPv4 Address is 10.0.0.11.

7. Select IPv4 WINS Settings. Verify that WINS Is Not Required For Applications On This Network is selected.

8. Select DHCP Scopes.

   Only IPv4 scopes can be defined on this page, so the scope list should be empty.

9. Select DHCPv6 Stateless Mode. Select Disable DHCPv6 Stateless Mode For This Server.

   This enables you to use the DHCP Management Console to configure DHCPv6 after the DHCP server role has been installed. Figure 1-17 shows this setting.

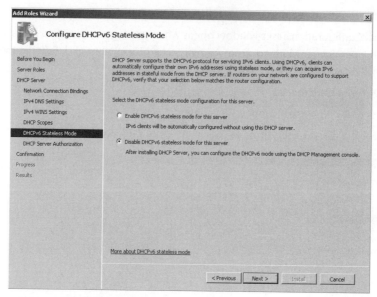

FIGURE 1-17 Disabling DHCPv6 stateless mode.

10. Select DHCP Server Authorization. Ensure that Use Current Credentials is selected.

11. Select Confirmation and check your settings.

12. Click Install. Click Close when installation completes.

13. Restart the domain controller. Note that a reboot is always a good idea after you have installed a server role, even if you are not prompted to do so, and especially if you are using virtual machines.

EXERCISE 2 Set Up a DHCPv6 Scope

In this exercise, you configure a DHCPv6 scope. You need to have configured the IPv6 settings on your client and domain controller computers and installed the DHCP server role on your domain controller before you carry out this exercise.

1. If necessary, log on to the domain controller with the Kim_Akers account.

2. In Administrative Tools, click DHCP.

3. If a UAC dialog box appears, click Continue to close it.

4. Expand glasgow.contoso.internal. Expand IPv6. Ensure that a green arrow appears beside the IPv6 icon.

   This confirms that the DHCPv6 server is authorized.

5. Right-click IPv6 and click New Scope to open the New Scope Wizard. Click Next.

6. Give the scope a name (such as Private Network Scope) and type a brief description. Click Next.

7. Set Prefix to **fec0::fffe**.

   You are configuring only one IPv6 scope on this subnet and do not need to set Prefer-ence. Your screen should look similar to Figure 1-18.

8. Click Next.

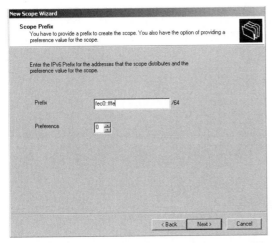

FIGURE 1-18 Setting a DHCPv6 prefix.

9. You want to exclude fec0:0:0:fffe::1 through fec0:0:0:fffe::ff IPv6 addresses from the scope. Specify a Start Address of **0:0:0:1** and an End Address of **0:0:0:ff** on the Add Exclusions page and click Add, as shown in Figure 1-19. Click Add.

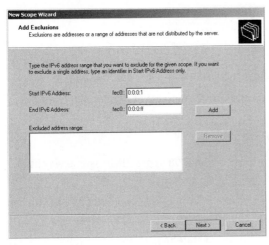

FIGURE 1-19 Configuring scope exclusions.

10. Click Next.

You can set the scope lease on the Scope Lease page. For the purposes of this practice, the lease periods are acceptable.

11. Click Next. Check the scope summary, ensure that Activate Scope Now is selected, and then click Finish.

12. In the DHCP tool, expand the scope, right-click Scope Options, click Configure Options, and examine the available options. Select Option 0023 DNS Recursive Server IPv6 Address List. Specify **fec0:0:0:fffe::1** as the DNS Server IPv6 address, as shown in Figure 1-20.

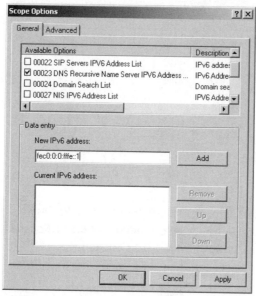

FIGURE 1-20 Specifying a DNS server for DHCPv6 configuration.

13. Click Add, and then click OK. Close the DHCP tool.

14. Close the Remote Desktop connection by logging off of the domain controller.

Lesson Summary

- DHCPv4 is implemented in Windows Server 2008 in exactly the same way as in Windows Server 2003.

- You need to install the DHCP server role in Windows Server 2008 before you can configure DHCPv4 and DHCPv6. You can install the role on a full server or on Server Core.

- IPv6 addresses can be configured through stateful (DHCPv6) and stateless (autoconfiguration) methods. DHCPv6 can also be used statelessly to configure (for example) DNS servers while hosts are autoconfigured.

- Problems can occur when using DHCP on a Hyper-V virtual cluster or on a multihomed DHCP server.

Lesson Review

Use the following questions to test your knowledge of the information in Lesson 2, "Configuring DHCP." The questions are also available on the companion DVD if you prefer to review them in electronic form.

> **NOTE ANSWERS**
>
> Answers to these questions and explanations of why each answer choice is right or wrong are located in the "Answers" section at the end of the book.

1. Which of the following commands should you run to configure the DHCP Server service to start automatically on a Server Core installation of Windows Server 2008?

    A. *start /w ocsetup DHCPServerCore*

    B. *sc config dhcpserver start= auto*

    C. *servermanagercmd -install dhcp*

    D. *net start DHCPServer*

2. Northwind Traders' Chicago office network has two private IPv6 VLANs that have been allocated the following site-local networks:

    - VLAN1: fec0:0:0: 80ca::1 through fec0:0:0:80ca::fffe
    - VVLAN2: fec0:0:0: 80cb::1 through fec0:0:0:80cb::fffe

    Exceptions are defined so that IPv6 addresses on the VLANS can be statically allocated to servers. You want to implement the 80:20 rule. What DHCPv6 scopes do you configure on the DHCP server on VLAN1?

    A. fec0:0:0:80ca::1 through fec0:0:0:80ca::cccb and fec0:0:0: 80cb::cccc through fec0:0:0: 80cb::fffe

    B. fec0:0:0:80cb::1 through fec0:0:0:80cb::cccb and fec0:0:0: 80ca::cccc through fec0:0:0: 80ca::fffe

    C. fec0:0:0:80ca::1 through fec0:0:0:80cca::8887 and fec0:0:0: 80cb::8888 through fec0:0:0: 80cb::fffe

    D. fec0:0:0:80ca::1 through fec0:0:0:80cb::cccb and fec0:0:0: 80ca::cccc through fec0:0:0: 80cb::fffe

3. You are deploying a DHCPv4 server on your network to supply addresses in the 172.16.10.0/24 range. You have 150 DHCP client computers on the local subnet. The subnet includes a domain controller that is also a DNS server with a statically assigned address of 172.16.10.100. How can you create a scope on the DHCPv6 server that does not conflict with the existing DNS server address?

   A. Configure two address ranges in the DHCP scope, 172.16.10.1 through 172.16.10.99 and 172.16.10.101 through 172.16.10.254.

   B. Use the 006 DNS Servers option to assign the address of the DNS server to clients.

   C. Create an exclusion for the address 172.16.10.100.

   D. Create a reservation that assigns the 172.16.10.100 address to the DNS server.

Chapter Review

To further practice and reinforce the skills you learned in this chapter, you can perform the following tasks:

- Review the chapter summary.
- Complete the case scenarios. These scenarios set up real-world situations involving the topics in this chapter and ask you to create a solution.
- Complete the suggested practices.
- Take a practice test.

Chapter Summary

- IPv6 is fully supported in Windows Server 2008 and is installed by default. It supports unicast, multicast, and anycast addresses. It is backward-compatible with IPv4.
- IPv6 addresses can be configured through stateful and stateless configuration. Both GUI and CLI tools are available to configure IPv6 and check network connectivity.
- The features of DHCPv4 on Windows Server 2008 are unchanged from Windows Server 2003. Many of these features are also relevant to DHCPv6. DHCPv6 is implemented by default on Windows Server 2008.

Case Scenarios

In the following case scenarios, you apply what you have learned about configuring Internet protocol addressing. You can find answers to these questions in the "Answers" section at the end of this book.

Case Scenario 1: Implementing IPv6 Connectivity

You are a senior network administrator at Wingtip Toys. Your corporate network consists of two subnets with contiguous private IPv4 networks configured as virtual local area networks (VLANs) connected to a layer-3 switch. Wingtip Toys accesses its ISP and the Internet through a dual-homed Internet Security and Acceleration (ISA) server that provides NAT and firewall services and connects through a peripheral zone to a hardware firewall and, hence, to its ISP. The company wants to implement IPv6 connectivity. All the network hardware supports IPv6, as does the ISP. Answer the following questions:

1. What options are available for the type of unicast address used on the subnets?
2. You decide to use stateful configuration to allocate IPv6 configuration on the two subnets. How should you configure your DHCPv6 servers to provide failover protection?

Case Scenario 2: Configuring DHCP

You are working as a consultant for Northwind Traders. The company has recently upgraded all its domain controllers and member servers at its head office to Windows Server 2008. The DHCP server role is implemented on a member server on each of the company's two networks. IPv4 scopes and options have been configured, and the 80:20 rule is implemented. The company is planning to implement IPv6 addresses. Answer the following questions:

1. Northwind Traders' network manager wants to know whether she can use DHCP to allocate IPv6 configuration and whether she needs to purchase any additional hardware or software. She is not keen to have IPv6 addresses configured manually on client machines. What do you tell her?

2. The technical director has heard of Hyper-V and sees it as an economical way of implementing virtual clusters on the network and providing a high-availability solution at little extra cost. He wants to know if there are any problems combining Hyper-V with the DHCP server service. What do you tell him?

Suggested Practices

To help you successfully master the exam objectives presented in this chapter, complete the following tasks.

Configure IPv4 and IPv6

Perform the following practice.

- **Practice**   The *netsh* command structure provides you with many powerful commands. In particular, use the help function in the command console to investigate the *netsh interface ipv6 set*, *netsh interface ipv6 add*, and *netsh interface ipv6 show* commands. Also, investigate the *netsh dhcp* commands.

Configure DHCP

Perform Practice 1. Practice 2 is optional.

- **Practice 1**   Use the DHCP administrative tool to list the DHCP scope and server options. Access Windows Server 2008 Help and the Internet to find out more about these options. In the process, you should learn something about Network Integration Service (NIS) networks. Although the objectives of the upgrade examinations do not cover NIS, you should, as a network professional, know what it is.

- **Practice 2**   If you have access to additional computers with suitable client operating systems, connect them to your network and configure them to obtain IPv6 configuration automatically. Ensure that the DHCPv6 scope you have configured provides configuration for these computers. Ensure that the host IPv6 addresses configured fall outside the fec0:0:0:fffe::1 through fec0:0:0:fffe::ff range, which includes the IPv6 addresses for the Glasgow and Melbourne computers.

Take a Practice Test

The practice tests on this book's companion DVD offer many options. For example, you can test yourself on just one exam objective, or you can test yourself on all of the Windows Server 2008 upgrade exam content. You can set up the test so that it closely simulates the experience of taking a certification exam, or you can set it up in study mode so that you can look at the correct answers and explanations after you answer each question.

> ***MORE INFO***   **PRACTICE TESTS**
>
> For details about all the practice test options available, see the "How to Use the Practice Tests" section in this book's Introduction.

CHAPTER 2

Configuring IP Services

As a Microsoft Windows Server 2003 administrator, you will have studied Routing and Remote Access Service (RRAS) for your Windows Server 2003 examinations. You might not be aware, however, of the Windows Server 2008 Network Policy Server, the Routing and Remote Access Services role service, and the Network Policy and Access Services server role. This chapter discusses the additions, enhancements, and changes that Windows Server 2008 introduces in RRAS. It goes on to discuss the Microsoft software routing solution and the Internet Protocol Security (IPsec) protocol.

Exam objectives in this chapter:
- Configure routing.
- Configure IPSec.

Lessons in this chapter:

Before You Begin

To complete the lessons in this chapter, you must have done the following:

- Installed Windows Server 2008 Enterprise edition configured as a domain controller in the contoso.internal domain as described in Chapter 1, "Configuring Internet Protocol Addressing." To function as a software router, your server must be multihomed. Most modern computers have an Ethernet and a wireless connection, but you can install virtual server software. You might already have implemented a virtual client in Chapter 1. Virtual server software implements virtual adapters that enable you to create additional subnets and route between them. To run computers as virtual machines within Windows, you can use Virtual PC 2007, Virtual Server 2005 R2, or third-party virtual machine software. To download Virtual PC 2007, visit *http://www.microsoft.com /windows/downloads/virtualpc/default.mspx*. To download an evaluation of Virtual Server 2005 R2, visit *http://www.microsoft.com/technet/virtualserver/evaluation /default.mspx*.

- Installed a Windows Server 2008 Enterprise edition member server in the contoso. internal domain. The server name is Boston, its IPv4 address is 10.0.0.31, its IPv4 default gateway is 10.0.0.11, and its Domain Name System (DNS) server address is also 10.0.0.11. Accept the defaults for all other settings. File sharing should be enabled on this server. It is highly recommended that you use a virtual server.

Lesson 1: Configuring Routing

This lesson provides an overview of routing in Windows Server 2008, particularly the Routing component of RRAS that implements a software-based routing solution. The lesson describes how you configure static routing and how you use a routing protocol in more complex networks. It also describes the enhancements and additions that Windows Server 2008 makes to RRAS and the features that the operating system no longer supports. Finally, the lesson describes how to troubleshoot routing problems, using the *pathping* and *tracert* commands.

After this lesson, you will be able to:

- Describe the enhancements and additions to RRAS implemented in Windows Server 2008.
- List the Windows Server 2003 features that Windows Server 2008 no longer supports.
- Display, analyze, and statically configure a route table.
- Describe and configure routing protocols.
- Use *pathping* and *tracert* to examine network routes.

Estimated lesson time: 45 minutes

 REAL WORLD

Ian McLean

It might sometimes be convenient to use a computer, particularly a virtual server, as a router on a small test network, and you need to know how to configure Windows Server 2008 as a router for the upgrade examinations. In the real world, however, computers are very seldom used as routers, particularly in large, complex corporate networks or on the Internet.

Hardware-based routers offer better performance with a lower purchase cost and cheaper maintenance than software-based routers. They are also more reliable because they are designed to be only routers. A Windows Server 2008 server is designed to be multipurpose. For example, it can be a domain controller, a Web server, a mail server, or a router. Because a hardware router is not required to implement this multiple functionality, there's much less that can go wrong with it.

Understanding the Changes to Windows Server 2008 RRAS

As an experienced network administrator, you know that a router is a multihomed device that manages data flow between networks. It directs incoming and outgoing IPv4 or IPv6 packets based on the information it holds about the state of its own network interfaces and a list of possible sources and destinations for network traffic stored in a route table.

At the most basic, client computers send all communications not addressed to another station on the same subnet to a single router known as the default gateway. If, however, you use multiple routers in a single subnet, you might need to configure more complex routing.

In practice, dedicated hardware routers handle heavier routing demands, and subnetting within an organization is often implemented by level-3 switches and virtual local area networks (VLANs). However, on a small, segmented network with relatively light traffic between subnets, you can use a software-based routing solution such as RRAS in Windows Server 2008. The upgrade examinations are likely to test your knowledge of Windows Server 2008 RRAS because it is a Microsoft solution.

> **NOTE SERVER CORE**
>
> It is not possible to install the Network Policy Server role and hence not possible to install the Routing and Remote Access role service on computers running Windows Server 2008 that are installed using the Server Core option.

New Features and Enhancements in Windows Server 2008 RRAS

This chapter deals mainly with routing and IPsec. Chapter 3, "Configuring Network Access," discusses remote access. Nevertheless, routing and remote access are closely linked through RRAS, and it is appropriate to discuss the new features, enhancements, and changes introduced by Windows Server 2008 RRAS at this point in the book. Windows Server 2008 provides the following RRAS enhancements:

- **Network Policy and Access Services server role** The most obvious enhancement is that you install RRAS by adding the Network Policy and Access Services server role in Server Manager. You install this role in the practice session later in this lesson.

- **Secure Socket Tunneling Protocol** Secure Socket Tunneling Protocol (SSTP) implements a new form of virtual private networking (VPN) tunnel with features that allow traffic to pass through firewalls that block Point-to-Point Tunneling Protocol (PPTP) and Layer 2 Tunneling Protocol (L2TP)/IPsec traffic. SSTP provides remote access rather than routing functionality and is discussed in Chapter 3.

- **VPN enforcement for Network Access Protection** Network Access Protection (NAP) is a client health policy technology included in Windows Server 2008. NAP enables you to establish and enforce health policies, which can include software requirements, security update requirements, required computer configurations, and other settings.

VPN enforcement for NAP provides strong limited network access for all computers accessing the network through a VPN connection. It is associated with remote access rather than with routing and is discussed in more detail in Chapter 3.

NOTE **NETWORK ACCESS QUARANTINE CONTROL**

VPN enforcement with NAP replaces the Network Access Quarantine Control feature implemented in Windows Server 2003 and is easier to deploy.

- **Internet Protocol version 6 support** Windows Server 2008 supports enhancements to Internet Protocol version 6 (IPv6). For example, native IPv6 traffic can be sent over point-to-point protocol (PPP)–based connections. PPP version 6 (PPPv6) is supported. This enables you to connect to an IPv6-based Internet service provider (ISP) through dial-up or PPP over Ethernet (PPPoE)–based connections that can be used for broadband Internet access. You can use PPPv6 over dial-up or Ethernet connections as well as over VPN tunnels. L2TP over IPv6 is implemented, as is DHCPv6 relay agent. Remote Authentication Dial-In User Service (RADIUS) is implemented over IPv6 transport. Finally, stateless filtering can be based on various parameters that include source IPv6 address prefix, destination IPv6 address/prefix, the IP protocol type of the next hop, the Transmission Control Protocol (TCP) or User Datagram Protocol (UDP) source port number, and the TCP or UDP destination port number.

MORE INFO **PPPV6**

For more information about PPPv6, see *http://www.ietf.org/rfc/rfc2472.txt.*

MORE INFO **RADIUS**

For more information about RADIUS, see *http://www.ietf.org/rfc/rfc2865.txt.*

- **New cryptographic support** Windows Server 2008 supports the PPTP 128-bit RC4 encryption algorithm. Forty-bit and 56-bit RC4 support is removed. The L2TP Data Encryption Standard (DES) encryption algorithm with Message Digest 5 (MD5) integrity check support is also removed. IPsec Internet Key Exchange (IKE) Main Mode supports Advanced Encryption Standard (AES) 256 (new); AES 192 (new); AES 128 (new); and 3DES encryption algorithms, the Secure Hash Algorithm 1 (SHA1) integrity check algorithm and Diffie-Hellman (DH) groups 19 (new), and 20 (new) for Main Mode negotiation. IKE Quick Mode supports AES 256 (new), AES 192 (new), AES 128 (new), and 3DES encryption algorithms and the SHA1 integrity check algorithm.

MORE INFO **ENCRYPTION AND INTEGRITY CHECK ALGORITHMS**

For more information about encryption and integrity check algorithms, access *http://www.rsa.com/node.aspx?id=2898* and follow the links. If you are professionally interested in security solutions, add this site to your favorites.

NOTE **SUPPORT FOR LESS SECURE SOLUTIONS**

You can edit the registry in Windows Server 2008 to implement PPTP 40-bit and 56-bit RC4 support and L2TP DES encryption algorithm with MD5 integrity check support. However, Microsoft does not recommend this procedure.

Technologies Removed or Disabled in Windows Server 2008 RRAS

In addition to new features and enhancements introduced in Windows Server 2008, you need to know which features are no longer supported. It is likely that the upgrade examinations will test this knowledge, possibly by suggesting a discontinued feature as an incorrect answer. Support for the following technologies has been removed or disabled in Windows Server 2008:

- **Bandwidth Allocation Protocol (BAP)** BAP is disabled in Windows Server 2008. This protocol has become less relevant as broadband connections replace multiple dial-up modem connections.

- **X.25** X.25 is an International Telecommunication Union-Telecommunication Standardization Sector (ITU-T) protocol standard for wide area network (WAN) communications. It is typically used in packet-switched networks (PSNs). However, its use has declined as more modern protocols replace it.

- **Serial Line Interface Protocol (SLIP)** SLIP was never formally designated as a standard and is less efficient and much less secure than PPP. Windows Server 2008 automatically updates SLIP-based connections to PPP-based connections.

- **Asynchronous Transfer Mode (ATM)** ATM is a PSN protocol that encodes data traffic into small fixed-sized cells. This differs from IP or Ethernet, in which variable-sized packets are used. Windows Server 2008 does not support ATM.

- **IP over IEEE 1394** The IEEE 1394 multimedia connection, sometimes known as Firewire, enables isochronous (real-time) data interfacing. Microsoft has not identified any customer dependency on IP over IEEE 1394, and Windows Server 2008 does not support it.

- **NWLink IPX/SPX/NetBIOS Compatible Transport Protocol** Windows Server 2008 does not support NWLink IPX/SPX/NetBIOS Compatible Transport Protocol. Modern Novell networks use TCP/IP.

- **Services for Macintosh**   Services for Macintosh enables Apple Macintosh clients to share files and printers and remotely connect to a Microsoft network. Windows Server 2008 does not support this service. Modern Apple Macintosh computers use TCP/IP.

- **Open Shortest Path First (OSPF)**   Windows Server 2008 does not support the OSPF routing protocol component in RRAS. OSPF is used in large networks, and Microsoft has identified software-based routing as a solution for small, segmented networks with relatively light traffic between subnets.

- **Basic Firewall**   Windows Server 2008 replaces Basic Firewall in RRAS with Windows Firewall and Windows Firewall with Advanced Security (WFAS).

- **Static IP filter application programming interfaces (APIs)**   Windows Server 2008 replaces static IP filter APIs for RRAS with Windows Filtering Platform APIs.

- **SPAP, EAP-MD5-CHAP, and MS-CHAP**   Windows Server 2008 does not support the SPAP, EAP-MD5-CHAP, and MS-CHAP authentication protocols for PPP-based connections. These protocols are not considered secure enough to counter the threats posed by the modern network environment.

Configuring Static Routing

On most networks, client computers must be configured with a single default gateway that handles all communications to and from the subnet. Sometimes, for redundancy, network administrators might place two default gateways on a single subnet. Whether you use single or multiple default gateways, you do not need to configure static routing on a single subnet. You simply configure the default gateways on your hosts manually or by using standard network configuration techniques such as Dynamic Host Configuration Protocol (DHCP).

 Quick Check
- **Does Windows Server 2008 RRAS support OSPF?**

Quick Check Answer
- **No. Windows Server 2003 supports OSPF, but Windows Server 2008 does not.**

If a computer must use different routers to communicate with different remote networks and you do not want to use a routing protocol, you must configure static routing. For example, in the network shown in Figure 2-1, the client computer accesses the Internet through a wireless connection to a wireless access point (WAP) with the gateway address 192.168.123.254. The client is also connected to the 10.0.0.0/24 private network and needs to communicate with clients on the 10.0.1.0/24 network through the 10.0.0.11 gateway. In this network, an administrator would need to configure a static route for the 10.0.1.0/24 subnet that uses the 10.0.0.11 gateway.

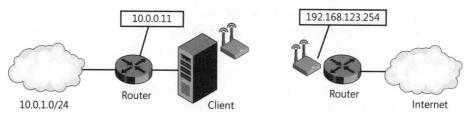

FIGURE 2-1 A network that requires static routing.

Typically, this configuration is performed by using the *route* command-line tool. For the example shown in Figure 2-1, you could allow the client to access the 10.0.1.0/24 network by using the following command:

route -p add 10.0.1.0 MASK 255.255.255.0 10.0.0.11

The client then routes traffic destined for the 10.0.1.0/24 subnet through the router at 10.0.0.11. All other communications would be sent through the default gateway.

> **NOTE PERSISTENT ROUTES**
>
> Using the -p parameter in the *route add* command makes a route persistent. A persistent route is not removed when you restart the computer. Typically, routes configured through static routing are persistent. Routes configured by a routing protocol such as Routing Internet Protocol (RIP) can change if the network is reconfigured and therefore are typically not persistent. If you want to remove a persistent route, you can use the *route delete* command.

The *route* command presents a number of options that help you configure static routing. In the practice session later in this lesson, you use the RRAS graphical tools to configure static routes.

> **NOTE ON-DEMAND NETWORK CONNECTIONS**
>
> Dial-up networks and VPNs can automatically change a client's routing configuration. They either change the default gateway so that all traffic travels through the on-demand connection, or they establish temporary routes so that only the traffic destined for the private network is sent through the on-demand connection. There is no need to set up this configuration manually.

Using the *Route* Command

The *route* command enables you to examine and configure static routing from a command prompt. To view the routing table, run the *route print* command. This command displays both the IPv4 and IPv6 route tables. For convenience, the output of the command is split, so Figure

2-2 shows the IPv4 route table and Figure 2-3 shows the IPv6 route table. In practice, you would combine the two figures to show the full output of the *route print* command. In this case, the command is run on the domain controller Glasgow that is connected to virtual clients on the 10.0.0.0/24 network and to the Internet through a wireless connection. The route table on your test domain controller will probably be different.

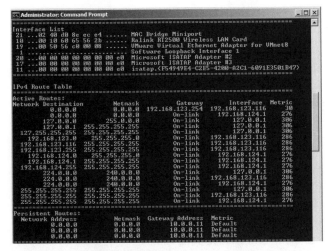

FIGURE 2-2 An IPv4 route table.

FIGURE 2-3 An IPv6 route table.

 Quick Check

- Which command would you use to define a persistent route from the 10.1.0.0/24 network to the 10.2.0.0/24 network when the persistent route uses the gateway address 10.1.0.1?

Quick Check Answer

- *route -p add 10.2.0.0 MASK 255.255.255.0 10.1.0.1*

The route table lists destination networks and the interface or router used to access them. Windows Server 2008 maintains separate routing tables for IPv4 and IPv6.

Looking for specific details helps you interpret the route table. For example, in the IPv4 route table, you can look at the following:

- Routes with a netmask of 0.0.0.0 show the IP address of the default gateway. For example, the first table entry shows that the address of the default gateway on the wireless network that connects to the Internet is 192.168.123.254.

- The Persistent Routes section displays any static routes to remote networks that have been added. For example, all external traffic sent from the 10.0.0.0/24 network goes through the 10.0.0.11 gateway.

- Routes with a netmask of 255.255.255.255 identify an interface.

- A network destination of 127.0.0.0 or 127.0.0.1 shows a loopback interface.

- A network destination of 224.0.0.0 is a multicast address. Multicasting enables you to send packages to more than one (but typically not all) clients on a network. It is used, for example, in Active Directory Domain Services (AD DS) replication.

For example, the following line from a *route print* output indicates that the computer is configured to send traffic destined for the 10.0.1.0/24 network to the router at 10.0.0.11 rather than to the default gateway to the Internet at 192.168.123.254:

```
10.0.1.0  255.255.255.0   On-link  10.0.0.11  21
```

The following line of output shows that the default gateway is configured to be 192.168.123.254 (for the interface with the IP address 192.168.123.116). You can identify this as the default gateway address because the subnet mask is set to 0.0.0.0.

```
0.0.0.0   0.0.0.0  192.168.123.254 192.168.123.116  30
```

You can also interpret the IPv6 route table by looking for specific details. Figure 2-3 lists individual IPv6 routes, which can be categorized as follows:

- Routes with a 128-bit prefix length (for example, fe80::4c81:2382:92ad:130f/128) are host routes for a specific IPv6 destination. By default, only host routes for locally configured IPv6 addresses are in the IPv6 route table.

- Routes with a 64-bit prefix length (for example, fe80::/64) are subnet routes for locally attached subnets.

- The ::/0 routes are default routes. No default routes are listed in Figure 2-3.

- The ff00::/8 routes are for multicast traffic.

Layer 2 and Layer 3 Addresses

The destination IP address (a Layer 3 address) of a packet never changes; it is always set to the IP address of the target computer. To forward packets to a router without changing the destination IP address, computers use the media access control (MAC) address (a Layer 2 address). Therefore, as the packet is forwarded between networks, the source and destination IP addresses never change. However, the source and destination MAC addresses are rewritten for every network between the client and server.

Configuring Static Routing with Routing and Remote Access

After installing the Network Policy and Access Services server role, you can view the IP routing table by right-clicking Roles\Network Policy and AccessServices\Routing And Remote Access\IPv4\Static Routes and then selecting Show IP Routing Table. Routing And Remote Access displays the static routing table (which does not include any dynamic routes added from RIP). You install the Network Policy and Access Services server role and view the IP route table in the practice session later in this lesson.

Using Routing Information Protocol

Static route table configuration is efficient if your network contains only a few (typically five or fewer) routers and the network configuration does not frequently change. For larger (but not very large) networks, typically containing up to 15 routers, or for networks in which the network topology is liable to change—for example, a dynamic corporate network used by a small but rapidly expanding organization—the use of a routing protocol is indicated.

The Microsoft software-based routing solution is not appropriate for large, complex networks in which hardware routers or layer 3 switches might be used. Consequently, Windows Server 2008 supports Routing Information Protocol (RIP), which is designed for exchanging routing information within a small to medium-size network.

RIP is simple to configure and deploy. However, it cannot scale to large or very large networks. The maximum hop count RIP routers can use is 15, and networks that are more than 15 hops away are considered unreachable. As networks grow larger in size, the periodic announcements that each RIP router generates can cause excessive traffic.

Compared to more sophisticated routing protocols (for example, OSPF), RIP has a high recovery time. When the network topology changes, it can take several minutes before the RIP routers reconfigure themselves to the new network topology. While the network reconfigures itself, routing loops might form that result in lost or undeliverable data. However, using RIP still results in less delay and lost traffic than manually reconfiguring route tables on 15 routers.

Initially, the route table for each router includes only the networks that are physically connected. A RIP router periodically sends announcements that contain its route table entries to inform other local RIP routers about the networks it can reach. RIPv1 uses IP broadcast packets for its announcements. RIPv2 uses either multicast or broadcast packets for its announcements. Figure 2-4 illustrates the route announcement process.

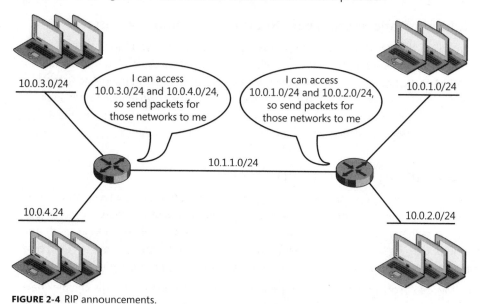

FIGURE 2-4 RIP announcements.

> **NOTE   SILENT RIP**
>
> Silent RIP accepts updates from other systems but does not respond to requests or send updates. By default, RIP sends a complete update to all neighbors and replies to all incoming requests (LAN only). This is sometimes known as periodic RIP.

RIP routers can also communicate routing information through triggered updates. Triggered updates occur when the network topology changes and updated routing information is sent that reflects those changes. RIP routers send triggered updates immediately and do not wait for the next periodic announcement. Suppose, for example, that a RIP router detects a link or router failure. It immediately updates its own route table and sends updated routes. Each router that receives the triggered update modifies its own route table and propagates the change.

Windows Server 2008 RRAS supports RIPv1 and RIPv2. RIPv2 supports multicast announcements, simple password authentication, and more flexibility in subnetted and classless interdomain routing (CIDR) environments and is the default routing protocol for Windows Server 2008.

The Windows Server 2008 implementation of RIP has the following features:

- You can select which RIP version to run on each interface for incoming and outgoing packets.
- Split-horizon, poison-reverse, and triggered-update algorithms are used to avoid routing loops and to speed recovery of the network when topology changes occur.
- You can use route filters to configure networks to ignore or accept announcements. On the Security tab of the RIP Properties dialog box (discussed in Lesson 2), you can configure the router to Accept Announcements From All Routers, Accept Announcements From Listed Routers Only, or Ignore Announcements From Listed Routers.
- You can use peer filters to choose which router's announcements to accept.
- Router announcements are configurable, and you can set route aging timers.
- Simple password authentication is supported.
- You can disable subnet summarization.

> **NOTE   CONFIGURING ROUTING FROM THE COMMAND PROMPT**
>
> You can use the routing context of the *netsh* command to control announcements and route advertisements from the command prompt. For example, the *netsh routing ip rip add peerfilter server=10.10.10.161* command configures RIPv2 to accept announcements from the router at 10.10.10.161. The *announcefilter* option filters specific advertised routes rather than accepting all updates from a particular router. You can use the *netsh routing ipv6 add persistentroute* command to add a static persistent IPv6 route to a particular interface. You can use *netsh routing ipv6 delete persistentroute* to remove a persistent route and *netsh routing ipv6 show persistentroute* to provide a list of all persistent routes. *Netsh routing ipv6 add filter* adds an IPv6 packet filter to a specified interface.

> **MORE INFO   COUNT TO INFINITY**
>
> Even if a routing protocol supports split horizon with poison reverse, count-to-infinity can still occur in a multipath internetwork because routes to networks can be learned from multiple sources. For more information about the count-to-infinity problem, see *http://www.microsoft.com/technet/prodtechnol/windows2000serv/reskit/intwork/inae_ips_vzbs .mspx?mfr=true*. This is an old link, but the problem has not changed and is well described here.

Split Horizon, Poison Reverse, and Triggered Updates

Split horizon helps reduce convergence time by not allowing routers to advertise networks in the direction from which those networks are learned. The information sent in RIP announcements is for those networks that are beyond the neighboring router in the opposite direction. Networks learned from the neighboring router are not included.

Split horizon eliminates count-to-infinity and routing loops during convergence in single-path internetworks and reduces the chances of count-to-infinity in multipath internetworks. Split horizon helps reduce convergence time because the only information sent in RIP announcements is for those networks that are beyond the neighboring router in the opposite direction.

Split horizon with poison reverse differs from simple split horizon because it announces all networks. However, networks learned in the direction prohibited by split horizon are announced with a hop count of 16, indicating that the network is unreachable. In a single-path internetwork, split horizon with poison reverse has no benefit beyond split horizon. However, in a multipath internetwork, split horizon with poison reverse reduces count-to-infinity and routing loops.

Triggered updates enable a RIP router to announce changes in metric values almost immediately rather than waiting for the next periodic announcement. A change to a metric in an entry in the routing table triggers the update. For example, networks that become unavailable can be announced with a hop count of 16 through a triggered update. This update is sent almost immediately. However, a small time interval to wait is specified on the router. If triggered updates were sent by all routers immediately, each triggered update could cause a cascade of broadcast traffic across the IPv4 network.

Triggered updates improve the convergence time of RIP internetworks but at the expense of additional broadcast traffic as the triggered updates are propagated.

Examining Network Routes

You can use the *pathping* and *tracert* commands to determine how packets travel between your computer and a destination. *Tracert* provides a quicker response, but *pathping* provides a more detailed analysis of network performance. Figure 2-5 and Figure 2-6 demonstrate how *pathping* displays a route to the *www.microsoft.com* destination.

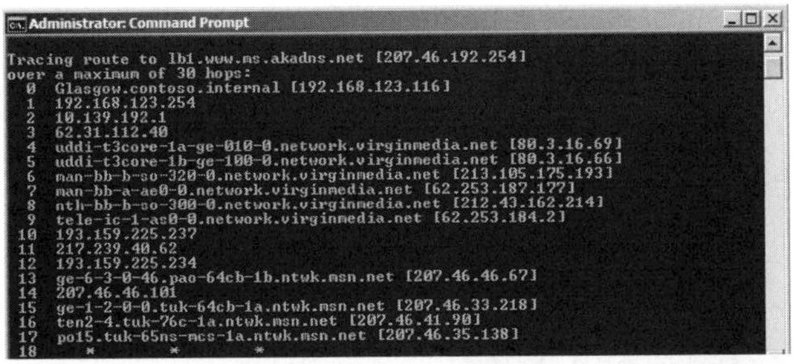

FIGURE 2-5 Route from source to destination.

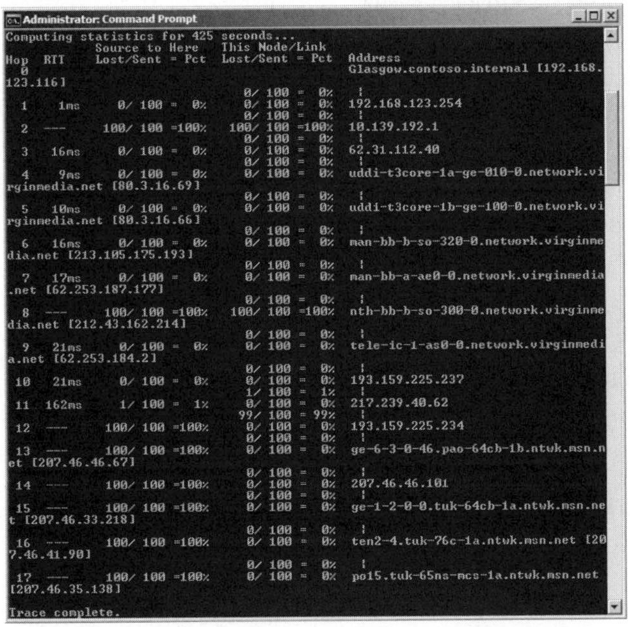

FIGURE 2-6 Latency to each router.

Pathping shows the data in two sections. The first shows the route from the source to the destination. The second shows the latency in milliseconds to each router.

The last line of the first section shows three asterisk (*) symbols. This occurs when a node does not respond to the Internet Control Message Protocol (ICMP) requests. Sometimes servers are configured to ignore ICMP. Consequently, they will not appear in the list even though they might be online and responding to other requests.

Figure 2-7 shows the output from the *tracert www.microsoft.com* command. The *tracert* command completes quicker than *pathping* but gives less information.

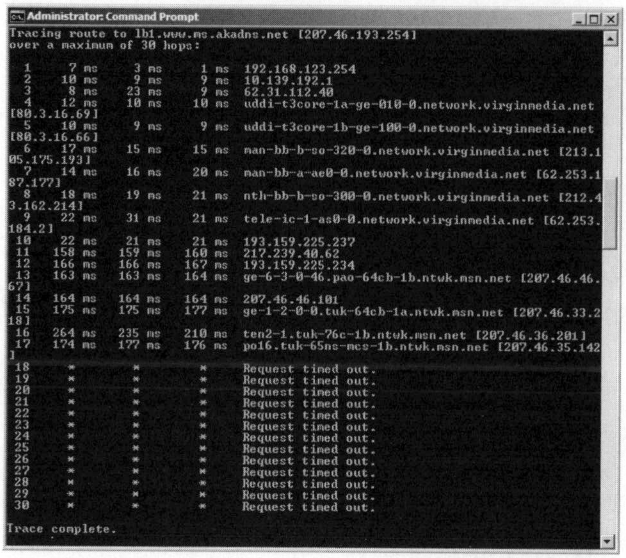

FIGURE 2-7 Using tracert.

PRACTICE **Installing and Configuring Routing**

In this practice session, you install the Network Policy and Access Services server role and Routing and Remote Access Services role service. You then configure your Windows Server 2008 server as a router.

EXERCISE 1 Install the Network Policy and Access Services Server Role

To install the Network Policy and Access Services server role, follow these steps:

1. Log on to your domain controller with the Kim_Akers account.

2. If Server Manager does not open automatically, click Start, and then select Server Manager.

3. In the left pane, select Roles, and then, in the right pane, click Add Roles.

4. If the Before You Begin page appears, click Next.

5. On the Select Server Roles page, select the Network Policy and Access Services check box, as shown in Figure 2-8, and then click Next.

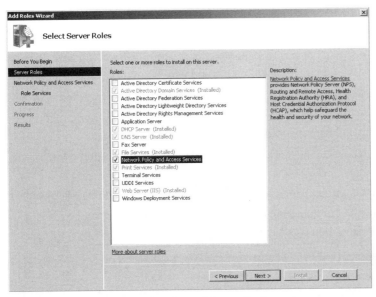

FIGURE 2-8 Adding the Network Policy and Access Services role.

6. On the Network Policy and Access Services page, click Next.

7. On the Role Services page, select the Routing and Remote Access Services check box.

   The wizard automatically selects the Remote Access Service and Routing check boxes, as shown in Figure 2-9.

8. Click Next.

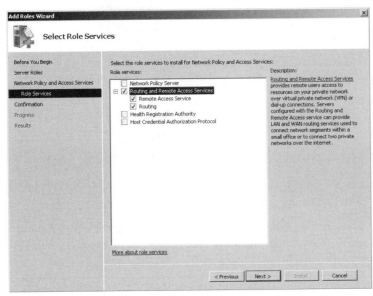

FIGURE 2-9 Specifying the Routing and Remote Access Services role service.

9. On the Confirm Installation Selections page, click Install.

10. After the Add Roles Wizard completes the installation, click Close.

11. In the left-side pane of Server Manager, expand Roles, expand Network Policy and Access Services, and then select Routing and Remote Access.

12. Right-click Routing and Remote Access, and then select Configure and Enable Routing And Remote Access.

    The Routing and Remote Access Server Setup Wizard appears.

13. On the Welcome To The Routing And Remote Access Server Setup Wizard page, click Next.

14. On the Configuration page, select Custom Configuration, and then click Next.

15. On the Custom Configuration page, select the LAN Routing check box, as shown in Figure 2-10, and then click Next.

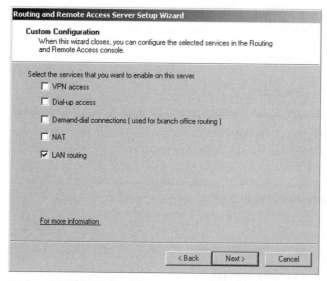

FIGURE 2-10 Selecting the check box to configure LAN routing.

16. On the Completing The Routing And Remote Access Server Wizard page, click Finish.

17. Click Start Service. If you do not see this button, right-click Routing and Remote Access, select All Tasks, and click Start.

EXERCISE 2 Use RRAS Graphical Tools to View and Configure Static Routes

In this exercise, you use the RRAS graphical tools in Server Manager to view the static route table and to add and then remove a static route. You must perform Exercise 1 before you attempt this exercise. To view, add, and delete static routes, follow these steps:

1. In the Server Manager console tree, expand Roles, expand Network Policy and Access Services, expand Routing and Remote Access, expand IPv4, right-click Static Routes, and then select Show IP Routing Table.

   The IPv4 route table is displayed as shown in Figure 2-11. The route table on your domain controller will probably show different routes.

GLASGOW - IP Routing Table

Destination	Network mask	Gateway	Interface	Metric	Protocol
0.0.0.0	0.0.0.0	10.0.0.11	Local Area C...	286	Network ma...
0.0.0.0	0.0.0.0	0.0.0.0	VMware Net...	276	Network ma...
127.0.0.0	255.0.0.0	127.0.0.1	Loopback	51	Local
127.0.0.1	255.255.255.255	127.0.0.1	Loopback	306	Local
169.254.0.0	255.255.0.0	0.0.0.0	Local Area C...	286	Network ma...
169.254.11.167	255.255.255.255	0.0.0.0	Local Area C...	286	Network ma...
169.254.255.255	255.255.255.255	0.0.0.0	Local Area C...	286	Network ma...
192.168.124.0	255.255.255.0	0.0.0.0	VMware Net...	276	Network ma...
192.168.124.1	255.255.255.255	0.0.0.0	VMware Net...	276	Network ma...
192.168.124.255	255.255.255.255	0.0.0.0	VMware Net...	276	Network ma...
224.0.0.0	240.0.0.0	0.0.0.0	Local Area C...	286	Network ma...
255.255.255.255	255.255.255.255	0.0.0.0	Local Area C...	286	Network ma...

FIGURE 2-11 The IPv4 route table displayed through Server Manager.

2. Close the route table display. Right-click Static Routes, and then select New Static Route.

3. In the IPv4 Static Route dialog box, select the network interface that will be used to forward traffic to the remote network. In the Destination box, type the network ID of the destination network. In the Network Mask box, type the subnet mask of the destination network. In the Gateway box, type the router that packets for the destination network should be forwarded to. Adjust metric only if you have multiple paths to the same destination network and want to prefer one gateway over the others. In this case, configure the preferred routes with lower metrics. The IPv4 Static Route dialog box should look similar to Figure 2-12. Click OK.

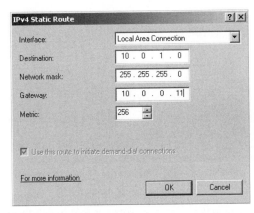

FIGURE 2-12 Adding a static route.

Routing and Remote Access adds the static route, which is displayed in the Static Routes pane.

4. Right-click the static route you have created, and then select Delete.

EXERCISE 3 Enable RIP

In this exercise, you enable RIP. This allows Windows Server 2008 to advertise routes to neighboring routers and to detect neighboring routers and remote networks automatically. You must perform Exercise 1 before you attempt this exercise. To enable RIP, follow these steps:

1. In the Server Manager console tree, expand Roles, expand Network Policy and Access Services, expand Routing and Remote Access, expand IPv4, right-click General, and then select New Routing Protocol.

2. In the New Routing Protocol dialog box, select RIP Version 2 For Internet Protocol, and then click OK.

   RIP appears under IPv4 in the left-side pane.

3. Right-click RIP, and then select New Interface.

4. In the New Interface for RIP Version 2 For Internet Protocol dialog box, select the interface you want to advertise with RIP, as shown in Figure 2-13.

   The interfaces on your domain controller might differ from those in the figure.

5. Click OK.

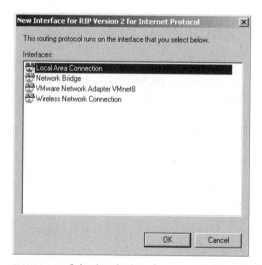

FIGURE 2-13 Selecting the interface you want to advertise with RIP.

6. Configure the RIP settings by using the RIP Properties dialog box.

   In practice, on a production network, you would choose settings that match those of neighboring routers. The default settings work in most environments. You can adjust settings by using the four tabs of the dialog box. On the General tab, you can choose whether RIPv1 or RIPv2 is used and whether authentication is required. On the Security tab, you can choose whether to filter router advertisements. The Neighbors tab enables you to list manually the neighbors with which the computer communicates. The Advanced tab configures announcement intervals, which define how frequently a router announces its routes, time-outs, and other infrequently used settings.

7. Click OK when you have completed the configuration. Repeat this process for every interface that has routing enabled.

> **NOTE   FILTERING ROUTER ADVERTISEMENTS**
>
> Because RIP can be used to advertise a route to a malicious computer, it can be used as part of a man-in-the-middle attack. Therefore, restrict the advertised routes that are accepted whenever possible.

Lesson Summary

- You can configure software-based routing on a Windows Server 2008 server to allow software-based routers to forward traffic between each other and enable clients and servers on different subnets to communicate.
- You can use static routing to allow computers with multiple routers connected to their subnet to forward traffic with different destinations to the correct subnet.
- You can use *pathping* and *tracert* to identify the routers between a source and a destination. You can use both tools to identify routing problems.
- Windows Server 2008 supports RIP, which you can enable by installing the Routing and Remote Access Services role service.

Lesson Review

You can use the following questions to test your knowledge of the information in Lesson 1, "Configuring Routing." The questions are also available on the companion DVD if you prefer to review them in electronic form.

> **NOTE   LESSON REVIEW ANSWERS**
>
> Answers to these questions and explanations of why each answer choice is right or wrong are located in the "Answers" section at the end of the book.

1. Currently, client computers on the 10.0.0.0/24 subnet are configured with the 10.0.0.11 default gateway. You connect a second router to both the 10.0.0.0/24 subnet and the 10.0.1.0/24 subnet. You would like clients on the 10.0.0.0/24 subnet to connect to the 10.0.1.0/24 subnet by using the new router, which has the 10.0.0.21 IP address on the 10.0.0.0/24 subnet. Which command should you run?

A. *route add 10.0.1.0 MASK 255.255.255.0 10.0.0.11*

B. *route add 10.0.1.0 MASK 255.255.255.0 10.0.0.21*

C. *route add 10.0.0.0 MASK 255.255.255.0 10.0.0.21*

D. *route add 10.0.0.21 MASK 255.255.255.0 10.0.1.0*

2. Which of the following are supported by Windows Server 2003 but not by Windows Server 2008? (Choose all that apply.)

A. RIPv2

B. NWLink

C. Services for Macintosh

D. Basic Firewall

E. OSPF

F. SSTP

3. You configure a computer running Windows Server 2008 with two network interfaces. Each interface is connected to a different subnet. One of those subnets has four other routers connected to it, and each router provides access to several subnets. You would like the computer running Windows Server 2008 to automatically identify the routers and determine which remote subnets are available using each router. What should you do?

A. Enable NAT on the interface.

B. Enable RIP on the interface.

C. Enable OSPF on the interface.

D. Add a static route to the interface.

4. You use the *route print* command on a Windows Server 2008 server and examine the IPv6 route table. Which of the following are host routes for a specific IPv6 destination? (Choose all that apply.)

A. fe80::4c81:2382:92ad:130f/128

B. fe80::8860:8bf:9cb8:80eb/128

C. fe80::/64

D. ff00::/8

5. You are experiencing intermittent connectivity problems accessing an internal Web site on a remote network. You would like to view a list of routers between the client and the server. Which tools can you use? (Choose all that apply.)

A. *ping*

B. *ipconfig*

C. *pathping*

D. *tracert*

Lesson 2: Configuring IPsec

By enforcing trusted communication, you can use IPsec to secure communication between two hosts or to secure traffic across external networks, including the Internet in VPN scenarios. IPsec is invisible to the end user and secures communication over the entire path between the source and the destination. You can manage IPsec through Local Security Policy, Group Policy, or command-line tools. This lesson discusses how you deploy IPsec and concentrates mainly on deployment through Group Policy.

After this lesson, you will be able to:

- Describe the various methods by which you can deploy IPsec.
- Deploy IPsec on a network through Group Policy.
- Distinguish between encryption and authentication and know which protocols and methods can be used to secure network communication.
- Understand *netsh* contexts and use *netsh* commands, particularly commands in the *netsh advfirewall consec* context, to manage IPsec rules.

Estimated lesson time: 60 minutes

 REAL WORLD

Ian McLean

I first came across IPsec in 1999, and it implemented some important security features. First, it could secure communication between a source and destination that could support it, even if intermediate stations did not. IPsec could secure all communications, whereas protocols such as Secure Sockets Layer (SSL) could secure only Web traffic. Most significant, IPsec was invisible to the user, and what users don't know about they don't complain about.

Those of us who had to configure and administer IPsec tended to be less keen on it. It was not easily understood or configured, you needed to understand soft and hard associations, and the debugging tools we used every day, for example, *ping* didn't work anymore (at least not until the association was established).

Windows Server 2008 introduces new methods of configuring IPsec through connection security rules. If you need to configure standard IPsec policies and do not require encryption, this greatly simplifies configuration. If you need to refine your configuration, you can do this through Windows Firewall with Advanced Security (WFAS) or *netsh advfirewall* commands. IPsec policies are retained and will undoubtedly still be used by those familiar with IPsec configuration in previous Windows operating systems, but now you have the choice.

L2TP/IPsec is now the standard way of encrypting and authenticating a VPN tunnel. Windows Server 2008 does not change IPsec fundamentally, but it introduces some important enhancements, discussed in this lesson. Love it or hate it, IPsec is here to stay, and IPsec configuration will almost certainly be tested in your upgrade examinations.

Implementing IPsec

As an experienced administrator, you know that IPsec provides a method of protecting data on an IP network by ensuring authenticity, confidentiality, or both. However, if you do not configure IPsec on a regular basis, you might need some review before you go on to look at the new features Windows Server 2008 introduces.

The Windows implementation of IPsec is based on standards developed by the Internet Engineering Task Force (IETF) IPsec working group. IPsec provides security for data sent between two computers on an IP network. It protects data between two IP addresses by providing the following services:

- **Data Authentication** IPsec provides data origin authentication. You can configure it to ensure that each packet you receive from a trusted party genuinely originates from that party and is not spoofed. The protocol also ensures data integrity and can ensure that data is not altered in transit. You can implement anti-replay protection by configuring IPsec to verify that each packet received is unique and not duplicated.
- **Encryption** You can use IPsec to encrypt network data so that the data is unreadable if captured in transit.

In Windows Server 2008, you configure IPsec through either IPsec policies or connection security rules. By default, IPsec policies attempt to negotiate both authentication and encryption services. Connection security rules, by default, attempt to negotiate only authentication services. You can, however, configure IPsec policies and connection security rules to provide any combination of data protection services.

NOTE **IPSEC BEYOND WINDOWS**

Because it is an interoperable standard, you can implement IPsec to secure communications between computers running Windows and those that don't.

In Windows Server 2008 networks, you typically implement IPsec through Group Policy, either by using IPsec policies or through connection security rules. The connection security rules method is new to Windows Server 2008 and is typically used in combination with WFAS. As a Windows Server 2003 administrator, you will be more familiar with the concepts behind IPsec policies.

Using Connection Security Rules

Windows Server 2008 refers to IPsec rules as connection security rules. They perform the same function as the IPsec rules available in previous versions of Windows but support more advanced authentication and encryption algorithms.

In previous versions of Windows, implementations of server or domain isolation sometimes required the creation of a large number of IPsec rules to make sure that required network traffic was protected while still permitting required network traffic that could not be secured with IPsec. Windows Server 2008 eases this complexity by a new default behavior that results in a more secure environment that is easier to troubleshoot.

MORE INFO **DOMAIN ISOLATION**

For more information about domain isolation in Windows Server 2008, see *http://technet .microsoft.com/en-us/library/cc770610.aspx.*

Windows Server 2008 introduces connection security rules, which facilitate implementing IPsec for authenticated communication on a network. Windows Server 2008 gives you the option of enforcing connection security rules through a Group Policy object (GPO) in the WFAS node.

Connection security rules evaluate network traffic and then block, allow, or negotiate security for messages based on the criteria you configure. Unlike IPsec policies, connection security rules do not include filters or filter actions. The features provided by filters and filter actions are built into each connection security rule, but the filtering capabilities in connection security rules are not as powerful as those of IPsec policies. If further, more complex filtering is required, you can use WFAS or *netsh* to implement this. By default, connection security rules do not apply to *types* of IP traffic such as IP traffic that passes over port 23. Instead, they apply to *all* IP traffic originating from or destined for certain IP addresses, subnets, or servers on the network.

A connection security rule first authenticates the computers defined in the rule before they begin communicating and then secures the information sent between these two authenticated computers. If you have configured a connection security rule that requires security for a given connection, and the two computers in question cannot authenticate each other, the connection is blocked.

By default, connection security rules provide only data authentication security (data origin authentication, data integrity, and anti-replay security). For this reason, connection security rules typically authenticate only connections. You can, however, also configure data encryption for connection security rules (typically through WFAS) so that the connections in question are truly *secured* and not merely authenticated.

 REAL WORLD

Ian McLean

The advantage of connection security rules lies in their simplicity. Most administrators choose to use connection security rules to perform only their default functions and implement more complex functions, such as port or IP filtering, through WFAS. You can also use IPsec policies when you require (for example) data encryption, and those familiar with IPsec configuration in Windows Server 2003 might be more comfortable with this method. It is difficult to say for certain whether the new methods of IPsec configuration will be more comprehensively tested in the upgrade examinations than will be the more familiar methods, although in my experience, examiners often concentrate on new features. My advice: know both methods.

Connection security rules are configured in the WFAS console. You can enforce specific WFAS console settings on a network by using Group Policy. Figure 2-14 shows a GPO that defines connection security rules for many computers on a network.

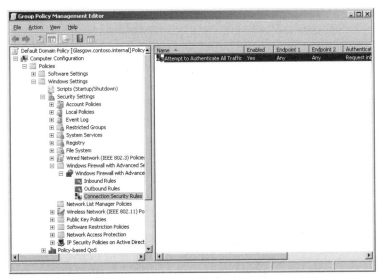

FIGURE 2-14 Connection security rules can be defined in Group Policy.

NOTE **EXPORTING CONNECTION SECURITY RULES**

You can use the Export Policy and Import Policy functions in the WFAS console to create a set of connection security rules and export them to other computers or GPOs.

Using Windows Firewall with Advanced Security

In Windows Server 2008, you can use a single tool, the WFAS MMC snap-in, to configure both Windows Firewall and IPsec. The new WFAS builds on the default configuration implemented by the connection security rules described in the previous section. By combining IPsec connection security rules and firewall filters into a single policy, Windows Firewall implements policy-driven network access, resulting in more intelligent authenticating firewall actions.

MORE INFO **POLICY-DRIVEN NETWORK ACCESS**

Do not confuse policy-driven network access with IPsec configuration through IPsec policies. For more information about policy-driven network access, see *http://technet.microsoft.com/en-us/magazine/cc194389.aspx*.

WFAS is on by default and consolidates and enhances the two functions, which were managed separately in previous versions of Windows Server. In addition to the new graphical user interface (GUI) tool, you can also manage both Windows Firewall and IPsec from the command-line *netsh advfirewall* context as discussed in the next section of this lesson.

By default, all IPv4 and IPv6 incoming traffic is blocked unless it is a response to a previous outgoing request from the computer (solicited traffic) or specifically allowed by a rule created to allow that traffic. All outgoing traffic is allowed by default, except where service-hardening rules prevent standard services from communicating in unexpected ways. You can allow traffic based on port numbers, IPv4 or IPv6 addresses, the path and name of an application, the name of a service that is running on the computer, or other criteria.

You can protect network traffic entering or exiting the computer by using the IPsec protocol to verify the integrity of the network traffic, to authenticate the identity of the sending and receiving computers or users, and, optionally, to encrypt traffic to provide confidentiality. You set up a rule by creating a WFAS inbound rule—for example, a rule that identifies an incoming port such as 443, specifying that the connection is allowed only if it is secure, and requiring encryption. You can then finish the rule creation and edit the WFAS rule you have created to specify to which IP addresses it applies. This method enables you to specify the source and destination IP address as well as the ports that require IPsec encryption and specific authentication methods. Figure 2-15 shows the dialog boxes you would use to create a rule by this method. These include the Custom Data Protection Settings dialog box together with the WFAS GUI and the Customize IPsec Settings dialog box.

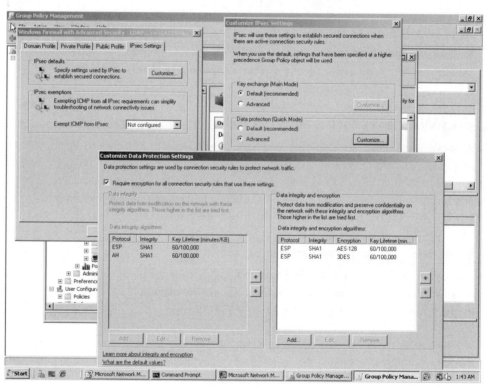

FIGURE 2-15 IPsec rule configuration dialog boxes.

MORE INFO **CONFIGURING IPSEC TO USE NETWORK ACCESS POLICY (NAP) RULES**

Using connection security rules and refining IPsec policy through WFAS enables you to specify a NAP rule together with or instead of an IPsec rule as part of IPsec policy. For more information, see *http://www.microsoft.com/windowsserver2008/en/us/security-policy.aspx*. For more information about NAP, see Chapter 4, "Configuring Network Access Security."

Netsh Commands for IPsec

As with almost all administrative functions, you can use the *network shell* command (*netsh*) instead of graphical tools to administer IPsec. However, the *netsh ipsec* context, which you might have used to administer Windows Server 2003 IPsec, is not the best tool for Windows Server 2008. The *netsh ipsec static* and *netsh ipsec dynamic* contexts are still provided, but they are for compatibility with previous versions of Windows. They do not enable you to manage or interact with any of the IPsec features that are new to Windows Server 2008. Microsoft recommends that you use the *netsh advfirewall* context instead.

MORE INFO **NETSH IPSEC**

If you want to remind yourself about how the tools provided in the *netsh ipsec static* and *netsh ipsec dynamic* contexts work, see *http://technet.microsoft.com/en-us/library /cc725926.aspx*.

MORE INFO **HOW TO USE *NETSH ADVFIREWALL***

For more information about the *netsh advfirewall* commands that replace the *netsh ipsec* commands in Windows Server 2008, see *http://support.microsoft.com/kb/947709*. For examination purposes, investigate *netsh advfirewall* and ascertain how you would verify that IPsec is enabled.

Administering IPsec from the command line is especially useful when you want to accomplish the following:

- Script IPsec configuration
- Extend the security and manageability of IPsec by configuring the following features, which are not available in the IP Security Policy Management snap-in:
  - IPsec diagnostics
  - Default traffic exemptions
  - Strong certificate revocation list (CRL) checking
  - IKE (Oakley) logging

- Logging intervals
- Computer startup security
- Computer startup traffic exemptions

NOTE **RUN AS ADMINISTRATOR**

If you are using *netsh* to configure IPsec (and for most other *netsh* configurations), you must run the Command Prompt console as an administrator.

Netsh advfirewall is a command-line context for WFAS by which you create, administer, and monitor Windows Firewall and IPsec settings. The tool is especially useful in the following situations:

- You are deploying WFAS settings to computers on a wide area network (WAN). You can use the commands interactively at the *netsh* command prompt to provide better performance than graphical utilities across slow-speed network links.
- When deploying WFAS settings to a large number of computers, you can use *netsh advfirewall* commands in batch mode at the *netsh* command prompt to help script and automate administrative tasks.

NOTE **NETSH** **FIREWALL**

The *netsh* firewall context is supplied for backward compatibility. Microsoft recommends that you do not use this context on a computer that is running Windows Server 2008.

The available contexts for managing Windows Firewall with Advanced Security are as follows:

- *Netsh advfirewall*
- *Netsh advfirewall consec*
- *Netsh advfirewall firewall*
- *Netsh advfirewall monitor*

The *Netsh Advfirewall* Context

Netsh advfirewall can be regarded as a separate context from the other three previously listed, although the other contexts are actually subcontexts of *netsh advfirewall*. This context provides commands that are common to all WFAS settings, including IPsec settings. For example, you might want to export a WFAS configuration that includes IPsec settings from one computer and import the configuration into other computers. The following commands are available at the *netsh advfirewall>* prompt:

- *dump*
- *export*

- *import*
- *reset*
- *set*
- *show*

Dump   The *dump* command is available but not implemented for the *netsh advfirewall* context or any of its three subcontexts. It produces no output but also generates no error.

Export   The *export* command exports the WFAS configuration in the current store to a file. This file can be used with the *import* command to restore the WFAS service configuration to a store on the same computer or to a different computer. The WFAS configuration on which the *export* command works is determined by the *set store* command. This command is equivalent to the Export Policy command in the WFAS Microsoft Management Console (MMC) snap-in.

Import   The *import* command imports a WFAS service configuration from a file created by using the *export* command to the local service. The command is equivalent to the *Import Policy* command in the WFAS MMC snap-in.

Reset   The *reset* command restores WFAS to its default settings and rules. Optionally, it first backs up the current settings by using the *export* command to export them to a configuration file. The command is equivalent to the *Restore Defaults* command in the WFAS MMC snap-in.

If the current focus of your commands is the local computer object, the default settings and rules immediately take effect on the computer. If the current focus of your commands is a GPO, the *reset* command resets all policy settings in that object to *Not Configured* and deletes all connection security and firewall rules from the object. Changes do not take place until that policy is refreshed on those computers to which the policy applies. To modify a GPO rather than the local computer's configuration store, you would use the *set store* command.

Set   The *netsh advfirewall* context provides three set commands that configure settings that apply either globally or to the per-profile configurations of WFAS. The *set* commands available at the netsh advfirewall prompt are:

- *set {ProfileType}*
- *set global*
- *set store*

> **NOTE   DEFAULT PROFILE STATE**
>
> The default state for all profiles on computers that are running a new installation of Windows Server 2008 is *on*. For computers that were upgraded to Windows Server 2008 from an earlier version of Windows Server, the state of WFAS is preserved from the state of Windows Firewall on the previously installed operating system.

Show The *show* command displays settings that apply either globally or to the per-profile configurations of WFAS. The following *show* commands are available at the netsh advfirewall> prompt:

- *show {ProfileType}*
- *show global*
- *show store*

The *Netsh AdvFirewall Consec* Context

The *netsh advfirewall consec* context enables you to view, create, and modify connection security rules specifically related to IPsec. This context is the command-line equivalent of the *Connection Security Rules* node of the WFAS MMC snap-in. The following commands are available in this context:

- *add*
- *set*
- *show*
- *delete*

Add In the *netsh advfirewall consec* context, the *add* command is used as the *add rule* command to add a connection security rule that defines IPsec requirements for network connections. For example, the following command creates a rule that you could use in a domain isolation scenario in which incoming traffic is permitted from other domain member computers only:

```
netsh advfirewall consec add rule name="Only Domain Members" endpoint1=any endpoint2=any
action=requireinrequestout
```

> **CAUTION   DO NOT USE ALL AS A NAME**
>
> Do not create a connection security rule with the name *all*. This creates a conflict with the *netsh* option.

Set In the *netsh advfirewall consec* context, the *set* command is used as the *set rule* command to modify an existing connection security rule identified by name or found by matching the criteria specified. Criteria that precede the keyword *new* identify the rule(s) to be modified. Criteria that follow the keyword *new* indicate properties that are modified or added. For example, the following command modifies the action in the Only Domain Members rule so that the criteria for incoming traffic are requested rather than required.

```
set rule name="Only Domain Members" new action=requestinrequestout
```

Show   In the *netsh advfirewall consec* context, the *show* command is used as the *show rule* command. For example, the following command displays all existing connection security rules:

```
netsh advfirewall consec show rule name=all
```

Delete   In the *netsh advfirewall consec* context, the *delete* command is used as the *delete rule* command to delete a connection security rule or a number of rules, all of which match the criteria specified in the command. For example, the following command deletes the Only Domain Members rule that you created earlier:

```
netsh advfirewall consec delete rule name="Only Domain Members"
```

Other *Netsh Advfirewall* Contexts

The *netsh advfirewall firewall* and *netsh advfirewall monitor* contexts are not relevant to IPsec configuration.

> **MORE INFO**   **NETSH COMMANDS FOR WFAS**
>
> For more information about *netsh* commands for WFAS, including syntax information and examples, see *http://technet.microsoft.com/en-us/library/cc771920.aspx#BKMK_2*. For more information about WFAS, see Chapter 4, "Network Access Security."

Using IPsec Policies

You can use IPsec policies to define how a computer or group of computers handle IPsec communication. You assign an IPsec policy to an individual computer by using Local Security Policy or to a group of computers by using Group Policy. You can specify several IPsec policies for use on a computer or network, but only one policy is assigned to a computer at any given time. Figure 2-16 shows a GPO in which an IPsec policy is assigned.

An IPsec policy contains one or more IPsec policy *rules*. These rules determine when and how IP traffic is protected. Each policy rule, in turn, is associated with one *IP filter list* and one *filter action*.

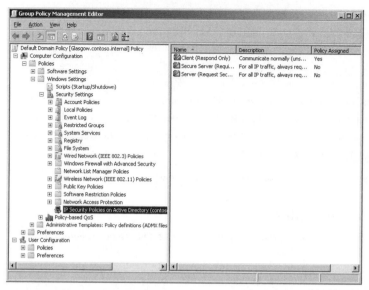

FIGURE 2-16 IPsec policies assigned in a GPO.

An IP filter list contains one or more IP filters that define the IP traffic affected by an IPsec policy. An IP filter can define a source or destination address, an address range, a computer name, a TCP/UDP port, or a server type (DNS, WINS, DHCP, or default gateway). If traffic leaving or arriving at a computer on which a policy is assigned matches a filter in one of the assigned policy's policy rules, the filter action associated with that rule is applied. Possible filter actions for a rule include *block*, *permit*, or *negotiate security*. When matching a source or destination address, the most specific IPsec filter always takes precedence.

Security Negotiation

*N*egotiate Security is a general filter action option. If you specify this option, you can then specifically choose the way security is negotiated for the filter action. For example, should encryption be negotiated or merely authentication? What is the order of preference for encryption technologies or hashing algorithms? Is it permissable to use unsecured communications if the source and destination cannot agree on a common protocol for security?

You can choose many ways to negotiate security for a filter action, and it is therefore possible to define many distinct rules when you select the Negotiate Security option. Security can be successfully negotiated only when both ends of an IPsec connection can agree on the particular services and algorithms used to protect the data.

Figure 2-17 illustrates an IPsec policy and how that policy is composed of rules, filters, and filter actions. In the figure, the IPsec policy consists of three rules. The first rule has priority because it defines traffic most specifically—both by type (Telnet or IMAP4) and by address (from 10.0.0.11 or from 10.0.0.31). The second rule is the next most specific, defining traffic by type (Telnet or IMAP4). The third rule is the least specific because it applies to all traffic. It, therefore, has the lowest priority.

A computer to which the IPsec policy illustrated in Figure 2-17 is assigned will attempt to authenticate (but not encrypt) all data except Telnet and IMAP4 traffic. Telnet and IMAP4 traffic are blocked by default unless the Telnet traffic originates from 10.0.0.11 or the IMAP4 traffic originates from 10.0.0.31, in which case, the traffic is allowed if encryption can be successfully negotiated.

IPsec Policy

		IP Filter Lists	Filter Actions
	Policy Rule #1	Filter #1: Telnet Traffic from 10.0.0.11 Filter #2: IMAP4 Traffic from 10.0.0.31	Negotiate Security (Require Encryption)
	Policy Rule #2	Filter #1: All Telnet Traffic Filter #2: All IMAP4 Traffic	Block
	Policy Rule #3	Filter #1: All Traffic	Negotiate Security (Request Authentication)

Less specific/Lower priority

FIGURE 2-17 An IPsec policy that consists of three rules.

Quick Check

1. What are the possible filter actions for an IPsec rule?

2. What does a filter action within an IPsec policy do?

Quick Check Answers

1. Block, permit, negotiate security.

2. A filter action determines whether the traffic captured by an IP filter in a given policy rule is permitted, blocked, encrypted, or authenticated.

Security Associations

After a source and a destination computer negotiate an IPsec connection, either through IPsec policies or connection security rules, the data sent between those computers is secured in a security association (SA). Security for an SA is provided by two IPsec protocols—*Authentication Header* (AH) and *Encapsulating Security Payload* (ESP). AH and ESP provide data and identity protection for each IP packet in an SA. AH provides data origin authentication, data integrity, and anti-replay protection for the entire IP packet. ESP provides data encryption, data origin authentication, data integrity, and anti-replay protection for the ESP payload. You can use AH alone, ESP alone, or AH and ESP together to secure data within an SA.

EXAM TIP

If you need encryption, use ESP. If you need to authenticate the data origin or verify data integrity, use AH.

Establishing an IPsec Connection

The Internet Key Exchange (IKE) protocol establishes SAs dynamically between IPsec peers. IKE sets up a mutually agreeable policy that defines the SA. This policy defines security services, protection mechanisms, and cryptographic keys between communicating peers. In establishing the SA, IKE provides the security keys and negotiation for the AH and ESP IPsec security protocols.

IKE performs a two-phase negotiation operation, each phase with its own SAs. Phase 1 negotiation is known as *main mode* negotiation, and Phase 2 is known as *quick mode* negotiation. The IKE main mode SAs secure the second IKE negotiation phase. The second IKE negotiation phase creates quick mode SAs and these are used to protect application traffic. When quick mode SAs are established, data can be safely sent between source and destination.

Using IPsec in Tunnel Mode

By default, IPsec operates in *transport mode* and provides end-to-end security between computers. Most IPsec-based VPNs use IPsec in transport mode and use L2TP to tunnel the IPsec connection through the public network.

However, if a VPN gateway is incompatible with L2TP/IPsec, you can use IPsec in *tunnel mode*, in which the entire IP packet is protected and then encapsulated with an additional, unprotected IP header. The IP addresses of the outer IP header represent the tunnel endpoints, and the IP addresses of the inner IP header represent the ultimate source and destination addresses.

Tunnel mode is an advanced IPsec feature that provides interoperability with routers, gateways, or end systems that do not support L2TP/IPsec or PPTP connections. However, IPsec tunnels are not supported for remote access VPN scenarios and, in practice, tunnel mode is rarely used. Chapter 3 provides more information about remote access VPNs.

EXAM TIP

For the upgrade examinations, you need to know when tunnel mode is used and in what scenarios it is not supported. However, IPsec tunnel mode is unlikely to be extensively tested in the examinations.

IPsec Authentication Methods

IPsec requires a shared authentication mechanism between communicating computers. The following three methods can be used to authenticate the hosts communicating through IPsec:

- **Kerberos** Kerberos is the default authentication protocol in an Active Directory environment and can be used if you implement IPsec within a single Active Directory forest. When the two IPsec endpoints can be authenticated by AD DS, IPsec authentication requires no configuration beyond joining the hosts to the domain. If your network environment includes a Kerberos realm that is not part of an Active Directory forest, you can also use this Kerberos realm to provide authentication for IPsec communications.

- **Certificates** In a production environment in which Kerberos authentication is not available, you can use a certificate infrastructure to authenticate the IPsec peers. In this solution, each host must obtain and install a computer certificate from a public or private certification authority (CA). The computer certificates do not need to originate from the same CA, but each host must trust the CA that has issued the certificate to the communicating peer. Chapter 7, "Active Directory Certificate Services," discusses security certificates in detail.

- **Preshared Key** A preshared key is a password known to both peers. It can be used to encrypt and decrypt data. You can specify a preshared key on IPsec endpoints to enable encryption between hosts. Although this authentication method enables IPsec SAs to be established, preshared keys do not provide the same level of authentication as do certificates or Kerberos. In addition, preshared keys for IPsec are stored in plaintext on each computer or in AD DS. Microsoft recommends that you use preshared keys in nonproduction environments only, such as in test networks.

EXAM TIP

Kerberos authentication is preferable in an Active Directory environment (or a Kerberos realm). If Kerberos authentication is unavailable, a certificate infrastructure is the best option.

Assigning a Predefined IPsec Policy

Group Policy predefines three IPsec policies. You can configure an IPsec policy for a domain or organizational unit (OU) by assigning any one of the following predefined policies through a GPO:

- **Client (Respond Only)** If you assign this policy, the computer will never initiate a request to establish an IPsec communications channel with another computer. However, any computer to which you assign the Client (Respond Only) policy will negotiate and establish IPsec communications when requested to by another computer. You typically assign this policy to intranet computers that need to communicate with secured servers but that do not need to protect all traffic.

- **Server (Request Security)** You assign this policy to computers for which encryption is preferred but not required. The computer accepts unsecured traffic but always attempts to secure additional communications by requesting security from the original sender. This policy allows the entire communication to be unsecured if the other computer is not IPsec-enabled. Typically, you would assign this policy if a server needs to communicate with different types of clients, some of which support IPsec and some of which do not.

- **Secure Server (Require Security)** You should assign this policy to servers that transmit highly sensitive data and require secure communications. The server will not communicate with computers that do not understand IPsec. Only the initial communication request is permitted to be insecure.

You assign an IPsec policy within a GPO by right-clicking the policy and then clicking Assign from the shortcut menu, as shown in Figure 2-18.

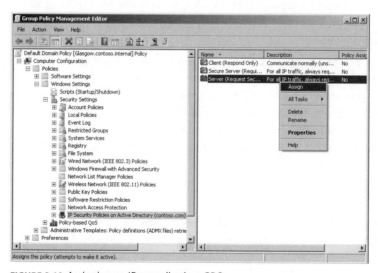

FIGURE 2-18 Assigning an IPsec policy in a GPO.

You can assign only one IPsec policy to a computer at a time. If you assign a second IPsec policy, the first IPsec policy automatically becomes unassigned. If Group Policy assigns an IPsec policy to a computer, the computer ignores any IPsec policy assigned in Local Security Policy.

Creating a New IPsec Policy

To create a new custom IPsec policy, you open Local Security Policy or a GPO. In the console tree below Security Settings, right-click the IP Security Policies node, and then select Create IP Security Policy, as shown in Figure 2-19. (You can find Security Settings in a GPO in the Computer Configuration\Policies\Windows Settings container.) This procedure launches the IP Security Policy Wizard.

The IP Security Policy Wizard enables you to create a blank policy, to name that policy, and to enable the Default Response Rule. After you create and name the IPsec policy, you can configure it through its Properties dialog box. You can add rules to the policy by clicking Add on the Rules tab, as shown in Figure 2-20. This procedure launches the Create IP Security Rule Wizard.

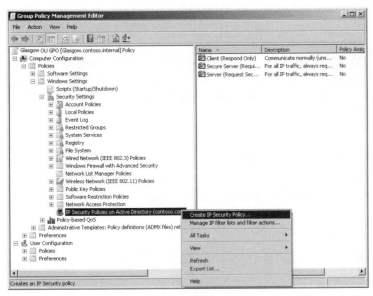

FIGURE 2-19 Creating a new IPsec policy in a GPO.

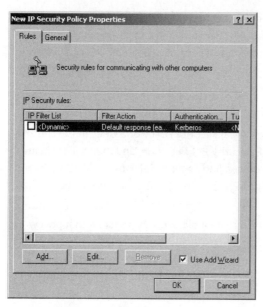

FIGURE 2-20 The Rules tab of the Security Policy Properties dialog box.

> **NOTE** **THE DEFAULT RESPONSE RULE**
>
> The Default Response rule is read-only by versions of Windows earlier than Windows Vista. For those operating systems, the rule provides a default action for an IPsec policy when no other IPsec policy filters apply.

Using the Create IP Security Rule Wizard

You use the Create IP Security Rule Wizard (also known as the Security Rule Wizard) to create and configure IPsec rules. The five main pages of the Create IP Security Rule Wizard are as follows:

- Tunnel Endpoint page
- Network Type page
- IP Filter List page
- Filter Action page
- Authentication Method page

Tunnel Endpoint page   You need to configure this page only when you want to use IPsec in tunnel mode.

Network Type page   You should use this page if you want to limit the rule to either the local area network (LAN) or to remote access connections.

IP Filter List page   You use this page to specify the set of IP filters you want to attach to the rule. Two IP filter lists in Group Policy are predefined for IPsec policy rules. These are All ICMP Traffic and All IP Traffic. To create a new IP filter list, click Add on the IP Filter List page, as shown in Figure 2-21. This procedure opens the IP Filter List dialog box.

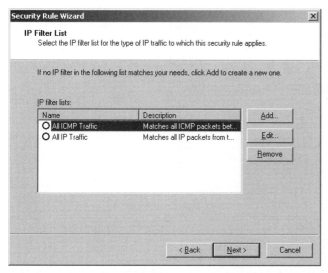

FIGURE 2-21 The IP Filter List page.

To specify a new IP filter to add to the IP filter list you are creating, click Add in the IP Filter List dialog box, as shown in Figure 2-22. This launches the IP Filter Wizard.

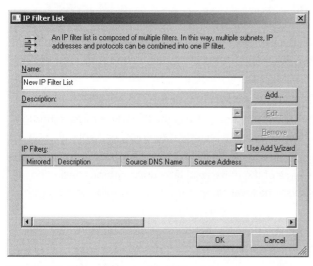

FIGURE 2-22 Adding a filter to the IP filter list.

Using the IP Filter Wizard, you specify IP traffic by source and destination. You can select a source and destination by using the IP address, DNS name, server function, and IP protocol type.

You can also use the IP Filter Wizard to create a mirrored filter. A mirrored filter matches the source and destination with the exact opposite addresses, so that, for example, you can easily configure a filter that captures Telnet traffic sent both to and from the local address. To configure your filter as a mirrored filter, select the Mirrored check box (selected by default) on the first page of the IP Filter Wizard, as shown in Figure 2-23.

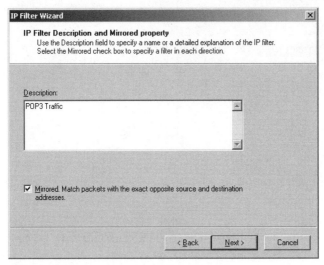

FIGURE 2-23 Specifying a mirrored IP filter.

Filter Action Page   When you have attached an IP filter list to a rule, you can specify a filter action for the rule in the Security Rule Wizard. In Group Policy, the following IP filters are predefined for IPsec policy rules:

- **Permit**   This filter action permits the IP packets to pass through unsecured.
- **Request Security (Optional)**   This filter action permits the IP packets to pass through unsecured but requests that clients negotiate security (preferably encryption).
- **Require Security**   This filter action triggers the local computer to request secure communications from the client source of the IP packets. If security methods (including encryption) cannot be established, the local computer will stop communicating with that client.

To create a new filter action, click Add on the Filter Action page, as shown in Figure 2-24. This procedure launches the Filter Action Wizard.

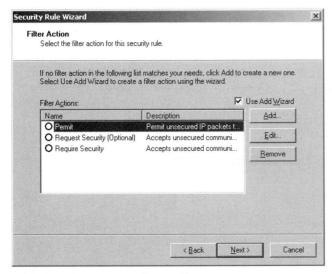

FIGURE 2-24 Creating a new filter action.

Authentication Method page Security can be negotiated only after IPsec clients are authenticated. By default, IPsec rules rely on AD DS and the Kerberos protocol to authenticate clients. You can, however, also specify a certificate infrastructure or a preshared key as a method of authenticating IPsec clients. You can use the Authentication Method page of the Security Rule Wizard, as shown in Figure 2-25, to specify the authentication method.

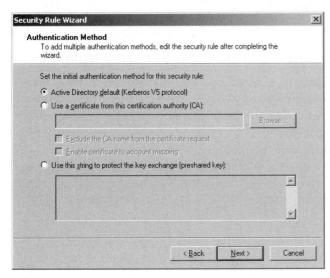

FIGURE 2-25 Specifying an authentication method.

Managing IP Filter Lists and Filter Actions

You can copy the IP filters, IP filter lists, and filter actions you create for an IPsec rule into other IPsec rules. You can also create and configure these features outside of the Security Rule Wizard. To do so, right-click the IP Security Policies node in Local Security Policy or a GPO, and then click Manage IP Filter Lists And Filter Actions, as shown in Figure 2-26.

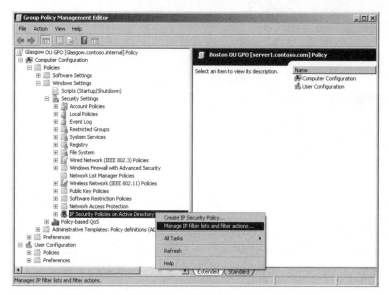

FIGURE 2-26 Managing IP filter lists and filter actions.

Creating and Configuring a Connection Security Rule

To create a Connection Security Rule in a GPO, right-click the GPO in the Group Policy Management console and select Edit. In the console tree of Group Policy Editor, expand Computer Configuration\Policies\Windows Settings\Security Settings\Windows Firewall With Advanced Security\Windows Firewall With Advanced Security – LDAP://*address*. You then select and right-click the Connection Security Rules node and then select New Rule from the shortcut menu, as shown in Figure 2-27. This launches the New Connection Security Rule Wizard.

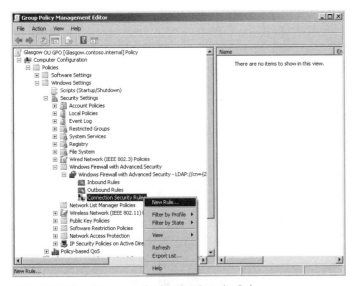

FIGURE 2-27 Creating a new Connection Security Rule.

The pages you see when you use the New Connection Security Rule Wizard depend on the type of rule you choose to create. The following pages appear when you create a custom rule:

- Rule Type page
- Endpoints page
- Requirements page
- Authentication Method page
- Profile page
- Name page

Rule Type page   The Rule Type page is shown in Figure 2-28. It enables you to create one of five rule types.

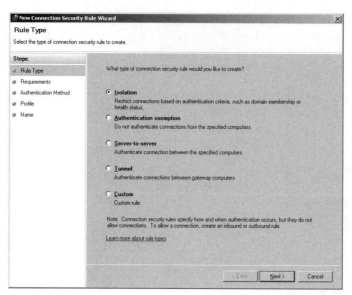

FIGURE 2-28 Choosing a Connection Security Rule type.

These five rule types are as follows:

- **Isolation rule**   This rule type authenticates all traffic for selected network profiles (network location types). When the network type defined for the local computer in Network and Sharing Center corresponds to one of the profiles selected for the rule, the local computer attempts to negotiate security as defined in the rule. The three profiles defined are Domain, Private, and Public.

- **Authentication Exemption rule**   This rule type exempts specific computers or a group or range of IP addresses from requiring to authenticate themselves, regardless of other connection security rules. Typically, you would use this rule type to grant access to infrastructure computers that a local host must communicate with before authentication can be performed. It is also used for computers that cannot use the form of authentication you configured for this policy and profile.

- **Server-To-Server rule**   This rule type enables you to authenticate communications between IP addresses or sets of addresses, including specific computers and subnets.

- **Tunnel rule**   You can use this rule type to configure IPsec tunnel mode for VPN gateways.

- **Custom rule**   This rule type enables you to create a rule that requires special settings or a combination of features from the various other rule types.

Endpoints Page   You can use this page to specify remote computers with which you want to negotiate an IPsec connection.

Requirements Page   You can use this page to specify whether authenticated communication should be *required* or merely *requested*. Alternatively, you can require authentication for inbound connections and request it for outbound connections. Also on this page, you can configure an authentication exemption for the endpoints specified.

Authentication Method Page   This page enables you to specify the method by which computer endpoints are authenticated. The first option is Default. When you choose this option, the authentication method used by the connection is that specified for the profile in the Profile tabs in the properties of the *WFAS* node.

You can also select Kerberos (Active Directory) authentication for both computers and users, Kerberos authentication for computers only, a computer certificate from a certificate infrastructure, or the Advanced authentication option. The Advanced option enables you to configure an order of preference for authentication methods for both users and computers. It also enables you to specify these authentication methods as optional.

Profile Page   This page enables you to limit the local network location types to which the rule will apply. The profiles you can enable for the rule are Domain, Private, and Public.

Name Page   This page enables you to name the new Connection Security Rule and (optionally) provide a description.

Configuring IPsec Settings for Connection Security Rules

You can define IPsec settings in the *WFAS* node of a GPO or in the WFAS console. To access these settings, first open the Properties dialog box of the Windows Firewall with Advanced Security node, as shown in Figure 2-29.

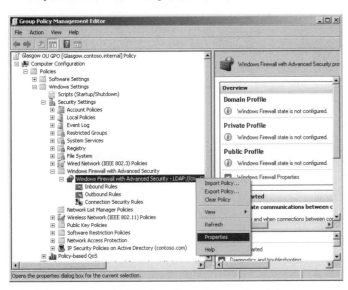

FIGURE 2-29 Opening the Windows Firewall Properties dialog box.

In the dialog box, click the IPsec Settings tab, as shown in Figure 2-30.

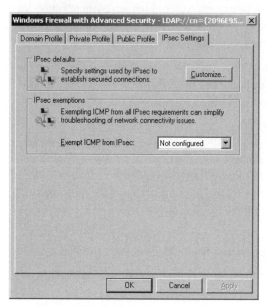

FIGURE 2-30 Configuring IPsec settings.

You can then configure two aspects of IPsec: IPsec defaults and ICMP exemptions.

IPsec Defaults Click Customize to open the Customize IPsec Settings dialog box, shown in Figure 2-31. From this dialog box, you can set new default parameters for key negotiation, data protection, and authentication method.

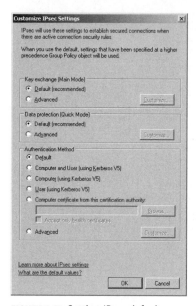

FIGURE 2-31 Setting IPsec defaults.

ICMP Exemptions   You can use this setting on the IPsec Settings tab to prevent ICMP messages from being authenticated, encrypted, or both. Keeping ICMP messages unprotected enables you to perform basic network troubleshooting when IPsec cannot be negotiated successfully.

PRACTICE **Deploying IPsec Through IPsec Policies and Connection Security Rules**

In the first exercise of this practice, you install Telnet services and then configure an IPsec policy to encrypt Telnet traffic between *boston.contoso.internal* and *glasgow.contoso.internal*. In the second exercise, you create a Connection Security Rule that authenticates all network traffic between the same two computers.

EXERCISE 1   **Install Telnet Services**

In this exercise, you install Telnet services on both the Glasgow and Boston computers.

1. If necessary, log on at the Glasgow domain controller by using the Kim_Akers account.

2. Insert your Windows Server 2008 Enterprise product DVD into the local DVD drive.

3. If Server Manager does not open automatically, click Start, click Administrative Tools, and select Server Manager. If a User Account Control (UAC) dialog box appears, click Continue. In the Server Manager window, under Features, click Add Features.

    The Select Features page of the Add Features Wizard opens.

4. In the list of features, select both the Telnet Client and Telnet Server check boxes, as shown in Figure 2-32, and then click Next.

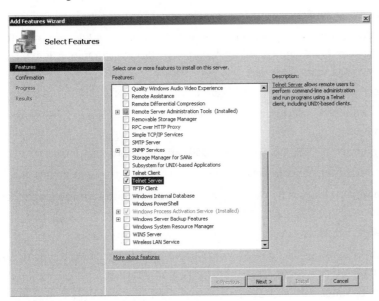

FIGURE 2-32 Selecting to install Telnet Server and Telnet Client.

5. On the Confirm Installation page of the Add Features Wizard, click Install.

6. After the installation has completed, click Close on the Installation Results page.

7. Open the Services console by clicking Start, clicking Administrative Tools, and then clicking Services. If a UAC dialog box appears, click Continue.

8. On the Services console, double-click Telnet to open its properties.

9. In the Telnet Properties dialog box, on the General tab, change the Startup Type to Automatic, and then click Apply.

10. In the Service Status area, click Start.

11. When the Service Status has changed to Started, click OK to close the Telnet Properties dialog box, and then close the Services console.

12. On the Start menu, select Administrative Tools and open Active Directory Users and Computers. If a UAC dialog box appears, click Continue.

13. If necessary, expand *contoso.internal*. Select Users.

14. In the details pane, double-click Telnet Clients.

15. In the Telnet Clients Properties dialog box, click the Members tab, and then click Add.

16. In the Select Users, Contacts, Computers, Or Groups dialog box, in the Enter The Object Names To Select text box, type **Domain Admins**, and then click OK.

17. In the Telnet Clients Properties dialog box, click OK.

18. Log off Glasgow.

19. Log on to the *contoso.internal* domain at the Boston server by using the Kim_Akers account.

20. Insert your Windows Server 2008 Enterprise product DVD into the local DVD drive.

21. If Server Manager does not open automatically, click Start, click Administrative Tools, and select Server Manager. If a UAC dialog box appears, click Continue. In the Server Manager window, under Features, click Add Features.

    The Select Features page of the Add Features Wizard opens.

22. In the list of features, select both the Telnet Client and Telnet Server check boxes, and then click Next.

23. On the Confirm Installation page of the Add Features Wizard, click Install.

24. After the installation has completed, click Close on the Installation Results page.

25. Open the Services console by clicking Start, clicking Administrative Tools, and then clicking Services. If a UAC dialog box appears, click Continue.

26. In the Services console, double-click Telnet to open its properties.

27. In the Telnet Properties dialog box on the General tab, change Startup Type to Automatic, and then click Apply.

28. In the Service Status area, click Start.

29. When the Service Status has changed to Started, click OK to close the Telnet Properties dialog box, and then close the Services console.

30. In the Start Search area of the Start menu, type **lusrmgr.msc**, and then press Enter. If a UAC dialog box appears, click Continue.

31. In the Local Users And Groups console tree, select Groups.

32. In the details pane, double-click Telnet Clients.

33. In the Telnet Clients Properties dialog box, click Add.

34. In the Select Users, Computers, Or Groups dialog box, in the Enter The Object Names To Select text box, type **Domain Admins**, and then click OK.

35. In the Telnet Clients Properties dialog box, click OK.

36. Log off from Boston.

EXERCISE 2   Create an IPsec Policy

In this exercise, you create a GPO and an IPsec policy that you will later configure to encrypt Telnet traffic in the *contoso.internal* domain.

1. Log on to the Glasgow domain controller by using the Kim_Akers account.

2. Open the Group Policy Management console (GPMC) by clicking Start, pointing to Administrative Tools, and then clicking Group Policy Management. If a UAC dialog box appears, click Continue.

3. In the console tree of GPMC, expand the Domains container, and then select the *contoso.internal* node.

4. Right-click the *contoso.internal* node and click Create A GPO In This Domain, And Link It Here.

5. In the New GPO dialog box, in the Name text box, type **IPsec GPO**, and then click OK.

6. In GPMC, in the details pane, right-click the IPsec GPO, and then click Edit from the shortcut menu.

7. In the Group Policy Management Editor window, expand Computer Configuration, expand Policies, expand Windows Settings, expand Security Settings, and select IP Security Policies On Active Directory (*contoso.internal*).

8. Right-click IP Security Policies On Active Directory (*contoso.internal*) and select Create IP Security Policy on the shortcut menu.

    The IP Security Policy Wizard opens.

9. Click Next.

10. On the IP Security Policy Name page, type **Contoso IPsec Policy**.

11. In the Description field, type **This IPsec policy encrypts Telnet traffic**.

12. Click Next.

13. On the Requests For Secure Communications page, read all the text on the page, and then click Next.

14. Click Finish.

    The Contoso IPsec Policy Properties dialog box appears.

15. Leave all windows open and continue to Exercise 3.

EXERCISE 3 **Create an IPsec Policy Rule and Filter**

In this exercise, you configure the newly created Contoso IPsec policy with rules that require high security for Telnet traffic. In the process, you run the Security Rule Wizard, the IP Filter Wizard, and the Filter Action Wizard.

1. While you are still logged on to Glasgow, in the Contoso IPsec Policy Properties dialog box, click Add.

    The Create IP Security Rule Wizard opens (also known as the Security Rule Wizard).

2. Read all the text on the first page, and then click Next.

3. On the Tunnel Endpoint page, read all the text on the page, and then click Next.

4. On the Network Type page, read all the text on the page, and then click Next.

5. On the IP Filter List page, read all the text on the page, and then click Add.

    The IP Filter List dialog box opens.

6. In the Name text box, type **Encrypt Telnet Filter List**, and then click Add.

    The IP Filter Wizard opens.

7. Click Next.

8. On the IP Filter Description And Mirrored Property page, read all the text on the page, and then click Next.

9. On the IP Traffic Source page, leave the default selection of Any IP Address, and then click Next.

10. On the IP Traffic Destination page, leave the default of Any IP Address, and then click Next.

11. On the IP Protocol Type page, select TCP from the Select A Protocol Type drop-down list box, and then click Next.

12. On the IP Protocol Port page, select To This Port, and then type **23** in the accompanying text box. Note that Telnet runs on TCP port 23, so you must specify both TCP and the appropriate port. (Leave From Any Port selected.)

13. Click Next, and then click Finish to close the IP Filter Wizard.

14. In the IP Filter List dialog box, click OK.

    The IP Filter List page of the Security Rule Wizard reappears.

15. In the IP Filter Lists area, select Encrypt Telnet Filter List, and then click Next.

16. On the Filter Action page, read all the text on the page, and then click Add.

    The Filter Action Wizard opens.

17. Leave this wizard open and continue to Exercise 4.

EXERCISE 4   Use the Filter Action Wizard

In this exercise, you use the Filter Action Wizard to configure a custom filter action to apply to Telnet traffic. Although the default filter actions available in Group Policy are usually adequate for creating IPsec rules, it is a good idea to configure higher security for Telnet. In addition, you should be familiar with the IP Security Filter Action Wizard for the upgrade examinations.

1. On the Welcome To The IP Security Filter Action Wizard page, read all the text on the page, and then click Next.

2. On the Filter Action Name page, in the Name text box, type **Require High Authentication and Encryption**.

3. In the Description field, type **Require AH authentication and 3DES encryption**.

4. Click Next.

5. On the Filter Action General Options page, ensure that Negotiate Security is selected, and then click Next.

6. On the Communicating With Computers That Do Not Support IPsec page, ensure that Do Not Allow Unsecured Communication is selected, and then click Next.

7. On the IP Traffic Security page, select Custom, and then click Settings.

8. In the Custom Security Method Settings dialog box, select the Data And Address Integrity Without Encryption (AH) check box.

9. In the Session Key Settings area, select both Generate A New Key Every check boxes.

10. Ensure that the Data Integrity And Encryption (ESP) check box is selected and that 3DES is the selected encryption algorithm. Figure 2-33 shows the required settings in the Custom Security Methods Settings dialog box. Click OK.

FIGURE 2-33 Custom security methods settings.

11. On the IP Traffic Security page, click Next.

12. On the Completing The IP Security Filter Action Wizard page, click Finish.

13. On the Filter Action page of the Security Rule Wizard, in the list of Filter Actions, select Require High Authentication And Encryption, and then click Next.

14. On the Authentication Method page of the Security Rule Wizard, leave the default Active Directory Default (Kerberos V5 Protocol), and then click Next.

15. On the Completing The Security Rule Wizard page, click Finish.

16. In the Contoso IPsec Policy Properties dialog box, click OK.

17. In the right-side pane of Group Policy Management Editor, right-click Contoso IPsec Policy, and then click Assign from the shortcut menu.

18. On both Glasgow and Boston, run the *gpupdate* command at a command prompt. You will need to run the Command Prompt console as an Administrator.

EXERCISE 5   Test the New IPsec Policy

In this exercise, you initiate a Telnet session from Glasgow to Boston. You then verify that data authentication and encryption are applied to the Telnet session.

1. On Glasgow, open a command prompt.

2. At the command prompt, type **telnet Boston**.

   A Telnet session to the Telnet server on Boston begins.

3. On Glasgow, from the Start menu, point to Administrative Tools, and then click Windows Firewall With Advanced Security. If a UAC dialog box appears, click Continue.

4. In the WFAS console tree, expand the Monitoring node and expand the *Security Associations* node.

5. Beneath the Security Associations node, select the Main Mode folder and then the Quick Mode folder.

   You will see that an SA appears in the details pane when you select each folder.

6. Spend a few moments browsing the information displayed about these SAs. If the quick mode SA disappears, enter a command such as **dir** at the Telnet prompt to reestablish it.

7. At the Telnet prompt, type **exit**.

Lesson Summary

- IPsec provides data authentication, encryption, or both. AH provides data origin authentication, data integrity, and anti-replay protection for the entire IP packet. ESP provides data encryption, data origin authentication, data integrity, and anti-replay protection for the ESP payload.

- You can implement IPsec either through IPsec policies or through connection security rules. You can refine default connection security rules settings by using WFAS. You can also use *netsh* commands from the command prompt.

- IPsec policies are made up of a set of IPsec rules. Each IPsec rule comprises one IP filter list and one filter action. The filter list defines the type of traffic to which the filter action is applied.

- IPsec operates by default in transport mode, which is also used in most IPsec-based VPNs. However, if a particular VPN gateway is not compatible with L2TP/IPsec VPNs, you can use IPsec in tunnel mode instead.

- Connection security rules protect all traffic between a particular source and its destination. Connection security rules can be configured in the WFAS console on an individual computer or enforced through a GPO.

Lesson Review

You can use the following questions to test your knowledge of the information in Lesson 2, "Configuring IPsec." The questions are also available on the companion DVD if you prefer to review them in electronic form.

> **NOTE ANSWERS**
>
> Answers to these questions and explanations of why each answer choice is right or wrong are located in the "Answers" section at the end of the book.

1. Which of the following *netsh* commands should you use to create an IPsec rule on a Windows Server 2008 server?

   A. *netsh advfirewall add rule name="Only Domain Members" endpoint1=any endpoint2=any action=requireinrequestout*

   B. *netsh advfirewall consec add rule name="Only Domain Members" endpoint1=any endpoint2=any action=requireinrequestout*

   C. *netsh firewall add rule name="Only Domain Members" endpoint1=any endpoint2=any action=requireinrequestout*

   D. *netsh ipsec dynamic add rule name="Only Domain Members" endpoint1=any endpoint2=any action=requireinrequestout*

2. You need to require network communications to be encrypted in the *contoso.internal* domain. Which protocol or protocols should you use?

   A. IPsec with AH

   B. IPsec in tunnel mode

   C. IPsec with both AH and ESP

   D. IPsec with ESP

3. You want to enforce IPsec communications between two domains that do not belong to the same Active Directory forest. Which IPsec authentication method should you choose?

   A. Certificates

   B. Kerberos

   C. Pre-shared key

   D. ESP

Chapter Review

To further practice and reinforce the skills you learned in this chapter, you can:

- Review the chapter summary.
- Complete the case scenarios. These scenarios set up real-world situations involving the topics of this chapter and ask you to create solutions.
- Complete the suggested practices.
- Take a practice test.

Chapter Summary

- You can configure software-based routing on a Windows Server 2008 server by using static routing to allow computers to forward traffic with different destinations to the correct subnet.
- You can use *pathping* and *tracert* to identify routing problems.
- Windows Server 2008 supports RIP, which you can enable by installing the Routing and Remote Access Services role service.
- IPsec enables you to protect network traffic by providing data authentication, encryption, or both.
- In Windows Server 2008 networks, you can implement IPsec through IPsec policies, through connection security rules, or by using *netsh* commands.

Case Scenarios

In the following case scenarios, you apply what you have learned about configuring IP services. You can find answers to these questions in the "Answers" section at the end of this book.

Case Scenario 1: Adding a Second Default Gateway

You are a systems administrator for Litware, Inc. A second gateway has been recently added to Litware's network for redundancy and fail-over protection. You need to configure client computers to connect through the second gateway if the first default gateway is unavailable. Litware's computers all have static IP configurations.

Answer the following question:

- How will you configure the client computers to use the second default gateway?

Case Scenario 2: Adding a New Subnet

You are a systems administrator working for Tailspin Toys. Recently, the 10.0.2.0/24 subnet was added to your company's network to be used for internal servers. This network is illustrated in Figure 2-34. Answer the following questions.

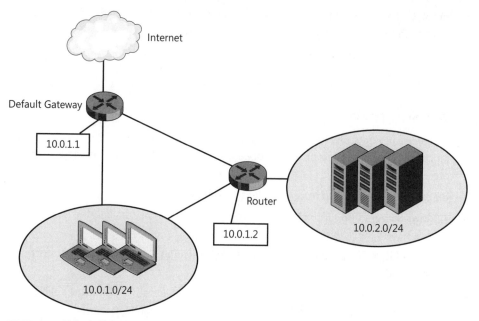

FIGURE 2-34 Tailspin Toys' network architecture.

1. How can client computers on the 10.0.1.0/24 subnet send traffic for the 10.0.2.0/24 subnet through the new router gateway (10.0.1.2) while sending traffic destined for every other network through the current default gateway (10.0.1.1)?

2. Which command do you run on the client computers to implement your solution?

Case Scenario 3: Implementing IPsec

You are a network administrator for Contoso, Ltd. Your company's network consists of a single Active Directory domain, *contoso.com*. Management has asked you to implement mandatory IPsec-based data authentication on all finance servers.

1. Which authentication method should you use for IPsec?

2. Contoso's Marketing manager needs to connect to a finance server but cannot do so. Which predefined IPsec policy can you assign in Group Policy to allow appropriate users to communicate with the finance servers?

Suggested Practices

To help you successfully master the exam objectives presented in this chapter, do all of the following practices:

- **Practice 1**   Use *pathping* and *tracert* to check the path to well-known Web sites. Note the differences in output.
- **Practice 2**   Use the *route print* command on any computer to which you have access and attempt to interpret the resulting route tables.
- **Practice 3**   Investigate the syntax of the *route* command and how you can configure both IPv4 and IPv6 routing from the Command Prompt console.
- **Practice 4**   In the *contoso.internal* domain, configure and assign an IPsec policy that requires the most secure methods of authentication and encryption. Note any disruptions or difficulty in network communication. Then, unassign the IPsec policy.
- **Practice 5**   Investigate the *netsh advfirewall* and *netsh advfirewall consec* contexts and their associated commands. In general, professional network administrators and engineers use command-line rather than graphics tools.

Take a Practice Test

The practice tests on this book's companion DVD offer many options. For example, you can test yourself on just the content covered in this chapter, or you can test yourself on all Windows Server 2008 upgrade certification exam content. You can set up the test so that it closely simulates the experience of taking a certification exam, or you can set it up in study mode so that you can look at the correct answers and explanations after you answer each question.

> **MORE INFO**   **PRACTICE TESTS**
>
> For details about all the practice test options available, see "How to Use the Practice Tests" in this book's Introduction.

CHAPTER 3

Network Access Configuration

This chapter discusses network access configuration, from allowing clients to access the network from locations outside the office to ensuring that only authorized clients within the office are able to connect to the existing network infrastructure. The first part of the chapter deals with remote access, which enables people to connect to their workplace from home or when travelling on business. In the past, people made these remote connections by using a modem and telephone line. Today, with Internet access now provided in hotel rooms, coffee shops, and airport lounges, remote connections to the office use virtual private networks (VPNs). Lesson 1, "Setting Up Remote Access," covers how you can configure Windows Server 2008 both to support dial-up connections and to provide VPN services. The second part of the chapter deals with local area network authentication. Windows Server 2008 enables you to configure network authentication policies that ensure that only authorized clients and devices are able to plug into your network infrastructure and use it to communicate. You can configure things so that if a device does not forward legitimate credentials to the switch it connects to, the switch will block it from accessing the network. By reading this chapter, you learn how to configure Windows Server 2008 network authentication and access settings to provide the type of secure access that best meets the needs of your organization.

Exam objectives in this chapter

- Configure remote access.
- Configure network authentication.

Lessons in this chapter:

Before You Begin

To complete the lessons in this chapter, you must have done the following:

- Installed and configured the evaluation edition of Windows Server 2008 Enterprise Edition in accordance with the instructions listed in the Introduction.

 **REAL WORLD**

Orin Thomas

Giving remote access to people in your organization can be both a blessing and a curse. I spent many hours in the early 1990s taking support calls related to remote access problems. Back then, people who were having problems with dial-up access generally had one phone line and no mobile phone. They would often call with a problem they were unable to reproduce because they were unable talk on the phone and use their modem at the same time. Some would attempt to describe the errors and some would even attempt to imitate the noises their modem made when it failed to connect. A couple of them would even go to the effort of bringing their entire desktop computers into the office from home where, of course, according to the universal law of tech support (things mysteriously work when an ordinary user tries to demonstrate a fault to an IT professional), they would be able to connect with the modem perfectly. There are many factors that influence whether someone can successfully make a dial-up connection, and most of them weren't at the end that I had any control over. Later, as I moved from help desk support toward systems administration, the remote access problems I had to deal with became more delicate. In one instance, examination of the proxy logs indicated that the CFO of the organization I worked for was accessing rather explicit material on the Web through his remote access dial-up connection to our company modem bank. The issue was resolved when my manager and I worked out that the explicit material tended to be accessed between 4 and 5 PM, a time when the CFO was still at work in his office, hence not accessing our network through a modem, but also the time when his teenage son arrived home from school. Luckily for me, explaining what was going on to the CFO was my manager's problem and not mine. Granting remote access, the topic of this chapter, is generally simple. Ensuring that people can connect and what they do when they do connect from the privacy of their own homes is another thing entirely!

Lesson 1: Setting Up Remote Access

Traditionally, remote access involved users connecting through modems to organizations so that they could gain after-hours access. Today, remote access is more likely to occur through VPN connections with dial-up connections used only as a means of last resort. In this lesson, you learn how to configure Windows Server 2008 to function as both a dial-up and a VPN access server. You learn how to configure remote access policies to limit access based on a set of conditions and how to configure Windows Server 2008 to function as a network address translation (NAT) or Internet Connection Sharing (ICS) server.

After this lesson, you will be able to:

- Configure remote access policies and VPNs.
- Manage ICS and NAT.
- Administer Routing and Remote Access.
- Configure RADIUS servers and proxies.
- Select remote access protocols.
- Set up Connection Manager.
- Configure RAS Authentication, using MS-CHAPv2 and EAP.

Estimated lesson time: 40 minutes

Configuring a Dial-Up Server

Although dial-up connections are significantly slower than most VPN connections, many organizations retain dial-up servers as a failsafe form of remote access if their Internet connection fails. People also use dial-up in areas that do not have cheap and reliable broadband connections. Windows Server 2008 is able to function as a dial-up server after you connect and install a modem.

You configure Routing and Remote Access, which, as you learned in Chapter 2, "Configuring IP Services," is installed as part of the Network Policy and Access Services (NPAS) server role to function as a dial-up server by selecting Dial-Up when running the Routing and Remote Access Server Setup Wizard, as shown in Figure 3-1.

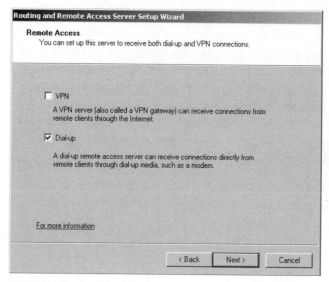

FIGURE 3-1 Configuring dial-up.

When running the wizard, you must specify the following information:

- Which network adapter successful dial-up connections will use to interact with the internal network when a server has multiple adapters.

- Whether a Dynamic Host Configuration Protocol (DHCP) server will assign IP addresses to dial-up clients or whether the dial-up server will assign them from a static pool. If you choose to use a DHCP server, you must configure a DHCP relay agent on the dial-up server.

- Whether you want the dial-up server to perform authentication or forward requests to another RADIUS or Network Policy Server (NPS) role service server. When the dial-up server forwards authentication requests, it functions as a RADIUS client. You learn more about configuring Windows Server 2008 as a RADIUS server later in this lesson.

Additionally, you must configure the Routing and Remote Access server to function as an IPv4 (or IPv6 if you are using IPv6 with dial-up) router. You must also set up Routing and Remote Access to enable IPv4 forwarding, as shown in Figure 3-2. When you use a DHCP server to provide IP addresses to dial-up clients, ensure that you select the Dynamic Host Configuration Protocol option. Alternatively, if you have chosen to assign IPv4 addresses from a pool, you can configure the address pool through this tab. If you are assigning IPv6 addresses to dial-up clients, you must configure settings on the IPv6 tab.

The final step, when configuring Windows Server 2008 to function as a dial-up server, is to configure each modem to accept inbound remote access connections. To do this, right-click the Ports node in the Routing and Remote Access console, select Properties, select each modem, and then click Configure. This displays the Configure Device dialog box, shown in Figure 3-3, in which you select Remote Access Connections (Inbound Only) and enter the phone number assigned to the modem.

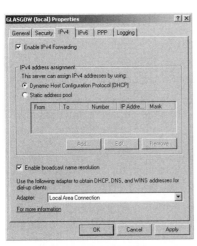

FIGURE 3-2 IPv4 Routing and Remote Access Service (RRAS) Properties dialog box.

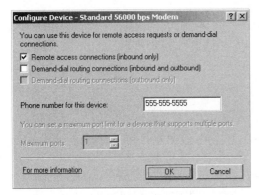

FIGURE 3-3 Configuring the dial-up server modem.

> **NOTE SERVER CORE AND NPAS**
>
> The NPAS role cannot be installed on computers running Windows Server 2008 configured with the Server Core installation option, which means that computers running Server Core cannot function as remote access servers.

> **MORE INFO CONFIGURING A DIAL-UP REMOTE ACCESS SERVER**
>
> To learn more about configuring Windows Server 2008 to function as a dial-up server, see the following page on TechNet: *http://technet.microsoft.com/en-us/library/cc753083.aspx*.

Configuring a VPN Server

VPN servers provide access to internal networks for external clients connected to the Internet. You can configure Windows Server 2008 to function as a VPN server by installing the Network Policy and Access Services server role and choosing the Routing and Remote Access Services and Remote Access Service role services. Windows Server 2008 can function as both a VPN server and a dial-up server concurrently, but most deployments have it functioning in one role or the other. To configure Windows Server 2008 to function as a VPN server, perform the following steps:

1. Run the Routing And Remote Access Server Setup Wizard from the Routing And Remote Access console. Choose the Remote Access (Dial-Up Or VPN) option.

2. Select the network interface connected to the Internet. This interface should be configured with a public IP address or, if NAT is in use, have the appropriate ports forwarded to it from the NAT server's public IP address.

3. Specify whether the server will assign IP addresses to VPN clients from a static pool or from a DHCP server on the internal network.

4. Specify whether the VPN server will perform authentication locally or as a RADIUS client that forwards authentication requests to a RADIUS server.

You perform the detailed steps to configure Windows Server 2008 to function as a VPN server in the practice at the end of this lesson.

VPN Protocols

Windows Server 2008 supports three VPN protocols: SSTP, L2TP, and PPTP. These protocols have the following properties:

- **Secure Socket Tunneling Protocol (SSTP)** SSTP uses an HTTPS channel for encapsulation and encryption and point-to-point protocol (PPP) for user authentication. SSTP uses TCP port 443, which is used for SSL traffic, meaning that it will rarely be blocked by firewalls in public access points such as those in hotels or in airport lounges. SSTP can also traverse NAT gateways without a problem. The drawback to SSTP is that only Windows Server 2008 and Windows Vista SP1 support it. SSTP requires you to install a Secure Sockets Layer (SSL) certificate on the VPN server that matches the hostname assigned to the VPN server's public IP address. Clients must connect using this hostname and must trust the certification authority (CA) that issued the SSL certificate. You must open TCP port 443 to allow SSTP access to the VPN server when it is located behind a firewall.

- **Layer 2 Tunneling Protocol with IPsec (L2TP/IPsec)** L2TP uses PPP user authentication and IPsec for the protection of data. The default L2TP/IPsec configuration requires a public key infrastructure (PKI) to issue computer certificates to each VPN client. It is possible to use preshared keys, but this is less secure. L2TP/IPsec is supported by Windows Server 2008, Windows Vista, Microsoft Windows XP, and Microsoft Windows Server 2003. Only Windows XP SP2 and later can use L2TP/IPsec through NAT gateways because they support NAT Traversal (NAT-T). L2TP/IPsec offers data encryption, origin authentication, and integrity protection. You must open User Datagram Protocol (UDP) ports 1701, 500, and 4500 to allow L2TP/IPsec access to the VPN server when it is located behind a firewall.

- **Point to Point Tunneling Protocol (PPTP)** PPTP uses Microsoft Point-to-Point Encryption (MPPE) for encryption and PPP for user authentication. PPTP is not as secure as L2TP/IPsec or SSTP. PPTP can traverse some, but not all, NAT gateways. PPTP does encrypt data but does not provide data integrity or data origin authentication. You must open TCP port 1723 to allow PPTP access to the VPN server when it is located behind a firewall.

> **MORE INFO** **VPN PROTOCOLS**
>
> To learn more about VPN protocols supported by Windows Server 2008, see the following page on TechNet: *http://technet.microsoft.com/en-us/library/cc771298.aspx.*

When you configure Windows Server 2008 as a VPN server, clients can make connections by using all three protocols. You can configure separate network policies that apply different connection settings based on which protocol is used. To disable a particular protocol, clear the Remote Access Connections (Inbound Only) and Demand-Dial Routing Connections (Inbound And Outbound) check boxes, as shown in Figure 3-4, by editing the properties of the Ports node in the Routing And Remote Access console.

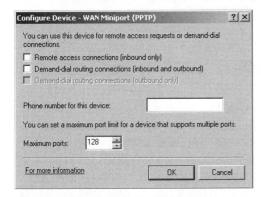

FIGURE 3-4 Disabling PPTP on a VPN server.

VPN Authentication

Windows Server 2008 supports the following authentication protocols for VPN connections:

- **MS-CHAPv2** A password-based authentication protocol supported by Windows Vista, Windows Server 2008, Windows Server 2003, and Windows XP.
- **EAP-MS-CHAPv2** A password-based authentication protocol supported only by Windows Vista and Windows Server 2008 VPN clients.

- **EAP-TLS** A certificate-based authentication protocol supported by Windows Vista, Windows XP, Windows Server 2008, and Windows Server 2003 VPN clients.

- **PEAP-MS-CHAPv2** A password-based authentication protocol that requires the installation of a computer certificate on the authentication server (either the VPN server or the RADIUS server). Clients must trust the CA that issued the computer certificate. Only Windows Vista and Windows Server 2008 VPN clients support this authentication protocol.

- **PEAP-TLS** A certificate-based authentication protocol, supported by Windows Vista and Windows Server 2008 clients, that can be used with smart cards or other digital certificates.

Windows Server 2008 does not support MS-CHAP, SPAP, or EAP-MD5, protocols that were supported in earlier versions of Windows. Windows XP and Windows Server 2003 VPN clients can use only the MS-CHAPv2 and EAP-TLS protocols for authentication, so bear this in mind when working with these older operating systems. When you deploy NAP with VPN enforcement, you must use a Protected Extensible Authentication Protocol (PEAP)-based authentication protocol. NAP with VPN enforcement is covered in detail in Chapter 4, "Network Access Security."

> **MORE INFO** **CONFIGURING REMOTE ACCESS VPN SERVERS**
>
> To learn more about configuring Windows Server 2008 to function as a remote access VPN server, see the following page on TechNet: *http://technet.microsoft.com/en-us/library /cc725734.aspx*.

Windows Server 2008 and RADIUS

Through the Network Policy Server role service, Windows Server 2008 can function as a RADIUS server, proxy, or client. In Windows Server 2003, this role was performed by the Internet Authentication Service (IAS). When functioning as a RADIUS server, it provides authentication services for RADIUS clients. When functioning as a RADIUS client, it sends authentication traffic to a designated RADIUS server. When functioning as a RADIUS proxy, it forwards authentication traffic from RADIUS clients to RADIUS servers based on the properties of the forwarded authentication traffic. Figure 3-5 shows a basic RADIUS infrastructure in which the RADIUS server provides authentication directly for the VPN server and indirectly, through a RADIUS proxy, for the dial-up server. Both the VPN server and the RADIUS proxy are RADIUS clients of the RADIUS server. The dial-up server, in turn, is a RADIUS client of the RADIUS proxy. A RADIUS server can use Active Directory Domain Services (AD DS) as a user account database or its local account database if it is a member of a domain. If the RADIUS server is not a member of a domain, you can configure it to use a local account database or Lightweight Directory Access Protocol (LDAP) instance for authentication lookups.

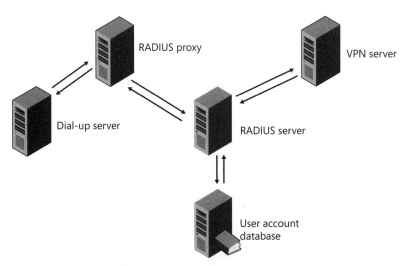

FIGURE 3-5 Basic RADIUS infrastructure.

Windows Server 2008 Enterprise and Datacenter enable you to configure an unlimited number of RADIUS clients and remote RADIUS server groups. With these editions, you can specify RADIUS clients by hostname, IP, and IP address range, enabling you to configure multiple RADIUS clients quickly. Windows Server 2008 Standard is limited to a maximum of 50 radius clients and two remote RADIUS server groups. When using Windows Server 2008 Standard with NPS, you can define RADIUS clients either by host name or IP address, but you cannot define them by IP address range. You can define RADIUS clients by address range when using Windows Server 2008 Enterprise or Datacenter editions.

RADIUS Client

Windows Server 2008 can function as a RADIUS client. You can also configure other servers and network devices to be RADIUS clients of a computer running Windows Server 2008 with the Network Policy Server role service installed in conjunction with the Network Policy and Access Services server role.

RADIUS clients can include dial-up servers or access points, VPN servers, wireless local area network (WLAN) access points, or 802.1x-compliant switches and RADIUS proxies. Configuring local area network (LAN) authentication with 802.1x-compliant switches is covered in Lesson 2, "Managing Network Authentication." Configuring RADIUS and WLAN access points is covered in Chapter 4. When adding a RADIUS client, you do not need to specify how the access works; RADIUS clients function in the same manner whether they are dial-up servers or wireless access points. To configure a computer running Windows Server 2008 with a RADIUS client, perform the following steps:

1. Open the Network Policy Server console.
2. In the console tree, navigate to the NPS (Local)\RADIUS Clients And Servers\RADIUS Clients node. Right-click the RADIUS Clients node, and then select New RADIUS Client.

This opens the New RADIUS Client dialog box, shown in Figure 3-6.

3. Enter the details of the RADIUS client, and then click OK.

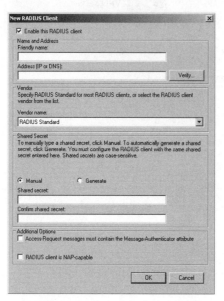

FIGURE 3-6 New RADIUS Client dialog box.

RADIUS clients and servers must authenticate with each other by using a shared secret. You can have Windows Server 2008 automatically generate the shared secret, which you then configure on the RADIUS client, or enter your own shared secret.

RADIUS Server

When you configure Windows Server 2008 to function as a RADIUS server, it performs authentication itself rather than forwarding authentication to another RADIUS server. If the RADIUS server is a member of a domain, it can perform authentication by using AD DS, the local account database, or an LDAP instance. If the RADIUS server is not a member of a domain, it can use the local account database or an LDAP instance for authentication.

RADIUS servers accept authentication traffic forwarded to them by RADIUS clients. Authentication decisions are made based on network policies configured on the RADIUS server. RADIUS clients can be access servers, such as VPN or dial-up servers, or RADIUS proxies that route authentication traffic to the RADIUS server from access servers. RADIUS servers authenticate clients on the basis of a shared secret. You configure a RADIUS client for a RADIUS server in the first exercise at the end of Lesson 2. In this exercise, the RADIUS client is a switch, but the process is the same for all RADIUS clients.

MORE INFO   **CONFIGURING NPS AS A RADIUS SERVER**

To learn more about configuring NPS to function as a RADIUS server, see the following document on TechNet: *http://technet.microsoft.com/en-us/library/cc755248.aspx.*

RADIUS Proxy

RADIUS proxies route RADIUS authentication requests between RADIUS clients and RADIUS servers. A RADIUS proxy makes decisions on where it will route RADIUS connection requests based on information contained in the RADIUS message. It is possible to have multiple RADIUS proxies between a RADIUS client and a RADIUS server.

When you want to forward connection requests to a remote NPS or RADIUS server, you must create a remote RADIUS server group and configure a connection request policy that forwards requests to that remote server group based on the properties of the connection request. This way, you can have multiple RADIUS server groups with the RADIUS proxy routing connection requests to each one, based on the connection request policies that you configured. It is possible for a computer running Windows Server 2008 to function both as a RADIUS server and as a RADIUS proxy, authenticating some requests locally and forwarding other requests to a remote RADIUS server group, based on configured connection request policies.

To create a RADIUS proxy group, perform the following steps:

1. Open the Network Policy Server console and expand the Radius Clients And Servers node.

2. Right-click the Remote RADIUS Server Groups node, and then select New.

    This launches the New Remote Radius Server Group dialog box shown in Figure 3-7.

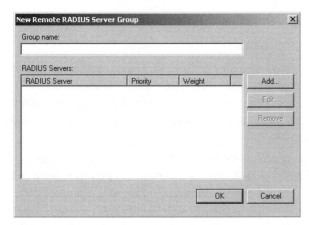

FIGURE 3-7 New Remote RADIUS server group.

3. Enter a name for the RADIUS server group and click Add.

   This opens the Add RADIUS Server dialog box.

4. Enter the host name or IP address of the remote RADIUS server on the Address tab and a shared secret on the Authentication/Accounting tab to use between the RADIUS proxy and the RADIUS server.

> **MORE INFO**   **CONFIGURING NPS AS A RADIUS PROXY**
>
> To learn more about configuring NPS to function as a RADIUS proxy, see the following document on TechNet: *http://technet.microsoft.com/en-us/library/cc731320.aspx*.

 Quick Check

1. Which password-based authentication protocols can you use with a Windows Server 2008 VPN server?

2. Which two things must you configure to enable an existing RADIUS server to function also as a RADIUS proxy?

Quick Check Answers

1. MS-CHAP v2, EAP-MS-CHAP v2, and PEAP-MS-CHAP v2 are the password-based authentication protocols you can use with a Windows Server 2008 VPN server.

2. To configure an existing RADIUS server to function also as a RADIUS proxy, configure a remote RADIUS server group and a connection request policy that routes traffic to that server group.

Network Address Translation

NAT enables you to use a host that has two (or more) network adapters to share an Internet connection with hosts on a private network. NAT differs from routing in that, whereas it allows hosts on the private network, it does not allow hosts on the Internet direct access to hosts on the private network. Port forwarding is an exception to this rule. You learn about port forwarding later in this lesson.

Windows Server 2008 provides two types of NAT: NAT through Routing and Remote Access and NAT through ICS. NAT through Routing and Remote Access enables you to use any internal network addresses that you desire, can be used with multiple subnets, and enables you to use separate DHCP servers to provide addresses to hosts on the internal network. NAT through Routing and Remote Access can be deployed in conjunction with Network Access Protection (NAP) with DHCP enforcement.

NAT through ICS supports only a single subnet with the addresses on the 192.168.0.0/24 network. When using ICS, you must use the ICS server's DHCP server. You cannot use ICS in conjunction with NAP with DHCP enforcement, although it is possible to use NAP with IPsec enforcement and NAP with 802.1x enforcement. You generally deploy NAT through ICS on networks with fewer than ten hosts, such as at a retail outlet or small branch office location.

Configuring NAT

To configure NAT through Routing and Remote Access, run the Routing And Remote Access Server Setup Wizard and select Network Address Translation, as shown in Figure 3-8. When proceeding through the wizard, you are asked to specify which interface connected to the server is addressable from the Internet, or you can create a new demand-dial interface so that RRAS can initiate a connection through a modem.

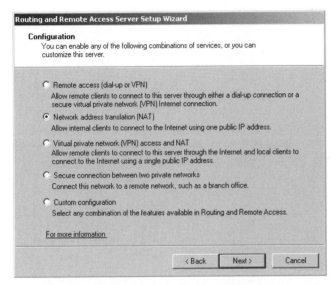

FIGURE 3-8 Set up NAT through the Routing And Remote Access Server Setup Wizard.

To configure NAT through ICS, perform the following steps:

1. Open the Network And Sharing Center and click Manage Network Connections.

2. Right-click the network interface that connects to the Internet, and then select Properties. Click Continue to dismiss the User Account Control dialog box.

3. In the Network Interface Connection Properties dialog box, click the Sharing tab and select the Allow Other Network Users To Connect Through This Computer's Internet Connection check box, as shown in Figure 3-9.

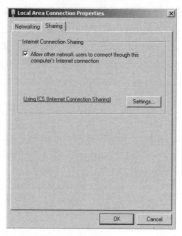

FIGURE 3-9 Enabling ICS.

Port Forwarding

Port forwarding enables you to redirect traffic targeted at a port on the NAT server's public interface to a host on the internal network. For example, you could map port 80 on the NAT server's public interface so that it redirects to a Web server located on your internal network. Port forwarding works based on interface address rather than on hostname. This means that you cannot forward requests to different hosts on the internal network that arrive on the same interface based on the hostname used with the request.

To configure port forwarding from the Routing and Remote Access console, perform the following steps:

1. Open the Routing And Remote Access console and navigate to the Server\IPv4\NAT node.

2. Right-click the network interface connected to the Internet, and then select Properties.

   This opens the Network Interface Connection Properties dialog box.

3. On the Services And Ports tab, select the check box for the service you want forwarded from the network interface connected to the Internet to a host on the internal network and click Edit.

   This displays the Edit Service dialog box.

4. In the Edit Service dialog box, shown in Figure 3-10, specify the IP address of the internal network host to which NAT will forward traffic on this port.

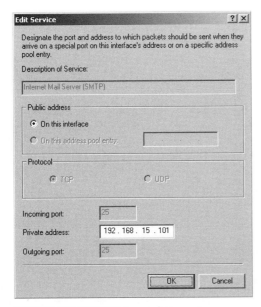

FIGURE 3-10 NAT SMTP forwarding.

You can also configure port forwarding from the *netsh* command-line tool. To configure port forwarding from *netsh* for Routing and Remote Access–enabled NAT, use the following command:

```
Netsh routing IP NAT add portmapping name="Public" tcp 0.0.0.0 X Y.Y.Y.Y Z
```

where "Public" is the interface name, X is the external port, Y is the IP address of the internal host, and Z is the port on the internal host. Use 0.0.0.0 if the NAT server has a single public IP address. If there are multiple public IP addresses, you can specify them individually. For example, to map port 80 on the NAT server's public interface to port 80 on host 192.168.15.151 on the internal network, issue this command:

```
Netsh routing IP NAT add portmapping name="Public" tcp 0.0.0.0 80 192.168.15.151 80
```

> **MORE INFO** **CONFIGURING NAT USING NETSH**
>
> To learn more about configuring NAT using *netsh*, see the following document on TechNet:
> *http://technet.microsoft.com/en-us/library/cc754535.aspx.*

To configure port forwarding when using ICS-enabled NAT, open the properties of the Internet-facing network interface, click the Sharing tab, and then click the Settings button. This opens the Advanced Settings dialog box, shown in Figure 3-11. From here, you can enable specific services running on an internal network. By selecting the check box for a service and clicking Edit, you can specify the internal IP address of the computer that hosts the service.

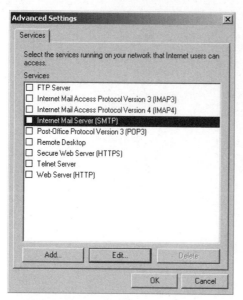

FIGURE 3-11 ICS port forwarding.

> **MORE INFO**   **NETWORK ADDRESS TRANSLATION**
>
> To learn more about configuring Windows Server 2008 with NAT, see the following docu-
> ment on TechNet: *http://technet.microsoft.com/en-us/library/cc731838.aspx.*

Configuring Packet Filters

Filters are similar to firewall rules in that they enable you to restrict traffic passing in and out
of a Routing and Remote Access server. You would use a filter, for example, to block clients
that connect to your internal network through a VPN from accessing particular subnets on
that internal network. The filter shown in Figure 3-12, when applied to an interface that
connects to the internal network on a VPN server, blocks VPN clients from accessing the
10.0.100.0 /24 network.

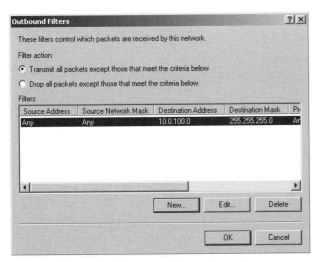

FIGURE 3-12 Outbound filter on a VPN server.

Packet filters are exception-based. You can block all traffic except that which you explicitly allow or allow all traffic except that which you explicitly block. Inbound filters apply to traffic coming into the network interface; outbound filters apply to traffic passing across the interface. VPN traffic is inbound on the Internet network interface and outbound on the internal network interface, so if you want to block VPN clients from accessing specific hosts on your internal network, apply an outbound filter on your internal network interface. To add a packet filter by using the *netsh* command-line tool, use the *netsh routing ip add filter* command. The following command creates the filter shown in the preceding figure:

```
Netsh routing ip add filter name="Internal Interface" filtertype=output srcaddr=0.0.0.0
srcmask=0.0.0.0 dstaddr=10.0.100.0 dstmask=255.255.255.0 proto-any
```

> **MORE INFO   PACKET FILTERS**
>
> To learn more about configuring filtering on Windows Server 2008 Routing and Remote Access, see the following document on TechNet: *http://technet.microsoft.com/en-us/library /cc732746.aspx.*

Connection Manager

The Connection Manager Administration Kit (CMAK) is a Windows Server 2008 feature that simplifies the configuration of remote client connections. You can add CMAK by using the Add Features Wizard. Rather than having to walk users through the process of configuring a remote access connection on their client computers, CMAK creates an installable file you can distribute to users. These installer files can be e-mailed or placed on a Web server or an accessible file share. When installed, all necessary settings for a remote access configuration are set up.

Creating a CMAK profile is a wizard-driven process that involves the following steps:

1. Specifying whether the profile will be for a computer running Windows Vista or Windows Server 2003, Windows XP, or Windows 2000.

2. Choosing whether to create a new profile or modify an existing profile.

   This enables you to update profiles quickly that you have already deployed to clients in your organization.

3. Specifying a Kerberos realm name (if necessary).

4. Specifying a VPN server or a list of VPN servers to which the client can choose to connect.

5. Configuring the properties of a VPN connection. This includes the following options:

   - Disabling file and printer sharing.

   - Limiting connectivity to IPv4, IPv6, or both.

   - Configuring VPN Domain Name System (DNS).

   - Configuring authentication and encryption settings, as shown in Figure 3-13. This includes the ability to limit VPNs to a particular protocol.

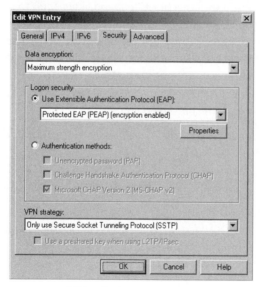

FIGURE 3-13 Editing CMAK VPN settings.

6. Adding a phone book file with a list of numbers a client can use as a dial-up connection to the Internet prior to accessing the VPN or, if your organization has a dial-up server, the phone number used to access that server.

7. Configuring proxy settings for Microsoft Internet Explorer.

8. Configuring custom icons, graphics, and help files for the connection.

Users of client computers do not need administrative privileges to install CMAK profiles because they already have the rights necessary to create dial-up and VPN connections. You are unlikely to use a CMAK profile in configuring a computer running Windows Server 2008. You use CMAK profiles primarily to simplify the process of configuring client computers that use the Windows Vista and Windows XP operating systems.

> **MORE INFO** **CONNECTION MANAGER**
>
> To learn more about Connection Manager, see the following document on TechNet:
> *http://technet.microsoft.com/en-us/library/cc753977.aspx*.

EXAM TIP

Remember that SSTP uses port 443 and almost always works through hotel and airport lounge firewalls.

PRACTICE Configuring a VPN Server

In this practice, you perform tasks similar to those you would perform when configuring Windows Server 2008 to function as a remote access server. The first exercise configures Windows Server 2008 to function as a VPN server; the second exercise configures filters and connection restrictions.

EXERCISE 1 Configure a VPN Server

In this exercise, you configure Windows Server 2008 to function as a VPN server.

1. Log on to server Glasgow with the Kim_Akers user account.

2. If you have not already performed Exercise 1 of Lesson 1 in Chapter 2, perform those exercises, and then proceed with step 3.

3. Open the Routing And Remote Access console from the Administrative Tools menu. Click Continue when presented with the User Account Control dialog box.

4. Right-click server Glasgow, and then select Disable Routing And Remote Access. When presented with the dialog box informing you that you will need to re-enable the router, click Yes.

   This step is necessary because you want to reconfigure Routing and Remote Access.

5. Right-click server Glasgow, and then select Configure And Enable Routing And Remote Access.

   This launches the Routing And Remote Access Server Setup Wizard.

6. Click Next.

7. On the Configuration page, select Virtual Private Network (VPN) Access And NAT, as shown in Figure 3-14, and then click Next.

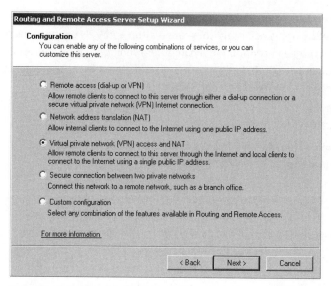

FIGURE 3-14 Configuring Routing and Remote Access as a VPN server.

8. On the VPN Connection page, select the network interface with the 10.0.0.11 IP address.

   This interface will function as a stand-in for one that is accessible from the Internet.

9. Click Next.

10. On the IP Address Assignment page, select From A Specified Range Of Addresses, and then click Next.

11. On the Address Range Assignment page, click New.

    This opens the New IPv4 Address Range dialog box.

12. Enter the values shown in Figure 3-15, click OK, and then click Next.

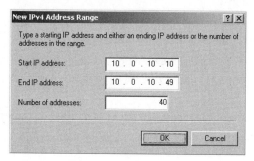

FIGURE 3-15 VPN address range.

13. On the Managing Multiple Remote Access Servers page, select No, Use Routing And Remote Access To Authenticate Connection Requests, click Next, and then click Finish.

After being presented with information about having created a default connection request policy and the necessity to set up a DHCP relay agent, the Routing and Remote Access service starts.

EXERCISE 2   Configure VPN Packet Filters and Connection Restrictions

In this exercise, you configure VPN packet filters and set up connection restrictions on incoming VPN clients.

1. If you have not done so already, log on to server Glasgow, using the Kim_Akers user account, and open the Routing And Remote Access console from the Administrative Tools menu.

2. Expand Routing And Remote Access\Glasgow\IPv4, and then select the General node (for IPv4 traffic). Right-click the interface that does not have the 10.0.0.11 IP address, and then select Properties.

3. Click the Outbound Filters button.

   This opens the Outbound Filters dialog box.

4. Click New.

   This opens the Add IP Filter dialog box.

5. Configure the dialog box as shown in Figure 3-16, and then click OK.

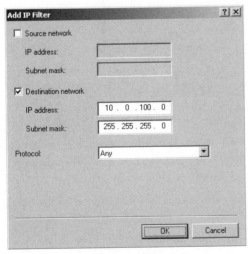

FIGURE 3-16 Creating an IP filter.

6. Verify that the Transmit All Packets Except Those That Meet The Criteria Below check box is selected, and then click OK. Click OK again to close the Properties dialog box.

   You have now created a filter that blocks traffic from VPN clients reaching the 10.0.100.0 /24 subnet.

7. Using Active Directory Users And Computers, create a new security group with a global scope named **VPN-Users**.

8. Close the Routing And Remote Access console. From the Administrative Tools menu, open the Network Policy Server console. Click Continue when prompted by the User Account Control dialog box.

9. Right-click the Network Policies node under NPS (Local)\Policies, and then select New. This launches the New Network Policy wizard.

10. On the Specify Network Policy Name And Connection Type page, enter **VPN_Access** as the policy name and, in the Type Of Network Access Server drop-down list, select Remote Access Server (VPN-Dial Up), as shown in Figure 3-17. Click Next.

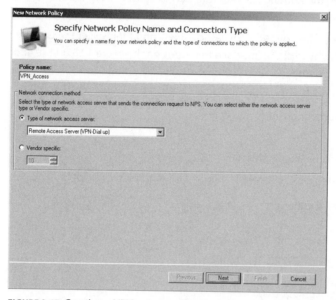

FIGURE 3-17 Creating a VPN access policy.

11. On the Specify Conditions page, click Add, select Windows Groups, click Add again, and then click Add Groups. In the Select Group dialog box, enter **VPN-Users** as the group name, and then click OK twice.

12. On the Specify Conditions page, click Add, select Day And Time Restrictions, and then click Add.

    This opens the Day And Time Restrictions dialog box.

13. Configure the Day And Time Restrictions dialog box so that VPN access is allowed only outside of regular business hours, and then click OK.

14. Verify that the Specify Conditions page matches what is displayed in Figure 3-18, and then click Next.

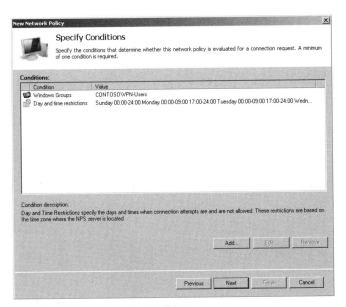

FIGURE 3-18 Network policy conditions.

15. Verify that the Access Granted option is selected, and then click Next.

16. On the Configure Authentication Methods page, clear the Microsoft Encrypted Authentication (MS-CHAP) check box, and then click Next.

17. On the Configure Constraints page, click Next. On the Configure Settings page, click Next.

18. On the Completing New Network Policy page, verify that the settings match those in Figure 3-19, and then click Finish.

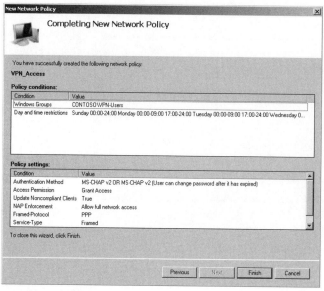

FIGURE 3-19 Completed policy.

Lesson Summary

- You can configure Windows Server 2008 as a dial-up server or as a RADIUS server that authenticates connection requests from dial-up access points configured as RADIUS clients.

- You can configure Windows Server 2008 as a VPN server. Connection requests can be authenticated locally or forwarded to a RADIUS server.

- Windows Server 2008 supports three VPN protocols, PPTP, L2TP/IPsec, and SSTP. L2TP /IPsec supports client and server certificates. SSTP can be used only by Windows Vista SP1 and Windows Server 2008 clients. It uses port 443 and can traverse NAT gateways.

- MS-CHAPv2, EAP-MS-CHAPv2, and PEAP-MSCHAPv2 are password-based authentication protocols. PEAP-TLS and EAP-TLS are certificate-based authentication protocols. EAP-MS-CHAPv2, PEAP-TLS, and PEAP-MS-CHAPv2 are supported by Windows Vista and Windows Server 2008 only.

- NAT through RRAS supports multiple subnets. NAT through ICS supports a single subnet. Port forwarding allows ports on a NAT server's public interface to be forwarded to hosts on the private network.

- You can use Connection Manager Administration Kit (CMAK) to create executable files that will automatically set up remote access connections on client computers.

Lesson Review

You can use the following questions to test your knowledge of the information in Lesson 1, "Setting Up Remote Access." The questions are also available on the companion DVD if you prefer to review them in electronic form.

NOTE ANSWERS

Answers to these questions and explanations of why each answer choice is right or wrong are located in the "Answers" section at the end of the book.

1. Several executives in your organization are having problems accessing your VPN server when they visit hotels or airport lounges across the country on business. The executives all have Windows XP Professional SP2–based laptop computers. Which of the following steps can you take to resolve this problem? (Choose two. Each correct answer presents part of a complete solution.)

   A. Configure the VPN server to support PPTP.

   B. Configure the VPN server to support SSTP.

   C. Configure the VPN server to support L2TP/IPsec.

   D. Upgrade the laptop computers to Windows XP SP3.

   E. Upgrade the laptop computers to Windows Vista SP1.

2. Your organization has a Windows Server 2008 VPN server located on the perimeter network. All clients connect to the VPN server by using SSTP. You want to block VPN clients from connecting to a sensitive subnet on your internal network with the 192.168.101.0/24 address. You want to allow VPN clients access to all other subnets on your organization's internal network. Which of the following should you do to accomplish this goal?

   A. Configure the external firewall to block traffic to 192.168.101.0/24.

   B. Configure a Routing and Remote Access filter on the VPN server.

   C. Configure an inbound firewall rule on the VPN server.

   D. Configure an authentication exemption rule on the VPN server.

3. You are configuring an NPS to authenticate connections made to a dial-up access server. You are configuring the dial-up access server as a RADIUS client on the NPS. In which of the following ways can you authenticate the RADIUS client and the NPS RADIUS server?

   A. Shared secret

   B. Digital certificate

   C. NTLMv2

   D. EAP-TLS

4. You have just installed three dial-up access server appliances. Clients connecting to the dial-up access server appliances should be able to authenticate using their domain credentials. You will configure the computer running Windows Server 2008 named GAMMA to perform this function. Which of the following must you do when configuring GAMMA after adding the Network Policy and Access Services server role and the Network Policy Server role service? (Choose three. Each correct answer presents part of a complete solution.)

   A. Configure GAMMA as a RADIUS server that authenticates against AD DS.

   B. Configure each dial-up access server appliance as RADIUS clients on GAMMA.

   C. Configure each dial-up access server to forward authentication requests to a domain controller.

   D. Configure each dial-up access server appliance as a RADIUS server on GAMMA.

   E. Configure each dial-up access server appliance as a RADIUS proxy on GAMMA.

   F. Configure each dial-up access server to forward authentication requests to GAMMA.

5. What does the *netsh routing IP NAT add portmapping name="Public" tcp 0.0.0.0 110 10.100.0.101 110* command do when executed on a Windows Server 2008 Routing and Remote Access Server that is configured as a NAT server?

   A. Forwards incoming IMAP4 traffic directed to the NAT server's public interface to the IMAP4 port on host 10.100.0.101

   B. Forwards incoming HTTP traffic directed to the NAT server's public interface to the HTTP port on host 10.100.0.101

   C. Forwards incoming POP3 traffic directed to the NAT server's public interface to the POP3 port on host 10.100.0.101

   D. Forwards incoming SSTP traffic directed to the NAT server's public interface to the SSTP port on host 10.100.0.101

Lesson 2: Managing Network Authentication

In highly secure environments, not only must clients provide authentication credentials before they access network services such as shared folders and printers, credentials must be passed to switches before access is granted to the network. Credentials can include digital certificates such as those found in smart cards or issued to user or computer accounts. It is also possible to use traditional usernames and passwords. When using usernames and passwords in your environment, ensure that strong password policies are applied and that users change their passwords regularly.

After this lesson, you will be able to:

- Manage LAN authentication by using NTLMv2 and Kerberos.
- Manage WLAN authentication by using 802.1x.

Estimated lesson time: 40 minutes

Configuring Password Policies

You use password policies to define the properties of user passwords in your Windows Server 2008 Active Directory environment. The basic set of password policies is found under the Computer Configuration\Policies\Windows Settings\Security Settings\Account Policies \Password Policy node of a Group Policy object (GPO). The policies this node contains are visible in Figure 3-20.

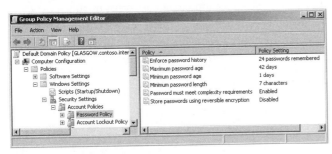

FIGURE 3-20 Password policies.

Password policies are set in the default domain GPO. Generally, only one set of password policies applies in a domain. The exception to this is fine-grained password policies, covered later in this lesson. Password policies control the following settings:

- **Enforce Password History**   This policy determines how many of the user's prior passwords AD DS remembers. Use this policy to stop users from reusing the same short list of passwords. The default setting is to remember 24 passwords.

- **Maximum Password Age**   This policy determines how long a user can retain the same password. The default setting is 42 days. This policy does not apply when you configure a password not to expire through the account's Active Directory properties.

- **Minimum Password Age**   This policy determines how long a user must retain a password before he or she can change it. This policy stops users from cycling through password changes when their password expires so that they can continue to use the same password. For example, it stops users from changing their password 25 times in a row every 42 days so that they can return to the same password. The default setting requires a user to wait one day after changing a password before they can change it again.

- **Minimum Password Length**   This policy determines the minimum length of a password that can be set in an Active Directory environment. The default setting is that passwords must be at least seven characters.

- **Password Must Meet Complexity Requirements**   This policy is active by default and requires all passwords to be more than six characters in length, not contain portions of the user or account name, and contain at least three of the following elements: symbols, uppercase characters, lowercase characters, and numbers.

- **Store Passwords Using Reversible Encryption**   This policy determines whether the operating system can store passwords by using reversible encryption. It is required only for older applications and authentication protocols, and activating this policy significantly reduces password security. This policy is not active by default.

Password policies apply during password changes only. When you want a new password policy to take effect immediately, you must force all users to change their passwords. You can force all users in an organizational unit (OU) to change their passwords by running a Microsoft PowerShell script. The following PowerShell script, when run by a user with sufficient privileges, will force each user account stored in the Management OU of the *contoso.internal* domain to change his or her password when he or she next logs on.

```
Set objOU = GetObject("LDAP://ou=Management,dc=contoso,dc=internal")
objOU.Filter = Array("user")
For Each objUser in objOU
    objUser.pwdLastSet = 0
    objUser.SetInfo
Next
```

Users who are logged on when you run the script will not have to change their passwords until they log on again.

Account Lockout Policies

Account lockout policies determine how long an account lock remains in place when a user fails to authenticate successfully for the number of times specified in the password policy. You can configure the Account Lockout Duration policy from not locking accounts to locking accounts for between 1 and 99,999 minutes (approximately 70 days). The default setting is that accounts are not locked no matter how many invalid logon attempts occur. The Account Lockout Threshold policy governs the number of sequential invalid logon attempts that must occur before AD DS locks an account. The default setting is zero, which means that account locks do not trigger. The Reset Account Lockout Counter After policy determines the period of time in which sequential invalid logons must occur to trigger account lockout. For example, if you configure this policy with a setting of 10 minutes, and the Account Lockout Threshold policy is set to a value of *3*, AD DS will trigger account lockout only if three invalid logons occur within 10 minutes. Only sequential invalid logons that occur within the threshold value count; activity that occurs outside that window does not count. The Reset Account Lockout Counter After policy is not configured by default.

Fine-Grained Password Policies

Until the release of Windows Server 2008, AD DS did not support having different password and account lockout policies for different sets of users in a domain. Fine-grained password policies enable you to apply different restrictions for password and account lockout policies to different groups of users in a single domain. Fine-grained password policies apply to user objects and global security groups only. By default, only members of the Domain Admins group can configure and apply fine-grained password policies.

You cannot apply fine-grained password policies directly to an OU. It is possible to create a security group that mirrors the membership of an OU and then use that as the basis for applying a fine-grained password policy. Fine-grained password policies do not interfere with password filters. You can use both fine-grained password policies and password filters to enforce restrictions on passwords.

> **MORE INFO   PASSWORD FILTERS**
>
> For more information on password filters, see the following document on MSDN:
> *http://msdn.microsoft.com/en-us/library/ms721882(VS.85).aspx*.

You can configure all the Active Directory settings that relate to password policies and account lockout settings by using fine-grained password policies. The other two fine-grained password settings determine which users or groups the settings link to and a precedence value used to resolve conflicts. All these settings are stored within a Password Settings Object (PSO). PSOs are stored in the Password Settings container, which you can view using Active Directory Users and Computers if you enable the Advanced Features view option. A single PSO can apply to multiple users and groups. Although it is possible to link PSOs to groups other than global security groups, only links to user accounts or global security groups are included when performing a Resultant Set of Policy (RSoP) calculation.

You can create PSOs by using ADSI Edit or *ldifde*. When using ADSI Edit, right-click the domain name\CN=System\CN=Password Settings container and create a new object of the *msDS-PasswordSettings* class. Then define each setting in the PSO.

MORE INFO **FINE-GRAINED PASSWORD POLICIES**

To learn more about fine-grained password policies, see the following TechNet document: *http://technet.microsoft.com/en-us/library/cc770394.aspx.*

Kerberos

Kerberos is the AD DS default authentication protocol. When a computer running Windows 2000, Windows XP, Windows Server 2003, Windows Vista, or Windows Server 2008 authenticates against AD DS, it will first attempt to use Kerberos. Five Kerberos policies directly relate to authentication. Figure 3-21 shows these policies. Like general, rather than fine-grained, password policies, you configure Kerberos policies in the Default Domain policy configuration rather than in other GPOs attached to Active Directory objects.

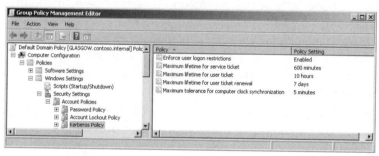

FIGURE 3-21 Active Directory Kerberos policies.

These policies have the following functions:

- **Enforce User Logon Restriction** Use this policy to ensure that every request for a user ticket is validated against user rights settings on the target computer. A user ticket is a limited term certificate issued by AD DS that allows the user to request service tickets. Service tickets access a specific network resource. A user requesting a user ticket must have either the Allow Log On Locally right or the Access This Computer From The Network right on the target computer. This policy is enabled by default.

- **Maximum Lifetime For Service Ticket** Use this policy to set the maximum amount of time in minutes that a service ticket is valid. The default setting is 600 minutes. When set to zero, service tickets never expire.

- **Maximum Lifetime For User Ticket** Use this policy to specify the maximum amount of time that a user ticket is valid. The default setting is 10 hours, which is the same as the validity for service tickets. When set to zero, user tickets never expire.

- **Maximum Lifetime For User Ticket Renewal** AD DS can renew a user ticket when it nears the end of its validity period. This policy specifies how long an existing user ticket can be renewed before a new user ticket must be reissued. The default setting is seven days.

- **Maximum Tolerance For Computer Clock Synchronization** This policy specifies the maximum time difference that can exist between the time on a client computer and the time on the authenticating domain controller. Computers measure this difference in universal time rather than by using local time zone settings. The default allowable difference is five minutes.

The default policy settings are appropriate for all but the highest-security environments. In high-security environments, consider decreasing user and session ticket lifetimes. The drawback of decreasing ticket lifetimes is an increased load on domain controllers.

> **MORE INFO   KERBEROS INTEROPERABILITY**
>
> To learn more about configuring Windows Server 2008 Group Policy settings for interoperability with non-Microsoft Kerberos realms, see the following document on the Microsoft Web site: *http://support.microsoft.com/kb/947706*.

NTLMv2

Windows uses NTLMv2 as a fallback authentication protocol when a client cannot authenticate using Kerberos. Windows Vista and Windows Server 2008 deprecate NTLM, an earlier version, in favor of NTLMv2. Windows Server 2008 still supports NTLM for inbound authentication but uses NTLMv2 for outbound authentication.

NTLM (version 1) is required only if computers with the Windows 95, Windows 98, or Windows NT operating systems are attempting to authenticate against a Windows Server 2008 domain controller. If your environment still has Windows 95 and Windows 98 clients, you must also install Active Directory Client Extension so that they can authenticate against Windows Server 2008 domain controllers.

The Network Security: LAN Manager Authentication Level policy, which you can find under the Computer Configuration\Policies\Windows Settings\Security Settings\Local Policies \Security Options node and can see in Figure 3-22, enables you to specify the minimum level of authentication that must be supported by clients in your organization. The strongest option, refusing LM and NTLM, will ensure that only NTLMv2 is used in your environment.

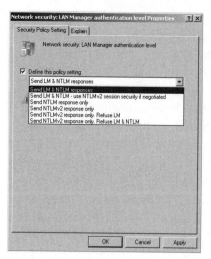

FIGURE 3-22 LAN Manager authentication level policy.

MORE INFO **WINDOWS AUTHENTICATION**

To learn more about Windows authentication, see the following page on TechNet: *http://technet.microsoft.com/en-us/library/cc755284.aspx.*

 Quick Check

1. What is the default authentication protocol Windows Server 2008 uses in a domain environment?

2. To which Active Directory objects can you apply fine-grained password policies?

Quick Check Answers

1. Kerberos version 5 is the default authentication protocol. NTLMv2 is used when Kerberos version 5 cannot be used.

2. Fine-grained password policies can be applied to user accounts and global security groups.

Configuring 802.1x LAN Authentication

802.1x-compatible switches support port-based network access control. This technology limits a host from communicating on the switch port it connects to until it successfully authenticates. This adds an additional layer of security because only authorized people and devices are able to connect to the network. Nefarious third parties will be unable to plug devices in to access the network because when you configure an 802.1x-compatible switch properly, network access is not possible without successful authentication.

802.1x-compatible switches do not authenticate the connections themselves but forward authentication to a RADIUS server. This is essentially the same process as RADIUS authentication of VPN or dial-up connections except that the access point is an 802.1x-compatible switch.

Configuring an 802.1x-compatible switch as a RADIUS client involves taking exactly the same steps as you would to configure any other RADIUS client.

1. Open the Network Policy Server console and expand the NPS (Local)\Radius Clients And Servers node.

2. Right-click the Radius Clients node, and then select New RADIUS Client.

3. Enter the following information about the 802.1x-compatible switch in the New RADIUS Client dialog box. (This is the same dialog box shown earlier, in Figure 3-6.)

   - Friendly Name
   - IP Address or Hostname
   - Shared Secret

> **NOTE   NAP WITH 802.1X ENFORCEMENT**
>
> NAP with 802.1x enforcement uses 802.1x-compatible switches and is covered in more detail in Chapter 4.

802.1X Authentication Protocols

Windows Server 2008 and Windows Vista support the following protocols for 802.1x authentication:

- **EAP-TLS**   This is a certificate-based authentication protocol, meaning you can use smart cards or computer or user certificates for authentication. This protocol is compatible with client computers running Windows XP, Windows Vista, Windows Server 2003, and Windows Server 2008. It requires a computer certificate to each RADIUS server and a computer certificate, user certificate, or smart card to all wired clients. The clients and the RADIUS servers must trust the CA that issued each other's certificates.

- **PEAP-MS-CHAPv2**   This is a password-based authentication protocol by which authentication is protected by an encrypted Transport Layer Security (TLS) session. When you deploy this protocol for authentication, you must install a computer certificate, trusted by all clients, on the authenticating RADIUS server.

- **PEAP-TLS**   This is a certificate-based authentication protocol, meaning you can use smart cards or computer or user certificates for authentication. This protocol is compatible with client computers running Windows Vista and Windows Server 2008 only. Like EAP-TLS, this protocol requires a computer certificate to each RADIUS server and a computer certificate, user certificate, or smart card to all wired clients. The clients and the RADIUS servers must trust the CA that issued each other's certificates.

Because EAP-TLS and PEAP-TLS require both client and authenticating servers to have certificates, both protocols require the deployment of some form of PKI, usually Active Directory Certificate Services (AD CS). Using AD CS vastly simplifies the issues related to ensuring that the appropriate certificate trusts are established.

> **NOTE 802.1X AUTHENTICATION PROTOCOLS**
>
> You also read the authentication protocols you can use for 802.1x LAN authentication in Lesson 1.

Configuring 802.1x Clients

You can configure 802.1x clients to authenticate, using the following modes:

- **User-Only**   802.1x authentication occurs using user credentials after the user logon process has completed unless Single Sign On is enabled within Group Policy.

- **Computer-Only**   802.1x authentication occurs using computer credentials prior to displaying the Windows Logon screen.

- **Computer-or-User**   802.1x authentication occurs twice, first using computer credentials before logon occurs and again, using user credentials after logon. This is the default authentication method.

The default authentication mode is Computer-or-User. This enables computers that provide resources to the network, such as file and print servers, to communicate with the network without requiring anyone to log on. Computer-only authentication also allows computers that can authenticate to access the network without direct user intervention.

Single Sign On allows wired network authentication to occur using cached user credentials prior to logon. This is a way around the problem of logon not occurring when the computer cannot contact a domain controller for authentication because it has yet to authenticate to the switch. Windows Vista SP1 and Windows Server 2008 support Single Sign On. You enable Single Sign On for users through the Wired Network (IEEE 802.3) Policies Group Policy, as shown in Figure 3-23, or by using the *netsh lan set profileparameter authmode=useronly ssomode=preLogon* command.

From the Computer Configuration\Policies\Windows Settings\Security Settings\Wired Network (IEEE 802.3) Policies node of a Windows Server 2008 GPO, you can create a wired network policy that applies to client computers running Windows Vista. This policy enables you to start the Wired AutoConfig service automatically on computers, which then enables you to configure settings so that you can deploy 802.1x-compatible authentication. The Security tab of the Wired Network Policy Properties dialog box, shown in Figure 3-24, enables you to configure authentication settings for clients, including Network Authentication Method and Authentication Mode settings.

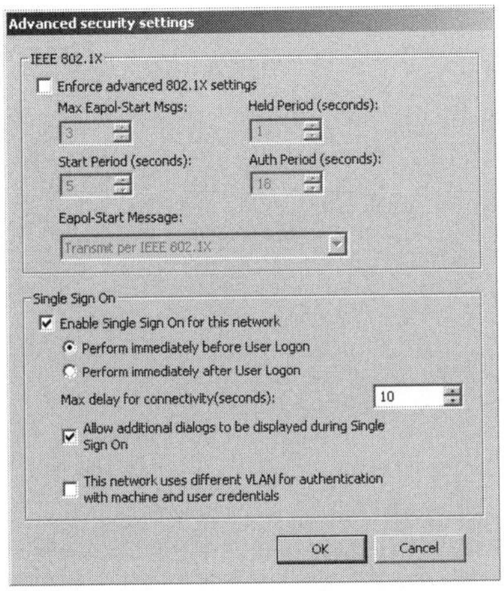

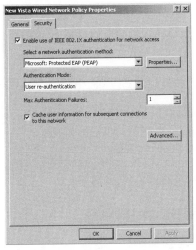

FIGURE 3-23 Enabling Single Sign On.

FIGURE 3-24 The Windows Vista Wired Network Policy dialog box.

When setting up individual computers running Windows Server 2008 or Windows Vista, configure the Wired AutoConfig service to start automatically. When you start this service, the Authentication tab becomes available on each network adapter's Properties tab, as shown in Figure 3-25. You can use this tab to configure authentication settings just as you do through Group Policy.

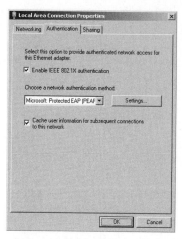

FIGURE 3-25 Configuring 802.1x authentication manually.

Configuring LAN Access Policies in NPS

To configure NPS to support 802.1x-authenticated wired access, you must create a network access policy. To do this, perform the following steps:

1. Open the Network Policy Server console from the Administrative Tools menu and select the NPS (Local) node.

2. In the Standard Configuration area, from the drop-down menu, select RADIUS Server For 802.1X Wireless Or Wired Connections, as shown in Figure 3-26, and then click Configure 802.1X.

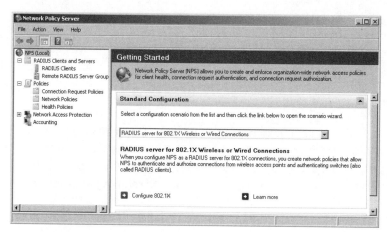

FIGURE 3-26 Network policy creation.

3. Specify that you want to configure a policy for secure wired rather than wireless connections and enter a policy name.

4. Specify which RADIUS clients, in this case 802.1x-compatible switches, the policy will process requests from.

5. Select which authentication method is used with the policy, EAP-TLS (Smart Card or Other Certificate), PEAP-TLS, or PEAP-MSCHAP v2.

6. Specify which user groups the policy applies to. If you choose no groups, it applies to all users.

7. If you are using virtual local area networks (VLANS) with your 802.1x-compatible switch, configure NPS to supply RADIUS clients with VLAN configuration information.

You create a network access policy for 802.1x-authenticated wired access in the practice at the end of this lesson.

> **MORE INFO** **802.1X-AUTHENTICATED WIRED ACCESS**
>
> To learn more about 802.1x-authenticated wired access, see the following document on TechNet: *http://technet.microsoft.com/en-us/library/cc753354.aspx*.

EXAM TIP

Remember which 802.1x authentication protocol enables you to use passwords instead of certificates for client authentication.

PRACTICE Configuring Network Authentication

In this practice, you perform tasks similar to those you would perform when configuring Windows Server 2008. The first exercise configures a switch as a RADIUS client; the second exercise configures a network policy for managing access to this switch.

EXERCISE 1 Add a Switch as a RADIUS Client

In this exercise, you add a switch as a RADIUS client. The switch does not actually have to exist; the exercise is about learning the process you go through to add the switch.

1. Log on to server Glasgow with the Kim_Akers user account. Use Active Directory Users And Computers to create a global security group named **Authenticating_Switch _Users**.

2. Open the Network Policy Server console from the Administrative Tools menu. Click Continue when prompted by the User Account Control dialog box.

3. Select the NPS (Local) node. In the Getting Started pane, use the drop-down menu to select RADIUS Server For 802.1X Wireless Or Wired Connections, and then click Configure 802.1X.

4. On the Select 802.1X Connections Type page, select Secure Wired (Ethernet) Connections. Accept the default policy name, Secure Wired (Ethernet) Connections, and click Next.

5. On the Specify 802.1X Switches page, click Add. Enter the address details in the New RADIUS Client dialog box as shown in Figure 3-27. Ensure that you select Generate, and then click Generate to generate a shared secret automatically. Click OK, and then click Next.

   Please note that this is only a hypothetical switch, which you will pretend exists for this practice exercise.

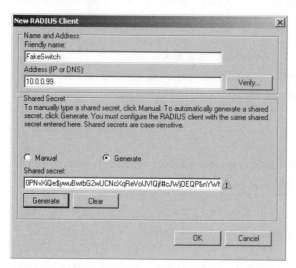

FIGURE 3-27 New RADIUS Client dialog box.

6. In the Configure An Authentication Method dialog box, select Microsoft: Secured Password (EAP-MS-CHAPv2) in the drop-down list, and then click Configure. Set the number of authentication retries to 3 and ensure that the Allow Client To Change Password After It Has Expired check box is selected. Click OK, and then click Next.

7. On the Specify User Groups page, click Add. In the Select Group dialog box, type **Authenticating_Switch_Users**, and then click OK. Click Next.

8. On the Configure A Virtual LAN (VLAN) page, click Next.

9. Verify that the Completing New IEEE 802.1X Secure Wired And Wireless Connections And RADIUS Clients policy matches that shown in Figure 3-28, and then click Finish.

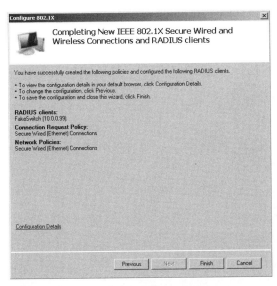

FIGURE 3-28 Secure wireless policy summary.

EXERCISE 2 Configure a Network Policy for 802.1x Switch Access

In this exercise, you create a network policy to manage access to an 802.1x switch.

1. If you have not already done so, log on to server Glasgow, using the Kim_Akers user account.

2. Open the Group Policy Management console from the Administrative Tools menu. Click Continue to dismiss the User Account Control dialog box.

3. Right-click the Group Policy Objects node, located under the Group Policy Management\Forest: Contoso.internal\Domains\contoso.internal node, and then select New. In the New GPO dialog box, in the Name text box, enter **802.1x_Wired** and click OK.

4. In the list of Group Policy objects, right-click the 802.1x_Wired policy, and then select Edit.

5. Navigate to the Computer Configuration\Policies\Windows Settings\Security Settings node. Right-click the Wired Network (IEEE 802.3) Policies node, and then select Create A New Windows Vista Policy.

6. In the New Vista Wired Network Policy Properties dialog box, click the Security tab. Configure the settings on this tab so that they match Figure 3-29.

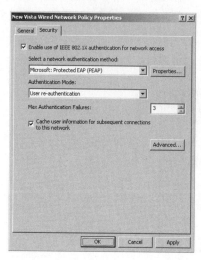

FIGURE 3-29 New Wired Network Policy properties.

7. Click Advanced. Select the Enable Single Sign On For This Network check box, and then select Perform Immediately After User Logon. Click OK twice.

Lesson Summary

- Password policies enable you to configure how often users must change their passwords and how secure those passwords are.

- Fine-grained password policies enable you to apply password policies on a per-user and per-group basis.

- Account lockout policies enable you to specify how long a user's account is locked out when he or she has entered an incorrect password a specific number of times.

- Kerberos v5 is the default LAN authentication protocol Windows Server 2008 uses. NTLMv2 is a fallback protocol if Kerberos v5 is not supported.

- 802.1x LAN authentication enables you to configure switches to authenticate clients through a RADIUS server prior to granting them access to the network.

- PEAP-MS-CHAPv2 enables 802.1x LAN authentication clients to authenticate using a password. EAP-TLS and PEAP-TLS enable 802.1x LAN authentication clients to authenticate using a computer certificate.

- 802.1x clients authenticate using the Computer-or-User method by default. The computer account authenticates with the switch prior to logon; the user account authenticates with the switch after logon.

Lesson Review

You can use the following questions to test your knowledge of the information in Lesson 2, "Managing Network Authentication." The questions are also available on the companion DVD if you prefer to review them in electronic form.

> **NOTE   ANSWERS**
>
> Answers to these questions and explanations of why each answer choice is right or wrong are located in the "Answers" section at the end of the book.

1. You want to ensure that all computers plugged into your organization's 802.1x-compliant switches have been authenticated before being granted access to the network. Which of the following must you do on your NPS to ensure that this can occur?

    A. Configure all 802.1x-compliant switches as RADIUS clients.

    B. Configure all 802.1x-compliant switches as RADIUS servers.

    C. Configure all 802.1x-compliant switches as RADIUS proxies.

    D. Configure all client computers as RADIUS clients.

2. Which of the following 802.1x wired authentication methods do not necessitate the deployment of certificates to clients?

    A. EAP-TLS

    B. PEAP-MS-CHAPv2

    C. PEAP-TLS

    D. NTLMv2

3. You are planning an 802.1x wired authentication strategy. You will be using PEAP-MS-CHAPv2 as an authentication method and a Windows Server 2008 NPS. All connecting client computers are members of the Active Directory domain. Which of the following certificates must you obtain from your organization's enterprise root CA to support this configuration?

    A. A computer certificate for the NPS server.

    B. Computer certificates for each authenticating switch.

    C. Computer certificates for each client computer.

    D. No computer certificates are necessary.

4. You want to ensure that your wired 802.1x network profile is configured to perform authentication against the switch before a user logs on to any computer, even if he or she has not logged on before. Which of the following commands creates a profile that meets these requirements?

A. *Netsh lan set profileparameter authmode=useronly ssomode=preLogon*

B. *Netsh lan set profileparameter authmode=machineonly ssomode=postLogon*

C. *Netsh lan set profileparameter authmode=MachineorUser ssomode=postLogon*

D. *Netsh lan set profileparameter authmode=machineonly ssomode=preLogon*

5. Which of the following Group Policy settings can you configure to enable computers that are members of an Active Directory domain to authenticate automatically with 802.1x-compatible switches?

   A. Wired Network (IEEE 802.3) policies

   B. Wireless Network (IEEE 802.11) policies

   C. IPsec policies

   D. Network Access Protection policies

6. Which of the following tools can you use to create a Password Settings Object (PSO) so that you can implement fine-grained password policies?

   A. Group Policy Management console

   B. *Ntdsutil*

   C. ADSI Edit

   D. Active Directory Users and Computers

Chapter Review

To further practice and reinforce the skills you learned in this chapter, you can perform the following tasks:

- Review the chapter summary.
- Complete the case scenarios. These scenarios set up real-world situations involving the topics of this chapter and ask you to create solutions.
- Complete the suggested practices.
- Take a practice test.

Chapter Summary

- When installed, the Network Policy and Access Services server role and the Routing and Remote Access role service enable Windows Server 2008 to function as both a dial-up and a VPN server.
- Windows Server 2008, with the Network Policy and Access Services server role and the Network Policy Server role service installed, can be configured as a RADIUS server, a RADIUS client, or a RADIUS proxy.
- Password policies enable you to configure the properties of passwords used throughout your network environment.
- You can configure Windows Server 2008 with the Network Policy Server role installed to authenticate clients connected to 802.1x-compatible switches prior to granting them network access.

Case Scenarios

In the following case scenarios, you apply what you've learned about network access configuration. You can find answers to these questions in the "Answers" section at the end of this book.

Case Scenario 1: Configuring a VPN Solution at Fabrikam, Inc.

You are upgrading your existing VPN solution so that all incoming VPN traffic connects to a computer running Windows Server 2008 located on your organization's perimeter network. VPN clients at Fabrikam, Inc., are a mixture of laptop computers running Windows XP SP3 and Windows Vista SP1. You want to retain the use of a password-based authentication protocol for VPN logons because you do not have the budget to deploy a full certificate services solution. You do not want to use PPTP as a VPN protocol. After you encountered some security problems earlier in the year, the CFO has asked you whether it is possible to block clients connecting to the network remotely from accessing the accounting database server. With this in mind, you must find answers to the following questions:

1. Which ports must be open on the firewall to support the VPN protocols used at Fabrikam?

2. Which authentication protocols can you use to authenticate all VPN clients?

3. How can you ensure that VPN clients cannot access the accounting database server?

Case Scenario 2: Network Access at Contoso, Ltd.

You are planning the rollout of 802.1x-compatible switch authentication at Contoso, Ltd. You want authentication to occur by using passwords rather than through digital certificates. Most of the computers at Contoso are members of the domain, but several standalone computers running Windows Server 2008 also must authenticate to the 802.1x-compatible switches. With this in mind, you must find answers to the following questions:

1. Which 802.1x authentication protocol should you use at Contoso?

2. Where should you deploy computer certificates?

3. How should you configure the standalone computers running Windows Server 2008?

Suggested Practices

To help you successfully master the exam objectives presented in this chapter, complete the following tasks.

Configure Remote Access

To get a thorough understanding of configuring remote access, complete both practices in this section.

- **Practice 1** Create a new remote access policy for VPN users that allows members of the Executives group to access the VPN server at all times, not just after business hours.

- **Practice 2** Modify the remote access policy that you created at the end of Lesson 1 so that VPN sessions that are idle for one hour are automatically disconnected.

Configure Network Authentication

To get a thorough understanding of configuring a network, complete both practices in this section.

- **Practice 1** Create a new network policy for a group named Smart_Card Users that requires 802.1x authentication using smart cards.

- **Practice 2** Modify the domain's password policy to ensure that the maximum length of time a person can have a password is 21 days and the minimum password length is eight characters.

Take a Practice Test

The practice tests on this book's companion DVD offer many options. For example, you can test yourself on just one exam objective, or you can test yourself on all the upgrade exam content. You can set up the test so that it closely simulates the experience of taking a certification exam, or you can set it up in study mode so that you can look at the correct answers and explanations after you answer each question.

> **MORE INFO**   **PRACTICE TESTS**
>
> For details about all the practice test options available, see the "How to Use the Practice Tests" section in this book's Introduction.

CHAPTER 4

Network Access Security

As a systems administrator, you understand that threats to network security exist on both sides of the organizational firewall. Attacks against your organization's computers can come from hosts on the Internet or hosts on the local area network (LAN). Whereas, in the past, computers were rarely removed from a controlled network environment, today the workers in your organization are less likely to be bound to a desktop workstation and are more likely to use a laptop computer or Tablet PC. In this chapter, you learn about technologies that give you a greater degree of control in providing secure access to your organization's network. These include authentication technologies, firewalls for use on the LAN, and Windows Server 2008 roles and features that you can use to limit network access based on the health status of a host.

Exam objectives in this chapter

- Configure wireless access.
- Configure firewall settings.
- Configure Network Access Protection (NAP).

Lessons in this chapter:

Before You Begin

To complete the lessons in this chapter, you must have done the following:

- Installed and configured the evaluation edition of Windows Server 2008 Enterprise Edition in accordance with the instructions listed in the Introduction.

REAL WORLD

Orin Thomas

One of the biggest shifts in thinking that has gone on since I became an IT professional is the shift in thinking about the LAN as a protected network environment. When I started out, firewalls were placed only at the border between a protected network environment and the Internet. Today's thinking is different in that it recognizes that the LAN is also potentially hostile to the health of systems. This shift of thinking is evident in the features shipped with Windows Vista and Windows Server 2008, namely the improved firewall and technologies such as Network Access Protection (NAP). Despite our best intentions, not every host that connects to the network we are responsible for managing is entirely under our control. Nothing is stopping a member of the sales team who has been overseas at trade shows for the past three months from connecting his or her laptop computer to the company network upon return. This is not problematic if the member of the sales team has ensured that antivirus protection, antispyware, and Windows Updates have been applied to that computer while he or she was away from the network. But what if, when the laptop computer was away from an environment in which harmful Web content is automatically filtered by Microsoft Internet Security and Acceleration (ISA) Server 2006, that laptop became infected? Without the technologies in Windows Server 2008, the act of connecting that computer to the LAN might activate a virulent worm. As IT professionals, we always need to be able to shift our thinking. Today, if we want to remain secure, we must consider the local area network as potentially hostile as we consider the Internet.

Lesson 1: Wireless Access

In the past decade, wireless network speeds have grown from painfully slow to fast enough that wireless technology is an acceptable replacement for traditional cabling. As wireless networking technology has matured, so have the methods through which administrators manage wireless clients in Windows Server network environments. Windows Server 2008 Group Policy gives you a way to automate the configuration of wireless network connections, ensuring that the people who use mobile computers within your organization can do so in a seamless and secure manner. In this lesson, you learn about the wireless technologies Windows clients and servers support, how you can configure secure authentication and encryption for wireless network connections, and how to deploy connection information automatically to clients through Group Policy.

After this lesson, you will be able to:

- Understand wireless network concepts.
- Understand the difference between ad hoc and infrastructure modes.
- Configure Group Policy related to wireless networks.
- Understand the difference between wireless authentication methods.
- Configure wireless local area network (WLAN) authentication, using 802.1x.

Estimated lesson time: 40 minutes

Wireless Network Components

The first part of this lesson covers the basic concepts behind WLANs. If you are an experienced administrator and already know the most commonly used IEEE 802.11 standards, what a service set identifier (SSID) does, the difference between ad hoc and infrastructure modes, and what a wireless access point (WAP) is, you should move forward to the section titled, "Wireless LAN Authentication."

IEEE 802.11 Standards

IEEE 802.11 is a collection of standards for WLANs developed by the Institute of Electronic and Electrical Engineers (IEEE), a professional organization that develops industry standards related to information technology, electricity, and electronics. The standards you are most likely to encounter in a modern network environment are as follows:

- **802.11b** This is an older wireless networking standard that has a maximum theoretical network throughput of 11 megabits per second (Mbps) and an approximate range of 35 meters (about 100 feet).

- **802.11g**   This is a newer standard than 802.11b and has a maximum theoretical network throughput of 64 Mbps and an approximate range of 35 meters. WAPs that use this standard can be configured to work in mixed mode, which supports both 802.11b and 802.11g clients at the cost of reduced network throughput.

- **802.11n**   Although this standard is awaiting formal approval, vendors sell products that use a draft version of the standard. It has a maximum theoretical network throughput of 300 Mbps and an approximate range of 70 meters (about 200 feet) and is backward compatible with 802.11b and 802.11g. This means that clients that support the older standards can connect to an 802.11n wireless network.

When considering the purchase of WAPs, remember that access points that support the 802.11n standard will be able support connections from clients that use 802.11b and 802.11g as well as 802.11n. Purchasing a WAP that is not compatible with existing wireless client hardware will mean that you have to replace that hardware for it to work with the new WLAN.

WAPs

WAPs are hardware devices that allow wireless clients, such as laptop computers, to access wireless networks directly and, through routing and switching, to access traditional physical networks, as shown in Figure 4-1. In many small businesses, a single hardware device functions as an external firewall, internal switch, and wireless access point. In most larger organizations, WAPs function as a bridge that allows wireless computers, such as laptops and Tablet PCs, to access resources such as servers that are connected to traditional wired networks.

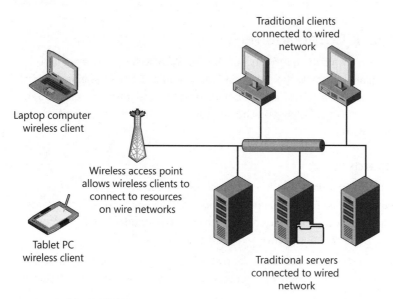

FIGURE 4-1 A basic WLAN.

NOTE **802.11 WIRELESS TO 3G/HSPDA**

Although WAPs have been defined earlier as connecting to traditional wired networks, some new-model mobile phones have software that can function as WAPs connecting to 3G/HSPDA data networks. This technology enables multiple 802.11 wireless clients to connect to a mobile phone WAP and to share the mobile phone's data connection.

SSID

SSID (service set identifier) is a wireless network name that can be up to 32 characters in length. You assign SSIDs to WAPs when you run a WAP's configuration utility. Some WAPs enable you to configure multiple SSIDs, with each SSID assigned to a different wireless network. It is customary to configure access points to broadcast SSIDs so that wireless clients can detect which wireless networks are available in a particular location. As with creating names for servers and client workstations, in large organizations it is essential to have a coherent and meaningful naming scheme for SSIDs. It is far easier for staff to locate a malfunctioning WAP named "CONTOSO-RM435-WAVERLEY" than it is to locate "ORINS-NEW-WIRELESS-ROUTER." With 32 characters, you can be descriptive, so there is no need to be cryptic when deploying SSIDs in your organization.

Although it is possible to configure WAPs not to broadcast SSIDs, Microsoft does not recommend this as a form of security because even when SSIDs are not broadcast, it is possible to detect a hidden SSID by using an appropriate set of tools. You should secure wireless networks by configuring strong authentication methods, not by hiding the network ID and hoping that an attacker is not proficient enough to figure it out.

MORE INFO **MORE ON NONBROADCAST WIRELESS NETWORKS**

To learn more about why Microsoft recommends broadcasting SSIDs, consult the following article on TechNet: *http://technet.microsoft.com/en-au/library/bb726942.aspx*.

AD Hoc Mode vs. Infrastructure Mode

Wireless networks in most Windows Server 2008 network environments will function in what is known as infrastructure mode as opposed to what is termed ad hoc mode. An infrastructure mode network has a wireless access point that manages communication between wireless clients. Ad hoc networks are created between wireless clients themselves and do not pass through a WAP. Infrastructure mode WLANs are more prevalent in business environments and typically connect wireless clients to traditional wired networks. Because the 70-648 and 70-649 exams concentrate on the server rather than on client operating systems, the focus of this lesson is on infrastructure mode rather than on ad hoc mode wireless networks.

NOTE WIRELESS NETWORKING ON WINDOWS SERVER 2008

By default, WLAN service is not installed on Windows Server 2008. You can add it through the *Features* node of the Server Manager console.

WLAN Authentication

You can restrict access to a wireless network by configuring WAPs to authenticate clients before allowing connections. It is also possible to protect wireless network traffic through encryption. The strength of WLAN encryption depends on the wireless standard used, although it is possible to use other network traffic encryption technologies in conjunction with WLAN encryption. Ensure that you encrypt wireless traffic because anyone within range of the WAP is able to capture all network communication between the access point and the client. Windows clients support the following wireless security standards:

- **Unsecured**   Unsecured wireless access points allow connections from any client with compatible hardware. When connecting to an unsecured wireless network, Windows Vista and Windows Server 2008 will warn users that it is possible for third parties to access transmissions sent to the WAP from the client. SSL and IPsec-encrypted traffic transmitted across networks with no security remains encrypted because this encryption is occurring at a higher layer of the Open Systems Interconnection (OSI) model.

- **Wired Equivalent Protection (WEP)**   WEP is an older wireless security standard that has vulnerabilities in its cryptographic design. WEP can be configured to use either 64-bit or 128-bit encryption. Tools are available that enable attackers to learn a WAP's WEP key by intercepting and analyzing existing wireless traffic. WEP is often used to deter people from casually connecting to an access point without authorization but will not deter a sophisticated attacker who is determined to get access. The WAP performs authentication when WEP is in use.

- **Wi-Fi Protected Access with Preshared Key (WPA-PSK/WPA2-PSK, WPA-Personal /WPA2-Personal)**   This standard uses a preshared key similar to WEP. Although the cryptography behind WPA-PSK is more sophisticated, making it more difficult to compromise than WEP, it is possible to calculate WPA-PSK preshared keys by using brute-force techniques, given enough time. With WPA-PSK, the access point performs authentication. WPA2-PSK (802.11i) uses stronger cryptography and is more secure than WPA-PSK, but the preshared key can still be calculated, given enough time and data.

- **Wi-Fi Protected Access with Extensible Authentication Protocol (WPA-EAP/WPA 2-EAP, WPA-Enterprise/WPA2-Enterprise)**   When this standard is used, the WAP forwards authentication requests to a RADIUS server. On computers configured with the Windows Server 2008 operating system, the Network Policy Server (NPS) role provides RADIUS authentication functionality. You can learn more about RADIUS by reviewing Chapter 3, "Network Access Configuration." WPA2-Enterprise supports smart-card, certificate-based, and password-based authentication. WPA2-Enterprise (802.11i) is more cryptographically secure than WPA-Enterprise; deploy WPA2-Enterprise if all clients in your network environment support this protocol.

When comparing these protocols from a security standpoint, Microsoft recommends deploying the WPA2-Enterprise or WPA-Enterprise authentication methods ahead of others that are available. These wireless standards are much more difficult to compromise than standards that use preshared keys. If a preshared key is compromised, it is necessary to update all clients and access points with new preshared keys to re-secure the network. If you are going to deploy WPA2-Enterprise and WPA-Enterprise in a Windows Server 2008 environment, you must deploy a Public Key Infrastructure (PKI) as well as enable auto-enrollment within Group Policy. Chapter 7, "Active Directory Certificate Services," covers these topics in detail.

> ***MORE INFO*** **WIRELESS NETWORKING TECHCENTER**
>
> To find out more about wireless networking in Microsoft operating systems, consult the wireless networking TechCenter on TechNet at: *http://technet.microsoft.com/en-us /network/bb530679.aspx*.

 Quick Check

1. Which wireless authentication protocol is the most secure out of the following: WPA2-EAP, WPA-EAP, WPA2-PSK, WPA-PSK, and WEP?
2. Which wireless authentication protocols do not use a preshared key to authenticate the client to the WAP?

Quick Check Answers

1. WPA2-EAP is more cryptographically secure than WPA-EAP, WPA2-PSK, WPA-PSK, and WEP.
2. WPA2-Enterprise (WPA2-EAP) and WPA-Enterprise (WPA-EAP) do not use preshared keys to authenticate the client to the access point.

Wireless Group Policy

Wireless network (IEEE 802.11) policies enable clients within your organization to connect to wireless networks with a minimum amount of end-user intervention and enable you to configure properties for specific access point identifiers, called SSIDs, in your organization. A wireless network policy consists of a collection of profiles. A profile addresses how the client should address specific SSIDs in your organization. A single profile can address multiple SSIDs, and the specific authentication methods and encryption technologies each access point supports. For example, you might create one profile for WAP1, WAP2, and WAP3 SSIDs, specifying the WPA2-Enterprise authentication method, the Microsoft PEAP network authentication method, and the AES encryption algorithm. You might create another profile for SSID WAP4 that specifies the WPA2-Personal authentication method and the TKIP encryption algorithm.

When you select the WPA/WPA2-Enterprise authentication method, you must also specify a network authentication method, as shown in Figure 4-2. It is necessary to specify the network authentication method because authentication occurs against an NPS/RADIUS server rather than against the WAP. Four basic authentication modes are available: Computer Authentication, User Re-authentication, User Authentication, and Guest Authentication. When the computer-only authentication mode is selected, the computer account authenticates the WAP connection prior to logon, allowing users transparent access to the network, similar to using a wired network. When the User Authentication mode is selected, authentication occurs after the users log on to their computers. You should not select this option unless the Single Sign On option is enabled in Advanced Properties because errors can occur during the authentication process if logon details are not cached.

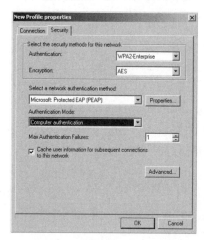

FIGURE 4-2 Wireless authentication policy.

When you select the User Re-authentication option, authentication is performed using computer credentials when a user is not logged on and user credentials when a user is logged on. You can configure this method so that a computer has limited access to the network until user credentials are provided. It is not necessary for a network authentication method to be specified when the WPA/WPA2-Personal method is selected because no network authentication is required, due to the use of preshared keys. The advanced security settings, shown in Figure 4-3, enable you to enforce advanced cryptography settings, enable Single Sign On, enable Fast Roaming, and use only cryptography that uses the FIPS 140-2 certified standard. Enable Single Sign On if you have chosen to implement the User Authentication mode because this will allow sign-on when a user's credentials have not been cached.

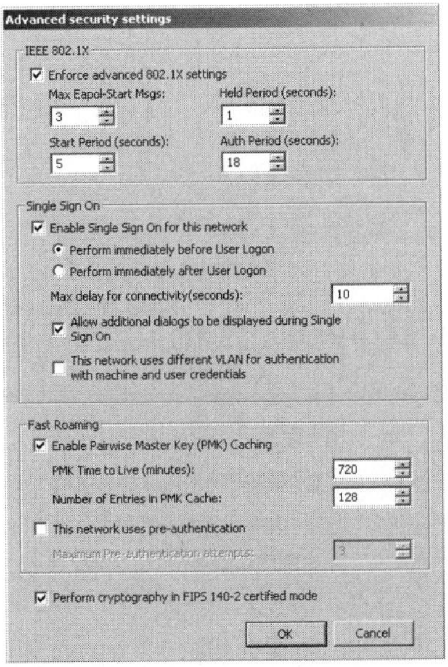

FIGURE 4-3 Advanced Security Settings.

Wireless network policies are configured on a per-client–operating system basis. You can configure a wireless network policy for Windows Vista or for Windows XP. It is important to note that computers running Windows XP are not influenced by the Windows Vista policy and vice versa. Although you can apply policies for both client operating systems in the same GPO, many network administrators find it simpler to separate client computers into different organizational units (OUs) and to apply separate policies if the settings for one operating system are significantly different from the settings for the other.

Wireless authentication policies also enable you to restrict wireless clients from connecting to either infrastructure or ad hoc mode networks. It is also possible to configure policies that allow users to view networks that they are denied access to, to use Group Policy profiles only for allowed networks, and to allow any user to create a wireless network profile. You configure some of these settings in the practice at the end of this lesson.

If it is necessary to troubleshoot wireless network policies, the commands available when *netsh* is in the *wlan* context are useful. It is also possible to use the *netsh wlan* commands to examine currently applied Group Policy settings. The *netsh wlan* commands enable you to configure wireless clients by using commands or scripts rather than through Group Policy. The command that provides the most information is *netsh wlan show all*, and you can use this command as a starting point to debug problems with wireless access policies.

MORE INFO   **MORE ON** *NETSH WLAN*

To find more detailed information on using *netsh wlan* to configure wireless connectivity and security settings, consult the following TechNet document: *http://technet2 .microsoft.com/windowsserver2008/en/library/f435edbe-1d50-4774-bae2 -0dda33eaeb2f1033.mspx?mfr=true.*

Configuring Network Policy and Access Services for Wireless Authentication

You can configure the Network Policy and Access Services role in Windows Server 2008 as a RADIUS server to authenticate WPA2-Enterprise and WPA-Enterprise connections to WAPs. Although NPS as a RADIUS server for remote access connections is covered in Chapter 3, this lesson focuses specifically on using NPS to support the WPA/WPA2-Enterprise protocols on WAPs.

You must add each access point as a RADIUS client. Configuring an access point as a RADIUS client involves setting up a shared secret password that you configure on both the access point and the RADIUS server. This shared secret can be generated automatically, as shown in Figure 4-4. The practice at the end of this lesson involves setting up a hypothetical access point as a RADIUS client.

FIGURE 4-4 Configuring an access point as a RADIUS client.

After you add each WAP in your organization as a RADIUS client, you can select from the following authentication methods:

- **Microsoft: Smart Card Or Other Certificate**   This method requires a user to provide a certificate by using a smart card. The user is prompted to insert the smart card when he or she attempts to connect to the wireless network.

- **Microsoft: Protected EAP (PEAP)**   This method requires the installation of a computer certificate on both the RADIUS/NPS server and the installation of a computer or user certificate on all wireless clients. Clients must trust the certification authority (CA) that issued the certificate on the RADIUS/NPS server, and the RADIUS/NPS server must trust the CA that issued the client certificates. You accomplish this most easily by deploying certificates issued by Active Directory Certificate Services (AD CS).

- **Microsoft: Secured Password (EAP-MSCHAP v2)**   This method requires a computer certificate to be installed on the RADIUS/NPS server and the issuing CA to be trusted by all wireless clients. Clients authenticate by using domain logon and password.

These authentication methods should be the same as those you specified in the profiles for each access point's SSID when configuring 802.11 wireless access Group Policy. Check the WAP documentation for details on how to configure the device to forward authentication information to a RADIUS server.

MORE INFO   **WINDOWS SERVER 2008 AND 802.1X**

To learn more about Windows Server 2008 and 802.1x wireless authentication, consult the following article on TechNet: *http://technet2.microsoft.com/windowsserver2008/en /library/710a912a-0377-414a-91d1-47698e4629361033.mspx?mfr=true.*

EXAM TIP

Remember that if an authentication method relies on a preshared key, you will not need a RADIUS server, but if you are pairing an access point with a RADIUS server, you will need a shared secret.

PRACTICE **Configuring Wireless Access**

In this practice, you perform tasks similar to those you would perform when configuring a Windows Server 2008 network environment to support wireless access by client computers running Windows Vista. The first exercise configures NPS for wireless access; the second exercise configures Group Policy to support wireless access.

EXERCISE 1   Configure NPS for Wireless Access

In this exercise, you configure server Glasgow to function as a Network Policy/RADIUS server so that it is able to process WPA2-Enterprise authentication traffic. You also configure a hypothetical access point named *wap1.contoso.internal* with a shared secret that will pair it with the RADIUS server.

1. Log on to server Glasgow with the Kim_Akers user account.

2. Open the Server Manager console, right-click the *Roles* node. If you have already installed the Network Policy and Access Services role in a prior practice, proceed to step 8; otherwise, select Add Roles.

    This starts the Add Roles Wizard.

3. Click Next on the Before You Begin page.

4. Select the Network Policy And Access Services check box and click Next.

5. Click Next on the Introduction To Network Policy And Access Services page.

6. On the Role Services page, ensure that the Network Policy Server and Routing And Remote Access Services check boxes are selected, as shown in Figure 4-5, and then click Next.

7. On the Confirm Installation Selections page, click Install. When the installation process finishes, click Close.

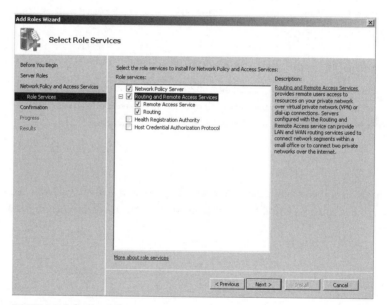

FIGURE 4-5 Selecting roles.

8. Open a command prompt and issue the command:

    ```
    dnscmd /recordadd contoso.internal wap1 A 10.50.0.1
    ```

9. Close the command prompt.

10. Open the Network Policy Server console from the Administrative Tools menu.

11. Select the *NPS (Local)* node. Use the drop-down menu in the Standard Configuration section of the Getting Started pane to select RADIUS Server For 802.1X Wireless Or

Wired Connections, as shown in Figure 4-6, and then click Configure 802.1X. This will open the Configure 802.1X Wizard.

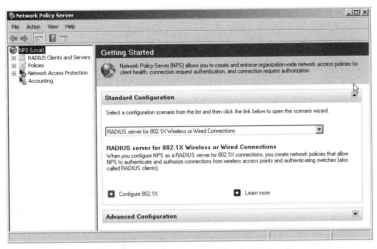

FIGURE 4-6 Getting started on configuring wireless authentication.

12. On the Select 802.1X Connections Type page, select Secure Wireless Connections, as shown in Figure 4-7, and then click Next.

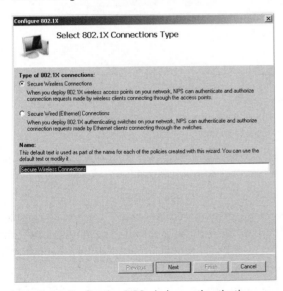

FIGURE 4-7 Configuring NPS wireless authentication.

13. On the Specify 802.1X Switches Or Wireless Access Points (RADIUS Clients) page, click Add.

This opens the New RADIUS Client dialog box.

14. In the New RADIUS Client dialog box, enter a friendly name for the access point, such as WAP-ONE. In the Address (IP or DNS) area, enter **wap1.contoso.internal**.

15. Select Generate, and then click the Generate button.

    This generates the shared secret that is entered on the WAP to bind it to the RADIUS server.

16. Click OK to close the dialog box. Click Next.

17. On the Configure An Authentication Method page, select Microsoft: Secured password (EAP-MSCHAP v2) from the drop-down list, and then click Next.

18. On the Specify User Groups page, click Next. On the Configure A Virtual LAN (VLAN) page, click Next.

19. Click Finish to close the Configure 802.1X Wizard.

20. Expand the *RADIUS Clients And Servers* node, and then select RADIUS Clients. Verify that WAP-ONE appears, as shown in Figure 4-8, and then close the Network Policy Server console.

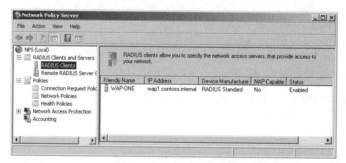

FIGURE 4-8 Wireless access point configured as RADIUS client.

EXERCISE 2 Configure Wireless Access Policies

In this exercise, you configure Wireless Access Group Policy and apply it to an OU in which you could then place the computer accounts of computers that have wireless cards.

1. Log on to server Glasgow, using the Kim_Akers user account.

2. From the Administrative Tools menu, open the Group Policy Management console. Expand the *Forest: contoso.internal* node and the *domain* node. Right-click the contoso. internal domain, and then select New Organizational Unit. Enter the organizational unit name as **Wireless_Computers**, and then click OK.

3. Right-click the new Wireless_Computers OU, and then select Create A GPO In This Domain And Link It Here. In the New GPO dialog box, enter the GPO name as **Wireless_Computer_Policy**, and then click OK.

4. Select the Wireless_Computers OU, right-click the Wireless_Computer_Policy GPO, and then select Edit.

    This opens the Group Policy Management Editor.

5. Right-click the *Computer Configuration\Policies\Windows Settings\Security Settings \Wireless network (IEEE 802.11) Policies* node, and then select Create A New Windows Vista Policy.

This opens the New Windows Vista Network Policy Properties dialog box, shown in Figure 4-9.

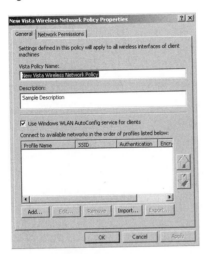

FIGURE 4-9 Vista wireless policy.

6. Click Add, and then select Infrastructure.

This opens the New Profile properties dialog box.

7. In the Profile Name area, enter **WAP-ONE**. In the Network Name(s) (SSID) text box, enter **WAP-ONE**, and then click Add.

8. Click the Security tab. Verify that the settings on the Security tab match those of Figure 4-10, and then click OK.

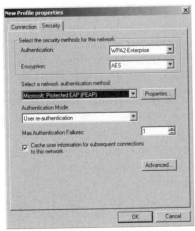

FIGURE 4-10 Authentication and encryption settings.

9. Click the Network Permissions tab. Ensure that the settings on the Network Permissions tab match those in Figure 4-11, and then click OK.

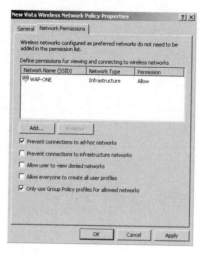

FIGURE 4-11 Wireless network permissions.

10. Close the Group Policy Management Editor, and then close the Group Policy Management console.

Lesson Summary

- Access points that support the 802.11n standard can support connections from clients that use 802.11b and 802.11g as well as 802.11n.

- SSID (service set identifier) is a wireless network name that can be up to 32 characters in length.

- An infrastructure mode network has a WAP that manages communication between wireless clients. Ad hoc networks are created between wireless clients.

- WEP is an older wireless security standard that uses a preshared key but is vulnerable to attack. WPA-Personal/WPA2-Personal uses preshared keys. WPA-Enterprise/WPA2-Enterprise forwards authentication requests to RADIUS servers. It supports smart card-, certificate-, and password-based authentication.

- Wireless Network (IEEE 802.11) Group Policy allows clients within your organization to connect to wireless networks with a minimum of end-user intervention. Wireless network policies enable you to configure properties for specific access point identifiers. A single profile can address multiple SSIDs and addresses the specific authentication methods and encryption technologies each access point supports.

Lesson Review

You can use the following questions to test your knowledge of the information in Lesson 1, "Wireless Access." The questions are also available on the companion DVD if you prefer to review them in electronic form.

> **NOTE ANSWERS**
>
> Answers to these questions and explanations of why each answer choice is right or wrong are located in the "Answers" section at the end of the book.

1. Which of the following authentication protocols enables you to deny access to wireless networks based on an Active Directory user or computer account?

    A. WPA2-Enterprise

    B. WEP

    C. WPA-PSK

    D. WPA2-Personal

2. You are configuring Network Policy and Access Services on a computer running Windows Server 2008 so that it responds to authentication traffic forwarded from WAPs in your organization. Which of the following must you do as part of this process?

    A. Configure WAPs as RADIUS servers.

    B. Configure wireless clients as RADIUS clients.

    C. Configure WAPs as RADIUS clients.

    D. Configure wireless clients as RADIUS proxies.

3. Which of the following must you ensure when configuring a wireless access policy that uses EAP-MSCHAP v2 as an authentication method?

    A. That the CA that issued the computer certificate to the NPS server is trusted by the RADIUS server

    B. That the CA that issued the computer certificates to the clients is trusted by the NPS server

    C. That the CA that issued the computer certificate to the NPS server is trusted by the clients

    D. That the CA that issued the computer certificates to the WAPs is trusted by the clients

4. All the clients at your organization use the Windows Vista Enterprise edition operating system. The Wireless_Clients OU hosts the computer accounts of those computers that have wireless network adapters. A group of executives is planning to have a weekly morning informal strategy meeting in the basement, where there is currently no WAP. The executives want to use the Windows Meeting Space application, included with Windows Vista, to set up a temporary network so that they can share documents. They are currently unable to do this. Which of the following configuration changes should you make to the GPO applied to the Wireless_Clients OU to enable them to meet their goals?

A. Configure the policy to allow users to view denied networks.

B. Configure the policy to allow connections to infrastructure networks.

C. Configure the policy to allow everyone to create wireless profiles.

D. Configure the policy to allow connections to ad hoc networks.

5. When configuring wireless network Group Policy profiles for specific SSIDs, which of the following WAP authentication protocols require you also to specify a network authentication method?

A. WEP

B. WPA2-Personal

C. Open

D. WPA2-Enterprise

Lesson 2: Windows Firewall with Advanced Security

Windows Server 2008 ships with a firewall enabled by default. In this lesson, you learn about Windows Firewall with Advanced Security and the features it includes that differentiate it from earlier firewall software included with Microsoft Windows operating systems such as Microsoft Windows Server 2003. You learn how to create inbound and outbound firewall rules, configure rule scope, and configure connection security rules, a technology that is new to Windows Vista and Windows Server 2008.

After this lesson, you will be able to:

- Configure incoming and outgoing traffic filtering.
- Configure Active Directory account integration.
- Identify common ports and protocols.
- Understand the difference between Microsoft Windows Firewall and Windows Firewall with Advanced Security.
- Configure firewalls by using Group Policy.
- Manage isolation policies.

Estimated lesson time: 40 minutes

Windows Firewall and Windows Firewall with Advanced Security

Windows Server 2008 uses two firewalls that work in concert, Windows Firewall and Windows Firewall with Advanced Security. The primary difference between these two firewalls is the complexity of the rules you can apply. Windows Firewall, accessible through Control Panel and shown in Figure 4-12, allows the application of only basic rules. When creating a rule, you can specify an exception based on program or port, but you cannot create advanced exceptions that work based on network location awareness, individual network interfaces, or specific incoming or outgoing addresses. With its limited ability to allow for the refinement of exceptions, Windows Firewall is a blunt instrument when compared to Windows Firewall with Advanced Security. As a server administrator, you are more likely to be interested in the expanded functionality of Windows Firewall with Advanced Security, and the rest of this lesson concentrates on this more complicated technology.

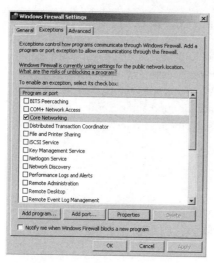

FIGURE 4-12 The Exceptions tab of Windows Firewall.

Network Location Awareness

Before covering Windows Firewall with Advanced Security, it is important to come to terms with the concept of network location awareness. Network location awareness, also known as network profiles, is a technology included in Windows Vista and Windows Server 2008 that enables network-aware applications and services to alter behavior, depending on how a computer is connected to the network. Whenever you connect a computer running Windows Server 2008 to a new network, you are queried as to whether the network is public, private, or domain based. Depending on how you classify the network, Windows Server 2008 will assign the following network location categories:

- **Public** The public network category is set by default. When set or configured, all inbound traffic is dropped. Outgoing connections are allowed when the public profile is active. Any untrusted network, including the Internet, should be classified as a public network.

- **Private** A user can select the private network category manually and use it for a network that is not directly accessible to public networks such as the Internet. Private networks are segmented from public networks by firewall or NAT devices. This does not include Windows Firewall or Windows Firewall with Advanced Security on the host itself. If a computer running Windows Server 2008 is configured as a standalone server on a protected network, assign the network connection the private network designation.

- **Domain** Select the domain network category when a computer has authenticated to an Active Directory domain. This category is selected automatically after domain authentication through a network interface has occurred and a domain controller is available.

When multiple interfaces are connected to network locations that have different categories, the least secure category will be assigned to the computer. Hence, if one network interface is connected to the Internet and another connects to a protected network with a domain controller, the Public category will be set, and the firewall will block incoming network connections.

MORE INFO **NETWORK LOCATION AWARENESS**

For more information about network location awareness, consult the following TechNet Article.

Configuring WFAS Rules

Windows Firewall with Advanced Security (WFAS) enables you to configure firewall rules that are applied based on which network location-awareness profile is active (Domain, Public, or Private) and whether a connection is a secure network interface. You can also configure firewall rules based on a protocol, port, source, and destination IP address as well as apply rules based on specific user and computer accounts. The WFAS console can import and export firewall configurations. This is very useful if you are responsible for managing a large number of standalone computers running Windows Server 2008 and need to replicate the same WFAS configuration quickly.

Configuring Inbound Rules

Inbound rules allow a specific type of traffic specified by the rule. When the firewall intercepts an incoming packet, it evaluates the packet against the list of inbound rules. If the packet matches any one of those inbound rules, it is processed according to that rule. If it matches no inbound rules, the packet is dropped. Windows Server 2008 automatically enables appropriate inbound rules when you install or enable a role or feature that requires incoming connections. For example, if you enable the Web Server (IIS) role, WFAS is automatically configured to allow inbound HTTP traffic on port 80 and inbound HTTPS traffic on port 443. Windows Server 2008 ships with a set of preconfigured inbound rules, or you can use the Inbound Rules Wizard to create your own.

The first page of the Inbound Rules Wizard, shown in Figure 4-13, enables you to select which type of rule you create. Your options are Program, Port, Predefined, and Custom. The list of predefined rules is extensive and covers almost every type of feature or role service you can install on a computer running Windows Server 2008. Custom rules enable you to define all aspects of a rule, and you can add both programs and ports as well as scope. If you want to block connections on a specific port to a specific program from a particular range of IP addresses, you configure a custom rule. In general, it is not necessary to specify both a program and a port because a single port can be bound to only one program or service. If you want to create a rule for a specific service, rather than for a program, you must create a custom rule. Configuring scope for firewall rules is covered later in this lesson.

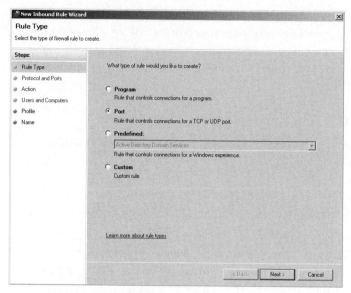

FIGURE 4-13 Inbound Rules Wizard.

If you decide to create a rule for a program, you must specify the path of the program on the server. If multiple versions of the program are installed on the server, you must create a separate program rule for each location. If you create a port rule, you must specify whether the rule applies to TCP or UDP connections and the specific ports the rule covers. You can specify multiple ports, separating each port by a comma. You create an inbound rule in one of the exercises at the end of this lesson.

Port Numbers

As a holder of the MCSA certification, MCSE certification, or both, it is likely that you are already familiar with the TCP port numbers of the most common networking protocols. In case you have forgotten some, remember that FTP uses ports 20 and 21, SSH uses port 22, Telnet uses port 23, SMTP uses port 25, DNS uses port 53, HTTP uses port 80, Kerberos uses port 88, POP3 uses port 110, IMAP uses port 143, LDAP uses port 389, and HTTPS uses port 443. You can find a list of all registered port numbers at *http://www.iana.org/assignments/port-numbers*.

The Action page of the New Inbound Rule Wizard enables you to configure how WFAS responds after a traffic match is found. As Figure 4-14 shows, the options are to allow the connection, to allow the connection if it is secure, and to block the connection. Allowing the connection is straightforward. If the traffic matches the rule, the traffic passes across WFAS. When you select the Allow The Connection If It Is Secure option, an extra page is added—on which you can specify users and computers using Active Directory—to the wizard. It is also possible to require that the connection be encrypted using IPsec and to override any existing block rules. By default, block rules have precedence over allow rules. Enabling the Override Block Rules option is the only way to bypass an existing block rule.

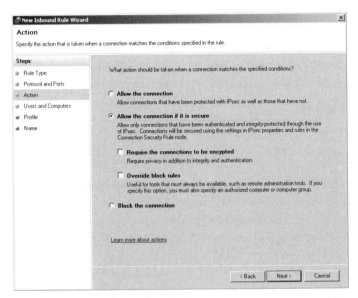

FIGURE 4-14 Configuring a rule action.

Although you can configure an inbound rule to block a specific sort of traffic, this is generally not necessary because Windows Firewall with Advanced Security automatically blocks any traffic that does not match an allow rule by default anyway. The main reason to implement block rules is to allow a certain type of traffic from specific hosts but block it from all other hosts. You can accomplish the same thing by configuring the scope of a rule. Configuring rule scope is covered later in this lesson.

After you have specified a rule action, you must specify to which profiles the rule will apply. You can apply the rule to one, two, or all available domain profiles. The last step in the New Inbound Rule Wizard is to provide a rule name and description. The information that you enter here should be meaningful because another administrator might need to inspect your configuration in the future; that administrator should not have to examine each custom rule's properties to figure out exactly what the rule is supposed to do.

 Quick Check

1. How is Windows Firewall limited compared to Windows Firewall with Advanced Security?

2. Under what conditions is the domain network location awareness profile set?

Quick Check Answers

1. Windows Firewall enables you to specify exceptions based on program or port, but you cannot specify exceptions based on network location awareness, individual network interfaces, specific incoming or outgoing addresses, or protocol.

2. The domain network location profile is set when a computer's network interface is connected to an Active Directory domain and a domain controller is accessible.

Configuring Outbound Rules

Outbound rules apply to traffic leaving the computer for a remote host. The default configuration of WFAS allows all outbound traffic. Blocking all outbound traffic will stop many built-in Windows features and applications from communicating with other hosts on the network. This can have unintended side effects; for example, a computer cannot retrieve updates from a local WSUS server when all outbound communication is blocked unless a rule related to this type of traffic is enabled. If you do decide to block all outbound traffic and then create exceptions for approved programs and services, you must carefully test your deployment prior to putting the server into a production environment because you might miss one or more vital services and applications you should allow.

Outbound Rules and Viruses

A common argument for applying outbound rules is that it can stop worms and viruses from replicating out from an infected computer. Unfortunately, if a virus or worm has infected a computer, it most likely has enough privileges in the operating system to configure its own firewall rules, hence bypassing any outbound filters. If firewalls are properly implemented on other computers in your environment, malicious worm traffic from an infected host will have minimal impact anyway. Where outbound rules can be useful is in specifically blocking unapproved programs that users might install on their computers, such as instant messaging clients or peer-to-peer programs. In a controlled desktop environment, ordinary users would not be able to install these programs in the first place.

To create an outbound rule, perform the following steps:

1. Open the Windows Firewall With Advanced Security console, and then select and right-click the *Outbound Rules* node. Select New Rule.

   The New Outbound Rule Wizard starts.

2. Select the Rule type from Program, Port, Predefined Or Custom, and then click Next.

3. If you select Program, browse to the program's path. If you select Port, select the protocol type (TCP/UDP) and type the appropriate port or port range.

4. On the Action page, choose between Allow The Connection, Allow The Connection If It Is Secure, and Block The Connection.

5. On the Profile page, select the network profile or profiles to which th e rule should apply.

6. Finish the wizard by entering a name for the rule.

Rule Scope

When you configure an inbound or an outbound firewall rule, you are unable to configure the scope of the rule. The scope of the rule enables you to apply a rule based on the IP address of the source or destination host. For example, in Figure 4-15, a firewall rule is given the scope of 10.0.0.1–10.10.10.254. Scope can enable you to fine-tune a rule. For example, you might use the scope option to configure a rule to block outbound SMTP traffic except to a specific SMTP server's IP address. When applying multiple rules to the same type of traffic, remember that a block rule always overrides an allow rule. Hence, if you wanted to block access to all Web servers except those on subnet 10.10.10.0 /24, you would need to configure the scope of the rule to apply to remote IP addresses 0.0.0.1-10.10.9.255 and 10.10.11.0-255.255.255.255 rather than configuring a block of all port 80 traffic and another rule allowing it for subnet 10.10.10.0 /24.

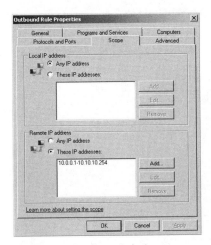

FIGURE 4-15 Configure Rule Scope.

Connection Security Rules

Connection security rules define how and under what conditions computers are able to communicate with each other. Connection security rules generally involve a list of computers, whether the connection will request or require authentication, and the methods of authentication the connection can use. Each category of connection security rule is appropriate to a specific type of scenarios. As with Inbound and Outbound rules, you can apply connection security rules by using the WFAS console, *netsh* in the *advfirewall firewall* context, or Group Policy. The next few pages cover the different types of connection security rules.

Isolation Policies

Through isolation policies, you can partition sets of computers on the network by using network authentication and encryption policies. Only computers that meet a specific set of criteria are able to communicate with computers subject to isolation policies. Although it is possible to configure isolation policies on a computer-by-computer basis, using either the WFAS console or *netsh* in the *advfirewall consec* context because isolation policies usually apply to multiple computers, it is best to configure and enforce them through the application of Group Policy.

The simplest form of isolation policy is the server isolation policy, which requires all communication with a server to be authenticated and encrypted. As shown in Figure 4-16, authentication can occur, using Kerberos V5, for computer and user accounts if the server is a member of a domain, through a computer certificate or a system health certificate issued by a trusted certificate authority (CA). By selecting Advanced Authentication, it is also possible to enable authentication by using the NTLMv2 protocol or a preshared key.

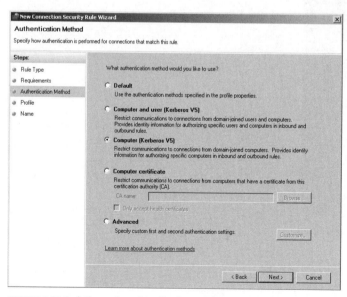

FIGURE 4-16 Isolation rule authentication options.

MORE INFO **SERVER ISOLATION**

To learn more about server isolation on Windows Server 2008 networks, consult the following TechNet link: *http://technet2.microsoft.com/windowsserver2008/en /library/13e8dad2-c99f-415b-a38a-669418d765c61033.mspx?mfr=true.*

Domain isolation restricts contact to computers on the basis of domain membership. When strictly applied, computers and users that are members of a specified domain or forest are able to perform successful authentication under a domain isolation rule. Domain isolation policies apply to all computers that are members of the domain rather than to a select set of computers, as is the case with a server isolation policy. When domain isolation policies are in effect, traffic can be protected using IPsec. You learned about configuring IPsec in conjunction with connection security policies in Chapter 2, "Configuring IP Services."

MORE INFO **DOMAIN ISOLATION**

To learn more about domain isolation on Windows Server 2008 networks, consult the following TechNet link: *http://technet2.microsoft.com/windowsserver2008/en /library/135110b6-23ab-45f2-8cd1-8b76b2e38b3d1033.mspx?mfr=true.*

Authentication Exemption

Authentication exemptions enable you to specify a group of computers, either through their Active Directory computer account name or IP address, to which existing connection security rules do not apply. Administrators primarily use authentication exemptions to ensure communication with infrastructure servers the computer must communicate with prior to the completion of the authentication process. Examples of such infrastructure servers include Dynamic Host Configuration Protocol (DHCP) servers, DNS servers, and domain controllers (DCs). To create an authentication exemption, perform the following steps:

1. Start the New Connection Security Rule Wizard.
2. Select the Authentication Exemption rule type and click Next.
3. On the Exempt Computers page, click Add.
4. In the IP Address dialog box, enter a single IP address or subnet address or an IP address range or select from a predefined set of computers in the drop-down list. Click OK, and then click Next.
5. Select the network profiles the authentication exemption applies to, and then click Next.
6. Give the exemption a name, and then click Finish.

Server-to-Server Rules

Server-to-server rules enable you to configure authentication for two different groups of computers. As Figure 4-17 shows, you specify computers by IP address or IP address range. As is the case with other connection security rules, it is possible to configure the rule to request authentication for inbound and outbound connections, require authentication for inbound connections and request it for outbound connections, or require authentication for all connections.

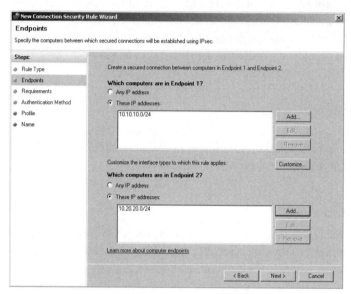

FIGURE 4-17 Server-to-server rule.

After you have specified the connection authentication request requirements, you must specify how authentication occurs for connections that match this rule. The options are a computer certificate issued by a commonly trusted CA; a preshared key; or a combination of authenticating computer accounts using Kerberos V5, NTLMv2, computer certificate, or preshared key. It is possible when choosing the computer certificate option to limit computer certificates to health certificates, such as those issued as part of the NAP process.

Tunnel

Tunnel rules are similar to server-to-server rules except that they allow you to specify lists of computers at different ends of a tunnel and addresses of local and remote gateways. These gateways are usually the beginning and endpoints of a virtual private network (VPN) or L2TP /IPsec connection across the Internet. When creating a tunnel rule, you specify which computers are located behind endpoint 1 and which computers are located behind endpoint 2. In a way, a tunnel rule works like a routing table that allows two groups of computers to communicate through a specifically defined set of gateway endpoints. Figure 4-18 shows groups of computers, specified as IP address ranges, at each end of a hypothetical tunnel. The authentication request requirements and the authentication options are the same as those available for the server-to-server rule type.

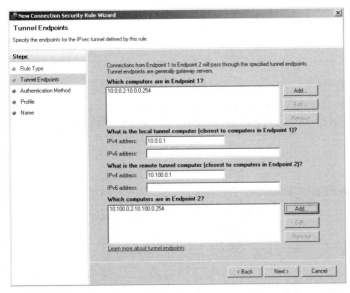

FIGURE 4-18 Configuring a tunnel rule.

> **NOTE CUSTOM**
>
> The custom rule type enables you to mix and match components of the preceding rule types. For example, you could create an authentication exemption rule that uses tunnel endpoints.

WFAS Command Line

You can also manipulate Windows Firewall with Advanced Security from the command line. This can be important if you are configuring a standalone computer running Windows Server 2008 that is configured using the Server Core installation option. You can use the *netsh firewall* and *netsh advfirewall* commands to create rules and show current configurations as well as to import and export those configurations. You can use the import and export functionality to quickly configure multiple standalone computers running Windows Server 2008 Server Core. Although complete coverage of the *netsh advfirewall* commands is beyond the scope of this book, some examples of commands that you can use to configure WFAS include:

- **Netsh advfirewall show allprofiles** Displays the properties of all advanced firewall profiles
- **Netsh advfirewall dump** Dumps the current firewall configuration to a script that can restore firewall configuration

- **Netsh advfirewall reset**   Returns a firewall to the default configuration
- **Netsh advfirewall consec**   Switches to the connection security context, enabling the creation of connection security rules
- **Netsh advfirewall firewall add rule**   Can create an advanced firewall rule, using all the categories available for creating a rule by using the GUI

> **MORE INFO   CONFIGURING WFAS**
>
> For more information on configuring WFAS by using the *netsh* command, consult the following article on the Microsoft Web site: *http://support.microsoft.com/kb/947709.*

EXAM TIP

Keep clear in your mind the differences between Windows Firewall and WFAS.

PRACTICE   Configuring Firewall Through Group Policy

In this practice, you create a Windows Firewall with Advanced Security policy that involves enabling the firewall for all profiles, configuring a rule for a specific type of traffic, and configuring a connection security rule.

EXERCISE 1   Create and Apply a WFAS Policy

In this exercise, you create a policy to enable WFAS for all network location profiles and configure the policy to enable IPsec encryption if any connection security rules are enforced. Finally, you create a rule that allows inbound HTTP and HTTPS traffic when the Domain profile is active.

1. Log on to Glasgow, using the Kim_Akers user account.
2. Open the Group Policy Management console from the Administrative Tools menu.
3. Under the *contoso.internal domain*, create a new organizational unit called Firewall_Clients.
4. Right-click the Firewall_Clients OU, and then select Create a GPO In This Domain And Link it Here. Name the GPO **WFAS_Policy** and click OK. Verify that the Group Policy Management console window on Glasgow resembles Figure 4-19.

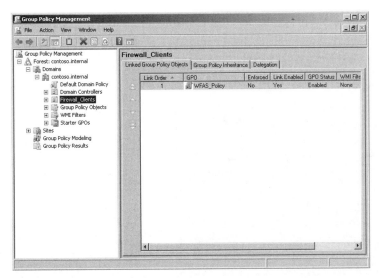

FIGURE 4-19 Creating a GPO.

5. Right-click WFAS_Policy in the Linked Group Policy Objects window, and then select Edit.

The Group Policy Management Editor opens.

6. Navigate to the *Computer Configuration\Policies\Windows Settings\Security Settings\ Windows Firewall with Advanced Security\Windows Firewall With Advanced Security* node.

7. Click the Windows Firewall Properties link in the Overview pane to open the Windows Firewall With Advanced Properties dialog box. On the Domain Profile tab, set Firewall State to On, set Inbound Connections to Block (Default), and the Outbound connections to Allow (Default), as shown in Figure 4-20, and then click Apply.

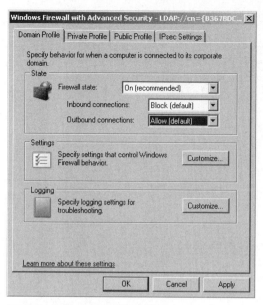

FIGURE 4-20 Domain profile settings.

8. Repeat step 7 on the Private Profile and Public Profile tabs.

9. Click Customize on the IPsec Settings tab. In the Customize IPsec Settings dialog box, shown in Figure 4-21, in the Data Protection (Quick Mode) section, select Advanced, and then click the Customize button. Select the Require Encryption For All Connection Security Rules That Use These Settings check box and click OK.

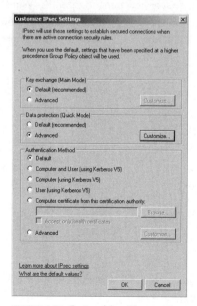

FIGURE 4-21 Customizing IPsec settings.

10. Click OK twice to close all open dialog boxes.

11. In the Group Policy Management Editor, under the *Windows Firewall With Advanced Security* node, select and then right-click Inbound Rules. Select New Rule.

    The New Inbound Rule Wizard opens.

12. On the Rule Type page, select Port, and then click Next.

13. On the Protocols And Ports page, select Specific Local Ports. Type **80, 443** in the ports text box, as shown in Figure 4-22, and then click Next.

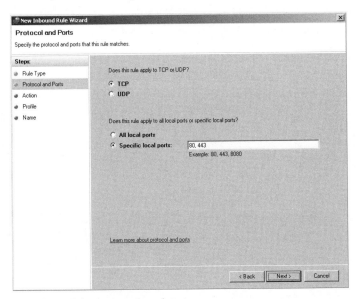

FIGURE 4-22 Select protocols and ports.

14. On the Action page, select Allow The Connection and click Next.

15. On the Profile page, ensure that only the Domain profile check box is selected, and then click Next.

16. On the Name page, enter Domain Web Traffic Rule, and then click Finish.

17. Verify that the Domain Web Traffic rule is listed when the Inbound Rules pane has focus, and then close Group Policy Management Editor.

EXERCISE 2   Create an Isolation Policy

In this exercise, you create a connection security policy, which forms the backbone of an isolation policy. Isolation policies ensure that only computers that have performed a specified type of authentication are able to communicate with each other.

1. If you closed the Group Policy Management console at the end of Exercise 1, "Create and Apply a WFAS Policy," reopen this console and select the Firewall_Clients OU.

    This OU was created in the preceding exercise.

2. Right-click the WFAS_Policy GPO located in the Linked Group Policy Objects pane of the Group Policy Management console, and then select Edit.

    The Group Policy Management Editor opens.

3. Expand the *Computer Configuration\Policies\Windows Settings\Security Settings \Windows Firewall with Advanced Security\Windows Firewall With Advanced Security* node.

4. Select and then right-click Connection Security Rules, and then select New Rule.

    This launches the New Connection Security Rule Wizard, as shown in Figure 4-23.

5. Ensure that the Isolation item is selected, and then click Next.

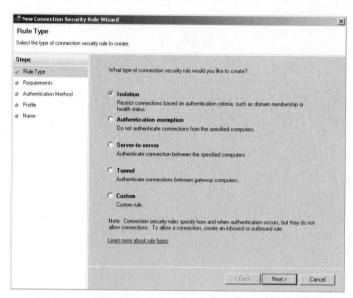

FIGURE 4-23 Select rule type

6. On the Requirements page, select Require Authentication For Inbound And Outbound Connections and click Next.

7. On the Authentication Method page, select Computer (Kerberos V5), as shown in Figure 4-24, and then click Next.

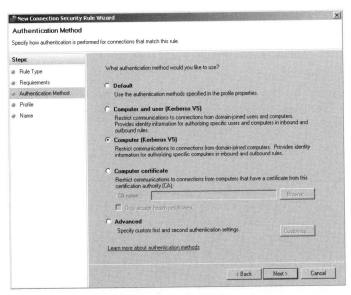

FIGURE 4-24 Configure authentication method.

8. Verify that the rule applies to all profiles, and then click Next.

9. On the Name page, enter Domain Isolation Policy, and then click Finish.

10. Verify that the Connection Security Rule Domain Isolation Policy is present and enabled in the Group Policy Management Editor. Close the Group Policy Management Editor and the Group Policy Management Console.

Lesson Summary

- If the packet matches any inbound rules, it is processed according to that rule. If it matches no inbound rules, the packet is dropped.
- Windows Server 2008 will automatically enable appropriate inbound rules when you install or enable a role or feature that requires incoming connections.
- Enabling the Override Block Rules option is the only way to bypass an existing block rule.
- The default configuration of WFAS allows all outbound traffic.
- The scope of the rule enables you to apply a rule based on the IP address of the source or destination host.
- Connection security rules define how and under what conditions computers are able to communicate with each other.
- Isolation policies enable you to partition sets of computers on the network by using network authentication and encryption policies.

- Authentication exemptions enable you to specify a group of computers to which existing connection security rules do not apply.
- Server-to-server rules enable you to configure authentication for two different groups of computers.
- Tunnel rules are similar to server-to-server rules except that they enable you to specify lists of computers at different ends of a tunnel and addresses of local and remote gateways.

Lesson Review

You can use the following questions to test your knowledge of the information in Lesson 2, "Windows Firewall with Advanced Security." The questions are also available on the companion DVD if you prefer to review them in electronic form.

> **NOTE ANSWERS**
>
> Answers to these questions and explanations of why each answer choice is right or wrong are located in the "Answers" section at the end of the book.

1. Which of the following should you configure if you want to ensure that all the Windows Server 2008 file servers in your organization will respond only to network traffic initiated by hosts that are members of the domain?

   A. Inbound firewall rule

   B. Outbound firewall rule

   C. Isolation rule

   D. Authentication exemption

2. You want to ensure that only computers that have authenticated to the domain are able to communicate with your organization's file servers. Which of the following would you configure in a GPO linked to the OU that hosts the file server's computer accounts?

   A. Isolation connection security rule

   B. Server-to-server connection security rule

   C. Authentication exemption connection security rule

   D. Tunnel connection security rule

3. An organization has two branch offices. Each branch office has an Internet connection. An L2TP/IPsec VPN connects these two branch offices. Which type of connection security rule would you create so that all computers in the first branch office can connect to all computers in the second branch office by using a computer certificate issued by a common CA as an authentication mechanism?

   A. Authentication exemption

   B. Isolation rule

   C. Server-to-server rule

   D. Tunnel rule

4. You are preparing the deployment of 30 computers running Windows Web Server 2008. Each of these computers will be configured as a standalone computer and will not be a member of a domain. Each computer will be connected to the Internet and will need an identical WFAS configuration. Which of the following options should you employ to provide each computer with the same set of WFAS rules? (Choose two. Each correct answer presents part of a complete solution.)

   A. Place all the Windows Web Server 2008 computer accounts in the same OU.

   B. Configure all WFAS rules on one computer running Windows Web Server 2008. Export the firewall policy by using the WFAS console.

   C. Import the firewall policy into a Group Policy object and apply it to the OU.

   D. Configure all WFAS rules on one computer running Windows Web Server 2008. Use the *netsh firewall dump* command to export the firewall configuration.

   E. Import the firewall policy by using the WFAS console on each of the other 29 computers running Windows Web Server 2008.

5. You must configure firewall rules on a computer running Windows Server 2008 to allow DNS, HTTPS, and SMTP traffic. Which of the following ports correspond to these protocols? (Choose three. Each correct answer presents part of a complete solution.)

   A. 53

   B. 110

   C. 80

   D. 25

   E. 443

Lesson 3: Network Access Protection

Network Access Protection (NAP) is a new Windows Server 2008 technology you can use to limit network access based on whether a client computer has up-to-date antivirus definitions as well as the most recent updates installed. As an experienced administrator, you are aware that most viruses and worms rely on operating system and application vulnerabilities for which vendors have already released patches. NAP enables you to block computers that are not up to date from joining your network, either by denying VPN access, by allowing DHCP leases to healthy computers only, or by using technologies such as VLANs or IPsec. In this lesson, you learn about NAP and the steps you must take to deploy and manage this technology in your own environment.

> **After this lesson, you will be able to:**
> - Describe how NAP works.
> - Install and configure NAP infrastructure.
> - Configure NAP enforcement methods.
>
> **Estimated lesson time: 40 minutes**

Introduction to Network Access Protection

NAP enables you to restrict access to the organizational network based on whether a client computer meets a set of predefined health standards. You can use several NAP methods to restrict access to the LAN. Each method has benefits and drawbacks. The simplest method, DHCP enforcement, requires no special infrastructure other than Windows Server 2008 DHCP servers. The 802.1X method requires network hardware that supports 802.1X authentication. The IPsec method requires no special hardware but does require complex Certificate Services and Group Policy configuration. NAP can also restrict VPN access and access to Terminal Services (TS) Gateway servers. This lesson begins by covering the core components of NAP and then moves on to cover each available enforcement method.

Configuring Health Policies

One of the first steps you must perform when rolling out NAP in your environment is determining your criteria for a healthy host. You do this by configuring health policies that use System Health Agents (SHAs) and System Health Validators (SHVs). SHAs are installed on a client computer and generate statements of health, which are forwarded to the NAP health policy server. Windows Vista, Windows Server 2008, and Windows XP with Service Pack

3 include a default SHA that monitors Windows Security Center settings. This allows the forwarding of data to health policy servers. This data indicates whether the latest updates are installed and whether antivirus and antispyware software are installed and up to date. Third-party vendors can also create their own SHAs that allow the assessment of other elements of client health.

SHVs are a configurable set of standards against which the NPS server assesses the statement of health forwarded by the client. Figure 4-25 shows the default Windows Security Health Validator for Windows Vista. An administrator can set options that determine how strictly health standards are enforced. For example, some administrators can simply choose to require an antivirus application to be active on the client computer; other administrators might allow clients to connect only when the antivirus application is enabled and up to date.

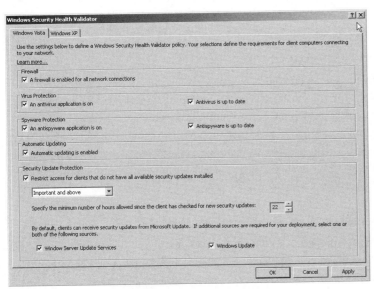

FIGURE 4-25 Security Health Validator.

Although Windows Vista, Windows Server 2008, and Windows XP with Service Pack 3 support NAP, the NAP client must be enabled, and the NAP Agent service must be configured to start automatically. The most common way of configuring client computers for NAP is through GPO settings in the *Computer Configuration\Policies\Windows Settings\Security Settings\Network Access Protection\NAP Client Configuration* node. From there, you can configure the NAP interface, Health Registration settings, and which NAP enforcement method is enabled. Figure 4-26 shows the DHCP Quarantine Enforcement Client enabled.

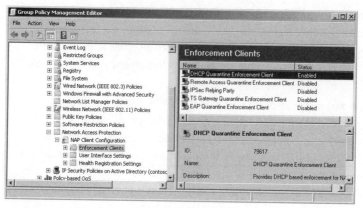

FIGURE 4-26 DHCP Quarantine Enforcement Client enabled.

Health Registration Authority

Install the Health Registration Authority (HRA) role service when the IPsec enforcement method is to be deployed. The HRA manages the issuance of system health certificates, digital certificates that are used for connection authentication when you deploy the IPsec enforcement method. Deploy your PKI prior to installing the HRA. If your organization's PKI is based on Windows Server 2003 rather than on Windows Server 2008, you must create some custom certificate templates to support NAP with IPsec. Alternatively, you can upgrade your certificate servers to Windows Server 2008.

> **MORE INFO   HOST CREDENTIAL AUTHORIZATION PROTOCOL**
>
> Health Credential Authorization Protocol (HCAP) enables NAP to be integrated with Cisco's Network Admission Control. You can find out more about this technology by consulting the following document: *http://www.microsoft.com/presspass/events/ssc/docs /CiscoMSNACWP.pdf*.

Remediation Server Groups

A remediation server group, shown in Figure 4-27, is a collection of servers, usually defined by IP address, that noncompliant computers can access. These servers should provide noncompliant client computers with all the resources they need to become compliant. This usually includes servers from which the latest software updates can be downloaded, such as a Windows Software Update Services (WSUS) server as well as servers hosting the latest anti-virus and antispyware software and definitions. You can create multiple remediation server groups—for example, remediation server groups for each site your company has—and then configure different NAP policies to direct noncompliant clients to these groups if the need arises.

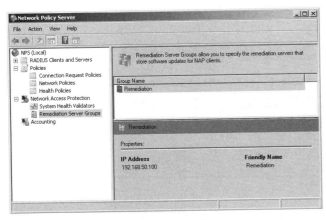

FIGURE 4-27 Remediation server groups.

✓ **Quick Check**

1. NAP uses SHAs and SHVs. Which of these do you configure on an NPS server?

2. What type of group should you configure on the NPS server to direct noncompliant computers so that they can become compliant?

Quick Check Answers

1. You configure an SHV (System Health Validator) on the NPS server.

2. Remediation server groups are listings of server addresses through which noncompliant computers can obtain the necessary files and updates to become compliant.

NAP Enforcement

Although Windows Vista and Windows XP SP3 clients already have basic SHA and NAP clients installed, you still have to configure the NAP client before the NAP process will work. You configure the NAP enforcement client through Group Policy. It is possible to enable an enforcement client on a computer that is not managed by Group Policy by using the *netsh nap client set enforcement* command and specifying the enforcement client ID, but configuring NAP through Group Policy is easier. The appropriate node in Group Policy is *Computer Configuration\Policies\Windows Settings\Security Settings\Network Access Protection*. Under this node, you can configure an enforcement client, as shown in Figure 4-28. It is also possible to configure a user interface for NAP so you can create both a text and an image that are presented to the client during the NAP process. You can also specify the settings for the HRA if you choose the NAP with IPsec enforcement method.

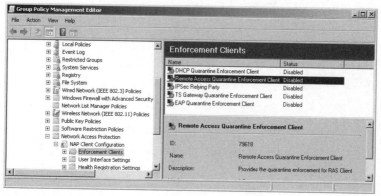

FIGURE 4-28 NAP enforcement clients.

It is also generally a good idea to configure Group Policy so that the NAP agent is set to start automatically on client computers. The remaining text of this lesson is devoted to describing how to implement and configure the different methods of NAP enforcement.

> **NOTE   NAP-INELIGIBLE CLIENT COMPUTERS**
>
> Part of deploying NAP is developing a way to deal with NAP-ineligible client computers. Although NAP clients have been released for many non-Microsoft operating systems, some clients cannot be subjected to the process. When you configure a NAP policy, you have the option of allowing full network access to NAP-ineligible client computers.

NAP Enforcement by Using DHCP

Of the NAP enforcement methods available to Windows Server 2008 administrators, the DHCP enforcement method is the simplest method to implement. When you enforce NAP with DHCP, you use a DHCP server to provide one set of IPv4 addresses to computers that meet compliance requirements and provide another set of IPv4 addresses to computers that do not meet compliance requirements. The IPv4 addresses provided to compliant computers allow unlimited access to other hosts on the network. The IPv4 addresses provided to noncompliant computers allow access to only a limited range of hosts, usually to hosts that can be used for remediation.

When the DHCP NAP enforcement method is used, enforcement occurs during initial address assignment or renewal only. Because a host can fall out of compliance after initial address assignment, configure short DHCP leases. Short DHCP leases mean that the client must renew its address information often, each subsequent renewal prompting a new NAP compliance check.

NAP enforcement using DHCP requires that DHCP servers have the DHCP Enforcement Service (ES). Only the Windows Server 2008 DHCP service currently supports DHCP ES. This means that you must upgrade all DHCP servers in your organization to Windows Server 2008 before you can deploy the DHCP NAP enforcement method. The DHCP enforcement client is included in the Windows Vista and Windows Server 2008 operating systems and Windows XP SP3. To enable NAP on all DHCP scopes, right-click the IPv4 node under the DHCP console, and then select Properties. On the Network Access Protection tab, shown in Figure 4-29, click Enable On All Scopes.

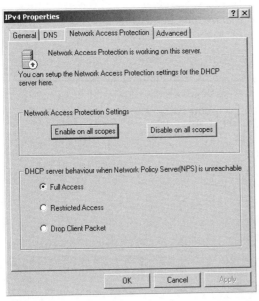

FIGURE 4-29 Enabling NAP on all scopes.

When deploying the DHCP NAP enforcement method, you must ensure that users do not have local administrator privileges on their computers. If users have local administrator privileges, they can circumvent the DHCP NAP enforcement method by manual IPv4 address assignment. DHCP NAP enforcement is not supported for IPv6 on Windows Server 2008 DHCP servers. Similarly, the presence of a rogue DHCP server on a network might also allow noncompliant clients access to the protected network. The practice at the end of this lesson provides a walkthrough on how to configure NAP with DHCP enforcement.

NAP with IPsec Enforcement

NAP with IPsec enforcement works in conjunction with connection security policies. Briefly, NAP with IPsec enforcement works by issuing system health certificates to compliant clients. You enforce connection security policies, covered in Lesson 2, on all hosts on the network and ensure that connections can be authenticated only with system health certificates. Administrators install these certificates manually on important servers that are not subject to the NAP process so they can be authenticated by connection security policies applied throughout the domain.

The IPsec enforcement method requires you to deploy the Health Registration Authority (HRA) role service and have an existing PKI. You learn about deploying Windows Server 2008 Certificate Services in Chapter 7. The HRA role service is responsible for managing the distribution of system health certificates to NAP-compliant clients through a Web application called DomainHRA. If you are using IPsec enforcement as well as enabling the IPsec Relying Party enforcement client, you must specify the Health Registration Authority Web site location for clients through Group Policy. In large organizations, deploy multiple HRAs for fault tolerance.

You use the Configure NAP Wizard on the Network Policy server and then select the IPsec with Health Registration Authority (HRA) network connection method, as shown in Figure 4-30. You then specify the NAP enforcement servers that have the HRA installed, select the computer groups the policy applies to (select no computer groups to apply the policy globally), select the SHVs you want to use and whether you want to enable auto-remediation, and then finish the wizard.

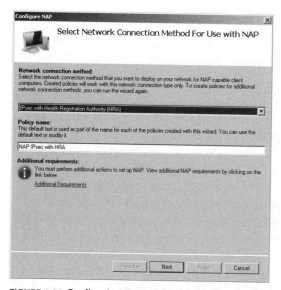

FIGURE 4-30 Configuring IPsec enforcement.

You must configure an isolation connection security rule that uses System Health certificates for authentication, as shown in Figure 4-31. When beginning a deployment of NAP with IPsec enforcement, you can have the connection security rule use the request authentication option, but for strict NAP with IPsec enforcement, use the Require Authentication for Inbound and Outbound Connections option. This ensures that only healthy clients are able to communicate with critical servers on the network.

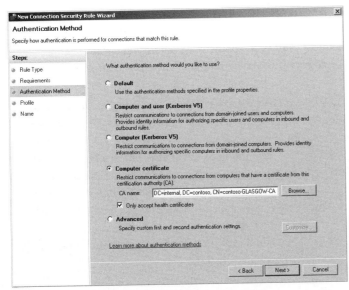

FIGURE 4-31 Using health certificates for authentication.

NAP with 802.1X Enforcement

NAP with 802.1X enforcement relies upon Ethernet switches and WAPs that support 802.1x authentication. WAPs that support 802.1x authentication are also necessary when you use the WPA2-Enterprise authentication method that was discussed in Lesson 1. If a WAP supports WPA2-Enterprise, it also supports the 802.1X NAP enforcement method. Unlike the DHCP enforcement method, in which a compliance check occurs only when the DHCP lease is renewed, the 802.1X enforcement method allows for an immediate change of conditions if the computer falls out of compliance. When you use the 802.1X method of NAP enforcement, there are two ways you can control how compliant, noncompliant, and unauthenticated computers access the network.

- **Virtual local area network (VLAN)**   A VLAN is a collection of ports on one or more switches that function as separate partitioned networks. For example, if you have three switches, ports 1–5 on switch 1, ports 5–10 on switch 2, and ports 20–30 on switch 3 can all be configured to be part of the same VLAN. You can configure switch software to change the VLAN assigned to a particular switch port. NAP enforcement works by assigning the port to which a NAP-compliant computer is connected to one VLAN and the port to which a noncompliant computer is connected to a different VLAN. When the computer switches compliance states, the VLAN assignment of the port it is connected to changes.

- **Access control lists (ACLs)** The second method of control involves applying packet filters, which essentially function as firewalls on the switch port, that limit the IP addresses a noncompliant computer can contact. The packet filters allow traffic only to remediation servers. The packet filters are removed after the computer becomes compliant.

If you want to deploy 802.1X enforcement, you must be able to configure the switch as well as configure the appropriate Windows Server 2008 NAP infrastructure. Organizations that have older switch hardware will need to investigate whether existing switch infrastructure supports 802.1X enforcement before attempting to deploy this enforcement method. Switches must be configured to perform Protected Extensible Authentication Protocol (PEAP)–based authentication, using either PEAP-TLS or PEAP-MS-CHAP v2, and be configured to forward RADIUS requests to the Network Policy and Access server. Switches must be configured as RADIUS clients, using the same method described earlier in this chapter for configuring WAPs as RADIUS clients. You should also configure reauthentication intervals so that clients that remain connected reauthenticate regularly.

> **MORE INFO** **DETAILED 802.1X ENFORCEMENT**
>
> For detailed information on how to implement 802.1X NAP enforcement, consult the following Step-by-Step guide on TechNet: *http://go.microsoft.com/fwlink/?LinkId=86036*.

NAP with VPN Enforcement

When you configure NAP with VPN enforcement, Windows Server 2008 Routing and Remote Access servers allow remote access connections only to computers that pass system health checks. You will recall that the topic of configuring remote access in Chapter 3 covered how you can configure Windows Server 2008 to support VPN connections. The primary difference between the configuration you learned about in Chapter 3 and NAP with VPN enforcement is that only NAP-compliant computers are granted unlimited network access. You can also create a set of packet filters that apply to noncompliant computers that limit network access to servers through which the remediation can occur. To configure NAP with VPN enforcement, perform the following steps:

1. Start the Configure NAP wizard from the Network Policy Server console. Select the Virtual Private Network (VPN) connection method.

2. Select Network Access Servers, the user groups that the policy applies to, and whether you want VPN clients to use PEAP-MS CHAPv2 or Smart Cards with EAP-TLS to authenticate.

3. Specify the Remediation Server Group that you want VPN clients to access if they are not in compliance. You can also specify a troubleshooting URL that users can access for more information.

4. On the Define NAP Health Policy page, shown in Figure 4-32, determine whether you want to allow access to NAP-ineligible clients and whether you want to enable auto-remediation.

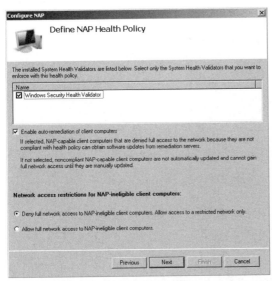

FIGURE 4-32 Configuring auto-remediation for VPN clients.

> **MORE INFO DETAILED VPN NAP ENFORCEMENT**
>
> For detailed information on how to implement VPN NAP enforcement, consult the following Step-by-Step guide on TechNet: *http://go.microsoft.com/fwlink/?LinkId=85896*.

NAP with TS Gateway

A new feature of Windows Server 2008 is Terminal Services Gateway, a role service that enables clients to make secure RDP connections, without the need for a VPN, from locations on the Internet to hosts on a protected network. Just as you do not want unhealthy VPN clients connecting to a protected internal network, you do not want unhealthy TS Gateway clients connecting to terminal servers on a protected internal network. You must carry out five steps when configuring NAP for TS Gateway servers. These are:

1. Enable NAP health policy checking on the TS Gateway server by selecting the Request Clients To Send A Statement Of Health check box on the TS CAP Store tab of the TS Gateway server's properties, as shown in Figure 4-33. You should also specify which NPS server manages TS Connection Authorization Policy (CAPs).

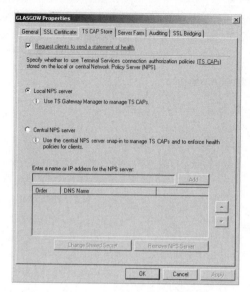

FIGURE 4-33 Enabling NAP on TS Gateway.

2. Remove existing TS CAPs, and then create a new TS CAP on the TS Gateway server. Create a TS Resource Authorization Policy (RAP) if none exists.

    The creation of TS CAPs and TS RAPs is covered in detail in Chapter 12, "Terminal Services."

3. Configure a Windows SHV on the NPS server that you specified in step 1.

    If you have NAP deployed using another enforcement method in your organization, you can use the health validator you created for that implementation.

4. Create NAP policies for the TS Gateway server by using the Configure NAP Wizard on the NPS server. When running the wizard, specify the Terminal Services Gateway (TS Gateway) network connection method, as shown in Figure 4-34. You then specify the TS Gateway servers the policy applies to and the acceptable authentication methods and add the User Groups that are able to use the TS Gateway server to make connections. On the Define NAP Health Policy page, specify whether access will be allowed or denied to NAP-ineligible clients. Access is denied to noncompliant clients.

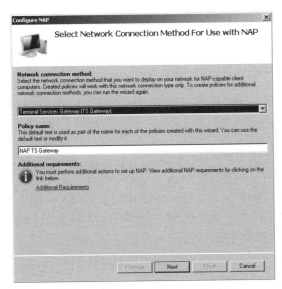

FIGURE 4-34 Creating a TS Gateway NAP policy.

5. Run a configuration script, which you can download from the Microsoft Web site, to configure the Terminal Services client software as a NAP enforcement client.

> **MORE INFO   NAP FOR TS GATEWAY**
>
> To learn more about configuring NAP for TS Gateway, consult the following TechNet article: *http://go.microsoft.com/fwlink/?linkid=85872*. To obtain the script that configures clients, go to: *http://go.microsoft.com/fwlink/?LinkId=103093*.

Debugging NAP

You can configure NAP logging on the NPS server by editing the properties of the NPS server and enabling logging. By default, NPS servers log both rejected and successful authentication requests. NPS writes event data to the Security log under the Network Policy Server task category. Successful NAP checks generate events with ID 6278, and failed NAP checks generate events with ID 6276. When first deploying NAP, you are more likely to be interested in the clients that are failing checks than in those that are successful because failing clients have proven system health problems.

Use the *netsh nap client show state* command on the client when attempting to determine why the NAP process is not successful. This command provides information about the state of the NAP client, including which clients are active. If NAP is not working properly, also examine the Network Access Protection\Operational log under the *Applications and Services Logs \Microsoft\Windows* node in Event Viewer. If you find that the data in this log does not give you enough information to resolve the problem, you can issue the *netsh nap client set tracing enable level=verbose* command to enable verbose logging. Logs are stored in text file format in the \%SystemRoot%\Tracing folder.

MORE INFO   MORE ON *NETSH NAP CLIENT*

You can find a complete list of NAP client–related *netsh* commands in the following Tech-Net article: *http://technet2.microsoft.com/windowsserver2008/en/library/d5779814-e2e1-404a-ad49-e5573f94f54a1033.mspx?mfr=true*.

EXAM TIP

Before the exam, remind yourself of the prerequisite infrastructure for each NAP enforce-ment method and the types of situations that might best suit the deployment of that method.

PRACTICE   **Preparing NAP with DHCP Enforcement**

In this practice, you prepare the necessary computer roles to support a NAP with DHCP enforcement rollout. NAP with DHCP enforcement is the easiest of the NAP enforcement methods to implement. NAP with DHCP enforcement can serve as a useful trial of the technology if your organization is considering implementing this or other NAP enforcement methods.

EXERCISE 1   Configure NAP with DHCP Enforcement Infrastructure

In this exercise, you configure the Windows Server 2008 server roles necessary to support NAP with DHCP enforcement. This involves creating a special DHCP scope and installing the Network Policy Server role.

NOTE   DHCP REQUIRED

This practice assumes that you installed the DHCP service on server Glasgow when you completed the practice at the end of Lesson 2, "Configuring DHCP," of Chapter 1. If the DHCP service is not installed on Glasgow, install the DHCP service, using the default settings.

---

1. Log on to server Glasgow with the Kim_Akers user account and open the DHCP console from the Administrative Tools menu.

2. Expand the *glasgow.contoso.internal* node, and then right-click the IPv4 node. Select New Scope.

    This launches the New Scope Wizard.

3. Click Next.

4. On the Scope Name page, enter the scope name, NAP_Compliant_Hosts, and then click Next.

5. On the IP Address Range page, set the start IP address to 192.168.100.10, the end IP address to 192.168.100.254, and the subnet length to 24, as shown in Figure 4-35. Click Next twice.

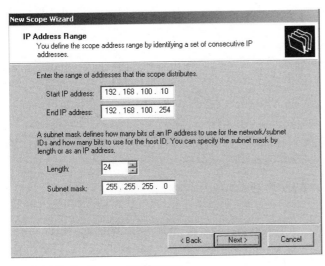

FIGURE 4-35 Configure a DHCP scope.

6. On the Lease Duration page, set the lease duration to **0** days, **8** hours, and **0** minutes, and then click Next.

7. On the Configure DHCP Options page, select No, I Will Configure These Options Later, and then click Next. Click Finish to close the New Scope Wizard. Close the DHCP console.

> **NOTE   LESSON ONE PRACTICE**
>
> **If you have completed the practice at the end of Lesson 1, skip the rest of the steps in this practice and move on to Exercise 2.**

8. Open the Server Manager console. Select and then right-click the *Roles* node. Select Add Roles. Click Next.

9. On the Select Server Roles page, select the Network Policy And Access Services check box, and then click Next.

10. Review the information on the Network Policy And Access Services page, and then click Next.

11. On the Role Services page, select Network Policy Server, click Next, and then click Install.

12. After the role has installed, minimize the Server Manager console. Open the Group Policy Management console from the Administrative Tools menu.

13. In the Group Policy Management console, right-click the *contoso.internal* node, and then select New Organizational Unit. Enter the organizational unit name, **DHCP_NAP_Clients**, and then click OK.

14. Right-click the DHCP_NAP_Clients OU, and then select Create A GPO In This Domain, And Link It Here.

15. In the New GPO dialog box, enter **DHCP_NAP**, and then click OK.

16. Select the DHCP_NAP_Clients OU. Right-click the DHCP_NAP GPO, and then select Edit.

17. Select the *Computer Configuration\Policies\Windows Settings\Security Settings \Network Access Protection\NAP Client Configuration* node. In the NAP Client Configuration window, click the Enforcement Clients link.

18. In the Enforcement Clients window, right-click DHCP Quarantine Enforcement Client, and then select Enable, as shown in Figure 4-36.

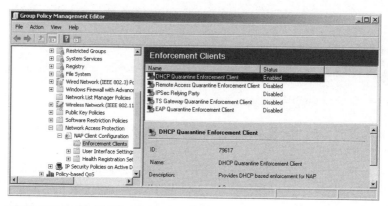

FIGURE 4-36 Enable DHCP enforcement client.

19. Close the Group Policy Management Editor, and then close the Group Policy Management console.

EXERCISE 2 Configure NAP with DHCP Enforcement Policies and Settings

In this exercise, you configure the policies that support NAP with DHCP enforcement. You create a health policy, configure a remediation server group, and then configure a NAP policy.

1. Open the Network Policy Server console from the Administrative Tools menu.

2. Expand the *Policies* node. Right-click the *Health Policies* node, and then select New.

3. In the Create New Health Policy dialog box, enter the policy name, **Healthy_NAP_Client**, ensure that the Client Passes All SHV Checks option is selected and that the Windows Security Health Validator SHV check box is selected, as shown in Figure 4-37, and then click OK.

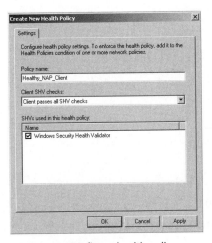

FIGURE 4-37 Configure health policy.

4. Open a command prompt, type **dnscmd /recordadd contoso.internal remediation A 192.168.50.100**, and then press Enter. Close the command prompt.

5. Expand the *Network Access Protection* node in the Network Policy Server console. Right-click Remediation Server Group, and then select New.

   This opens the New Remediation Server Group dialog box.

6. In the New Remediation Server Group dialog box, enter **Contoso_Remediation** in the Group Name text box. Click Add.

7. In the Add New Server dialog box, enter the friendly name, **Remediation**, and then enter the IP address, **192.168.50.100**, and click OK twice.

8. Select the *NPS (Local)* node. In the Getting Started pane, click the Configure NAP link.

   This launches the Configure NAP Wizard.

9. On the Select Network Connection Method For Use With NAP page, select Dynamic Host Configuration Protocol (DHCP) from the drop-down list, as shown in Figure 4-38, and then click Next.

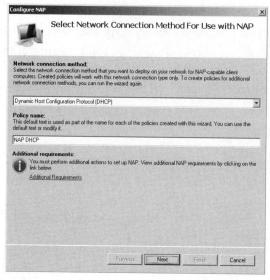

FIGURE 4-38 Configure NAP method.

10. Click Next on the RADIUS clients page. On the Specify DHCP Scopes page, click Add.

11. In the MS-Service Class dialog box, enter **NAP_Compliant_Hosts**, and then click OK. Click Next.

12. On the Machine Groups page, click Next.

13. On the Remediation Server Group page, use the drop-down list to select the group named Contoso_Remediation, and then click Next.

14. On the Define NAP Health Policy page, accept the default settings and click Next. Click Finish to complete the Configure NAP Wizard.

15. Close the Network Policy Server console.

Lesson Summary

- An SHV is a set of conditions that a computer must meet to be considered healthy.
- An SHA is what the Network Policy server checks with to determine whether a connecting client meets all the conditions of the SHV.
- DHCP NAP enforcement uses IP address assignment to separate compliant computers from noncompliant computers.

- IPsec enforcement uses connection security policies authenticated by using system health certificates to separate compliant computers from noncompliant computers.

- You can use VPN enforcement to block noncompliant computers from making successful VPN connections to protected networks.

- 802.1X enforcement uses VLANs or IPsec filters to block noncompliant computers from communicating with hosts on the organizational network.

- TS Gateway NAP blocks noncompliant computers from accessing terminal servers.

- Network Policy servers are installed as part of the Network Policy and Access Server roles. These servers are where you configure health policies and SHVs that dictate the health compliance benchmark.

Lesson Review

You can use the following questions to test your knowledge of the information in Lesson 3, "Network Access Protection." The questions are also available on the companion DVD if you prefer to review them in electronic form.

> **NOTE ANSWERS**
>
> Answers to these questions and explanations of why each answer choice is right or wrong are located in the "Answers" section at the end of the book.

1. NAP using the IPsec enforcement method has been deployed at your organization. You are attempting to resolve a problem. A computer, running Windows Vista, that you are working on has antivirus software that is six weeks out of date, yet the computer is able to obtain a system health certificate and can successfully connect to protected servers. When you disable the antivirus software, the computer falls out of compliance and is unable to contact the protected servers. Which steps must you take to ensure that NAP clients in your organization fall out of compliance if the antivirus definitions are not up to date?

    A. Update the SHA configuration on all clients.

    B. Update the SHV configuration on the Network Policy server.

    C. Update the SHA configuration on the Network Policy server.

    D. Update the SHV configuration on all clients.

2. For historical reasons, several of the developers in your organization have been added to the local Administrators group of their desktop computers running Windows Vista Enterprise. You are in the process of deciding which NAP enforcement method to deploy in your organization. Which of the following methods for local network access should you avoid deploying to ensure that these developers cannot bypass the NAP process when using their desktop computers?

A. IPsec enforcement

B. DHCP enforcement

C. 802.1X enforcement

D. VPN enforcement

E. TS Gateway NAP enforcement

3. Your organization is in the process of migrating from a Windows Server 2003 network infrastructure to Windows Server 2008. You have been asked to implement NAP, using the DHCP enforcement method in your organization. Although Windows Server 2008 domain controllers have been deployed in each domain in the forest, numerous Windows Server 2003 domain controllers are still in each domain. All DNS zones are Active Directory integrated. All DHCP servers are currently installed on Windows Server 2003 member servers. Which of the following changes must you make before NAP with DHCP enforcement can be successfully deployed in your organization?

A. Configure each domain to run at the Windows Server 2008 functional level.

B. Configure the forest to run at the Windows Server 2008 functional level.

C. Upgrade all domain controllers to Windows Server 2008.

D. Upgrade all DHCP servers to Windows Server 2008.

4. Which of the following methods are used to control the level of access that compliant, noncompliant, and unauthenticated computers receive when the 802.1X NAP enforcement method is used? (Choose two. Each correct answer presents a complete solution.)

A. IPsec certificate

B. IP address lease

C. Access point ACL

D. Virtual local area network

E. Subnet mask

Chapter Review

To further practice and reinforce the skills you learned in this chapter, you can perform the following tasks:

- Review the chapter summary.
- Complete the case scenarios. These scenarios set up real-world situations involving the topics of this chapter and ask you to create solutions.
- Complete the suggested practices.
- Take a practice test.

Chapter Summary

- Wireless networks between clients are known as ad hoc; wireless networks that use WAPs are known as infrastructure. A wireless network is identified by its SSID.
- WEP is a wireless access protocol that uses a shared key but is cryptographically weak. WPA/WPA2-Personal also uses shared keys. WPA/WPA2-Enterprise uses RADIUS servers for authentication and support smart cards, digital certificates, and username and password.
- Each incoming packet is evaluated against a firewall rule and dealt with according to the rule properties. If an incoming packet does not match a rule, it is dropped. By default, all outbound traffic is allowed.
- You can apply firewall rules, using Group Policy. Firewall rules are automatically enabled when an appropriate role service or feature is installed on a computer running Windows Server 2008.
- Connection security rules govern how connections are established between computers. Isolation rules isolate hosts based on authentication criteria. Authentication exemptions bypass connection security rules. Server and tunnel rules govern how set groups of computers communicate with each other.
- NAP uses a computer's health as a benchmark for allowing network access. There are various methods through which you can enforce NAP, and the one you use depends on the circumstances of network access.

Case Scenarios

In the following case scenarios, you apply what you've learned about Windows Firewall, Wireless Network Access, and Network Access Protection. You can find answers to these questions in the "Answers" section at the end of this book.

Case Scenario 1: Contoso, Ltd., Wireless Access

You are part of a team that is planning the deployment of a wireless network at the new Copenhagen office of Contoso, Ltd. The building that hosts the Contoso office is five floors high, with the top two floors devoted to executive offices. Recently, several stories have been published in the Danish press about unauthorized access to corporate networks by attackers who compromise preshared keys. The executives at Contoso do not want their network to be vulnerable to this type of attack. Executives also do not want wireless users to use smart cards or to type in logon credentials to gain access to the Contoso wireless network. Finally, executives want to ensure that only their computers are able to connect to wireless networks on the top two floors. As part of planning the Contoso wireless deployment, your team must find answers to the following questions:

1. What steps should you take to ensure that none of the WAPs at your organization authenticate connections by using preshared keys?

2. Which method of authentication must you select when configuring wireless access policies?

3. How can you accommodate the executives' desire for exclusive access to WAPs on the building's top two floors?

Case Scenario 2: Protecting Critical Infrastructure at Fabrikam, Inc.

You are part of the team planning the configuration and deployment of NAP using the IPsec enforcement method on the corporate network of Fabrikam, Inc. You are to develop server connection security policies. You have been told that only computers that have passed a system health check should be able to communicate with file and print servers. All computer accounts for the file and print servers are located in the FilePrint OU. A standalone WSUS server is used for updates and remediation. All computers should be able to connect to it without authenticating. At the main site, all servers are located in a single server room. All 20 servers located in the server room are rack mounted. Although a KVM switch is available, it can be connected to only five servers at any one time. Unless there is a dire emergency, servers are usually managed using remote desktop protocol. There is a spare workstation in the server room that members of the systems administration team often use when they need to work directly with the servers. With that in mind, you must develop solutions for the following problems:

1. What type authentication should you configure for a domain isolation connection security policy?

2. How should incoming and outgoing network connections to the file and print servers be authenticated?

3. If there is a critical failure in the NAP infrastructure (such as the CA not being available for a short period of time), how can you ensure that connection is possible over the network to servers located on racks from the workstation located in the server room if authentication policies are still in place?

Suggested Practices

To help you successfully master the exam objectives presented in this chapter, complete the following tasks.

Configure Wireless Access

Do both practices in this section.

- **Practice 1** Using the Group Policy settings that you configured in Lesson 1, "Wireless Access," configure a Windows XP Wireless Network policy to use infrastructure networks only and to use the SSID WAPTWO and Microsoft PEAP for authentication.

- **Practice 2** Using the Group Policy settings that you configured in Lesson 1, configure a Windows XP Wireless Network policy to use infrastructure networks only and to use the SSID WAPTWO and Microsoft PEAP for authentication.

Configure Firewall Settings

To get a thorough understanding about configuring WFAS settings, complete both practices in this section.

- **Practice 1** Use the Group Policy settings that you created in the practice at the end of Lesson 2 to create an authentication exemption for computers on the 10.120.0.0 /24 network.

- **Practice 2** Use the Group Policy settings that you created in the practice at the end of Lesson 2 to create a server-to-server rule. One group of servers is located in the 10.140.0.0 /24 network; the second group is located in the 192.168.140.0 /24 network.

Configure NAP

To get a thorough understanding of NAP, complete both practices in this section.

- **Practice 1** If you have access to a switch that supports 802.1X authentication and can use it in a test lab environment, download the "NAP with 802.1X Step-by-Step" guide referenced earlier in this chapter and use it to deploy a test lab, using this technology.

- **Practice 2** Configure a test network, using the instructions in the "NAP with IPsec enforcement Step-by-Step" guide referenced earlier in this chapter to deploy a test lab, using this technology. No special hardware is required to complete this exercise.

Take a Practice Test

The practice tests on this book's companion DVD offer many options. For example, you can test yourself on just one exam objective, or you can test yourself on all the upgrade exam content. You can set up the test so that it closely simulates the experience of taking a certification exam, or you can set it up in study mode so that you can look at the correct answers and explanations after you answer each question.

> *MORE INFO* **PRACTICE TESTS**
>
> For details about all the practice test options available, see the "How to Use the Practice Tests" section in this book's Introduction.

Configuring Active Directory Lightweight Directory Services and Read-Only Domain Controllers

Active Directory Lightweight Directory Services (AD LDS) is a subset of Active Directory Domain Services (AD DS). Both use the same core code, and both provide a similar feature set. AD LDS is new to Windows Server 2008, and you will not have come across it when studying for your Microsoft Windows Server 2003 examinations.

Windows Server 2008 also introduces the read-only domain controller (RODC), specifically for use in the branch office scenario. In this chapter, you learn how to configure AD LDS and about the functionality this feature provides. You also explore the issues related to branch office authentication and domain controller placement and learn how to implement and support a branch office RODC.

Exam objectives in this chapter:

- Configure Active Directory Lightweight Directory Service (AD LDS).
- Configure the read-only domain controller (RODC).

Lessons in this chapter:

Before You Begin

To complete the lessons in this chapter, you must have done the following:

- Installed a Windows Server 2008 Enterprise server configured as a domain controller in the *contoso.internal* domain as described in Chapter 1, "Configuring Internet Protocol Addressing."

- Installed a Windows Server 2008 Enterprise server in the *contoso.internal* domain as described in Chapter 2, "Configuring IP Services." This server should have a separate 10-gigabyte (GB) hard disk partition on which to store the data for the AD LDS instances. If it is not practical to add a hard disk partition, you can use an external USB drive. You cannot use a USB flash memory device for this purpose.

- Optionally, installed a second Windows Server 2008 member server, Chicago, in the *contoso.internal* domain. This computer should have the same IPv4 settings as the Boston server except that its IPv4 address is 10.0.0.35. It should have a separate 10-GB hard disk partition on which to store the data for the AD LDS instances. This server is optional, and you need to install it only if you want to configure AD LDS replication.

Lesson 1: Configuring Active Directory Lightweight Directory Services

AD LDS was formerly called Active Directory Application Mode (ADAM), and this name is still used in the Windows Server 2008 folder structure. It supports directory-enabled applications on an application-by-application basis without the need to modify the database schema of the network operating system (NOS) directory running on AD DS. With AD LDS, you can use directory-enabled applications without integrating them in the NOS directory. This lesson discusses the function and functionality of AD LDS and describes how you install it on a Windows Server 2008 server and configure the service.

After this lesson, you will be able to:

- Understand when to use AD LDS.
- Install AD LDS onto a member server.
- Locate and view the AD LDS directory store.
- Work with AD LDS tools.
- Create AD LDS instances.
- Create and configure an AD LDS replica.
- Configure AD LDS replication.
- Manage replication between AD LDS instances.

Estimated lesson time: 50 minutes

 REAL WORLD

Ian McLean

'm a great believer in defaults.

After all, the people who design the software specify the defaults and are likely to choose values that will work in the majority of cases. Also, if you know the defaults, you know what you have specified. It's much easier to document the exceptions to default settings than to document all settings.

Knowing and using defaults saves you time because you don't need to determine the values you used during setup. Also, accepting defaults speeds up configuration. Another advantage to knowing the default settings is that they are often tested in examinations. So unless I have a very good reason not to, I use default values.

As a result, the first time I used AD LDS, it jumped up and bit me. Because AD LDS is a subset of AD DS, it uses the same ports and default port settings. So if you install AD LDS on a member server in a domain and take the defaults, you have problems, particularly when AD DS and AD LDS both try to use the same LDAP ports. So, the wizened old network engineer got it wrong and his less experienced colleagues got it right. They put it about that it was because I couldn't count past 50,000.

The moral is obvious. No matter how much you think you know, read the Help Files and TechNet, especially the bits marked Important.

Understanding AD LDS and its Relationship with AD DS

To determine whether you must use AD DS to support an application or whether you can (and should) use AD LDS, you need to understand the functional differences between the two services. AD DS supports directory-enabled applications that extend the AD DS schema. If this functionality is not required, consider AD LDS.

For example, all user information in Microsoft Exchange Server 2007 is provided by the directory and, when you install this application, it significantly extends the AD DS schema. Adding to the schema for an application such as Exchange Server is appropriate because it provides a core networking service. AD LDS is not the correct choice in this case.

If, however, you add an object or an attribute to the AD DS schema, it is added forever and cannot be removed (although it can be deactivated or renamed and reused). Microsoft recommends that for less mission-critical applications, especially applications that are provided by third-party software manufacturers, avoid expanding the schema. In other words, use AD LDS rather than AD DS.

AD LDS, unlike AD DS, can support multiple AD LDS instances on a single server. It can meet the requirements of any directory-enabled application and provide instances on an application-by-application basis. You can differentiate between instances by instance name, which is typically based on the name of the application the instance supports (for example, MyApp_Instance). You do not need Enterprise Administrator or Schema Administrator credentials to work with AD LDS, as you do with AD DS. AD LDS can run on member or standalone servers, and you require only local administration access rights to manage it. It can also be used in a perimeter network to provide application or Web authentication services.

When you install AD LDS on a server, it does not change the configuration of the server to the extent that AD DS does when you create a domain controller. AD LDS is an application and, when you install it, you do not need to reboot the server.

For the Windows Server 2008 upgrade examinations, you need to understand what constitutes an AD LDS instance, how AD LDS instances should be used, and what their relationship is or can be with AD DS directories. You need to know how to install and configure the AD LDS service.

AD LDS instances are based on the Lightweight Directory Access Protocol (LDAP) and provide hierarchical database services. LDAP directories are optimized for specific purposes and should be used whenever you need to rely on fast lookups of information that will support given applications.

> **NOTE RELATIONAL AND HIERARCHICAL DATABASES**
>
> Briefly, from the point of view of the user, a hierarchical database provides fast lookup, but it takes longer to modify the database because it needs to be placed in a specific hierarchical position dependent on its characteristics. A relational database has a slower lookup than a hierarchical database, but it is quicker to insert data. Relational databases are preferred when database contents change frequently.

Comparing AD LDS and AD DS

AD LDS is based on AD DS but does not include all the features of AD DS. Both AD LDS and AD DS rely on multimaster replication for data consistency and support the LDAP application programming interface (API) and the Active Directory Services Interface (ADSI) APIs. Both services support schema extensions and application directory partitions. Both can install a replica from removable media and are integrated into the Windows Server 2008 backup tools. Both services support object-level security and delegation of administration. Although both AD DS and AD LDS can run on a domain controller, Microsoft recommends that you run AD LDS on a member or standalone server. You can start and stop both services without rebooting the computer, but AD DS, unlike AD LDS, requires a reboot after installation or removal.

Unlike AD LDS, AD DS can include security principals to provide access to a Windows Server network and includes a global catalog; it can manage objects such as workstations, member servers, and domain controllers; and it supports and integrates with public key infrastructures (PKIs) and X.509 certificates. Again, unlike AD LDS, AD DS supports Group Policy, the Messaging API (MAPI), trusts between domains and forests, and Domain Name System (DNS) service (SRV) records for locating directory services. AD DS can authenticate domain security principals to provide access to applications and Web Services, whereas AD LDS can be used for Web authentication but does not support domain security principals.

Unlike AD DS, AD LDS can include more than one instance on a server and supports independent schemas for each instance. This enables the service to support schema extensions without amending the AD DS schema. Under AD LDS, directory partitions can rely on X.500 naming conventions, and the service can be installed or removed without a reboot. AD LDS runs on client operating systems such as Windows Vista or Windows Server 2008 member or standalone servers.

In summary, AD LDS provides much of the same functionality as AD DS but does not amend the AD DS schema. In some cases (for example, in Exchange Edge Transport servers),

AD LDS can replicate data from AD DS for local storage, but it cannot access Active Directory features such as Group Policy. You can install several AD LDS instances on a server, and each instance has its independent schema. As its name implies, AD LDS is a lightweight version of AD DS.

> ### ✔ Quick Check
>
> 1. Can you install both AD LDS and AD DS on a computer with a client operating system?
> 2. Do both AD LDS and AD DS support schema extensions and application directory partitions?
> 3. Do both AD LDS and AD DS support object-level security and delegation of administration?
> 4. Can both AD LDS an AD DS be installed without a reboot?
>
> ### Quick Check Answers
>
> 1. No, you can install AD LDS on a computer with a client operating system. AD DS needs to run on a domain controller.
> 2. Yes, both AD LDS and AD DS support schema extensions and application directory partitions.
> 3. Yes, both AD LDS and AD DS support object-level security and delegation of administration.
> 4. No, you can install AD LDS without a reboot, but you must reboot when you install AD DS.

When You Should Use AD LDS

As a network administrator, you will be called on to decide when it is appropriate to use AD LDS and when AD DS is required. Consider using AD LDS in the following situations:

- **You need to provide support for departmental applications that require additional identity information that is of no relevance to any other department within the organization.** By integrating the additional information in an AD LDS instance, you can ensure that the relevant department has access to it without affecting the directory service for the entire organization.

- **You need to provide support for distributed applications that require access to data in several locations.** AD LDS provides the same multimaster replication capabilities as AD DS and can be used to support distributed applications.

- **Your organization is running earlier applications that rely on an LDAP directory.** You can migrate earlier data to an AD LDS instance and standardize it by using Active Directory technologies.

- **Your applications rely on an LDAP directory.** AD LDS can often be hosted on the same server as the application, providing high-speed and local access to directory data. This reduces replication traffic because all required data is local. Also, you can bundle the AD LDS instance along with the application when you deploy it. For example, if you are installing an accounting application that relies on custom policies to ensure that users can access only specific content when their user object contains a set of particular attributes, you can store these attributes and policies within AD LDS.

- **You need to provide authentication services for a Web application such as Microsoft SharePoint Portal Server in a perimeter network or extranet.** AD LDS can query the internal AD DS structure through a firewall to obtain user account information and store it securely in the perimeter network. This avoids the need to deploy AD DS in the perimeter. Note that you could deploy either AD LDS or Active Directory Federation Services (AD FS) in this scenario.

- **You need to provide data associated with user accounts in AD DS and require extensions to the AD DS schema to support this data.** Using AD LDS in this scenario, you can provide the additional user data without modifying the AD DS schema. For example, if you are installing an application that provides biometric data for each employee in your organization and associates each set of data with the relevant user's AD DS account, you can store the data in an AD LDS instance in a central location. The data sets are associated with the user accounts in AD DS, but because they are in AD LDS, they are not replicated with other AD DS data, hence reducing bandwidth requirements for replication.

- **You need to provide support for local development.** AD LDS can be installed on client workstations. This enables you to provide your application developers with portable single-instance directories they can use to develop custom applications that require access to identity data.

Typical applications in which you might use AD LDS include white-page directories, security-oriented applications, and policy store applications. AD LDS is more portable and manageable than AD DS and, if an AD DS solution requires schema modifications, consider using AD LDS instead.

EXAM TIP

The upgrade examinations are unlikely to ask a large number of questions about AD LDS, but when they do test the subject, they are likely to pose scenarios in which you choose between AD LDS and other Active Directory technologies such as AD DS.

Authentication (Binding) and Access Control in AD LDS

Access control in AD LDS consists of two parts. AD LDS first authenticates the identity of users requesting access to the directory, allowing only successfully authenticated users into the ADAM directory. Then, AD LDS uses security descriptors, called access control lists (ACLs), on directory objects to determine to which objects an authenticated user has access.

Users, or security principals, request directory data from AD LDS through directory-enabled applications, which in turn make requests to AD LDS, using LDAP. Before requesting data, the directory-enabled application presents the user's credentials to AD LDS for authentication, or binding. This request includes a username, password, and—depending on the type of bind—a domain name or computer name.

AD LDS can accept bind requests from both AD LDS security principals and Windows (local and domain) security principals. AD LDS security principals are authenticated directly by AD LDS. Local Windows security principals are authenticated by the local computer. Domain security principals must be authenticated by an AD DS domain controller.

Installing AD LDS

AD LDS can be installed on both the full Windows Server 2008 installation and Server Core. Also, AD LDS is a good candidate for virtualization through Windows Server 2008 Hyper-V. AD LDS can easily run within a virtual instance of the Windows Server 2008 operating system, and you should consider doing so unless the application that is tied to the AD LDS instance has specific requirements for physical installation.

Microsoft recommends that you avoid installing AD LDS on domain controllers whenever possible. Although AD LDS can fully coexist with the domain controller role and the RODC role, you should treat domain controller roles as special roles within your network that whenever possible should be tied only to the DNS service. You can use host servers running Hyper-V to create virtualized instances of both domain controllers and member servers running other services; virtualize domain controllers as much as possible. You can ensure that no other roles are hosted on a virtual domain controller because all other roles can also be virtualized within their own instances of Windows Server 2008.

AD LDS cannot authenticate domain security principals to provide access to applications, but it can authenticate Web applications and AD LDS security principals. This makes it suitable for authentication on a perimeter network or for external clients on an extranet. If you need to provide an authentication directory service on a perimeter network or an extranet, consider deploying AD LDS on a Server Core installation. Server Core installations enhance security by reducing the number of components included in Windows Server 2008.

Requirements for AD LDS Installation and Removal

AD LDS installation requirements include the following:

- A supported operating system such as Windows Server 2008 Standard, Enterprise, or Datacenter
- An account with local administration access rights

You install AD LDS on a full installation of a Windows Server 2008 member server in the practice session later in this lesson.

To remove AD LDS from a Windows Server 2008 server, you must log on to the server by using an account that has local administrator rights. You then do the following:

- Use Programs And Features in Control Panel to uninstall any instance of AD LDS you created after the role installation.
- Use Server Manager to remove the AD LDS role.

Take care to ensure that you remove all AD LDS instances from a server before you remove the role itself.

EXAM TIP

Remember that you need to remove all instances of AD LDS from a server before you can remove the role from the server.

Installing AD LDS on Server Core

To install AD LDS on a Server Core installation of Windows Server 2008, log on with local administrative credentials to a Windows Server 2008 member or standalone server running Server Core and enter the following command:

```
start /w ocsetup DirectoryServices-ADAM-ServerCore
```

Note that this command is case-sensitive. Using the start /w command ensures that the command prompt does not return until the role installation is complete. You can verify that the role is installed and discover the role name (DirectoryServices-ADAM-ServerCore) by using the following command:

```
oclist | more
```

Files Created on a Full Installation of Windows Server 2008 and on Server Core

On a full installation of Windows Server 2008, AD LDS creates the ADAM folder and populates it with 20 files and two subfolders. You view the contents of this folder in the practice later in this lesson. The two subfolders include localization information. The files contained in the ADAM folder include:

- The AD LDS program files, including .dll, .exe, .cat, .ini, and .xml files.
- The AD LDS directory store, *adamntds.dit*.
- Lightweight directory format (.ldf) files that are used to populate AD LDS instances when they are created.

The installation of AD LDS on Server Core does not include the same files and folders as on a full installation of Windows Server 2008. Server Core creates only one folder for localization, whereas the full installation creates two. In addition, the full installation includes an additional tool: the AD Schema Analyzer, which is not installed on Server Core. Figure 5-1 shows the files created on Server Core.

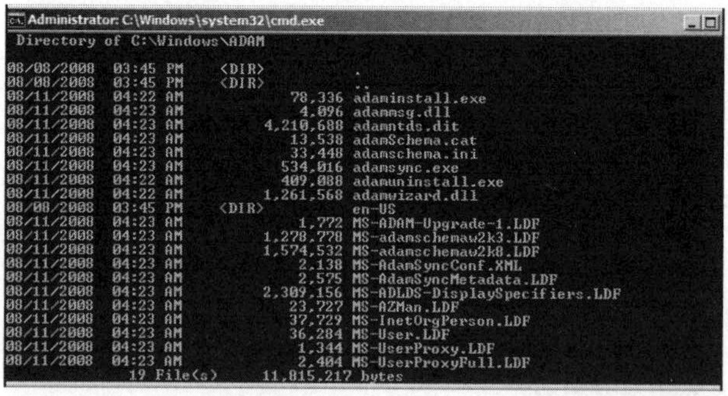
```
Administrator: C:\Windows\system32\cmd.exe
 Directory of C:\Windows\ADAM

08/08/2008  03:45 PM    <DIR>          .
08/08/2008  03:45 PM    <DIR>          ..
08/11/2008  04:22 AM            78,336 adaminstall.exe
08/11/2008  04:23 AM             4,096 adammsg.dll
08/11/2008  04:23 AM         4,210,688 adamntds.dit
08/11/2008  04:23 AM            13,538 adamSchema.cat
08/11/2008  04:23 AM            33,448 adamschema.ini
08/11/2008  04:23 AM           534,016 adamsync.exe
08/11/2008  04:22 AM           409,088 adamuninstall.exe
08/11/2008  04:22 AM         1,261,568 adamwizard.dll
08/08/2008  03:45 PM    <DIR>          en-US
08/11/2008  04:23 AM             1,772 MS-ADAM-Upgrade-1.LDF
08/11/2008  04:23 AM         1,278,778 MS-adamschemaw2k3.LDF
08/11/2008  04:23 AM         1,574,532 MS-adamschemaw2k8.LDF
08/11/2008  04:23 AM             2,138 MS-AdamSyncConf.XML
08/11/2008  04:23 AM             2,575 MS-AdamSyncMetadata.LDF
08/11/2008  04:23 AM         2,309,156 MS-ADLDS-DisplaySpecifiers.LDF
08/11/2008  04:23 AM            23,727 MS-AZMan.LDF
08/11/2008  04:23 AM            37,729 MS-InetOrgPerson.LDF
08/11/2008  04:23 AM            36,284 MS-User.LDF
08/11/2008  04:23 AM             1,344 MS-UserProxy.LDF
08/11/2008  04:23 AM             2,404 MS-UserProxyFull.LDF
              19 File(s)     11,815,217 bytes
```

FIGURE 5-1 The AD LDS installation on Server Core includes only 19 files and one subfolder.

> ***MORE INFO*** **AD LDS INSTALLATION PROCESS**
>
> **For a step-by-step guide to the installation of AD LDS, see *http://technet2.microsoft.com/windowsserver2008/en/library/141900a7-445c-4bd3-9ce3-5ff53d70d10a1033.mspx?mfr=true*.**

Configuring and Using AD LDS

When you have installed AD LDS, you can use it to store directory-related data for different applications. To do this, you must first become familiar with the AD LDS tool set. You then create AD LDS instances and secure them to ensure that they are properly protected. You can then create replicas for these instances, install them on various other systems, and control replication so that instances located on different computers are updated through multimaster replication.

Using AD LDS Tools

Many of the tools you use to configure and manage AD LDS are the same tools you use to administer AD DS. The following GUI tools are available:

Active Directory Schema snap-in   Modifies the schema for AD LDS instances. You must first use the *Regsvr32.exe* command to register the Schmmgmt.dll file.

ADSI Edit   Interactively manages AD LDS content through ADSI.

AD LDS Setup   Creates AD LDS instances.

You can also use the following general-purpose graphical user interface (GUI) tools in the process of managing AD LDS:

Active Directory Sites and Services   Configures and manages replication scopes for AD LDS instances. You must first update AD LDS instances to support replication objects.

Event Viewer   Audits AD LDS changes and logs old and new values for both objects and attributes.

Server Manager   Manages existing AD LDS instances.

Windows Server Backup   Backs up or restores AD LDS instances and their contents.

The following command-line tools are available if you change the directory to the %SystemRoot%\ADAM folder. (You need to run these tools in an elevated command prompt.)

ADAMInstall.exe   Creates AD LDS instances.

ADAMSync.exe   Synchronizes data from AD DS forest to AD LDS instance. You must first update the AD LDS instance to the AD DS schema.

ADAMUninstall.exe   Removes AD LDS instances.

ADSchemaAnalyzer.exe   Copies schema contents from AD DS to AD LDS or from one AD LDS instance to another. The tool supports third-party LDAP directory schema copies.

The following tools are available directly from an elevated command prompt:

Csvde.exe   Imports data into AD LDS instances.

DCDiag.exe   Diagnoses AD LDS instances. You must use the */n:NamingContext* switch to name the instance to diagnose.

DSACLS.exe   Controls ACLs on AD LDS objects.

DSAMain.exe   Mounts Active Directory store (*.dit*) backups or snapshots to identify their contents.

DSDBUtil.exe   Performs database maintenance, configures AD LDS ports, and views existing instances. The tool also creates one-step installations for transporting AD LDS instances through the install from media (IFM) generation process.

DSMgmt.exe   Supports application partition and AD LDS policy management.

Ldifde.exe   Imports data into AD LDS instances.

Ldp.exe   Interactively modifies content of AD LDS instances through LDAP.

NTDSUtil.exe   Manages AD LDS instances but only if AD DS is also installed. (Microsoft recommends that you use *dsbdutil.exe* instead.)

RepAdmin.exe   Analyzes replication so you can view potential issues.

You can also use the LDAP Data Interchange Format (LDIF) files as an instance creation and configuration tool. AD LDS installations can dynamically import LDIF files (.ldp) during instance creation and automatically configure the instance.

> **MORE INFO   AD LDS AUDITING**
>
> For more information on auditing AD LDS instances or AD DS domains, see *http://technet .microsoft.com/en-us/library/cc731764.aspx*.

Creating and Using AD LDS Instances

To create AD LDS instances, you install the AD LDS binaries, and then create instances to use the AD LDS service. Many of the tools you use to manage AD LDS instances can also be used to manage AD DS instances.

Preparing to Create an AD LDS Instance

You use the Active Directory Lightweight Directory Services Setup Wizard to create AD LDS instances. First, however, you must carry out the following tasks:

Create a data drive on your server   The server will be hosting directory stores; you must place these stores on a drive that does not contain the operating system.

Decide what name you will use when you create the instance   Use meaningful names to identify instances, for example, the name of the application tied to an instance. The instance name identifies the instance on the local computer as well as naming the files that make up the instance and the service that supports it.

Create a group to contain the user accounts that will administer the instance   The best practice for permission assignments is always to use groups even if only one account is a member of the group. If personnel changes, you can add or change group members without adding or changing permissions. Create a domain group if you are in a domain; otherwise, create a local group. Give the group the same name as the instance. This makes it easier to identify the group's purpose. Add your own account to the group as well as the service account you created earlier.

Decide the Active Directory application partition name you will use for the instance You must use a distinguished name (DN) to create the partition. For example, you could use CN=AppPartition1,DC=contoso,DC=internal. Depending on how you intend to use the instance, you might or might not need the application partition. Application partitions control the replication scope for a directory store. For example, when you integrate DNS data within the directory, AD DS creates an application partition to make DNS data available to appropriate domain controllers. Application partitions for AD LDS can be created in one of three ways: when you create the instance, when you install the application that will be tied to the instance, or when you create the partition manually through the *ldp.exe* tool. If your application does not create application partitions automatically, create them with the wizard.

Decide which ports you will use to communicate with the instance AD LDS and AD DS use the same ports for communication. These ports are the default LDAP (389) and LDAP over Secure Sockets Layer (SSL), or Secure LDAP (636), ports. AD DS uses two additional ports, 3268, which uses LDAP to access the global catalog, and 3269, which uses Secure LDAP to access the global catalog. Because AD DS and AD LDS use the same ports, do not install both roles on the same server (although it is possible to do so). However, when the wizard detects that ports 389 and 636 are already in use, it proposes 50,000 and 50,001 for each port, and then proposes other ports in the 50,000 range for additional instances.

> **NOTE USING PORTS 389 AND 636**
>
> If you are creating AD LDS instances within a domain, do not use ports 389 or 636 even if you are not creating the first instance on a domain controller. AD DS uses these ports by default and, because of this, some consoles, such as those using the Active Directory Schema snap-in, will not bind to local instances because they bind to the AD DS directory by default. As a best practice, always use ports beyond the 50,000 range for your AD LDS instances.

EXAM TIP

Make note of the default ports (in particular, 389 and 636) because they are likely to be tested in the examination, even though you should avoid using them in production environments.

Select or create a service account to run the instance You can use the Network Service account, but if you intend to run multiple instances, it might be best to use named service accounts for each instance. Remember to follow the service accounts guidelines and requirements listed in the Service Accounts Guidelines and Requirements sidebar.

Service Account Guidelines and Requirements

You should use the following guidelines when creating a service account to run an AD LDS instance:

- Create a domain account if you are in a domain; otherwise (for example, in a perimeter network), use a local account.
- Name the account with the same name as the instance.
- Assign a complex password to the account.
- Set User Cannot Change Password in the account properties. You assign this property to ensure that no one can appropriate the account.
- Set Password Never Expires in the account properties. You assign this property to ensure that the service does not fail because of password policy.
- Assign the Log On As A Service user right in the Local Security Policy of each computer that will host the instance.
- Assign the Generate Security Audits user right in the Local Security Policy of each computer that will host this instance. This supports account auditing.

Create any additional LDIF files you need for the instance   Place these files in the %SystemRoot%\ADAM folder. These files will be imported during the creation of the instance. Importing LDIF files extends the schema of the instance you are creating to support additional operations. For example, to synchronize AD DS with AD LDS, you would import the MS-AdamSyncMetadata.ldf file. If your application requires custom schema modifications, create the LDIF file ahead of time and import it as you create the instance. Note that you can always import LDIF files after the instance is created. The following LDIF files are available by default:

- **MS-adamschemaw2k3.ldf** A prerequisite for synchronizing an instance with Active Directory directory services in Windows Server 2003.
- **MS-adamschemaw2k8.ldf** A prerequisite for synchronizing an instance with AD DS in Windows Server 2008.
- **MS-AdamSyncMetadata.ldf** Synchronizes data between an AD DS forest and an AD LDS instance through *ADAMSync*.
- **MS-ADAM-Upgrade-1.ldf** Upgrades the AD LDS schema to the latest version.
- **MS-ADLDS-DisplaySpecifiers.ldf** Required for Active Directory Sites And Services snap-in operation.
- **MS-AZMan.ldf** Required to support the Windows Authorization Manager.
- **MS-InetOrgPerson.ldf** Creates *inetOrgPerson* user classes and attributes.
- **MS-User.ldf** Creates user classes and attributes.

- **MS-UserProxy.ldf** Creates a simple *userProxy* class.
- **MS-UserProxyFull.ldf** Creates a full *userProxy* class. You need to import MS-UserProxy.ldf first.

EXAM TIP

Watch out for filenames that contain the 2k3 string, for example, MS-adamschemaw2k3. ldf. These are Windows Server 2003 files and are probably the incorrect choice in questions about Windows Server 2008.

Creating an AD LDS Instance

You create an AD LDS instance in the practice session later in this lesson, and you follow the detailed steps for doing so there. In summary, you log on at the computer on which you want to create the instance by using an account with local administrator rights and start the Active Directory Lightweight Directory Services Setup Wizard. On the Setup Options page, shown in Figure 5-2, you select A Unique Instance to create a new instance. If you want to create a distributed AD LDS instance, you instead select A Replica Of An Existing Instance. On the next page, you provide an instance name as well as the name of the service that will run that instance.

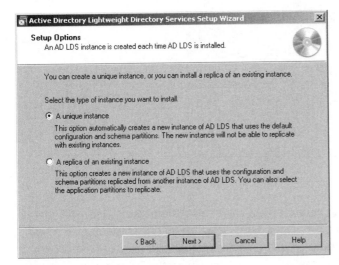

FIGURE 5-2 Selecting to create a new instance.

NOTE INSTANCE NAME

The service name will be ADAM_*instancename*, but the name listed in the Services console will be *instancename*.

On the Ports page, you specify the ports to use to communicate with this instance, typically (but not necessarily) 50000 and 50001. Note that you cannot change the ports after you have created the instance—you must delete it and re-create it. You then specify that the wizard is to create an Active Directory partition and name the partition. You must supply a distinguished name. You then specify the folder in which the instance's files will be located. Because this is a directory store, you should place it on a disk that does not contain the operating system, for example, a second internal hard disk or an external USB hard disk.

You then specify the service account that will run the instance's service. By default, Windows Server 2008 selects the Network Service account, but it is preferable to use a named account. Next, you select the group that will be responsible for administering the instance and the LDIF files you want to import. You review your selections on the Ready To Install page, shown in Figure 5-3, and then click Next to create the instance. If you choose to import LDIF files, you are asked for the credentials of an administrative-level account as installation proceeds.

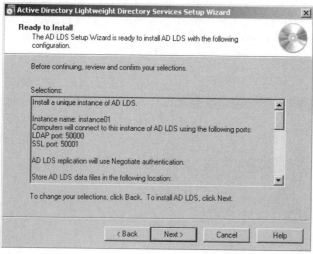

FIGURE 5-3 Reviewing your selections before installation.

AD LDS creates log files during the creation of an instance. These files are located in the %SystemRoot%\Debug folder and are named ADAMSetup.log and ADAMSetup_loader.log. You can review them if you encounter issues during the creation of the instance. Also, creating an instance creates a service for the instance. You can launch the Services console from the Administrative Tools program group to verify the existence of this service.

Unattended AD LDS Instance Creation

You can also perform unattended AD LDS instance creations. For example, you must use an unattended instance creation process on a Server Core installation because there is no GUI to run the wizard. You can also use unattended instance creation when you need to create an instance for a distributed application on multiple servers. Make sure you prepare all the prerequisites for the instance as described in the "Preparing to Create an AD LDS Instance" section earlier in this lesson.

The %SystemRoot%\ADAM folder includes an additional command, *adaminstall.exe*, which you can use to perform unattended instance setups. As with the *dcpromo.exe* command, this command requires a text file as input for the creation of the instance. You can run *adaminstall.exe* on either a full installation or Server Core. Your first step is to create a text file by using the following template:

```
[ADAMInstall]
InstallType=Unique
InstanceName=InstanceName
LocalLDAPPortToListenOn=PortNumber
LocalSSLPortToListenOn=PortNumber
NewApplicationPartitionToCreate=PartitionName
DataFilesPath=D:\ADAMInstances\InstanceName\Data
LogFilesPath=D:\ADAMInstances\InstanceName\Data
ServiceAccount=DomainorMachineName\AccountName
ServicePassword=Password
Administrator=DomainorMachineName\GroupName
ImportLDIFFiles="LDIFFilename1" "LDIFFilename2" "LDIFFilename3"
SourceUserName=DomainorMachineName\AccountName
SourcePassword=Password
```

You must replace all the items in italics with the appropriate values, save the file in the %SystemRoot%\ADAM folder, and name it with the name of the instance you want to create.

NOTE **THE TEXT FILE CONTAINS CLEAR-TEXT PASSWORDS**

Use caution with the ADAMInstall file because it includes passwords displayed in clear text. The passwords are removed as soon as the file is used by the AD LDS instance creation tool. Create the file just before you use the tool, and do not back it up until after you use the tool. Do not print it out in its initial state, and do not let anyone else read it.

MORE INFO **AD LDS INSTANCE CREATION**

For more information on AD LDS instance creation, see *http://technet.microsoft.com/en-us /library/cc725619.aspx*.

To create your instance by using the unattended creation process, log on with local administrative rights to the appropriate server, open an elevated command prompt, and move to the %SystemRoot%\ADAM folder by entering **cd\windows\adam**.

You then enter the command, **adaminstall /answer:filename.txt**, where filename.txt is the name of your text file. Use quotation marks around the filename if it contains spaces. This command creates your instance. You can verify that the instance files have been created by viewing the target folder's contents.

Migrating an Existing LDAP Instance to AD LDS

You can migrate existing LDAP directories to AD LDS or upgrade instances of ADAM to AD LDS by importing the contents of the older instances into a new instance of AD LDS.

You can import data either when you create the instance or after the instance is created. Both processes rely on LDIF files or files with the .ldf extension. If you choose to import data after the instance is created, use the *ldifde.exe* command. You must first export the data from the existing instance and place it into a file in LDIF format before you can import the data into the new instance. The *ldifde* command to export the data has the following syntax:

```
ldifde -f filename -s servername:portnumber -m -b username domainname password
```

The *ldifde* command to import the data has the following syntax:

```
ldifde -i -f filename -s servername:portnumber -m -b username domainname password
```

If you want to import passwords from the older instance, you use the *-h* switch. This switch will encrypt all passwords, using simple authentication and security layer (SASL).

> **MORE INFO** **LDIFDE**
>
> For more information on the *ldifde.exe* command, see *http://technet2.microsoft.com /windowsserver/en/library/32872283-3722-4d9b-925a-82c516a1ca141033.mspx?mfr=true*.

 Quick Check

1. Which three modes can you use to create application partitions for AD LDS instances?

2. What is the purpose of the LDIF files included with AD LDS?

3. How do you debug an AD LDS instance creation process that goes wrong?

Quick Check Answers

1. The three ways to create application partitions for AD LDS instances are as follows:

   - You can create them during the creation of an instance with AD LDS Setup.

   - You can create them through the installation of the application that will be tied to an AD LDS instance.

   - You can create them manually by using the *ldp.exe* tool.

2. The LDIF files included with AD LDS serve several purposes, depending on the actual file, but generally, they extend the schema of an instance to support specific functionality.

3. AD LDS creates log files during the creation of the instance. These files are located in the %SystemRoot%\Debug folder and are named ADAMSetup.log and ADAMSetup_loader.log. You can review them to find and resolve issues during the creation of the instance.

Working with AD LDS Instances

Earlier, this lesson listed the tools you can use to work with AD LDS instances. These include graphical tools such as ADSI Edit, *ldp.exe*, the Schema snap-in, and Active Directory Sites and Services and command-line tools such as *ADAMSync.exe* and *ADSchemaAnalyzer.exe*. Command-line tools are useful for automating processes and data input for AD LDS instances.

Using ADSI Edit to Work with Instances

ADSI Edit is a general administration tool for AD LDS instances. If you want to use ADSI Edit to work with an instance, you must first connect and bind to that instance. To use ADSI Edit, launch it from the Administrative Tools program group and, in the tree pane, right-click ADSI Edit and select Connect To. This opens the Connection Settings dialog box. You specify the following values:

Name The name of the instance you want to connect to.

Connection Point Choose Select Or Type A Distinguished Name Or Naming Context and type in the distinguished name of the instance.

Computer Choose Select Or Type A Domain Or Server and type in the server name with the port number, for example, **Boston:50000**. Select the Use SSL-based Encryption check box if you are using a Secure LDAP port.

Your Connection Settings dialog box should look similar to Figure 5-4.

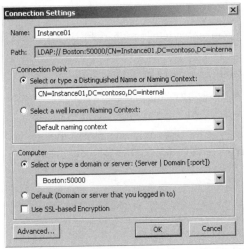

FIGURE 5-4 Connecting to an AD LDS instance with ADSI Edit.

When you click OK, this binds you to the instance. You can expand all entries to view the instance contents and explore the context menus to understand the operations you can perform with ADSI Edit on AD LDS instances.

When you are bound to an instance, you can create and manage objects within that instance. To do this, carry out the following procedure:

1. Right-click the application partition distinguished name, select New, and choose Object.

   This opens the Create Object dialog box, which lists all the available object classes in the instance's schema.

2. To create a user group, scroll to the Group object, select it, and click Next.

3. Type the name of the group, for example, AD LDS Usergroup, and click Next.

   On the next screen of the dialog box, you can click More Attributes to assign more values to this new object. For example, you can assign a description to the group.

4. From the Select A Property To View drop-down list, select adminDescription. Type a description in the *Edit Attribute* field, for example, **Group to contain AD LDS** users, click Set, and then click OK.

5. Click Finish to create the group.

   By default, this creates a security group.

6. To create a user, right-click the application partition distinguished name, select New, and then choose Object.

7. Scroll to the User object, select it, and then click Next.

8. Type the name of the user and click Next.

   You can click More Attributes if you want to assign more values to this new object.

9. Click Finish to create the user.

10. To add the user to the group, locate the group in the details pane, right-click it, and select Properties.

11. In the Properties dialog box, select the *Member* property, and then click Edit.

12. In the Multi-valued Distinguished Name With Security Principal Editor dialog box, click Add DN.

13. In the Add Distinguished Name dialog box, type the distinguished name of the user you created. For example, type **cn=Don Hall,cn=Instance01,dc=contoso,dc=internal**, and click OK.

   The user is now listed in the members list.

14. Click OK to complete the operation.

If you now view the properties of the group, you will see that the user has been added to the group. It is quite cumbersome to add large numbers of users and groups to an instance in this manner, but you can use it for single modifications. Ideally, you would create user and group lists, and then use either *csvde.exe* or *ldifde.exe* to add them in batches.

Using *Ldp.exe* to Work with Instances

The *ldp.exe* console enables you to view and edit instance contents. As with the ADSI Edit tool, you must connect and then bind to the instance you need to work with. You must be administrator of the instance to perform administrative operations on it. To view and edit instance contents by using *ldp.exe*, carry out the following procedure:

1. Launch *ldp.exe* from the command line or from Server Manager by selecting Active Directory Lightweight Directory Services in the console tree and then clicking Ldp.exe in the Advanced Tools section.

2. Click Connect on the Connection menu.

3. Type the name of the server you want to connect to and the port number to use. Select the SSL check box if you are using a Secure LDAP port. Click OK.

4. Click Bind on the Connection menu, as shown in Figure 5-5.

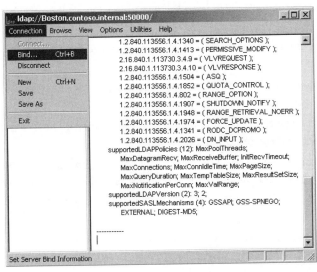

FIGURE 5-5 Binding to an instance with LDAP.

5. If your account has local administrator permissions on the server, select Bind As Currently Logged On User. If not, select Bind With Credentials and type in the appropriate credentials. Click OK.

6. Select Tree from the View menu.

7. In the BaseDN dialog box, click the down arrow to view the list of distinguished names and select the name of your instance. Click OK.

You can use the tree pane to identify where you want to work inside the instance. Explore the various menus to see which operations you can perform with *ldp.exe* and then close *ldp.exe*.

MORE INFO **USING *LDP.EXE* WITH AD LDS INSTANCES**

For more information on using *ldp.exe* with AD LDS instances, see *http://technet2.microsoft
.com/windowsserver2008/en/library/141900a7-445c-4bd3-9ce3-5ff53d70d10a1033.mspx*.

Using the Schema Snap-in to Work with Instances

You can use the Active Directory Schema snap-in to create custom consoles to manage AD
LDS instance schemas. If you want to use this snap-in, you must first register it on the server.
To register and use the Active Directory Schema snap-in, carry out the following procedure:

1. In an elevated command prompt, enter **regsvr32 schmmgmt.dll**.

2. Click Start and type **mmc** in the Search box. Press Enter.

3. In the empty console, click Add/Remove Snap-in from the File menu.

4. Select Active Directory Schema Snap-In from the Available Snap-ins list, click Add, and
   then click OK.

5. Save the console with an appropriate name. Make sure you save it in an appropriate
   location.

   The Schema snap-in binds to the Active Directory Domain Services directory by
   default.

6. To bind to an AD LDS instance, right-click Active Directory Schema in the tree pane
   and select Change Active Directory Domain Controller.

7. In the Change Directory Server dialog box, select This Domain Controller Or AD LDS
   Instance, click Type A Directory Server Name[:Port] Here, type the server name with
   the port number separated by a colon, as shown in Figure 5-6, and press Enter. Click
   OK.

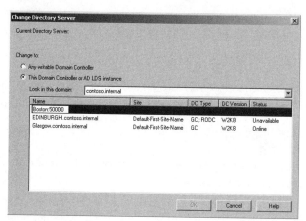

FIGURE 5-6 Binding the Schema snap-in to an LDS instance.

8. In the warning dialog box, click Yes to change servers.

You can now view the schema for this instance. Save the console again to save these settings.

NOTE **CREATING A MULTI-AD LDS CONSOLE**

If you want to create one console with multiple AD LDS instance schemas, add additional Schema snap-ins to your console. Use one snap-in for each instance to which you want to connect. When you reopen the console, it will link to each instance and save you time.

Using Active Directory Sites and Services to Work with Instances

You can manage AD LDS instances with the Active Directory Sites and Services console. However, before you can do so, you must import the MS-ADLDS-DisplaySpecifiers.ldf file. This updates the instance's schema to support the appropriate objects. To manage AD LDS instances with the Active Directory Sites and Services console, carry out the following procedure:

1. Open an elevated command prompt.

2. Enter **cd \windows\adam** to move to the %SystemRoot%\ADAM folder.

3. Import the LDIF file into the instance by entering the following command (with the parameters in italics replaced by your own values): **ldifde –i –f MS-ADLDS-DisplaySpecifiers.ldf –s *servername:portnumber* –m –a *username domainname password*.**

4. Close the command prompt.

5. Launch Active Directory Sites And Services from the Administrative Tools program group.

   The console binds to the Active Directory Domain Services directory by default.

6. To bind to an AD LDS instance, right-click Active Directory Sites And Servers in the tree pane and select Change Domain Controller.

7. In the Change Directory Server dialog box, select This Domain Controller Or AD LDS Instance and click Type A Directory Server Name[Port] Here. Type in the server name with the port number separated by a colon and press Enter. Click OK.

8. In the warning dialog box, click Yes to change servers.

   You can now work with the replication parameters for the instance. Note that the server name uses the *Servername$InstanceName* format to illustrate that it is not a domain controller.

MORE INFO **AD LDS TOOLS AND INSTANCES**

For more information on AD LDS tools and instances, see *http://technet2.microsoft.com /windowsserver2008/en/library/141900a7-445c-4bd3-9ce3-5ff53d70d10a1033.mspx.*

EXAM TIP

Remember that you cannot use graphical tools on Server Core. To manage instances located on Server Core installations, use the command-line tools. If you want to use graphical tools, use them from a full Windows installation and bind to the Server Core server, or use them from a client system running Remote Server Administration Tools (RSAT).

PRACTICE **Installing and Working with AD LDS Instances**

In this practice, you install the AD LDS role on a server running the full installation of Windows Server 2008 and browse the contents of the installation folder to identify which files have been installed. You then create your first AD LDS instance. Optionally, if you have two member servers on your test network, you can create a replica and manage replication between the two instances.

EXERCISE 1   Install AD LDS

In this exercise, you install the AD LDS server role and view the installed files.

1. Ensure that your domain controller, Glasgow, and your member server, Boston, are both running. If you created a second member server, Chicago, make sure it is running also.

2. Log on to the *contoso.internal* domain at Boston by using the Kim_Akers account.

3. If Server Manager does not open automatically, open it from Administrative Tools on the Start menu. In Server Manager, right-click the *Roles* node and select Add Roles.

4. Review the Before You Begin page and click Next.

5. On the Select Server Roles page, select the Active Directory Lightweight Directory Services check box, as shown in Figure 5-7, and click Next.

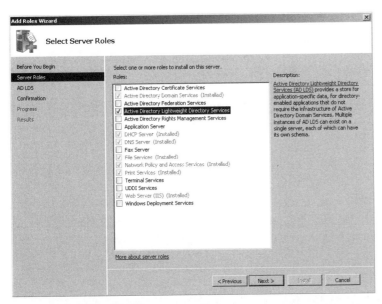

FIGURE 5-7 Installing AD LDS.

6. Review the information on the Active Directory Lightweight Directory Services page and click Next.

7. Confirm your choices and click Install.

8. Review the installation results.

9. When the installation is complete, click Close.

   The role appears in Server Manager, as shown in Figure 5-8.

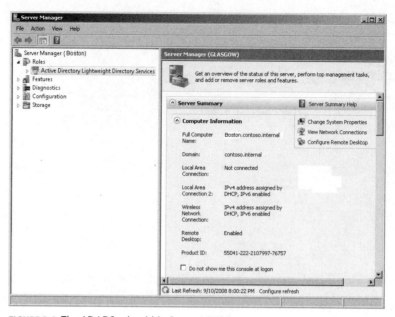

FIGURE 5-8 The AD LDS role within Server Manager.

10. Close Server Manager.

11. Open Windows Explorer and view the %SystemRoot%\ADAM folder, as shown in Figure 5-9.

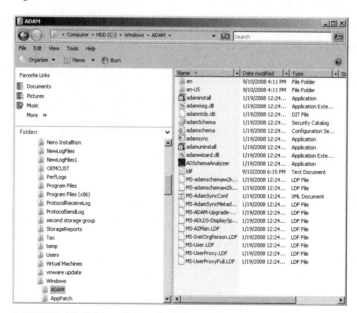

FIGURE 5-9 AD LDS installs into the %SystemRoot%\ADAM folder and creates the AD LDS database.

12. If you have created a second member server, Chicago, log on to the domain at that server by using the Kim_Akers account and repeat the procedure to install the AD LDS server role on that server.

EXERCISE 2   Create an AD LDS Instance

In this exercise, you create your first AD LDS instance. You need to have completed Exercise 1, "Install AD LDS," before you attempt this exercise. Use the values in Table 5-1 to perform this exercise.

TABLE 5-1 Instance Creation Values

ITEM	VALUE
Instance Name	MYADLDSInstance
Ports	50,000 for LDAP 50,001 for Secure LDAP
Application Partition Name	CN=MYADLDSInstance,dc=contoso,dc=internal
Data Paths	D:\ADLDS\MYADLDSInstance\Data
Service Account	Network Service
Administration Account	Contoso\Kim_Akers
LDIF Files for Import	MS-AdamSyncMetadata.ldf MS-ADLDS-DisplaySpecifiers.ldf MS-AZMan.ldf MS-InetOrgPerson.ldf MS-User.ldf MS-UserProxy.ldf MS-UserProxyFull.ldf

1. Ensure that your domain controller, Glasgow, and your member server, Boston, are running. If you installed the member server, Chicago, ensure that it is running also.

2. Log on to the *contoso.internal* domain at Boston with the Kim_Akers account.

3. Launch the Active Directory Lightweight Directory Services Setup Wizard from the Administrative Tools program group.

4. Review the information on the Welcome page and click Next.

5. On the Setup Options page, verify that A Unique Instance is selected, and then click Next.

6. On the Instance Name page, type **MYADLDSInstance** and click Next.

7. On the Ports page, specify the ports to use to communicate with this instance. Use 50000 for LDAP and 50001 for the SSL port number. Click Next.

8. On the Application Directory Partition page, select Yes, Create An Application Directory Partition. In the Partition Name text box, specify the application partition name, in this case, CN=MYADLDSInstance,dc=contoso,dc=internal, and then click Next.

9. On the File Locations page, change the paths to *<DriveLetter:>*ADLDS \MYADLDSInstance\Data, where *<DriveLetter:>* identifies the hard disk partition you want to hold the data for the AD LDS instances, and then click Next.

10. On the Service Account Selection page, verify that Network Service Account is selected, and then click Next.

> **NOTE USING THE NETWORK SERVICE ACCOUNT**
>
> In a production environment, you should create and use a service account, but Network Service is sufficient for the purpose of the exercise.

11. On the AD LDS Administrators page, verify that Currently Logged On User is selected and click Next.

> **NOTE USING AN ADMINISTRATIVE GROUP AND DELEGATING CONTROL**
>
> In a production environment, you should create and use an administrative group, but the Kim_Akers account is sufficient for the purpose of the exercise. Note that you can use the AD LDS Administrators page to delegate control of an instance. If you want to, you can delegate control of one instance to one group of users and a control of a second instance to another group of users.

12. On the Importing LDIF Files page, select the check boxes for the LDIF files listed in Table 5-1, and then click Next.

13. On the Ready To Install page, review your selections, and then click Next.

    AD LDS installs the new instance.

14. Click Finish.

    Your first instance is ready to use.

EXERCISE 3 Create an AD LDS Replica Instance (Optional)

You should carry out this exercise if you configured the (optional) Chicago server as described in the "Before You Begin" section at the start of this chapter. You must have successfully completed Exercise 1 on both member servers and Exercise 2, "Create an AD LDS Instance," on the Boston member server. In this exercise, you create an AD LDS replica instance on the Chicago member server.

1. Make sure your domain controller, Glasgow, and your member servers, Boston and Chicago, are running.

2. Log on to the *contoso.internal* domain at Chicago with the Kim_Akers account.

3. Launch the Active Directory Lightweight Directory Services Setup Wizard from the Administrative Tools program group.

4. Review the information on the Welcome page and click Next.

5. On the Setup Options page, select A Replica Of An Existing Instance, and then click Next.

6. On the Instance Name page, type **MYADLDSInstance** and click Next.

7. On the Ports page, specify the ports to use to communicate with this instance. Use 50000 for LDAP and 50001 for the SSL port number. Click Next.

8. On the Joining A Configuration Set page, under Server, type **Boston** and click Check Names. Click OK and type **50000** into the *LDAP Port* field. Click Next.

9. On the Administrative Credentials For The Configuration Set page, select Currently Logged On User and click Next.

10. On the Copying Application Directory Partitions page, select the CN=MYADLDSInstance,dc=contoso,dc=internal partition and click Next.

11. On the File Locations page, change the paths to ***<DriveLetter:>*\ADLDS \MYADLDSInstance\Data**, and then click Next.

12. On the Service Account Selection page, select Network Service Account, and then click Next.

13. On the AD LDS Administrators page, select Currently Logged On User and click Next.

14. On the Ready To Install page, review your selections, and then click Next.

    AD LDS installs the new instance.

15. Click Finish.

    Your replica has been created.

EXERCISE 4 Manage Replication Between AD LDS Replicas (Optional)

In this exercise, you view the replication parameters between your two instances. Carry out this exercise only if you installed the Chicago member server and have completed Exercises 1, 2, and 3, "Create an AD LDS Replica Instance (Optional)." You do not need to update the instances to support Active Directory Sites and Services objects because you imported all LDIF files in Exercise 2 when you created the source instance.

1. Ensure that your domain controller, Glasgow, and your member servers, Boston and Chicago, are running.

2. Log on to the *contoso.internal* domain at Chicago with the Kim_Akers account.

3. Launch Active Directory Sites And Services from the Administrative Tools program group.

    The console binds to the Active Directory Domain Services directory by default.

4. To bind to the AD LDS instance, right-click Active Directory Sites And Services in the tree pane and select Change Domain Controller.

5. In the Change Directory Server dialog box, select This Domain Controller Or AD LDS Instance and click Type A Directory Server Name[:Port] Here. Type **Boston:50000**, and then press Enter. Click OK.

6. In the warning dialog box, click Yes to change servers.

7. Fully expand the Active Directory Sites And Services tree by pressing the asterisk key (*) on your numerical keypad several times.

   This displays the replication structure for this instance.

8. To create a new site and move one of the instance objects into this site, right-click Sites in the tree pane and select New Site.

9. Name the site **Replication01**, select DEFAULTIPSITELINK, and click OK.

   Your new site link is created, and Active Directory Sites And Services outlines the next steps you must perform, as shown in Figure 5-10.

10. Click OK to close the dialog box.

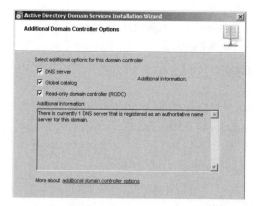

FIGURE 5-10 Required tasks to complete a replication partnership.

In this exercise, you do not need to perform all the activities listed in Figure 5-10. You only move Chicago to the new site link.

11. Expand Replication01.

12. Click Chicago$MYADLDSInstance and drag it to the Servers container under Replication01.

13. In the Moving Objects warning box, click Yes to move the object.

    The object now appears under the Replication01 site.

> **NOTE ADDITIONAL REPLICATION TASKS**
>
> This exercise demonstrates how to work with instances and control replication. On a production network, you must perform all the tasks listed in Figure 5-10 to create replication partnerships.

MORE INFO **AD LDS REPLICATION**

For more information on AD LDS replication, see *http://technet2.microsoft.com /windowsserver2008/en/library/9d4b4004-9f26-4545-a1e4-8e527102f0a71033.mspx*.

Lesson Summary

- AD LDS supports directory-enabled applications on an application-by-application basis and without having to modify the database schema of the NOS directory running on AD DS.

- You install AD LDS by using the Add Roles Wizard. To remove AD LDS, you first remove all instances through Programs and Features in Control Panel and then remove the role in Server Manager.

- You can create instances both with the graphical interface through the AD LDS Setup tool and through the command line with the *ADAMInstall.exe* command. In both cases, you must plan beforehand. When using the *ADAMInstall.exe* tool, you must prepare an answer file that contains the instance prerequisite values beforehand.

- You can create replicas of instances and configure replication.

Lesson Review

You can use the following questions to test your knowledge of the information in Lesson 1, "Configuring Active Directory Lightweight Directory Services." The questions are also available on the companion DVD if you prefer to review them in electronic form.

NOTE **ANSWERS**

Answers to these questions and explanations of why each answer choice is right or wrong are located in the "Answers" section at the end of the book.

1. What are the default LDAP and LDAP over SSL, or Secure LDAP, ports AD LDS uses for communication? (Choose two. Each answer presents a complete solution.)

    A. 3268

    B. 636

    C. 50000

    D. 389

    E. 3269

    F. 50001

2. A full installation member server currently hosts five AD LDS instances, and you want to uninstall AD LDS from this server. You log on to the server with local administrative rights and launch an elevated command prompt. You use the *ocsetup* command with

the /uninstall switch, but this does not work. Which of the following actions will resolve the problem?

A. Use the *oclist* command to verify the syntax of the option you are trying to remove with the *ocsetup* command. Then retry the *ocsetup* command with the correct syntax.

B. Restart the server to make sure all running setup processes are complete, and then run the *uninstall* command again.

C. First uninstall all existing instances of AD LDS by using Programs and Features in Control Panel, and then execute *ocsetup /uninstall* from the elevated command prompt.

D. Use Server Manager to remove all AD LDS instances and the role.

3. You are installing AD LDS on a Server Core installation of Windows Server 2008. You have determined that the service name for AD LDS is DirectoryServices-ADAM-ServerCore. Which command do you use to install AD LDS?

A. *start /w ocsetup DirectoryServices-ADAM-ServerCore*

B. *oclist/more*

C. *start /w ocsetup DirectoryServices-ADLDS-ServerCore*

D. *start /w oclist DirectoryServices-ADAM-ServerCore*

4. Recently, you installed four AD LDS instances on Boston, a member server in your domain. You used the default settings for the port selections of each instance. You need to modify the schema of the first instance you installed, Instance01. You register the Active Directory Schema snap-in on the server and create a custom Active Directory Schema console. When you try to connect to the schema of the first instance, you get an error message. Which of the following is most likely to be the problem?

A. You cannot modify the schema of an instance with the Active Directory Schema snap-in. You modify the schema of an instance by importing LDIF files with the *ldifde.exe* command.

B. You cannot modify the schema of an instance with the Active Directory Schema snap-in. You must use the *ldp.exe* command.

C. Instance01 does not include a schema, and you therefore cannot edit it.

D. You cannot connect to the instance with the AD Schema snap-in because, by default, it uses the same port as your AD DS directory.

Lesson 2: Configuring Read-Only Domain Controllers

Traditionally, the existence of branch offices on a network posed a question that had no easy answer: Where do you locate your domain controllers? A branch office is typically separated from the hub site by a wide area network (WAN) link. Should you place a domain controller in the branch office so that logon is local and users are not authenticated over the WAN? Can branch office staff support a domain controller? Can a branch office offer the same physical security as a hub site? Does replication traffic use more bandwidth than authentication traffic?

Windows Server 2008 tackles this problem by introducing the read-only domain controller (RODC). In this lesson, you explore the issues related to branch office authentication and domain controller placement, and you learn how to implement and support a branch office RODC.

After this lesson, you will be able to:

- Identify the business requirements for RODCs.
- Install an RODC.
- Configure password replication policy.
- Monitor the caching of credentials on an RODC.

Estimated lesson time: 50 minutes

 REAL WORLD

Best practices can be a great comfort.

They might not always be appropriate to your particular situation, but this happens less often than most people believe. (We all think our own networks are special.) So, unless there's a very good reason for not doing so, experienced administrators tend to follow best practices. To be cynical (I frequently am), it gives you an out if something goes wrong. You can show management that you acted as a professional and followed best practices—there it is in black and white.

Over the years, I've had many a discussion about domain controller placement and other topics for which there is no standard answer and no best practice. Discussions can be heated because all participants have suffered. The CEO is visiting a branch office and it takes him or her five minutes to log on. That's my fault. A domain controller in a branch office breaks down and nobody there can maintain it. That's my fault, too. I can't produce a document that says I've done the right thing and followed the best practice, and what happened was merely bad luck.

So I was relieved and pleased when I first heard about RODCs. Finally, Microsoft designers were addressing a problem that had haunted me (and many others) for a very long time. My only quibble is that they hadn't thought of it years ago. Now whose fault is that?

Authentication and Domain Controller Placement in a Branch Office

Many organizational structures consist of a hub site and several branch offices that connect to the hub site over WAN links. These links can be congested, expensive, slow, or unreliable. Users in the branch office must be authenticated by AD DS to access resources in the domain. One or more domain controllers placed in the branch office would avoid the need to authenticate over a WAN link and would speed up authentication.

Typically, a hub site is maintained by qualified IT staff and includes secure facilities for services. The branch offices, however, might offer inadequate physical security for servers and might have insufficient skilled IT staff to support the domain controllers.

If domain controllers are not placed in the branch office, authentication and service ticket activities will be directed to the hub site over a WAN link. Authentication occurs when a user logs on to his or her computer. Service tickets are a component of the Kerberos authentication mechanism used by Windows Server 2008 domains that allow users to connect to a service such as the File and Print services on a file server. Authentication and service ticket activity over the WAN link between a branch office and a hub site can result in slow or unreliable performance.

MORE INFO **KERBEROS AND SERVICE TICKETS**

As a Windows Server 2003 professional, you should be familiar with Kerberos authentication and server tickets. If, however, you want to review these topics, more information is available at *http://technet.microsoft.com/en-us/library/cc772815.aspx*.

If a domain controller is placed in a branch office to make authentication more efficient, this introduces several significant risks. A domain controller maintains a copy of all attributes of all objects in its domain, including confidential information related to user passwords. If an attacker can access or steal a domain controller, it is possible (although not easy) to identify valid usernames and passwords. At the very least, you would need to reset the passwords of every user account in the domain. In a large hub site, domain controllers, and other significant servers such as certificate servers, can be kept in a secure room. However, the physical security of servers at branch offices is often less than ideal.

Another concern is that the changes to the Active Directory database on a branch office domain controller replicate to the hub site and to all other domain controllers in the environment. Therefore, corruption of the branch office domain controller poses a risk to the integrity of the enterprise directory service. For example, if a branch office administrator performs a restore of the domain controller from an outdated backup, there can be significant repercussions for the entire domain. If, as is often the case, branch office IT employees are less experienced than the team at the head office, an inexperienced administrator can compromise the entire site.

A branch office domain controller might require maintenance such as the installation of a new device driver. To perform maintenance on a standard domain controller, you must log on as a member of the Administrators group on the domain controller, which means you are an administrator of the domain. It might not be appropriate to grant permissions at that level to a support team at a branch office.

Using Read-Only Domain Controllers

The RODC is designed to address the branch office scenario. An RODC is a domain controller that maintains a copy of all objects in the domain and all attributes except confidential attributes (secrets) such as password-related properties. When a user in the branch office logs on, the RODC receives the request and forwards it to a domain controller in the hub site for authentication.

You are able to configure a password replication policy (PRP) for the RODC that specifies user accounts the RODC is allowed to cache. If the user logging on is included in the PRP, the RODC caches that user's credentials so that the next time the user requests authentication, the RODC can perform the task locally. As users who are included in the PRP log on, the RODC builds its cache of credentials so that it can perform authentication locally for those users. These concepts are illustrated in Figure 5-11.

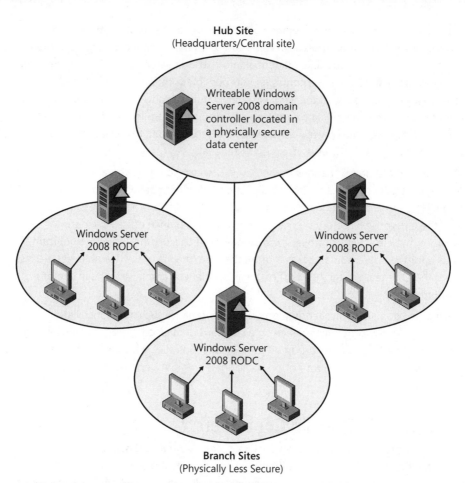

Hub Site
(Headquarters/Central site)

Writeable Windows Server 2008 domain controller located in a physically secure data center

Windows Server 2008 RODC

Windows Server 2008 RODC

Windows Server 2008 RODC

Branch Sites
(Physically Less Secure)

FIGURE 5-11 A branch office scenario supported by RODCs.

RODCs can support technologies such as AD FS, Dynamic Host Configuration Protocol (DHCP), DNS, Group Policy (GP), distributed file system (DFS), Microsoft Operations Manager (MOM), and System Center Configuration Manager 2007 (SMS). They are prime candidates for virtualization through technologies such as Hyper-V because they do not support a large amount of network traffic.

If the RODC is compromised or stolen, the effect of the security exposure is limited. You need to change the passwords only for the user accounts that were cached on the RODC. Writable domain controllers maintain a list of all cached credentials on individual RODCs. When you delete the account of the stolen or compromised RODC from AD DS, you can reset the passwords of all user accounts that were cached on the RODC.

Using BitLocker and Syskey in Combination with RODCs

B itLocker is a full-drive encryption solution that runs on Trusted Platform Model (TPM) 1.2-based hardware to store encryption keys and can be configured through Group Policy. It is particularly valuable for servers stored in branch offices, which are often less well protected physically than the machines in the hub site. A thief who steals a BitLocker-protected server will not be able to access any of the data stored on the system's hard drives.

BitLocker also works well in combination with Server Core installations and RODCs. If you combine RODC with Windows Server 2008 technologies such as BitLocker and Server Core, you can configure the most secure remote server possible. Even malicious users who gain physical control of the server cannot take over your network.

Although BitLocker provides full-drive encryption, the *syskey* tool enables you to configure the Windows account database—sometimes known as the Security Account Management (SAM) database—to enable additional encryption, further protecting account name and password information from compromise. You can use the *syskey* utility to secure the Windows account database further by moving the Windows Account database encryption key off the Windows-based computer. You can also use the *syskey* utility to configure a start-up password that must be entered to decrypt the system key so that Windows can access the database.

Unlike BitLocker, which is introduced in Windows Server 2008, *syskey* has been around for some considerable time—one of the options it gives you is to move the encryption key to a floppy disk. Take care if you are using *syskey* on a modern computer that does not have floppies. If you then select the move to floppy option, no error message is displayed, but you will subsequently be unable to reboot the computer.

MORE INFO **TPM 1.2, *SYSKEY*, AND BITLOCKER**

The TPM 1.2 specification is unlikely to be tested in the upgrade examinations, but if you are interested in it professionally and want more information, see *https://www .trustedcomputinggroup.org/groups/tpm/TPM_1_2_Changes_final.pdf. Syskey* is also unlikely to be tested in detail, but you can get more information at *http://support.microsoft .com/kb/310105*. This is not a Windows Server 2008 link, but the information it contains is valid. Questions about BitLocker probably will appear in the examination. For more information, see *http://technet.microsoft.com/en-us/windows/aa905065.aspx*.

An RODC replicates changes to AD DS from domain controllers in the hub site. Replication is one way. No changes to the RODC are replicated to any other domain controller. The directory service can no longer be corrupted through changes made to a compromised branch office domain controller. Finally, RODCs, unlike writable domain controllers, have a local Administrators group. You can give one or more local support personnel the ability to maintain an RODC without granting them the rights of domain administrators.

> **NOTE** **USING BITLOCKER ON RODCS**
>
> RODCs do not require you to install BitLocker Drive Encryption because they do not store account information for the full domain. If, however, you deploy an RODC in a location from which it might be stolen, you might want to install BitLocker as an additional precaution to help safeguard data on the server.
>
> One possible disadvantage to using BitLocker on an RODC is that you have to provide a password and restart the RODC each time you apply an operating system update to it. Weigh the potential security benefits BitLocker provides against this additional administrative requirement to determine whether to use BitLocker on a specific RODC.

Deploying an RODC

The high-level steps to install an RODC are as follows:

1. Ensure that the forest functional level is Windows Server 2003 or higher.
2. If the forest has any domain controllers running Microsoft Windows Server 2003, run *adprep /rodcprep.*
3. Ensure that at least one writable domain controller is running Windows Server 2008.
4. Install the RODC.

Configuring a Forest Functional Level of Windows Server 2003 or Higher

Functional levels enable features unique to specific versions of Windows and are therefore dependent on the versions of Windows running on domain controllers. If all domain controllers are Windows Server 2003 or later, you can set the domain functional level to Windows Server 2003. If all domains are at Windows Server 2003 domain functional level, you can set the forest functional level to Windows Server 2003. Similarly, if all domain controllers in a domain are Windows Server 2008, you can raise the domain functional level to Windows Server 2008, and if all domains in a forest are at the Windows Server 2008 domain functional level, you can raise the forest functional level to Windows Server 2008. However, you do not need the Windows Server 2008 functional levels to install an RODC.

NOTE DO NOT BE TOO HASTY IN RAISING DOMAIN AND FOREST FUNCTIONAL LEVELS.

It is easy to raise a functional level. It is difficult to reduce one—this requires a re-install or a restore from backups of the lower functional level. If, for example, you raised the domain functional level to Windows Server 2008 and then found you needed to add a Windows Server 2003 domain controller to your domain, you have a serious problem. Similarly, if you raised your organization's forest functional level to Windows Server 2008 and your organization acquired another that had a domain that included Windows Server 2003 domain controllers, you would have problems integrating your network. Raise functional levels only enough to enable the features you need.

MORE INFO DOMAIN AND FOREST FUNCTIONAL LEVELS

For more information about domain and forest functional levels, see *http://technet .microsoft.com/en-us/library/cc754918.aspx*.

RODCs require a forest functional level of Windows Server 2003 or higher. To determine the functional level of your forest, open Active Directory Domains And Trusts from the Administrative Tools group, right-click the name of the forest, choose Properties, and verify the forest functional level, as shown in Figure 5-12. Any user can verify the forest functional level in this way.

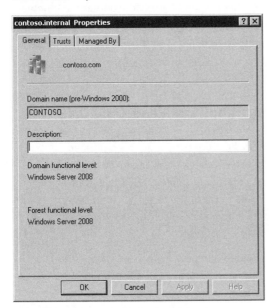

FIGURE 5-12 The Forest Properties dialog box.

If the forest functional level is not at least Windows Server 2003, examine the properties of each domain to identify any domains for which the domain functional level is not at least Windows Server 2003. If you find such a domain, ensure that all domain controllers in the domain are running Windows Server 2003. Open Active Directory Domains And Trusts, right-click the domain, and choose Raise Domain Functional Level.

When you have raised each domain functional level to at least Windows Server 2003, right-click the root node of the Active Directory Domains And Trusts snap-in and choose Raise Forest Functional Level. In the Select An Available Forest Functional Level drop-down list, choose Windows Server 2003 and click Raise. You must be a domain administrator to raise the domain's functional level. To raise the forest functional level, you must be either a member of the Domain Admins group in the forest root domain or a member of the Enterprise Admins group.

Running *adprep /rodcprep*

If you are upgrading an existing forest to include domain controllers running Windows Server 2008, you must run *adprep /rodcprep*. This command configures permissions so that RODCs are able to replicate DNS application directory partitions. If you are creating a new Active Directory forest that contains only domain controllers running Windows Server 2008, you do not need to run *adprep /rodcprep*.

You can find the *adprep* command in the cdrom\Sources\Adprep folder of the Windows Server 2008 installation DVD. Copy the folder to the domain controller acting as the schema master, log on to the schema master as a member of the Enterprise Admins group, open a command prompt, change directories to the Adprep folder, and enter **adprep /rodcprep** in an elevated command prompt.

DNS Application Directory Partitions and Read-Only DNS

When DNS data is stored within AD DS directory databases, it is replicated by default with the directory data with which it is associated. You can also define a custom replication scope for DNS data. For example, DNS data that belongs to a root domain in a forest must be available to the entire forest, whereas DNS data for a specific domain is required only for that domain. You control DNS data replication scopes through DNS application directory partitions.

To support the RODC role, DNS has been updated to provide read-only DNS data for primary zones hosted on the RODC. This further secures the role and ensures that no one can create records from potentially unprotected servers to spoof the network. A DNS server running on an RODC does not support dynamic updates, but clients are able to use the DNS server to query for name resolution.

Because the DNS is read-only, clients cannot update records on it. If, however, a client wants to update its own DNS record, the RODC sends a referral to a writable

DNS server. The single updated record will be replicated from the writable DNS server to the DNS server on the RODC. This is a special single object (DNS record) replication that keeps the RODC DNS servers up to date and gives the clients in the branch office faster name resolution.

The Schema Master Role

The domain controller holding the schema master role is responsible for making any changes to the forest's schema. All other domain controllers hold read-only replicas of the schema. If you want to modify the schema or install an application that modifies the schema, Microsoft recommends you do so on the domain controller holding the schema master role. Otherwise, the changes you request must be sent to the schema master to be written into the schema.

Placing the Writable Windows Server 2008 Domain Controller

An RODC must replicate domain updates from a writable domain controller running Windows Server 2008, and the RODC must be able to establish a replication connection with the writable Windows Server 2008 domain controller. Ideally, the writable Windows Server 2008 domain controller should be in the closest site—the hub site. If you want the RODC to act as a DNS server, the writable Windows Server 2008 domain controller must also host the DNS domain zone.

 Quick Check

- Your domain consists of a central site and four branch offices. The central site has two domain controllers. Each branch office site has one domain controller. All domain controllers run Windows Server 2003. Your company decides to open a fifth branch office and you want to configure it with a new Windows Server 2008 RODC. What must you do before configuring the first RODC in your domain?

Quick Check Answer

- You must ensure that the forest functional level is Windows Server 2003. Then you need to upgrade one of the existing domain controllers to Windows Server 2008 so there is one writable Windows Server 2008 domain controller on the network. You must then run *adprep /rodcprep* on the writable Windows Server 2008 domain from the Windows Server 2008 installation DVD.

Installing an RODC

After you complete the preparatory steps, you can install an RODC on either a full or Server Core installation of Windows Server 2008. On a full installation of Windows Server 2008, you can use the Active Directory Domain Services Installation Wizard to create an RODC. You select Read-Only Domain Controller (RODC) on the Additional Domain Controller Options page of the wizard, as shown in Figure 5-13.

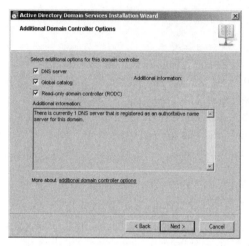

FIGURE 5-13 Creating an RODC with the Active Directory Domain Services Installation Wizard.

Alternatively, you can use the *dcpromo* command with the */unattend* switch to create the RODC. On a Server Core installation of Windows Server 2008, you must use the *dcpromo /unattend* command. You can also delegate the installation of the RODC, which enables a user who is not a domain administrator to create the RODC, by adding a new server in the branch office and running *dcpromo*.

EXAM TIP

Remember that if you create an RODC by using delegated installation, the server must be a member of a workgroup, not of the domain.

Installing an RODC on Server Core

Microsoft recommends deploying RODCs that run on the Server Core installa-tion whenever practicable. This improves the security of branch office domain controllers.

GUI tools are not available in Server Core, but you can use the *dcpromo /unattend* command at an elevated command prompt in exactly the same way as you can to install an RODC on a full Windows Server 2008 installation. The following example creates an RODC in the *contoso.internal* domain in the MyBranch site, creates a global catalog, and installs and configures the DNS Server service:

```
dcpromo /unattend /InstallDns:yes /confirmGC:yes
/replicaOrNewDomain:ReadOnlyReplica /replicaDomainDNSName:contoso.internal
/sitename:MyBranch /databasePath:"e:\ntds" /logPath:"e:\ntdslogs"
/sysvolpath:"f:\sysvol" /safeModeAdminPassword:P@ssw0rd
/rebootOnCompletion:yes
```

Alternatively, you can choose to use an answer file. In this case, first create your answer file by using a text editor, and then enter the command dcpromo / unattend:<path to answer file>. Your answer file would be similar to the following:

```
[DCInstall]

Username=Kim_Akers

Password=P@ssw0rd

UserDomain=contoso.internal

InstallDns=yes

ConfirmGC=yes

ReplicaOrNewDomain=ReadOnlyReplica

ReplicaDomainDNSName=contoso.internal

Sitename=MyBranch

databasePath="e:\ntds"

logPath="e:\ntdslogs"

sysvolpath:"f:\sysvol"

SafeModeAdminPassword:P@ssw0rd

RebootOnCompletion:yes
```

MORE INFO   **SERVER CORE FEATURES**

For more information about the features that you can install with a Server Core installation, see *http://technet.microsoft.com/en-us/library/cc771345.aspx*.

MORE INFO   OPTIONS FOR INSTALLING AN RODC

For more information about RODC installation, including delegated installation, see "Step-by-Step Guide for Read-only Domain Controllers" at *http://technet2.microsoft.com /windowsserver2008/en/library/ea8d253e-0646-490c-93d3-b78c5e1d9db71033. mspx?mfr=true.*

Password Replication Policy

PRP determines which users' credentials can be cached on a specific RODC. If PRP allows an RODC to cache a user's credentials, that user's authentication and service ticket activities can be processed by the RODC. If a user's credentials cannot be cached on an RODC, authentication and service ticket activities are referred to a writable domain controller by the RODC.

An RODC PRP is determined by two multivalued attributes of the RODC computer account. These attributes are known as the Allowed List and the Denied List. If a user's account is on the Allowed List, the user's credentials are cached. You can include groups on the Allowed List, in which case, all users who belong to the group can have their credentials cached on the RODC. If a user is on both the Allowed List and the Denied List, that user's credentials will not be cached—the Denied List takes precedence.

Configuring Domain-Wide Password Replication Policy

To facilitate the management of PRP, Windows Server 2008 creates two domain local security groups in the Users container of AD DS. The first, named Allowed RODC Password Replication Group, is added to the Allowed List of each new RODC. By default, the group has no members. Therefore, by default, a new RODC will not cache any user's credentials. If there are users whose credentials you want all domain RODCs to cache, add those users to the Allowed RODC Password Replication Group.

The second group is named Denied RODC Password Replication Group. It is added to the Denied List of each new RODC. If there are users whose credentials you want to ensure domain RODCs never cache, add those users to the Denied RODC Password Replication Group. By default, this group contains security-sensitive accounts that are members of groups such as Domain Admins, Enterprise Admins, and Group Policy Creator Owners.

NOTE   CACHING COMPUTER CREDENTIALS

In addition to branch office users, branch office computers also generate authentication and service ticket activity. To improve performance of systems in a branch office, allow the branch RODC to cache both user and computer credentials.

Configuring an RODC-Specific Password Replication Policy

The Allowed RODC Password Replication Group and Denied RODC Password Replication Group provide a method of managing PRP on all RODCs. However, you typically need to allow the RODC in each branch office to cache user and computer credentials for that specific location. Therefore, you must configure the Allowed List and the Denied List of each RODC.

To configure an RODC PRP, open the properties of the RODC computer account in the Domain Controllers OU. On the Password Replication Policy tab, shown in Figure 5-14, you can view the current PRP settings and add or remove users or groups from the PRP.

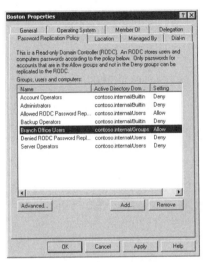

FIGURE 5-14 The Password Replication Policy tab of an RODC.

Administering Credentials Caching on an RODC

When you click the Advanced button on the Password Replication Policy tab, shown in Figure 5-14, the Advanced Password Replication Policy dialog box shown in Figure 5-15 appears.

The drop-down list at the top of the Policy Usage tab enables you to select one of the following RODC reports:

Accounts Whose Passwords Are Stored On This Read-Only Domain Controller   This report displays the list of user and computer credentials currently cached on the RODC. You can use this list to determine whether credentials are being cached that you do not want to be cached on the RODC and modify the PRP accordingly.

Accounts That Have Been Authenticated To This Read-Only Domain Controller   This report displays the list of user and computer credentials that have been referred to a writable domain controller for authentication or service ticket processing. You can use this list to identify users or computers that are attempting to authenticate with the RODC. If any of these accounts are not being cached and you want them to be, add them to the PRP.

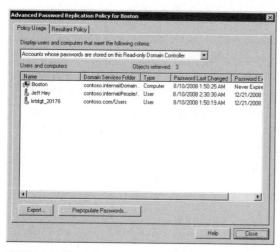

FIGURE 5-15 The Advanced Password Replication Policy dialog box.

The Resultant Policy tab of the Advanced Password Replication Policy dialog box enables you to evaluate the effective caching policy for an individual user or computer. Click Add to select a user or computer account for evaluation.

You can also use the Advanced Password Replication Policy dialog box to prepopulate credentials in the RODC cache. If a user or computer is on an RODC Allowed list, the account credentials can be cached on the RODC, but not until the authentication or service ticket events cause the RODC to replicate the credentials from a writable domain controller. You can ensure that authentication and service ticket activity will be processed locally by the RODC even when the user or computer is authenticating for the first time by prepopulating credentials in the RODC cache for users and computers in the branch office. To prepopulate credentials, click Prepopulate Passwords and select the appropriate users and computers. Typically, you would do this if a new employee is starting work at a branch office (or if you know that a senior manager is visiting a branch office and will want to log on).

Administrative Role Separation

RODCs in branch offices can require maintenance such as the installation of an updated device driver. Additionally, small branch offices might combine the RODC with (for example) the file server role on a single computer, in which case, it is important that a staff member at the branch office can back up the system. RODCs support local administration through a feature called *administrative role separation*. Each RODC maintains a local database of groups for specific administrative purposes. You can add domain user accounts to these local roles to enable support for a specific RODC.

You can configure administrative role separation by using the *dsmgmt.exe* command. To add a user to the Administrators role on an RODC, follow these steps:

1. Open an elevated command prompt on the RODC.

2. Type **dsmgmt**.

3. Type **local roles**.

4. At the local roles prompt, you can type **?** to obtain a list of commands. You can also type **list roles** to obtain a list of local roles.

5. Type **add username administrators**, where *username* is the pre-Windows 2000 logon name of a domain user.

You can repeat this process to add other users to the various local roles on an RODC.

MORE INFO **IMPROVING AUTHENTICATION AND SECURITY**

For more information about how RODCs improve authentication and security in branch offices, see *http://technet2.microsoft.com/windowsserver2008/en/library/ea8d253e-0646 -490c-93d3-b78c5e1d9db71033.mspx*.

PRACTICE   **Configuring an RODC**

In this practice, you configure an RODC to simulate a branch office scenario. You install the RODC, configure password replication policy, monitor credential caching, and prepopulate credentials.

NOTE **RODC AND AD LDS**

In this practice, you promote the Boston server to an RODC. If you completed the practice in Lesson 1, the AD LDS server role is already installed on this server. In a production network, you would not promote a server that is running the AD LDS server role. In your test environment, the exercises work as written. However, you might decide to remove the AD LDS role on Boston before you promote the server. Lesson 1 details how to remove the AD LDS role.

EXERCISE 1   Create Active Directory Objects

In this exercise, you create Active Directory objects that you will use in the following exercises.

1. Log on to the Glasgow domain controller with the Kim_Akers account.

2. Open Active Directory Users And Computers.

3. Create the following Active Directory objects:

   - A global security group named Branch_Office_Users

   - A user named Jeff Hay

   - A user named Joe Healy

   - A user named Tanja Plate

- Put Jeff Hay and Joe Healy in Branch_Office_Users. Do not put Tanja Plate into this group. All three accounts will be members of Domain Users by default.

4. Add the Domain Users group as a member of the Print Operators group.

> **NOTE   PRINT OPERATORS GROUP**
>
> Adding standard user or group accounts to the Print Operators group enables users to log on interactively at a domain controller. You would not do this in a production environment.

5. Log off from the domain controller.

EXERCISE 2   Install an RODC

In this exercise, you configure the Boston server as an RODC in the *contoso.internal* domain.

1. Log on to the domain at Boston with the Kim_Akers account.
2. Click Start, click Run, and enter **dcpromo**.

   A window appears, informing you that the Active Directory Domain Services binaries are being installed. When installation completes, the Active Directory Domain Services Installation Wizard appears.
3. Click Next.
4. On the Operating System Compatibility page, click Next.
5. On the Choose A Deployment Configuration page, select Existing Forest, and then select Add A Domain Controller To An Existing Domain. Click Next.
6. On the Network Credentials page, type **contoso.internal**.
7. Click Set.
8. In the User Name box, type **Kim_Akers**.
9. In the Password box, type the password for the Kim_Akers account. Click OK.
10. Click Next.
11. On the Select A Domain page, select contoso.internal, and then click Next.
12. On the Select A Site page, select Default-First-Site-Name, and then click Next.

    Note that in a production environment, you would select the site for the branch office in which the RODC is being installed.
13. On the Additional Domain Controller Options page, select Read-Only Domain Controller (RODC). Ensure that DNS Server and Global Catalog are selected. Click Next.
14. On the Delegation Of RODC Installation And Administration page, click Next.
15. On the Location For Database, Log Files, And SYSVOL page, click Next.
16. On the Directory Services Restore Mode Administrator Password page, type a password in the Password and Confirm Password text boxes, and then click Next.

    Choose a secure password that you will remember but others are unlikely to guess.

17. On the Summary page, click Next.

18. In the progress window, select the Reboot On Completion check box.

EXERCISE 3   Configure Password Replication Policy

In this exercise, you configure PRP at the domain level and for an individual RODC. PRP determines whether the credentials of a user or computer are cached on an RODC.

1. Log on to Glasgow as Kim_Akers.

2. Open the Active Directory Users And Computers snap-in.

3. Expand the domain name and select Users.

4. Examine the default membership of the Allowed RODC Password Replication Group.

5. Open the properties of the Denied RODC Password Replication Group.

6. Add the DNSAdmins group as a member of the Denied RODC Password Replication Group, and then click OK twice.

7. Select the Domain Controllers OU.

8. Open the properties of Boston.

9. Click the Password Replication Policy tab.

10. Identify the PRP settings for the two groups, Allowed RODC Password Replication Group and Denied RODC Password Replication Group.

11. Click Add.

12. Select Allow Passwords For The Account To Replicate To This RODC and click OK.

13. In the Select Users, Computers, Or Groups dialog box, type **Branch_Office_Users** and click OK.

14. Click OK.

EXERCISE 4   Monitor Credential Caching

In this exercise, you simulate the logon of several users to the branch office server. You then evaluate the credentials caching of the server.

1. Log on to Boston as Jeff Hay, and then log off.

2. Log on to Boston as Tanja Plate, and then log off.

3. Log on to Glasgow as Kim_Akers and open the Active Directory Users And Computers snap-in.

4. Open the properties of Boston in the Domain Controllers OU.

5. Click the Password Replication Policy tab.

6. Click Advanced.

7. On the Policy Usage tab, in the Display Users And Computers That Meet The Following Criteria drop-down list, select Accounts Whose Passwords Are Stored On This Read-Only Domain Controller.

8. Locate the entry for Jeff Hay. Check that because you configured the PRP to allow caching of credentials for users in the Branch_Office_Users group, Jeff Hay's credentials were cached when he logged on. Check that Tanja Plate's credentials were not cached.

9. In the drop-down list, select Accounts That Have Been Authenticated To This Read-Only Domain Controller.

10. Locate the entries for Jeff Hay and Tanja Plate.

11. Click Close, and then click OK.

EXERCISE 5   **Prepopulate Credentials Caching**

In this exercise, you prepopulate the cache of the RODC with the credentials of a user.

1. Log on to Glasgow as Kim_Akers and open the Active Directory Users And Computers snap-in.

2. Open the properties of Boston in the Domain Controllers OU.

3. Click the Password Replication Policy tab.

4. Click Advanced.

5. Click Prepopulate Passwords.

6. Type **Joe Healy** and click OK.

7. Click Yes to confirm that you want to send the credentials to the RODC.

8. On the Policy Usage tab, select Accounts Whose Passwords Are Stored On This Read-Only Domain Controller.

9. Locate the entry for Joe Healy. Check that Joe Healy's credentials are now cached on the RODC.

10. Click OK.

Lesson Summary

- RODCs are designed for use in branch offices and contain a read-only copy of the Active Directory database. An RODC replicates domain updates from a writable domain controller, using inbound-only replication.

- PRP defines whether the credentials of the user or computer are cached on an RODC. The Allowed RODC Password Replication Group and Denied RODC Password Replication Group are in the Allowed List and Denied List, respectively. You can use the two groups to manage a domain-wide password replication policy. You can further configure the individual PRP of each domain controller.

- An RODC can be supported by configuring administrator role separation to enable one or more users to perform administrative tasks without granting those users permissions to other domain controllers or to the domain. The *dsmgmt* command implements administrator role separation.

- An RODC requires a Windows Server 2008 writable domain controller in the same domain. Additionally, the forest functional level must be at least Windows Server 2003, and the *adprep /rodcprep* command must be run prior to installing the first RODC.

Lesson Review

You can use the following questions to test your knowledge of the information in Lesson 2, "Configuring Read-Only Domain Controllers." The questions are also available on the companion DVD if you prefer to review them in electronic form.

> **NOTE   ANSWERS**
>
> Answers to these questions and explanations of why each answer choice is right or wrong are located in the "Answers" section at the end of the book.

1. You want to display in report format a list of user and computer credentials that an RODC has referred to a writable domain controller for authentication or service ticket processing. How do you do this?

   A. In Active Directory Users And Computers, open the properties of the RODC computer account in the Domain Controllers OU. Click Advanced on the Password Replication Policy tab. In the Advanced Password Replication Policy dialog box, select Accounts That Have Been Authenticated To This Read-Only Domain Controller from the drop-down list at the top of the Policy Usage tab.

   B. In Active Directory Users And Computers, open the properties of the RODC computer account in the Domain Controllers OU. Click Advanced on the Password Replication Policy tab. In the Advanced Password Replication Policy dialog box, select Accounts Whose Passwords Are Stored On This Read-Only Domain Controller from the drop-down list at the top of the Policy Usage tab.

   C. In Active Directory Users And Computers, expand the domain name and select Users. Examine the membership of the Allowed RODC Password Replication Group.

   D. In Active Directory Users And Computers, expand the domain name and select Users. Examine the membership of the Denied RODC Password Replication Group.

2. A new employee is joining one of the branch offices of Tailspin Toys. The branch office contains an RODC. You want to ensure that when the user logs on for the first time, she does not experience problems authenticating over the WAN link. You create an account for the new user. Which other steps should you perform? (Choose two. Each step presents part of a complete solution.)

   A. Add the user's account to the Password Replication Policy tab of the branch office RODC.

   B. Add the user's account to the Allowed RODC Password Replication Group.

C. Click Prepopulate Passwords.

D. Add the user's account to the Log On Locally security policy on the Default Domain Controllers Policy GPO.

3. During a recent burglary at a branch office of Litware, Inc., the RODC was stolen. Where can you find out which users' credentials were stored on the RODC?

A. The Policy Usage tab of the Advanced Password Replication Policy dialog box

B. Active Directory Domains and Trusts

C. The Resultant Policy tab of the Advanced Password Replication Policy dialog box

D. The Password Replication Policy tab of the RODC computer account Properties dialog box

4. Your domain consists of seven domain controllers, one of which is running Windows Server 2008. All other domain controllers are running Windows Server 2003. What must you do before you install an RODC?

A. Run *dsmgmt.*

B. Run *adprep /rodcprep.*

C. Run *dcpromo /unattend.*

D. Run *syskey.*

Chapter Review

To further practice and reinforce the skills you learned in this chapter, you can perform the following tasks:

- Review the chapter summary.
- Complete the case scenarios. These scenarios set up real-world situations involving the topics of this chapter and ask you to create a solution.
- Complete the suggested practices.
- Take a practice test.

Chapter Summary

- You can use AD LDS rather than AD DS where Active Directory features such as Group Policy are not required and you do not want to extend the AD DS schema. AD LDS can be installed and configured on both full installation and Server Core.
- After you have installed the AD LDS service, you can create an AD LDS instance. You can create replicas of instances on other servers and configure replication. You can create more than one AD LDS instance on the same server.
- RODCs support branch office scenarios and reduce security risks by authenticating users in the branch office without needing to store the entire account database. You can configure which credentials an RODC will cache. You can also delegate both installation and administration of an RODC without granting permissions to other domain controllers or to the domain.

Case Scenarios

In the following case scenarios, you apply what you have learned about AD LDS and RODCs. You can find answers to the questions in these scenarios in the "Answers" section at the end of this book.

Case Scenario 1: Create AD LDS Instances

Trey Research has upgraded all its domain controllers to Windows Server 2008, and the company wants to use AD LDS to support its applications. Specifically, they want each application to be an AD LDS instance. Trey has employed you as a consultant to carry out this task. Answer the following questions.

1. How should you name each instance?
2. Where should you store the files related to each instance?
3. Why should you use application directory partitions?
4. Which ports should you use to connect to the instances?

5. Which type of account should you use to run each instance?

6. How would you prevent an attacker from tampering with or detecting AD LDS data?

Case Scenario 2: Prepare to Install an RODC at a Branch Office

You are an administrator at the A. Datum Corporation and maintain the domain's directory service on five domain controllers at your hub site. All five domain controllers run Windows Server 2003. A. Datum has decided to open an overseas branch office. Initially, fifteen salespersons and one desktop-maintenance technician will be employed at the office. You decide to place an RODC in the branch office. Answer the following questions.

1. What preliminary tasks must you complete before installing an RODC or configuring your network so that a non–domain administrator can install one?

2. You do not want to send one of your IT staff overseas to install an RODC. How do you enable the local desktop-maintenance technician to create an RODC without making this technician a domain administrator?

3. You want the technician to be able to log on to the RODC to perform regular maintenance. How do you configure administrator role separation?

4. You want the RODC to cache the credentials of each of the salespersons the first time he or she logs on. How do you achieve this?

5. You do not want the technician's credentials to be cached. How do you achieve this?

6. Your CEO will be visiting the new branch office. How do you ensure that there is no authentication delay over the WAN link even when he or she logs on for the first time?

Suggested Practices

To help you successfully master the exam objectives presented in this chapter, complete the following tasks.

Work with AD LDS Instances

Do both suggested practices.

- **Practice 1** Practice connecting and working with the AD LDS instance you created earlier in this chapter. Use the following tools to explore the instance and view its content:
  - Active Directory Schema snap-in
  - Active Directory Sites and Services
  - *Ldp.exe*
  - ADSI Edit

- **Practice 2** Practice creating objects within the instance. For example, create an OU and add both a group and a user within the OU.

Recover from a Stolen RODC

In this practice, you perform the processes to recover from a stolen or compromised RODC. In this situation, any user credentials cached on the RODC should be considered suspect and reset. You must identify the credentials that had been cached on the RODC and reset the password of each account. Do both practices.

- **Practice 1** Determine the user and computer accounts that had been cached on Boston by examining the Policy Usage tab of the Boston Advanced Password Replication Policy dialog box. Use the steps in Exercise 4, "Monitor Credential Caching," in the Lesson 2 practice, "Configuring an RODC," to identify accounts whose passwords were stored on the RODC. Export the list to a file on your desktop.

- **Practice 2** Open the Active Directory Users And Computers snap-in and, in the Domain Controllers OU, select Boston. Press Delete and click Yes. Examine the options for resetting user and computer passwords automatically.

Take a Practice Test

The practice tests on this book's companion DVD offer many options. For example, you can test yourself on just one exam objective, or you can test yourself on all the upgrade exam content. You can set up the test so that it closely simulates the experience of taking a certification exam, or you can set it up in study mode so that you can look at the correct answers and explanations after you answer each question.

> **MORE INFO** **PRACTICE TESTS**
>
> For details about all the practice test options available, see the "How to Use the Practice Tests" section in this book's introduction.

Active Directory Federation Services and Active Directory Rights Management Services Server Roles

Active Directory Federation Services (AD FS) is designed to extend the authority of your internal network and facilitate the formation of partnerships with other organizations. AD FS communicates over HTTPS port 443 so that sensitive data can be secured and encrypted. It enables single sign-on (SSO) so that—for example—Don Hall, a user logged on to the Contoso domain, can access a collaboration application hosted by Contoso's partner organization, Northwind Traders, without needing to supply additional credentials.

Active Directory Rights Management Services (AD RMS) protects intellectual property through the integration of several Active Directory technologies such as Active Directory Domain Services (AD DS) and Active Directory Certificate Services (AD CS). AD FS extends AD RMS policies beyond the firewall and protects your organization's intellectual property among your business partners.

This chapter aims to give a deeper understanding of AD FS and AD RMS, discusses their installation and configuration, and explains how they interact with each other and with other Active Directory technologies.

Exam objectives in this chapter:

- Configure Active Directory Federation Services (AD FS).
- Configure Active Directory Rights Management Services (AD RMS).

Lessons in this chapter:

Before You Begin

To complete the lessons in this chapter, you must have done the following:

- Installed a Windows Server 2008 Enterprise server configured as a domain controller in the *contoso.internal* domain as described in Chapter 1, "Configuring Internet Protocol Addressing."

- Installed a Windows Server 2008 Enterprise server in the *contoso.internal* domain as described in Chapter 2, "Configuring IP Services." If you completed the practices in Chapter 5, "Configuring Active Directory Lightweight Directory Services and Read-Only Domain Controllers," this server might currently have the Active Directory Lightweight Directory Services (AD LDS) server role installed and be configured as a read-only domain controller (RODC). In this case, remove the AD LDS role as described in Chapter 5 and then run the *dcpromo* command to demote the computer to a member server.

> **NOTE TESTING AD FS FUNCTIONS**
>
> To test AD FS and AD RMS functions fully, you need two forests and at least seven servers, two of them domain controllers, plus several client computers. Even with Hyper-V virtualization, this is a requirement that is probably beyond the capability of most test setups. The considerable time taken to configure such a test network would almost certainly be better spent answering practice test questions. In this chapter, the practices are kept brief and straightforward, and the AD FS and AD RMS server roles are installed on a domain controller. This is not recommended in a production network. A case study is included to give you a feel for full AD FS installation.

Lesson 1: Installing, Configuring, and Using AD FS

Securing an organizational network against attacks from external networks—typically but not exclusively the Internet—presents problems about which every network engineer is aware and which have led to the development of firewalls, virtual private networks (VPNs), perimeter networks, and security technologies such as intrusion detection systems. Possibly the most difficult problem that faces a network professional is to secure a network without impairing potential partnerships such as those created through forest trusts.

You will almost certainly have studied forest trusts for your Windows Server 2003 examinations and will be aware that they enable organizations to extend the security contexts of their own internal forests to trust partner forests. However, implementing forest trusts requires an administrator to set up complex, semipermanent VPN links between disparate organizations or to open specific ports in a firewall to support AD DS. Also, forest trusts can be difficult to manage, particularly in multiple partnerships.

Trust relationships are powerful entities and have their place in fully featured inter-organizational relationships. However, there existed a perceived need for partners to access a specific and limited set of resources without all the facilities and complexity involved in a full trust relationship.

To address this need, Microsoft introduced AD FS—which is often described as a limited trust relationship. The AD FS service provides external support for the internal identity and access (IDA) services that AD DS requires and extends the authority of your internal network to external networks. In this lesson, you learn how AD FS authenticates a user, how you install and configure the service, and how you manage the trusts and certificates it requires.

After this lesson, you will be able to:

- Describe the AD FS authentication process.
- List the components used in an AD FS implementation.
- Install the AD FS server role.
- Manage AD FS certificates.
- Configure AD FS servers.
- Configure AD FS trust policies.

Estimated lesson time: 60 minutes

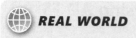

REAL WORLD

Ian McLean

A few years ago I was involved in a very large project that involved collaboration between a number of organizations that strongly defended the security, integrity, and independence of their networks. I've no problems with defending security and integrity, but sometimes independence can be a problem when collaboration is required.

For reasons far too complex to go into here, VPNs were not seen as an appropriate solution. Trust relationships required collaboration so they could be set up at both ends. I lost count of the number of times I had to tell network administrators that I wasn't asking them to trust me. I was asking them to permit me to trust them. And when it came to anything whatsoever that involved a firewall—well, I'd rather not go into that can of worms.

So when it came to a second project that required SSO and involved the same set of organizations, I was wary about trusts, VPNs, and firewalls. The central organization for which I was working was the resource organization. It was not asking to be able to access resources owned by its partner organizations; it was permitting them to use its resources. I needed a solution that allowed account partners to access a specific and limited set of resources and required little or no network reconfiguration on their part.

AD FS wasn't around at the time, which was a pity because that's exactly what it does.

Understanding AD FS

AD FS is an SSO facility that allows users of external Web-based applications to access and authenticate through a browser. It relies on the internal authentication store of the user's own domain to authenticate a client and does not have a store of its own. It also relies upon the original authentication clients perform in their own networks and passes this authentication to Web applications that are AD FS–enabled. To return to the example earlier in this chapter, Don Hall from Contoso, Ltd., should be able to log on to the password-protected Northwind Traders Web site by using his *d.hall@contoso.com* account and without needing to supply additional credentials.

With AD FS, organizations need to manage only a single authentication store for their own users. If you use an AD LDS directory for extranet authentication, this adds administrative overhead because the organization then needs to manage its own internal store and an external store or stores. Users must remember several access codes and passwords to log on to each of these stores. It is difficult enough for most users to remember a single name and password, never mind several. AD FS, alternatively, federates a user's internal AD DS identity and submits it to external networks. Users need to authenticate only once.

For example, David Hamilton, Nancy Anderson, and Jeff Hay buy supplies for Wingtip Toys from Wide World Importers, an organization with which their company has a long-standing relationship. David, Nancy, and Jeff need to log on to Web applications at World Wide Importers. Unfortunately, Wide World Importers has different username and password policies, and David, Nancy, and Jeff need to remember two sets of logon names and passwords, which regularly change. AD FS allows Wingtip Toys and World Wide Importers to set up a partnership so that David, Nancy, and Jeff can log on to these Web applications using their Wingtip Toys credentials and do not need to log on twice and remember two usernames and two passwords to do their jobs.

Unlike forest trusts, AD FS does not use Lightweight Directory Access Protocol (LDAP) ports but rather the common HTTP ports, specifically port 443, so all AD FS trust communications can be secured and encrypted. AD FS relies on AD CS to manage certificates for each server in the AD FS implementation. AD FS can also extend AD RMS deployment and provide federation services for intellectual property management between partners.

> **NOTE NAMED SERVICE ACCOUNTS**
>
> AD FS, like all Active Directory services, can use a named service account. However, if you install the AD FS role on a Windows Server 2008 server, or if you upgrade Federation Services running under Windows Server 2003 R2 to AD FS, the service runs by default under the Network Service account.

EXAM TIP

Windows Server 2003 R2 introduced AD FS, and you might or might not have studied it for your Windows Server 2003 examinations. Even if you did, you should spend some time looking at the service again because Windows Server 2008 introduces some significant enhancements.

AD FS provides extensions to internal forests and enables your organization to create partnerships without needing to open any additional ports on its firewall. It relies on each partner's internal AD DS directory to provide authentication for extranet or perimeter services. When a user attempts to authenticate to an application integrated to AD FS, the AD FS engine polls the internal directory for authentication data. Users who have access provided through the internal directory are granted access to the external application. This means that each partner needs to manage authentication data only in its internal network. The federation services of AD FS do all the rest.

Use AD FS whenever you want to implement a partnership with other organizations that also rely on internal AD DS directories. If, however, you need to provide authentication services in your perimeter network but the users or organizations with which you want to interact do not have internal AD DS directories, or the scope of the partnership does not warrant an AD FS deployment, use (for example) AD LDS. Account partners can have stores in AD DS, AD LDS, or ADAM and do not need AD DS to work with AD FS.

> **NOTE AD LDS, AD CS, AND AD RMS**
>
> You will find more information about AD LDS in Chapter 5; more information about AD CS in Chapter 7, "Active Directory Certificate Services"; and more information about AD RMS in Lesson 2, "Installing, Configuring, and Using AD RMS," of this chapter.

Business-to-Business Partnerships

You can use AD FS to form business-to-business (B2B) partnerships. In this arrangement, partners can be account or resource organizations (or both). These can be described as follows:

- **Account organizations**   Manage the accounts used to access the shared resources in SSO scenarios. Account organizations join partnerships created by resource organizations and access the resources in these organizations.

- **Resource organizations**   Form the partnerships in SSO scenarios. An organization that has resources (such as a collaboration Web site) can use AD FS to simplify the authentication process to these resources by forming partnerships that account organizations then join. The organization that initially forms the partnership is deemed the resource organization because it hosts the shared resources in its perimeter network.

> **NOTE ACCOUNT AND RESOURCE ORGANIZATIONS**
>
> In the example given earlier in this lesson, David, Nancy, and Jeff are logged on to the Wingtip Toys forest and can access Web applications at Wide World Importers without needing to supply additional credentials. In this case, Wingtip Toys is the account organization (or account partner) and Wide World Importers is the resource organization (or resource partner).

> **NOTE WEB SSO DESIGN**
>
> In a Web SSO design, discussed later in this lesson, AD FS can authenticate users from anywhere on the Internet. After a user accessing from the Internet has been authenticated, AD FS examines the user's attributes in AD DS or in AD LDS directories to identify what rights the user has to the application to which he or she is authenticating.

AD FS Components

AD FS uses the following components:

- Claims
- Cookies
- Certificates

CLAIMS

A claim is a statement the federation server makes about a user or client. Claims are stored as AD DS attributes that each partner in an AD FS relationship attaches to its user accounts. They can be based on several values—for example, usernames, certificate keys, membership of security groups, and so on. Claims are included in the signed security token AD FS sends to the Web application and are used for authorization. They can be based on user identity (the identity claim type) or on security group membership (the group claim type). Claims can also be based on custom information (the custom claim type), for example, a custom identification number such as employee number or bank account number. The federation server filters claims as part of the AD FS authentication process. This greatly reduces the overall number of claims an organization needs to manage.

> **MORE INFO** **AD FS CLAIMS**
>
> For more information on AD FS claims, see *http://technet.microsoft.com/en-us/library /cc730612.aspx*.

COOKIES

User browsers hold cookies that are generated during Web sessions authenticated through AD FS. AD FS uses authentication cookies, account partner cookies, and sign-out cookies. When a user is authenticated through AD FS, an authentication cookie is placed within the user's browser to support SSO for additional authentications. This cookie includes all the claims for the user. It is a session cookie and is erased after the session is closed.

The AD FS process writes an account partner cookie when a client announces its account partner membership during authentication, so it does not need to perform partner discovery again the next time the client authenticates. An account partner cookie is long-lived and persistent.

Each time the federation service assigns a token, it adds the resource partner or target server linked to the token to a sign-out cookie. The authentication process uses sign-out cookies for various purposes, for example, for cleanup operations at the end of a user session. A sign-out cookie is a session cookie and is erased after the session is closed.

MORE INFO **AD FS COOKIES**

For more information on AD FS cookies, see *http://technet.microsoft.com/en-us/library
/cc770382.aspx.*

CERTIFICATES

AD FS communications must be encrypted at all times, and this requires several certificate types. The type of certificate required by the role depends on its purpose.

A federation server requires both a server authentication certificate and a token-signing certificate. In addition, the trust policy requires a verification certificate. The server authentication certificate is a Secure Sockets Layer (SSL) authentication certificate that is typically requested and installed through IIS Manager.

A token-signing certificate is made up of a private and public key pair. When a federation server generates a security token, it digitally signs the token with its token-signing certificate. A verification certificate is used during the verification process that takes place between servers when there is more than one federation server in a deployment. It contains only the public key of the token-signing certificate.

A Federation Service Proxy requires a server authentication certificate to support SSL-encrypted communications with Web clients. It also needs a client authentication certificate (known as a Federation Service Proxy certificate) to authenticate the federation server during communications. Both private and public keys for this certificate are stored on the proxy. The public key is also stored on the federation server and in the trust policy. A Web server hosting the AD FS Web agent also requires a server authentication certificate to secure its communications with Web clients.

NOTE **CERTIFICATES AND OUTWARD-FACING ROLES**

Many AD FS roles are outward-facing. Therefore, your certificates should be from a trusted certification authority (CA). If you use Active Directory–generated certificates, you need to modify the Trusted CA store on each Web client. AD FS relies on AD CS to manage these certificates.

MORE INFO **AD FS CERTIFICATES**

For more information on AD FS certificates, see *http://technet.microsoft.com/en-us/library
/cc730660.aspx.*

✔ **Quick Check**

- Which claim types does AD FS support?

Quick Check Answer

- AD FS supports three claim types:

  - **Identity claims**   These can be user principal name, e-mail address, or common name.

  - **Group claims**   These consist of membership in specific distribution or security groups in AD DS.

  - **Custom claims**   These can include custom information such as a user's bank account number.

AD FS Role Services

Federated identity is the process of authenticating a user's credentials across multiple IT systems and organizations. Identity federation enables users in one domain to access data or systems of another domain securely by using SSO. AD FS relies on the following role services to support identity federation:

- **Federation Service**   A server running the Federation Service (a federation server) routes authentication requests to the appropriate source directory to generate security tokens for the user requesting access. Servers that share a trust policy use this service.

- **Federation Service Proxy**   A federation server relies on a proxy server that is located in the perimeter network to obtain authentication requests from a user. The proxy collects authentication information from the user's browser through the WS-Federation Passive Requestor Profile (WS-F PRP), an AD FS Web service, and passes it on to the Federation Service.

WS-Federation

WS-Federation is an Identity Federation specification that was developed by BEA Systems; BMC Software; CA, Inc.; IBM; Layer 7 Technologies; Microsoft; Novell; and VeriSign. It is part of the larger Web Services Security framework and defines mechanisms for allowing disparate security realms to broker information on identities, identity attributes, and authentication. For more information about WS-Federation, see *http://msdn.microsoft.com/en-us/library/bb498017.aspx*.

- **Windows token-based agent**   A Windows token-based agent converts an AD FS security token into an impersonation-level Windows NT access token that is recognized by applications that rely on Windows authentication rather than on Web-based authentication.

- **Claims-aware agent**   A claims-aware agent on a Web server initiates queries of security token claims to the Federation Service. Each claim is used to grant or deny access to a given application. (For example, ASP.NET applications that examine the various claims contained in the user's AD FS security token are claims-aware applications.) These applications rely on the claims to determine user access to the application. Claims are discussed later in this lesson. AD RMS, discussed in Lesson 2, is a claims-aware application, as is Microsoft Office SharePoint Server 2007.

AD FS is based on a Web service and does not rely only on AD DS to support federated identities. Any directory service that adheres to the WS-Federation standard can participate in an AD FS identity federation.

Federation Services existed in Windows Server 2003 R2, but Windows Server 2008 improves AD FS significantly to facilitate its installation and administration processes. Windows Server 2008 AD FS also supports a wider variety of Web applications than did the original AD FS release.

> *MORE INFO*   **AD FS**
>
> For more information about AD FS and the enhancements Windows Server 2008 introduces, see *http://technet2.microsoft.com/windowsserver2008/en/servermanager /activedirectoryfederationservices.mspx* and follow the links.

AD FS Architectural Designs

AD FS supports three configurations or architectural designs, depending on the type of B2B partnership you need to establish. Each supports a particular partnership scenario. These architectural designs are:

- **Federated Web SSO**   This is the most common AD FS deployment scenario and typically spans several firewalls. It links applications contained within an extranet in a resource organization to the internal directory stores of account organizations. The federation trust is the only trust used in this model. A federation trust is a one-way trust from the resource organization to the account organization(s).

MORE INFO   **FEDERATION TRUSTS**

For more information about federation trusts, see *http://technet.microsoft.com/en-us /library/cc770993.aspx*.

- **Web SSO**   Web SSO is deployed when all users of an extranet application are external. This model allows users to authenticate using SSO to multiple Web applications. It relies on multihomed Web servers that are connected to both the internal and external network and that are part of the AD DS domain. The Federation Service Proxy is also multihomed to provide access to both the external and the internal network.

- **Federated Web SSO with Forest Trust**   In this model, a forest trust is established between an external forest in the perimeter network and an internal forest, and a federation trust is established between the resource federation server located within the perimeter and the account federation server located in the internal network. Internal users have access to the applications from both the internal network and the Internet, whereas external users have access to the applications only from the Internet. Microsoft does not recommend hosting an AD DS forest in a perimeter network. You should instead use AD FS and AD LDS to achieve the same user experience.

The most common scenarios are Web SSO and Federated Web SSO. Ideally, all members of an identity federation deployment have their own AD DS directory and act as account organizations to simplify the deployment strategy.

EXAM TIP

You should not ignore the Federated Web SSO with Forest Trust architectural model, even though Microsoft does not recommend it. It could appear in an upgrade examination, possibly as an incorrect answer.

AD FS Authentication

When an AD FS partnership is in place, users can log on transparently to external Web applications included in the partnership. In a typical AD FS scenario, a user logs on to a claims-aware Web application in an extranet, and AD FS automatically provisions the user's credentials and outlines the claims included in the user's AD DS account attributes. Figure 6-1 illustrates the process.

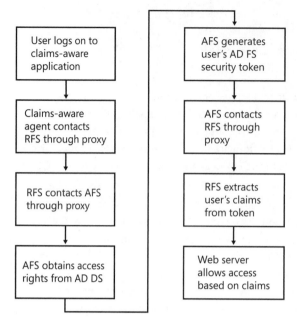

FIGURE 6-1 AD FS authentication.

A more detailed high-level description of the process is as follows:

1. A user attempts to log on to a claims-aware application in an extranet.

2. The claims-aware agent on the Web server contacts a resource federation server (RFS) in the resource organization through a Federation Service Proxy (FSP).

3. The RFS accesses an account federation server (AFS) in the account organization's internal network, again through a proxy, to identify the user's access rights.

4. The AFS obtains access rights from AD DS through an LDAP query. These access rights are listed in the form of claims linked to the user's account object in AD DS.

5. The AFS generates the user's AD FS security token. This includes the claims linked in the user's AD DS account. Security tokens also identify the user and include the AFS digital certificate.

6. The AFS contacts the RFS through the proxy server and sends the security token.

7. The RFS decrypts the token and extracts the user's claims. It filters them, depending upon the access requirements of the Web application and generates a signed security token. The signature for the token is based either on the RFS digital certificate or on a Kerberos session key.

8. The signed security token is sent to the Web server in the resource organization's extranet. The claims-aware agent on the Web server decrypts the token and grants access to the Web application based on the claims in the token. A local authentication cookie is generated in the user's browser so the process is not repeated if the user needs to authenticate again during this session.

✔ **Quick Check**

1. What are the four role services and features that make up the AD FS server role?

2. What are the three AD FS architectural designs?

Quick Check Answers

1. AD FS includes the following role services:

   - The Federation Service role service provides the core AD FS functionality. It manages resource access, claims filtering, and security token generation.

   - The Federation Service Proxy role service is an Internet relay that passes requests on to internal Federation Service servers.

   - The Windows token-based agent supports the integration of Windows applications to AD FS processes.

   - The claims-aware agent supports the integration of Web applications with AD FS processes.

2. AD FS supports three architectural designs: Federated Web SSO, Web SSO, and Federated Web SSO with Forest Trust.

Configuring AD FS

Servers in an AD FS relationship rely on certificates to create a chain of trust and ensure that all traffic transported over the relationship is encrypted at all times. To ensure that the chain of trust is valid and trusted in all locations, you can obtain certificates from a trusted third-party CA or through the creation of a linked implementation of AD CS that uses a trusted third-party CA as its root.

When you deploy AD FS, you need to configure AD FS–aware applications, trust policies between partner organizations, and claims for your users and groups. After you install and deploy AD FS, you need to carry out the following configuration tasks:

- Configure the Web service on each AD FS server to use SSL/TLS encryption on the Web site that hosts the AD FS service. You will learn more about this in Chapter 13, "Configuring a Web Services Infrastructure."

- Configure IIS on servers that host claims-aware applications.

- Export certificates from each server and import them on the other servers in the relationship.

- Create and configure the claims-aware applications you are hosting.

- On the federation servers in both account and resource organizations, configure the trust policy, create claims for users, and configure the AD DS account store for identity federation. In a resource organization, you also then enable the claims-aware applications.

- Create the federation trust to enable identity federation by exporting the trust policy from the account organization and importing it into the resource organization, creating and configuring a claim mapping in the resource organization, and exporting the partner policy from the resource organization so you can import it into the account organization.

Details about the configurations you require in both account and resource partners are given in the case study later in this lesson. Much of the configuration process involves certificate mapping from one server to another. You need to be able to access the certificate revocation lists (CRL) for each certificate. CRLs indicate to a member of a trust chain whether a certificate is valid.

In AD FS, CRL checking is enabled by default. Typically, CRL checking is performed for security token signatures, but Microsoft recommends that you rely on it for all digital signatures. For more information about certificates, CRLs, and trust chains, see Chapter 7.

AD CS Online Responder

I f it is supported, you can use the AD CS Online Responder implemented by the Microsoft Online Responder service from AD CS to configure and manage Online Certificate Status Protocol (OCSP) validation and revocation checking in Windows-based networks. The Online Responder snap-in enables you to configure and manage revocation configurations and Online Responder Arrays to support public key infrastructure (PKI) clients in diverse environments.

For more information about AD CS Online Responder and the Microsoft Online Responder service, see *http://technet.microsoft.com/en-us/library/cc774575.aspx*. For more information about OCSP, see *http://www.ietf.org/rfc/rfc2560.txt*. For more information about Online Responder Arrays, see *http://technet.microsoft.com/en-us /library/cc731175.aspx*. For more information about PKI and the Enterprise PKI snap-in, see *http://technet.microsoft.com/en-us/library/cc771400.aspx*. Chapter 7 also discusses Online Responders.

Managing AD FS

When you have configured the identity federation, you need to administer and manage AD FS services and server roles. You can use the Active Directory Federation Services console in Server Manager to perform these tasks. Administration and management tasks include the following:

- Configuring the Federation Service for each group of servers or federation server farm. A federation server farm can include several servers hosting the same role. You can also have a Federation Service Proxy farm and a claims-aware application server farm running IIS.

■ Administering account stores in AD DS or AD LDS.

■ Managing account partners and resource partners that trust your organization.

■ Managing claims.

■ Managing certificates on federation servers and in AD FS–protected Web applications.

Many federation server settings that you configure in Server Manager are stored in the Web.config file located in the Federation Service virtual directory in IIS. Figure 6-2 shows this file. As yet, no configuration has been added.

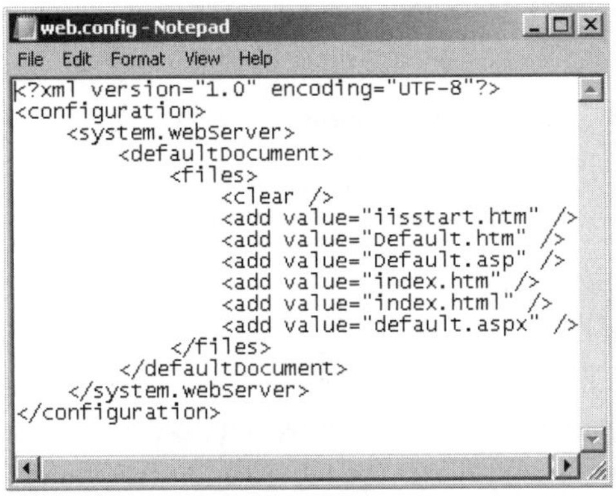

```
web.config - Notepad
File  Edit  Format  View  Help
<?xml version="1.0" encoding="UTF-8"?>
<configuration>
    <system.webServer>
        <defaultDocument>
            <files>
                <clear />
                <add value="iisstart.htm" />
                <add value="Default.htm" />
                <add value="Default.asp" />
                <add value="index.htm" />
                <add value="index.html" />
                <add value="default.aspx" />
            </files>
        </defaultDocument>
    </system.webServer>
</configuration>
```

FIGURE 6-2 The Web.config file.

Other configuration settings are stored in the trust policy file. You can use a text editor to edit the Web.config file directly and specify the following settings:

■ The path to the trust policy file

■ The path to the log files directory

■ The local token-signing certificate

■ The location of the ASP.NET Web pages that support the service

■ The debug logging level for the service

■ The access type specification

You can publish the Web.config file to other servers requiring the same configuration settings. When you restart the IIS service, the new configuration takes effect.

CAUTION **DO NOT EDIT THE TRUST POLICY FILE MANUALLY**

The Web.config file holds the path to the trust policy file. Microsoft recommends that, unlike the Web.config file, you should never edit the trust policy file manually. You should always configure the settings for this file through the AD FS console or through program settings that rely on the AD FS object model.

MORE INFO SCRIPTING SUPPORT AND THE AD FS OBJECT MODEL

For more information on scripting support and the AD FS object model, see *http://msdn2. microsoft.com/en-us/library/ms674895.aspx.*

You can use the AD FS console to configure the following on an FSP:

- The Federation Service that the FSP works with
- How the FSP collects user credentials from browsers and Web applications

Federation Service Proxy configurations are also stored in a Web.config file. The FSP does not host a trust policy file, and all its settings are stored within the Web.config file. These include the following:

- The URL for the Federation Service
- The client authentication certificate to be used by the federation server proxy to encrypt TLS/SSL communications with the Federation Service
- The path to the ASP.NET Web pages supporting the service

AD FS Deployment (Case Study)

On a production network, AD FS operates over a number of computers. Typically, the service works across at least two AD DS domains, each with a perimeter network, and AD FS servers distributed within each environment. The account organization hosts AD DS and at least one federation server internally and an FSP in its perimeter network. The resource organization(s) should each host at least one AD DS domain and at least one internal federation server. Their perimeter networks should include at least one AD FS–enabled Web server and one FSP. The deployment is based on considerations such as the number of partner organizations, the type of applications to share, and the requirement for high availability and load balancing.

Computer clocks need to be synchronized to the same time. If there is more than five minutes' time difference between servers, AD FS will not work because the token time stamps are invalid. AD FS involves a partnership between different organizations with separate forests, so you must rely on a third-party time server and use the Network Time Protocol (NTP). As a Windows Server 2003 professional, you should be familiar with NTP.

This case study discusses a minimum deployment. In the production environment, an organization would have multiple domain controllers (DCs), federation servers, and proxies to implement fail-over protection and a number of client computers at which users log on. Also, this case study does not include perimeter networks, which require complex TCP/IP configuration. AD FS deployments in a production network require proper server placement within perimeter networks.

NOTE **COMMUNICATE WITH THE OTHER ADMINISTRATOR**

If you are setting up a federation partnership with another organization, your first step should be to get in touch with your counterpart in that organization to determine how you will exchange policy files while setting up the partnership.

In the case study, the *tailspintoys.com* account domain uses the following Windows Server 2008 servers in its AD FS deployment:

- **TailspinToysDC** The AD DS domain controller for *tailspintoys.com*.
- **TailspinToysFed** The federation server for *tailspintoys.com*. This server is also a root CA.
- **TalispinToysProxy** The Federation Service Proxy for *tailspintoys.com*.

The *treyresearch.net* resource domain uses the following Windows Server 2008 servers in its AD FS deployment:

- **TreyResearchDC** The AD DS domain controller for *treyresearch.net*.
- **TreyResearchFed** The federation server for *treyresearch.net*.
- **TreyResearchProxy** The Federation Service Proxy and AD FS–enabled Web server for *treyresearch.net*.

In the simple configuration discussed in this case study, first configure cross–Domain Name System (DNS) references in each forest and then install the federation servers. Install the Federation Service Proxy role service in both forests and AD FS–enable the Web site in the resource forest.

Configuring Cross-DNS References

Each forest is independent of the other, and their DNS servers do not know about each other. You therefore need to configure the DNS servers in each forest with cross-DNS references that refer to the servers in the other forest. The simplest method is to specify forwarders from one domain to the other and vice versa. Figure 6-3 shows an IPv4 address of one DNS server being added to the Forwarders tab on the DNS server in the other forest.

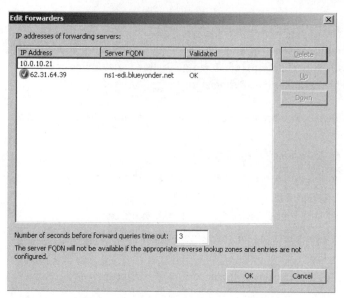

FIGURE 6-3 Specifying the IPv4 address of a DNS forwarder.

Installing the Federation Servers

To install the federation servers, install the AD FS server role plus the required role services on TailspinToysFed and TreyResearchFed. You install the AD FS role on a designated computer that will become a federation server in the practice later in this lesson.

> **IMPORTANT WINDOWS SERVER 2008 EDITIONS**
>
> The AD FS role can be installed only on Enterprise and Datacenter editions.

> **NOTE VIRTUALIZATION**
>
> In a production network federation, servers are good candidates for Hyper-V virtualization. Federation Service Proxies on the peripheral network have specific configuration and security requirements and are less frequently implemented as virtual machines.

Installing the Federation Service Proxies

Installing an FSP involves the installation of the AD DS server role plus the required support services for the role. You install an FSP in the practice later in this lesson.

NOTE FEDERATION SERVICE PROXY AND FEDERATION SERVER

You cannot add the Federation Service Proxy on the same server as the federation server. However, you can combine the FSP and the AD FS Web Agents role services on the same server.

Configuring SSL for the Federation Servers and the FSPs

Configure the IIS server to require SSL on each of the federation servers. Map certificates from one server to the other and configure the Web server. You can also create and configure the claims-aware Web application and then configure the federation servers for each partner organization. Finally, create the federation trust. Configure IIS to require SSL on the Default Web Site of the federation servers and the Federation Service Proxies on the SSL Settings page in Internet Information Services (IIS) Manager as shown in Figure 6-4.

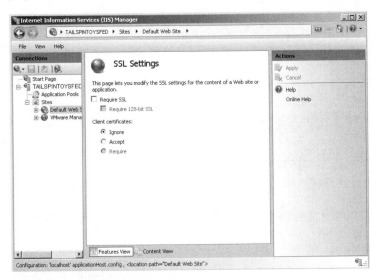

FIGURE 6-4 The SSL Settings page.

NOTE 128-BIT SSL

In a production environment, you would typically specify 128-bit SSL, which is more secure but requires additional processing overhead.

Exporting and Importing Certificates

When you set up federation partnerships, you need to integrate the certificates from each server to link to the server with which it needs to communicate. Create a file share that each server can access and export the token-signing certificate from the account federation server (TailspinToysFed) to a file in that share. Export the server authentication certificate of the same server (TailspinToysFed) to a file.

Export the server authentication certificate of the resource federation server (TreyResearchFed) to a file and import the server authentication certificate for both federation servers. In addition, export the client authentication certificate of the account Federation Service Proxy (TalispinToysProxy) to a file.

Now, export the client authentication certificate of the resource Federation Service Proxy (TreyResearchProxy) to a file and import the client authentication certificate on the respective federation servers. To do all these tasks, create the file share you will use to store the certificates. Ensure that you use DER Encoded Binary X.509 (.cer) format when you export the certificates. You do this on the Export File Format page of the Certificate Export Wizard, shown in Figure 6-5.

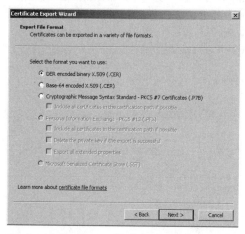

FIGURE 6-5 The Export File Format page.

Table 6-1 outlines which certificates must be exported and where they must be imported.

TABLE 6-1 AD FS Certificate Mappings

SERVER NAME	CERTIFICATE NAME	CERTIFICATE TYPE	IMPORT LOCATION
TailspinToysFed	TailspinToysFedToken-Signing.cer	Token Signing	TreyResearchFed
TailspinToysFed	TailspinToysFedSSL.cer	SSL Server Authentication	TalispinToysProxy
TalispinToysProxy	TalispinToysProxySSL.cer	SSL Client Authentication	TailspinToysFed
TreyResearchFed	TreyResearchFedSSL.cer	SSL Server Authentication	TreyResearchProxy
TreyResearchProxy	TreyResearchProxySSL.cer	SSL Client Authentication	TreyResearchFed

NOTE   TOKEN-SIGNING CERTIFICATES

As described earlier in this lesson, a token-signing certificate contains a public and private key pair. You can obtain a token-signing certificate from a third-party CA and install it according to the CA's instructions. Even if you use third-party CAs for other certificates, you can generate a self-signed token-signing certificate in the account organization and export it to the resource organization. For more information about creating a self-signed token-signing certificate, see *http://technet.microsoft.com/en-us/library/cc780178.aspx*.

MORE INFO   CODE-SIGNING OBJECT IDENTITY (OID)

Your examinations are unlikely to test you on specific certificate OIDs, but if you are look-ing for more information about the code-signing OID used for token-signing certificates through professional interest, see *http://www.alvestrand.no/objectid/1.3.6.1.5.5.7.3.3.html/.*

Exporting the SSL Server and Client Certificates and Importing an SSL Authentication Certificate

Now, export the SSL server and client authentication certificates to a file on TaispinToysFed and TailspinToysProxy. Do not export the private keys and (as before), select DER Encoded Binary X.509 (.cer) as the export format. Store the certificate files in the shared folder you cre-ated earlier.

Use the Certificates MMC snap-in on TailSpinToysFed to access the Certificate Import Wiz-ard. On the File To Import page, click Browse and select the shared folder (in this case, C:\MyTemp), as shown in Figure 6-6.

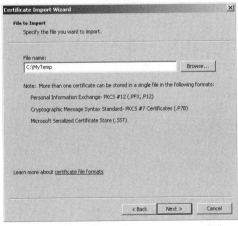

FIGURE 6-6 Selecting the folder that contains the file to import.

On the Certificate Store page, select Place All Certificates In The Following Store and ensure that the selected store is Trusted Root Certification Authorities. Repeat the procedure for all the servers on which you need to import certificates (see Table 6-1). The required certificate files should have been exported to the shared folder on TailSpinToysFed.

Configuring the Web Server

When you set up a claims-aware application on a Web server, you must configure IIS and create the application. In this case study, you create the application on TreyResearchProxy. In Internet Information Services (IIS) Manager, access the Site Bindings dialog box and select the HTTPS binding. Verify that the TreyResearchProxy.Treyresearch.net certificate is bound to port 443, as shown in Figure 6-7.

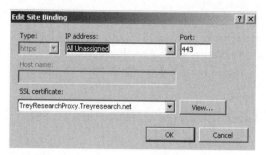

FIGURE 6-7 TreyResearchProxy.Treyresearch.net certificate is bound to port 443.

Configure SSL settings: specify that the settings require SSL and accept client certificates. Right-click Default Web Site and select Add Application to create and configure a claims-aware application. In the Alias field, type the application name (for example, **myclaim-application**). Click Select, select Classic .NET AppPool from the drop-down list, and click OK. Under Physical Path, click the ellipsis button (...), select the C:\inetpub\wwwroot folder, click Make A New Folder, type **myclaimapplication**, and click OK. The Add Application dialog box should look similar to Figure 6-8.

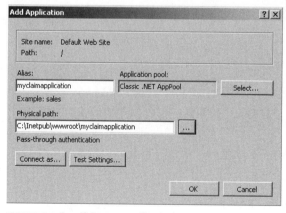

FIGURE 6-8 Specifying an application to add.

Configuring the Federation Servers

You need to configure a trust policy on the account federation server, TailspinToysFed. You must also identify the AD DS account store and create claims for your users. On the resource federation server, TreyResearchFed, you must create a trust policy, claims for the users in the resource domain, a configured account store, and enabled claims-aware applications.

In the Active Directory Federation Services GUI on TailspinToysFed, access the trust policy Properties dialog box; specify the Federation Service URI as **urn:federation:Tailspintoys**, and ensure that the Federation Service endpoint URL lists *https://TailspinToysFed.Tailspintoys.com/adfs/ls/*. Provide a display name that does not depend on a single server (for example, Tailspintoys).

To create claims for your users, expand Trust Policy\My Organization and create a new organization group claim, as shown in Figure 6-9.

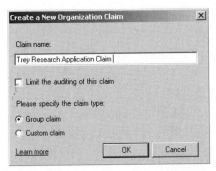

FIGURE 6-9 Creating a new organization claim.

To add the account store for *Tailspintoys.com*, access the *Account Stores* node in the tree pane and create and enable a new AD DS account store. Only one AD DS store can be associated with an AD FS implementation. To map a group to the group claim, create a new group claim extraction and add the name of the security group you want to map to the claim.

Ensure that Trey Research Application Claim is selected. Figure 6-10 shows the Group Claim Extraction Properties dialog box for Trey Research Application Claim.

Now, configure the resource federation server, TreyResearchFed, by carrying out a very similar procedure. Figure 6-11 shows the application details.

Enable the new claim, and the resource federation server is now ready to process claims. You can add several identity claim types that are then processed in order.

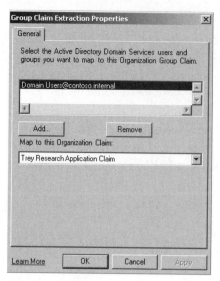

FIGURE 6-10 The Group Claim Extraction Properties dialog box.

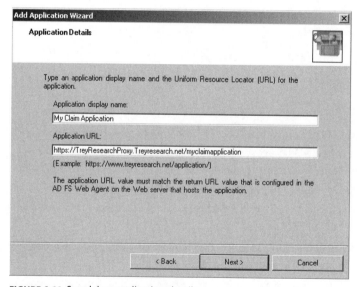

FIGURE 6-11 Supplying application details.

Configuring the Federation Trust

When you have configured both federation servers, you can configure the federation trust. You must export the trust policy from the AFS, import it into the RFS, create a claim mapping based on this policy, and then export the partner policy from the RFS and import it into the AFS. This completes the AD FS implementation.

NOTE **WINDOWS SERVER 2008 ENHANCEMENT**

In Windows Server 2003 R2, the export and import of policies in Federation Services was performed manually. This could lead to errors. In Windows Server 2008 AD FS, you use the graphical interface to perform the task.

Hiding an Organization Name

Sometimes an organization that is an account partner in a federation partnership wants to support user access from the Internet but, for privacy and security reasons, does not want to list its name in a drop-down list. If you do not want to include your organization name in the organization drop-down list on the federation server's Web page, you can use the *whr* parameter to include your organization name directly within the query used to access the application. The syntax of the query is as follows:

```
https://webserver/appname/apppage.aspx?whr=urn:federation:accountpartner
```

For more information about the *whr* parameter, see *http://technet.microsoft.com/en-us/library/cc784321.aspx*.

PRACTICE **Preparing an AD FS Deployment**

In this practice, you install Certificate Services on the Boston server, enabling you to install AD FS and an AD FS proxy on the Windows Server 2008 servers (Boston and Glasgow) in the *contoso.internal* domain as servers in the *contoso.internal* resource domain. You install a CA root server, a federation server, and an FSP in this domain. In a production environment, you would not install AD FS on a domain controller.

EXERCISE 1 Install a Root CA

The root CA certificate establishes the foundation and basic rules that govern certificate issuance and use for your entire PKI. In this exercise, you install an enterprise root CA on the Boston server. This enables you to install and configure AD FS on the *contoso.internal* resource domain.

1. Log on to the domain at Boston with the Kim_Akers account.

2. If necessary, open Server Manager and click Add Roles. If the Before You Begin page appears, click Next, and then select the Active Directory Certificate Services check box on the Select Server Roles page, as shown in Figure 6-12. Click Next, and then click Next again.

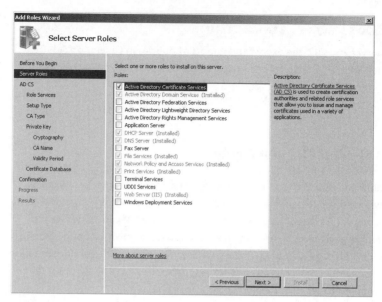

FIGURE 6-12 Selecting Active Directory Certificate Services.

3. On the Select Role Services page, ensure that the Certification Authority check box is selected. Click Next.

4. On the Specify Setup Type page, select Enterprise. Click Next.

5. On the Specify CA Type page, shown in Figure 6-13, select Root CA. Click Next.

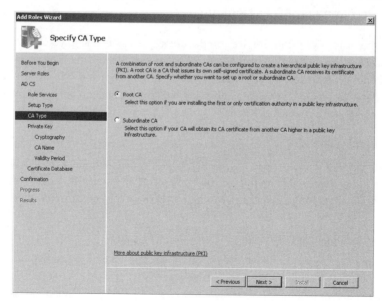

FIGURE 6-13 Specifying a root CA.

6. On the Set Up Private Key page, click Create A New Private Key. Click Next.

   On the Configure Cryptography page, you can select a cryptographic service provider, key length, and hash algorithm.

7. Accept the defaults and click Next.

8. On the Configure CA Name page, create a unique name to identify the CA, in this case, **contoso-BOSTON-CA**. Check that the Distinguished Name Suffix is DC=contoso,DC=internal. Click Next.

9. On the Set Validity Period page, you can specify the number of years or months that the root CA certificate will be valid. Accept the default (5 years) and click Next.

10. On the Configure Certificate Database page, accept the default locations and click Next.

11. On the Confirm Installation Options page, review the configuration settings and click Install. When the setup process finishes, click Close.

EXERCISE 2   Install the Resource Federation Server

In this exercise, you install AD FS on the Glasgow domain controller. Glasgow is the federation server in the *contoso.internal* resource domain. In a production environment, you would not add the AD FS role on a domain controller.

1. Log on to Glasgow with the Kim_Akers account.

2. If necessary, open Server Manager.

3. Right-click the *Roles* node in the tree pane and select Add Roles.

4. If the Before You Begin page appears, click Next.

5. On the Select Server Roles page, select the Active Directory Federation Services check box and click Next.

6. Read the information and click Next.

7. On the Select Role Services page, select the Federation Service check box, as shown in Figure 6-14. Click Next.

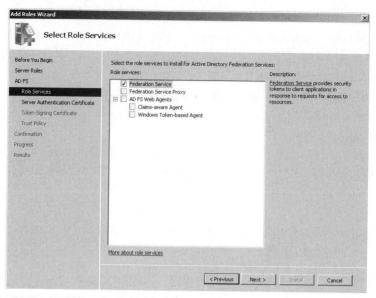

FIGURE 6-14 Adding the Federation Service role service.

8. On the Choose A Server Authentication Certificate For SSL Encryption page, select Create A Self-Signed Certificate For SSL Encryption and click Next.

   Note that if you have already installed a certificate for server authentication, this page does not appear.

9. On the Choose A Token-Signing Certificate page, select Create A Self-Signed Token-Signing Certificate and click Next.

10. On the Select Trust Policy page, select Create A New Trust Policy and click Next.

   Make a note of the path you use to save this trust policy (typically, C:\Windows \systemdata\adfs\trustpolicy.xml). Your federation relationship will use this policy.

11. On the Confirm Installation Selections page, review your choices and click Install.

12. When the installation is complete, click Close.

EXERCISE 3   Install the Federation Service Proxy

In this exercise, you install the FSP for the resource domain. You install this role and role services on the Boston member server. In a production network, your FSP would typically be a standalone server on a peripheral network.

1. Log on to the *contoso.internal* domain at Boston with the Kim_Akers account.

2. If necessary, open Server Manager.

3. Right-click the *Roles* node in the tree pane and select Add Roles.

4. If the Before You Begin page appears, click Next.

5. On the Select Server Roles page, select the Active Directory Federation Services check box and click Next.

6. Read the information about the role and click Next.

7. On the Select Role Services page, select the Federation Service Proxy and AD FS Web Agents check boxes. Click Next.

8. On the Choose A Server Authentication Certificate For SSL Encryption page, select Create A Self-Signed Certificate For SSL Encryption and click Next.

9. On the Specify Federation Server page, type **glasgow.contoso.internal** and click Validate.

10. Click Next.

11. On the Choose A Client Authentication Certificate page, select Create A Self-Signed Client Authentication Certificate and click Next.

12. Review the information on the Web Server (IIS) page and click Next.

13. On the Select Role Services page, accept the default values and click Next.

14. On the Confirm Installation Selections page, review your choices and click Install.

15. When the installation is complete, click Close.

Lesson Summary

■ AD FS extends your internal authentication store to external environments through identity federation and federation trusts. Federation partnerships always involve a resource and one or more account partners.

■ AD FS uses SSL authentication certificates to verify the identity of servers and clients. All communications occur through port 433 over HTTPS. AD FS can interact with partners using third-party operating systems, for example, UNIX and Linux.

■ AD FS relies on secure communications, and each server in an AD FS partnership trusts the root certificate. Typically, you install third-party certificates obtained from a trusted CA.

■ When you configure a partnership, you create claims-aware applications and assign specific claims to each partner in the partnership. You identify the directory store that each federation server will use and create a federation trust between the two partners. You use the trust policy to assign claims to the account organization. Finally, you export the partner policy from the RFS and import it into the AFS.

Lesson Review

You can use the following questions to test your knowledge of the information in Lesson 1, "Installing, Configuring, and Using AD FS." The questions are also available on the companion DVD if you prefer to review them in electronic form.

> **NOTE ANSWERS**
>
> Answers to these questions and explanations of why each answer choice is right or wrong are located in the "Answers" section at the end of the book.

1. Users at Trey Research, Woodgrove Bank, Tailspin Toys, and Northwind Traders want to use a Web-based collaboration application hosted by Litware, Inc. Users at Litware, Trey Research, Tailspin Toys, and Northwind Traders want to use a Web-based account-ing application hosted by Woodgrove Bank. All organizations have Windows Server 2008 servers and domain controllers. SSO is a requirement. How best can you imple-ment this setup?

   A. Create a single AD FS federation. Make Litware Inc., and Woodgrove Bank resource partners. Make Trey Research, Tailspin Toys, and Northwind Traders account partners.

   B. Create two AD FS federations. In the first, make Litware, Inc., the resource partner and Trey Research, Woodgrove Bank, Tailspin Toys, and Northwind Traders the account partners. In the second, make Woodgrove Bank the resource partner and Litware, Trey Research, Tailspin Toys, and Northwind Traders the account partners.

   C. Create multiple AD FS partnerships, each with a single resource partner and a single account partner. For example, make Litware the resource partner and Trey Research the account partner; make Litware the resource partner and Woodgrove Bank the account partner, and so on.

   D. Do not use AD FS partnerships. Instead, use forest trusts.

2. You attempt to add an AD DS account store on the federation server in an AD FS fed-eration account partner's network. You are unable to do so. What is the likely reason?

   A. You cannot add an account store on an AFS. You can do this only on the RFS.

   B. You cannot add an account store on an AFS. You need to do this on an FSP.

   C. AD DS is not an appropriate type of account store.

   D. An account store has already been added on the federation server.

3. Your employer, Litware, Inc., wants to create a federation partnership with Northwind Traders so that Litware employees can access a Web-based collaboration application in Northwind Trader's perimeter network. You install federation servers and FSPs at Litware, and you now must configure the federation trust to enable identity federation. Northwind Traders is already a resource partner in AD FS federation partnerships with other organizations. Which steps must you perform? (Choose five. Each correct answer presents part of a complete solution.)

   A. Export the trust policy from Litware and import it into Northwind Traders.

   B. Export the trust policy from Northwind Traders and import it into Litware.

   C. Export the partner policy from Northwind Traders and import it into Litware.

   D. Export the partner policy from Litware and import it into Northwind Traders.

   E. Communicate with the administrator at Northwind Traders to establish how you will exchange information.

   F. Create and configure a claim mapping in Northwind Traders.

   G. Configure the DNS servers in each forest with cross-DNS references that refer to the DNS servers in the other forest.

Lesson 2: Installing, Configuring, and Using AD RMS

Active Directory Rights Management Services (AD RMS), formerly known as Rights Management Services, extends the control of intellectual property rights from your internal network to the outside world. Digital rights management (DRM) has been a difficult topic since the early days of computers. Some software vendors require the use of hardware keys, whereas others use a Web-based approval and validation process.

AD RMS is designed to protect intellectual property through the integration of a number of features. In addition to direct integration with AD DS, AD RMS uses both AD CS and AD FS. AD CS generates the PKI certificates that AD RMS embeds in documents. AD FS extends AD RMS policies beyond the firewall and supports external organizations. It also protects against misuse or theft of important data by malicious or careless internal users and protects data in transit. (For example, if someone loses a USB key with a file that has AD RMS protection, the file cannot be opened.)

After this lesson, you will be able to:

- List and explain the components that make up AD RMS services.
- List and explain different AD RMS deployment scenarios.
- List the AD RMS prerequisites for deployment.
- Install an AD RMS cluster.
- Configure extranet URLs.
- Prepare for integration with partners.
- Work with AD RMS certificates.
- Prepare user accounts for AD RMS.
- Prepare exclusion policies.
- Work with policy templates.
- Work with the AD RMS databases.

Estimated lesson time: 55 minutes

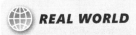
Ian McLean

Even with the best motives in the world, you can fall foul of intellectual property considerations.

A good few years ago, I worked for a government-funded organization linked to a well-regarded university. This was the dawn of the personal computer revolution, and university and college lecturers had started to look at the new, relatively cheap, and readily available personal computer as a possible teaching aid. Not just computing lecturers—this was the real revolution—but lecturers in chemistry, physics, and even literature and languages saw computer-aided training as the way forward. It was an exciting time.

But there were hills to climb. Even the cleverest professors with their doctorate certificates hanging proudly on their walls were, in those days, less computer-aware than the average seven year old is today. My job was to slay each successive dragon as the technologies emerged. I had to write papers, articles, and other documents telling my academic colleagues, in nontechnical language, how they could use these new devices to teach their subjects.

Public money paid for our efforts in investigating and explaining a new personal computing system weeks, and sometimes days, after it was released. Our publications were copyright-free—available to our fellow academics to copy, print, or amend as they thought fit.

I saw the downside of this when I was asked to evaluate a thesis written for a Masters degree. I read this document with growing horror. At the end, I said that I had to agree with every word because I had written all of them. As far as my academic colleagues were concerned, the student had done her research and included copyright-free material from a reputable source. As far as I was concerned, I would rather have given the master's degree to the photocopier she had used.

This totally changed my philosophy toward intellectual property. Yes, I still write for the public domain. But I make sure my work's protected and that nobody can take it, reproduce it without acknowledgement, and claim it as their own. OK, I know AD RMS won't stop plagiarism of work that is published in the public domain and to which everyone has free access (as in the case I described). However, it will stop people from accessing and copying documents when they don't have the right to do so. What has changed is my attitude and, I think, the attitude of society in general. We're all more interested in protecting our intellectual property. I believe in DRM. I'm an AD RMS aficionado.

Implementing AD RMS

The most straightforward implementation of AD RMS controls the internal use of intellectual property. You create access rights for the documentation you produce, and your colleagues can view, read, and manage only the content with which they are professionally involved. Content cannot be copied except under strict conditions. You can use AD RMS internally to protect confidential company information from being accessed by malicious or careless employees who do not have the right to do so. It can also protect confidential data when (for example) a user loses a USB key. Microsoft Exchange Server can use AD RMS to stop e-mail messages from being distributed to unauthorized people.

EXAM TIP

The obvious applications that generate data that needs to be protected are Microsoft Office applications such as Office Word, Office Access, and Office Excel. However, it is worth remembering that Exchange Server 2007 and Microsoft SharePoint Server 2007 can use AD RMS to enforce document rights and protect e-mail communication. You can also use AD RMS to enforce document expiry dates.

The next stage involves sharing content with partner organizations. Partners can view and access protected documents but cannot copy or share the information. The third stage involves the distribution of your content to third parties, possibly over the Internet. You do this in a protected mode, and your content cannot be copied or distributed unless you give the required authorization.

Whatever implementation model you choose, you must communicate your document protection policy to the people who will be working with your data. Work colleagues need to understand the problems caused by divulging information to unauthorized persons. Partners require policy statements that explain how they should protect your information. When you reach wider audiences, you must ensure that they fully understand your protection policies so they can work with your information properly. A remarkable number of people believe that anything they download from the Internet is free from copyright and can be used however they want.

AD RMS works with an AD RMS client to protect sensitive information. Windows Vista and Windows Server 2008 include the AD RMS client, and you can download Windows RMS Client with SP2 for Windows XP, Microsoft Windows 2000 Server, and Microsoft Windows Server 2003 from the Microsoft Web site. The precise URL is given later in this lesson.

Windows Protection is provided through the AD RMS server role, which provides certificate and licensing management. Configuration and logging information is held in a database. In test environments, you can use the Windows Internal Database (WID) included in Windows Server 2008. However, WID does not support remote connections, and only one server can use it. In production environments, use a fully featured database engine such as Microsoft SQL Server 2005 or SQL Server 2008 running on a separate server to load balance AD RMS through the installation of multiple SQL servers.

MORE INFO **WINDOWS INTERNAL DATABASE**

For more information about WID, see *http://technet.microsoft.com/en-us/library
/cc754405.aspx*.

Internet Information Services (IIS) 7.0 provides the Web services that AD RMS requires, and the Microsoft Message Queuing service implements transaction coordination in distributed environments.

The AD RMS client provides access to AD RMS features on the desktop. In addition, an AD DS directory provides integrated authentication and administration. AD RMS uses AD DS to authenticate users and verify that they are allowed to use the service. This makes up the AD RMS infrastructure, which can be summarized as follows:

- The AD RMS server role provides certificate and licensing management.
- A database (WID or SQL Server) holds configuration and logging information.
- IIS 7.0 provides Web services.
- An AD RMS client provides access to AD RMS features.
- An AD DS directory provides integrated authentication and administration.
- The Microsoft Message Queuing service implements transaction coordination in distributed environments.

AD RMS Clusters

The first time you install an AD RMS server, you create an AD RMS root cluster by default. A root cluster handles both certification and licensing requests, and only one root cluster can exist in an AD DS forest. If you install licensing-only servers, these automatically form a licensing cluster. Clusters are available only if you deploy the AD RMS database on a different server from the one on which you install AD RMS.

Each time you add a new AD RMS server with either the root or the licensing-only role, it is automatically integrated into the corresponding existing cluster. Microsoft recommends using the root role rather than the licensing-only role because root clusters handle all AD RMS operations and because root and licensing-only clusters cannot share load balancing. If you install all your AD RMS servers as root servers, they automatically load balance each other.

When the AD RMS infrastructure is in place, applications that generate information (for example, word processors) can use AD RMS to provide information protection services. When users create information, they define who will be able to access and manipulate that information. AD RMS policy templates can apply a given configuration to documents as these documents are created.

EXAM TIP

Any server installation of AD RMS automatically creates a cluster. AD RMS clusters provide high availability and load balancing to ensure that the service is always available. Do not confuse AD RMS clusters with the Failover Clustering or Network Load Balancing services provided by Windows Server 2008.

If you send an AD RMS-protected document to a user in another organization that is not within your organization's forest, the information remains protected because AD RMS settings are persistent. This means that the document remains encrypted, and a user with the appropriate license can open it and work with it on his or her home computer. AD RMS Web services enable you to extend AD RMS protection and integrate its features in information-producing applications. Organizations can use these Web services to integrate AD RMS features in both Windows and non-Windows environments.

MORE INFO   **AD RMS**

For more information about AD RMS, see *http://technet.microsoft.com/en-us/library /cc534988.aspx.*

Windows Server 2008 Enhancements

AD RMS is an enhanced version of the Microsoft Windows Rights Management Services, available in Microsoft Windows Server 2003. Microsoft has included enhancements that extend AD RMS functionality. The enhancements introduced by Windows Server 2008 include the following:

- AD RMS integrates with AD FS, which enables you to extend your rights management policies to partners beyond your firewall. Partners do not need their own AD RMS infrastructure and can use yours to access AD RMS features.

- AD RMS is a Windows Server 2008 server role. Using Server Manager to install the role provides all the necessary dependencies and component installations. If a remote database server is not specified during installation, Server Manager will automatically install WID.

- You can administer AD RMS through an MMC snap-in. In previous versions, you could use only a Web interface.

- When you create an AD RMS server, it is self-enrolled. Enrollment creates a server licensor certificate (SLC), which grants the server the right to participate in the AD RMS structure. You can run AD RMS in an isolated network without requiring Internet access.

- AD RMS includes administration roles that enable you to delegate specific AD RMS tasks without needing to grant extensive administration rights. The local administrative roles include AD RMS Enterprise Administrators, AD RMS Template Administrators, AD RMS Auditors, and AD RMS Service.

AD RMS Local Administrative Roles

Installing AD RMS creates the following local security groups on your server:

- **AD RMS Enterprise Administrators**   Members of this group can manage all aspects of AD RMS. The group includes the user account that installed the role in addition to the local Administrators group.

- **AD RMS Template Administrators**   Members of this group can read information about the AD RMS infrastructure and create, modify, and export rights policy templates.

- **AD RMS Auditors**   Members of this group can manage logs and reports and have read-only access to AD RMS infrastructure information.

- **AD RMS Service**   This group contains the AD RMS service account identified during the role installation.

Because these groups are local, you must create corresponding groups in your AD DS directory and insert these groups within the local groups on each AD RMS server. When you need to grant rights an administrative role to a user, you add the user's account to the group in AD DS.

EXAM TIP

AD RMS local administrative roles and rights delegation are likely to be tested in the upgrade examinations.

User Rights and Certificates

AD RMS protects information by using rights account certificates. These certificates identify trusted entities (such as users, groups, computers, applications, or services) that create and publish rights-enabled content. If a user establishes a protection policy, AD RMS issues a publishing license and integrates it in the content. The license is permanently attached and does not require access to AD RMS to provide content protection.

Protected content is encrypted, and users need to access it through an AD RMS–enabled browser or application. When users access the rights-protected content, their AD RMS clients request a usage license from the server. If the user is also a trusted entity, the AD RMS server issues this license. The usage (or use) license reads the protection license and applies the appropriate rights to the document. Trusted users can create protection licenses from pre-defined templates.

Installation Scenarios

AD RMS provides the following deployment scenarios:

- **Single server deployment** You can install AD RMS on a single server. This installs the WID as the support database.

- **Internal multiple-server deployment** You can install AD RMS on multiple servers tied to an AD DS directory. You must use a separate server to host the AD RMS database.

- **Extranet deployment** You can deploy AD RMS in an extranet. You must configure appropriate firewall exceptions and add an extranet URL on an external-facing Web server to allow external client connections.

> **MORE INFO** **AD RMS DEPLOYMENT IN AN EXTRANET**
>
> For more information on how to deploy AD RMS on an extranet, see *http://technet. microsoft.com/en-us/library/cc753490.aspx.*

- **Multiple forest deployment** If you have existing partnerships based on AD DS trusts, you must configure a multiforest deployment. This requires multiple AD RMS installations, one in each forest. You must assign an SSL certificate to each Web site that hosts AD RMS clusters in each forest. You must also extend the AD DS forest schema to include AD RMS objects, and your AD RMS service account needs to be trusted in each forest.

> **MORE INFO** **MULTIPLE FOREST DEPLOYMENT**
>
> For more information on multiple forest deployment, see *http://technet.microsoft.com /en-us/library/cc772182.aspx.*

- **AD RMS with AD FS deployment** You can extend an AD RMS root cluster to other forests through AD FS. You must assign an SSL certificate to the Web site hosting the AD RMS root cluster, install the root cluster, set up a federated trust relationship, and install the AD RMS Identity Federation Support role service. Next, create a claims-aware application on the AD FS resource partner server, assign the Generate Security Audits user right to the AD RMS service account, and define the extranet cluster URL in AD RMS. Finally, install the AD RMS Identity Federation Support role service.

> **MORE INFO** **AD RMS AND AD FS DEPLOYMENT**
>
> For more information on the AD RMS with AD FS deployment, see *http://technet .microsoft.com/en-us/library/cc771425.aspx.*

- **Licensing-only server deployment** You can deploy a licensing-only AD RMS cluster in addition to the root cluster. In this case, assign an SSL certificate to the Web site hosting the AD RMS root cluster and then install the root cluster. You can then install a licensing-only server.

MORE INFO **SETTING UP A LICENSING-ONLY AD RMS CLUSTER**

For more information on how to deploy a licensing-only AD RMS cluster, see *http://technet.microsoft.com/en-us/library/cc730671.aspx*.

 Quick Check

- Distinguish between a root AD RMS cluster and a licensing-only cluster. Why should you use the former whenever possible?

Quick Check Answer

- The root cluster provides all AD RMS facilities, whereas the licensing-only cluster manages only licenses. If you can choose, deploy only one type of cluster because root and licensing-only clusters do not load-balance. You must deploy a root cluster to implement AD RMS, and a root cluster can do everything a licensing-only cluster can do.

Installing AD RMS

Before you install the AD RMS role, you must ensure that the necessary prerequisites are in place. These depend on whether your deployment is internal only or requires interaction with outside partners. You must also decide whether to use only root clusters or both root and licensing-only clusters.

MORE INFO **AD RMS CLUSTER INSTALLATION**

For more information on AD RMS cluster installation, see *http://technet.microsoft.com /en-us/library/cc726041.aspx*.

AD RMS Installation Prerequisites

You can install AD RMS in a test environment with very little preparation, and you do this in the practice session later in this lesson. In a production environment, however, you need to satisfy the following prerequisites to AD RMS installation:

- You can install AD RMS on any Windows Server 2008 edition except Windows Server Web and Itanium-based systems. However, Microsoft recommends Windows Server Enterprise or Windows Server Datacenter.
- You require Message Queuing and IIS (preferably, IIS 7.0) with ASP.NET enabled.
- You must reserve Web server URLs that will not change and do not include a computer name or localhost. Use different URLs for internal and external connections.

- AD RMS requires an AD DS domain. Preferably, all your domain controllers should run Windows Server 2008. Microsoft recommended best practice is to install AD RMS in the child production domain in a multidomain forest.

- Install AD RMS in the same domain as its potential users. Domain user accounts require e-mail addresses configured in AD DS. This implies that in a multidomain forest, your user accounts should also be in a child production domain to follow the Microsoft recommendation.

- The installation account must be domain-based and have local administrator privileges. If you need to generate service connection points, this account must be a member of Enterprise Admins. If you must use an external database (which you should do in a production environment), the installation account must be a member of the System Administrators role on the database server. For security reasons, the account must not be on a smart card. (If you use a smart card account, installation will fail.)

- You need a service account that is either a standard domain user account that is a member of the local Administrators group or a domain-based service account that is assigned the Generate Security Audits user right.

- You must obtain an SSL certificate from an external third-party commercial CA for the AD RMS cluster. Self-signed certificates are not appropriate in a production environment. You must install the certificate prior to AD RMS installation.

- You should not use WID in a production environment and should instead configure a SQL Server 2005 server with SP2 or later, or a SQL Server 2008 server, that includes stored procedures to perform operations. You must create and name the AD RMS database instance and start the SQL Server Browser service before AD RMS installation. SQL Server must be installed on a separate server from AD RMS.

- You need to configure DNS and create custom CNAME records for the root cluster URL and the database server.

- You must decide on an SLC name before you install AD RMS—for example, the name of your organization.

- You need a cluster key stored in the AD RMS configuration database. Microsoft recommends that you use a hardware protection device to store the cluster key and install it on each server before you install the AD RMS role.

NOTE   RMS CLIENT

Microsoft Windows Vista and Windows Server 2008 include the AD RMS client by default. Microsoft Windows XP, Windows 2000 Server, and Windows Server 2003 require Windows RMS Client with SP2, which you can download from *http://www.microsoft.com/downloads /details.aspx?familyid=02da5107-2919-414b-a5a3-3102c7447838&displaylang=en*.

MORE INFO **CLUSTER KEY PROTECTION AND STORAGE**

For more information about how to store and protect an AD RMS cluster key, see *http://technet.microsoft.com/en-us/library/cc754905.aspx*.

IMPORTANT **AD RMS VIRTUALIZATION**

AD RMS is not supported on Server Core installations of Windows Server 2008. However, AD RMS servers are good candidates for virtualization under Hyper-V.

MORE INFO **AD RMS INSTALLATION PREREQUISITES**

For more information about AD RMS installation prerequisites, see *http://technet.microsoft.com/en-us/library/cc771789.aspx*.

AD RMS Installation Procedure

When the prerequisites are in place, you can install the AD RMS server role and create an AD RMS cluster. You do this in the practice later in this chapter. The high-level steps to install AD RMS are as follows:

1. Create a CNAME record in DNS. You use this in the AD RMS cluster URL.

2. Create a service account and four global security groups for AD RMS administration delegation. The groups you need to create are listed and described later in this lesson.

NOTE **CREATING GLOBAL SECURITY GROUPS**

Installing the AD FS role automatically creates four local security groups on the server on which it is installed. However, for a full implementation of AD FS, you must manually create four global security groups with the same names in AD DS. The practice later in this lesson describes how you use these groups.

3. Create and install a Web server certificate. You need to do this because AD RMS requires SSL-encrypted Web connections. You must have installed a root CA (installed the AD DS role and selected the Certification Authority role service) to manage this process.

4. Install the AD RMS server role. This creates an AD RMS root cluster.

NOTE **INSTALL AD RMS ON A MEMBER SERVER**

Microsoft recommends that you install AD RMS on a member server rather than on a domain controller. A Hyper-V virtual server with a full installation of Windows Server 2008 is the ideal candidate. AD RMS does not run on a Server Core installation.

AD RMS Certificates and Licenses

AD RMS requires certificates to encrypt and sign data. It also requires licenses in Extensible Rights Markup Language (XrML) format. These licenses are embedded in user-created content. The AD RMS hierarchy forms a chain of trust that validates the certificate or license when it is used. You require the following certificates and licenses in an AD RMS infrastructure:

- **Server licensor certificate (SLC)**   A self-signed certificate generated when you set up the first server in an AD RMS root cluster. If you create a licensing-only cluster, it will also generate an SLC. The SLC is assigned to the cluster as a whole. Other cluster members will share the SLC when they are installed.

- **Rights account certificate (RAC)**   Generated when a trusted user who has an e-mail–enabled account in AD DS first accesses rights-protected content. An RAC contains both the user's public and private keys.

- **Client licensor certificate (CLC)**   Automatically requests a CLC from the AD RMS cluster when a user receives an RAC and launches an AD RMS–enabled application. After a CLC is obtained, the user can apply AD RMS policies both online and offline. The CLC private key encrypts content.

- **Machine certificate**   Created the first time an AD RMS–enabled application is used. The AD RMS client automatically manages this process with the AD RMS cluster. The machine certificate creates a lockbox on the computer that correlates the machine certificate with the user's profile.

> **MORE INFO   LOCKBOXES**
>
> For more information about lockboxes, see *http://msdn.microsoft.com/en-us/library /aa362637(VS.85).aspx*.

- **Publishing license**   Created when a user saves content in a rights-protected mode. This license lists which users can use the content and under what conditions. It also lists the rights each user has to the content.

- **Use license**   Assigned to a user who opens rights-protected content. The use license is tied to the user's RAC and lists the access rights the user has to the content.

EXAM TIP

Know the different certificates and licenses used in AD RMS and what each is used for.

 Quick Check

- Which type of certificate is self-signed, is generated during setup of the first server in a root cluster, and is assigned to the cluster as a whole?

Quick Check Answer

■ A server licensor certificate (SLC). Other cluster members share the SLC when they are installed.

Configuring and Using AD RMS

When you have installed AD RMS, configure the AD RMS cluster and prepare the usage policies you want to implement in your network. If you want to make AD RMS available outside your network, add an extranet cluster URL to your configuration. If you want to integrate AD RMS services with partners, configure proxy settings and install Identity Federation Support. You can (if you want to) configure AD RMS certificates and change the default validation periods. Configure trust policies so your AD RMS cluster interoperates with other clusters.

You can configure exclusion policies so that some rights-protection policies do not apply to the entire organization but only to specified users or departments. Prepare user accounts for integration with AD RMS and configure policy templates that facilitate the rights-protection process for your users. You can also configure exclusion policies for applications.

Become familiar with the various AD RMS clients you need to support and with the databases required for AD RMS operation.

You can configure AD RMS by using the Active Directory Rights Management Services console that is integrated with Server Manager or accessed through Remote Server Administration Tools (RSAT). Figure 6-15 shows this console.

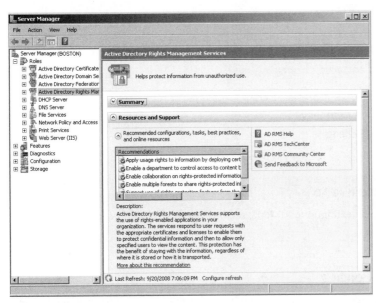

FIGURE 6-15 The Active Directory Rights Management Services console accessed from Server Manager.

Add the AD RMS cluster you have created to the Active Directory Rights Management Services console. Figure 6-16 shows the AD RMS cluster tool in Server Manager.

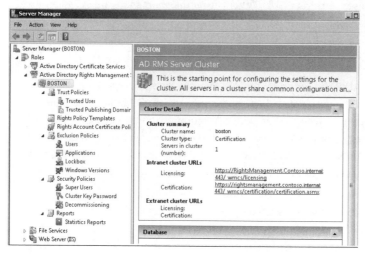

FIGURE 6-16 The AD RMS cluster tool in Server Manager.

You can use this tool to carry out the following tasks:

- Configure trust policies
- Manage AD RMS certificates
- Configure an extranet URL
- Export the SLC
- Configure exclusion policies
- Prepare accounts and access rights
- Configure a Super Users group
- Create and use policy templates
- Work with AD RMS clients
- Manage databases

MORE INFO **CONFIGURING AD RMS**

For more information on configuring AD RMS, see *http://technet.microsoft.com/en-us /library/cc771603.aspx*.

Configuring Trust Policies

You cannot enable federation support unless you have a working AD FS infrastructure in place (as described in Lesson 1). AD RMS supports four trust models:

- **Windows Live ID trusts** These enable users who have a valid Windows Live ID (or a Microsoft Passport) to use rights-protected content (but not to create it).
- **Federated trusts** These are established through AD FS to extend the operation of an AD RMS cluster to forests with which you establish a federated trust.
- **Trusted publishing domains** These enable your AD RMS cluster to issue use licenses for content protected in another AD RMS cluster.
- **Trusted user domains** These enable your AD RMS cluster to process requests for other AD RMS clusters located in different AD DS forests.

> **MORE INFO**   **CREATING AD RMS TRUSTS**
>
> For more information about AD RMS trusts, see *http://technet.microsoft.com/en-us/library /cc754459.aspx*.

Managing AD RMS Certificates

When you install the of AD RMS server role, you create certificates by default. You must configure certificate durations based on your rights-protection policies. You can specify the duration of rights account certificates, enable certification of server services, enable certification for mobile devices, and authenticate clients through smart cards.

In particular, you must set the validation period for the RAC. To modify RAC duration, you log on to a server that is a member of the root cluster with an account that has AD RMS Enterprise Administrators credentials, start Server Manager (if necessary), expand Roles\Active Directory Rights Management Services, and click the server name.

You click Change Standard RAC Validity Period in the details pane, select the Standard RAC tab, and set the number of days to enable the certificate in the Standard RAC Validity Period section of the dialog box. You then click the Temporary RAC tab and set the number of minutes to enable the certificate in the Temporary RAC Validity Period section of the dialog box and click OK.

Standard RACs are, by default, valid for 365 days. Temporary RACs, by default, last only 15 minutes. If you use federated trusts, you modify the RAC validity period under the *Federated Identity Support* node rather than under the root cluster node.

> **MORE INFO**   **MANAGING CERTIFICATES**
>
> For more information about managing the certificates AD RMS requires, see *http://technet .microsoft.com/en-us/library/cc730842.aspx*.

Quick Check

- What trust models does AD RMS support?

Quick Check Answer

- AD RMS supports the following trust models:
    - Windows Live ID trusts
    - Federated trusts
    - Trusted publishing domains
    - Trusted user domains

Configuring an Extranet URL

When you want to extend your AD RMS infrastructure to (for example) mobile users external to your network, configure an extranet URL. Do this on a server that is a member of the root cluster, using an account that has AD RMS Enterprise Administrators credentials. The account you used to install the AD RMS roles has these credentials, provided you subsequently logged off and then logged back on again.

To configure an extranet URL, open Server Manager, expand Roles\Active Directory Rights Management Services, right-click RootClusterServerName, and choose Properties. Select the Cluster URLs tab, enable Extranet URLs, and add the appropriate URL data for both licensing and certification.

Extranet URLs must point to a valid IIS installation in the extranet. You must configure DNS registration and use SSL encryption. You also need to create virtual directories to host the AD RMS data.

> **NOTE AN EXTRANET URL NEEDS A CERTIFICATE FROM A TRUSTED CA**
> When users try to access an extranet URL, the server certificate is validated. If the certificate is not from a trusted third-party CA, access is denied. If you used a self-signed certificate, the URL works when you access it from the server because the server trusts its own certificate, but it will not work from user browsers because they do not trust the self-signed certificate.

Exporting the SLC

To work with either trusted publishing domains or trusted user domains, you need to export the SLC from your root cluster or from a trusted root cluster. You export certificates and use them to establish trusts. To do this, log on with an account that is a member of the local AD RMS Enterprise Administrators group. In Server Manager, expand Roles\Active Directory Rights Management Services, right-click RootClusterServerName, and click Properties.

On the Server Certificate tab, click Export Certificate. In the Export Certificate As dialog box, type a valid name (for example, the name of your cluster) and select a location, such as your Documents folder, in which to create the .bin file. Click Save and close the Properties dialog box. Protect this certificate because it controls access to your AD RMS cluster.

Configuring Exclusion Policies

Exclusion policies specify the entities you do not want to participate in your AD RMS implementation. After you decide the scope of your rights-protection policy, you can create exclusion policies for users, applications, lockboxes, and Windows operating systems.

To create an exclusion policy, log on to a server that is a member of the root cluster with an account that has AD RMS Enterprise Administrators credentials. In Server Manager, expand Roles\Active Directory Rights Management Services*RootClusterServerName*\Exclusion Policies and click Users. In the Actions pane, select Enable User Exclusion.

To exclude users, click Exclude User in the Actions pane. This launches the Exclude User Account Wizard. You can identify the users to exclude by specifying their e-mail addresses (for users included in your AD DS directory) or their assigned public keys (for external users). Use the same process for other exclusion types.

> **MORE INFO** **EXCLUSION POLICIES**
>
> For more information about exclusion policies, see *http://technet.microsoft.com/en-us /library/cc771228.aspx.*

Preparing Accounts and Access Rights

AD DS provides authentication for users of AD RMS, and this information is written to the directory services database. If the AD RMS cluster receives a user account request, the user's RAC is written to the configuration database, and the request is recorded in the logging database if logging is enabled.

When you remove an account, AD RMS disables the account but does not automatically remove the database entry in the user key table for the user's RAC. In a production environment, this can cause the directory services database to become large and store obsolete data. Remove the appropriate database entries by creating a stored procedure in SQL Server that will automatically remove the account entry when you remove the account or by creating a script that will do so on a regular basis.

EXAM TIP

The upgrade examinations are unlikely to ask you to create an SQL stored procedure or script. However, be aware that you do this for SQL databases, and this is one of the reasons you use SQL Server and not WID in a production environment.

Configuring a Super Users group

A Super Users group contains the accounts of users who have full access to all content protected by your AD RMS implementation. These users can recover or modify any data that is managed by your AD RMS infrastructure as well as recover data generated by users who have subsequently left the organization. The Super Users group is typically a Universal Group.

To configure a Super Users group, log on to a server that is a member of the root cluster with an account that has AD RMS Enterprise Administrators credentials. In Server Manager, expand Roles\Active Directory Rights Management Services*RootClusterServerName*\Security Policies and click Change Super Users Settings in the detail pane.

In the Actions pane, click Enable Super Users. In the details pane, click Change Super Users Group to view the Super User Group Property sheet and then specify the e-mail address of a mail-enabled Universal distribution group in your forest (or use the Browse button to select the group).

> **MORE INFO   ACCOUNT PREPARATION**
>
> For more information about account preparation, see *http://technet.microsoft.com/en-us /library/cc754120.aspx*.

Using Policy Templates

Policy templates facilitate rights-protection applications by your users. These templates save time and ensure that you maintain the standards you set in your rights-protection policies. When you create a template, you specify its location, typically a shared folder within your network. You must configure the offline folder settings for the shared folder so that the content of the folder will automatically be available locally to offline users. Ensure that offline folders are automatically updated on the client computer each time the user connects to the network.

Offline folders, however, do not work for external users who do not have access to your internal network. In this case, consider an alternate delivery method (for example, a collaboration application) if you choose to allow external users to create content. Note that users who have access only to pre-created content do not require access to policy templates.

Creating Policy Templates

To create a policy template, log on to a server that is a member of the root cluster, using AD RMS Template Administrators credentials. In Server Manager, expand Roles\Active Directory Rights Management Services*RootClusterServerName*\Rights Policy Templates and, in the Actions pane, select Create Distributed Rights Policy Template. This starts the Create Policy Template Wizard.

On the Add Template Identification Information page, click Add, specify the language, specify the name and description for the new template, click Add, and then click Next. On the Add User Rights page, click Add and select the user or group that should have access to the template. Selecting Anyone enables any user to request a use license for the content. If you want to select a specific group, you can use the Browse button.

Under Users And Rights, select a user or group, and then assign the rights to that particular user or group in the Rights For User pane. You can also create a custom right for a user. The Grant Owner (Author) Full Control right with no expiration option is selected by default. In the Rights Request URL text box, type the appropriate URL. This enables users to request additional rights by going to the URL.

Click Next and, on the Specify Expiration Policy page, select one of the available options and type in a value in days. If you need to ensure that content expires automatically after a number of days, select Expires After The Following Duration (Days) and type in the number of days. Click Next.

On the Specify Extended Policy page, you can assign the following settings:

- Choose Enable Users to view protected content, using a browser add-on. This enables users who do not have AD RMS–enabled applications to view protected content by automatically installing the required add-on.

- Select Request A New Use License Every Time Content Is Consumed (Disable Client-Side Caching) if you need authentication against the AD RMS servers each time content is consumed. This will not work for offline users.

- Select If You Would Like To Specify Additional Information For Your AD RMS-Enabled Applications, You Can Specify Them Here As Name-Value Pairs if you need to add specific data to the protected content. This option is typically used only by developers.

When you have configured the appropriate settings, click Next. On the Specify Revocation Policy page, you can enable revocation by selecting Require Revocation and then selecting Location Where The Revocation List Is Published (URL or UNC) and typing the path to the revocation file. If you use a URL and you have both internal and external users, the URL should be accessible from both internal and external network locations.

You can determine when users need to update their revocation list when viewing content by selecting Refresh Interval For Revocation List (Days) and specifying the number of days for which the revocation list will be maintained. Select File Containing Public Key Corresponding To The Signed Revocation List and click Finish. It is a good idea to publish the revocation list on a regular basis.

MORE INFO POLICY TEMPLATES

For more information about policy templates, see *http://technet.microsoft.com/en-us /library/cc731599.aspx*.

Additional Permissions and Settings on an AD RMS-Enabled Application

A policy template specifies the AD RMS settings for applications to which it is required. However, you can configure additional permissions and settings to a specific application or group of applications (for example, Microsoft Office applications). You can specify, for example, which users have changed permission to a document and which can only read it.

How you access the Permissions dialog for a specific application depends on the application. For example, for Microsoft Office 2007 applications, you click the Office button, point to Prepare, and then point to Restrict Permission. This lets you select a template and opens the Permissions dialog box. If you click the More Options button, you can specify additional settings and options for a policy template as described in Table 6-2.

TABLE 6-2 Additional Settings and Options

PERMISSION OR SETTING	DESCRIPTION
Restrict Permission To This Document	Enables or disables the permissions applied to a specific document.
The Following Users Have Permission To This Document	Modifies the list of users who have the permissions and settings configured in the dialog box.
This Document Expires On	Sets an expiration date for the document. After the expiration date, users will no longer have the right to open the document.
Print Content	Specifies whether users can print the document.
Allow Users With Read Access To Copy Content	Specifies whether users with Read permission can also copy content.
Access Content Programmatically	Specifies whether services or scripts can access the content.
Users Can Request Additional Permissions From	Provides the e-mail address of the individual from whom users can request additional permissions for content access and modification.
Require A Connection To Verify A User's Permission	Ensures that only AD RMS–verified users can open the document. This verification is done every time the file is opened, and you should not enable this setting for offline users.
Set Defaults	Restores default settings.

When you have configured the additional permissions and settings, click OK to apply them and close the dialog box.

MORE INFO **EXPORTING AND DISTRIBUTING RIGHTS POLICY TEMPLATES**

You need to be able to export rights policy templates to a location from which they can be distributed to clients. For more information, see *http://technet.microsoft.com/en-us/library /cc730997.aspx*.

Working with AD RMS Clients

Local clients implement user access to AD RMS. The Windows Vista client is also included in Windows Server 2008. A second client, which runs on Windows 2000 Server, Windows Server 2003, and Windows XP, is available as a download.

Clients automatically discover the AD RMS cluster by one of the following methods:

- They use the AD DS Service Connection Point created during the AD RMS installation.
- In complex, multiforest AD RMS deployments, registry overrides are placed directly on the client computer. This method is used mostly for earlier versions of Windows operating systems.
- They use the URLs included in the issuance licenses for the content.

Each of these methods provides redundancy to ensure that clients can always access content.

MORE INFO **AD RMS AND WINDOWS RMS CLIENTS**

For more information about AD RMS clients and to download Windows RMS clients, see *http://technet.microsoft.com/en-us/library/cc771050.aspx*.

Managing Databases

AD RMS uses the following three databases:

- **The configuration database**   This database stores all AD RMS configuration data. AD RMS servers access the configuration database to provide rights-protection services and information to clients.
- **The logging database**   This database stores data about every activity in either a root or a licensing-only cluster. You can use the logging database to audit AD RMS events.
- **The directory services database**   This database stores information about users and all their related data. This information is accessed from AD DS directories through LDAP. The directory services database requires regular maintenance, particularly if you remove users from AD RMS (as mentioned earlier in this lesson).

AD RMS uses the Microsoft Message Queuing service to send events to the logging database. If you want to audit AD RMS usage, you must perform regular checks and verifications of this service to ensure its proper operation.

MORE INFO RIGHTS MANAGEMENT SERVICES ADMINISTRATION TOOLKIT

Microsoft provides an RMS toolkit that contains a series of utilities for AD RMS administration and operation. You can download this toolkit with utilities for RMS management at *http://www.microsoft.com/downloads/details.aspx?FamilyID=bae62cfc-d5a7-46d2-9063 -0f6885c26b98&DisplayLang=en.*

MORE INFO ADDITIONAL AD RMS RESOURCES

You can access additional AD RMS resources at *http://technet.microsoft.com/en-us/library /cc771334.aspx.*

Active Directory Metadirectory Services

Windows Server 2008 includes the Windows Server 2003 Identity Integration Feature Pack as Active Directory Metadirectory Services (AD MDS). AD MDS manages identities and coordinates user details across AD LDS. You can use AD MDS to combine identity information for a given user or resource into a single, logical view. AD MDS also automates the provisioning of new and updated identity data. This eliminates repetitive administration and the need to add, delete, or update identity information, groups, and user accounts manually.

PRACTICE Installing AD RMS

In this practice, you install AD RMS into a new cluster. First, you add a DNS CNAME record. Then you create the service account and the AD RMS role groups in the directory. Your next task is to create and install a Web Server certificate, and you then install the AD RMS server role. Before you attempt this practice, you should have completed Exercise 1, "Install a Root CA," in the practice in Lesson 1 and installed a root CA server.

You must do all the exercises in order. Ensure that both your Glasgow domain controller and your Boston member server are running for all exercises.

EXERCISE 1 Create a CNAME DNS Record

In this exercise, you create a CNAME record to use in the AD RMS cluster URL.

1. Log on to the Glasgow domain controller with the Kim_Akers account.
2. In the Administrative Tools group, open DNS.

3. Expand DNS\Glasgow\Forward Lookup Zones and right-click *contoso.internal*.

4. Select New Alias (CNAME).

5. In the New Resource Record dialog box, type an alias name of **Rights_Management** and assign it to *boston.contoso.com* in the Fully Qualified Domain Name (FQDN) For Target Host section of the dialog box, as shown in Figure 6-17.

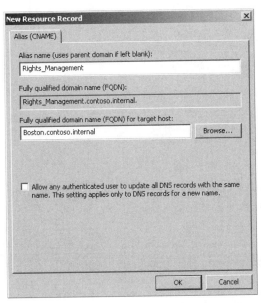

FIGURE 6-17 Creating a CNAME record.

6. Click OK.

   This creates a CNAME record for the AD RMS cluster URL.

EXERCISE 2   Add the AD RMS Service Account and Global Security Groups

In this exercise, you create a service account and four groups for AD RMS administration delegation.

1. If necessary, log on to the Glasgow domain controller with the Kim_Akers account.

2. Open Active Directory Users And Computers in the Administrative Tools group.

3. If necessary, expand Active Directory Users And Computers.

4. Expand *contoso.internal*.

5. Right-click Users, select New, and then click User.

6. Name the user **ADRMSServiceAccount** and use this name for both the logon and the pre-Windows 2000 logon names, as shown in Figure 6-18. Click Next.

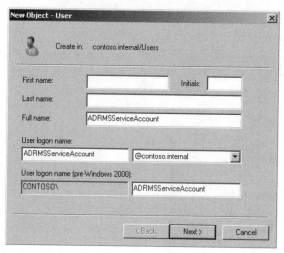

FIGURE 6-18 Creating the service account.

7. Assign the complex password **P@ssw0rd**, clear the User Must Change Password At Next Logon check box, and select the Password Never Expires check box. Click Next, and then Finish to create the account.

8. To create the AD RMS administration groups, right-click the Global Group OU, select New, and click Group. Create the following four global security groups:

   - AD RMS Enterprise Administrators
   - AD RMS Template Administrators
   - AD RMS Auditors
   - AD RMS Service

9. Right-click the AD RMS Service group and select Properties. Click the Members tab. Click Add and specify ADRMSServiceAccount. Click OK.

   The service account is added to this group, as shown in Figure 6-19.

10. Click OK.

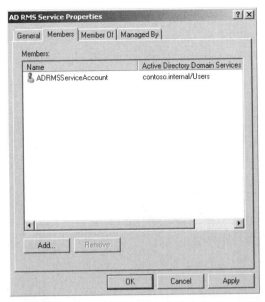

FIGURE 6-19 Adding the AD RMS service account to the AD RMS Service group.

11. Log on to the *contoso.internal* domain at the Boston member server, with the Kim_Akers account.

12. If necessary, open Server Manager.

13. Expand Configuration\Local Users and Groups\Groups.

14. Right-click the Administrators group and select Properties.

15. On the Members tab, add the AD RMS Service group to the Administrators group.

EXERCISE 3 **Prepare a Web Server Certificate**

AD RMS requires SSL-encrypted Web connections, and you must create and install a Web server certificate before you proceed with the installation.

1. If necessary, log on to *contoso.internal* at Boston with the Kim_Akers account and open Server Manager.

2. Expand Roles\Active Directory Certificate Services\ and select Certificate Templates (Boston.contoso.internal).

3. Right-click the Web Server template in the details pane and select Duplicate Template.

4. Select Windows Server 2008, Enterprise Edition and click OK.

5. On the General tab, type in the Template Display Name as **Web Server WS08**. The template name is then WebServer08.

6. Select the Publish Certificate In Active Directory check box.

Figure 6-20 shows these settings.

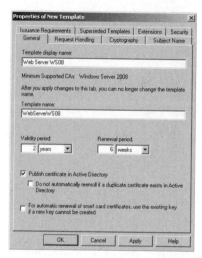

FIGURE 6-20 General template settings.

7. On the Security tab, click Add, click Object Types, select the Computers check box, and click OK. Type **Boston**, click Check Names, and click OK. Grant Boston Allow Read and Allow Enroll permissions and click OK.

8. Click OK to close the New Templates Properties box.

You now issue the template.

9. In Server Manager, expand Roles\Active Directory Certificate Services and select Contoso-BOSTON-CA.

10. Right-click Certificate Templates, select New, and then select Certificate Template To Issue.

11. In the Enable Certificate Templates dialog box, select Web Server WS08, as shown in Figure 6-21. Click OK.

You have created the Web server certificate. Now you must install it.

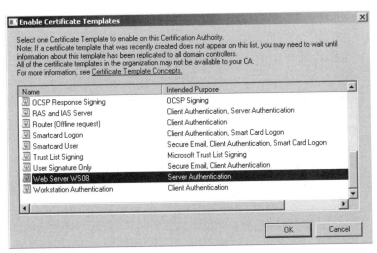

FIGURE 6-21 Creating the Web server certificate.

EXERCISE 4 Install the Web Server Certificate

In this exercise, you install the Web server certificate you created.

1. If necessary, log on to *contoso.internal* at Boston, with the Kim_Akers account.

2. On the Start menu, enter **mmc** in the Search box.

3. Select Add/Remove Snap-in from the File menu, select the Certificates snap-in, and click Add.

4. Select Computer Account and click Next.

5. Ensure that Local Computer is selected, click Finish, and then click OK.

6. Select Save As from the File menu, navigate to your Documents folder, and name the console **Computer Certificates**. If you are informed that a console of that name already exists, choose to save your console.

7. In the Computer Certificates console, expand Certificates (Local Computer)\Personal and right-click Certificates.

8. Select All Tasks, and then click Request New Certificate, as shown in Figure 6-22.

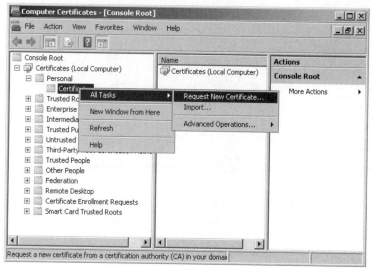

FIGURE 6-22 Requesting a new certificate.

9. Click Next on the Before You Begin page.

10. Select the Web Server WS08 certificate, and then click More Information Is Required To Enroll For This Certificate. Click Here To Configure Settings.

11. In the Certificate Properties dialog box, on the Subject tab, in the Subject Name Value field, ensure that Full DN is selected in the Type drop-down list. Type **CN=Boston,DC= Contoso,DC=internal** in the Value box under Subject Name, and then click Add.

12. Click the Alternative Name section, select URL in the Type drop-down list, enter **Rights_Management.contoso.internal** in the Value field, and then click Add.

The settings on the Subject tab are shown in Figure 6-23.

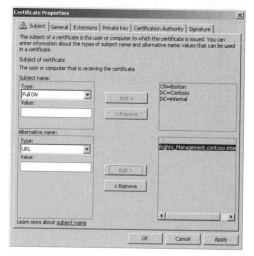

FIGURE 6-23 Subject settings for the Web Server WS08 certificate.

13. Click the General tab and type **Contoso DRM** in the Friendly Name field **and Web Server Certificate** in the Description field.

14. Click the Private Key tab, expand the Key Options section, and select the Make Private Key Exportable and Allow Private Key To Be Archived check boxes.

15. Click OK, and then click Enroll. When you see the STATUS: Succeeded message, click Finish.

16. To verify that the certificate has been issued, click Certificates and identify the certificate by its friendly name in the details pane. Right-click the certificate and select Properties. Click OK to close the Properties dialog box.

17. Close the Computer Certificates console. Do not save the console settings.

    You can now install AD RMS.

EXERCISE 5 Install the AD RMS Server Role

You now install AD RMS on the Boston member server. You do not have a SQL server on your test network and therefore use WID.

1. If necessary, log on to *contoso.internal* at Boston, with the Kim_Akers account, and open Server Manager.

2. In the tree pane, right-click the *Roles* node and select Add Roles.

3. If the Before You Begin page appears, click Next.

4. On the Select Server Roles page, select the Active Directory Rights Management Services check box.

    The Add Role Wizard asks you to add the Web Server (IIS) role with the required management tools.

5. Click Add Required Role Services.

6. On the Select Server Roles page, click Next.

7. On the Active Directory Rights Management Services page, review the information about the selected role and click Next.

8. On the Select Role Services page, ensure that the Active Directory Rights Management Server check box is selected and click Next.

9. On the Create Or Join An AD RMS Cluster page, ensure that Create A New AD RMS Cluster is selected and click Next.

10. On the Select Configuration Database page, ensure that Use Windows Internal Database On This Server is selected and click Next.

11. On the Specify Service Account page, click Specify, type the username **ADRMSServiceAccount** and the password **P@ssw0rd**, click OK, and then click Next.

12. On the Configure AD RMS Cluster Key Storage page, select Use AD RMS Centrally Managed Key Storage and click Next.

> **NOTE PROTECTING THE AD RMS CLUSTER KEY**
>
> The option chosen in this exercise is sufficient for a test scenario. In a production environment, you would use the stronger protection for this key, typically through a cryptographic service provider (CSP).

13. On the Specify AD RMS Cluster Key Password page, type **P@ssw0rd,** confirm the password, and click Next.

    In a production environment, you would not use the same password as the service account.

14. On the Select AD RMS Cluster Web Site page, ensure that Default Web Site is selected and click Next.

15. On the Specify Cluster Address page, select Use An SSL-Encrypted Connection (https://). In the Fully Qualified Domain Name text box in the Internal Address section, type **Rights_Management.contoso.internal**. Do not change the port number. Click Validate.

    Figure 6-24 shows the validated settings on the Specify Cluster Address page.

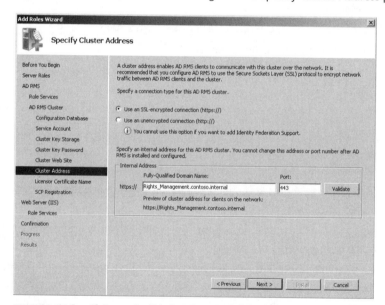

FIGURE 6-24 Specifying and validating the cluster URL and port number.

16. Click Next.

17. On the Name The Server Licensor Certificate page, type **Contoso DRM** in the Name text box and click Next.

18. On the Register AD RMS Service Connection Point page, ensure that Register The AD RMS Service Connection Point Now is selected and click Next.

    This registers the AD RMS service connection point (SCP) in AD DS.

> **NOTE YOU CAN DEPLOY ONLY A SINGLE AD RMS ROOT CLUSTER IN A FOREST.**
> Because AD RMS creates an SCP during installation and only one SCP can exist per forest, you can deploy only a single AD RMS root cluster in an AD DS forest.

19. On the Web Server (IIS) page, read the information and click Next.

20. On the Select Role Services page, do not change the role services settings. Click Next.

21. On the Confirm Installation Selections page, review your choices and click Install.

22. When the installation is complete, click Finish to close the installation wizard.

23. Log off from Boston and log back on with the same account.

    This updates the permissions granted the Kim_Akers account, which is added to the AD RMS Enterprise Administrators group.

24. If necessary, open Server Manager.

25. Expand Configuration\Local Users and Groups\Groups.

26. Add each of the administrative groups you created in AD DS to its corresponding local group on Boston.

> **MORE INFO AD RMS INSTALLATION**
> For more information on how to install an AD RMS cluster, see *http://technet.microsoft .com/en-us/library/cc771627.aspx*. For a step-by-step installation guide, see *http://technet .microsoft.com/en-us/library/cc753531.aspx*. For more information about installing additional cluster members, see *http://technet.microsoft.com/en-us/library/cc753417.aspx*.

EXERCISE 6 Remove Server Roles

Do not carry out this exercise unless you have finished studying the AD LDS, AD FS, and AD RMS server roles. When you have done so and are ready to move on to the next chapter, ensure that you start with a clean slate by removing the roles you installed on both Boston and Glasgow in this chapter and the previous one. You should already have removed the RODC role from Boston. Chapter 5 gives instructions on how to remove the AD LDS role.

1. In Server Manager, remove the AD FS role from both Glasgow and Boston.

2. Remove the AD CS role from Boston so the server is no longer a root CA and remove the AD RMS role from Boston.

    You need Glasgow to remain a domain controller. Do *not* remove the AD DS role from this server.

Lesson Summary

- AD RMS provides support for data protection services through digital rights management. A user must have an e-mail–enabled account in an AD DS domain to use AD RMS services. AD RMS–enabled applications (for example, Office Word) enable users to generate and work with protected content.

- Windows Vista includes the AD RMS client by default. In Windows XP, you must download and install Windows Rights Management Client with SP2.

- After you install AD RMS, you must create an extranet URL and configure trust policies if you want to give external users access to your DRM system. If you want to work with other AD RMS infrastructures, you must exchange SLCs. If you want to exclude users from your DRM system, you must create exclusion policies.

- Rights policy templates facilitate user content creation. These templates simplify the user experience and ensure that your DRM strategy is used in a standard manner.

 Quick Check

- How many root clusters can you deploy in an AD DS forest?

Quick Check Answer

- You can deploy only a single AD RMS root cluster in an AD DS forest. AD RMS creates an SCP during installation, and only one SCP can exist per forest.

Lesson Review

You can use the following questions to test your knowledge of the information in Lesson 2, "Installing, Configuring, and Using AD RMS." The questions are also available on the companion DVD if you prefer to review them in electronic form.

> *NOTE* **ANSWERS**
>
> Answers to these questions and explanations of why each answer choice is right or wrong are located in the "Answers" section at the end of the book.

1. You want to enable users to recover or modify any data that is managed by your AD RMS infrastructure. These users should have full access to all content protected by an AD RMS implementation and should be able to recover data generated by other users who have subsequently left the organization. How best would you accomplish this?

   A. Add the users to the AD RMS Template Administrators global security group.

   B. Add the users to the Enterprise Admins Universal group.

   C. Create a Universal Super Users group and add the user accounts to this group.

   D. Add the users to the AD RMS Auditors global security group.

2. You have just installed the AD RMS server role, and you want to configure it. The *AD RMS* node is available in Server Manager. You have specified a root cluster and AD RMS. Setup has completed without any errors. When you begin working with AD RMS, you get an error message. What is likely to be the problem?

   A. The AD RMS server role is not properly installed on your server.

   B. An AD RMS root cluster already exists in your AD DS forest.

   C. Your account does not have appropriate privileges to manage AD RMS.

   D. Your server is not a member of an AD DS domain.

3. You have installed the AD RMS server role and configured an extranet URL. You have tested this URL successfully from the server you were using to set it up. The URL uses the HTTPS protocol. When users try to access AD RMS from outside your network, they cannot do so. What is likely to be the problem?

   A. The server certificate is invalid.

   B. Your users should be using the HTTP protocol, not HTTPS.

   C. Users require AD DS domain accounts to access the URL.

   D. You provided an incorrect URL to users.

Chapter Review

To further practice and reinforce the skills you learned in this chapter, you can perform the following tasks:

- Review the chapter summary.
- Complete the case scenarios. These scenarios set up real-world situations involving the topics of this chapter and ask you to create solutions.
- Complete the suggested practices.
- Take a practice test.

Chapter Summary

- AD FS uses identity federation partnerships and federation trusts to extend AD DS internal IDA services to external networks. It relies on secure communications, and each server in an AD FS partnership trusts the root certificate.
- In AD FS, claims-aware applications allow access based on the claims assigned to each partner in the partnership. You create a federation trust between the two partners and assign claims to the account organization.
- AD RMS uses DRM to support data protection services. AD RMS–enabled applications enable users to generate and work with protected content. You can create an extranet URL and configure trust policies to give external users access to your DRM system.
- You can use exclusion policies, rights policy templates, and the Super User group to implement additional AD RMS configuration. If you want to work with other AD RMS infrastructures, you must exchange SLCs.

Case Scenarios

In the following case scenarios, you apply what you've learned about AD FS and AD RMS. You can find answers to the questions in these scenarios in the "Answers" section at the end of this book.

Case Scenario 1: Using Active Directory Technologies

You are a consultant currently working for Margie's Travel. This company has recently upgraded all its domain controllers to Windows Server 2008 and wants to implement AD DS technologies. The company's requirements are as follows:

- To update the central authentication and authorization store.
- To support applications running in the extranet. Three of these are Windows-based and rely on Windows NT authentication. Two are Web-based and rely on the authentication models supported by IIS. Clients for the extranet applications are located on the

internal network and in partner organizations and include the general public accessing from the Internet.

You must have secure communications at all times. You have been asked to identify which Windows Server 2008 Active Directory technologies should be used and how they should be implemented. Answer the following questions.

1. Which technology should you use to upgrade the internal directory service and update the central authentication and authorization store?

2. How do you support applications in the extranet?

3. Which AD FS federated Web SSO design should you implement?

4. Would Margie's Travel be the resource or the account partner in this setup?

5. How do you support the Windows-based and Web-based applications?

6. How do you implement communications security?

Case Scenario 2: Implementing an External AD RMS Cluster

You are a systems administrator with Litware, Inc. You have recently implemented an AD RMS deployment within the organization. External and internal uses can access your rights management policies and ensure content protection. Answer the following questions.

1. Litware wants to share rights protection policies with Contoso, Ltd., but does not want to put an AD FS infrastructure in place. How do you do this?

2. Currently, only users with Windows Vista clients can create and access rights-protected content. Users with Windows XP clients cannot. How do you solve this problem?

3. You monitor database sizes on Litware's SQL Server 2005 server and find that the size of the directory services database is unacceptably large. You have been careful to delete AD RMS users when staffing changes make this necessary. What do you need to do?

Suggested Practices

To help you successfully master the exam objectives presented in this chapter, complete the following tasks.

- **Practice 1**   Carry out the exercises outlined in the Microsoft Step-by-Step Guide for Active Directory Federation Services, available at *http://www.microsoft.com/downloads /details.aspx?familyid=062F7382-A82F-4428-9BBD-A103B9F27654&displaylang=en*. Note that the Step-by-Step Guide (and this chapter) asks you to install AD FS on a domain controller. Be aware that this is not recommended on a production network.

- **Practice 2**   Review the activities you need to carry out to create or modify a rights policy template. Rights policy templates are an important part of the AD RMS administration process.

- **Practice 3**   Use TechNet and the Windows Server 2008 Help files to obtain more information about DRM implementations in Windows Server 2008.
- **Practice 4**   Practice using the various console settings for AD RMS. These are available in Server Manager.

Take a Practice Test

The practice tests on this book's companion DVD offer many options. For example, you can test yourself on just one exam objective, or you can test yourself on all the upgrade exam content. You can set up the test so that it closely simulates the experience of taking a certification exam, or you can set it up in study mode so that you can look at the correct answers and explanations after you answer each question.

> **MORE INFO**   **PRACTICE TESTS**
>
> For details about all the practice test options available, see the "How to Use the Practice Tests" section in this book's Introduction.

CHAPTER 7

Active Directory Certificate Services

Certificate servers are as important to a Windows Server 2008 Active Directory network infrastructure as Domain Name System (DNS) and Dynamic Host Configuration Protocol (DHCP) servers. Certificate servers enable you to issue certificates that support smart card logons, encrypt network traffic through IPsec, encrypt Web traffic by using Secure Sockets Layer (SSL), and encrypt files and folders through encrypting file system (EFS). This chapter discusses the different types of certificate servers, how you can configure the settings of a certificate authority (CA), how you can manage certificate templates, the options you have for configuring certificate enrollment, and the technologies available in Windows Server 2008 to manage certificate revocation.

Exam objectives in this chapter

- Install Active Directory Certificate Services.
- Configure CA server settings.
- Manage certificate templates.
- Manage enrollments.
- Manage certificate revocations.

Lessons in this chapter:

Before You Begin

To complete the lessons in this chapter, you must have done the following:

- Installed and configured the evaluation edition of Windows Server 2008 Enterprise Edition in accordance with the instructions listed in the Introduction.

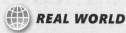 **REAL WORLD**

Orin Thomas

When I started working in IT, few of my colleagues would have considered a certificate server a necessary part of network infrastructure. An organization needed DNS and DHCP servers (though to be honest, we used BOOTP because DHCP hadn't been introduced yet), but certificate servers were seen as an infrastructure novelty rather than as a necessity. The important place that digital certificates hold in a Windows Server 2008 network infrastructure is indicative of how the role of Certificate Services has changed over the past decade and a half. Whereas certificate servers were once an oddity on a corporate network, today you would be hard pressed to find a large corporate network that doesn't have Certificate Services deployed to some extent. As an experienced systems administrator, you need to be as familiar with the functionality of Active Directory Certificate Services (AD CS) as you are with the functionality of DNS, DHCP, and Active Directory Domain Services (AD DS) itself.

Lesson 1: Managing and Maintaining Certificate Servers

In this lesson, you learn about the four types of certificate servers: enterprise root, enterprise subordinate, standalone root, and standalone subordinate. You learn which type of certificate server you should deploy to meet a specific set of needs and how to configure key archiving and set up user accounts to function as key recovery agents. You also learn how to configure Certificate Services roles, a method through which you can divide the responsibilities for managing certificate servers and managing certificates between different groups of people.

After this lesson, you will be able to:

- Install standalone and enterprise certificate authorities.
- Configure certificate authority hierarchies.
- Configure key archiving, recovery, and CA backup.
- Assign CA administrative roles.

Estimated lesson time: 40 minutes

Active Directory Certificate Services

Unlike Active Directory integrated DNS servers or domain controllers, which have an architecture in which each server is essentially equal, AD CS, known just as Certificate Services in prior versions of Microsoft Windows, is strictly hierarchical in nature. Certificate Services, also called public key infrastructure (PKI), is all about trust and, in an AD CS infrastructure, trust flows from the top down. The certificate server at the top of the hierarchy is known as the root CA. Every certificate server under the root CA is a subordinate CA. The root CA signs the signing certificate of the subordinate CAs directly under it in the hierarchy. If you trust the root CA, you also, by implication, trust the subordinate CA because the certificates issued by the subordinate CA are authorized indirectly by the root CA. Subordinate CAs can issue their own signing certificates, allowing further levels to be added to the Certificate Services hierarchy. If the administrator of a certificate server higher up the chain has reason to believe that a CA lower down the hierarchy has become compromised, he or she can revoke the signing certificate issued to that CA. This marks the CA as untrustworthy, and certificates issued by that CA and all CAs under it in the hierarchy become invalid.

You can configure Windows Server 2008 certificate servers as either enterprise CAs or standalone CAs. This leads to four possibilities, the enterprise root CA, the enterprise subordinate CA, the standalone root CA, and the standalone subordinate CA. Enterprise CAs interact directly with AD DS and use Group Policy to propagate certificate trust and revocation data to clients throughout the Active Directory forest. Enterprise CAs use customizable certificate templates. Each certificate template has a configurable set of security permissions that enable administrators to specify which clients are able to enroll in certificates generated from that template. Other advantages of enterprise CAs are that the client data required to generate the certificate is automatically extracted from AD DS and that you can use auto-enrollment to automate the deployment of certificates from certificate servers of this type. You learn more about certificate templates and the auto-enrollment process in Lesson 2, "Managing and Maintaining Certificates and Templates."

Standalone CAs can function on computers that are not members of an Active Directory domain. You can also install a standalone CA on a computer that is a member of the domain. If you do this using an account that is a member of the Domain Admins group, information about the CA is automatically added to the Trusted Root Certificate Authorities certificate store. Standalone CAs can also publish revocation data to AD DS. What standalone CAs cannot do is automatically extract information needed for certificate enrollment from AD DS. When a client submits a request to a standalone CA, it must manually provide all relevant identification information. The administrator of the CA must then manually verify this registration information before deciding whether to issue the certificate. It is possible to use both enterprise and standalone CAs in the same infrastructure. Many organizations deploy a standalone CA as the root CA and then have a group of enterprise CAs to manage certificates for AD DS. Standalone CAs can be taken offline, and having an offline root CA is considered the most secure way of deploying a root CA. Offline root CAs are covered in more detail later in this lesson.

The type of CA you can deploy depends on the edition of Windows Server 2008 you have available. You cannot install the AD CS role on a computer running Windows Web Server 2008. Enterprise CAs are supported on Windows Server 2008 Enterprise and Datacenter only. Windows Server 2008 Standard supports the installation of a standalone CA but does not support other features such as network device enrollment, the Online Responder service, key archival, role separation, delegated enrollment agent, or certificate manager restrictions.

Deploying AD CS

You must decide about the type of CA you deploy before you install the role. After you have installed the role, you cannot convert the CA type. You cannot promote a subordinate CA to a root CA, and you cannot convert a standalone CA to an enterprise CA; nor can you demote a root CA or change an enterprise CA to a standalone CA. It is important to note that other than needing to be installed on a computer that is a member of the domain, an enterprise CA can perform the same tasks as a standalone CA. During the installation of the AD CS role, you must select whether you want to install an enterprise or a standalone CA, as shown in Figure 7-1. As mentioned earlier, an enterprise CA requires access to AD DS. When you deploy an enterprise CA, certificate trust and revocation lists are automatically published through AD DS. The publication of revocation lists is one of those necessary housekeeping tasks that many administrators neglect, so having the process automated is a benefit.

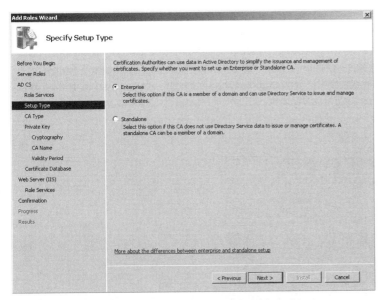

FIGURE 7-1 Selecting between an enterprise and standalone CA.

During the setup of a CA, you can choose to create a new private key or use an existing key, as shown in Figure 7-2. Select only the Use Existing Private Key option when you are recovering or reinstalling a CA and you have access to a preexisting private key. Restoring CAs is covered later in this lesson.

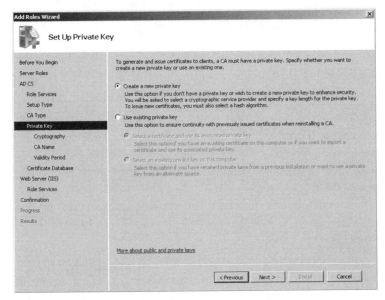

FIGURE 7-2 Setting up a private key.

During the installation of AD CS, you can also specify the location of the certificate database, as shown in Figure 7-3. On certificate servers that process a lot of certificate requests, consider placing the certificate database on a separate volume protected by redundant disks. Many important certificate servers use RAID 1+0 arrays to store the Certificate Services logs and database. Use care in selecting the location of the Certificate Services database and logs because it is difficult to change these locations if your original choice proves problematic. During the practice at the end of the lesson, you put what you have learned into practice by installing an enterprise root CA.

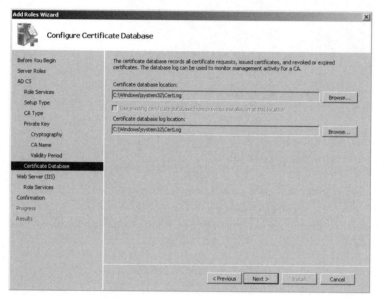

FIGURE 7-3 The default certificate database location.

Offline Root CA

One method of ensuring that a CA is not susceptible to attack is to take it offline. In many PKI deployments, the root CA is not only offline, but its hard disk drive is removed and stored in a secure area. If an attacker compromises a root CA, consider every CA in the hierarchy under the root CA suspect. However, if you want to take your organization's root CA offline, you must ensure that the root CA in your hierarchy is a standalone CA. Because of its tight integration with AD DS, you cannot take an enterprise CA offline without causing significant network disruption. Microsoft recommends that you perform the following steps when you are deploying an offline root CA.

1. Install a root CA on a standalone computer running Windows Server 2008 that is not a member of a domain.

2. Configure the CA so that the default action on the receipt of any certificate request is to set the status of the request to pending.

3. Configure the URL location of the certificate revocation list (CRL) distribution point to a location that is accessible after the server is offline. Similarly, modify the URL location for the authority information access (AIA) distribution points.

   This is necessary because an offline root CA's default CRL and AIA distribution points are not accessible when the server is offline. If you do not do this, CRL checks will fail because clients are unable to locate the CRL, and certificate chain verification will fail because the AIA cannot be located.

4. Publish the CRL. Export the CA certificate. Migrate the CRL and CA certificate to all CRL distribution point locations. You can now shut down the standalone root CA.

5. If deploying PKI with AD DS, publish the CA certificate to the enterprise root store and the certificate to the AIA points, using *certutil.exe*.

6. If you are setting up subordinate enterprise CAs, or even standalone subordinate CAs, save certificate requests to a removable media location, boot up the standalone root CA, manually process the requests, and then shut the standalone root down.

> **MORE INFO**   **MORE ON OFFLINE ROOT CAS**
>
> For more information on creating a certification hierarchy with an offline root certification authority, see the following TechNet document: *http://technet2.microsoft.com /windowsserver/en/library/45c28bf8-9952-4ca1-b124-7d86afb83f691033.mspx?mfr=true*.

Offline root CAs are not necessary, and many organizations that deploy AD CS will use an enterprise root CA because it is far simpler to set up than the offline standalone alternative.

Certificate Practice Statements

A certificate practice statement is a policy document that defines the process through which a CA issues certificates. Committees that include systems administrators and the company legal team usually create certificate practice statements. Certificate practice statements are created in conjunction with certificate policies. A certificate policy is a formal document that describes the certificates issued by the CA and the responsibility of the organization that manages the CA with respect to those certificates. It generally includes information about the conditions under which a certificate can be used, issuance and enrollment procedures, and the legal liabilities that exist for all parties involved. Certificate practice statements and policies generally do not need to be formally drawn up if your organization is not issuing digital certificates to anyone outside the organization. For example, if your CA issues certificates only to support IPsec Network Access Protection (NAP) enforcement, the company legal team need not be involved. Consider the creation of certificate practice statements and certificate policies if there are legal issues or liabilities that arise if the CA is compromised or misused. In such circumstances, develop and finalize these policy documents prior to deploying the CA hierarchy.

MORE INFO **CERTIFICATE POLICIES AND PRACTICES WHITE PAPER**

For more detail on the definition and development of certificate policy and practice documents, see the following document on TechNet: *http://technet2.microsoft.com /windowsserver/en/library/78c89e0f-44f8-452a-922c-5dd5b8eaa63b1033.mspx?mfr=true*.

 Quick Check

1. What are the names of the policy documents you should develop in conjunction with your organization's legal team if there are potential liability issues related to the issuance of digital certificates from CAs that you will manage?

2. Which one of these policies relates to the issuance of certificates and which one relates to the management of the CA?

Quick Check Answers

1. Certificate policies and certificate practice statements.

2. Certificate policies relate to the issuance of certificates. Certificate practice statements relate to the management of the CA.

Managing Certificate Services Roles

AD CS is an integral component of an organization's security infrastructure. Many organizations assign the responsibility for different aspects of security infrastructure to different people. Partitioning these responsibilities works as a set of checks and balances, ensuring that no one single person is in control of everything. The label assigned to this division of important responsibility is *role separation*. AD CS supports role separation, so organizations can partition the responsibility of administering the server from the responsibility of issuing actual certificates.

NOTE **AUDITING AND RESTRICTED GROUPS**

Not only is it necessary to set up role separation in high-security environments, it is also necessary to set up an auditing and alerts infrastructure so that necessary personnel can detect any attempt to subvert the process. Use restricted Group Policy to limit the membership of sensitive groups used in role separation.

There are four Certificate Services roles: CA Administrator, Certificate Manager, Backup Operator, and Auditor. The two critical roles are CA Administrator and Certificate Manager. You designate Certificate Services roles by assigning permissions on the Security tab of the CA properties. You assign the CA Administrator role by granting the Manage CA permission, as shown in Figure 7-4. You assign the Certificate Manager role by granting the Issue and Manage Certificates permission. If you plan to implement role separation on your organization's

CAs, remember that the Domain Admins, the Enterprise Admins, and the Administrators local groups have the Issue and Manage Certificates and the Manage CA permissions by default.

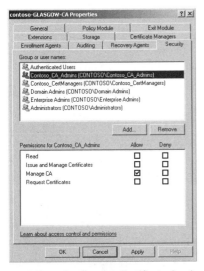

FIGURE 7-4 Configuring Certificate Services roles.

Assign the CA Administrator role to people in your organization who are responsible for configuring and maintaining the CA itself. When you assign this role to users, they are able to start and stop the certificate server, renew CA keys, define key recovery agents, configure certificate manager restrictions, configure extensions, and—very important—assign Certificate Services roles. Auditing is very important when using role separation because you want to ensure that your CA Administrators do not assign themselves the Certificate Manager role.

Assign the Certificate Manager role to the people in your organization who are responsible for approving certificate enrollments and making decisions about revocations. It is also possible to restrict the Certificate Managers role to specific templates. For example, you can assign one group of users the permission to manage the Web Server certificate template, as shown in Figure 7-5.

Assign the auditor role to people in your organization who are responsible for checking the use of the CA. Auditors are able to view the CA's Security event log and can review auditing events related to AD CS. To assign this role, edit the Local Security Policy on the CA. Under the *User Rights Assignment* node, add the user accounts or groups responsible for auditing the CA to the Manage Auditing and Security Log policy. Assign the Backup Operator role to people who are responsible for backing up the CA database, the CA configuration, and the CA's public and private key pairs. Like the Auditor role, you assign the Backup Operator role by editing the Local Security Policy on the CA and adding the appropriate user accounts or groups to the Backup Files and Directories policy under the *User Rights Assignment* node, as shown in Figure 7-6.

FIGURE 7-5 Configuring the Certificate Managers role.

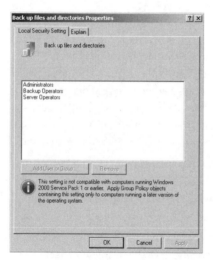

FIGURE 7-6 Configuring backup operators.

Role separation is employed on a CA-by-CA basis. In a CA hierarchy, permissions related to role separation are not inherited. For example, a group assigned the Issue and Manage Certificates permission on the root CA does not automatically gain the Issue and Manage Certificates permission on a subordinate CA. Role separation permissions are not assigned through Group Policy. If you need to enforce strict Certificate Services role separation in your organization for a small number of certificate templates, consider deploying an issuing CA just for these templates. You should do this because, generally, only a few certificate templates are sensitive enough to justify the administrative overhead of role separation.

When you take this approach, remove these sensitive templates from other CAs in your organization.

> **MORE INFO** **MORE ON ROLE SEPARATION**
>
> For more on archiving encryption keys, consult Chapter 13, "Role Separation," in *Windows Server 2008 PKI and Security*, by Brian Komar (Microsoft Press, 2008).

Key Archiving and Recovery

Key archiving allows for the recovery of a private key if a user's private key becomes corrupted or is lost. Key recovery is often necessary if a user profile is accidently deleted, a hard disk fails or becomes corrupted, a smart card fails, or a computer is stolen or lost. You can avoid some of these situations if you enable credential roaming. When you enable credential roaming through the Certificate Services Client policy, private keys are stored within AD DS.

You must configure certificate templates to support key archival. You do this on the Request Handling tab of a certificate template's properties by selecting the Archive Subject's Encryption Private Key check box, as shown in Figure 7-7. You learn more about editing the properties of certificate templates in Lesson 2.

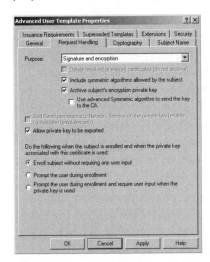

FIGURE 7-7 Enabling private key archiving.

You enable key archival on the Recovery Agents tab of the CA Properties in the CA console by selecting the Archive The Key option and specifying a key recovery agent, as shown in Figure 7-8. In the number of recovery agents to use, select the number of key recovery agent (KRA) certificates you have added to the CA. This ensures that each KRA can be used to recover a private key. If you specify a smaller number than the number of KRA certificates installed, the CA will randomly select that number of KRA certificates from the available total and encrypt the private key, using those certificates. This complicates recovery because you then have to figure out which recovery agent certificate was used to encrypt the private key before beginning recovery.

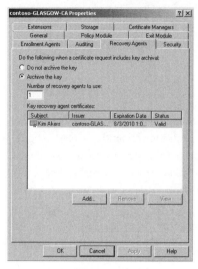

FIGURE 7-8 Enabling a recovery agent.

You assign the KRA role to people in your organization responsible for recovering private keys archived in the CA database. For example, a user with the KRA role is able to retrieve the private key and certificate used for EFS if he or she must recover another user's encrypted files. Before you assign the key recovery agent role to a user, ensure that you have issued that user account a certificate with the Key Recovery Agent OID (object identifier). The default KRA certificate template has this OID. You can secure this template by limiting which users and groups have enrollment permissions to it. If you decide to deploy key recovery in your organization, minimize the number of people who can function as key recovery agents. Lesson 2 discusses editing permissions on security templates in more detail.

Recovering a private key involves determining the serial number of the certificate in question and using *certutil –getkey* to extract an encrypted version of the key from the CA database. This functionality is also available from the Certification Authority console by right-clicking the appropriate certificate in the list of issued certificates. A user with a KRA certificate can then use the *certutil –recoverkey* command to extract the private key, which he or she can then import or allow others to import as required.

> **MORE INFO** **MORE ON ARCHIVING ENCRYPTION KEYS**
>
> For more on archiving encryption keys, consult Chapter 18, "Archiving Encryption Keys," in *Windows Server 2008 PKI and Security*, by Brian Komar (Microsoft Press, 2008).

Certificate Database Backup and Recovery

Certificate servers are a critical component of your organization's network infrastructure, and you must back them up regularly. The most common method of backing up AD CS is the system state backup. When you perform a system state backup on a CA, the following Certificate Services components are backed up:

- **CA database**   The CA database stores information on all certificates that have been issued and revoked by the CA.

- **CA key pairs**   If you back up the CA key pair, you can rebuild the CA in the event of its failure, so that all currently issued certificates remain valid. If you renew the CA's certificate, generating a new version of the key pair, you must not only back up the new CA keys but previous versions as well. It is important to note that if a hardware security module is present, the CA's key pair might be excluded from the system state backup. If you have one of these devices installed on your CA, check the documentation.

- **Certificate Services registry settings**   During a system state backup, the computer's entire registry is backed up. This includes the registry changes made during the installation of Certificate Services.

You can perform a system state backup on a computer running Windows Server 2008 by installing Windows Server Backup and then issuing the *wbadmin start systemstatebackup –backuptarget:driveletter* command. You cannot initiate system state–only backups from the Windows Server Backup GUI, although when you back up a volume or perform a full backup, the system state data is automatically included.

It is also possible to perform backups of the CA database, key pairs, and log files, using the Certification Authority console and using the *certutil* command. To perform a backup using the CA console, right-click the CA, select All Tasks, and then select Back Up CA. This launches the Certification Authority Backup Wizard. As Figure 7-9 shows, you are able to back up both the private key and the CA certificate as well as the certificate database and certificate database log. The directory that you perform the backup to must be empty. For security reasons, you must enter a password if you are backing up the private key and CA certificate. Store any written record of this password in a secure location separate from the location in which you store the backup containing the private key and CA certificate. To achieve the same result from the command line, issue the *certutil –backup C:\BackupLocation* command.

To restore Certificate Services from a system state backup, use the *wbadmin start systemstaterecovery –version:VersionID –backuptarget:DriveLetter –machine:ComputerName* command. The DriveLetter option is the letter of the drive storing the system state backup. The ComputerName option is the name of the CA for which you are restoring the system state backup. The VersionID option is the version identifier of the backup. You can get a list of all the version identifiers of previous backups taken by issuing the *wbadmin get versions* command.

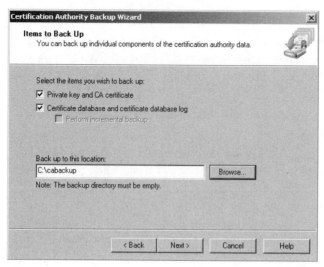

FIGURE 7-9 Backing up the CA.

You can restore a private key and CA certificate by using the CA console or the *certutil* command. To restore using the CA console, right-click the CA, select All Tasks, and then select Restore CA. This starts the Certification Authority Restore Wizard. You can choose to restore the private key and CA certificate and the certificate database and database log. During the restoration process, you are asked for the password that was supplied when the original backup of the private key and CA certificate was taken. AD CS is stopped while you are performing the restoration process and restarts automatically after the restoration is successful. If the restoration process is unsuccessful, you must restart AD CS manually. To restore AD CS from the command line, issue the *certutil –restore BackupDirectory* command.

If you are restoring Certificate Services from scratch on a new computer with the same name as the original CA, first import the CA certificate and private key to the local machine store and verify that CAPolicy.inf is imported to the %Winddir% folder. Add the AD CS role, selecting Use Existing Private Key and the original CA's certificate.

> **MORE INFO**   **MORE ON CA BACKUP AND RECOVERY**
>
> For more on archiving encryption keys, consult Chapter 14, "Planning and Implementing Disaster Recovery," in *Windows Server 2008 PKI and Security*, by Brian Komar (Microsoft Press, 2008).

EXAM TIP

Remember which steps you must perform before you take a standalone root CA offline.

PRACTICE **Installing a CA and Assigning Administrative Roles**

In this practice, you install an enterprise root CA in the *contoso.internal* domain and then configure a key recovery agent.

EXERCISE 1   Install an Enterprise Root CA

In this exercise, you install Active Directory Certificate Services on server Glasgow. Glasgow then functions as an enterprise root CA.

1. Log on to server Glasgow, using the Kim_Akers user account.

2. Open the Server Manager console. Right-click the *Roles* node, and then select Add Roles.

   This launches the Add Roles Wizard.

3. On the Before You Begin page, click Next.

4. On the Select Server Roles page, select the Active Directory Certificate Services check box, and then click Next. Review the information on the Introduction To Active Directory Certificate Services page, and then click Next.

5. On the Role Services page, select the Certification Authority and Certification Authority Web Enrollment check boxes.

6. When you select the Certification Authority Web Enrollment items, you are prompted by the Add Role Services dialog box. Click Add Required Role Services, and then click Next.

7. On the Specify Setup Type page, verify that Enterprise is selected, and then click Next.

8. On the Specify CA Type page, select Root CA, and then click Next.

9. On the Set Up Private Key page, select Create A New Private Key, and then click Next.

10. On the Configure Cryptography For CA page, change the character length to 4096 and select the Use Strong Private Key Protection Features Provided By The CSP check box, as shown in Figure 7-10, and click Next.

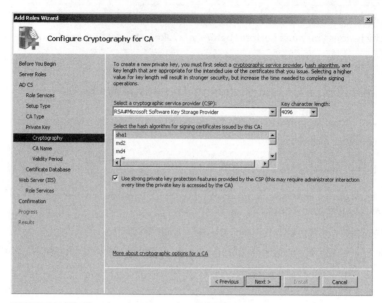

FIGURE 7-10 Configuring cryptography settings.

11. On the Configure CA Name page, verify that the common name is set to Contoso-GLASGOW-CA and the distinguished name suffix is set to DC=Contoso,DC=internal, and then click Next.

12. Verify that the validity period is set to 5 years, and then click Next.

13. Verify the certificate database location, and then click Next.

14. Review the information on the Confirm Installation Selections page, and then click Next twice. Click Install to install Active Directory Certificate Services and support role services from the Web Server (IIS) role. Click Close to dismiss the Add Roles Wizard when the installation completes.

EXERCISE 2 Configure Enterprise Root CA Settings

In this exercise, you configure key archival settings and assign administrative roles.

1. Log on to Glasgow, using the Kim_Akers user account.

2. Open the Certification Authority console from the Administrative Tools menu. Click Continue to dismiss the User Account Control dialog box.

3. Expand the *Contoso-Glasgow-CA* node, and then right-click the *Certificate Templates* node. Select New, and then select Certificate Template To Issue.

4. From the list of available certificate templates, select Key Recovery Agent, as shown in Figure 7-11, and then click OK.

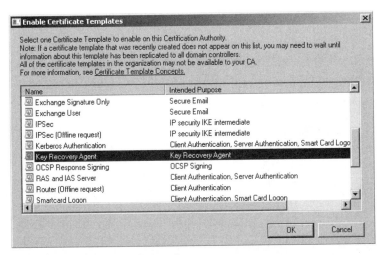

FIGURE 7-11 Enabling the KRA template.

5. From the Start menu, click Run, type **mmc**, and then click OK. Dismiss the UAC dialog box and add the Certificates snap-in for your user account.

6. Expand the *Certificates – Current User* node.

7. Right-click the Personal store, select All Tasks, and then select Request New Certificate. In the Certificate Enrollment Wizard, select the Key Recovery Agent check box and click Enroll. Click Finish when the certificate installation completes.

8. Return to the Certificate Authority console and select the *Pending Requests* node. In the details pane, right-click the pending certificate request, select All Tasks, and then select Issue.

9. In the Certification Authority console, right-click Contoso-GLASGOW-CA, and then select Properties.

10. On the Recovery Agents tab, select Archive The Key, and then click Add. Select the certificate issued to Kim Akers, and then click OK. Click Apply. In the dialog box asking whether you want to restart Active Directory Certificate Services, click Yes.

11. Open Active Directory Users And Computers. Create a new global security group called **KRA_CertManagers** in the Users container. Close Active Directory Users And Computers.

12. In the Certificate Authority console, right-click Contoso-GLASGOW-CA, and then select Properties.

13. On the Security tab, click Add. Add the KRA_CertManagers group, as shown in Figure 7-12, and assign the group the Allow Issue And Manage Certificates permission. Click Apply.

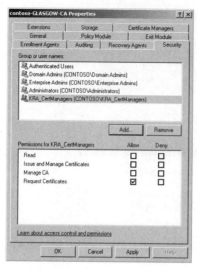

FIGURE 7-12 Assigning the Cert Manager role.

14. On the Certificate Managers tab, select Restrict Certificate Managers. Verify that the CONTOSO\KRA_CertManagers group is listed and, in the Certificate Templates area, click Add.

15. In the Enable Certificate Templates dialog box, select the Key Recovery Agent template, and then click OK.

16. In the Certificate Templates list, select <All>, and then click Remove. Verify that the CA Properties dialog box matches Figure 7-13, and then click OK.

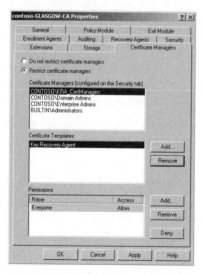

FIGURE 7-13 Certificate Managers configuration.

Lesson Summary

- Enterprise CAs are tightly integrated into AD DS. They can use custom certificate templates, and you can configure them to auto-enroll certificates. Standalone CAs cannot use custom certificate templates, and certificate request data must be entered manually rather than automatically extracted from AD DS.

- You can take a standalone root CA offline and physically secure it. You cannot take an enterprise root CA offline. An enterprise CA can be a subordinate of a standalone root CA.

- You must configure key archiving on the CA and from within a certificate template. You can configure a key recovery agent (KRA) by issuing a user a key recovery agent certificate.

- You can back up certificate services by using a normal system state backup, by using the Certification Authority Console, or by using the *certutil.exe* command-line utility.

- The Certificate Manager role allows users granted the role the ability to issue and manage certificates. The CA Administrator role allows users to start and stop Certificate Services, configure extensions, assign roles, and define key recovery agents.

Lesson Review

You can use the following questions to test your knowledge of the information in Lesson 1, "Managing and Maintaining Certificate Servers." The questions are also available on the companion DVD if you prefer to review them in electronic form.

> **NOTE ANSWERS**
>
> Answers to these questions and explanations of why each answer choice is right or wrong are located in the "Answers" section at the end of the book.

1. You are planning the deployment of Active Directory Certificate Services in your Windows Server 2008 functional level forest. You want to be able to take the root CA offline but also integrate Certificate Services fully with AD DS. Which of the following deployments should you recommend for the first CA in your organization?

   A. Enterprise root CA

   B. Enterprise subordinate CA

   C. Standalone root CA

   D. Standalone subordinate CA

2. On which of the following versions of Windows Server 2008 can you install an enterprise subordinate CA?

A. Windows Web Server 2008

B. Windows Server 2008 Standard

C. Windows Server 2008 Enterprise

D. Windows Server 2008 Datacenter

3. You want to implement key archiving in your organization. Two users will have the responsibility for restoring private keys from the certificate server's database. Which step must you take to ensure that these users will be able to restore archived keys?

A. Ensure that you issue the users a certificate with the Key Recovery Agent OID.

B. Ensure that you issue the users a certificate with the Enrollment Agent OID.

C. Ensure that you issue the users a certificate with the Subordinate Certification Authority OID.

D. Ensure that you issue the users a certificate with the EFS Recovery Agent OID.

E. Ensure that you issue the users a certificate with the OCSP Response Signing OID.

4. Your CA hierarchy will involve an offline standalone root CA with three enterprise subordinate CAs. You have just installed AD CS on the standalone root CA. Which of the following steps must you take prior to issuing signing certificates to the enterprise subordinate CAs? (Choose four. Each correct answer presents part of a complete solution.)

A. Change the CRL distribution point URL.

B. Change the AIA distribution point URL.

C. Add the standalone root CA certificate to the enterprise root store in AD DS.

D. Set the standalone root CA to offline mode.

E. Configure the AIA points in AD DS, using *certutil.exe*.

5. You want to ensure that the SSLCertManagers group is the only group able to issue certificates based on the Web Server template from a specific issuing CA. When you navigate to the Certificate Managers tab on the CA in question, the SSLCertManagers group is not present in the Certificate Managers list. Which step should you take to resolve this problem?

A. Assign the SSLCertManagers group the Request Certificates permission on the Security tab of CA properties.

B. Assign the SSLCertManagers group the Manage CA permission on the Security tab of CA properties.

C. Assign the SSLCertManagers group the Issue and Manage Certificates permission on the Security tab of CA properties.

D. Edit the Web Server certificate template properties. Assign the SSLCertManagers group the Read permission to this template.

E. Edit the Web Server certificate template properties. Assign the SSLCertManagers group the Write permission to this template.

Lesson 2: Managing and Maintaining Certificates and Templates

This lesson discusses managing certificate revocations, including publishing certificate revocation lists and configuring online responders, and the different methods of enrollment, such as Web and automatic enrollment. The lesson also covers certificate templates, which enable you to create advanced digital certificates that might be a better fit for your organization than the default certificate templates that ship with Windows Server 2008.

> **After this lesson, you will be able to:**
> - Manage certificate revocations and configure online responders.
> - Manage certificate templates.
> - Manage and automate certificate enrollments.
>
> **Estimated lesson time: 40 minutes**

Managing and Maintaining Certificate Revocation Lists

Certificate revocation lists are just what they sound like: lists of revoked certificates. You trust a certificate issued by a CA because you trust the policies under which the CA issues certificates. If you did not trust the CA, you would not trust any certificates issued by that CA. A certificate revocation list shows you which certificates issued by the CA are no longer trustworthy. There are many reasons a certificate might be placed on a CRL list, such as a signing certificate issued to a subordinate CA being revoked because the subordinate CA has been compromised, but the primary statement made by a certificate being placed on a CRL list is "This certificate is no longer trustworthy."

Each time a new certificate is encountered, or an existing certificate is used, a check is made to see whether that certificate is listed on the issuing CA's CRL list. If the CA is part of a hierarchy, another check occurs to see whether the upstream CA that issued the signing certificate still trusts the CA that issued the certificate against which the check is occurring. This is because you should not trust a certificate issued by an untrustworthy CA! The location of the CRL is included with the certificate so that the software performing the CRL check knows where to access this information. The name for the location of the CRL is the CRL distribution point. It is possible for you to designate multiple CRL distribution points for a single CA.

CRL Distribution Points

You can configure the CRL distribution point for a specific certificate server by modifying the properties listed on the Extensions tab of the issuing CA's properties. To edit CRL distribution point information, you must assign the user the CA Administrator role as described in Lesson 1. As shown in Figure 7-14, you can specify CRL distribution points as HTTP, FTP, or

Lightweight Directory Access Protocol (LDAP) addresses or by file and folder location. Note that any changes to a certificate server's CRL distribution points do not apply retroactively. This information is included in the certificate at the time of issue. If you change the CRL distribution point, clients checking previously issued certificates will be unable to locate the new distribution point. If it becomes necessary to change a distribution point, develop a transition strategy that either keeps the old distribution point available over the lifetime of already issued certificates or renews all existing certificates with the updated CRL distribution point information.

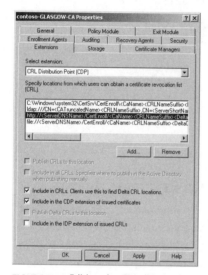

FIGURE 7-14 Editing the CRL distribution point.

CRLs are a single file that, over time, can become very large. This size is important because each time a client performs a check, it has to download the full CRL if it does not already have a copy in its cache. If you frequently update your CRL, clients must always download the entire CRL because it will not already be present in their cache. As a way of dealing with this problem, it is possible for you to publish a smaller CRL, known as a delta CRL. The delta CRL includes information only about certificates revoked since the publication of the CRL. The client downloads the delta CRL and appends it to the CRL in its cache. Because delta CRLs are smaller, you can publish them more often with less of an impact on the certificate server than would occur if you published the full CRL by using a similar schedule.

To configure the CRL and delta CRL publication interval, open the Certificate Authority console, right-click the *Revoked Certificates* node, and then select Properties. This displays the Revoked Certificate Properties dialog box shown in Figure 7-15. The default CRL publication interval is one week, and the default delta CRL publication interval is one day. Use the *certutil −CRL* command to force the publication of a new CRL or delta CRL.

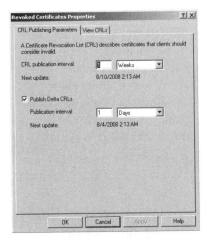

FIGURE 7-15 Revoking a certificate.

Overlap periods describe the amount of time after the end of a published CRL's lifetime that the CRL is still considered valid. Consider increasing the overlap period if you are using multiple CRL distribution points (CDPs) and replication of CRL data does not occur immediately, such as if you use a distributed file system (DFS) share as a CDP and it takes a significant amount of time for replication to complete. You can configure overlap periods for both CRLs and delta CRLs by using the *certutil –setreg ca\CRLOverlapUnits* command.

> **MORE INFO**   **CONFIGURING CERTIFICATE REVOCATION**
>
> For more information on configuring certificate revocation, see the following TechNet article: *http://technet2.microsoft.com/windowsserver2008/en/library/336d3a6a-33c6-4083 -8606-c0a4fdca9a251033.mspx?mfr=true*.

Authority Information Access

The authority information access (AIA) extension contains the URLs at which the issuing CA's certificate is published. The client uses these URLs when creating a certificate chain to retrieve the CA certificate if it does not have a copy of this certificate in a copy of the client cache. Modify the AIA extension to an alternate location if you want to take the CA offline. You must also export the CA certificate and place it in this alternate location to support certificate chain requests. The AIA also contains the URL of any online responders that you have configured to support revocation checks. You learn more about online responders later in this lesson.

Revoking a Certificate

A user must hold the Certificate Manager role to be able to revoke certificates. Just as you should not issue certificates in an arbitrary manner, you should not revoke certificates in an arbitrary manner. If possible, your organization should develop a certificate revocation policy that clearly details the reasons and situations for which issued certificates are revoked. These policies are a necessity for organizations that might be legally liable for the consequences of certificate revocation. For example, if a CA issues an SSL certificate to an e-commerce site, revoking that certificate will have an impact on the function of that business. If the revocation cannot be justified, your organization can be legally liable for loss of income. To revoke a certificate, right-click it in the list of issued certificates in the Certification Authority console and, from All Tasks, select Revoke Certificate. As Figure 7-16 shows, a dialog box asks you to provide a reason when you revoke a certificate. You can provide the following reasons:

- **Key Compromise** Select this reason if you suspect that the private key associated with the certificate has been compromised. Use this reason to revoke all keys related to a laptop that had been lost or stolen, for instance.

- **CA Compromise** Select this reason if you suspect that a subordinate CA has been compromised and want to revoke that CA's signing certificate. This invalidates all certificates issued by that CA, including the certificates of any CA below it in the hierarchy.

- **Change of Affiliation** Select this reason when the person to whom you issued the certificate leaves or changes his or her role within your organization.

- **Superseded** Select this reason when an updated certificate has been issued, perhaps with improvements to the certificate template, and you want to invalidate any previously issued certificates used for the same purpose.

- **Cease of Operation** Select this reason when revoking a computer certificate assigned to a computer that is being decommissioned. For example, your organization is decommissioning an e-commerce Web site because of a brand-name change, and you want to revoke the SSL certificate assigned to that site.

- **Certificate Hold** Select this reason to place certificates on hold status. This means that the certificate is not validated, but it also has not been fully revoked. It is possible to undo this status by assigning the RemoveFromCRL status, which can be assigned only to certificates placed on hold.

- **Unspecified** This reason is assigned when a specific revocation code is not applicable. The drawback of this category is that it does not allow auditors to determine why a particular certificate has been revoked if that decision is queried later.

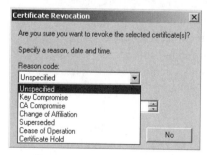

FIGURE 7-16 Certificate Revocation Wizard.

Remember that a revocation does not take effect until you publish the CRL or delta CRL. This does not mean that you should automatically force the publication of a new CRL every time you revoke a certificate, but you should make the people responsible for revoking certificates aware that there is a delay before the revocation will propagate out to the CRL.

Managing and Maintaining Online Responders

When a CRL check occurs, and the CRL does not exist in the client's cache, the entire CRL must be downloaded as well as the most recent delta CRL. The longer a CA has been active, the larger the CRL will be. During peak activity, for example, when a large number of users are logging on using smart cards, significant delays can occur due to bandwidth limitations. By implementing the Online Certificate Status Protocol (OCSP), you can deal with this problem.

A traditional revocation check involves accessing the entire CRL. An online responder check responds directly to requests about the status of specific certificates. Rather than transmitting all the data in the CRL across the network, only data about a specific certificate is transmitted. A single CA's revocation data can be distributed across multiple online responders in a responder array. Similarly, a single online responder or array can provide revocation status data for certificates issued by multiple CAs. Implementing Online Responders significantly reduces delays that occur due to CRL checks.

You can install the Online Responder role service only on computers running Windows Server 2008. Microsoft recommends that you not deploy the Online Responder role service on the computer that hosts the CA, although it is possible do to so; this is the likely configuration in small AD CS deployments. Deploy the Online Responder role service after you have deployed your initial CA infrastructure but prior to issuing any certificates. This ensures that an online responder, rather than traditional CDPs, handles all revocation checks.

To deploy an online responder, ensure that you have configured and enabled an OCSP response signing certificate template on the CA online responder servers. You must also use auto-enrollment to issue OCSP response signing certificates to all computers that host the Online Responder role service. An online responder that services multiple CAs needs OCSP response signing certificates for each CA it services. You must also modify the CA's AIA extension by adding the URL for the online responder.

You use the Online Responder management console, shown in Figure 7-17, to manage the Online Responder role service. You can use this console to create revocation configurations for every CA and CA certificate serviced by the responder. A revocation configuration includes all information necessary to reply to requests from clients about certificates issued from a specific CA. It is necessary to ensure that an online responder has a key and signing certificate for each CA it supports.

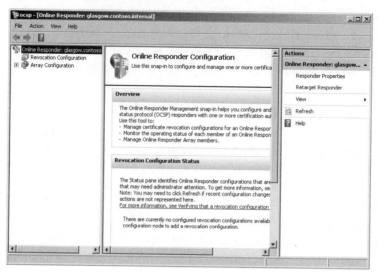

FIGURE 7-17 Online Responder management console.

> **MORE INFO**   **MORE ON CERTIFICATE REVOCATION AND ONLINE RESPONDERS**
>
> For a more detailed look at revoking certificates and the Online Responder role service, consult Chapter 10, "Certificate Revocation," in *Windows Server 2008 PKI and Security*, by Brian Komar (Microsoft Press, 2008).

 Quick Check

1. What is the difference between a CRL and a delta CRL?
2. Which types of addresses can you use to specify CDPs?

Quick Check Answers

1. A CRL contains a list of all revoked certificates. A delta CRL contains a list of certificates revoked since the publication of the last full CRL.
2. CDPs can be specified using HTTP, FTP, and LDAP addresses or by file and folder location.

Managing Certificate Templates

Certificate templates define the format and content of certificates issued by enterprise certificate authorities. A template determines which user or computer accounts can enroll for a certificate, and it defines the enrollment process (automatic, manual, or enrollment with authorized certificates). A discretionary access control list (DACL) is associated with each certificate template, which governs which users and groups have permission to access and configure the template. Certificate templates are stored within AD DS. A modification to a template will replicate through the directory to all enterprise CAs in the forest. Only the Enterprise and Datacenter editions of Microsoft Windows Server 2003 and Windows Server 2008 support customizable certificate templates.

Although Windows Server 2008 ships with a number of certificate templates that you can deploy to meet a general set of needs, the settings on the default set of certificates might not precisely suit your needs for digital certificates in your own environment. By creating your own certificate templates, you can address your organization's needs more directly.

There are three versions of the certificate template, two of which you can create for use with Windows Server 2008 Enterprise. Version 1 templates are compatible with Windows 2000 Server, Windows Server 2003, and Windows Server 2008 CAs. You cannot modify or remove a version 1 template. When you create a duplicate of a version 1 template, the duplicate becomes a version 2 or 3 template to which you can make modifications. You can customize version 2 templates, and they are compatible with Windows Server 2003 and Windows Server 2008 Enterprise and Datacenter CAs. Version 3 certificate templates support Windows Server 2008 features such as Cryptography Next Generation (CNG) and Suite B cryptographic algorithms such as elliptic curve cryptography. You can use only version 3 certificate templates with enterprise CAs installed on Windows Server 2008.

You create a new template by creating a duplicate of an existing template that best matches the function of what you want to achieve with the new digital certificate type. For example, if you want to create a more advanced type of EFS certificate, you duplicate the EFS certificate template. When you duplicate the template, you are asked whether you want to set the minimum supported CA as Windows Server 2003 Enterprise or Windows Server 2008 Enterprise, as shown in Figure 7-18.

FIGURE 7-18 Selecting template compatibility.

After you have selected the minimum supported CA, enter a name for the template. After you have set this name, you will be unable to change it. The General tab of a certificate template's properties enables you to specify the certificate's validity period, renewal period, whether to publish certificates in AD DS, whether automatic reenrollment should occur if a valid certificate exists in AD DS, and whether to use the existing key for smart card certificate renewal if a new key cannot be created. Figure 7-19 shows these settings.

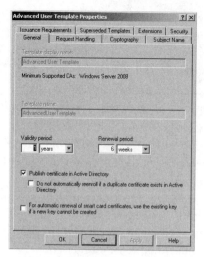

FIGURE 7-19 General tab of a certificate template's properties.

On the Request Handling tab, shown in Figure 7-20, you can define the purpose of the certificate. The available purposes are Signature and Encryption, Encryption, Signature, and Signature and Smart Card Logon. If you want to use Key Recovery in your environment for this certificate type, enable the Archive Subject's Encryption Private Key option. This enables designated key recovery agents to recover the private key if necessary. You learned about key recovery agents in Lesson 1. You can also use the options on this tab to determine the level of user input when the private key is used and whether the private key can be exported.

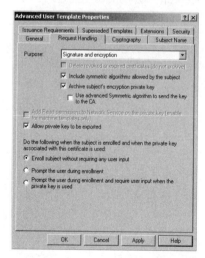

FIGURE 7-20 Certificate template request handling.

On the Cryptography tab, you can specify the algorithm and key size. You can also specify whether any cryptographic provider on the subject's computer, or a specific provider, is used for the certificate request. On the Subject Name tab, you can specify whether the CA extracts the certificate's subject name from Active Directory information or whether the subject supplies this information in the certificate request. On the Issuance Requirements tab, you can specify whether a user who holds the Certificate Manager role must approve the certificate. You can also configure whether more than one digital signature is required before enrollment can occur. If more than one signature is required, auto-enrollment is not possible for this template. Use this setting when multiple people must authorize the issuing of a certificate.

On the Superseded Templates, you can specify existing templates that the new template replaces. You must ensure that any templates specified perform the same function as the new template. The Extensions tab, shown in Figure 7-21, enables you to configure the application policies, certificate template information, issuance policies, and key usage. Application policies define the purposes for which the certificate can be used, certificate template information provides data on the OID of the certificate, issuance policies describe the rules implemented when issuing the certificate, and key usage is a restriction method that determines what a certificate can be used for.

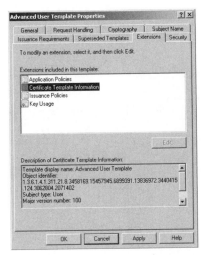

FIGURE 7-21 Certificate template extensions.

The Security tab, shown in Figure 7-22, enables you to specify the accounts and groups that can enroll and auto-enroll certificates issued from the template. You can also use this dialog box to block specific accounts and groups from enrolling or auto-enrolling. Finally, you can use this dialog box to specify which accounts and groups are able to make modifications or view the certificate template itself.

To configure a CA to issue a custom template or a template that it does not already issue that is stored within AD DS, open the Certificate Authority console, right-click the *Certificate Templates* node, select New, and then select Certificate Template To Issue. From the Enable Certificate Templates dialog box, shown in Figure 7-23, select the templates you want the CA to issue, and then click OK. You can also use the *Templates* node of the Certificate

Authority console to remove templates from a CA, stopping that CA from issuing certificates of that type.

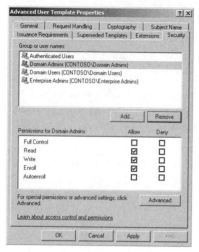

FIGURE 7-22 Certificate template security.

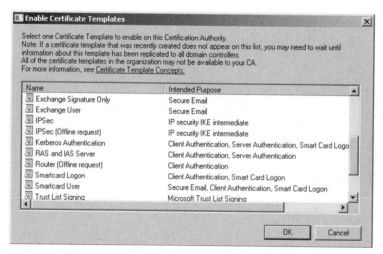

FIGURE 7-23 Select templates to issue.

MORE INFO **MORE ON CERTIFICATE TEMPLATES**

For more information on implementing and administering certificate templates, see the following TechNet link: *http://technet2.microsoft.com/windowsserver2008/en /library/9354c9b0-f4da-440c-8b2c-fb84c534e0351033.mspx?mfr=true.*

Managing Enrollment

Enrollment is the process through which users or computers acquire certificates. Traditionally, there have been two certificate enrollment methods: the Certificates console and Web enrollment. Through the Certificates console, you can run the Certificate Enrollment Wizard. The wizard provides a list of all certificates for which the security principal is eligible, as shown in Figure 7-24. You can run the Certificates console for your user account, a service account, or a computer account with the list of available certificates reflecting the context in which you run the wizard. You learn about Web enrollment later in this lesson.

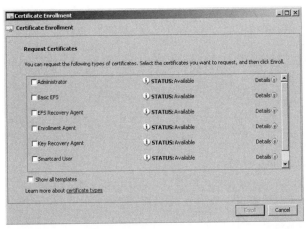

FIGURE 7-24 Certificate Enrollment Wizard.

Auto-enrollment

Although you can implement enrollment by using the Certificates console, the enrollment process is cumbersome to nontechnical users. Auto-enrollment enables you to deploy certificates automatically to users, computers, and service accounts in your organization. It minimizes the necessity for user interaction, greatly simplifying the process of certificate deployment.

You must configure a certificate template to support auto-enrollment. Only level 2 and level 3 certificate templates support auto-enrollment. Configure a template to support auto-enrollment by modifying the permissions on the certificate template's Security tab, giving the desired user or group accounts the Autoenroll permission. Figure 7-25 shows that the Accountants group has the Autoenroll permission to the Advanced User certificate template.

After configuring a certificate template's permissions to support autoenrollment, you must configure the Default Domain policy for all domains in your forest to support auto-enrollment. Do this by configuring the Certificate Services Client – Autoenrollment policy, as shown in Figure 7-26. This policy setting is available in both the Computer Configuration and User Configuration sections of a GPO and whether you enable the policy in either section depends on the types of certificates you are attempting to deploy automatically. You can also use the auto-enrollment policy to configure automatic renewal of expired certificates, updating certificates that use superseded templates. It is also possible, when configuring the policy for User certificates, to display expiration notifications.

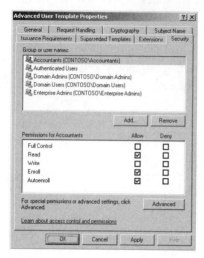

FIGURE 7-25 Configuring auto-enrollment in the template.

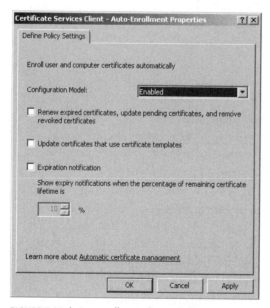

FIGURE 7-26 Auto-enrollment Group Policy.

MORE INFO   **MORE ON CONFIGURING AUTO-ENROLLMENT**

For more information on configuring autoenrollment, see the following TechNet document: *http://technet.microsoft.com/en-us/library/cc731522.aspx*.

Web Enrollment

You can configure Web enrollment to enable users of Microsoft Internet Explorer 6.x or later to use a Web application to submit certificate requests. Web enrollment enables users to request certificates and review the status of existing requests, gain access to the CRL and delta CRL, and perform smart card enrollment. Web enrollment enables you to provide a certificate enrollment mechanism for users and computers that are not part of an Active Directory environment. Web enrollment also provides certificate enrollment functionality to users of non-Microsoft operating systems. Users of alternative browsers must first create a PKCS #10 certificate request and then submit that request through the Web enrollment application. After a request has been processed, a user can reconnect to the Web enrollment application and download and install the issued certificates.

You can configure a server to support Web enrollment by installing the Certification Authority Web Enrollment role service. You can install this role service on the same computer as the CA or on a separate host. When you collocate Web enrollment with the CA, the wizard automatically configures the role service to support the local CA. When installed on a separate host, you must provide additional details to pair the Web application with a CA. Although you can install Web enrollment on enterprise CAs, you cannot use it with version 3 certificate templates. Also, you cannot request computer certificates through Web enrollment against a Windows Server 2008 CA.

MORE INFO   **MORE ON CONFIGURING WEB ENROLLMENT**

To learn more about configuring Web enrollment support for Windows Server 2008 CAs, see the following TechNet link: *http://technet.microsoft.com/en-us/library/cc732895.aspx*.

Enrollment Agents

Restricted enrollment agents are users who are able to enroll for a certificate on behalf of another client. Restricted enrollment agents often enroll smart card certificates for other users. For example, staff in the HR department might be designated enrollment agents because they need to issue smart cards as part of the process of preparing all the resources a new employee needs to start work. Enrollment agents can perform only enrollment tasks; they cannot approve pending requests or revoke existing certificates. This means an enrollment agent can be a normal user account, and you do not have to assign one of the Certificate Services roles.

To prepare a user to function as a restricted enrollment agent, issue that user an enrollment agent certificate. Two types of enrollment agent template are available on Windows Server 2008 CAs, one for computer certificates and one for user certificates. Configure enrollment agents for specific certificate templates on the Enrollment Agents tab of the CA properties. Figure 7-27 shows that the Sam Abolrous user account is an enrollment agent for the Smartcard User certificate template.

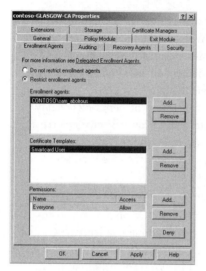

FIGURE 7-27 Configuring enrollment agents.

MORE INFO   **MORE ON ENROLLMENT AGENTS**

To learn more about enrollment agents, see the following link on TechNet: *http://technet2 .microsoft.com/windowsserver2008/en/library/56d66319-2e49-447b-92a3 -1ca2a674fb8d1033.mspx?mfr=true.*

MORE INFO   **MORE ON SMART CARD ENROLLMENT**

For a more detailed look at smart card enrollment, see Chapter 21, "Deploying Smart Cards," in *Windows Server 2008 PKI and Security*, by Brian Komar (Microsoft Press, 2008).

Network Device Enrollment Service

The Network Device Enrollment Service enables you to deploy and manage certificates to routers, switches, and wireless access points that would otherwise not have Active Directory accounts. The Network Device Enrollment Service sends Simple Certificate Enrollment Protocol (SCEP) requests on behalf of each device to a Windows Server 2008 CA, retrieves issued certificates, and then forwards them to the network device. The number of network devices that can participate in the enrollment process at any one time is five.

> **MORE INFO** **NETWORK DEVICE ENROLLMENT SERVICE**
>
> For more information about the Network Device Enrollment Service, see the following TechNet link: *http://technet2.microsoft.com/windowsserver2008/en/library/f3911350 -ab45-494d-a07e-d0b9696a651e1033.mspx?mfr=true.*

EXAM TIP

Understand the benefits of using Online Responder as opposed to using a CRL.

PRACTICE Certificate Templates and Auto-enrollment

In this practice, you configure a custom certificate template and configure the certificate revocation infrastructure.

EXERCISE 1 Creating a Certificate Template for System Health Certificates

In this exercise, you create a certificate template for system health certificates. You deploy these certificates when implementing NAP with IPsec enforcement. NAP issues these certificates to compliant computers, and they authenticate connection security policies. You manually enroll NAP-exempt clients with these certificates.

1. Log on to server Glasgow, using the Kim_Akers user account.
2. Use Active Directory Users And Computers to create a new security group called Non_NAP_Secure_Computers.
3. From the Start menu, click Run, type **mmc**, and then click OK.

   After dismissing the User Account Control dialog box, Microsoft Management Console opens.
4. From Add/Remove Snap-in, add the Certificate Templates snap-in to the console.
5. Select the *Certificate Templates* node. Right-click the Workstation Authentication template, and then select Duplicate Template.
6. In the Duplicate Template dialog box, select Windows Server 2008, Enterprise Edition, and then click OK.
7. On the General tab, enter **System Health Authentication** in the Template Display Name text box. Select the Publish Certificate In Active Directory check box. Verify that the dialog box matches what you see in Figure 7-28, and then click Apply.

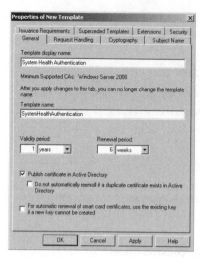

FIGURE 7-28 Creating a system health authentication template.

8. Click the Extensions tab. Select Application Policies, and then click Edit. In the Edit Application Policies Extension dialog box, click Add.

9. From the list of application policies, select System Health Authentication, and then click OK. Verify that the Edit Application Policies Extension dialog box matches Figure 7-29, and then click OK. Click OK again to return to the Properties Of New Template dialog box.

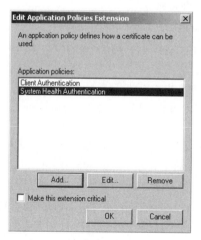

FIGURE 7-29 Configure the Application Policies extension.

10. On the Security tab, click Add. In the Select Users, Computers, Or Groups dialog box, in the Enter The Object Names To Select text box, type **Non_NAP_Secure_Computers**, and then click OK. Assign this group the Allow Enroll permission, and then click OK.

11. Open the Certification Authority console from the Administrative Tools menu. Click Continue to dismiss the User Account Control dialog box.

12. Expand the *contoso-GLASGOS-CA* node. Right-click the *Certificate Templates* node, select New, and then select Certificate Template To Issue.

13. In the Enable Certificate Templates dialog box, select the System Health Authentication template, and then click OK.

EXERCISE 2 Configure CRL Settings and Online Responder

In this exercise, you configure CRL settings and set up an online responder.

1. Log on to server Glasgow with the Kim_Akers user account.

2. Open the Server Manager console. Right-click Active Directory Certificate Services under the *Roles* node, and then select Add Role Services.

3. On the Select Role Services page, select the Online Responder role service check box, and then click Next. Click Install to install the Online Responder role service and click Close when the role service installation process completes.

4. Add the Certificate Templates snap-in to a custom MMC. Edit the properties of the OCSP Response Signing Template. On the Security tab, click Add. Click Object Types, select the Computers check box, and click OK. Enter **Glasgow** as the object name and click OK. Give the Glasgow Computer account the Allow Enroll permission, and then click OK.

5. Open the Certificate Authority console from the Administrative Tools menu. Right-click the *Certificate Templates* node, and then select New and Certificate Template To Issue. Select the OCSP Response Signing template, and then click OK.

6. Add the Certificates console, set to the local Computer Account, to a custom MMC. Right-click the Personal store, select All Tasks, and then select Request New Certificate.

7. From the list of certificates, select the OCSP Response Signing certificate check box, and then click Enroll. Click Finish to dismiss the Certificate Enrollment Wizard.

8. In the Certificate Authority console, right-click Contoso-GLASGOW-CA, and then select Properties. On the Extensions tab, select Authority Information Access (AIA) from the Select Extension drop-down list.

9. Click Add. In the Add Location dialog box, type **http://glasgow.contoso.internal /ocsp**, and then click OK.

10. Select the Include In The AIA Extension Of Issued Certificates and Include In The Online Certificate Status Protocol (OCSP) Extension check boxes, as shown in Figure 7-30, and then click OK.

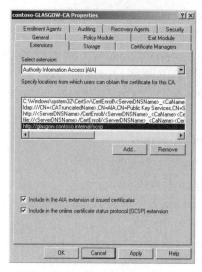

FIGURE 7-30 Configuring extensions.

11. Click Yes in the Certification Authority dialog box that asks whether you want to restart Active Directory Certificate Services.

12. In the Certification Authority console, right-click the *Revoked Certificates* node and then select Properties. Change the CRL publication interval to 2 weeks and the Delta CRL publication interval to 2 days, and then click OK.

Lesson Summary

- You cannot customize Level 1 certificate templates, but you can use them on Windows 2000 Server, Windows Server 2003, and Windows Server 2008 CAs. You can use level 2 certificate templates on Windows Server 2003 and Windows Server 2008 CAs and you can customize them. You can use level 3 certificate templates only on Windows Server 2008 CAs, and you can use advanced cryptographic methods such as elliptic curve cryptography.

- By configuring template permissions, you can specify which security principals can enroll or auto-enroll a particular certificate. You can also specify which security principals can modify a particular template.

- Auto-enrollment is a process by which you can deploy certificates automatically to security principals without intervention on the part of the user or an administrator.

- You can install Web enrollment on a CA or on a separate host. It enables clients using Microsoft and non-Microsoft operating systems to submit certificate requests as well as retrieve certificates generated by approved requests.

- Restricted enrollment agents can create certificate enrollments on behalf of other users. This is most often used by users who are responsible for enrolling other users with smart card certificates.

- Certificate Revocation Lists (CRL) are lists of certificates revoked on the CA. A delta CRL is a list of certificates revoked since the publication of the last CRL.

- Online Responder enables certificate revocation checks to be handled in a less bandwidth–intensive manner.

Lesson Review

You can use the following questions to test your knowledge of the information in Lesson 2, "Managing and Maintaining Certificates and Templates." The questions are also available on the companion DVD if you prefer to review them in electronic form.

> **NOTE ANSWERS**
>
> Answers to these questions and explanations of why each answer choice is right or wrong are located in the "Answers" section at the end of the book.

1. You have just created a customized level 2 certificate template based on the default level 1 user certificate template. On which of the following operating systems can you install a CA that supports this customized template? (Choose three. Each correct answer presents a complete solution.)

   A. Windows 2000 Advanced Server

   B. Windows Server 2008 Standard

   C. Windows Server 2008 Enterprise

   D. Windows Server 2008 Datacenter

   E. Windows Server 2003 Enterprise

2. You are creating a level 3 template to support encrypting file system (EFS). You will name this template Advanced EFS. Currently, all EFS certificates that have been issued by your enterprise CAs have used the Basic EFS certificate template that is included with Windows Server 2008 by default. You want to ensure that all future EFS certificates issued by enterprise CAs use the new level 3 template. Which step must you take to ensure that this occurs?

   A. Configure the Advanced EFS certificate template so that the certificate is published in AD DS.

   B. Configure the Advanced EFS certificate template as a superseded template in the Basic EFS certificate template properties.

   C. Configure the Basic EFS certificate template so that the certificate is published in AD DS.

   D. Configure the Basic EFS certificate template as a superseded template in the Advanced EFS certificate template properties.

3. Rooslan works in the HR department at your organization. You are rolling out smart cards for user authentication, and you want Rooslan to be able to enroll new employees for their user certificates. Which of the following must you do as part of this process?

   A. Grant Rooslan's account the Certificate Manager role.

   B. Issue Rooslan an enrollment agent certificate.

   C. Grant Rooslan's account the CA Administrator role.

   D. Grant Rooslan's account the CA Auditor role.

4. You have created an advanced computer certificate template and configured the template's security so that the Secure_Workstations group has the Enroll and Auto-enroll permissions. You add the computer accounts of 20 computers to this group and publish the advanced computer certificate template on your organization's enterprise CA. You check back later and find that none of the 20 computers has been issued the certificate. Which of the following steps should you take to resolve this issue?

   A. Edit the certificate template properties and disable the Enroll permission for the Secure_Workstations group.

   B. Edit the certificate template properties and disable the Autoenroll permission for the Secure_Workstations group.

   C. Edit the certificate template properties and enable CA certificate manager approval.

   D. Edit the certificate template properties and enable the Allow Private Key To Be Exported option.

   E. Configure the auto-enrollment policy in the Default Domain Policy GPO.

5. At present, your organization publishes a new CRL every 48 hours. On average, five certificates are revoked every day. The current CRL is 30 MB in size. Traffic analysis shows that 1,000 unique clients contact the CA every 48 hours to retrieve the latest version of the CRL. What steps can you take to minimize the amount of network traffic generated by CRL checks while ensuring that information about revoked certificates is disseminated every 48 hours? (Choose two. Each correct answer presents part of a complete solution.)

   A. Change the publication interval of the CRL to once every 24 hours.

   B. Change the publication interval of the CRL to once every two weeks.

   C. Publish a delta CRL once every 48 hours.

   D. Publish a delta CRL once a week.

   E. Publish a delta CRL once every two weeks.

6. You are responsible for managing an enterprise subordinate CA. The CA has been in operation for some time, and the CRL has become very large. The CRL publication interval is two weeks, and the delta CRL publication interval is three days. Revocation check traffic is causing delays. You want to minimize the amount of pressure of checks against newly issued certificates on the current CDPs. Which of the following should you do while ensuring that clients are still notified within 72 hours if a certificate has been revoked?

   A. Configure Online Responder.

   B. Increase the frequency at which you publish the CRL.

   C. Increase the frequency at which you publish the delta CRL.

   D. Decrease the frequency at which you publish the delta CRL.

Chapter Review

To further practice and reinforce the skills you learned in this chapter, you can perform the following tasks:

- Review the chapter summary.
- Complete the case scenarios. These scenarios set up real-world situations involving the topics of this chapter and ask you to create solutions.
- Complete the suggested practices.
- Take a practice test.

Chapter Summary

- You can install an enterprise CA only on Windows Server 2008 Enterprise or Datacenter. You can install a standalone CA on Windows Server 2008 Standard.
- Root CAs are at the apex of a Certificate Services hierarchy. There can be multiple levels of subordinate CA, with each CA higher in the hierarchy generating the signing certificates for CAs lower in the hierarchy. There can be only one root CA.
- Key archival enables you to recover private keys. Certificate managers approve and revoke certificates. CA administrators manage certificate servers.
- You can customize certificate templates to meet specific needs. Only enterprise CAs can issue customized templates.
- Auto-enrollment enables you to deploy certificates automatically.
- Online responders are the most efficient way of distributing CRL information.

Case Scenarios

In the following case scenarios, you apply what you've learned about managing and maintaining certificate servers, certificates, and certificate templates. You can find answers to these questions in the "Answers" section at the end of this book.

Case Scenario 1: Tailspin Toys Certificate Services

You are consulting with Tailspin Toys over the deployment of Active Directory Certificate Services on their network. After discussion with the principals at the company, you have decided to secure the root CA by installing it as a virtual machine under Hyper-V on a removable disk. This removable disk will be kept in a safe except when the root CA needs to issue a certificate. The subordinate CA will integrate with AD DS. Eventually, this CA will be used to issue certificates based on custom certificate templates. Management at Tailspin Toys does not want the systems administration team to be responsible for approving the issuing of certificates.

Instead, management would like members of a special security group named CertApprove to have this responsibility. With that in mind, you must find answers to the following questions.

1. With licensing costs in mind, which edition of Windows Server 2008 should you use for the root CA?

2. With licensing costs in mind, which edition of Windows Server 2008 should you use for the subordinate CA?

3. What steps can you take to ensure that only members of the CertApprove security group can approve the issuance of certificates?

Case Scenario 2: Contoso Online Responder

You work for Contoso, Ltd.'s Copenhagen office. You are rolling out smart cards to use for logon and EFS. You are concerned that your current system of publishing a CRL every week and a delta CRL every 24 hours will not cope well with the amount of traffic generated by the newly deployed certificates. With this in mind, you are considering the deployment of the Online Responder role service. Before management approves this project, they have asked you to address the following questions:

1. What steps must you take to configure Online Responder?

2. What impact will configuring Online Responder have on revocation checks against previously issued certificates?

3. What steps can you take to reduce the load on Online Responder if revocation check traffic overwhelms it?

Suggested Practices

To help you successfully master the exam objectives presented in this chapter, complete the following tasks.

Install and Configure AD CS

Do both practices in this section.

- **Practice 1** Install Windows Server 2008 on another computer and join it to the *contoso.internal* domain. Name this computer **Copenhagen** and give it the IP address of 10.0.0.42. Install AD CS and configure this computer as an enterprise subordinate CA.

- **Practice 2** Modify the configuration of the subordinate enterprise CA that you created so that only members of the Certificate Managers global group are able to issue and revoke certificates.

Configure Certificate Templates, Enrollments, and Certificate Revocations

Do both practices in this section.

- **Practice 1** Make a copy of the Web Server certificate template that can be issued only from Windows Server 2008 CAs. Configure the template to require Certificate Manager approval and give members of the Enterprise Admins group Autoenroll permissions.

- **Practice 2** Create a new shared folder on server Glasgow. Reconfigure the CA's properties and add this new shared folder as a CDP. Use the *certutil* command-line utility to force the publication of a delta CRL. Verify that the delta CRL is published to the new shared folder you specified as a CDP.

Take a Practice Test

The practice tests on this book's companion DVD offer many options. For example, you can test yourself on just one exam objective, or you can test yourself on all the upgrade exam content. You can set up the test so that it closely simulates the experience of taking a certification exam, or you can set it up in study mode so that you can look at the correct answers and explanations after you answer each question.

> **MORE INFO** **PRACTICE TESTS**
>
> For details about all the practice test options available, see the "How to Use the Practice Tests" section in this book's Introduction.

CHAPTER 8

Maintaining the Active Directory Environment

As a Microsoft Windows network professional, you are familiar with backup and recovery processes. Typically, some form of backup process occurs in an organization every day. Recovery is (hopefully) much less frequent, but you need to know exactly what to do when everyone else is panicking. It would be unprofessional to wait until Windows Server 2008 is installed and then start to draw up a backup and recovery plan.

You need to learn about Windows Server 2008 backup and recovery, including the backup of server roles, applications, the Active Directory database (*Ntds.dit*), Active Directory Domain Services (AD DS) objects, and Group Policy objects (GPOs). You need to formulate your disaster recovery plans and carry them out on your test network *before* your production network is upgraded. From the point of view of the examinations, because backup and recovery are universally important and because Windows Server 2008 introduces significant changes and enhancements, these topics are likely to be extensively tested.

In addition to securing your data and Active Directory settings through disaster recovery plans, you must ensure that AD DS operation is fast and efficient. Formulate plans for offline maintenance that include AD DS database defragmentation and compaction. Because AD DS is a service in Windows Server 2008, it can be stopped and restarted; consider the advantages and implications of restartable AD DS. If you are updating domain controller hardware, consider Active Directory database storage allocation and how you relocate Active Directory database files.

The monitoring process is not the same as troubleshooting, although monitoring logs can sometimes be used as troubleshooting tools. The aim of monitoring is to solve problems before they happen, to check that all systems are working the way they should be, and to identify resources that are coming under pressure before the problem becomes critical.

This chapter discusses the enhanced tools and techniques Microsoft Windows Server uses to back up and restore both user data and Active Directory settings. It looks at offline Active Directory maintenance in Windows Server 2008 and considers the use of monitoring tools and the enhancements introduced in the new operating system.

Exam objectives in this chapter:

- Configure backup and recovery.
- Perform offline maintenance.
- Monitor Active Directory.

Lessons in this chapter:

Before You Begin

To complete the lessons in this chapter, you must have done the following:

- Installed a Windows Server 2008 Enterprise server configured as a domain controller in the *contoso.internal* domain as described in Chapter 1, "Configuring Internet Protocol Addressing."

- Provided an extra disk that can store at least 25 gigabytes (GB) of data attached to the Glasgow domain controller. This disk can be an additional virtual disk if you are using virtual machine software, an internal physical disk, or an attached external USB 2.0, SATA, or IEEE 1394 disk. This disk will be used to store backup data.

- Installed the Windows Server 2008 Enterprise server Boston in the *contoso.internal* domain as described in Chapter 2, "Configuring IP Services."

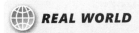

REAL WORLD

Ian McLean

Beware of anything you know really well and do every day.

It happened to me a few years ago when Software Upgrade Services (SUS) was replaced by Windows Server Update Services (WSUS). Of course I knew all about server-based software updates. I assessed and applied them on a regular basis. WSUS couldn't be all that different from SUS, could it? It could.

Fortunately, my years of experience rescued me from my natural-born stupidity. I installed WSUS and the WSUS administration console on my test network and found that, yes, I did need to change the way I did things.

Don't fall into the trap I almost fell into when it comes to backup and restore. Of course you back up regularly and perform trial restores. Probably you don't need to do a restore for real very often, but you know exactly how to do this. As a professional, you have written procedures and scripts and tested them thoroughly. You are undoubtedly an expert . . . Maybe . . .

For a start, you probably designed your procedures and wrote your scripts a few years ago. As a professional, you made sure they were easy to follow. A regular procedure should be a no-brainer. So you probably haven't actually looked at Windows Server 2003 backup and restore features since. . . 2003?

Then along comes Windows Server 2008. Things are different—in some instances, radically different. Don't rely on half-remembered Windows Server 2003 theory and the scripts and procedures that have worked well for the past five years. You could lose all your data *and* fail your exams! Be warned.

Lesson 1: Configuring Backup and Recovery

Backup and recovery have always been a core component of a systems administrator's job. Although more reliable hardware has meant that the amount of time that a systems administrator spends on backup and recovery has decreased, it has also meant that management's expectations about server availability have also changed. Management now expects fail-over or, at worst, very short server downtimes, and it is your job to meet these expectations.

In this lesson, you learn what is new in the process of backing up Windows Server 2008 and the data and services that it hosts for your organization. You also learn how to plan and implement disaster recovery for your organization's Windows Server 2008 environment. You learn how to recover everything from single Active Directory objects through to files, folders, roles, volumes, and even entire servers.

After this lesson, you will be able to:

- Use the *wbadmin.exe* utility and Windows Server Backup to back up servers.
- Perform a complete server and a volume backup.
- Back up system state data that includes Active Directory and server role data.
- Recover entire servers, selected files and folders, server role data, and AD DS.

Estimated lesson time: 55 minutes

Windows Server Backup

The Windows Server Backup tool replaces, but is significantly different from, the Windows 2000 Server and Windows Server 2003 tool, *ntbackup.exe*. As a Windows Server 2003 professional, you should be familiar with the *ntbackup.exe* tool, and you need to familiarize yourself with the capabilities and limitations of the new Windows Server Backup utility and the functional differences between this tool and its predecessor.

The following list summarizes these differences:

- A volume is the smallest object you can back up using Windows Server Backup.
- You can back up only local NTFS-formatted volumes.
- Windows Server Backup cannot write to tape drives.
- You cannot write to network locations or optical media during a scheduled backup.
- Windows Server Backup files are created as virtual hard disk (VHD) files. You can mount and read VHD files with the appropriate software, either directly or through virtual machine software such as Hyper-V.

Windows Server Backup is not installed by default. You must install it as a feature, using Add Features under the Features node of the Server Manager console. You do this in the practice session later in this lesson. When the feature is installed, the *Windows Server Backup* node becomes available under the *Storage* node of the Server Manager console; you can also open the Windows Server Backup console from Administrative Tools. The *wbadmin.exe* command-line utility, discussed later in this lesson, is also installed during this process.

To use Windows Server Backup or *wbadmin* to schedule backups, the computer requires an extra internal or external disk. External disks need to be USB 2.0, IEEE 1394 (Firewire), or Serial Advanced Technology Attachment (SATA) compatible. You can also use an external SCSI disk, although typically the SCSI interface is used for internal disks. When you deploy disks to host scheduled backup data, ensure that the volume can hold at least 2.5 times the amount of data that you want to back up.

When you configure your first scheduled backup, the disk that will host backup data is hidden from Windows Explorer, and any volumes and data on the disk are removed. This applies only to scheduled backups and not to manual backups—you can use a network location or external disk for a manual backup without losing data already stored on the device. Formatting and repartitioning happens only when a device is first used to host scheduled backup data and does not happen when subsequent backup data is written to the same location.

For example, Don Hall, an administrator at Northwind Traders, has tested manual backup on his production network. He used a 250-GB USB disk drive and experienced no problems whatsoever. He implements backup on his company's production network and backs up Microsoft SQL 2005 Server T-SQL routines and databases to a local Firewire 3TB drive that has over 90 percent of its capacity available. Management requires regular backups, and Don implements scheduled backups. Suddenly, he loses all his T-SQL routines and SQL databases. Fortunately, Don has the routines backed up elsewhere. The moral of the story—never have only one copy of anything.

A volume can store a maximum of 512 backups. If you need to store a greater number of backups, you must use a second volume. In practice, you are unlikely to specify a disk that can store 512 server backups. To permit a scheduled backup, Windows Server Backup will automatically remove the oldest backup data on the target volume. You do not need to clean up or remove old backup data manually.

> **MORE INFO   RECOVERING NTBACKUP BACKUPS**
>
> You cannot, by default, recover backups that were made using *ntbackup.exe*. If you need to do this, you can download a read-only version of *ntbackup.exe* compatible with Windows Server 2008 at *http://go.microsoft.com/fwlink/?LinkId=82917*.

Performing a Scheduled Backup

Scheduled backups enable you to automate the backup process. You set the schedule, and Windows Server Backup implements the backup. Scheduled backups occur at 9 P.M. by default, but you can change this if your organization still has people regularly working on documents at that time. Ensure that backups occur at a time when users have left work and the most recent day's changes to data can be captured.

Only members of the local Administrators group can configure and manage scheduled backups.

TO CONFIGURE A SCHEDULED BACKUP

1. Open Windows Server Backup and click Backup Schedule in the Actions pane.

   This will start the Backup Schedule Wizard.

   The wizard asks whether you want to perform a full server or a custom backup. As shown in Figure 8-1, volumes that contain operating system components are always included in custom backups. Volume F is excluded in this case because this is where backup data will be written.

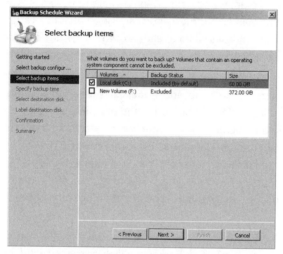

FIGURE 8-1 Selecting volumes to back up.

2. Specify the backup schedule.

   By default, backups occur once a day at 9 P.M. Optionally, you can configure multiple backups during a single day. You would do this if data on the server you are backing up changes rapidly. On servers on which data changes less often, for example, on a Web server on which pages are updated only once a week, you would configure a more infrequent schedule.

3. On the Select Destination Disk page, shown in Figure 8-2, select the disk to which backups are written.

   If you select multiple disks, multiple copies of the backup data are written. Because this is a scheduled backup, the entire disk is used, and all existing volumes and data are removed. The backup utility will format and hide the disks prior to writing the first backup data.

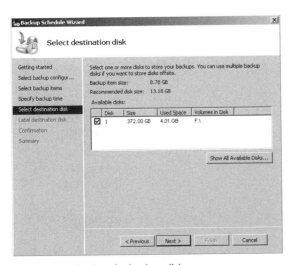

FIGURE 8-2 Selecting the backup disk.

4. On the next page, label the destination disk.

   If you configure multiple disks, this helps you locate quickly where your backups are stored.

5. When you finish the wizard, the target destination disk is formatted, and the first backup occurs at the scheduled time.

   Windows Server Backup can schedule only one backup job. Jobs that you scheduled in earlier versions of Windows, such as a full backup on Saturday night with a series of incremental backups every other day of the week, cannot be scheduled using Windows Server Backup. You can configure Windows Server Backup to perform incremental backups, although this process is different from what you might be used to with other backup applications. Windows Server Backup uses Volume Shadow Copy Service (VSS) and block-level backup technology to back up and recover your operating system, files and folders, and volumes. After the first full backup is created, you can configure Windows Server Backup to run incremental backups automatically by saving only the data that has changed since the last backup. You can, if you want to, configure Windows Server Backup to run incremental backups automatically before you make the first backup. In this case, Windows Server Backup will take the first backup as a full image backup and subsequently take incremental backups. VSS is discussed later in this lesson.

   For example, Sam Abolrous of Contoso, Ltd., schedules backups of a Windows Server 2003 file server that holds mission-critical data. On Sundays at 13:00 hours, a full backup occurs. On every other day of the week at 3:00 hours, an incremental backup is scheduled. When Sam upgrades the server to Windows Server 2008, he is concerned to find that it appears as if he cannot schedule the same backup routine. However, he discovers that he can schedule the backups he requires and can use backup performance settings (discussed later in this lesson) to specify whether each backup is full or incremental.

> **MORE INFO**   **ACTIVE DIRECTORY BACKUP AND RESTORE**
>
> For more information about Active Directory backup and restore, see *http://technet .microsoft.com/en-us/magazine/cc462796.aspx*. This link provides some good general information in addition to specific Active Directory backup information. For a step-by-step guide, see *http://technet.microsoft.com/en-us/library/cc770266.aspx*.

Manual Backup to Media

You can write unscheduled single backups, also known as manual backups, to network locations, local and external volumes, and local DVD media. If a backup encompasses more than the space available on a single DVD, you can span the backup across multiple DVDs. Otherwise, if the calculated size of a backup exceeds the amount of free space available on the destination location, the backup fails. The facility to back up volumes manually directly to optical media drives offers a solution if you want to create backups that you can move easily offsite. You perform a manual backup in the practice session later in this lesson.

When you perform a manual backup, you select one of two types of VSS backup:

- **VSS copy backup**   Used when another backup product is also used to back up applications on volumes in the current backup. Application log files are retained when you perform this type of manual backup. This is the default when implementing a backup.
- **VSS full backup**   Used when no other backup products are used to back up the host computer. This option updates each file's backup attribute and clears application log files.

When you perform a manual backup, you can back up a single volume without backing up the system or boot volumes by clearing the Enable System Recovery option when selecting backup items. You can use this option to back up the data on a specific volume when you intend to perform maintenance on the volume or suspect that the disk hosting the volume might fail but you do not want to wait for a full server backup to complete.

Performing Incremental Backups by Configuring Backup Performance

Incremental backups work in a different way than they did in earlier versions of Windows. In Windows Server Backup, you do not select whether to make an individual backup full, differential, or incremental when you create the backup job. Whether full backups or incremental backups are taken is configured separately as a general backup performance option. All backups are configured as either Full or Incremental. The first backup image taken in a schedule will be the equivalent of a full backup.

You configure backup performance by clicking Configure Performance Settings in the Actions pane of the Windows Server Backup console. You can then select from the options shown in Figure 8-3. The custom backup option allows you to choose full or incremental backups on a per-volume basis. Selecting the incremental backup option will enable you to store more scheduled backups on the same media and, consequently, gives you a greater time window from which you can restore data. With Windows Server Backup, you do not need to hunt around for specific incremental backup sets when performing a restore because the appropriate backup images are located based on your restoration selections. Restoration is covered in more detail later in this lesson.

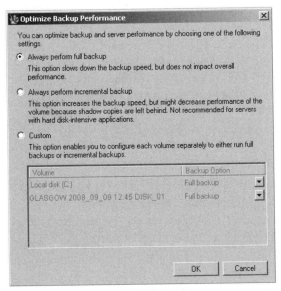

FIGURE 8-3 Optimizing backup performance.

Backing Up Computers Remotely

You can use the Windows Server Backup tool to connect to another computer running Windows Server 2008 and perform backup tasks as though the backup were being performed on the local computer. This enables users who have the Remote Systems Administration Tools (RSAT) installed on their Windows Vista workstations to connect to computers running Windows Server 2008 and perform backup operations as though they were logged on locally. To perform this operation, the user making the connection must be a member of the Backup Operators or local Administrators group on the remote computer running Windows Server 2008.

The same limitations that apply to a locally run instance also apply to remote connections when you use the Windows Server Backup console. A user who is a member only of the Backup Operators local group will be unable to schedule backups but can perform unscheduled backups. A user who is a member of the local Administrators group on the server that is the target of the remote Windows Server Backup connection can perform all normal backup tasks.

For example, all the servers at Litware, Inc., are located in a secure server room, and none of them have keyboards or monitors. Backup operators on a specific server are not permitted to use Remote Desktop to connect to the server. A backup operator on the Dundee server wants to back up all volumes on the server. From her Windows Vista Enterprise workstation, she uses the appropriate RSAT tool to connect to the Dundee server. She can now carry out an unscheduled manual backup. One advantage of this is that you can permit someone to perform backups without giving that person local logon access to the server (or access through Remote Desktop). If, however, she needs to configure scheduled backups, she should ask her network administrator to make her a member of the local Administrators group on the server.

Windows Server Backup does not allow you to schedule backup data generated on remote computers to be written to a local source. You can write to a local source when performing an unscheduled backup only if the computer to which you are attempting to write data has a shared folder configured. You cannot use the *wbadmin.exe* utility to manage backups on remote computers.

Backing Up Server Roles and Applications

To back up a particular server role, such as the DHCP Server or DNS Server role and its associated data, you back up system state data. System state data is automatically included in backups whenever you perform a full server backup or a scheduled backup. You also back up system state data when you perform a manual backup by using Windows Server Backup and select the Enable System Recovery option.

System State Data

On a server running the AD DS role, system state data includes:

- Registry settings
- COM+ Class Registration database
- Boot files
- System files that are under Windows Resource Protection
- The AD DS database (*Ntds.dit*)
- The SYSVOL directory

When other server roles are installed on a system, the system state will include the first four objects listed previously plus the following files:

- For the Active Directory Certificate Services role, the AD CS database
- For the Failover Cluster feature, cluster service information
- For the Web server role, Microsoft Internet Information Services (IIS) configuration files

If an application is VSS-aware and Windows Server Backup–aware, it is registered with Windows Server Backup automatically during the application's installation. You can then restore just the application and its associated data from a full server or volume backup. This functionality applies only to applications that are designed to run on Windows Server 2008. (If an application does not register itself with Windows Server backup, you can still back up and restore data related to it.) This feature simplifies the application restoration process, ensuring that all application data, including executable files and registry settings, is packaged so you can restore just that application, its dependencies, and its data.

Backing up AD DS

Multimaster replication provides both failover support and Active Directory protection. A copy of the AD DS database is stored on all domain controllers within a domain, so if one is lost and you do not have access to backup data, you can perform a recovery by reinstalling the domain controller from scratch and replicating the database from other domain controllers. In addition, methods exist for retrieving deleted or tombstoned items in AD DS. Also, you can configure items so they cannot be deleted and monitor attribute changes. All these topics are discussed in Lesson 2, "Performing Offline Maintenance." However, these techniques do not always provide the best method for data recovery. For example, objects you restore from tombstone containers do not include all their previous attributes.

When you restore AD DS data from a backup created by Windows Server Backup, you restore all object attributes, and you do not need to reassign attributes such as group membership. AD DS is automatically backed up whenever you back up the critical volumes on a domain controller. You can also perform an Active Directory backup by performing a system state backup.

Although performing a system state backup backs up all Active Directory objects, the nature of Active Directory replication means that a recovered AD DS object is likely to be deleted again unless it is marked as authoritative. The process of performing an authoritative restore is covered later in this lesson. However, you should be aware that the technique for restoring a deleted GPO is significantly different from restoring a user account or organizational unit (OU) tree. GPOs are backed up using the Group Policy Management console, and you should use this console, rather than Directory Services Restore Mode, to recover deleted GPOs.

To back up GPOs, open the Group Policy Management console so that the Group Policy Objects container is visible. Right-click Group Policy Objects, shown in Figure 8-4, and select Back Up All. As part of this process, you must specify a location and a description for the backup. You should choose a location that is normally backed up as part of the Windows Server Backup routine.

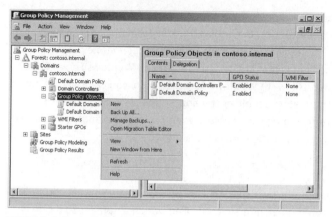

FIGURE 8-4 Group Policy backup.

MORE INFO **ACTIVE DIRECTORY BACKUP**

For more information on backing up AD DS, see *http://technet.microsoft.com/en-us/library /cc753359.aspx*.

The *wbadmin* Command-Line Tool

The *wbadmin* utility is available on both the standard and the Server Core installations of Windows Server 2008. It enables you to do everything you can do with Windows Server Backup and more. When you install the Windows Server Backup feature and select Command-Line Tools, as shown in Figure 8-5, the *wbadmin* utility is installed on a standard installation of Windows Server 2008.

On a Server Core installation, *wbadmin* is the only direct backup utility you can use, although it is possible to connect to the computer remotely by using the Windows Server Backup console. You can install *wbadmin* on a computer running in the Server Core con-figuration by running the Command Prompt console as an administrator and entering the command:

```
Ocsetup WindowsServerBackup
```

The following *wbadmin.exe* commands are useful for backing up Windows Server 2008 files:

- **wbadmin enable backup** Enables you to create and manage scheduled backups
- **wbadmin start systemstatebackup** Performs a system state data backup
- **wbadmin start backup** Starts a single manual backup
- **wbadmin get versions** Displays details of backups that have already been taken
- **wbadmin get items** Enables you to determine which items are contained in a specific backup image

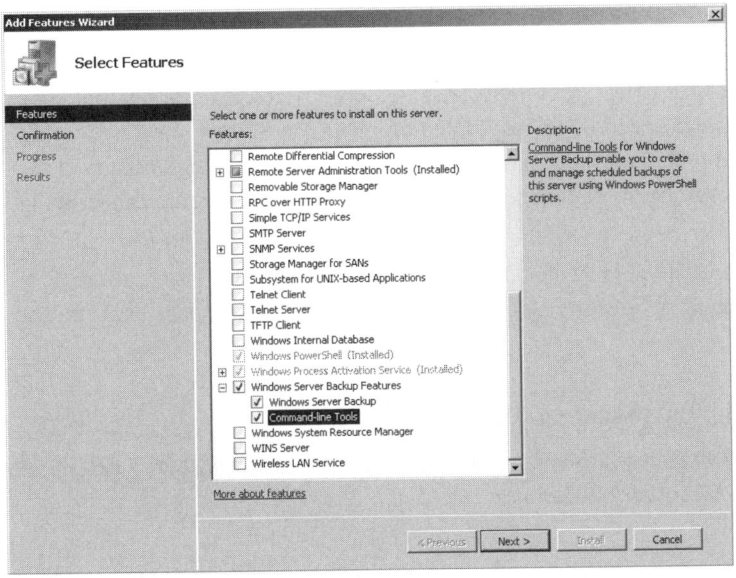

FIGURE 8-5 Installing command-line tools.

With the *wbadmin start backup* command, you carry out manual backups to shared folders by using the *–backuptarget:\\Share\Folder* syntax where the shared folder location is expressed as a UNC pathname. If it is necessary to provide authentication credentials to write data to the shared folder, you can use the *–user:* and *–password:* options. For example, to back up volume E to the shared folder store on the server Glasgow, using Kim Aker's credentials, you would enter the command:

```
Wbadmin start backup -backuptarget:\\Glasgow\Store -include:E:-User:Kim_Akers@contoso.
internal -Password:P@ssw0rd
```

You can issue *wbadmin.exe* commands from a batch file, and you can schedule batch file operation with the Scheduled Tasks utility. Using this method, you can schedule the execution of more accurately timed backups than is possible using Windows Server Backup scheduling options. You can configure scheduled backups to network locations. For example, the following command creates a batch file named ssbackup.bat in the c:\scripts directory that will perform a system state backup to the \\Server\Share network share, using the credentials of RemoteUser:

```
Echo wbadmin start systemstatebackup -backupTarget:\\Server\Share -user:RemoteUser
-password:RemotePassword -quiet >> c:\scripts\ssbackup.bat
```

You can use Scheduled Tasks to configure this batch file to run according to a schedule. If you plan backups by using this method, note the following points:

- The *–quiet* option is required in the *wbadmin* command because you do not want a scheduled task to halt while waiting for input.

- The scheduled task must be run using the local Administrator account because *wbadmin.exe* runs with elevated privileges.

- If the scheduled task is writing to a network share, you need to put user account credentials into the script called by the scheduled task. You can protect these credentials by using encrypting file system (EFS) or Active Directory Rights Management Service (AD RMS) to encrypt the file so that only the local Administrator account can view the script contents.

- Scripted backups fail if the target location is full. Backups scheduled using *wbadmin. exe* will automatically remove the oldest backup when not enough space exists for the current backup.

> **MORE INFO**   **FULL LIST OF *WBADMIN* OPTIONS**
>
> To learn more about *wbadmin* syntax and to obtain a list of options, see *http://technet .microsoft.com/en-us/library/cc754015.aspx*.

EXAM TIP

Upgrade examinations assume a high level of professionalism and frequently test your knowledge of command-line administration.

Backing Up System State Data Only with *wbadmin*

If you want to back up only system state data, use *wbadmin.exe* with the *start systemstatebackup* option. If you use *wbadmin.exe* with this option, system state data can be written only to a local volume. To perform a backup of system state data only, open a command prompt as Administrator and enter the command:

```
Wbadmin start systemstatebackup –backuptarget:F: -quiet
```

where F: is the volume identifier. Performing a system state data recovery is covered in detail later in this lesson.

> **Quick Check**
>
> 1. Which command installs *wbadmin.exe* on a computer running Windows Server 2008 with the Server Core configuration?
>
> 2. What happens to any volumes and data stored on a disk that you select as a target to store backup data generated by a Windows Server Backup scheduled backup?

Quick Check Answers

1. Ocsetup WindowsServerBackup

2. All volumes and data on the target disk are removed before Windows Server Backup writes its first set of backup data.

Configuring Backup Settings

In Windows Server 2003, you can back up individual files and folders, but the smallest unit of backup in Windows Server 2008 is the volume. This affects how you configure servers prior to their deployment. The deployment of file servers, bearing in mind how they are going to be backed up and restored, can be considered the first step in your disaster recovery planning. Because backup works at the per-volume level, you might consider creating separate volumes for each share rather than placing several shares on each volume. This also facilitates mounting a per-volume backup image within a virtual machine if you are unable to restore it immediately to its original server in the event of a hardware failure.

> **NOTE PROVIDING BACKUP REDUNDANCY**
>
> If you have multiple external disks connected to a server, you can write the same backup to each disk during the same backup operation. This provides redundancy if a target disk fails.

You must also decide how frequently particular volumes are backed up. You can use Storage Reports to discover how often files on a particular volume are altered. A folder that holds marketing brochures that are updated only occasionally does not need to be backed up every night. If you move this shared folder to its own volume partition, you can back up its contents less frequently. Alternatively, if data in a shared folder is updated frequently and is mission critical, you can move the folder into its own volume and back this up every few hours.

You need to plan an offsite strategy so that if the building that hosts your servers is destroyed by flood, fire, or earthquake, your organization can still recover its data. When planning an offsite backup strategy, consider the following:

- Ensure that if data is encrypted, the recovery keys are included in the offsite backup data set.
- Store offsite backup media in a secure location. Do not permit staff members to take backup data home because this environment is not secure.
- Ensure that you have enough equipment at your recovery site to recover your servers.

System Center Data Protection Manager

System Center Data Protection Manager 2007 (DPM 2007) is the Microsoft advanced backup solution. Windows Server Backup is suitable for most simple backup and restore situations, whereas DPM 2007 targets more complex backup scenarios such as backing up production Microsoft Exchange Server 2007 or SQL Server 2008 servers. DPM 2007 offers the following benefits:

- It provides byte-level backups. In an incremental backup, only files that have changed since the most recent backup are backed up. In a byte-level backup, only those bytes in the files that have changed are backed up. This significantly reduces the amount of data that needs to be written to a backup (and the amount of time required for both backup and restore).

NOTE **BLOCK-LEVEL INCREMENTAL BACKUPS**

Conflicting information exists on TechNet about the savings provided by DPM 2007 as compared to Windows Server Backup. Windows Server Backup incremental backups are block level and based on changes to the disk image, and byte-level backups might not give as much of an advantage as they would initially seem to.

- It can provide zero data loss restoration of Exchange, SQL Server, and Microsoft Office SharePoint Server by integrating point-in-time database backups with existing application logs. This permits application data to be restored to the point in time when the failure occurred rather than to the point when the last backup was taken.

- You can install agent software on branch office servers, allowing backup data to be forwarded over wide area network (WAN) links. You can also use agent software to forward backup data over your local area network (LAN), allowing remote backups to be written to local media.

- It supports backup to direct attached storage, Fibre Channel SAN, and iSCSI SAN. It does not support USB, SATA, and IEEE 1394 devices.

- It provides comprehensive reporting, including protection success and failure as well as backup media use.

- Management Pack is available for System Center Operations Manager 2007. This enables centralized management of the state of data protection and recovery for multiple DPM 2007 servers and servers with DPM 2007 agent software installed. Management Pack is best used in environments with many DPM 2007 servers and clients.

MORE INFO   **DPM 2007**

To learn more about DPM 2007, read the DPM 2007 FAQ at *http://technet.microsoft.com/en-us/library/bb795549.aspx*.

EXAM TIP

Remember that if a question specifies a scheduled backup, the locations to which you can write backup data are more restricted than the locations that you can write backup data to when performing a manual backup.

Windows Server Backup Recovery

Recovery operations using Windows Server Backup permit the following recovery modes:

- File and folder recovery
- Application and application data recovery
- Volume recovery
- Full server and operating system recovery
- System state recovery

Recovering Files and Folders

You can perform recovery at the file and folder level to restore a set of files and folders or even an individual file. Figure 8-6 shows how you select the items to restore.

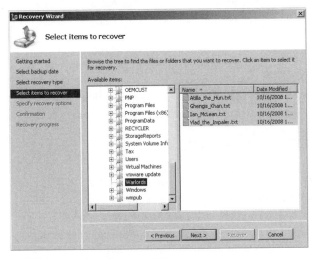

FIGURE 8-6 Selecting items to restore.

Windows Server Backup in Windows Server 2008 manages your backup files so that if backup data needs to be read from several files, for example, when several volumes on a folder that has been backed up incrementally need to be restored, the process occurs automatically. Determining which backups are required when restoring from incremental backups was a problem in previous operating systems, but now this is done for you. You perform a file and folder recovery during the first practice exercise at the end of this lesson.

> **MORE INFO** **RECOVERING FILES AND FOLDERS**
>
> For more information on recovering files and folders and a step-by-step guide, see *http://technet.microsoft.com/en-us/library/cc772028.aspx.*

Recovering Applications and Application Data

Windows Server Backup in Windows Server 2008 can perform application-specific restorations that restore an application, its settings, and the associated application data. You can use Windows Server Backup to perform an application restoration only on applications that have been registered with Windows Server Backup. Registration occurs during application installation.

When you perform an application recovery, you are presented with a list of applications that are registered with Windows Server Backup and can be recovered. This list is based on the backup date you have selected. If you are performing a restore from the most recent backup taken of an application according to the data stored in the backup catalog, you have the option of rolling forward the application database. The default option is to allow roll forward. You can select Do Not Perform A Roll-Forward Recovery Of The Application Database if you want to block rolling forward. You would choose this option if, for example, you had accidently dropped a table in a SQL Server database and wanted to restore the database, with the lost table, from a backup.

> **MORE INFO** **RECOVERING APPLICATIONS**
>
> For more information on recovering Windows Server Backup–aware applications, including a step-by-step guide, see *http://technet.microsoft.com/en-us/library/cc725726.aspx.*

Recovering Volumes

Volume recovery is used when, for example, you have lost a volume because of a disk failure but you do not need to perform a full operating system or server recovery. Remember that if you recover a volume from backup, all existing data at the destination location will be overwritten when you perform the recovery. You can recover one or more volumes during a volume recovery.

MORE INFO **VOLUME RECOVERY**

For more information about volume recovery, including a step-by-step guide, see
http://technet.microsoft.com/en-us/library/cc753186.aspx.

Full Server and Operating System Recovery

Full server recovery, also known as bare metal recovery, enables you to restore the server
completely by booting from the Windows Server 2008 installation media or Windows Recovery Environment. Full server recovery goes further than the Automated System Recovery
(ASR) feature in Windows Server 2003 because a full server recovery restores all operating
system, application, and other data stored on the server. With ASR, it was necessary to restore
further data from backup after the ASR process was complete.

An operating system recovery is similar to a full server recovery except that you recover
only critical volumes. For example, if you have a file server on which the disks that host critical operating system volumes are separate from the disks that host shared folder volumes,
and the disks that host the operating system volumes fail, you would perform an operating
system recovery.

When performing either a full server or operating system recovery, you must ensure that
the disk you are recovering to is at least as large as the disk that contained the volumes you
backed up, irrespective of the size of the volumes on that disk. For example, if you performed
a full server backup on a server that was configured to use only a 30-GB partition on a
100-GB disk and that disk failed, you must perform a full server or operating system restore
to a disk that is at least 100 GB in size.

MORE INFO **OPERATING SYSTEM RECOVERY**

For more information about recovering the operating system, including a step-by-step
guide, see *http://technet.microsoft.com/en-us/library/cc755163.aspx*.

NOTE **BITLOCKER PROTECTION**

If a server is protected by BitLocker encryption when it is backed up and you perform
a volume, operating system, or full server restore, BitLocker settings are not restored.
You must reapply BitLocker after the restoration is complete to ensure that volumes are
encrypted. Chapter 5, "Configuring Active Directory Lightweight Directory Services and
Read-Only Domain Controllers," discusses BitLocker.

System State Recovery

A system state recovery is the most commonly used method of recovering corrupt server role data or restoring AD DS. You cannot perform a partial system state recovery; system state recovery must occur in its entirety. If you want to recover only the system state rather than perform a full server or volume recovery, use the *wbadmin* utility.

Your first step is to obtain a list of backups, with the most recent backup listed first. The command to do this is:

```
wbadmin get versions
```

You make a note of the backup version identifier, which will be in the MM/DD/YYYY-HH:MM format. Provide the entire backup version identifier when performing the restore. To start system state recovery, you use a command with this syntax:

```
wbadmin Start SystemStateRecovery -version:MM/DD/YYYY-HH:MM.
```

Type **Y** to accept the System State Recovery option, and then press Enter to start the recovery process. When the process completes, reboot the server. You might need to reboot the server several times, depending on which server roles were installed on Windows Server 2008 when the system state backup was taken.

> **MORE INFO**   **SYSTEM STATE RECOVERY**
>
> For more information about system state recovery, including a step-by-step guide, see *http://technet.microsoft.com/en-us/library/cc753789.aspx.*

 Quick Check

1. Which applications can be recovered with an application recovery?
2. How do you access the tool to perform a full server recovery?

Quick Check Answers

1. Applications that are registered with Windows Server Backup. Such applications can be restored without restoring any other nonapplication-related data.
2. Boot from the Windows Server 2008 installation media or boot into the Windows Recovery Environment.

Recovering AD DS

You recover AD DS when you recover a domain controller's system state data. This type of recovery is termed a nonauthoritative restore. It brings the Active Directory database on the server back to the point it was when the backup was taken. When you restart the domain controller at the end of the System State recovery process, it replicates with other domain controllers in the domain, and the Active Directory database is updated with changes that have occurred since the backup was taken. If, rather than merely wanting to recover the domain controller, you want to recover specific Active Directory objects that have been deleted from the database, perform an authoritative restore.

MORE INFO PERFORMING NONAUTHORITATIVE RESTORES

For more information on performing nonauthoritative restores of AD DS, see *http://technet.microsoft.com/en-us/library/cc816627.aspx.*

Authoritative Restore

After a nonauthoritative restore, objects deleted after the backup was taken will again be deleted when the restored domain controller replicates with other domain controllers in the domain. On every other domain controller, the object is marked as deleted, so when replication occurs, the local copy of the object will also be marked as deleted. The authoritative restore process marks the deleted object in such a way that when replication occurs, the object is restored across the domain. Remember that when an object is deleted, it is not instantly removed from AD DS but gains an attribute that marks it as deleted until the tombstone lifetime is reached and the object is removed. The tombstone lifetime is the amount of time a deleted object remains in AD DS and has a default value of 180 days.

Yesterday, for example, a member of your administrative team accidentally deleted the Senior Managers OU. You restore this OU on a domain controller from system state backup, but it is promptly deleted when Active Directory replication occurs. You therefore need not only to restore the group but to mark its restoration as authoritative.

You can use the Directory Services Restore Mode (DSRM) to perform an authoritative restore. DSRM enables you to perform the necessary restorations and mark the objects as restored before rebooting the domain controller and allowing those changes to replicate out to other domain controllers in the domain.

Alternatively, Windows Server 2008 restartable AD DS gives you the option of stopping AD DS if you need to mark an object or objects as authoritative. In previous versions of Windows Server, you had to start the domain controller in DSRM and then perform a nonauthoritative restore before you could mark an object as authoritative. Lesson 2 discusses restartable AD DS and the operations it enables you to carry out.

NOTE READ-ONLY DOMAIN CONTROLLERS

Because the AD DS database on an RODC is read-only, you cannot perform an authoritative restore on an RODC. If you perform a full server recovery on an RODC, this includes a nonauthoritative restore.

> **NOTE** **ONLY ONE DOMAIN CONTROLLER IN A DOMAIN**
>
> Authoritative restores are not necessary if there is only one domain controller in a domain because there is no other copy of the Active Directory database to replicate with the database you have restored. Suppose, for example, that you lose an OU from a domain controller that is the only writable domain controller in the domain but replicates its AD DS database to several RODCs. In this case, a nonauthoritative restore would restore the OU, which would then be restored to the RODCs on replication. However, if you had more than one writable domain controller, you would need to do an authoritative restore on one of them.

Booting into Directory Services Restore Mode

Three methods of booting into DSRM exist. The first is to press F8 during the boot process and then to select Directory Services Restore Mode from the prompt, as shown in Figure 8-7.

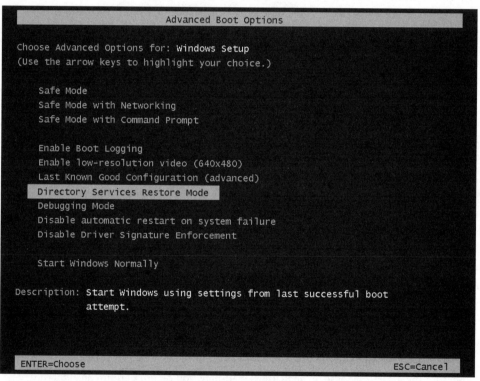

FIGURE 8-7 Using F8 to boot into DSRM.

Using F8 tends to be unpopular with administrators because you have only a very short time window during which you can press the key. If you press the key too late, you must let the server boot normally into Windows Server 2008 and then reboot.

NOTE **BITLOCKER AND DSRM**

If you have BitLocker applied, you must enter the BitLocker key when booting into DSRM.

The second method of booting into DSRM is to open an administrative command prompt and enter the command:

```
bcdedit /set safeboot dsrepair
```

This changes the boot option so that Windows Server 2008 automatically boots into DSRM. You typically use this option on domain controllers with a Server Core configuration. If you do not subsequently remove this option, the server will always boot into DSRM. To cancel the DSRM boot option, open an administrative command prompt and enter the command:

```
bcdedit /deletevalue safeboot
```

The third method of starting a Windows Server 2008 domain controller in DSRM is to open the System Configuration console from the Administrative Tools menu and select the Safe Boot check box and then the Active Directory Repair option, as shown in Figure 8-8.

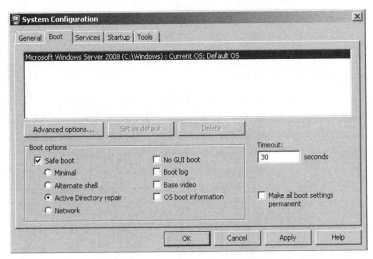

FIGURE 8-8 Using the System Configuration console to specify a boot into DSRM.

You need the DSRM password to log on to DSRM. You specify this password individually for each domain controller during the domain controller promotion process, and it is very easy to forget it. In this case, you can reset it as follows:

1. Log on to the domain controller with an account that is a member of the Domain Admins group.

2. Open an administrative command prompt and type **ntdsutil**.

3. At the *Ntdsutil* command prompt, type **set dsrm password**.

4. At the DSRM command prompt, do one of the following:
   - If you want to reset the DSRM password on the local domain controller, enter the command **reset password on server null**. Type and confirm the new password.
   - If you want to reset the DSRM password for another domain controller, enter the command **reset password on server servername** where *servername* is the FQDN of the server for which you are resetting the password.

5. At the DSRM prompt, type **q**. At the *Ntdsutil* command prompt, type **q** to exit.

When you reboot a domain controller into DSRM and you have logged on using the Administrator account and the DSRM password, you can perform a nonauthoritative restore by restoring the system state data by using the *wbadmin.exe* utility as described earlier in this lesson. If you need to perform an authoritative restore of SYSVOL, use the *–AuthSysVOL* option. Use this option only if it is necessary to roll SYSVOL back to an earlier version than currently exists. This option is not typically used as part of the authoritative restore process.

After the system state recovery process has completed, you can use the *ntdsutil* utility to enter the Authoritative Restore mode. Then, to restore an object, type **Restore Object** followed by the object's distinguished name. To restore a container and everything located under it, type **Restore Subtree** followed by the container's distinguished name. For example, to restore the Accounts OU and all its contents in the *adatum.com* domain, issue the command:

```
Restore Subtree "OU=Accounts,DC=Adatum,DC=com"
```

If objects have back links, a file is generated in the directory from which you have performed the authoritative restore operation. A back link includes information such as group memberships associated with the restored object that are not automatically included when you perform the authoritative restore operation. You must run the *ldifde* utility in each domain that might have group objects, (possibly) including the restored object at the time of its deletion. To perform this operation, execute the following command on a domain controller in each necessary domain:

```
Ldifde -I -k ldif.filename
```

> **MORE INFO**   **AUTHORITATIVE RESTORE AND LDIFDE FILES**
>
> For more information on performing an authoritative restoration of Active Directory objects, see *http://technet.microsoft.com/en-us/library/cc779573.aspx*. For more information about ldifde files, see *http://support.microsoft.com/kb/237677*.

Recovering Deleted Group Policy Objects

You cannot restore a deleted GPO by using an authoritative restore. You must instead recover GPOs by using the Group Policy Management Console (GPMC). Open the GPMC, right-click Group Policy Objects, and then select Manage Backups. Browse to where you store backed up

GPOs and select the GPO that you want to recover, as shown in the dialog box in Figure 8-9. Click Restore.

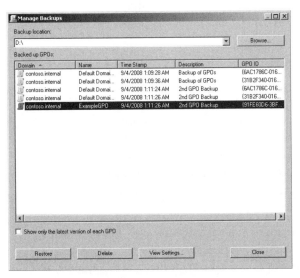

FIGURE 8-9 Choosing a GPO to restore.

Full Server Recovery on a Domain Controller

When you perform a full server recovery of a domain controller, you automatically perform a nonauthoritative restore of AD DS. It is difficult to use full server recovery to perform an authoritative restore because it is likely that the server will reboot and replicate before you have a chance to force it into DSRM (unless you pull out the network cable at the appropriate time—but this is possibly not the most elegant form of administration). Microsoft recommends that performing a full server recovery on a domain controller should not be considered a viable method of restoring deleted Active Directory objects.

> **NOTE** **LINKED VALUE REPLICATION**
>
> Windows Server 2003 introduced linked value replication, which continues to be used in Windows Server 2008. Linked value replication allows domain controllers to replicate individual values of a multivalued attribute separately. In previous operating systems when (for example) a change was made to a group member's account, the entire group had to be replicated. With linked value replication, only the altered group member is replicated. To enable linked value replication, raise the forest functional level to Windows Server 2003 (or higher).

MORE INFO FULL SERVER RECOVERY OF A DOMAIN CONTROLLER

For more information on performing a full server recovery of a domain controller, see *http://technet.microsoft.com/en-us/library/cc772519.aspx.*

The Active Directory Database Mounting Tool

The Active Directory Database Mounting Tool (*dsamain.exe*) enables you to create and view data stored within AD DS without needing to restart the domain controller in DSRM. You can use the tool to compare the state of AD DS as it exists in different snapshots without restoring multiple backups. This helps if you are trying to determine whether a particular backup of AD DS contains the objects that you want to restore.

You can use *dsamain.exe* with both the *ntdsutil* snapshot operation and a Windows Server 2008 system state data backup. You use *ntdsutil* to mount the snapshot of the directory and then use *dsamain* to view and modify the snapshot. Only members of the Domain Admins and Enterprise Admins groups can view these snapshots. Although you can use the *dsamain.exe* tool to re-create deleted objects, this process is laborious. Microsoft recommends that you use DSRM and an authoritative restore as your primary method of restoring deleted directory objects rather than attempting manual re-creation through *dsamain.exe*.

To learn more about the Active Directory Database Mounting Tool and how it can be used in Windows Server 2008 disaster recovery scenarios, see *http://technet .microsoft.com/en-us/library/cc753609.aspx.*

PRACTICE   **Backing Up and Restoring Windows Server 2008**

In this practice, you install Windows Server Backup and the command-line backup tools on your Glasgow domain controller. You then use *wbadmin.exe* to perform a simple volume backup and a system state–only backup. Your next task is to delete some folders you created earlier and restore them from the volume backup you created earlier. As it is written, this practice assumes your second hard disk is on drive F. If this is not the case on your computer, please amend the exercises accordingly.

EXERCISE 1   Install Windows Server Backup

In this practice, you install the Windows Server Backup feature and the command-line backup tools.

1. Log on to the domain controller Glasgow, using the Kim_Akers account.

2. If necessary, open Server Manager.

3. In the Server Manager console, select the *Features* node, and then click Add Features.

4. On the Select Features page of the Add Features Wizard, expand the *Windows Server Backup Features* node.

5. Select the Windows Server Backup and Command-line Tools check boxes, as shown previously in Figure 8-5, and then click Next.

> **NOTE   POWERSHELL**
>
> **You might be prompted to confirm the installation of PowerShell. If so, allow Windows Server 2008 to install this feature by clicking Add Required Features.**

6. On the Confirm Installation Selections page, shown in Figure 8-10, click Install. When the feature has been installed, click Close to exit the Add Features Wizard.

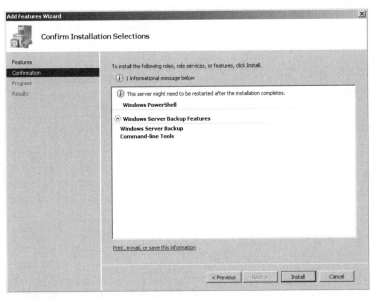

FIGURE 8-10 The Confirm Installation Selections page.

EXERCISE 2   Perform a Volume Backup

In this exercise, you perform a volume backup and a system state backup, using the *wbadmin. exe* command-line utility, and then you create a scheduled task. You must have completed Exercise 1, "Install Windows Server Backup," before you attempt this exercise.

1. If necessary, log on to the Glasgow domain controller with the Kim_Akers user account.

2. Verify that an extra disk is connected to your computer and that you know its volume name. If the disk is not formatted, format it using the NTFS file system.

> **NOTE   FAT32**
>
> You can write a manual backup to a FAT32 file system disk, but Microsoft does not recommend doing this.

3. Create a folder on volume C, named **Warlords**. Create four text files within this volume, named **Ghengis_Khan.txt**, **Attila_the_Hun .txt**, **Vlad_the_Impaler.txt**, and **Ian_McLean.txt**.

   You do not need to put any content in the text files.

4. Open Windows Server Backup in the Administrative Tools menu. If a UAC dialog box appears, click Continue to clear it. In the Actions pane, click Backup Once.

   The Backup Once Wizard opens.

5. Ensure that Different Options is selected, and then click Next.

6. On the Select Backup Configuration page, shown in Figure 8-11, select Custom, and then click Next.

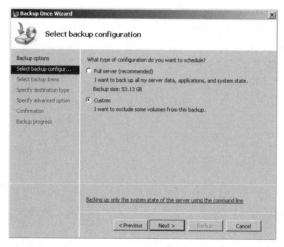

FIGURE 8-11 Selecting Custom backup.

7. On the Select Backup Items page, ensure that the Enable System Recovery check box is selected, as shown in Figure 8-12.

   This automatically selects all volumes that contain operating system components.

8. Click Next.

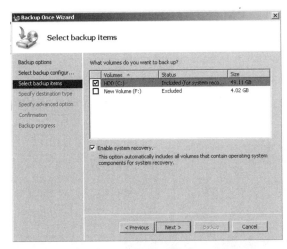

FIGURE 8-12 Enabling system recovery.

9. On the Specify Destination Type page, ensure that Local Drives is selected, and then click Next.

10. On the Select Backup Destination page, use the drop-down list to select the appropriate disk, as shown in Figure 8-13, and then click Next.

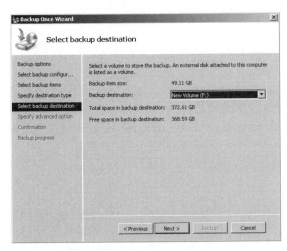

FIGURE 8-13 Selecting the backup destination.

11. On the Specify Advanced Option page, select VSS Full Backup, and then click Next.

12. On the Confirmation page, click Backup. When the backup process is complete, click Close.

13. After the backup completes, delete the C:\ Warlords folder.

    You now use the *wbadmin* utility to perform a system state–only backup.

14. Open a Command Prompt window with administrative privileges.

15. Enter **WBADMIN START SYSTEMSTATEBACKUP –backupTarget:f: -quiet**.

16. When the command completes, enter the command **WBADMIN GET VERSIONS**.

17. Verify that two backup jobs have been created, as shown in Figure 8-14.

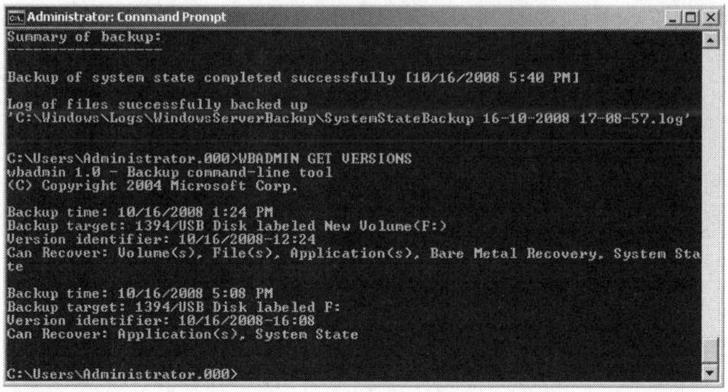

FIGURE 8-14 Verifying that backup jobs were created.

EXERCISE 3 Restore Windows Server 2008

You need to have completed Exercise 1 and Exercise 2, "Perform a Volume Backup," before you attempt this exercise, in which you use the Recovery Wizard to restore the deleted War-lords folder and the files that it hosted.

1. If necessary, log on to the Glasgow domain controller with the Kim_Akers account. Verify that the C:\Warlords directory is not present.

2. From the Administrative Tools menu, start Windows Server Backup. If a UAC dialog box appears, click Continue to clear it.

3. In the Actions pane, click Recover.

    This launches the Recovery Wizard.

4. On the Getting Started page, shown in Figure 8-15, select This Server (Glasgow) and click Next.

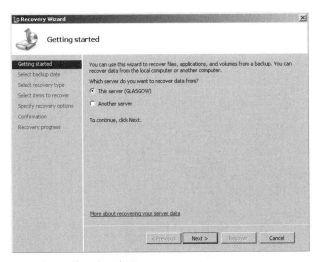

FIGURE 8-15 Choosing the server to recover.

5. On the Select Backup Date page, select the date on which you performed Exercise 2, and then click Next.

6. On the Select Recovery Type page, select Files And Folders, and then click Next.

7. On the Select Items To Recover page, expand Glasgow and Local Disk (C:), and then select the Warlords folder.

   By default, Windows Server Backup selects all files that were in this folder for recovery.

8. Click Next.

   This page was shown in Figure 8-6, earlier in this lesson.

9. On the Specify Recovery Options page, shown in Figure 8-16, set the Recovery Destination to Original Location and ensure that security settings are restored. Click Next.

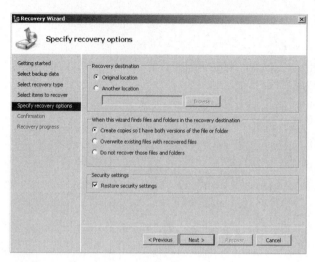

FIGURE 8-16 Choosing recovery options.

10. On the Confirmation page, click Recover. When the recovery is complete, click Close.
11. Check that the Warlords folder and the files it contains have been restored.

Lesson Summary

- You can use Windows Server Backup or the *wbadmin.exe* command-line tool to perform Windows Server 2008 backups. Only members of the Administrators local group can schedule backups on Windows Server 2008. Members of the Backup Operators group can perform manual backups.

- Scheduled backups can be written only to local disks or externally attached USB 2.0, SATA, or IEEE 1394 disks. Manual backups can also be written to network shares and local DVD writers. You can create scheduled backups to network locations by using the Scheduled Tasks tool to schedule a script file that uses a *wbadmin.exe* command.

- A system state backup backs up the AD DS database and Windows Server 2008 roles.

- When performing an operating system or full server recovery to a new hard disk, you must ensure that the disk is as big as the original disk that contained the volumes that were backed up.

- You can use the Recovery Wizard to recover a file, folder, or volume or to perform a full server recovery. A full server recovery also performs a nonauthoritative restore of system state data.

- You can perform a nonauthoritative restore of AD DS by booting into DSRM and restoring system state data. You can recover deleted Active Directory objects by using the *ntdsutil* utility to mark them as authoritative.

Lesson Review

You can use the following questions to test your knowledge of the information in Lesson 1, "Configuring Backup and Recovery." The questions are also available on the companion DVD if you prefer to review them in electronic form.

> **NOTE ANSWERS**
>
> **Answers to these questions and explanations of why each answer choice is right or wrong are located in the "Answers" section at the end of the book.**

1. You are scheduling a system state backup to be written to a shared network location every morning at 03:00 hours. The remote computer does not use the same Administrator password as the computer you are backing up. What steps must you take to schedule the backup? (Choose two. Each correct answer presents part of the solution.)

   A. Use the Scheduled Tasks tool to configure a job that runs the batch file once a day at 03:00 hours in the context of the local Administrator account credentials.

   B. Use the Scheduled Tasks tool to configure a job that runs the batch file once a week in the context of an account with credentials that have appropriate access to the share.

   C. Use the Scheduled Tasks tool to configure a job that runs a batch file once a week in the context of the local Administrator account credentials.

   D. Create a batch file that contains the *wbadmin start systemstatebackup* command and specifies the UNC path to the network share and the credentials of a user account that has appropriate access to the share.

   E. Create a batch file that contains the *wbadmin start systemstatebackup* command and specifies a local volume and the local Administrator account credentials.

2. You are attending a TechNet event and get into a discussion with a systems administrator who works for Tailspin Toys. He is dismissive of Windows Server Backup because he cannot use it to schedule backups of an important SQL Server 2005 server. Instead he uses System Center Data Protection Manager (DPM) 2007. Which of the following conclusions would you draw from this information?

   A. He is backing up his server to a local IEEE 1394 external disk.

   B. He is backing up his server to a local USB 2.0 external disk.

   C. He is backing up his server to an iSCSI SAN.

   D. He is backing up his server to an SCSI internal disk.

3. You want to back up server role settings and their associated data on a Windows Server 2008 member server. You do not want to carry out a critical volume backup. How do you proceed?

   A. Start Windows Server Backup. Do not specify a volume to back up. Perform a manual backup and select the Enable System Recovery option.

   B. Use *wbadmin.exe* with the *start systemstatebackup* option.

   C. Reboot the server into DSRM mode. Use the *ntdsutil* utility to enter the Authoritative Restore mode. Restore server role settings by using the *Restore Object* command.

   D. Open the System Configuration console from the Administrative Tools menu and select the Active Directory Repair Safe Boot option.

4. One of your trainee administrators has accidentally deleted the Boston computer account from the Windows_Server_2008_Servers OU in the *contoso.internal* domain. You reboot the Glasgow domain controller in this domain into DSRM, perform a system state recovery, start the *ntdsutil* utility, and specify Authoritative Restore mode. Which of the following commands would you use to restore the deleted computer account authoritatively?

   A. Restore Object
      "cn=Windows_Server_2008_Servers,OU=Boston,dc=contoso,dc=internal"

   B. Restore Computer
      "cn=Boston,OU=Windows_Server_2008_Servers,dc=contoso,dc=internal"

   C. Restore Object
      "cn=Boston,OU=Windows_Server_2008_Servers,dc=contoso,dc=internal"

   D. Restore Computer
      "cn=Windows_Server_2008_Servers,OU=Boston,dc=contoso,dc=internal"

5. Another administrator has accidentally deleted the Vista Workstations GPO in the *adatum.com* domain. Fortunately, you recently backed up the GPOs in this domain. How do you recover this GPO?

   A. Start the *ntdsutil* utility and specify Authoritative Restore mode. Enter the **Restore Object "GPO=Vista Workstations,dc=Adatum,dc=com"** command.

   B. Access the Restore Wizard and select the Vista Workstations GPO on the Select Items To Recover page.

   C. Access the Restore Wizard and select GPO Recovery on the Specify Recovery Options page.

   D. Open the GPMC, right-click the Group Policy Objects container, and then select Manage Backups. Browse to the location where backed up GPOs are stored and select the Vista Workstations GPO. Click Restore.

6. All RODCs deployed at Northwind Traders' branch office sites have BitLocker protection on all volumes. Full server backups of each RODC are taken once. The hard disk drive on the Denver branch office RODC fails. You replace the hard disk and perform a full server recovery. Which other step must you take to return the RODC to its original condition?

   A. Perform an authoritative restore.

   B. Perform a nonauthoritative restore.

   C. Perform a full server backup.

   D. Reapply BitLocker settings.

Lesson 2: Performing Offline Maintenance

One significant change in AD DS from previous versions is that AD DS is a server role that you can stop and restart. In previous versions of Windows Server, you needed to stop the entire domain controller to stop the Active Directory service. To perform maintenance on the *Ntds.dit* database, for example, you needed to shut down the domain controller and restart it in DSRM. This made it impossible to automate the Active Directory database maintenance.

When a database record is deleted, the allocated space is not automatically recovered; you must compact the database offline to recover it. The AD DS service carries out automatic online database maintenance, but this is limited. It rearranges data to facilitate access (defragmentation) but does not recover lost space within the database (compaction). To recover lost space, stop the AD DS service. This takes the database offline and enables you to run compaction and defragmentation operations against it. Windows Server 2008 introduces restartable AD DS, so you can perform offline operations without restarting a domain controller in DSRM.

> **NOTE** **AD DS WILL NOT STOP UNLESS IT IS AVAILABLE ON ANOTHER DOMAIN CONTROLLER**
>
> If you plan to stop the AD DS service, ensure that the domain controller can communicate with another writable Windows Server 2008 domain controller on which the service is running. If this is not the case, you will be unable to stop the AD DS service. AD DS automatically checks and ensures that at least one domain controller is available at all times so users can log on to the network.

EXAM TIP

Microsoft documentation states that you cannot stop the AD DS service on a domain controller unless another domain controller is available in the domain to service authentication requests. This is how this chapter is written and probably how the examinations will be assessed. However, although this is bad practice, it is physically possible to stop the AD DS service on a single domain controller in a domain. You can also move the Active Directory database to a new location after you have created a new OU and marked it as protected, although Microsoft says you cannot.

After this lesson, you will be able to:

- Stop and restart the AD DS service.
- Change the DRSM Administrator logon default.
- Protect AD DS objects from deletion and recover tombstoned objects.
- Allocate Active Directory storage.

Estimated lesson time: 40 minutes

Restartable AD DS

Restartable AD DS reduces the time to perform offline operations such as offline compaction and defragmentation. It also improves the availability of other services that do not depend on AD DS by keeping them running when AD DS is stopped.

You can use the Microsoft Management Console (MMC) Computer Management snap-in or the *net.exe* command-line utility to stop and restart AD DS. Other services that run on the server but do not depend on AD DS (for example, DHCP) remain available to service client requests while AD DS is stopped. You cannot stop AD DS if no other domain controller is running the service in your domain. As a result, users can continue to log on to the domain by using a domain account. Provided one or more other domain controllers are available to validate your credentials, you can log on to the domain when the domain controller is started in DSRM.

> **NOTE STOPPING AD DS ON AN RODC**
>
> Use the *net.exe* utility (*net stop "Active Directory Domain Services"*) to stop AD DS on an RODC unless you access the computer remotely by using RSAT.

Suppose, however, you stop AD DS on one domain controller and then the second domain controller in the domain goes offline. With no other domain controller available, you can log on to the first domain controller in DSRM only, and you must use the DSRM Administrator account and password. If you want to change this default, you can do so by modifying the *HKLM\System\CurrentControlSet\Control\Lsa\DSRMAdminLogonBehavior* registry entry, as shown in Figure 8-17.

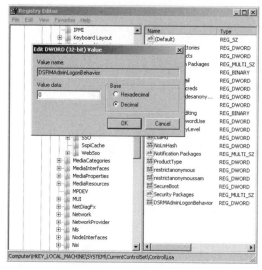

FIGURE 8-17 Modifying the default DSRM Administrator logon behavior.

If you change the value for this registry entry to 1, you can use the DSRM Administrator account to log on in normal startup mode to a domain controller that has AD DS stopped, even if no other domain controller is available. This can help prevent you from being inadvertently locked out of a domain controller to which you have logged on locally and stopped the AD DS service. The various settings for this registry entry are discussed later in this lesson when it discusses domain controller states.

> **MORE INFO** **MODIFYING THE DEFAULT LOGON BEHAVIOR**
>
> For more information, see "Modifying the Default Logon Behavior" in the Restartable AD DS Step-By-Step Guide at *http://technet.microsoft.com/en-us/library/cc732714 .aspx#BKMK_Mod*.

You cannot remove AD DS from a domain controller, while AD DS is stopped, by using the *dcpromo* command in the way you normally do. However, you can use the *dcpromo /forceremoval* command to demote a domain controller forcibly while AD DS is stopped.

> **MORE INFO** **FORCIBLY REMOVING AD DS**
>
> For more information about how to remove AD DS forcibly, access the AD DS Installation and Removal Step-by-Step Guide at *http://technet.microsoft.com/en-us/library/cc755258 .aspx* and follow the links.

Domain Controller States

Microsoft identifies three possible states for a domain controller running Windows Server 2008:

- **AD DS Started**   AD DS is started, and the computer is operating normally as a domain controller in its domain.

- **AD DS Stopped**   In this state, AD DS is stopped. The AD DS Stopped state is a feature of restartable AD DS. The AD DS database (*Ntds.dit*) on the domain controller is offline. The server is joined to the domain, and all services that do not depend on AD DS are running. If no other domain controller can be contacted to service a domain logon request, you can use the DSRM password to log on to the local domain controller in DSRM. If another domain controller can be contacted, users can continue to log on to the domain. In this state, you can run the *dcpromo /forceremoval* command to remove AD DS forcibly from the domain controller.

- **Directory Services Restore Mode**   In this state, the server has booted into DSRM. The features and functions of the DSRM state are unchanged from Windows Server 2003 except for one additional feature. In Windows Server 2008 you can run the *dcpromo /forceremoval* command to remove AD DS forcibly from a domain controller that is started in DSRM, just as you can in the AD DS Stopped state.

You cannot start a domain controller that is running Windows Server 2008 in the AD DS Stopped state, but you can restart it in DSRM. Although services that do not depend on AD DS continue to run when AD DS is stopped, services that depend on AD DS shut down before AD DS shuts down. These services include File Replication Service (FRS), Kerberos Key Distribution Center (KDC), and Intersite Messaging. If a dependent service was running when AD DS was stopped, that service restarts when AD DS restarts. You can stop and start AD DS, but you cannot pause it. The only startup type is Automatic.

 Quick Check

- A domain controller in your domain is servicing DHCP requests but is not authenticating user logons. When you reboot, it does not boot normally but instead boots into DSRM. It was not in the DSRM state before its reboot. What state was the domain controller in before you rebooted?

Quick Check Answer

- AD DS Stopped

If the domain controller is a DNS server, it will not respond to any queries for Active Directory–integrated zones while AD DS is stopped. To help prevent DNS lookup failures, configure the DNS client settings on member computers, application servers, and domain controllers to point to more than one DNS server. This is a good idea whether you intend to stop AD DS on a domain controller or not because it provides redundancy.

Options for logon in the AD DS Stopped state depend on whether another domain controller can service domain logon requests. If another domain controller services the logon request, the computer on which AD DS is stopped acts as a member server, and normal Group Policy settings apply to user and computer accounts. If another domain controller cannot service the domain logon request, you can (by default) only log on to the server in DSRM, which requires the DSRM Administrator account and password.

By default, you must start a domain controller in DSRM (the DSRM state) to log on by using the DSRM Administrator account. However, you can change this behavior by modifying the *DSRMAdminLogonBehavior* registry entry introduced earlier in this lesson. By changing the value for this entry, you can configure a domain controller so that you can log on to it with the DSRM Administrator account if the domain controller was started normally but the AD DS service has been stopped. You can also configure this registry entry so you can use the DSRM Administrator account to log on to a domain controller whether AD DS is stopped or running, but Microsoft does not recommend using this setting.

Table 8-1 shows the settings available for the *DSRMAdminLogonBehavior* registry entry. This table describes the options for using the DSRM Administrator account to log on when the domain controller is started normally. Remember that you can always use the DSRM admin account to log on to a domain controller in the DSRM state.

TABLE 8-1 *DSRMAdminLogonBehavior* Registry Entry Settings

VALUE	DESCRIPTION
0 (default)	You can log on only to a domain controller in the AD DS Stopped state with a domain account. This requires an additional domain controller to authenticate the request and functional connectivity, name resolution, authentication, and authorization services between the local domain controller and the authenticating domain controller.
1	You can use the DSRM Administrator account to log on only to a domain controller in the AD DS Stopped state. This value can improve functionality by allowing more options for logging on to a domain controller. However, the DSRM Administrator account password is not checked against any password policy.
2	You can use the DSRM Administrator account to log on to a domain controller whether it is in the AD DS Started or AD DS Stopped state. Microsoft does not recommend using this setting because the DSRM Administrator account password is not checked against any password policy.

Typically, you would change this registry setting in a domain that has a single domain controller or on a domain controller that is on an isolated network or that points to itself or other offline domain controllers exclusively for name resolution.

An example of how a domain controller could be locked out would be if you had logged on to a domain controller locally by using a Domain Admin account, stopped the AD DS service to perform maintenance, and then found that a password-protected screen saver had locked the domain controller. By default, in this situation, you could unlock the domain controller only if another domain controller is available to service the request. If, however, the registry setting had been changed, you could use a DSRM Administrator account to log on only to the domain controller in the AD DS Stopped state.

Performing Offline Database Operations

Windows Server 2008 restartable AD DS enables you to perform offline database operations more quickly than you could with previous versions of the operating system because you do not have to restart the domain controller in DSRM. When you stop AD DS, you can carry out tasks such as offline defragmentation and compaction and marking AD DS objects as authoritative.

PERFORMING AN OFFLINE DEFRAGMENTATION AND COMPACTION

You can compact the AD DS database by stopping AD DS instead of restarting the domain controller in DSRM. The *compact to* subcommand of the *ntdsutil* command-line utility both compacts and defragments the *Ntds.dit* database and places the compacted database either in a local folder or in a shared folder on another computer. When you have compacted the database, you can delete the relevant log files. The original database remains unchanged, and you first back this up into another folder before you replace it in its original location by the new compacted database. You perform this procedure in the practice session later in this lesson.

> **MORE INFO** **OFFLINE DEFRAGMENTATION**
>
> For step-by-step instructions for performing an offline defragmentation operation, see *http://technet.microsoft.com/en-us/library/cc772931.aspx*.

> **NOTE** **PROTECTING THE *NTDS* DATABASE**
>
> Perform a system state backup before you perform offline defragmentation and compaction.

MARKING AN OBJECT AS AUTHORITATIVE

You can stop AD DS if you need to mark an object or objects as authoritative, which is one step in the process for performing an authoritative restore to recover an object that you have accidentally deleted. In previous versions of Windows Server, you had to start the domain controller in DSRM and then perform a nonauthoritative restore before you could mark an object as authoritative. On a domain controller that runs Windows Server 2008, you can stop AD DS and mark the object as authoritative by using the *ntdsutil authoritative restore* command. You can then use the *restore object* or *restore subtree* command, depending on whether you want to restore a single object or a hierarchy.

For example, if you want to restore a deleted OU named Chicago Sales in the *houston. northwindtraders.com* domain, you would enter:

```
restore subtree "OU=Chicago Sales,DC=houston,DC=Northwindtraders,DC=com"
```

MORE INFO **MARKING OBJECTS AS AUTHORITATIVE**

For more information about using the *ntdsutil authoritative restore* command, see *http://technet.microsoft.com/en-us/library/cc757068.aspx*.

 Quick Check

- You want to be able to log on to a domain controller with the DSRM Administrator account when the domain controller is in the AD DS Stopped state but not when it is in the AD DS Started state. Which registry change do you make?

Quick Check Answer

- Change the value of the *HKLM\System\CurrentControlSet\Control\Lsa \DSRMAdminLogonBehavior* registry entry to 1.

Active Directory Database Storage Allocation

Active Directory database storage allocation generally involves relocating AD DS database files to a temporary location while hardware updates are being performed and then moving the files to a permanent location. On Windows 2000 Server and Windows Server 2003 domain controllers, this requires restarting the domain controller in DSRM. Windows Server 2008 introduces restartable AD DS, and you can instead stop the AD DS service before you move database files.

You would allocate storage for AD DS database files under the following circumstances:

- If the physical disk on which the database or log files are stored requires upgrading or maintenance, you must move the database files—either temporarily or permanently.

- If free disk space is low on the logical drive that stores the database file (*Ntds.dit*), the log files, or both, and the database file or log files are the cause of the growth, you must provide more disk space.

You can allocate disk storage for AD DS database files by expanding the partition or partitions on the disk that currently stores these files. This does not change the path to the files, and you do not need to update the registry.

If it is not possible or practicable to extend the partition, you can use *ntdsutil.exe* to move the database file, the log files, or both to a larger existing partition. Note that if you choose not to use *ntdsutil.exe* to move these files to a different partition, you must update the registry manually. Typically, the path to the database file or log files will change as a result of moving the files, and Microsoft recommends that you use *ntdsutil.exe* whenever you move AD DS database files—even when the move is temporary—because this ensures that the registry remains current.

Perform a system state or critical volume backup as soon as the move is complete so that the restore procedure uses the correct path. You also need to verify that the correct permissions are applied on the destination folder after the move.

> *NOTE* **AD DS OBJECTS PROTECTED FROM DELETION**
>
> **If you have protected AD DS objects from deletion as described later in this lesson, you cannot relocate them.**

Storage Allocation Requirements for Relocating Active Directory Database Files

If you are relocating AD DS database files, ensure that you have free space on the destination drive that is at least equivalent to the current size of the database file, the combined log files, or both, depending on which files you are moving. If you are moving the files to a permanent location, ensure that you have free space on the destination NTFS drive that is at least equivalent to the following specified size, plus space to accommodate anticipated growth, depending on which file or files you are moving:

- If you are moving the database file only, the free space should, at a minimum, equal the size of the database file plus 20 percent of the *Ntds.dit* file or 500 megabytes (MB)—whichever is greater.
- If you are moving log files only, the free space should, at a minimum, equal the size of the combined log files plus 20 percent of the combined logs or 500 MB—whichever is greater.
- If you are moving both database and logs and the database and log files are stored on the same partition, the free space available should be at least 20 percent of the combined *Ntds.dit* and log files or 1 GB—whichever is greater.

The levels stated in the previous list are minimum recommended levels. Microsoft recommends adding additional space, depending upon anticipated growth. Note that the drive that is the permanent location of the database file or log files must be formatted as NTFS. Note also that if you replace or reconfigure a drive that stores the SYSVOL folder, you must first move the SYSVOL folder manually.

Protecting AD DS Objects

Traditionally, you protect AD DS objects from accidental deletion or misconfiguration by taking regular system state backups and performing authoritative restores if required. However, Windows Server 2008 AD DS includes other features that enable you to recover information without resorting to backups. These include the following:

- AD DS object protection
- More granular AD DS access auditing
- The tombstone or deleted objects container

AD DS Object Protection

You can protect every new object you create in AD DS by specifically assigning the Object Protection feature to the object. Objects you create through a batch process or through migration will not be protected unless you assign the feature during the creation process, and if you create an object interactively, you must also explicitly assign protection. You can assign object protection on the Object tab of the AD DS objects Properties dialog box, shown in Figure 8-18. This tab is visible only if you have enabled Advanced Features in the View menu of the Active Directory Users and Computers console. Note that container objects such as OUs have object protection turned on by default because they form part of the directory structure. When object protection is assigned, you cannot delete the object or move it from one location to the other.

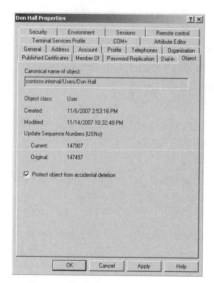

FIGURE 8-18 Protecting the Don Hall user account object from accidental deletion.

When object protection is assigned, you cannot delete the object or move it from one location to the other. This is a useful feature if you want to delegate object administration.

Under these circumstances, you could consider making object protection part of the user account template.

AD DS Access Auditing

This feature logs old and new values, enabling you to return to an original value if object properties are modified. When you audit directory changes in Windows Server 2008, AD DS access auditing logs old and new values of an attribute each time an object is modified. The AD DS audit policy in Windows Server 2008 logs four subcategories of service access, which enables you to control the assignment of this policy at a more granular level than in previous Windows Server operating system versions. The Directory Service Changes subcategory controls attribute captures. When enabled, it captures create, modify, move, and recover operations on an object. Each operation is assigned an Event ID in the Directory Services event log.

You can then use the Security event log to keep a record of directory changes. At least two events are logged when an object is modified. The first lists the former value, and the second lists the new value. This is useful for fixing erroneous modifications.

Recovering Tombstoned AD DS Objects

When you remove an AD DS object from the directory, it is tombstoned for a specific period of time (by default, 180 days, configurable by editing the registry). While the object is still in the tombstone (or deleted object) container, you can recover it by using the *ldp.exe* utility. You must be logged on with domain administrator credentials to perform this operation.

You can start the *ldp.exe* tool by typing **ldp.exe** in the Search bar and clicking OK. If you are not logged on at a domain controller, you can connect to one by specifying Connect and typing the domain controller's FQDN, for example, *glasgow.contoso.internal*. Select Bind and specify Bind As Currently Logged On User. Click Options and select Controls. Select Return Deleted Objects from the Load Predefined drop-down list, as shown in Figure 8-19. Ensure that Server is selected in the Control Type section of the dialog box, and then click OK.

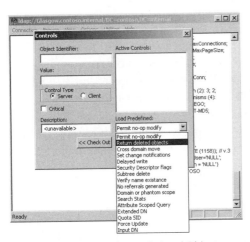

FIGURE 8-19 Selecting Return Deleted Objects.

Select View and then Tree and type in the distinguished name (DN) of the Deleted Objects container, for example, *cn=deleted objects,dc=contoso,dc=internal*. In the tree pane, double-click the Deleted Objects container to expand its contents. By default, *ldp.exe* returns only 1,000 objects, but this is usually enough. Locate the object you want to restore in the tree pane and double-click it. Right-click the object name in the tree pane and select Modify.

In the Modify dialog box, type **isDeleted** in the Edit Entry Attribute text box, select Delete as the Operation, and click Enter. Type **distinguishedName** in the Edit Entry Attribute text box, type the object's new DN in the Values text box, select Replace as the Operation, and click Enter. For example, to restore Sam Abolrous's account to the Users container in the *contoso.internal* domain, the DN is cn=Sam Abolrous,ou=Users,dc=contoso,dc=internal. Ensure that the Synchronous and Extended check boxes are both selected in the bottom left of the dialog box. The Modify dialog box is shown in Figure 8-20. Click Enter, and then click Run.

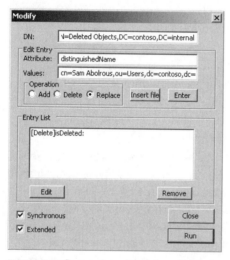

FIGURE 8-20 Recovering a tombstoned object.

You can then use Active Directory Users and Computers to access the OU to which you restored the object and refresh the OU contents. Reset the restored object's password, group memberships, and any other required settings and then enable the account. Note that this procedure recovers the object with its original SID but does not retain all group member-ships and other values. If you are restoring a complex AD DS object or container with a lot of settings (for example, an OU), you would probably carry out an authoritative restore instead. For an object that has fewer settings that are not a major task to restore (for example, a user account), you would probably use *ldp.exe*.

In this practice, you first promote your member server, Boston, to a domain controller in the *contoso.internal* domain. You cannot stop AD DS on a domain controller unless another domain controller is in the domain. You then stop AD DS on Boston and compact the *NTDS* database. Finally, you demote Boston to a member server.

EXERCISE 1   Stop AD DS

In this exercise, you promote Boston to a domain controller and stop the AD DS service. If you are using virtual machines, ensure that both Glasgow and Boston are running.

1. Log on to the *contoso.internal* domain at the Boston member server with the Kim_Akers account.

2. Use the *dcpromo* command to promote Boston to a domain controller in the *contoso. internal* domain.

3. Log on to the Boston domain controller with the Kim_Akers account.

4. Create folders **C:\CompactNTDS** and **C:\OriginalNTDS**.

5. If necessary, open Server Manager. Expand the *Configuration* node and select Services.

> **ALTERNATIVE METHOD**
>
> You can also open the Computer Management MMC snap-in, double-click Services And Applications, and then select Services.

6. Locate the Active Directory Domain Services service, right-click it, and select Stop, as shown in Figure 8-21.

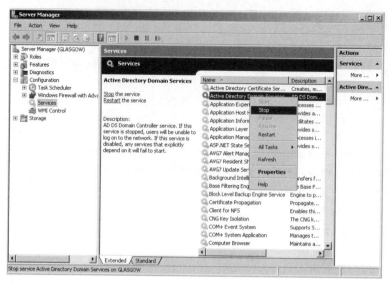

FIGURE 8-21 Stopping the AD DS service.

7. In the Stop Other Services dialog box, review the list of dependent services, and then click Yes.

   The AD DS service is now stopped. If you want to, you can go straight on to Exercise 2, "Compacting the *NTDS* Database." If you want to experiment, you can start the AD DS service again and observe that the dependent services start before AD DS starts. In this case, ensure that AD DS is stopped before you attempt Exercise 2.

EXERCISE 2   Compact the *NTDS* Database

In this exercise, you defragment and compact the *NTDS* database on the Boston domain controller. Bear in mind that this is an exercise to familiarize you with the procedure. The *NTDS* database on a newly created domain controller does not need to be defragmented and compacted. Before you start this exercise, be sure you have carried out Exercise 1, "Stop AD DS," that you are logged on to the Boston domain controller with the Kim_Akers account, and that you have stopped AD DS.

1. Open an elevated command prompt.
2. Enter **ntdsutil.cd**.
3. At the ntdsutil: prompt, enter **activate instance ntds**.
4. Enter **files**.
5. At the File Maintenance prompt, enter **compact to C:\CompactNTDS**.

   The *ntdsutil.exe* utility compacts the database and copies it to the new location.

6. When this operation is complete, enter **quit**.

7. Enter **quit** again to exit from the *ntdsutil* utility.

8. To delete all the log files, change to the *ntds* subdirectory. Enter **cd %systemroot%\ntds**.

9. Enter **del *.log**.

   This deletes the log files. You must do this because you will be replacing the *Ntds.dit* file with the newly compacted file, and the existing log files will not work with the new database.

10. To back up the original *Ntds.dit* file in case something goes wrong, enter **copy ntds.dit \originalNTDS**.

    You now copy the compacted database to the original NTDS folder.

11. Ensure that you are still in the %systemroot%\ntds (where %systemroot% will almost certainly be Windows) folder and enter **copy C:\CompactNTDS\ntds.dit**. Enter **y** when prompted.

    To verify the integrity of the compacted *Ntds.dit* file, you again use the *ntdsutil* utility.

12. Enter **ntdsutil**.

13. At the Ntdsutil prompt, enter **activate instance ntds**.

14. Enter **files**.

15. At the File Maintenance prompt, enter **integrity**.

    You should get an Integrity Check Successful message.

16. Enter **quit** to exit from file maintenance and **quit** again to exit from the *ntdsutil* utility.

    Your Command Prompt console should look similar to Figure 8-22.

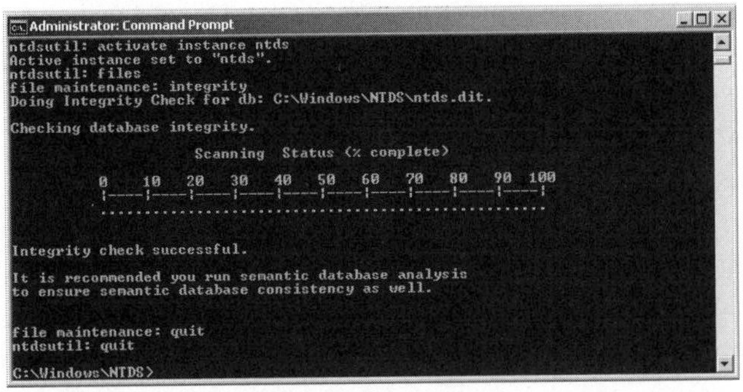

FIGURE 8-22 Checking AD DS database integrity

> **NOTE** **SEMANTIC DATABASE ANALYSIS**
>
> You can optionally carry out a further check on the *Ntds.dit* database by performing a semantic database analysis. This analyzes data with respect to Active Directory semantics—similar to checking a program file for syntax errors. To carry out this check directly after you have checked integrity, type **quit** to exit from the file maintenance prompt. At this point, the AD DS database is still stopped, and the activate instance is set to *ntds*. Enter **semantic database analysis**, followed by **go fixup**. When the analysis completes, enter **quit** twice to exit from the *ntdsutil* utility.

17. If the integrity check fails, copy the original *Ntds.dit* file in *C:\OriginalNTDS* back to the ntds folder and repeat the procedure. Otherwise, continue to the next step.

18. In Server Manager, expand the *Configuration* node and select Services.

19. Locate and right-click the Active Directory Domain Services service, and then select Start.

   Your Boston domain controller should now be fully operational. You can delete the *Ntds.dit* file located in the *C:\OriginalNTDS* folder because it is no longer valid. If, however, you encounter errors, do not delete the original *Ntds.dit* file but instead stop AD DS, restore the original *Ntds.dit* file, and restart AD DS.

   Do not demote the Boston domain controller at this stage. You will be exploring authoritative restore and restartable AD DS in the Suggested Practices section at the end of this chapter.

Lesson Summary

- You can stop the AD DS service to compact and defragment the AD DS database offline. You can also stop the service and mark restored AD DS objects as authoritative. You cannot stop the AD DS service if your domain controller is the only domain controller authenticating logons in the domain.

- You can protect AD DS objects from accidental deletion by using the Object tab in the Active Directory Users and Computers console. AD DS access auditing logs old and new values for AD DS objects in the Directory Services event log, enabling you to return to an original value if object properties are modified. You can use the *ldp.exe* utility to restore tombstoned AD DS objects. However, you might need to reconfigure some object properties manually.

- You can allocate disk storage for AD DS database files by expanding the partition or partitions on the disk that currently stores these files. If it is not possible or practicable to extend the partition, you can use *ntdsutil.exe* to move the database file, the log files, or both to a larger existing partition. You cannot move AD DS objects that are protected from deletion.

Lesson Review

You can use the following questions to test your knowledge of the information in Lesson 2, "Performing Offline Maintenance." The questions are also available on the companion DVD if you prefer to review them in electronic form.

> **NOTE ANSWERS**
>
> Answers to these questions and explanations of why each answer choice is right or wrong are located in the "Answers" section at the end of the book.

1. You want to perform an offline defragmentation of the *Ntds.dit* database on the LeedsDC1 domain controller. You stop AD DS and open an elevated command prompt. How do you defragment the database?

    A. Start the *ntdsutil* utility. At the Ntdsutil prompt, enter **activate instance ntds**, and then enter **compact to** and specify the directory that will hold the compacted database.

    B. Start the *ntdsutil* utility. At the Ntdsutil prompt, enter **activate instance ntds**, and then enter **files**. At the File Maintenance prompt, enter **compact to** and specify the directory that will hold the compacted database.

    C. Start the *ntdsutil* utility. At the Ntdsutil prompt, enter **defragment to** and specify the directory that will hold the defragmented database.

    D. Start the *ntdsutil* utility. At the Ntdsutil prompt, enter **files**. At the File Maintenance prompt, enter **defragment to** and specify the directory that will hold the defragmented database.

2. Trey Research has two Windows Server 2008 server domain controllers in its *chicago. treyresearch.com* domain, ChicagoDC1 and ChicagoDC2. You want to compact and defragment the *Ntds.dit* database on ChicagoDC2. You access the computer and open the Services console, but you cannot stop the Active Directory Domain Services service. What is the likely reason for this?

    A. You must use the *net stop* command to stop AD DS on a Windows Server 2008 domain controller.

    B. You need to boot ChicagoDC2 into DSRM.

    C. You cannot stop the AD DS service on a Windows Server 2008 domain controller.

    D. Someone has either stopped the AD DS service on ChicagoDC1 or has taken the computer offline.

3. You want to restore a deleted OU called Denver Computers in the *litwareinc.com* domain. As part of the restore process, you stop AD DS on a domain controller in the domain and open an elevated command prompt. How do you carry out an authoritative restore of the OU?

A. Enter **ntdsutil authoritative restore**. Enter **restore subtree "OU=Denver Computers,DC=Litwareinc,DC=com"**.

B. Enter **ntdsutil**. Enter **restore subtree "OU=Denver Computers,DC=Litwareinc, DC=com"**.

C. Enter **ntdsutil authoritative restore**. Enter **restore object "OU=Denver Computers,DC=Litwareinc,DC=com"**.

D. Enter **ntdsutil**. Enter **restore object "OU=Denver Computers,DC=Litwareinc, DC=com"**.

4. Which tool do you use to recover a tombstoned AD DS object?

   A. *Wbadmin.exe*

   B. *Ntdsutil. exe*

   C. *Ldp.exe*

   D. *Net.exe*

Lesson 3: Monitoring Active Directory

Windows Server 2008 is a stable and reliable operating system, but as with any software package, things can still go wrong. You can quickly notice and immediately deal with a catastrophic failure by using tested procedures (for example, restore from backup for a disk failure) that are already in place.

However, it is emphatically not good systems administration practice to lurch from one failure to the next. You need to monitor your Windows Server 2008 servers and, in particular, AD DS operation on your domain controllers proactively and continuously. A good administrator detects and fixes problems before anyone else notices them. Such vigilance can reveal which resources are under strain, and that administrator can present a business case for more resources to prevent a failure from happening next year rather than having to address preventable problems. This lesson discusses the tools and techniques that enable you to monitor Active Directory.

 REAL WORLD

Ian McLean

Good systems administration is mostly invisible. The last thing your users want is an interruption to their mission-critical work while you perform some systems task that they neither need nor want to understand. This is why many tasks are done at night and why you need to be good at scheduling them to start and run automatically.

Monitoring is possibly the least visible of all administrative tasks. You have systems set up to capture the data you need, but as a hard-working administrator, you might be short of the time required to look at the results. So who is to know if you haven't checked your event logs and performance counters for a couple of months? The answer is nobody—until your entire system crashes catastrophically.

This was brought home to me one evening when I was with my wife celebrating an anniversary in a restaurant that we could not normally afford. Now, I don't deliberately listen to other people's conversations, but the two gentlemen at the table beside us had particularly loud and strident voices.

"Our man's really good," said the first. "We've had three crashes this year and every time he's been right on the job and worked into the evening to get things running again. And he's always up at the Executive suite every morning to get us going, you know, something to do with trees."

"Log on," said the other. "The person we have insists we do that ourselves. I've told her several times I'm far too busy to remember—what's it called—my passport or something. Fortunately, my PA knows it. And we never seem to have crashes. I really don't know what she does all day, other than ask for more bits to plug into our machines."

"Oh, our man never does that. I don't think we've had to, what's it called—grade up—our computers for years."

At this point, I forced myself not to hear. It's a waste of good steak to choke on it. As a professional administrator, you won't be appreciated and you certainly won't become rich. Sometimes, though, you can have a good laugh.

After this lesson, you will be able to:

- Monitor performance and reliability.
- View Information, Warning, and Error events.
- Use Windows System Resource Manager.
- Create and use Data Collector Sets to generate reports.
- Check AD DS Replication.
- Use the Resultant Set of Policies tool.

Estimated lesson time: 45 minutes

Monitoring and Management Tools

Windows Server 2008 includes a number of tools that can identify potential system resource issues and where potential bottlenecks are likely to occur. If you identify a potential bottleneck on a physical system, you might need to shut the system down while you install new resources. If the system is virtual, you might be able to allocate new resources while the virtual machine is still running. When you have made the appropriate changes, you need to monitor system performance again to assess whether the additional resources solved the problem.

Tools that can identify performance bottlenecks and potential AD DS problems in Windows Server 2008 include the following:

- Task Manager.
- Resource Monitor and Resource View.
- Event Viewer.

- Windows System Resource Manager (WSRM).
- Windows Reliability and Performance Monitor (WRPM). This can be considered as two tools, Reliability Monitor and Performance Monitor.
- The *RepAdmin*, *Replmon*, and *Dcdiag* command-line tools.
- Resultant Set of Policies (RSoP).

Additional tools are available, such as Microsoft System Center Operations Manager, which continuously monitor the state of a system and automatically correct well-known issues. Operations Manager uses custom management packs to monitor specific applications.

> **MORE INFO** **MICROSOFT SYSTEM CENTER OPERATIONS MANAGER**
>
> **For more information about Microsoft System Center Operations Manager, see** *http://www* *.microsoft.com/systemcenter/operationsmanager/en/us/default.aspx.*

You seldom use other tools, such as Network Monitor, for AD DS monitoring in Windows Server 2008 because tools such as Reliability and Performance Monitor provide the required functionality. You use Network Monitor, discussed in Chapter 10, "Monitoring Performance and Events," for more general-purpose monitoring.

Other tools you might have used in previous versions of the Windows Server operating system are not provided in Windows Server 2008, for example, Server Performance Advisor (SPA). SPA functionality is now included in WRPM.

EXAM TIP

Even though SPA no longer exists, it is mentioned in the examination objectives. You are expected to know that its functions are now carried out by WRPM. If SPA appears in the examination, it will probably be an incorrect answer.

Using Task Manager

Task Manager provides real-time system status information and covers several key aspects of system performance, including:

- Applications
- Processes
- Services
- CPU performance and memory usage
- Network interface card (NIC) usage
- Logged-on users

You can access Task Manager by right-clicking the task bar and selecting Task Manager or by pressing the Ctrl+Alt+Delete key combination and clicking Task Manager. The second method accesses the tool on a Server Core installation, where there is no task bar.

The Task Manager Performance tab, shown in Figure 8-23, displays information about your system's key resource usage, including physical and kernel memory usage. This tab also provides access to Resource Monitor. You can launch Resource Monitor while keeping Task Manager open.

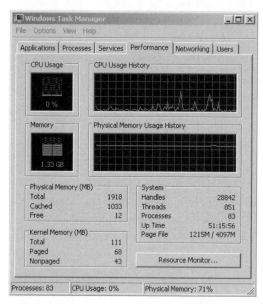

FIGURE 8-23 Task Manager Performance tab.

Resource Monitor

Resource Monitor combines the CPU, disk, memory, and network usage graphs into a single view, as shown in Figure 8-24. It provides expandable components for each resource so you can identify which process might be the culprit if problems are encountered. Task Manager and Resource Monitor are used for on-the-spot verifications of resource usage that can identify immediate problems. They are less suitable for periodic monitoring of resources that can identify potential bottlenecks and problems that could be developing.

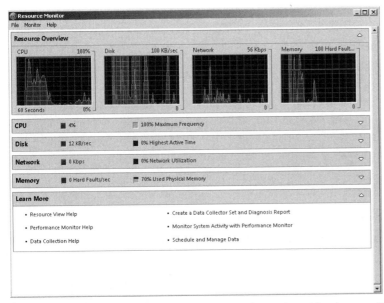

FIGURE 8-24 Resource Monitor (the Resource View of WRPM provides the same Window).

RESOURCE VIEW

Resource View, the home page of WRPM, provides the same functionality as Resource Monitor and displays information from the Windows Kernel Trace provider session. To use this tool, you must be a member of the local Administrators group on the server you are monitoring, or you can specify the credentials of an account with these privileges. In Resource View, you can monitor CPU, disk, network, and memory resources in real time, and you can expand each of these four resources to obtain more detail, in particular, which processes are using which resources.

> **NOTE RUNNING WRPM WITH INSUFFICIENT CREDENTIALS**
>
> If you attempt to run WRPM with insufficient credentials, the Resource View home page does not show current system information. If you click the Start button under these circumstances, you see the following message: "The Windows Kernel Trace Provider Is Already In Use By Another Trace Session. Taking Control Of It May Cause The Current Owner To Stop Functioning Properly."

You can ensure that Resource View is running in the context of an account with the appropriate privileges by starting it from an elevated Command Prompt console. If you are not currently logged on with the appropriate privileges, you will be prompted for credentials.

You can start WRPM by entering **perfmon.exe** in the Search box or in an elevated Command Prompt console. The facilities this powerful tool provides are discussed later in this lesson. If you prefer, you can start Resource View in its own window by entering **perfmon /res**.

For example, Don Hall wants to view CPU usage on the Boston member server. He is logged on interactively at that server and starts Resource View in its own window. Don sees four scrolling graphs in the Resource Overview pane that display the real-time usage of CPU, Disk, Network, and Memory, as shown in Figure 8-24. The CPU graph displays the total percentage of CPU capacity currently in use in green and the CPU Maximum Frequency in blue. Don clicks the CPU graph to view the following details (shown in Figure 8-25):

- **Image** Indicates the application that is using CPU resources.
- **PID** Displays the process ID of the application instance.
- **Description** Displays the application name.
- **Threads** Displays the number of threads currently active from the application instance.
- **CPU** Displays the CPU cycles currently active from the application instance.
- **Average CPU** Indicates the average CPU load, over the past 60 seconds, that resulted from the application instance. This is expressed as a percentage of the total capacity of the CPU.

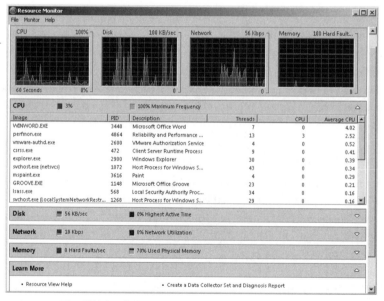

FIGURE 8-25 The CPU details in Resource View.

From the Average CPU readings, Don locates an application that is using 60 percent of the total CPU capacity. He can then determine whether this application runs frequently and is mission critical, in which case, he might consider it necessary to install a second CPU. If the server already has more than one CPU, Don can look at application affinity. Possibly, he can reschedule the task that requires the application so it runs in off-peak hours.

> **MORE INFO** **RESOURCE VIEW**
>
> For more information about the details available in Resource View in the disk, network, and memory categories, see *http://technet.microsoft.com/en-us/library/cc771692 .aspx#BKMK_Scen1*.

Using Event Viewer

Windows maintains several event logs that hold information about the services running on a server. On a member or standalone Windows Server 2008 server, these are the Application, Security, Setup, System, and Forwarded event logs (sometimes called collectors or collector views), all of which are located under the Windows Logs folder in the Event Viewer snap-in. On a domain controller, additional collectors are available that are specifically related to AD DS operation and other functions typically implemented by a domain controller (for example, DNS) and are located in the Applications and Services Logs folder. AD DS collectors include:

- **DFS Replication** DFS Replication is available in domains and forests operating in Windows Server 2008 functional mode. If your domains or forests run in an earlier functional mode, the collector will be for FRS replication.
- **Directory Service** Directory Service is a collector for operations specifically related to AD DS.
- **DNS Server** On a domain controller, the DNS Server collector holds all events related to Active Directory–integrated DNS.

Chapter 10 discusses Event Viewer in more detail.

Event Viewer is available on the Administrative Tools menu and in the Diagnostics section of Server Manager. Server Manager also provides custom collector views related to server roles. Of particular interest for monitoring AD DS operation is the collector view related to the Active Directory Domain Services role. If you select this role in the Server Manager console, you can obtain information that includes a summary view of key events related to AD DS, as shown in Figure 8-26.

Event logs hold three types of events: Information, Warning, and Error. Some logs also display Critical events. The summary view displayed under a server role lists the Error messages with a high priority, the Warning messages with a medium priority, and the Information messages with a low priority. Errors, therefore, appear at the top of the summary, so you can see immediately whether there is an issue with your system. You view event details by double-clicking the event or accessing Event Viewer under the *Diagnostics* node of the tree pane in Server Manager.

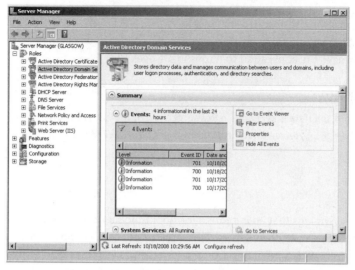

FIGURE 8-26 Viewing AD DS summary events.

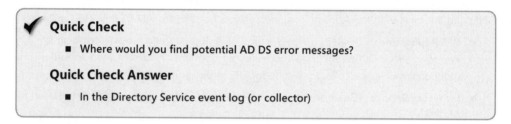

Quick Check

- Where would you find potential AD DS error messages?

Quick Check Answer

- In the Directory Service event log (or collector)

For example, Sam Abolrous views the following entry in the DNS log on a domain controller:

Error Event 4010

The DNS server was unable to load a resource record (RR) from the directory at *<data>* in zone *<zone name>*. Use the DNS console to re-create this RR or check that AD DS is functioning properly and reload the zone. The event data contains the error.

Sam accesses a third-party database, for example, at *http://kb.prismmicrosys.com/index. asp* or *http://www.eventid.net*. As a result of what he learns, he stops the netlogon service and deletes the netlogon.dns and netlogon.dnb files. He opens an elevated command prompt and enters **ipconfig /flushdns** and then **ipconfig /registerdns**. Finally, he starts netlogon and checks that the error does not recur.

Windows Server 2008 Event Viewer and event logs are considerably enhanced in Windows Server 2008, and you can typically obtain a full explanation of an event in Event Viewer. You can also link to an online database, maintained by Microsoft for each event, by clicking the Event Log Online Help link in the event's Properties dialog box.

This database does not provide information about every Windows event, but it covers the most frequently viewed events. There are also third-party event log databases (as specified in the example given earlier in this section) that you can use to obtain information about events.

Using Reliability Monitor

Reliability Monitor is a component of WRPM. You can access it through Server Manager by expanding Diagnostics, expanding Reliability And Performance, expanding Monitoring Tools, and then selecting Reliability Monitor. Reliability Monitor tracks system changes, software installs and uninstalls, application failures, hardware failures, and Windows failures, as shown in Figure 8-27.

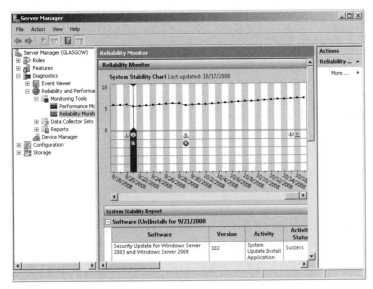

FIGURE 8-27 Reliability Monitor.

If an issue arises, Reliability Monitor helps you discover what might have made your system unresponsive. If, for example, it shows that a new device driver was recently installed, you can roll back the device installation and see whether that solves the problem.

Using Performance Monitor

Like Reliability Monitor, you can access Performance Monitor through Server Manager by expanding Diagnostics, expanding Reliability And Performance, expanding Monitoring Tools, and then selecting Performance Monitor. Reliability Monitor and Performance Monitor can be considered components of the WRPM tool.

Performance Monitor tracks performance counters that record the performance of system components either in real time or from log files created on a scheduled basis. It displays performance data as a graph, histogram, or report. You can use it as a troubleshooting tool, but its main function is to establish baselines for system performance and to determine whether system components are coming under stress and bottlenecks are developing.

The Windows Server 2008 Performance Monitor combines the functionality of Windows Server 2003 and Windows 2000 Server tools with which you are probably familiar, for example, Performance Logs and Alerts, Server Performance Advisor (SPA), and System Monitor. Performance Monitor enables you to create interactive collections of system counters or reusable data collector sets.

> **NOTE DATA COLLECTOR SETS**
>
> A data collector set groups data collectors into reusable elements that can be used to review or log performance. Data collector sets contain three types of data collectors: performance counts, event trace data, and system configuration information. Data collector sets are discussed in detail in Chapter 10.

You can use Performance Monitor in conjunction with the WRPM Reports tool, which generates preconfigured performance and diagnosis reports and can also be used to generate reports from data collected using a data collector set.

Windows Server 2008 introduces the built-in Performance Log Users group. This enables server administrators who are not members of the local Administrators group to perform tasks related to performance monitoring and logging. By default, this group has the Log On As A Batch Job right, so group members can initiate data logging or modify data collector sets.

Windows Server 2008 creates custom data collector set templates when a role is installed. You can find these templates under the System node of the Data Collector Sets section of WRPM. For example, the following collector sets are created for the AD DS role:

- **Active Directory Diagnostics**   This set collects data from registry keys, performance counters, and trace events related to AD DS performance on a local domain controller.

- **LAN Diagnostics**   This set collects data from network interface cards, registry keys, and other system hardware. It can be used to identify issues related to network traffic on the local domain controller.

- **System Diagnostics**   This set collects data from local hardware resources to generate data that helps streamline system performance on the local domain controller.

- **System Performance**   This set provides information about the status of hardware resources, system response times, and processes on the local domain controller.

Arguably, Active Directory Diagnosis is the most useful set for monitoring AD DS. You can also create a personalized data set. If you do, you should consider the following counters:

- LogicalDisk\% Free Space

- PhysicalDisk\% Idle Time

- PhysicalDisk\Avg. Disk Sec/Read

- PhysicalDisk\Avg. Disk Sec/
- PhysicalDisk\Avg. Disk Queue Length
- Memory\Cache Bytes
- Memory\% Committed Bytes in Use
- Memory\Available MBytes
- Memory\Free System Page Table Entries
- Memory\Pool Non-Paged Bytes
- Memory\Pool Paged Bytes
- Memory\Pages/Sec
- Processor\% Processor Time
- Processor\% User Time
- Processor\% Interrupt Time
- System\Processor Queue Length
- Network Interface\Bytes Total/Sec
- Network Interface\Output Queue Length
- Process\Handle Count
- Process\Thread Count Process\Private Bytes

> **MORE INFO** **PERFORMANCE COUNTERS**
>
> Find out what each of the listed performance counters does and how it can help you do your job. You can look up each individual counter in TechNet or the Windows Server 2008 Help files, but a good place to start is *http://technet.microsoft.com/en-us/magazine /cc718984.aspx*.

As a Windows Server 2003 professional, you should know how to add counters to Performance Monitor, but if you have forgotten, click the plus (+) sign on the toolbar at the top of the details pane. In some cases, you might need subcounters or instances under a specific heading; in others, you need the entire subset of counters. The Show Description facility shows you a description at the bottom of the dialog box. Use this facility shamelessly. No matter how often you use a counter, you can feel more comfortable when you have reminded yourself of exactly what it does. Figure 8-28 shows a counter being added to Performance Monitor.

If you want to store the values in the counters you added into a custom dataset, you can right-click Performance Monitor and select All Tasks. You then select New Data Collector Set and follow the prompts.

One of your first tasks in a newly installed system is to use Performance Monitor to create a performance baseline. As load increases, you compare the current load with the baseline and see what has changed. This helps you identify whether additional resources are required.

To create a performance baseline, you sample counter values for 30 to 45 minutes each day for at least a week during periods of peak, normal, and low activity.

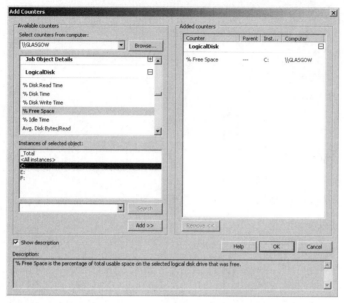

FIGURE 8-28 Adding a counter to Performance Monitor.

EXAM TIP

Performance Monitor is likely to be extensively tested in the upgrade examinations. It is worth repeating that SPA is not a separate tool in Windows Server 2008 but is now part of WRPM.

Quick Check
- Which data collector set collects data from registry keys, performance counters, and trace events related to AD DS performance on a local domain controller?

Quick Check Answer
- The Active Directory Diagnostics data collector set

When you want to view your results, use WRPM Reports. Right-click the collector set for which you want to view the report (either User Defined or System) and select Latest Report. This generates the report if it is not already available and provides extensive information on the status of your DC. You do this in the practice session later in this lesson.

MORE INFO **PERFORMANCE MONITOR**

For more information about Performance Monitor, see the Windows Reliability and Performance Monitor (WRPM) Step-by-Step Guide at *http://technet.microsoft.com/en-us/library /cc771692.aspx*.

Using WRSM

Install WSRM by using Add Features in Server Manager. This tool can help you identify the resources an application requires on a regular basis. In this mode, WSRM logs events in the application event log only when the application exceeds its allowed limits.

You can also use WSRM in Manage mode, in which the tool uses allocation policies to control how many resources an application can use on a server. If applications exceed their resource allocations, WSRM can stop the application from executing and make sure other applications on the same server continue to operate. WSRM, however, will not affect any application if combined processor resources do not exceed 70 percent usage.

WSRM also supports Alerts and Event Monitoring. This helps you control processor and memory usage on large multiprocessing servers. By default, WSRM includes four built-in management policies in addition to custom resources that you can use to define your own policies. WSRM ensures that high-priority applications always have enough resources available to them for continued operation.

 Quick Check

- You use WSRM to control processor and memory resources for a number of server applications. None of your policies are applied. What is the probable reason?

Quick Check Answer

- WSRM does not affect any application if combined processor resources do not exceed 70 percent usage.

You can use WSRM to evaluate how your applications are being used. You can then apply management policies. Do this initially on your test network and ensure that you thoroughly test your policies before applying them in a production environment. You can use the WSRM Calendar to determine when which policy should be applied.

NOTE **WSRM RESOURCE USAGE**

WSRM is resource-intensive. Consider placing it on a dedicated management server in a production network.

For example, Kim Akers is designing a WSRM scenario. She chooses to deploy predefined policies to manage system resources. She can allocate resources on a per-process, per-user, or per–Internet Information Services (IIS) application pool basis. She uses calendar rules to apply her policies at different times on different dates without manual intervention.

Kim can automate the resource policy selection process based on server properties, events, or changes to available physical memory or processor count. She chooses to collect resource usage information in local text files rather than storing them in a SQL database. As her network expands, she plans to create a central WSRM collection system to collate resource usage from several systems that run their own instances of WSRM.

Chapter 12, "Terminal Services," also discusses WSRM.

Monitoring AD DS Replication

Monitor AD DS replication regularly to help identify and fix problems before they affect your users. You can use the *repadmin.exe*, *dcdiag.exe*, and *replmon* utilities and the Directory Service event log to monitor replication.

REPADMIN

The *repadmin* command-line tool reports failures between replication partners. For example, the following command displays the replication partners and any replication failures for the domain controller Glasgow in the *contoso.internal domain*:

```
repadmin /showrepl Glasgow.contoso.internal
```

> **MORE INFO**   **REPADMIN/SHOWREPL**
>
> For more information about the repadmin /showrepl command syntax and parameters, see *http://technet2.microsoft.com/windowsserver2008/de/library/4f5de244-f996-4537-986a -50d0b361dcc01031.mspx?mfr=true.*

DCDIAG

The *dcdiag* command-line tool checks the DNS registration of a domain controller, verifies that the SIDs on the naming context heads have appropriate permissions for replication, and analyzes the state of domain controllers in a forest or enterprise. For example, the following command checks for any replication errors between domain controllers:

```
dcdiag /test:replications
```

REPLMON

The *replmon* GUI support tool displays the low-level status of AD DS replication, forces synchronization between domain controllers, displays the replication topology, and monitors the status and performance of domain controller replication. You must install this tool from the operating system DVD or from the Microsoft download site before you can use it.

The tool enables you to do the following:

- View the properties of directory replication partners and detect when a replication partner fails
- View the history of successful and failed replication changes
- View a snapshot of performance counters and registry configuration
- Create your own applications or scripts to extract specific data from AD DS
- Generate status reports
- Force replication
- Trigger the Knowledge Consistency Checker (KCC) to recalculate the replication topology
- Display changes from a given replication partner that have not yet replicated
- List the trust relationships maintained by the domain controller being monitored
- Display the metadata of an AD DS object's attributes
- Monitor the replication status of domain controllers from multiple forests

---

MORE INFO   **REPLMON**

For more information about the *replmon* support tool, see *http://technet.microsoft.com /en-us/library/cc772954.aspx and http://technet.microsoft.com/en-us/library/cc775394 .aspx.* These are Windows Server 2003 links but should give you the information you need.

THE DIRECTORY SERVICE LOG

The Directory Service log (in Event Viewer under Application Logs) reports replication errors that occur after a replication link has been established. Event logs were discussed earlier in this lesson.

The time required to replicate directory data between domain controllers is known as the replication latency. This can vary, depending on the number of domain controllers, the number of sites, the available bandwidth between sites, the replication frequency, and so on.

You can monitor replication to determine the normal replication latency on your network. If you know the normal replication latency, you can determine whether a problem is occurring. You also must check the Directory Service log and use the *repadmin /showrepl* command to discover recent replication errors.

MORE INFO   **SITE TOPOLOGY**

A good site topology design is important for replication efficiency. For more information about site topology design, see *http://technet.microsoft.com/en-us/library/cc772013.aspx.*

Using Resultant Set of Policy

You can use the Resultant Set of Policy (RSoP) snap-in to create detailed reports about applied policy settings in two modes: logging mode and planning mode. Logging mode displays policy settings applied to computers or users who have logged on. Planning mode simulates policy settings that you intend to apply to a computer or user. You can also use planning mode to check assigned policy settings for a computer that is not currently available or for a user who is not currently logged on.

To open RSoP as an MMC snap-in and display RSoP logging mode for the currently logged-on user and computer, type **rsop.msc** in the Search or Run box. Figure 8-29 shows the RSoP console.

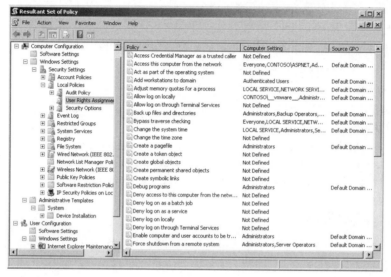

FIGURE 8-29 The RSoP console.

To open RSoP as an MMC snap-in and display RSoP logging mode for a specified namespace and target computer, type **rsop.msc /RsopNamespace:<NameSpace>/ RsopTargetComp:<*TargetComputer*>** (for example, *rsop.msc /RsopNamespace:contoso. internal /RsopTargetComp:Glasgow*) in the Search or Run box.

RoSP operation has not changed significantly from Windows Server 2003. What has changed is the introduction of fine-grained password policies in Windows 2008. This adds flexibility but makes it more important to have an automatic method of determining the result of actual or planned password policy settings.

MORE INFO   **ROSP AND FINE-GRAINED PASSWORD POLICIES**

For more information about the RSoP snap-in, see *http://technet.microsoft.com/en-us /library/cc736424.aspx*. This is a Windows Server 2003 link, but the information it contains also applies to Windows Server 2008. For more information about fine-grained password policies, see *http://technet.microsoft.com/en-us/library/cc770394.aspx*.

PRACTICE   **AD DS Performance Analysis**

In this practice, you install WSRM on the Glasgow domain controller and view the policies it provides. You then create a custom data collector set on the same computer, run the collector set, and use WRPM to view the diagnostics report.

EXERCISE 1   Install WSRM

In this exercise, you install the WSRM service and view WRSM policies.

1. Log on to Glasgow with the Kim_Akers account.

2. If necessary, start Server Manager.

3. In Server Manager, right-click Features and select Add Features.

4. Select the Windows System Resource Manager check box on the Select Features page of the Add Features Wizard, and then click Next.

5. If Server Manager prompts you to add Windows Internal Database, click Add Required Features. Click Next.

   Windows Internal Database (WID) was discussed in Chapter 6, "Configuring Active Directory Federation Services and Active Directory Rights Management Services Server Roles."

6. Review the Confirm Installation Selections page shown in Figure 8-30 and click Install.

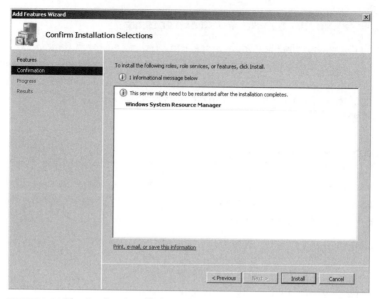

FIGURE 8-30 The Confirm Installation Selections page.

7. Click Close when your installation is complete.

8. Open the WRSM console in the Administrative Tools program group.

9. Select This Computer and click Connect.

10. View the WRSM interface shown in Figure 8-31 and experiment with the features it provides.

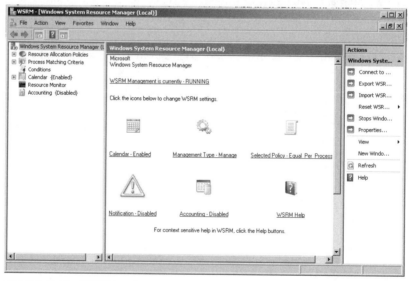

FIGURE 8-31 The WRSM interface.

EXERCISE 2 **Create a Custom Data Collector Set and Generate a Report**

In this exercise, you use a data collector template to create a data collector set. You configure this set for five minutes to generate report data. However, you choose to run an immediate report in the first instance.

1. If necessary, log on to Glasgow with the Kim_Akers account and start Server Manager.

2. In Server Manager, expand Diagnostics, expand Reliability And Performance, and expand Data Collector Sets.

3. Right-click User Defined, select New, and then select Data Collector Set.

4. On the Create New Data Collector Set page, type **My New Data Collector Set**. Ensure that Create From A Template (Recommended) is selected, and then click Next.

   The Create New Data Collector Set page is shown in Figure 8-32.

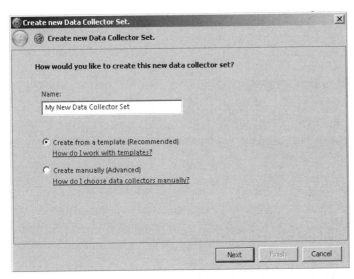

FIGURE 8-32 The Create New Data Collector Set page.

5. Select the Active Directory Diagnostics template and click Next.

   By default, the wizard selects %systemdrive%\PerfLogs\Admin as the root directory. In a production environment, you would probably keep your collector sets on a separate drive.

6. For the purposes of this exercise, accept the default and click Next.

7. In the Run As field on the Create The Data Collector Set page, you have the option to click Change and enter an account name and the password to run the Data Collector Set. Click Finish to accept the default.

   Your data collector set is created and is displayed in Server Manager.

NOTE **ACCOUNT TO RUN DATA COLLECTOR SETS**

When you create data collector sets on a production network, create an account to run your collector sets. This account should be a member of the Performance Log Users group. Note that the Performance Log Users group has the Log On As A Batch Job right assigned to it by default.

8. To schedule the start condition for your data collector set, right-click My New Data Collector Set and select Properties.

9. To create a start date, time, or day schedule, click the Schedule tab and click Add.

10. In the Folder Action dialog box, specify today's date as the beginning date, select Expiration Date, and set it for a week hence. Ensure that the report time is set to the current time.

   Your Folder Action dialog box should look similar to Figure 8-33.

11. Click OK.

FIGURE 8-33 Scheduling the start of your data collector set.

NOTE **FAILURE TO SCHEDULE A COLLECTOR SET**

If you do not configure a collector set to run on a schedule, it will stop as soon as you (or the specified account under which it is running) logs off.

12. Click the Stop Condition tab, select the Overall Duration check box, and ensure that it lists five minutes. Select the Stop When All Data Collectors Have Finished check box. Click OK.

Note that if you do not specify a stop condition, the collector set continues to gather data and could quickly fill up your allocated disk resource.

> **NOTE STOP WHEN ALL DATA COLLECTORS HAVE FINISHED**
>
> If you have configured an overall duration, select the Stop When All Data Collectors Have Finished check box to allow all data collectors to finish recording the most recent values before Data Collector Set is stopped.

My New Data Collector set appears in Server Manager. Note that it is currently stopped.

13. Right-click My New Data Collector Set and select Data Manager.

    Note the defaults on the Data Manager tab. If you are short of hard disk space, you might want to change the Minimum Free Disk setting.

14. Click the Actions tab. Select 1 Day(s), and then click Edit.

    Note the policy settings. In a production environment, you might change these settings, but in this exercise, you accept the defaults.

15. Click OK, and then click OK again.

16. To view an immediate report, right-click My New Data Collector Set, and then select Start.

17. Expand Reports under Reliability and Performance. Expand User Defined, and then expand My New Data Collector Set. Select the report name to view the report status, as shown in Figure 8-34.

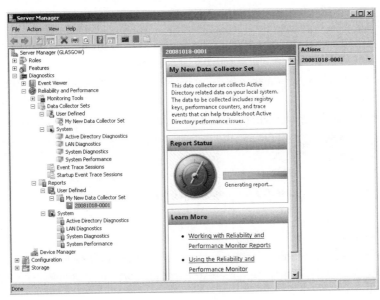

FIGURE 8-34 Generating a report.

When the report completes, you see a screen similar to Figure 8-35. On your small test network, it might not contain much of interest.

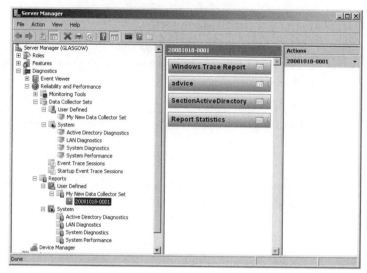

FIGURE 8-35 The report completes.

18. Under Data Collector Sets, select User Defined. Check that My New Data Collector Set is stopped.

If you do not want this data collector set to write to your hard disk for the rest of the week, it is a good idea to delete it.

Lesson Summary

- Tools to manage and monitor domain controller resource usage include Task Manager, Event Viewer, WRPM, WSRM, and command-line utilities.

- Windows Server 2008 Performance Monitor incorporates the functionality of other tools used in previous versions of Windows.

- WSRM controls how resources behave on a scheduled basis. It monitors resource usage over time and logs activity. It also controls access to resources based on specific policies.

- You can use the Directory Service log and the *repadmin* and *dcdiag* command-line tools to report and diagnose AD DS replication errors.

Lesson Review

You can use the following questions to test your knowledge of the information in Lesson 3, "Monitoring Active Directory." The questions are also available on the companion DVD if you prefer to review them in electronic form.

NOTE **ANSWERS**

Answers to these questions and explanations of why each answer choice is right or wrong are located in the "Answers" section at the end of the book.

1. You are an administrator for Northwind Traders. You want to display the replication partners for the Chicago domain controller in the *northwindtraders.com* domain. What command do you use?

   A. *Repadmin /showrepl Chicago. northwindtraders.com*

   B. *Dcdiag /test:replications*

   C. *Rsop.msc /RsopNamespace:northwindtraders.com/RsopTargetComp:Chicago*

   D. *Rsop.msc*

2. You access a collector set that a colleague has configured on one of your organization's domain controllers. You find that the set is running continuously and has filled the allocated storage area. What could be the problem? (Choose two. Each correct answer presents a complete solution.)

   A. Your colleague has not created a special account under which the collector set runs.

   B. Your colleague has not set the collector set to run on a schedule.

   C. Your colleague has not specified an expiration date.

   D. Your colleague has not specified a stop condition.

   E. Your colleague has not specified a duration limit.

3. Which data collector set template created for the AD DS role would you choose if you wanted your data collector set to collect data from registry keys, performance counters, and trace events related to AD DS performance on a local domain controller?

   A. LAN Diagnostics

   B. Active Directory Diagnostics

   C. System Performance

   D. System Diagnostics

4. You are investigating issues on a domain controller and believe that the performance of the AD DS service has deteriorated. Which of the following tools could help you diagnose the problem? (Choose four. Although each answer could present a complete solution, it is likely you would use several tools in combination.)

   A. Reliability Monitor

   B. *Repadmin.exe*

   C. Event Viewer

   D. SPA

   E. Task Manager

   F. Performance Monitor

Chapter Review

To further practice and reinforce the skills you learned in this chapter, you can perform the following tasks:

- Review the chapter summary.
- Complete the case scenarios. These scenarios set up real-world situations involving the topics of this chapter and ask you to create a solution.
- Complete the suggested practices.
- Take a practice test.

Chapter Summary

- You can use Windows Server Backup or the *wbadmin.exe* command-line tool to perform Windows Server 2008 backups. A system state backup backs up the AD DS database and Windows Server 2008 roles.

- A full server recovery performs a nonauthoritative restore of system state data. However, Microsoft recommends booting into DSRM to restore system state data. You recover deleted Active Directory objects by using the *ntdsutil* utility to mark them as authoritative.

- You can stop the AD DS service to compact and defragment the AD DS database offline and mark restored AD DS objects as authoritative. You cannot stop the AD DS service if your domain controller is the only domain controller authenticating logons in the domain.

- You can protect AD DS objects from accidental deletion. AD DS access auditing logs old and new values for AD DS objects in the Directory Services event log. You can use the *ldp.exe* utility to recover tombstoned AD DS objects.

- You can allocate disk storage by expanding the partition or partitions on the disk that currently stores these files. If this is not possible or practicable, you can use *ntdsutil.exe* to move a database or log file to a larger existing partition. You cannot move AD DS objects that are protected from deletion.

- Tools to manage and monitor domain controller resource usage include Task Manager, Event Viewer, WRPM, and WSRM. You can use the Directory Service log and the *repadmin* and *dcdiag* command-line tools to report and diagnose AD DS replication errors.

Case Scenarios

In the following case scenarios, you apply what you've learned about maintaining the Active Directory environmnent. You can find answers to the questions in this scenario in the "Answers" section at the end of this book.

Case Scenario 1: Designing Backup and Restore Procedures

Northwind Traders currently has a mixture of Windows 2000 Server and Windows Server 2003 member servers and Windows Server 2003 domain controllers on its domain. The company intends to upgrade all member servers to Windows Server 2003 and all domain controllers to Windows Server 2008. You need to develop consistent backup and restore procedures. Answer the following questions.

1. Six domain controllers that use *ntbackup* to write backup data to tape are to be upgraded to Windows Server 2008. What hardware is required so you can take scheduled daily backups, using the Windows Server Backup utility?

2. You are considering a future upgrade of your hardware storage solution for domain controller backups to Fibre Channel SAN. What Microsoft backup software do you need to use?

3. You need to ensure that you can restore accidentally deleted AD DS objects on the upgraded domain controllers. You do not want to protect AD DS objects against deletion because you might want to move them to another location during hardware maintenance. You know that restoring AD DS objects from the tombstone container does not restore all object attributes, and you want to restore accidentally deleted AD DS objects from backup. How best can you do this?

Case Scenario 2: Compacting and Defragmenting the AD DS Database

Tailspin Toys has made numerous changes to its AD DS objects and now needs to defragment and compact the *Ntds.dit* database, particularly in its Windows Server 2008 root domain. The organization has two domain controllers in its root domain. Answer the following questions.

1. You know that in a Windows Server 2008 domain, you can stop the AD DS service on a domain controller and perform an offline compaction and defragmentation. How do you stop the service, and which command defragments and compacts the database?

2. You attempt to stop the AD DS service on a domain controller and know that another administrator is currently working on the other domain controller. You cannot stop AD DS. What is the probable reason?

Case Scenario 3: Monitoring AD DS

Trey Research recently upgraded all its domain controllers to Windows Server 2008. You must generate baselines and schedule regular AD DS performance monitoring. You need to create data collector sets that enable you do this. Answer the following questions.

1. You want to log data from registry keys, performance counters, and trace events related to AD DS performance as well as information about the status of hardware resources, system response times, and processes on your domain controllers. Which templates should you select when creating your data collector sets?

2. How do you create performance baselines?

Suggested Practices

To help you successfully master the exam objectives presented in this chapter, perform all the following practices.

- **Practice 1** This practice assumes that both your Glasgow and your Boston servers are domain controllers. Boot a domain controller in DSRM and practice changing the DSRM password. Create an OU and some user accounts within that OU. Perform a system state backup and then delete the OU. Carry out a nonauthoritative restore. Check that after replication occurs, the OU is again deleted. Perform another nonauthoritative restore and mark the restored OU as authoritative. Confirm that the OU has been restored.

- **Practice 2** This practice also assumes that both Glasgow and Boston are domain controllers. Stop the AD DS service on Boston. Change the registry entry *HKLM\System \CurrentControlSet\Control\Lsa\DSRMAdminLogonBehavior* as described earlier in this chapter and test how this affects logging on with the DSRM Administrator account. Delete the OU you created earlier and investigate stopping AD DS and marking the restored OU authoritative. Investigate restoring the deleted OU from the tombstone container.

- **Practice 3** Work with the AD DS monitoring tools. Use Task Manager, WRSM, Event Viewer, Reliability Monitor, and Performance Monitor. Experiment with the various options. Create a data collector set, using a different template from the one you used in the practice in Lesson 3, and configure different scheduling options.

- **Practice 4** Stop AD DS on Boston. Use *dcpromo /forceremoval* to demote Boston to a member server.

Take a Practice Test

The practice tests on this book's companion DVD offer many options. For example, you can test yourself on just one exam objective, or you can test yourself on all the upgrade exam content. You can set up the test so that it closely simulates the experience of taking a certification exam, or you can set it up in study mode so that you can look at the correct answers and explanations after you answer each question.

> **MORE INFO** **PRACTICE TESTS**
>
> For details about all the practice test options available, see the "How to Use the Practice Tests" section in this book's Introduction.

CHAPTER 9

Managing Software Updates and Monitoring Network Data

Managing a network is more than just deploying computers and tuning servers. A big part of network management is network maintenance. As a Windows Server 2008 administrator, you will find a large amount of the time you allocate to network maintenance is spent managing software updates and monitoring network traffic. In this chapter, you learn about Microsoft Windows Server Update Services 3.0 SP1, a freely available application that many Windows Server 2008 administrators use to manage the deployment of software updates within their organizations. You also learn about the Microsoft Baseline Security Analyzer, a tool for auditing whether clients have updates installed and their security settings; Network Monitor, a tool for capturing and analyzing network traffic; and SNMP, a network management and reporting protocol.

Exam objectives in this chapter

- Configure Windows Server Update Services (WSUS) server settings.
- Gather network data.

Lessons in this chapter:

Before You Begin

To complete the lessons in this chapter, you must have done the following:

- Installed and configured the evaluation edition of Windows Server 2008 Enterprise Edition in accordance with the instructions listed in the Introduction.

In addition, you must download the following applications:

- The current version of WSUS from the WSUS TechCenter Web site at *http://www .microsoft.com/wsus*. You install this software during the first practice exercise at the end of Lesson 1, "Managing Windows Server Update Services."

- Report Viewer 2005 from the Microsoft Web site at *http://www.microsoft.com/downloads /details.aspx?familyid=8a166cac-758d-45c8-b637-dd7726e61367&displaylang=en*.

- Report Viewer 2005 SP1 from the Microsoft Web site at *http://www.microsoft.com /downloads/details.aspx?FamilyId=35F23B3C-3B3F-4377-9AE1 -26321F99FDF0&displaylang=en*.

- Network Monitor from the Microsoft Web site at *http://www.microsoft.com/downloads /details.aspx?familyid=18b1d59d-f4d8-4213-8d17-2f6dde7d7aac&displaylang=en*. You install this software during the first practice exercise at the end of lesson 2, "Gathering Network Data."

- The current version of the Microsoft Baseline Security Analyzer from the MBSA Web site at *http://technet.microsoft.com/en-us/security/cc184924.aspx*.

 REAL WORLD

Orin Thomas

If you haven't already learned this lesson the hard way, take it from me: Always test updates on nonproduction systems before deploying them on computers that are integral to the operation of your organization. Generally, you want to avoid explaining to your manager why an update you applied to a mission-critical server led to that server experiencing a couple of hours of downtime. Although Microsoft goes to all possible lengths to ensure that the updates it publishes do not conflict with existing software, it is possible that some special application or driver on your servers happens to react badly to the latest critical update. In environments in which you don't have the resources to test updates on configurations identical to those in production, you can use virtualization to attempt to replicate your production environment. Even when you test everything thoroughly, things can go wrong. Remember to have a rollback plan. Fully back up all servers prior to deploying updates. If an unforeseen conflict does arise, you are in a position to roll back to your previous configuration easily.

Lesson 1: Managing Windows Server Update Services

As an experienced administrator, you most likely already employ a patch management solution such as Windows Server Update Services (WSUS) on your organization's network. When you were completing your Windows Server 2003 certification exams, you learned about the ancestor of WSUS, Software Update Services (SUS). In some exams, you would have been examined on an earlier version of WSUS. WSUS 3.0 SP1 is the first version of WSUS that is compatible with Windows Server 2008 and is the version of the product that is tested in the 70-648 upgrade exam.

> **After this lesson, you will be able to:**
> - Manage update type selection.
> - Configure WSUS client settings.
> - Configure Group Policy related to software update.
> - Configure client targeting.
> - Test and approve updates.
> - Configure software updates for disconnected networks.
>
> **Estimated lesson time: 40 minutes**

WSUS Server Configuration

After you have installed WSUS, you configure the WSUS servers through the *Options* node of the Update Services console, shown in Figure 9-1. You can use Update Source and Proxy Server to configure the way the WSUS server retrieves updates. The Products and Classifications option enables you to specify the products for which the update server will provide updates. You use classifications settings to determine whether the WSUS server downloads critical, important, or other types of update for the products specified.

Through the Update Files and Languages item, you can specify the update languages you want to download and specify whether the WSUS server will retrieve and store update files. You can also specify the location to which the server saves these files. When you configure a WSUS server not to download updates, client computers use the WSUS server to determine which updates have been authorized. Clients then retrieve those updates from the Microsoft Update servers on the Internet.

Synchronization Schedule enables you to configure how often WSUS checks for new updates. Although Microsoft usually publishes new updates on the second Tuesday of each month, Microsoft sometimes releases urgent updates outside this schedule. The default setting is to synchronize manually. You can also configure a WSUS server to perform an update check multiple times a day. If you have configured a synchronization schedule, you can configure the WSUS server to e-mail you if a new update that requires approval becomes available.

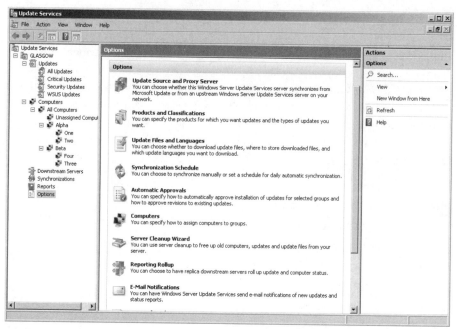

FIGURE 9-1 Configuring WSUS options.

When you deploy multiple WSUS servers within an organization, it is possible to configure the WSUS servers in a hierarchy. When configured in a hierarchy, WSUS servers download updates from the server above them in the hierarchy, with the WSUS server at the top of the hierarchy obtaining updates from the Microsoft Update servers. When you configure downstream servers in a WSUS hierarchy, you must decide which administrative mode they will use. There are two options, autonomous mode or replica mode. These modes work in the following manner:

- **Autonomous mode** When you configure a WSUS server in autonomous mode, you have complete control over the creation of computer groups and the approval of updates. Servers at the top of a WSUS hierarchy are always configured in autonomous mode.

- **Replica mode** When you configure a WSUS server to use replica mode, it inherits all update approval and computer group settings from a server above it in the WSUS hierarchy. Replica mode deployments enable you to place WSUS servers at branch office locations while still managing your WSUS server deployment centrally.

Software Updates

In the Update Services console, you use Products and Classifications to specify which update classifications the WSUS server will provide to clients. As Figure 9-2 shows, the WSUS server can provide Critical Updates, Definition Updates, Drivers, Feature Packs, Security Updates,

Service Packs, Tools, Update Rollups, and Updates. Organizations that want to provide only basic update services can limit the updates WSUS retrieves to only those classifications they deem necessary.

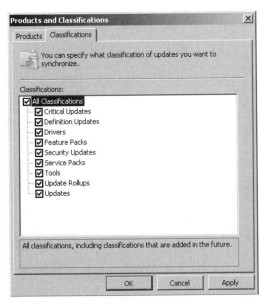

FIGURE 9-2 Update classifications.

The Products tab, also available through Products and Classifications, enables you to revise the products for which WSUS downloads updates. For example, if your organization upgrades from Office 2003 to Office 2007, you might want to reconfigure the Products settings so that WSUS downloads updates for Office 2007 but not for Office 2003. Through Products and Classifications, you can tailor your WSUS installation so that only the updates deployed to your organization are actually downloaded from the Internet rather than downloading updates for every Microsoft product in existence.

Automatic approvals enable you to configure WSUS so that the WSUS server automatically distributes some types of updates as soon as they become available. You configure automatic approvals from the *Options* node of the Update Services console. You create automatic approval rules that specify the update classification (Critical, Security, and so on) and the specific WSUS groups to which the server will automatically distribute the update. The default Automatic Update Approval Rule, shown in Figure 9-3, allows all Critical and Security updates to be distributed to all WSUS clients. Important to note is that this rule is not enabled by default. The benefit of automatic approval rules is that they ensure that WSUS will distribute updates to computers in your organization almost as soon as they become available. The drawback of automatic approval rules is that they do not allow you to test the update prior to deployment. Some organizations use automatic approval rules to deploy updates to a test group of computers. WSUS administrators then decide whether to deploy the update manually after they have reviewed the update's impact on the test group. Testing and approving updates is covered in more detail later in this lesson. By default, WSUS automatically approves updates to the WSUS software and automatically approves revisions to updates that an administrator has already approved.

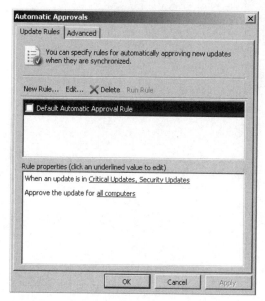

FIGURE 9-3 Automatic approvals.

Windows Update Group Policies

A Windows Server 2008 Group Policy object (GPO) contains 15 policies that relate to software updates. These policies are located under the *Computer Configuration\Policies\Administrative Templates\Windows Components\Windows Update* node. From the perspective of the WSUS administrator, the most important policies are Configure Automatic Updates, Specify Intranet Microsoft Update Service Location, and Enable Client-Side Targeting. These policies have the following functions:

- **Configure Automatic Updates**   You can enable automatic updates, determine the download and notification settings, and specify an automatic update schedule.

- **Specify Intranet Microsoft Update Service Location**   You can specify the location of the WSUS server the client will use with this policy, shown in Figure 9-4.

- **Enable Client-Side Targeting**   You can specify the WSUS group to which the computer will be assigned.

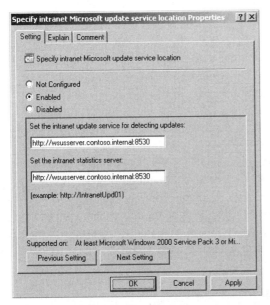

FIGURE 9-4 WSUS server location.

Although 12 other policies are related to software updates, these policies primarily relate to how the client will deal with updates rather than with WSUS directly. Although you can review these policies at your leisure, the upgrade exam concentrates more on the server aspect of WSUS configuration than on the specifics of client update configuration. You configure several of these Group Policy settings in the practice exercise at the end of this lesson.

 Quick Check

1. What sort of rule should you configure to ensure that new updates are automatically distributed to a group of test computers without requiring administrator approval?

2. Which Group Policy enables you to configure the WSUS group to which a computer belongs?

Quick Check Answers

1. Configure an automatic approval rule to approve updates automatically to the test group of computers.

2. The Enable Client-Side Targeting policy enables you to configure the WSUS group to which a computer belongs.

Client Targeting

Client targeting is a process through which you can segment the way updates are applied to computers in your organization. You accomplish this by using WSUS computer groups. A computer can be a member of only a single group. Groups work hierarchically, with the All Computers group representing all computers for which the WSUS server provides updates. It is possible to create tiered hierarchies of groups under the All Computers group. An update approved for a group at the top of the hierarchy is automatically approved for all groups under that group in the hierarchy unless the WSUS administrator overrides inheritance for specific groups. For example, when you approve an update for the All Computers group, the update is automatically approved for all groups under the All Computers group. It is possible to block the update for specific groups such as the Unassigned Computers group. When you set an approval to Not Approved, that approval setting flows on to groups further down the hierarchy. In Figure 9-5, the One and Three groups have inherited the Not Approved status from the approval setting assigned to the Alpha group. The administrator could override the status of groups One and Two if he or she so desired.

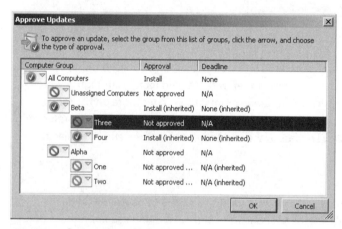

FIGURE 9-5 Group approval inheritance.

You can use one of two methods to assign computers to WSUS groups. Client-side targeting enables you to use Group Policy to assign computers to groups that you have already created on the WSUS server. You can configure client-side targeting by using the Enable Client-Side Targeting Properties policy displayed in Figure 9-6. When configuring this policy, you enter the name of the group on the WSUS server you want the computer to join. The group must already exist on the WSUS server. If the group does not exist, WSUS allocates the computer to the Unassigned Computers group. The alternative to client-side targeting is server-side targeting. When a computer first contacts a WSUS server for updates, and client-side targeting is not in effect, the WSUS server allocates the computer to the Unassigned Computers group. With server-side targeting, you assign the computer to a WSUS server group manually through the WSUS console. This works best on small networks, where manually assigning computers is practical. However, after your WSUS server has more than a few hundred clients, manually allocating them to WSUS groups becomes burdensome. You configure whether the WSUS server uses client-side or server-side targeting through the *Options* node on the Update Services console.

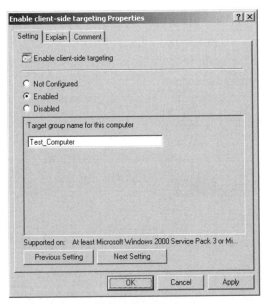

FIGURE 9-6 Enable client-side targeting.

> **MORE INFO   MORE ON TARGETING UPDATES**
>
> To learn more about using computer groups to target updates, see the following TechNet article: *http://technet.microsoft.com/en-us/library/cc708530.aspx.*

Testing and Approving Updates

Although Microsoft rigorously tests updates before publishing them, it is impossible to test updates against all possible software and hardware configurations. Thus, it is possible, however unlikely, that a published update might cause conflicts with your existing computer configurations. To avoid this type of situation, develop an update testing process. By distributing updates to a group of test computers prior to general distribution, you can catch possible conflicts before they impact all the computers in your organization.

The simplest way to do this is to create a separate computer group for the computers that will function as the test subjects. You first approve each update for the test subjects, as shown in Figure 9-7. If, after a suitable interval, no problems arise with the test subjects, you can then deploy the update more widely across your organization. Ensure that the test group reflects the diversity of software and hardware configurations that exist within your organization. You should also ensure that users of test group computers use their computers normally. Just having test group computers that have similar configurations to those in the production environment might not be enough to tease out conflicts caused by updates. You can be confident that an update does not cause conflicts with existing configurations only if conflicts do not become apparent over a period of normal use. The length of time that you devote to testing will depend on your environment. Many organizations roll out updates generally after a week of testing among a smaller group of computers, but your organization might have specific needs that require more rigorous testing before you deploy updates.

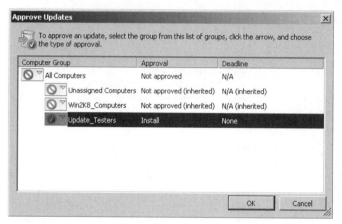

FIGURE 9-7 Using a test group.

If an update deployed to your test group does cause a conflict, you can use WSUS to remove the update by right-clicking the update under the *All Updates* node, selecting Approve Updates, right-clicking the computer group you wish to remove the update from, and selecting Approved For Removal. When you do this, WSUS assigns the update the Removal status as displayed in Figure 9-8. After you determine why there is a conflict, you can decide whether you want to let the update remain on the WSUS server in an unapproved state or decline the update. Declining the update removes it from the WSUS server.

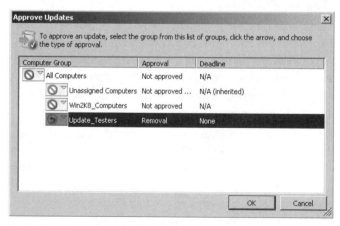

FIGURE 9-8 Removing a deployed update.

WSUS on Disconnected Networks

Some organizations have networks partitioned from the Internet but which also host computers that need updates regularly applied. Although you can apply updates to all these computers manually, some isolated networks have so many hosts on them that such an approach is impractical. In this situation, you can deploy WSUS in disconnected mode, which enables you to use WSUS when the WSUS server is unable to obtain updates from an upstream server. In essence, you transfer updates and metadata from an Internet-connected WSUS server to the disconnected WSUS server.

To use disconnected mode, you must do three things:

- **Configure Advanced Options**   Ensure that the options for express installation files and update languages are the same on both the connected and disconnected WSUS servers.

- **Copy Updates**   Copy updates from the \WSUS\WSUSContent\ folder on the connected server to a removable storage device. Connect the removable storage device to the disconnected server and copy updates from that device to the \WSUS\WSUSContent\ folder. You can also use Windows Backup to back up these files on the connected server and restore them on the disconnected server.

- **Export and Import Metadata**   Use the *wsusutil.exe* utility to export metadata from the connected WSUS server. Copy the export data to a removable storage device and use the *wsusutil.exe* utility to import the data to the disconnected WSUS server. WSUS metadata stores information about available updates, groups, and approval status.

> **MORE INFO   SETTING UP A DISCONNECTED WSUS SERVER**
>
> For more information on setting up a disconnected WSUS server, see the following TechNet article: *http://technet.microsoft.com/en-us/library/cc720486.aspx*.

PRACTICE   **Deploying and Managing WSUS**

In this practice, you install, configure, and manage Windows Server Update Services (WSUS). In a real-world deployment, you would be unlikely to collocate the WSUS server on your organization's domain controller (DC). It is a matter of practicality for this exercise.

To complete these practice exercises, you must have downloaded WSUS and Report Viewer from the Microsoft Web site. The "Before You Begin" section at the start of this chapter lists where you can obtain this software.

EXERCISE 1   Install and Configure WSUS

In this exercise, you install and configure WSUS 3.0 SP1 and have the option of downloading updates to the WSUS server; you download only updates relevant to Windows Server 2008 rather than downloading all possible updates.

NOTE **GLASGOW INTERNET CONNECTION**

The practice exercises in this training kit are written under the assumption that server Glasgow has only a single network card, and that network card is configured with a private IP address. To allow your practice computer to connect to the Internet, consider adding a second network card. If your practice server is a virtual machine, add a second virtual network adapter.

1. Log on to server Glasgow with the Kim_Akers user account and locate the folder to which you have downloaded the Report Viewer, Report Viewer SP1, and WSUS 3.0 SP1 executable files.

2. Install the Microsoft Report Viewer 2005 application by double-clicking the installer file and clicking Continue when prompted by the User Account Control dialog box.

3. Click Next to start the installation procedure, accept the terms of the license agreement, and then click Install. Click Finish to complete the installation process.

4. Install Microsoft Report Viewer 2005 SP1 by double-clicking the installer file and clicking Continue when prompted by the User Account Control dialog box.

5. Click OK when queried whether to install Hotfix For Microsoft Report Viewer Redistributable 2005. Click I Accept to accept the EULA and click OK when the hotfix successfully installs.

6. Open the Server Manager console. Click Continue in the UAC dialog box and right-click Roles. Select Add Roles and, when the Add Roles Wizard starts, click Next.

7. Select the Web Server (IIS) check box. When prompted by the Add Roles Wizard, click Add Required Features. Click Next.

8. Review the Introduction To Web Server (IIS) page, and then click Next.

9. On the Select Role Services page, select the ASP.NET check box. When prompted to install additional role services, click Add Required Role Services.

10. Under the *Security* node, select Windows Authentication and under Management Tools, select IIS 6 Metabase compatibility.

11. Click Next, and then click Install. At the end of the installation process, click Close. Close the Server Manager Console.

12. Open the WSUS setup file to begin installation. Click Continue to dismiss the UAC dialog box.

13. On the Welcome To The Windows Server Update Service 3.0 SP1 Setup Wizard page, click Next.

14. In the Installation Mode Selection dialog box, select Full Server Installation Including Administration Console, and then click Next.

15. On the License Agreement page, select I Accept The Terms Of The License Agreement, and then click Next.

16. On the Select Update Source page, shown in Figure 9-9, verify that the Store Updates Locally check box is selected and that the C:\WSUS directory is specified, and then click Next.

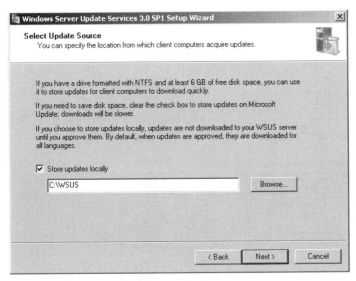

FIGURE 9-9 Store WSUS updates locally.

17. On the Database Options page, select Install Windows Internal Database On This Computer, and then click Next.

18. On the Web Site Selection page, select Create A Windows Server Update Services 3.0 SP1 Web Site, as shown in Figure 9-10.

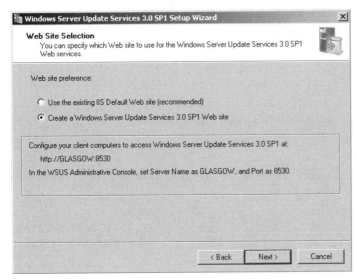

FIGURE 9-10 WSUS Web site location.

19. Click Next twice to begin the installation process. Click Finish to dismiss the setup wizard when the installation completes.

The Windows Server Update Services Configuration Wizard automatically begins.

20. If your computer, running Windows Server 2008, does not have a connection to the Internet, click Cancel at this point.

21. After the Windows Server Update Services Configuration Wizard launches, click Next twice.

22. On the Choose Upstream Server page, select Synchronize From Microsoft Update, as shown in Figure 9-11, and then click Next.

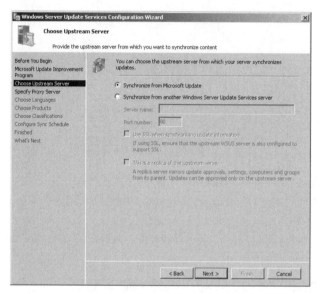

FIGURE 9-11 Choose upstream server.

23. If there is a proxy server between Glasgow and the Internet, enter the proxy server details on the Specify Proxy Server page, and then click Next. Otherwise, just click Next.

24. On the Connect To Upstream Server page, click Start Connecting. The server contacts the Microsoft Update servers on the Internet. When the connection completes, click Next.

25. On the Choose Languages page, ensure that your language is selected, and then click Next.

26. On the Choose Products page, scroll down and ensure that only updates for Windows Server 2008 are selected, as shown in Figure 9-12, and then click Next.

NOTE **ONLY WINDOWS SERVER 2008 UPDATES**

Selecting only updates for Windows Server 2008 minimizes the number of updates downloaded from the Microsoft Update servers.

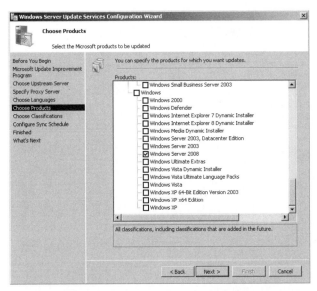

FIGURE 9-12 Selecting updates.

27. On the Classifications page, select only Critical Updates, and then click Next.

28. On the Set Sync Schedule page, verify that Synchronize Manually is set, click Next, and then click Finish.

    The Update Services console opens. You use this console in the following exercise.

EXERCISE 2 Manage WSUS and Configure Software Update Policies

In this exercise, you use the WSUS console to approve updates and configure client settings, using Group Policy.

1. If the Update Services console is not open already, open it from the Administrative Tools menu by selecting Microsoft Windows Server Update Services 3.0 SP1.

2. Right-click the *GLASGOW\Computers\All Computers* node, and then select Add Computer Group.

3. In the Add Computer Group dialog box, type **Win2K8_Computers**, and then click Add.

4. Select the *Glasgow\Updates\All Updates* node. Set the Approval drop-down list to Unapproved and the status to Any, and then click Refresh.

This displays a list of Windows Server 2008 updates similar to that shown in Figure 9-13.

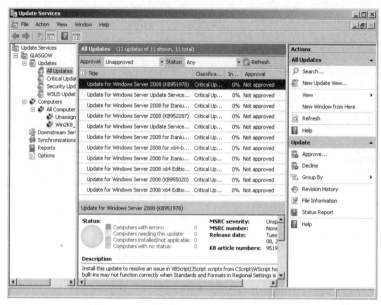

FIGURE 9-13 Updates awaiting approval.

5. Right-click the update at the top of the list, and then select Approve.

   This launches the Approve Updates dialog box.

6. Right-click the Win2K8_Computers group, and then select Approved For Install.

7. Right-click the Win2K8_Computers group again, click Deadline, and then select One Week. Verify that the Approve Updates dialog box is similar to Figure 9-14, and then click OK.

   This launches the Approval Progress dialog box.

8. Click Close when this dialog box completes.

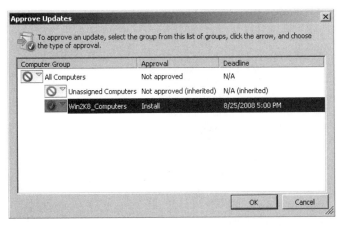

FIGURE 9-14 Approved update.

9. Open the Group Policy Management console from the Administrative Tools menu.

10. Right-click the *Forest:Contoso.inernal\Domains\Contoso.internal\Group Policy Objects* node, and then select New.

11. In the New GPO dialog box, enter **WSUS_Policy** in the Name text box, and then click OK.

12. In the Group Policy Objects In Contoso.internal pane, right-click WSUS_Policy, and then select Edit.

    This opens Group Policy Management Editor.

13. Navigate to the Computer *Configuration\Policies\Administrative Templates\Windows Components\Windows Update* node.

14. Edit the Specify Intranet Microsoft Update Service Location policy by setting the policy to Enabled. In the Set The Intranet Update Service For Detecting Updates and the Set The Intranet Statistics Server text boxes, type **http://GLASGOW:8530**, as shown in Figure 9-15, and then click OK.

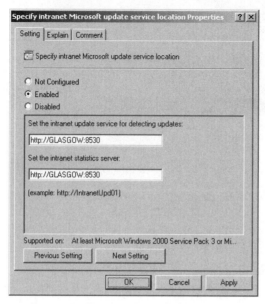

FIGURE 9-15 Configure WSUS server location policy.

15. Edit the Enable Client-Side Targeting policy by setting the policy to Enabled. In the Target Group Name For This Computer text box, enter **Win2K8_Computers**. Click **OK** to close the policy.

16. Close all open consoles.

Lesson Summary

- When configuring WSUS, you can choose which classification of update to download and the products for which WSUS will provide updates. Configure WSUS to download updates only for products your organization uses.

- You can deploy WSUS updates to WSUS computer groups. Update deployment works hierarchically, with all groups under a group for which an approval is made inheriting that approval. An administrator can override approval inheritance.

- You can configure Group Policy to segment computers into WSUS groups, using client-side targeting. Group Policy also enables you to specify a WSUS server and whether automatic updating is enabled.

- Test updates with a small group before deploying them generally so that you can resolve conflicts before updates are deployed across your organization.

- Disconnected WSUS servers are located on networks that are not connected to the Internet. An administrator manually copies the metadata and updates from a connected WSUS server to the disconnected WSUS server.

Lesson Review

You can use the following questions to test your knowledge of the information in Lesson 1, "Managing Windows Server Update Services." The questions are also available on the companion DVD if you prefer to review them in electronic form.

> **NOTE   ANSWERS**
>
> Answers to these questions and explanations of why each answer choice is right or wrong are located in the "Answers" section at the end of the book.

1. Prior to deploying updates to all computers in your organization, you want to deploy them to a group of update testers so that you can verify that there is no adverse impact to your existing software configuration. Which of the following steps should you take to meet this objective? (Choose three. Each correct answer presents part of a complete solution.)

   A. Place all the computers involved in the update testing group in a separate organizational unit (OU) called Update_Testing.

   B. Place all the computers involved in the update testing group in a new security group called Update_Testing.

   C. Create a new computer group called Update_Testing on the WSUS server.

   D. Create a GPO and apply it to the Update_Testing OU. Configure the Enable Client-Side Targeting Properties policy and specify Update_Testing as the target group.

   E. Create a new user group called Update_Testing on the WSUS server.

2. You want to ensure that computers in the Test_Computers WSUS group automatically install updates released by Microsoft without administrator intervention. You also want to ensure that all other computers in your organization receive and install updates only after their impact on the computers in the Test_Computers group has been assessed by the IT team. Which of the following steps should you take? (Choose two. Each correct answer presents part of a complete solution.)

   A. Create an automatic approval rule for the All Computers group.

   B. Create an automatic approval rule for the Test_Computers group.

   C. Configure the WSUS server to synchronize automatically.

   D. Configure the WSUS server to synchronize manually.

   E. Configure WSUS to work in replica mode.

3. Which of the following Group Policy settings should you configure to ensure that computers in your organization all use the local WSUS server rather than the Microsoft Update server as a source of updates?

   A. Configure Automatic Updates

   B. Automatic Updates Detection Frequency

   C. Enable Client-Side Targeting

   D. Specify Intranet Microsoft Update Service Location

   E. Allow Automatic Updates Immediate Installation

4. During testing, you have found that a recent update has caused conflicts with an application written by one of your organization's vendors. Users of test computers are unable to perform their job roles. The vendors promise a fix within three months. Which of the following should you do to resolve this situation?

   A. Use WSUS to remove the update from the Test_Group computers.

   B. Decline the update by using the WSUS console.

   C. Move all computer accounts out of the Test_Group until the vendor presents a fix.

   D. Set the approval for the update for 90 days away.

5. You are configuring a WSUS server for a separate network, which is completely isolated from the Internet, at your organization. Your organization has an existing network infrastructure that allows connections to the Internet. Clients on this network use a WSUS server located on a perimeter network. Which steps must you take to allow the WSUS server on the disconnected network to distribute the updates present on the WSUS server on the perimeter network? (Choose three. Each correct answer presents part of a complete solution.)

   A. Copy updates from the WSUS server on the disconnected network to the WSUS server on the perimeter network by using a removable USB disk.

   B. Use *wsusutil.exe* to export metadata from the WSUS server on the disconnected network, and then import the metadata to the WSUS server on the perimeter network.

   C. Configure the WSUS server on the disconnected network to have the same Advanced options as the WSUS server on the perimeter network.

   D. Copy updates from the WSUS server on the perimeter network to the WSUS server on the disconnected network by using a removable USB disk.

   E. Use *wsusutil.exe* to export metadata from the WSUS server on the perimeter network, and then import the metadata to the WSUS server on the disconnected network.

Lesson 2: Gathering Network Data

You can learn a lot about a network by actively probing it and by passively listening to it. This lesson concentrates on three technologies with which you perform these functions. With Microsoft Baseline Security Analyzer (MBSA), you can scan your network for clients that do not have security updates installed and have problematic security configurations. Network monitoring enables you to capture network traffic so you can learn exactly what a computer is hearing when plugged into the network. Simple Network Management Protocol (SNMP) enables you to monitor network-aware devices. In this lesson, you learn about these tools and what you can accomplish with them in a Windows Server 2008 network environment.

> **After this lesson, you will be able to:**
> - Gather information about the network, using SNMP.
> - Monitor client security by using Microsoft Baseline Security Analyzer.
> - Gather network information by using Network Monitor.
>
> **Estimated lesson time: 40 minutes**

Microsoft Baseline Security Analyzer

MBSA is a tool you can use to check that computers on your organization's network have all relevant updates installed and their security settings configured according to Microsoft best-practice guidelines. The MBSA tool can either use the list of updates published on the Microsoft Update servers or check against a list of approved updates on the local WSUS server. You can use the MBSA tool to scan a single computer, a continuous range of IPv4 addresses, or a domain, as shown in Figure 9-16.

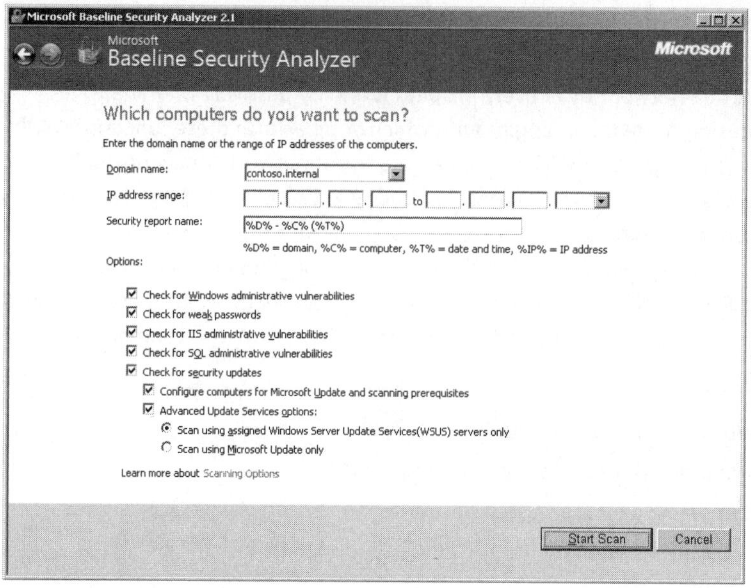

FIGURE 9-16 MBSA multiple computer scan.

When configuring an MBSA scan, you can check for the following:

- **Whether security updates are installed** Use this to check against Microsoft Update or a local WSUS server.

- **Administrative vulnerability check** This check includes examining the status of guest accounts, file system format, file share configuration, and the configuration of members of the administrative group (for example, a check to see whether any administrative accounts have passwords that do not expire).

- **Weak password check** This checks whether there are passwords that do not meet complexity requirements on the targeted computer.

- **IIS configuration vulnerabilities** Checks whether the IIS lockdown tool has been run and whether specific sample applications and virtual directories are present.

- **SQL configuration vulnerabilities** This check looks for vulnerabilities such as authentication mode and sa account status as well as service account memberships.

When using the MBSA tool, the account you initiate the scan with must have administrative privileges on both the scanning and the target computer. This stops malicious third parties from using the tool to scan Windows networks for exploitable vulnerabilities. The computer running the MBSA scan needs the Workstation service and the Client for Microsoft Networks enabled. Windows Update Agent 3.0 or later must be installed and, if the computer is going to perform a scan for IIS vulnerabilities, the IIS common files are required. Computers that are the remote targets of MBSA scans require the Remote Registry Service, Server service, File and Printer Sharing service, DCOM, and Windows Update Agent 3.0 or later. The MBSA uses ports 135, 139, and 445 to perform remote scans. If a firewall or packet filter exists between the scanning and target computers, you must allow traffic on UDP ports 137 and 138 so that authentication can occur.

As Figure 9-17 shows, you can use the MBSA tool from the command line by issuing the *mbsacli.exe* command. This command is located in the MBSA directory, and you must run it from an elevated command prompt. You can pipe the output of an *mbsacli.exe* command to a text file for later review. You can learn all the *mbsacli.exe* command-line options by typing **mbsacli.exe /?** into an elevated command prompt.

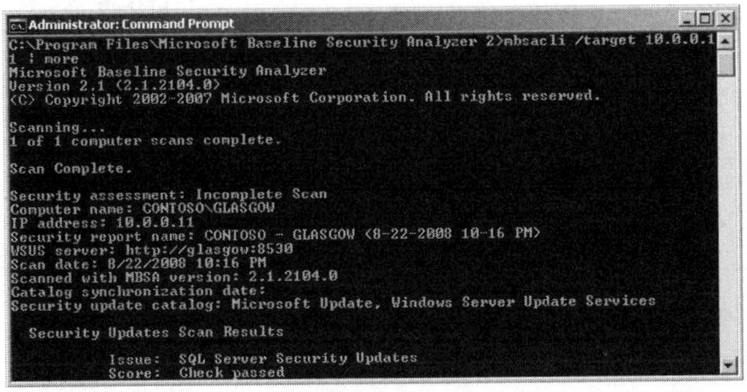

FIGURE 9-17 MBSA command-line output.

> **MORE INFO** **MORE ON MBSA**
>
> To learn more about the MBSA tool, consult the following article on the Microsoft Web site: *http://msdn.microsoft.com/en-au/library/aa302360.aspx.*

Simple Network Management Protocol

You can use SNMP to configure remote devices, detect network faults, measure network usage, and record network performance. The Windows Server 2008 SNMP service functions as an SNMP agent. SNMP works by having management applications and agent applications. To access the information the Windows Server 2008 SNMP service provides, you need an SNMP management application such as System Center Essentials 2007 or System Center Operations Manager 2007. Windows Server 2008 does not include an SNMP management application by default. SNMP uses Windows Internet Naming Service (WINS) for name resolution or, if a WINS server is not present, the hosts file.

> **MORE INFO** **SNMP AND SYSTEM CENTER ESSENTIALS 2007**
>
> To learn more about creating monitors for SNMP traps by using System Center Essentials 2007, see the following TechNet article: *http://technet.microsoft.com/en-us/library /bb437324.aspx.*

You can configure the SNMP service by editing the registry or through Group Policy. The settings relate to community names, managers, and trap locations. These settings have an impact only if you have installed the SNMP service. SNMP community names define a group of SNMP managers and agents. SNMP agents will not respond to requests from SNMP managers that are not members of the same community. You can configure SNMP community membership by configuring one of the following:

- The HKLM\SYSTEM\CurrentControlSet\Services\SNMP\ValidCommunities registry key
- The Computer Configuration\Policies\Administrative Templates\Network\SNMP \Communities policy

The Permitted Managers property enables you to specify a list of hosts who can initiate a query to which the SNMP agent will respond. You do not specify a username, and any person running the management software on a host that is in the permitted managers list will be able to send SNMP queries to the agent successfully. You can configure the SNMP managers by editing one of the following:

- The HKLM\SYSTEM\CurrentControlSet\Services\SNMP\Parameters\PermittedManagers registry key
- The Computer Configuration\Policies\Administrative Templates\Network\SNMP \Permitted Managers policy

The Trap Configuration property enables you to specify the hosts within the community that will be sent SNMP TRAP messages by the SNMP service. Traps report alert data to the SNMP management software and allow notifications to occur outside the normal SNMP querying process. To configure the hosts to which TRAP messages are sent, edit one of the following settings:

- The HKLM\SYSTEM\CurrentControlSet\Services\SNMP\Parameters\TrapConfiguration registry key
- The Computer Configuration\Policies\Administrative Templates\Network\SNMP\Traps For Public Community policy

---

MORE INFO   CONFIGURING SNMP

To learn more about configuring the SNMP service, consult the following article on Microsoft's Web site: *http://technet.microsoft.com/en-us/library/cc731328.aspx*.

 Quick Check

1. Which ports does the MBSA tool use to scan remote computers on the local area network?

2. What is the name of the MBSA command-line utility?

Quick Check Answers

1. The MBSA uses ports 135, 139, and 445 to perform remote scans.

2. *Mbsacli.exe.*

Network Monitor

Network Monitor is a tool you can download from the Microsoft Web site that can be used to capture and analyze network traffic. Unlike the MBSA tool, which actively probes other hosts on the network, Network Monitor is a passive tool that listens and records what it hears on the network. After you have installed Network Monitor on a computer running Windows Server 2008, you must add your user account to the Network Configuration Operators local group. On computers running Windows Vista, you must add your user account to the Netmon Users local group. On computers running Windows Server 2008, only members of the Network Configuration Operators local group can capture network data without elevating privileges through User Account Control.

Network Monitor can intercept only network traffic that the host network adapter receives. In older networks, this meant that Network Monitor could intercept traffic between other hosts. Today's networks almost always use OSI Layer 2 switches, which means that a host will intercept only network broadcasts and unicast messages directed specifically at the adapter's Ethernet address. On networks that use hubs instead of switches, it is possible for Network Monitor to see more traffic. To do this, you must configure Network Monitor to work in promiscuous mode. When Network Monitor is in promiscuous mode, (or P-mode), it will capture all traffic it sees, not just traffic directed to the host on which Network Monitor has been installed.

NOTE **MONITORING PORT**

Some layer 2 switches have a monitoring port. When configured, the switch forwards all traffic it processes to the monitoring port. If you connect a host running Network Monitor to the monitoring port, you will be able to capture and analyze all network traffic that passes across the switch.

Capturing Data with Network Monitor

To capture network data from the Network Monitor interface, click Create A New Capture Tab. Clicking Play starts a capture, clicking Pause pauses a capture, and clicking Stop finishes a capture. You are most likely to use Network Monitor when trying to diagnose a network-related problem with the server on which you have installed the network monitor. When doing this, start a Network Monitor capture, attempt to replicate the problem, finish the capture, and then analyze the capture data. Examining the capture data enables you to see what network data the server sent and received when you replicated the issue. This can lead you toward finding a solution for the problem. Figure 9-18 shows the results of a packet capture during a Domain Name System (DNS) request for *www.microsoft.com*. You are most likely to find the Frame Summary and Frame Details panes most informative when examining packet capture data. The Hex Details pane shows the contents of the frame, but you generally will not need this level of detail to diagnose network problems.

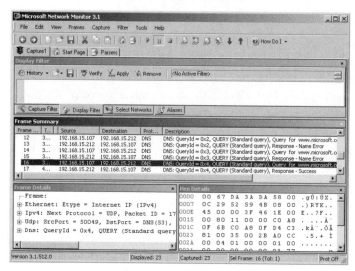

FIGURE 9-18 Packet capture.

You can perform network captures from the command prompt by using the *nmcap.exe* command, which is located in the Network Monitor installation folder. A simple capture, in which all data from all network interfaces is captured, uses this syntax:

```
Nmcap.exe /network * /capture /file c:\temp\filename.cap
```

The default capture size is 20 MB; you should ensure that *nmcap.exe* writes it to a location other than the Network Monitor folder. You can place *nmcap.exe* in promiscuous mode so that all traffic is captured, using the /disablelocalonly option. You can open a command-line capture from within the Network Monitor console.

Filtering Network Monitor Data

You can apply filters to packet captures performed either by using the Network Monitor GUI or through the *nmcap.exe* command-line utility. Capture filters limit the data that is recorded, and display filters limit what information is presented when looking at an existing capture. Many administrators prefer display filters because they retain the benefit of capturing all information and just hide data during the display process. If you use a capture filter, the data you can analyze is limited by the properties of the filter. It is often better to capture more and show less than it is to capture less and be limited by what you have captured. You load and apply both capture and display filters through the Filter Menu. To apply a filter using *nmcap. exe*, use the /filter option. For example, to capture only Terminal Server–related data, using *nmcap.exe*, issue the command:

```
Nmcap.exe /network * /capture "TerminalServer" /filename c:\temp\terminalservercapture.
cap
```

Network Monitor ships with over 40 standard filters. Each of these standard filters can be used as a display or capture filter. It is possible to modify these standard filters to create custom filters. Filters are strings of text that you can enter directly into the capture or display filter or load from the Filter menu. You can use the *AND* and *OR* logical operators to combine filters. When you use logical operators within a filter, the *AND* operator means that all conditions must be met, and the *OR* operator means that either condition must be met. You can also substitute the symbols && for *AND* and || for *OR*. For example, Figure 9-19 shows the results of the display filter DNS AND IPv4.Address == 192.168.15.107. You could also write this filter as DNS && IPv4 Address == 192.168.15.107. Display filters and capture filters use the same syntax. You can use the Export button to save a filter you have created for later use.

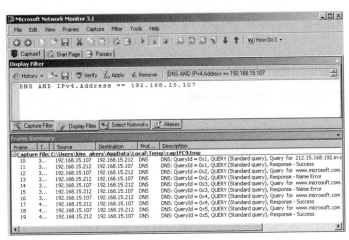

FIGURE 9-19 Display filter syntax.

It is also possible to create filters directly from capture data by right-clicking a frame in the Frame Summary windows and then selecting Copy Cell As Filter or Add Cell to Display Filter, as shown in Figure 9-20. You can also perform these functions from the Frame Details window. When you do this, you can then paste the filter text into the filter window. From here, you can either customize it or use the export function to save the filter data for later use.

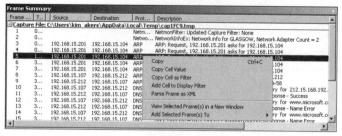

FIGURE 9-20 Create filters dynamically.

MORE INFO   **MORE ON NETWORK MONITOR**

For more information about how to capture network traffic using Network Monitor, see the following TechNet article: *http://support.microsoft.com/kb/148942*.

EXAM TIP

Understand the purpose of each technology and how it can be used to learn information about your network.

PRACTICE   **Gathering Data about the Network**

In this practice, you use MBSA and Network Monitor to perform tasks related to gathering network data.

To complete these exercises, you must have downloaded MBSA and Network Monitor software from the Microsoft Web site. The "Before You Begin" section at the start of this chapter lists where you can obtain this software.

EXERCISE 1   **Microsoft Baseline Security Analyzer**

In this exercise, you install and configure MBSA.

1. Log on to server Glasgow, using the Kim_Akers user account, and locate the folder to which you downloaded the MBSA installation file.

2. Double-click the installation file to begin the MBSA setup process. Click Run when presented with the security warning. On the Welcome To The Microsoft Baseline Security Analyzer page, click Next.

3. On the License Agreement page, select I Accept The License Agreement, and then click Next. Accept the default destination folder location, and then click Next. On the Start Installation page, click Install. When prompted by the User Account Control dialog box, click Continue. Click OK to dismiss the MBSA Setup dialog box when the installation process completes.

4. Open the Group Policy Management console from the Administrative Tools menu. Click Continue to dismiss the User Account Control dialog box.

5. Edit the default domain policy and configure the \Computer Configuration\Policies\ Administrative Templates\Windows Components\Windows Update\Specify Intranet Microsoft Update Service Location policy so that it points to *http://glasgow:8530* for both the intranet update service and intranet statistics server.

6. Apply the policy by running *gpupdate.exe* from the command prompt.

7. Open MBSA by clicking Start, All Programs, and then MBSA. Click Allow when the User Account Control dialog box appears.

8. Click Scan A Computer. On the Which Computer Do You Want To Scan page, verify that the selected options match those in Figure 9-21, and then click Start Scan.

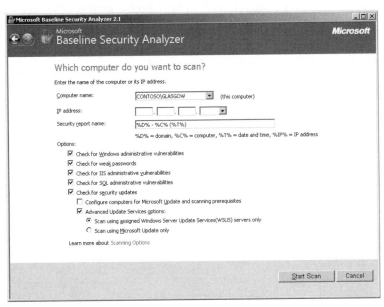

FIGURE 9-21 Configuring MBSA options.

9. Review the report details for the scan against Glasgow, and then dismiss the report by clicking OK.

10. Close all open consoles to end the practice exercise.

EXERCISE 2 Use Network Monitor to Capture Network data

In this exercise, you install and use Network Monitor.

1. Log on to server Glasgow with the Kim_Akers user account. Locate the folder to which you downloaded the Network Monitor installer file.

2. Double-click the Network Monitor installation file to initiate the setup process. Click Run in the Open File – Security Warning dialog box. Click Next when presented with

the Welcome page of the Network Monitor Setup Wizard. Accept the terms of the license agreement, and then click Next.

3. On the Use Microsoft Update To Help Keep Your Computer Secure And Up To Date page, select I Do Not Want To Use Microsoft Update, and then click Next. On the Customer Experience Improvement Program page, select I Do Not Want To Participate In The Program At This Time and click Next.

4. On the Choose Setup Type page, click Complete. Click Install. When prompted by the User Account Control dialog box, click Continue. Click Finish when the installation routine completes.

5. Use Active Directory Users And Computers to add the Kim_Akers user account to the Network Configuration Operators Builtin group.

6. Log off, and then log back on to server Glasgow, using the Kim_Akers user account.

7. Launch Network Monitor from the Microsoft Network Monitor 3.1 menu. Dismiss the Microsoft Update Opt-in dialog box. In the Microsoft Network Monitor 3.1 console, shown in Figure 9-22, click Create A New Capture Tab.

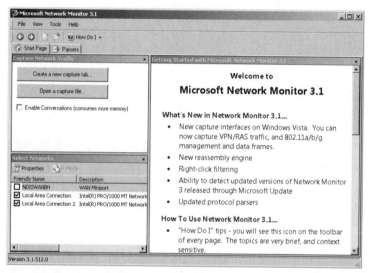

FIGURE 9-22 Network Monitor.

8. Click Play. After 30 seconds' worth of data has been collected, click Stop.

9. Click different frames that have been captured and examine the Frame Details pane for more information about the type of traffic that has been captured.

Lesson Summary

- You can use Microsoft Baseline Security Analyzer to check for missing updates and scan for security vulnerabilities in IIS, SQL, and administrative configuration.

- You can use Network Monitor to capture and analyze network traffic. Filters allow you to restrict the capture or display of data.
- You can enable the Simple Network Management Protocol agent on Windows Server 2008 by installing the SNMP service. SNMP agents are collected into communities. You can use SNMP management software, such as System Center Essentials 2007, to collect data from SNMP agents.

Lesson Review

You can use the following questions to test your knowledge of the information in Lesson 2, "Gathering Network Data." The questions are also available on the companion DVD if you prefer to review them in electronic form.

NOTE **ANSWERS**

Answers to these questions and explanations of why each answer choice is right or wrong are located in the "Answers" section at the end of the book.

1. Several users are having trouble connecting to a network application on one of your computers running Windows Server 2008. The application appears to be functioning correctly, and other users are able to make connections. Which of the following tools can you use to examine the network traffic that passes to the server from the trouble-some client computers?

    A. Microsoft Baseline Security Analyzer

    B. Telnet

    C. Network Monitor

    D. SNMP

2. One of the client computers on your network is having trouble resolving DNS addresses. The IP address of the client computer is 192.168.15.101. The IP address of the DNS server is 192.168.15.240. The DNS server also hosts an Intranet server. You install Network Monitor and perform a capture while attempting DNS resolution from the client. When you look at the capture data, there is far too much information, with DNS and Web server requests coming in from many clients over the same period. Which of the following display filters displays problematic traffic between the client and the server?

    A. DNS AND IPv4.Address == 192.168.15.240

    B. DNS OR IPv4.Address == 192.168.15.240

    C. DNS AND IPv4.Address == 192.168.15.101

    D. DNS OR IPv4.Address == 192.168.15.101

3. Your organization uses WSUS to distribute updates to client computers. Which of the following tools can you use to determine whether a client computer is missing important updates?

   A. *nmcap.exe*

   B. *ping.exe*

   C. *mbsacli.exe*

   D. *telnet.exe*

4. Which of the following must you enable on a remote computer for MBSA to scan it successfully?

   A. Server service

   B. Remote Registry service

   C. File and Print Sharing

   D. Workstation service

   E. Client for Microsoft Networks

5. Which of the following Group Policy settings enables you to specify the hosts that can query SNMP data from the SNMP service? (Choose two. Each correct answer presents part of a complete solution.)

   A. Dynamic Update

   B. Communities

   C. Traps For Public Community

   D. Permitted Managers

   E. Update Security Level

Chapter Review

To further practice and reinforce the skills you learned in this chapter, you can perform the following tasks:

- Review the chapter summary.
- Complete the case scenarios. These scenarios set up real-world situations involving the topics of this chapter and ask you to create solutions.
- Complete the suggested practices.
- Take a practice test.

Chapter Summary

- You can use WSUS to download and distribute software updates to your organization.
- You can use Network Monitor to capture and analyze network traffic.
- You can use Microsoft Baseline Security Analyzer to check for missing updates and scan for security vulnerabilities.

Case Scenarios

In the following case scenarios, you apply what you have learned about managing software updates and network data. You can find answers to these questions in the "Answers" section at the end of the book.

Case Scenario 1: Contoso, Ltd's WSUS Deployment

You are configuring and deploying WSUS for Contoso's Copenhagen head office. There are 300 client computers and 30 servers at the head office. All the client computers in the Copenhagen office use Windows Vista, and all the servers have the Windows Server 2008 operating system installed. Approximately 50 client computers and servers are located on an isolated network that is not connected to the Internet.

With that in mind, answer the following questions.

1. You want to ensure that when an update is approved for the organization's Windows Vista clients, it is not automatically approved for the organization's computers running Windows Server 2008, even if it is applicable to them. What steps should you take to meet this goal?

2. You want to ensure that all critical and security updates are automatically deployed to the computers running the Windows Vista client. What steps should you take to meet this goal?

3. What steps should you take to provide software updates to clients on the isolated network?

Case Scenario 2: Probing the Network at Fabrikam, Inc.

You are performing network maintenance as part of your ongoing duties as a systems administrator at Fabrikam. One of the computers is having persistent problems retrieving updates from the WSUS server. So far, you have been able to determine that the problem exists somewhere in the way the client is interacting with the WSUS server over the network. You also recently ran a scan with Microsoft Baseline Security Analyzer, but the results showed what you already knew. The computers you scanned were missing updates that you have yet to approve. With these things in mind, answers the following questions.

1. What steps should you take to diagnose the problem with the computer that cannot retrieve updates?

2. How can you ensure that you capture only data related to the problematic client?

3. How can you ensure that the update check looks only for updates that you have approved in WSUS?

Suggested Practices

To help you successfully master the exam objectives presented in this chapter, complete the following tasks.

Configure WSUS Server Settings

Do all the practices in this section.

- **Practice**   Install a standalone Windows Server 2008 server and install WSUS on this server. Configure WSUS to function as a replica server of the WSUS server that you installed on Glasgow.

Gather Network Data

Do all the practices in this section.

- **Practice 1**   Create a Network Monitor filter that displays only Web traffic data from a host at IP address 10.0.0.21. This is the Melbourne computer, running Windows Vista, which you have used for practice exercises in earlier chapters. Use Melbourne to check the default Web site at *http://glasgow.contoso.internal* when performing the capture.

- **Practice 2**   Perform a scan of a remote computer, using MBSA.

Take a Practice Test

The practice tests on this book's companion DVD offer many options. For example, you can test yourself on just one exam objective, or you can test yourself on all the upgrade exam content. You can set up the test so that it closely simulates the experience of taking a certification exam, or you can set it up in study mode so that you can look at the correct answers and explanations after you answer each question.

> **MORE INFO** **PRACTICE TESTS**
>
> For details about all the practice test options available, see the "How to Use the Practice Tests" section in this book's Introduction.

CHAPTER 10

Monitoring Performance and Events

M onitoring performance data and comparing it to established baselines is crucial to
determining the health of your servers and your network. You also need to keep a
close watch on events that occur on your network. Many events are informational, but
you should not ignore them because of that. It is possible to have too much information,
but, even so, some information is vital. Your skill and experience as an administrator must
determine what you should address and what you can safely ignore. What you should never
ignore are warning and error events that can indicate real and immediate problems in your
systems.

You will almost certainly have experience with Windows Reliability and Performance
Monitor (WRPM) and Event Viewer and have studied these tools for your Microsoft
Windows Server 2003 examinations. In addition, Chapter 8, "Maintaining the Active
Directory Environment," discussed these tools in the context of Active Directory Domain
Services (AD DS) monitoring. This chapter discusses the Windows Server 2008 enhance-
ments to the monitoring tools, for example, the data collector set tool, event forwarding,
and custom views.

Exam objectives in this chapter:

- Capture performance data.
- Monitor event logs.

Lessons in this chapter:

Before You Begin

To complete the lessons in this chapter, you must have done the following:

- Installed a Windows Server 2008 Enterprise server configured as a domain controller in the *contoso.internal* domain, as described in Chapter 1, "Configuring Internet Protocol Addressing."
- Installed the Windows Server 2008 Enterprise server Boston in the *contoso.internal* domain, as described in Chapter 2, "Configuring IP Services."

 REAL WORLD

Ian McLean

used to drive to work each morning along a particularly congested road that was undergoing improvement work. Wherever there was roadwork, there was a bottleneck. When one roadwork site was completed, the bottleneck didn't disappear. It simply moved a mile farther on to the next site. Even when the road upgrade was finished, there were still bottlenecks as a larger volume of traffic used the improved road.

It's the same with your network and your servers. You will never eliminate bottlenecks. You compare your current performance counters with your performance baselines and decide that a server needs an additional or a faster CPU. As soon as you improve processor performance, the server's memory looks like it's coming under pressure. Next, a disk upgrade is indicated. The process never stops.

What you are actually doing is not eliminating all bottlenecks; you likely never will. Just like the road engineers, you are ensuring an acceptable flow of traffic. You are solving problems before they become problems and certainly before your users see them as problems.

Hopefully, you are also planning for the future. You see that further down the line, your organization will need a new storage area network (SAN), and you prepare a business case for it. Management is most unlikely to authorize a budget for upgrades just because some administrator thinks they are a good idea. Managers need a sound economic justification—and quite rightly so.

When you are monitoring your systems, you are not attempting merely to eliminate bottlenecks. You are doing your job.

Lesson 1: Capturing Performance and Reliability Data

You monitor performance and reliability to improve server performance, identify potential bottlenecks, and upgrade the appropriate resources. You especially want to identify sources of critical performance problems that could make services unacceptably slow or completely unusable.

Reliability monitoring helps you correlate events, such as application installations, with failures. For example, if you find that reliability decreases and problems start to occur after the installation of a new device driver, you might consider rolling back this installation.

Data collector sets use performance counters to generate performance logs and can, in turn, be read by Performance Monitor and the Reports tool. The data collector set tool is a more fully featured replacement for Performance Logs and Alerts. In Windows Server 2008, WRPM includes the Performance Monitor, Reliability Monitor, data collector set, and Reports tools and replaces a number of Windows Server 2003 tools such as Performance Logs and Alerts, System Performance Advisor, and System Monitor. Chapter 8 introduced Performance Monitor, Reliability Monitor, and data collector sets. This lesson describes them in more detail.

> **After this lesson, you will be able to:**
> - Use Performance Monitor to view real-time performance data or performance logs.
> - Use Reliability Monitor to examine failures related to software installations.
> - Use the data collector set tool to record information about a computer's current state and to generate reports.
>
> **Estimated lesson time: 45 minutes**

Using Performance Monitor

Performance Monitor is part of WRPM but can be seen as a tool in its own right. You almost certainly studied this tool for your Windows Server 2003 examinations, in which case, much of this section will be review.

In Windows Server 2008, you typically access Performance Monitor by expanding Diagnostics in Server Manager, expanding Reliability And Performance, expanding Monitoring Tools, and selecting Performance Monitor. However, you can also select Reliability And Performance on the Administrative Tools menu and then select Performance Monitor within the Reliability and Performance Monitor console. You can choose to monitor either the local computer or a remote computer.

NOTE **MONITORING A REMOTE COMPUTER**

If you want to view performance counters on a remote computer, you must enable the Performance Logs and Alerts firewall exception on the remote computer. At a minimum, your account must be a member of the Performance Log Users group and the Event Log Readers group on the remote computer. A domain administrator can monitor any computer in the domain, provided the firewall exception is enabled on that computer.

You can add counters by clicking the green + button on the Performance Monitor toolbar, and you can specify whether you want to display a single instance of a counter or a total of all instances. For example, if a computer has more than one CPU, you could select a counter that monitors the usage of a single CPU or a counter that monitors total CPU usage. Figure 10-1 shows Performance Monitor displaying real-time data.

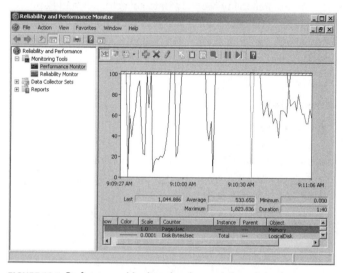

FIGURE 10-1 Performance Monitor showing real-time data.

Each line on the graph appears in a different color. To make it easier to view a specific graph, select its counter and press Ctrl+H. The selected counter appears bold and in black on the graph. To change the appearance and refresh rate of the chart, right-click Performance Monitor, and then select Properties. The five tabs of the Performance Monitor Properties dialog box provide access to different configuration options as follows:

- **General** In the Graph Elements group, you can adjust the Sample Every box to change how frequently the graph updates. If you specify a longer interval, your graph is updated less frequently and uses less bandwidth. You can adjust the value (in seconds) in the Duration box to change how much data is displayed in the graph before Performance Monitor begins overwriting the graph on the left portion of the chart. A Duration of 3,600 displays one hour of data in the graph, and a Duration of 86,400 displays one full day. You can also specify whether the Legend, Value Bar, and Toolbar are displayed and whether the Report and Histogram views show Default, Maximum, Minimum, Average, or Current values. Figure 10-2 shows the General tab.

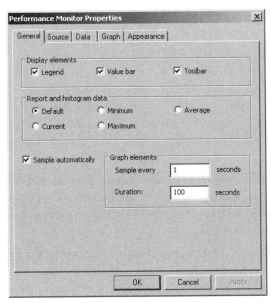

FIGURE 10-2 General tab of the Performance Monitor Properties dialog box.

■ **Source** On this tab, you can choose whether to display current activity in real time or show log files that you have saved using a data collector set. If you display a log file, you can use this tab to control the time range displayed in the Performance Monitor window.

■ **Data** On this tab, in the Counters list, select the counter you want to configure and adjust Color, Width, and Style. You can increase or decrease the Scale value to change the height of a counter's graph. You can also adjust the scale for all counters by clicking the Graph tab and changing the Maximum and Minimum values in the Vertical Scale group.

■ **Graph** By default, Performance Monitor begins overwriting graphed counter values on the left portion of the chart after the specified duration is reached. If you want to record counter values over a long period of time, you likely want to see the chart scroll from right to left. To do this, select the Scroll style. You can also select one of the following chart types by clicking the Change Graph Type button on the toolbar or by pressing Ctrl+G:

• **Line** This is the default setting and shows values as lines on the chart.

• **Histogram** This shows a bar graph with the current, maximum, minimum, or average counter values displayed. If you have a large number of counters, a histogram is easier to read than a line chart.

- **Report**   This lists the current, maximum, minimum, or average counter values in a text report.

■ **Appearance**   If you keep multiple Performance Monitor windows open simultaneously, you can use this tab to change the color of the background or other elements. This makes it easier to distinguish between the windows.

For example, Don Hall wants to view the current performance of a server called Glasgow in the *tailspintoys.com* domain. He suspects that the memory resource is currently under stress on the server. If he wanted to monitor memory-related counters over an extended period, he would create a data collector set but, for the moment, he wants a snapshot over five minutes when a particular application is open. Don starts Performance Monitor and adds the following counters:

■ **Memory\Pages/sec**   This counter measures the rate at which pages are read from or written to disk. Typically, if RAM is under stress, data is written to virtual paged memory on disk. If the value is greater than 1,000, this indicates excessive paging that, in turn, indicates inadequate memory resource.

■ **Memory\% Committed Bytes in Use**   This counter measures the ratio of Committed Bytes to the Commit Limit, which is a measure of the amount of virtual memory in use. If the value in this counter exceeds 80 percent, this indicates insufficient memory or a memory leak.

■ **Memory\Available MBytes**   This counter measures the amount of physical memory in megabytes available for running processes. If this value is less than 5 percent of the total physical RAM, it indicates insufficient memory.

■ **Memory\Free System Page Table Entries**   This counter measures the number of page table entries not currently in use by the system. If the number is less than 5,000, there could be a memory leak.

■ **Memory\Pool Non-Paged Bytes**   This counter measures the size of the nonpaged pool in bytes. The nonpaged pool is an area of system memory that holds objects that cannot be written to disk but instead need to remain in physical memory for as long as they are allocated. If this value is greater than 175 MB, there is a possible memory leak. Typically, an Event ID 2019 is recorded in the system event log if this counter exceeds its limit.

■ **Memory\Pool Paged Bytes**   This counter measures the size of the paged pool in bytes. The paged pool is an area of system memory used for objects that can be written to disk when they are not being used. If this value is greater than 250 MB, there is a possible memory leak. Typically, Event ID 2020 is recorded in the system event log.

Usually, instances are not required for memory counters. In the Performance Monitor Properties dialog box, Don configures the Sample Every setting to 5 seconds and the Duration setting to 300 seconds. He verifies that each counter displays in a different color and checks that the scale for each counter is set so the expected maximum values show histogram bars near (but not at) the top of the screen. (The default scale settings generally are acceptable.)

When he views the counter values in a histogram, as shown in Figure 10-3, Don sees that several counters are outside their permitted values, so the server has memory problems. Viewing the results in report format, as shown in Figure 10-4, Don deduces that the problem does not appear to be a memory leak. The server simply needs more memory.

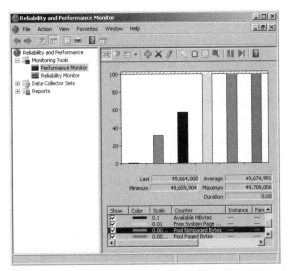

FIGURE 10-3 Performance monitoring results as a histogram.

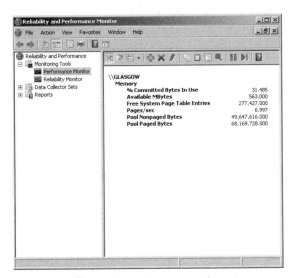

FIGURE 10-4 Viewing the results in report format.

✔ **Quick Check**

1. On which tab of the Performance Monitor Properties dialog box can you specify how often the graphs update?

2. Which rights does a user need to be able to monitor performance data remotely?

Quick Check Answers

1. On the General tab, in the Graph Elements group, you can adjust the Sample Every box to change how frequently the graph updates.

2. At a minimum, the user's account must be a member of the Performance Log Users group and the Event Log Readers group on the remote computer.

Using Reliability Monitor

Reliability Monitor, introduced in Chapter 8, tracks a computer's stability. Computers that have no reboots or failures are considered stable and can (eventually) achieve the maximum system stability index of 10. The more reboots and failures that occur on a computer, the lower the system stability becomes. The minimum index value is zero. The system stability index is not an exact measure of reliability because, sometimes, installing a new service pack or update requires a reboot, which initially lowers the index value but ultimately makes a system more reliable than it was before. However, Reliability Monitor provides valuable information about what system changes were made before a problem occurred.

You can use Reliability Monitor to diagnose intermittent problems. For example, if you install an application that causes the operating system to fail intermittently, it is difficult to correlate the failures with the application installation. Figure 10-5 shows how Reliability Monitor can be used to indicate that application failures and a general reduction in stability followed a system upgrade. If you obtained this result on a test network, you might consider obtaining more information before installing the upgrade on your production network.

You can open Reliability Monitor from Server Manager by expanding Diagnostics, expanding Reliability And Performance, expanding Monitoring Tools, and selecting Reliability Monitor. Alternatively, you can open Reliability And Performance Tools from Administrative Tools and select Reliability Monitor.

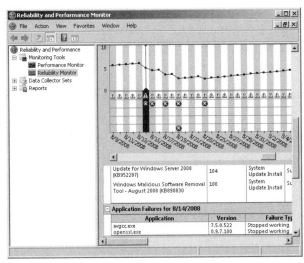

FIGURE 10-5 Reliability Monitor shows a drop in the system stability index.

Understanding the System Stability Index

The system stability index is based on data collected over the lifetime of a system. Each day in the system stability chart is associated with a graph point showing its system stability index rating. The system stability index is a weighted measurement calculated from the number of failures seen over a rolling historical period. The index value is calculated over the preceding 28 days, although the results for considerably more days are displayed. Reliability events in the System Stability Report describe the specific failures.

Recent failures are weighted more heavily than past failures so that improvement over time is reflected in an ascending system stability index when a reliability issue has been resolved. Days when the system is powered off or is in a sleep or hibernate state are not included when calculating the system stability index.

If there is not enough data to calculate a steady system stability index, the line on the graph is dotted. For example, until the Reliability Monitor has 28 days of data, the system stability index is displayed as a dotted line, indicating it has not yet established a valid baseline. When enough data has been recorded to generate a steady system stability index, the line is solid. If there are any significant changes to the system time, an Information icon appears on the graph for each day on which the system time was adjusted.

Reliability Monitor maintains up to a year of history for system stability and reliability events. The System Stability Chart displays a rolling graph organized by date.

✔ **Quick Check**

- What would a system stability index of 10 indicate?

Quick Check Answer

- The maximum value of the system stability index is 10. This value indicates that the system has been stable over the previous 28 days with no failures or reboots. It also indicates that no software updates and service packs that require a reboot have been applied during that time.

Using the System Stability Chart

The top section of the System Stability Chart displays a graph of the system stability index on a day-to-day basis. Rows in the lower half of the chart track reliability events that either contribute to the stability measurement for the system or provide related information about software installation and removal. When one or more reliability events of each type are detected, an icon appears in the column for that date.

For software installs and uninstalls, an information icon indicates a successful event, and a warning icon indicates a failure. For all other reliability event types, an error icon indicates a failure. If more than 30 days of data are available, you can use the scroll bar at the bottom of the System Stability Chart to find dates outside the visible range.

By default, Reliability Monitor displays the most recent data. To view data for a specific date, click the column for that date or use the drop-down date menu to select a different date, as shown in Figure 10-6. To view all available historical data, click the drop-down date menu and click Select All.

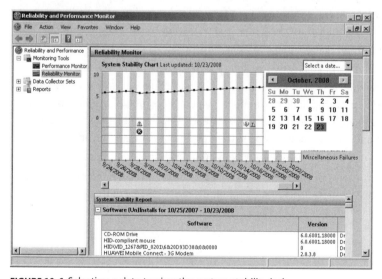

FIGURE 10-6 Selecting a date to view the system stability index.

The System Stability Report helps you identify changes that contribute to a lower system stability index by identifying reliability events. If you have clicked a date column in the System Stability Chart, the System Stability Report displays events for that date. Click the plus sign in the title bar of each reliability event category to view events. For example, Figure 10-5, shown earlier in this lesson, displays reports about software installations and application failures on August 13, 2008.

The following reliability events might be recorded in the System Stability Report:

- System clock changes
- Software installs and uninstalls
- Application failures
- Hardware failures
- Windows failures
- Miscellaneous failures

If Reliability Monitor reports consistent application failures, Microsoft Windows failures, or software installation or removal failures, consider updating the failing application or components of the operating system. Use the Windows Update and the Problem Reports And Solutions control panel icons to search for application updates that might resolve your problems. If the failing application is not a Microsoft product and a solution does not exist in the Problem Reports And Solutions control panel, search the application manufacturer's Web site for software updates.

If Reliability Monitor reports consistent hardware failures, the computer could have serious technical problems that cannot be resolved by a software update. Contact the manufacturer of the hardware device for additional troubleshooting information.

Gathering System Stability Data

The Reliability Monitor displays data gathered by the Reliability Analysis Component (RAC). This is implemented using *RACAgent.exe*, which is scheduled to run once an hour. Reliability Monitor starts displaying a system stability index rating and specific event information 24 hours after system installation, and the RACAgent scheduled task runs by default after the operating system is installed. If it has been disabled, it must be enabled manually from the Task Scheduler snap-in for Microsoft Management Console (MMC).

To enable the RACAgent scheduled task (assuming it has been disabled), you must use an account that is a member of the local Administrators group on the computer you are monitoring. In the Start Search box, enter **taskschd.msc**. In the navigation pane, expand Task Scheduler Library, expand Microsoft, expand Windows, and select RAC. Right-click RAC, select View, and select Show Hidden Tasks. In the Results pane, right-click RACAgent and select Enable, as shown in Figure 10-7.

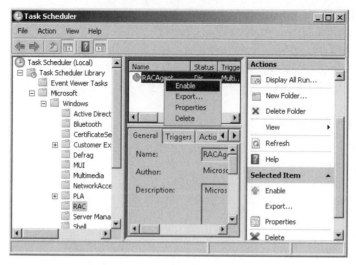

FIGURE 10-7 Enabling the RACAgent scheduled task.

Using Data Collector Sets

You used the data collector set tool in Chapter 8 when you created a data collector set based on the Active Directory Diagnostics template to gather information specific to AD DS operation. Data collector sets gather system information, including configuration settings and performance data, and store it in a data file. You can use Performance Monitor to examine the data file and analyze detailed performance data, or you can generate a report that summarizes this information.

Built-in Data Collector Sets

Windows Server 2008 includes the following built-in data collector sets:

- **Active Directory Diagnostics**   This data collector set is present only on domain controllers. It logs kernel trace data, Active Directory trace data, performance counters, and Active Directory registry configuration.

- **LAN Diagnostics**   You can use this data collector set when troubleshooting complex network problems such as network time-outs, poor network performance, or virtual private network (VPN) connectivity problems. It logs network performance counters, network configuration data, and diagnostics tracing data.

- **System Performance**   You can use this data collector set when troubleshooting a slow computer or intermittent performance problems. It logs processor, disk, memory, and network performance counters and kernel trace data.

- **System Diagnostics**   You can use this data collector set when troubleshooting reliability problems such as problematic hardware, driver failures, or STOP errors. It logs all the information included in the System Performance data collector set, plus detailed system information.

- **Wireless Diagnostics** This data collector set is present only on computers with wireless capabilities, and you should use it when troubleshooting network problems that occur when connected to a wireless network. It logs the same data as the LAN Diagnostics data collector set, plus information relevant to troubleshooting wireless network connections.

To use a data collector set, right-click it, and then select Start, as shown in Figure 10-8. The System Performance and System Diagnostics data collector sets stop automatically after a minute, the Active Directory Diagnostics data collector set stops automatically after five minutes, and the LAN Diagnostics and Wireless Diagnostics data collector sets run until you stop them. If you are troubleshooting a network problem, attempt to reproduce the problem after starting the data collector set. To stop a data collector set manually, right-click it, and then click Stop.

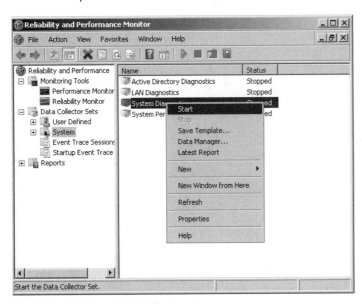

FIGURE 10-8 Starting a data collector set.

After running a data collector set, you can view a summary of the data it has gathered in the *Reliability and Performance\Reports* node. To view the most recent report for a data collector set, right-click the data collector set, and then click Latest Report, as shown in Figure 10-9. You can then view the report by accessing it in the *Reports* node, as shown in Figure 10-10.

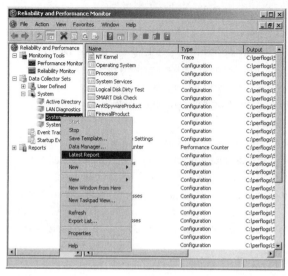

FIGURE 10-9 Specifying the latest report.

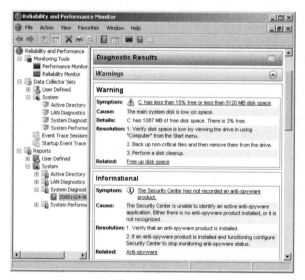

FIGURE 10-10 Viewing a report.

You can also add performance counter alerts to data collector sets. This enables you to monitor and detect an alert, which you can then use to start a batch file, send you an e-mail, or call you on a pager. For example, if you configured an alert to trigger when free space on a logical volume falls below 30 percent, you could add this to a data collector set and use it to trigger a batch file that archives the data on the volume.

Data logging uses a large amount of system resources, and performance log files can become very large. To minimize the performance impact of performance data logging, log the minimum amount of information you require. For example, use System Performance instead of System Diagnostics whenever possible because System Performance includes fewer counters.

Creating a Data Collector Set

You created a data collector set from a template in Chapter 8. Remember that your first task after creating one or more data collector sets is to use them to create baselines for periods of light, normal, and heavy traffic. Remember also that if you make a significant system change, you need to re-create your baselines. Chapter 8 discussed performance baselines.

If you have a performance problem or want to analyze and possibly improve the performance of a server, you can use data collector sets to gather performance data and compare it against your baselines. Chapter 8 introduced data collector sets, and you created and used one in a practice in that chapter. However, to remind you, the following high-level procedure creates a custom data collector set:

1. In the Reliability And Performance Monitor console, right-click Data Collector Sets \User Defined, select New, and then select Data Collector Set.

   This starts the Create New Data Collector Set wizard.

2. On the How Would You Like To Create This New Data Collector Set page, specify a name for the set. Ensure that Create From A Template is selected. Click Next.

3. On the Which Template Would You Like To Use page, choose from one of the standard templates. (Remember that Active Directory Diagnostics is available only on domain controllers.) Click Next.

4. On the Where Would You Like The Data To Be Saved page, click Next to accept the default location for the data.

5. On the Create New Data Collector Set page, leave Run As set to the default to create and run the data collector set, using the logged-on user's credentials. Alternatively, click the Change button and specify alternative administrative credentials.

6. Select one of the following three options before clicking the Finish button:

   - Open Properties For This Data Collector Set
   - Start This Data Collector Set Now
   - Save And Close

Custom data collector sets are located under the *User Defined* node within Data Collector Sets. You can schedule when a data collector set runs and configure its stop conditions as described in Chapter 8. You can also start a data collector set manually by right-clicking it and selecting Start.

MORE INFO **CREATING DATA COLLECTOR SETS**

For more information about the various methods of creating data collector sets, see *http://technet.microsoft.com/en-us/library/cc749337.aspx*.

Customizing Data Collector Sets

A custom data collector set logs only the performance data defined in the template you chose. To add your own data sources to a data collector set, you must update it after you create it.

To add a performance data source (such as a performance counter) to a data collector set, right-click the data collector set, select New, and then select Data Collector. The Create New Data Collector wizard opens. On the What Type Of Data Collector Would You Like To Create page, specify the data collector name, select the type, and then click Next. You can choose from the following types of data collectors:

- **Performance Counter Data Collector** This type of data collector enables you to collect performance statistics over long periods of time for later analysis. You can use it to set baselines and analyze trends. Its functionality is similar to the Performance Log component of the Performance Logs and Alerts tool in Windows Server 2003.

- **Event Trace Data Collector** This type of data collector enables you to collect information about system events and activities. Its functionality is similar to the Trace Log component of the Performance Logs and Alerts tool in Windows Server 2003.

- **Configuration Data Collector** This type of data collector stores information about registry keys, Windows Management Instrumentation (WMI) management paths, and the system state.

- **Performance Counter Alert** This type of data collector (sometimes termed an Alert data connector) enables you to configure an alert that is generated when a particular performance counter exceeds or drops below a specific threshold value. An alert can send information to you when it is triggered, or it can start a stored program. For example, an alert that triggers when data stored on a hard disk consumes more than 85 percent of disk capacity could trigger a program that archives the disk. This functionality is similar to the Alerts component of the Performance Logs and Alerts tool in Windows Server 2003.

You can add as many data collectors to a data collector set as you need. To edit a data collector, select it in the *Data Collector Sets\User Defined* node. In the Details pane, right-click the data collector and click Properties.

> **MORE INFO   DATA COLLECTOR SET PROPERTIES**
>
> For more information about configuring data collector set properties, see *http://technet.microsoft.com/en-us/library/cc749267.aspx*.

If a data collector set includes performance counters, you can view the counter values, using Performance Monitor, by right-clicking the report, clicking View, and then clicking

Performance Monitor. Performance Monitor then displays the data logged by the data collector set rather than real-time data.

Creating Data Collectors from the Command Prompt

You can create data collectors from an elevated command prompt by using the *logman* utility. This is especially useful for servers in Server Core configuration. For example, you can use the following commands to create the various types of data collector listed in the previous section:

- *Logman create counter* This command creates a Performance Counter data collector. For example, the *logman create counter my_perf_log -c "\Processor(_Total)\% Processor Time"* command creates a counter called my_perf_log that records values for the % Processor Time counter in the Processor(_Total) counter instance.

- *Logman create trace* This command creates an Event Trace data collector. For example, the *logman create trace my_trace_log -o c:\trace_log_file* command creates an event trace data collector called my_trace_log and outputs the results to the c:\trace_log_file location.

- *Logman create config* This command creates a Configuration data collector. For example, the *logman create config my_cfg_log -reg HKEY_LOCAL_MACHINE\SOFTWARE\Microsoft\Windows\CurrentVersion* command creates a configuration data collector called my_cfg_log using the HKEY_LOCAL_MACHINE\SOFTWARE\Microsoft\Windows\CurrentVersion registry key.

- *Logman create alert* This command creates an Alert data collector. For example, the *logman create alert my_alert -th "\Processor(_Total)\% Processor Time>90"* command creates an alert called my_alert that fires when the % Processor Time performance counter in the Processor(_Total) counter instance exceeds a value of 90.

You can also use the *logman* utility to query data collector output; for example, the *logman query "my_perf_log"* command lists the data collectors contained in the my_perf_log data collector set. You can start and stop data collector sets, for example, *logman start my_perf_log* and *logman stop my_perf_log*. You can delete a data collector set, for example, by using the *logman delete my_perf_log* command, and you can use *logman update* to update a performance counter, a trace counter, an alert, or a configuration. *Logman* enables you to export the information in data collector sets to and import information from an XML file.

> **MORE INFO** **LOGMAN**
>
> For more information about the logman utility, see *http://technet.microsoft.com/en-us/library/cc753820.aspx*.

Using Performance Monitor to Generate a Snapshot of Disk Performance Data

In this practice, you take a snapshot of performance data on your Glasgow domain controller. You then view this data in graph, histogram, and report format. The results illustrate that Glasgow is experiencing problems with its C volume. You will probably obtain different results from the domain controller in your practice network. Before you carry out this practice, connect a second storage device, such as a second hard disk or USB flash memory, to your computer.

EXERCISE 1   Add and Monitor Disk Counters

In this exercise, you add counters that enable you to monitor the performance of your system (C) hard disk volume. If you have additional volumes on a single hard disk or additional hard disks on your system, you can extend the exercise to monitor them also.

> **NOTE   DISKPERF**
>
> Both logical and physical disk performance counters are enabled on demand by default on Windows Server 2008. The *Diskperf* command still exists, and you can use it to enable or disable disk counters forcibly for previous applications that use *ioctl_disk_performance* to retrieve raw counters.

> **MORE INFO   LOCTL_DISK_PERFORMANCE**
>
> For more information about *loctl_disk_performance*, see *http://msdn.microsoft.com/en-us /library/ms804569.aspx*. Note, however, that this is an older feature and is unlikely to be tested in the upgrade examinations.

A bottleneck affecting disk usage and speed has a significant impact on a server's overall performance. To add counters that monitor disk performance, perform the following procedure.

1. Log on to your Glasgow domain controller, using the Kim_Akers account. If necessary, start Server Manager.

2. In Server Manager, expand Diagnostics, expand Reliability And Performance, expand Monitoring Tools, and select Performance Monitor.

3. In Performance Monitor, click the Add button (the green + symbol).

4. In the Add Counters dialog box, ensure that Local Computer is selected in the Select Counters From Computer drop-down list.

5. Select the Show Description check box.

6. In the Counter Selection pane, expand LogicalDisk and select % Free Space. In the Instances Of Dialog Box pane, select C: as shown in Figure 10-11.

The LogicalDisk\% Free Space counter measures the percentage of free space on the selected logical disk drive. If this falls below 15 percent, you risk running out of free space for the operating system to store critical files.

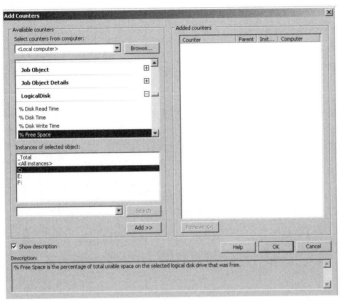

FIGURE 10-11 Specifying the C instance of the LogicalDisk\% Free Space counter.

7. Click Add to add this counter.

8. In the Counter Selection pane, expand PhysicalDisk and select % Idle Time. In the Instances Of Dialog Box pane, select C: as shown in Figure 10-12.

This counter measures the percentage of time the disk was idle during the sample interval. If this value falls below 20 percent, the disk system is said to be *saturated*, and you should consider installing a faster disk system.

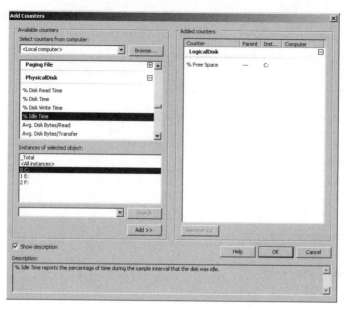

FIGURE 10-12 Specifying the C: instance of the PhysicalDisk\% Idle Time counter.

9. Click Add to add this counter.

10. Use the same technique to add the C: instance of the PhysicalDisk\Avg. Disk Sec/Read counter.

   This counter measures the average time in seconds to read data from the disk. If the value is larger than 25 milliseconds (ms), the disk system is experiencing latency (delay) when reading from the disk. In this case, consider installing a faster disk system.

11. Use the same technique to add the C: instance of the PhysicalDisk\Avg. Disk Sec/Write counter.

   This counter measures the average time in seconds to write data to the disk. If the value is larger than 25 ms, the disk system is experiencing latency (delay) when writing to the disk. In this case, consider installing a faster disk system.

> **NOTE** **MISSION-CRITICAL APPLICATION SERVERS**
>
> For mission-critical application servers hosting Microsoft SQL Server and Microsoft Exchange Server, the acceptable threshold of the PhysicalDisk\Avg. Disk Sec/Read and PhysicalDisk\Avg. Disk Sec/Write counters is much lower, typically 10 ms.

MORE INFO **PHYSICALDISK\% DISK TIME COUNTER**

Because the value in the PhysicalDisk\% Disk Time counter can exceed 100 percent, many administrators prefer to use PhysicalDisk\% Idle Time, PhysicalDisk\Avg. Disk sec /Read, and PhysicalDisk\Avg. Disk sec/write counters to obtain a more accurate indication of hard disk usage. For more information about the PhysicalDisk\% Disk Time counter, see *http://support.microsoft.com/kb/310067*.

12. Use the same technique to add the C: instance of the PhysicalDisk\Avg. Disk Queue Length counter.

    This counter indicates how many I/O operations are waiting for the hard drive to become available. If the value of this counter is larger than twice the number of spindles in a disk array, the physical disk itself might be the bottleneck.

13. Use the same technique to add the Memory\Cache Bytes counter.

    This counter indicates the amount of memory being used for the file system cache. There might be a disk bottleneck if this value is greater than 300 MB.

14. Check that the Add Counters dialog box shows the same counters and instances as Figure 10-13. Click OK.

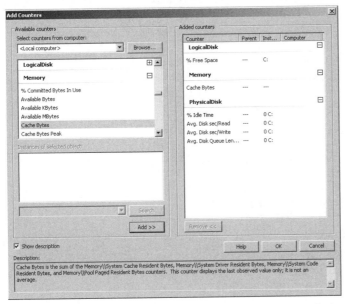

FIGURE 10-13 The required counters and instances have been specified.

15. Do not close Performance Monitor. Go directly to Exercise 2.

EXERCISE 2   Set Performance Monitor Properties and Monitor Disk Performance

In this exercise, you set the sample interval and duration, read data from and write data to the disk volume you are monitoring, and view the results in line, histogram, and report formats. Perform this exercise directly after Exercise 1.

1. In the Performance Monitor Action pane, click More Actions and select Properties.

2. On the General tab of the Performance Monitor Properties dialog box, in the Graph Elements section, change the Sample Every value to 5 and the Duration value to 300. Click OK.

3. Copy a file or folder (about 10 MB in size) from your C drive to your attached storage device.

4. Copy a file or folder (about 10 MB in size) from your attached storage device to your C drive.

5. View the line graph in Performance Monitor as shown in Figure 10-14.

    This might not easily provide the information you are looking for.

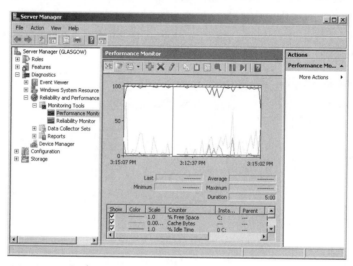

FIGURE 10-14 Performance Monitor line graph view.

6. In the Change Graph drop-down list, select Histogram Bar. Repeat the file copying operation you carried out before. View the histogram in Performance Monitor as shown in Figure 10-15. Note that because Windows Server 2008 caches the file after the first copy, the results reflect only the impact of writing the file to disk and retrieving it from RAM.

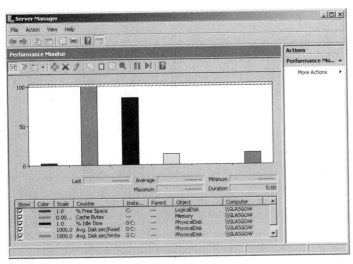

FIGURE 10-15 Performance Monitor histogram view.

7. In the Change Graph drop-down list, select Report. Repeat the file copying operation you carried out before. View the Report in Performance Monitor as shown in Figure 10-16.

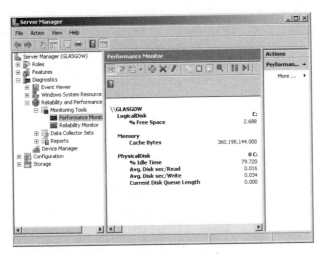

FIGURE 10-16 Performance Monitor report view.

8. Analyze the counter values in the light of the information given about each counter in Exercise 1. The results shown in the figures indicate that space on the C volume is very low. This will reduce performance significantly because the operating system will have problems writing to the disk. The results you obtain are likely to be different.

Lesson Summary

- You can use Performance Monitor to set baselines and compare current performance counter values with the baseline values. You can view performance counters in real time, or you can view log files created when you run a data collector set that records configuration settings, performance data, and events. Data collector sets enable you to gather information about a computer's current state for later analysis.

- Reliability Monitor records application installations and different types of failures. You can use this tool to correlate software installations with recurring problems.

Lesson Review

You can use the following questions to test your knowledge of the information in Lesson 1, "Capturing Performance and Reliability Data." The questions are also available on the companion DVD if you prefer to review them in electronic form.

> **NOTE** ANSWERS
>
> Answers to these questions and explanations of why each answer choice is right or wrong are located in the "Answers" section at the end of the book.

1. You want to use Performance Monitor to display performance data captured in a data collector set. You open the tool and access the Performance Monitor Properties dialog box. On which tab can you choose whether to display current activity in real time or log files that you have saved using a data collector set?

   A. General

   B. Source

   C. Data

   D. Graph

   E. Appearance

2. A Windows Server 2008 file server is experiencing intermittent performance problems. You suspect the problems might be caused by an application that you recently installed using Windows Installer, but you have forgotten exactly when you did this. Which tool would you use to determine when the application was installed?

   A. Reliability Monitor

   B. Network Monitor

   C. Data Collector Set

   D. Performance Monitor

3. Which of the following types of information are stored in Reliability Monitor? (Choose four. Each correct answer presents part of a complete solution.)

A. A Web page is misconfigured.

B. An application failed and needs to be restarted.

C. A Windows error occurred and the system was rebooted.

D. An application was uninstalled.

E. A service was stopped.

F. A device driver failed.

4. Users report slow response times on a Windows Server 2008 file server in your domain. You open Task Manager on the server and observe that the processor is operating at 100 percent capacity. Which of the following actions would you perform to gather additional data that would help diagnose the problem?

A. Use a data collector set to create a counter log that tracks processor usage.

B. Use a data collector set to create an alert that triggers when the usage of the processor exceeds 80 percent for more than five minutes.

C. Use Event Viewer to view the server's Application log.

D. Use the Resource View screen in Reliability and Performance Monitor to find out the percentage of processor capacity used by each application.

Lesson 2: Monitoring Event Logs

Chapter 8 introduced Event Viewer and event logs; you likely studied the tool for your Windows Server 2003 examinations and use it professionally in your job. The main difference in Windows Server 2008 is that Event Viewer is now available under Diagnostics in Server Manager as well as through the Administration Tools program group, the messages and event descriptions in Windows Server 2008 are much more informative, and access to an internal database is provided. A number of third-party databases also exist, as was discussed in Chapter 8. Additionally, Windows now includes many more event logs to make it easier to troubleshoot problems with a specific Windows component or application. Windows Server 2008 makes it easier to attach tasks to events and provides event log subscriptions so that event logs on one or more source computers can be displayed on a single collector computer.

Windows has always stored a great deal of information in event logs. Unfortunately, with versions of Windows released prior to Windows Server 2003 R2 and Windows Vista, that information could be difficult to access. Event logs were always stored on the local computer, and finding important events among the large number of events in an event log could be challenging.

With Windows Vista, Windows Server 2008, and Windows Server 2003 R2, you can collect events from remote computers (including computers running Windows XP) and detect problems, such as low disk space, before these problems become more serious. You might not have studied event forwarding for your Windows Server 2003 examinations, and you might not have used the feature extensively. This lesson, therefore, describes how to implement event forwarding in Windows Server 2008.

Windows Server 2008 also features Applications and Services logs and custom views and enables you to view DNS events directly from the Domain Name System (DNS) MMC snap-in. This lesson also covers these topics.

> **After this lesson, you will be able to:**
> - Use event forwarding.
> - Configure computers to support event forwarding and create a subscription.
> - Use Custom Views and Applications and Services logs.
>
> **Estimated lesson time 45 minutes.**

REAL WORLD

Ian McLean

While I was writing this lesson, I found myself typing "These events can some-times be difficult to interpret." I was referring to the Operational subtype of Applications and Services logs.

Oh dear.

Events are very useful if you know what they mean. Some very clever people designed the event logging and event reporting restrictions in previous versions of Windows Server. I suspect some of the same people wrote the explanations. They wrote them in terms that were perfectly clear and simple to themselves and their highly competent colleagues. To mere mortals, they were incomprehensible.

When I was clearing out some filing cabinets last week, I came across a document that explained how an obscure part of a telephony hardware design worked. It was dated 1969. I read it three times. Yes, it was in English, although few would recognize it as such. It was written by a young engineer who thought everyone would be just as familiar as he was with what he had been working on for three months. His name was McLean. Who am I to criticize?

When something is new, it is sometimes not very well explained. It seems to take several iterations before clear, concise explanations appear. There are many reasons for this, and I'm not criticizing Microsoft designers and developers in any way. It's how things have always been. I suspect the instruction manual for the first spear took about a hundred stone tablets to say, "Do not hold by the pointed end."

So Windows Server 2008 offers a significant improvement in explanations of the type of events that have been around for a while. New features tend to be more difficult to interpret—which usually means that their explanations are difficult to understand. If you come across this, don't panic. The fault is not with you. Type the incomprehensible text into a search engine. You will probably be directed to a blog or other discussion Web site where your peers will be describing what new features actually do and how best you can use them. This will help you do your job. It might also help you pass your exams.

Using Event Forwarding

Event forwarding enables you to transfer events that match specific criteria to an administrative (or collector) computer. This enables you to manage events centrally. A single event log on the collector computer holds important events from computers anywhere in your organization. You do not need to connect to the local event logs on individual computers.

Event forwarding uses Hypertext Transfer Protocol (HTTP) or (if you need to provide an additional encryption and authentication layer for greater security) Hypertext Transfer Protocol Secure (HTTPS) to send events from a source computer to a collector computer. Because event forwarding uses the same protocols that you use to browse Web sites, it works through Internet Security and Acceleration (ISA) Server and most firewalls and proxy servers. Event forwarding traffic is encrypted whether it uses HTTP or HTTPS.

To use event forwarding, you must configure both the source and collector computers. On both computers, start the Windows Remote Management and the Windows Event Collector services. On the source computer, configure a Windows Firewall exception for the HTTP protocol. You might also need to create a Windows Firewall exception on the collector computer, depending on the delivery optimization technique you choose. This is described in detail later in this lesson.

You can configure collector-initiated or source-initiated subscriptions. In collector-initiated subscriptions, the collector computer retrieves events from the computer that generated the event. You would use a collector-initiated subscription when you have a limited number of source computers and these are already identified. In this type of subscription, you configure each computer manually.

In a source-initiated subscription (sometimes termed a source computer–initiated subscription), the computer on which an event is generated (the source or source computer) sends the event to the collector computer. You would use a source-initiated subscription when you have a large number of source computers and you configure these computers through Group Policy. In a source-initiated subscription, you can add additional source computers after the subscription is established and you do not need to know immediately which computers in your network are to be source computers. In collector-initiated subscriptions, the collector computer retrieves events from one or more source computers. Collector-initiated subscriptions are typically used in small networks. In source-initiated subscriptions, the source computers forward events to the collector computer. Enterprise networks use source-initiated subscriptions.

A collector computer needs to run Windows Server 2008, Windows Vista, or Windows Server 2003 R2. A source computer needs to run Windows XP with Service Pack 2, Windows Server 2003 with Service Pack 1 or 2, Windows Server 2003 R2, Windows Vista, or Windows Server 2008.

MORE INFO **WS-MANAGEMENT 1.1**

To enable computers running Windows XP or Windows Server 2003 to act as source computers, you must install WS-Management 1.1. For more information, see *http://www.microsoft.com/downloads/details.aspx?FamilyID=845289ca-16cc-4c73-8934 -dd46b5ed1d33&displaylang=en*.

NOTE **FORWARDING COMPUTERS**

Much of the literature on this subject uses the term *forwarding computer* rather than *source computer*, sometimes inaccurately. In collector-initiated subscriptions, the collector computer retrieves events from the source computer. The source computer does not forward events. Only in source-initiated subscriptions does the source computer forward events and can accurately be called a forwarding computer. To prevent confusion, the term *source computer*, rather than *forwarding computer*, is used throughout this lesson.

Configuring a Collector-Initiated Subscription

In a collector-initiated subscription, you first manually configure one or more source computers and the collector computer. When the source computers and the collector computer are configured, you can create an event subscription to determine what events should be transferred.

CONFIGURING A SOURCE COMPUTER

To configure a computer running Windows Server 2008 so that a collector computer can retrieve events from it, open an elevated command prompt and use the *winrm* Windows Remote Management command-line tool to configure the Windows Remote Management service by entering the following command:

```
winrm quickconfig
```

You can abbreviate this to *winrm qc*. Windows will display a message similar to that shown in Figure 10-17. The changes that must be made depend on how the operating system is configured. You enter **Y** to make these changes.

FIGURE 10-17 Configuring the Windows Remote Management service.

Depending on the current configuration, *winrm* might make the following changes:

- Configure a Windows Remote Management HTTP listener.
- Create a Windows Firewall exception to allow incoming connections to the Windows Remote Management service, using HTTP. This exception applies only to the Domain and Private profiles. Traffic remains blocked while the computer is connected to public networks.

EXAM TIP

On computers running Windows Vista, the *winrm quickconfig* command also sets the Windows Remote Management (WS-Management) service to Automatic (Delayed Start) and starts the service. This service is already started on computers running Windows Server 2008.

Next, add the computer account of the collector computer to the local Event Log Readers group or the local Administrators group on the source computer. You can do this by using the Local Users and Groups MMC snap-in or by entering a *net* command in an elevated command prompt. For example, to add Glasgow as the collector computer on the Boston server in the *contoso.internal* domain, enter the following command on Boston:

```
net localgroup "Event Log Readers" glasgow$@contoso.internal /add
```

> **NOTE ADDING THE COLLECTOR COMPUTER ACCOUNT TO THE ADMINISTRATORS GROUP**
>
> You can add the collector computer account to the local Administrators group or the Event Log Readers group on the source computer. If you do not require the collector computer to retrieve events in Security Event logs, it is considered best practice to use the Event Log Readers group. However, if you do need to transfer Security Event log information, you must use the local Administrators group.

By default, the Local Users and Groups MMC snap-in does not permit you to add computer accounts. You must click the Object Types button in the Select Users, Computers, Or Groups dialog box and select the Computers check box. You can then add computer accounts.

Note also that you cannot use this MMC snap-in on a domain controller. You must use Active Directory Users And Computers and add the computer account to the local security group Event Log Readers. To do this, right-click the group, select Properties, click the Members tab, click Add, click Object Types, and select the Computers check box, as shown in Figure 10-18. Click OK, specify the computer account you want to add, click OK, and then click OK again.

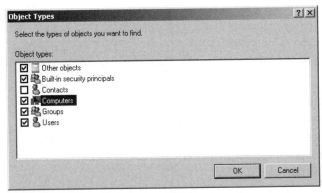

FIGURE 10-18 Specifying that the Event Log Users Group on a domain controller can contain computer accounts.

CONFIGURING THE COLLECTOR COMPUTER

To configure a computer running Windows Server 2008 to collect events, open a command prompt with administrative privileges and enter the following command to configure the Windows Event Collector service:

```
wecutil qc
```

In Windows Server 2008 (but not in Windows Vista), you can also select the *Subscriptions* node in Event Viewer. Event Viewer then prompts you to configure the Windows Event Collector service to start automatically, as shown in Figure 10-19.

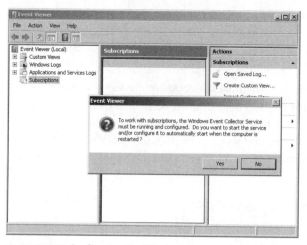

FIGURE 10-19 Configuring the Windows Event Collector service to start automatically in Event Viewer.

CONFIGURING THE EVENT SUBSCRIPTION

When you have configured the source and collector computers, configure the event subscription by specifying what events the collector computer needs to retrieve and the event sources (specifically the source computers) it must retrieve them from. You configure a collector-initiated subscription in the practice later in this lesson.

EXAM TIP

Distinguish between *winrm* and *wecutil*. *Winrm* is used to configure Windows Remote Management and is typically used on the source computer. *Wecutil* is used to configure the Windows Event Collector service and is typically used on the collector computer.

Configuring a Source-Initiated Subscription

To configure a source-initiated subscription, configure the collector computer manually. You can then use Group Policy to configure the source computers. When the collector computer and source computers are configured, you can create an event subscription to determine which events are forwarded.

Source-initiated subscriptions (sometimes termed source computer–initiated subscriptions) enable you to configure a subscription on a collector computer without defining the event source computers. You can then set up multiple remote event source computers by using Group Policy to forward events to the event collector computer. By contrast, in the collector-initiated subscription model, you must define all the event sources in the event subscription.

CONFIGURING THE COLLECTOR COMPUTER

You use command-line commands to implement this setup. This is useful if you are using servers in Server Core configuration. If the collector and source computers are in the same domain, you must create an event subscription XML file (called, for example, subscription.xml) on the collector computer, open an elevated command prompt on that computer, and configure Windows Remote Management by entering the following command:

```
winrm qc -q
```

Configure the Event Collector service on the same computer by entering this command:

```
wecutil qc /q
```

Create a source-initiated subscription on the collector computer by entering this command:

```
wecutil cs configuration.xml
```

Whenever you want to configure a source computer to use this subscription, first configure Windows Remote Management on that computer by entering the following command from an elevated command prompt:

```
winrm qc -q
```

USING GROUP POLICY TO CONFIGURE THE SOURCE COMPUTERS

You can use Group Policy to add the address of the event collector computer to the SubscriptionManager setting. From an elevated command prompt, enter the following command to configure Windows Remote Management:

```
winrm qc -q
```

Start Group Policy by entering the following command:

```
%SYSTEMROOT%\System32\gpedit.msc
```

In Local Group Policy Editor, under Computer Configuration, expand Administrative Templates, expand Windows Components, and select Event Forwarding. (Note that you do not have this option if you have already configured your computer as a collector computer.)

Right-click the SubscriptionManager setting and select Properties. Enable the SubscriptionManager setting and then click the Show button to add a server address to the setting. Add at least one setting that specifies the event collector computer. The SubscriptionManager Properties window contains an Explain tab that describes the syntax for the setting.

After the SubscriptionManager setting has been added, run the following command to ensure that the policy is applied:

```
gpupdate /force
```

MORE INFO **CONFIGURING A SOURCE-INITIATED SUBSCRIPTION**

Configuring a source-initiated subscription when the collector and source computers are in different domains is a complex procedure that involves the use of computer certificates and firewall configuration. For more information about this procedure as well as information about how to create an event subscription XML file, see *http://msdn.microsoft.com /en-s/library/bb870973(VS.85).aspx.*

Creating an Event Subscription

To receive events transferred from a source computer to a collector computer, you must create one or more event subscriptions. Before setting up a subscription, configure both the collector and source computers as previously described. To create a subscription on a collector computer running Windows Server 2008, perform the following procedure:

1. In Event Viewer, right-click Subscriptions and select Create Subscription.

2. If prompted, click Yes to configure the Windows Event Collector service to start automatically.

3. In the Subscription Properties dialog box, shown in Figure 10-20, type a name for the subscription. Optionally, you can also type a description.

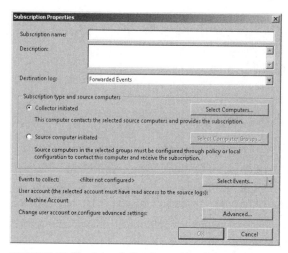

FIGURE 10-20 The Subscription Properties dialog box.

4. Select the type of subscription you want to create—Collector Initiated or Source Computer Initiated. You configure your chosen subscription type as follows:

    ■ If you select Collector Initiated, click the Select Computers button and, in the Computers dialog box, click Add Domain Computers, choose the computers you want to monitor as shown in Figure 10-21, and then click OK. You can click the Test button to verify that the source computer is properly configured and then click OK. If you have not run the *winrm qc* command on the source computer, the connectivity test fails. Click OK to return to the Subscription Properties dialog box.

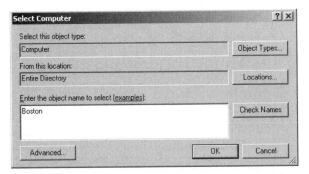

FIGURE 10-21 Specifying a source computer.

- If you select Source Computer Initiated, click Select Computer Groups. You can select either Add Domain Computer or Add Non-Domain Computers to determine the type of computer to add. If you add nondomain computers, they must have computer certificates installed. Click Add Certificates to add the certification authority that issued the certificates to the nondomain computers. If you add domain computers, you can use Group Policy to configure the computers as source computers. This is an appropriate procedure if you need to add a large number of source computers or if you want to add more source computers as they are installed on your domain. Using certificates to add nondomain computers is a manual procedure, and, typically, you would add only a small number of nondomain computers. For more information about computer certificates, see Chapter 7, "Active Directory Certificate Services."

5. Click the Select Events button in the Subscription Properties dialog box to open the Query Filter dialog box. Use this dialog box to define the criteria that forwarded events must match. Figure 10-22 shows an example configuration. Then click OK.

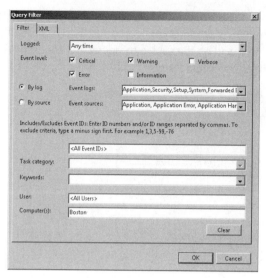

FIGURE 10-22 Defining the criteria for forwarded events.

6. Optionally, you can click the Advanced button in the Subscription Properties dialog box to open the Advanced Subscription Settings dialog box. You can configure three types of subscriptions:

- Selecting Normal ensures reliable delivery of events and does not attempt to conserve bandwidth. Choose this option unless you need tighter control over bandwidth usage or need events forwarded as quickly as possible. A normal subscription uses pull delivery mode (by which the collector computer contacts the source computer) and downloads five events at a time unless 15 minutes pass, in which case, it downloads any events that are available.

- Selecting Minimize Bandwidth reduces the network bandwidth consumed by event delivery. Choose this option if you are using event forwarding across a WAN or on a large number of computers on a local area network (LAN). It uses push delivery mode (by which the source computer contacts the collector computer) to forward events every six hours.

- Selecting Minimize Latency ensures that events are delivered with minimal delay. Choose this option if you are collecting alerts or critical events. It uses push delivery mode and sets a batch timeout of 30 seconds.

NOTE **SPECIFYING THE ACCOUNT THE SUBSCRIPTION USES**

Use the Advanced Subscription Settings dialog box to configure the account the subscription uses. Whether you use the default Machine Account setting or specify a user, you must ensure that the account is a member of the source computer's Event Log Readers group (or, if you are collecting Security Event log information, the local Administrators group).

7. Finally, click OK in the Subscription Properties dialog box to create the subscription.

Configuring the Subscription Interval

By default, normal event subscriptions check for new events every 15 minutes. You can decrease this interval to reduce the delay in retrieving events. No graphical interface exists to configure the delay, and you should use the command-line *wecutil* tool.

To adjust the event subscription delay (or subscription interval), create your subscription, and then enter the following two commands at an elevated command prompt:

```
wecutil ss <subscription_name> /cm:custom
wecutil ss <subscription_name> /hi:<milliseconds_delay>
```

For example, if you created a subscription named "Application Failures" and you wanted the delay to be one minute, you would run the following commands:

```
wecutil ss "Application Failures" /cm:custom
wecutil ss "Application Failures" /hi:60000
```

If you need to check the interval, run the following command:

```
wecutil gs "<subscription_name>"
```

For example, to verify that the interval for the "Application Failures" subscription is one minute, you would run the following command and look for the HeartbeatInterval value:

```
wecutil gs "Application Failures"
```

The Minimize Bandwidth and Minimize Latency options both batch a default number of items at a time. You can determine the value of this default by typing the following command at a command prompt:

```
winrm get winrm/config
```

Configuring Event Forwarding to Use HTTPS

The standard HTTP transport uses encryption for forwarded events. However, for added security, you can configure event forwarding to use the encrypted HTTPS protocol. When configuring the source computer, perform the following additional actions:

1. Configure the computer with a computer certificate. You can do this automatically in Active Directory environments by using an enterprise certification authority (CA).

2. Create a Windows Firewall exception for TCP port 443. Note that if you have configured Minimize Bandwidth or Minimize Latency event delivery optimization for the subscription, you must also configure a computer certificate and an HTTPS Windows Firewall exception on the collector computer.

3. Run the following command at an elevated command prompt with administrative privileges:

```
winrm quickconfig -transport:https
```

On the collector computer, open the Advanced Subscription Settings dialog box for the subscription and set Protocol to HTTPS, as shown in Figure 10-23. Additionally, the collector computer must trust the CA that issued the computer certificate for the source computer. This happens automatically if the certificate was issued by an enterprise CA and both the source computer and the collector computer are part of the same Active Directory domain.

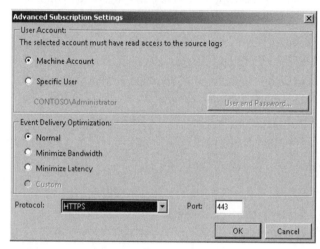

FIGURE 10-23 Specifying the HTTPS protocol.

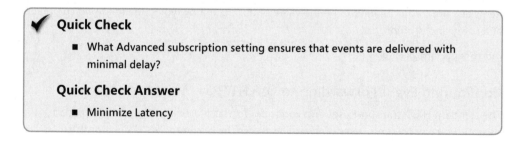

Quick Check

- What Advanced subscription setting ensures that events are delivered with minimal delay?

Quick Check Answer

- Minimize Latency

Using Custom Views

Event logs typically hold a very large number of events. Focus your attention on only those events that apply to the issue you are investigating and therefore need to filter. You saw an example of event filtering when you were specifying which events to transfer from a source to a collector computer in the previous section.

In previous versions of Event Viewer, you could filter the events in an event log by specifying a set of rules that determine which events in the log would be displayed. You could, for example, specify that only events with a level value of Error were visible. Windows Server 2008 Event Viewer extends the filtering beyond a single event log. It enables you to create a set of rules that select events from specified sources and display only the events from those sources whose property values satisfy the rules.

Creating a filter to display only the events you are interested in can be time-consuming, particularly when you must re-create the same filter you used before to filter another set of events. Custom Views provides a more efficient method. Filters are nonpersistent, whereas views are permanent. Filters can apply to only one log, whereas views can apply to multiple logs. When you have created a filter that displays only the records you are interested in, you can name the filter and save it to use later. That saved filter is a custom view.

EXAM TIP

Forwarding or retrieving events and creating subscriptions, in particular the use of the *wecutil* utility, are likely to be tested in the upgrade examinations.

Creating a Custom View

To create a custom view, first create a filter that includes events from multiple event logs that satisfy specified criteria; then, name and save the filter as a custom view. You apply the custom view by navigating to it in the console tree and clicking its name. You create a custom view in the practice later in this lesson. The high-level procedure for doing so is as follows:

1. On the Action menu in Event Viewer, select Create Custom View and, from the Logged drop-down list, select the time period you are interested in.

2. Select the check boxes for the event levels that you want included in the custom view. You can specify either the event logs or the event sources of the events that are displayed in the custom view. To specify event logs, select the event logs from which you want to include events in the Event Log drop-down list. To specify event sources, select the Event Source option and select the event sources in the Event Source drop-down list that you want to include in the custom view.

3. In the text box that displays <All Event IDs>, type the event IDs you want your custom view to display. You separate multiple event IDs by commas. Follow the instructions given to specify ranges of event IDs and to exclude event IDs. If you do not specify

event IDs, you can use the drop-down list in Task Category to select the task categories you want to include in the custom view.

4. In Keywords, optionally, select the keywords you want included in the custom view in the drop-down list. In User, enter the name of the user account(s) you want to display. You can enter multiple users by separating them with a comma. In Computer(s), enter the name of the computers you want your custom view to display. After completing these configurations, click OK.

5. Specify a name for the custom view. Optionally, you can add a description. Then click OK.

Exporting a Custom View

You can export custom views as XML files and then import them into other computers by using Event Viewer. This enables you to share custom views between users and computers.

To export a custom view, start Event Viewer and, in the console tree, select the custom view you want to export. In the Actions pane, click Export Custom View and, in the Save As dialog box, select a folder; enter a file name for the exported file and click Save.

If you want to save the custom view and make it accessible only to the currently logged-on user, ensure that the All Users check box is clear and click OK.

Importing a Custom View

You can import custom views as XML files by using Event Viewer. To import a custom view, start Event Viewer and select Import Custom View on the Action menu. Navigate to the location of the exported view, click the corresponding .xml file, and click Open.

In the Import Custom View File dialog box, in Name, enter a name for the imported custom view. In Description, enter a description of the custom view. This does not need to be the same as the description you specified when you created the custom view.

Custom views can be stored in the Custom Views folder or any subfolder of the Custom Views folder. If you want the custom view to be accessible to anyone using the computer, ensure that the All Users check box is selected and click OK. If you want the custom view to be accessible only to the currently logged-on user, ensure that the All Users check box is clear and click OK.

Saving a Filter as a Custom View

If you create a filter by using Filter Displayed Events in Event Viewer and then decide you might want to use it again at a later date, you can save it as a custom view. On the Event Viewer Action menu, click Save Filter As Custom View; specify a name, description, and location; and click OK.

Quick Check

- Which file format do you use when you import and export custom views?

Quick Check Answer

- XML

Locating Events

You can use filters and custom views to find the events in which you are interested from among the very large number of events in the event logs. You can also use Microsoft Power-Shell scripts and command-line utilities to specify and list events. This is especially useful in the Server Core installation, where GUI tools are not available.

You can use PowerShell scripts that contain the *Get-EventLog* cmdlet. This enables you to manage event logs and select events contained within those event logs. For example, the following cmdlet in a PowerShell script returns the four most recent events written to the Application log:

```
Get-EventLog application -newest 4
```

To obtain more detailed information, you can pipe your results into the *Format-List* cmdlet, for example:

```
Get-EventLog application -newest 4 | Format-List
```

You can also pipe events into the *Where-Object* cmdlet; for example, the following command returns all events with Event ID 5811 in the system log:

```
Get-EventLog system | Where-Object {$_.EventID -eq 5811}
```

> **MORE INFO USING *GET-EVENTLOG***
>
> For more information about *Get-EventLog*, see *http://www.microsoft.com/technet /scriptcenter/topics/msh/cmdlets/get-eventlog.mspx* and *http://technet.microsoft.com /en-us/library/bb978657.aspx*.

You can also query the event log in Windows Server 2008 by using the *wevtutil* command-line tool. For example, the following command displays configuration information about the system log in XML format:

```
wevtutil el
```

> **MORE INFO WEVTUTIL**
>
> For more information about *wevtutil*, see *http://technet.microsoft.com/en-us/library /cc732848.aspx*.

Typically, when you are searching for events, the most straightforward criterion to use is Event ID. You can find lists of event IDs on TechNet; for example, you can access a list of IDs for security log events at *http://support.microsoft.com/kb/947226*.

Using Applications and Services Logs

Applications and Services logs are a new category of event logs in Windows Server 2008. They store events from a single application or component. Applications and Services logs include four subtypes: Admin, Operational, Analytic, and Debug.

Events in Admin logs provide you with guidance about how to respond when you are troubleshooting problems. Events in the Operational log help you troubleshoot problems associated with server operations. These events can sometimes be difficult to interpret. Analytic logs store events that trace an issue and frequently log a high volume of events. Developers use Debug logs when debugging applications. Analytic and Debug logs are hidden and disabled by default. Details of these event types are as follows:

- **Admin** Admin events indicate a problem experienced by end users, administrators, and support personnel and provide a well-defined solution on which an administrator can act. For example, an Admin event might occur when an application fails to connect to a printer.

- **Operational** You can use Operational events to analyze and diagnose a problem. They can trigger tools or tasks based on the problem or occurrence. For example, an Operational event occurs when a printer is added or removed from a system.

- **Analytic** Analytic events describe program operation and identify problems that cannot be handled by user intervention.

- **Debug** Developers use Debug events to troubleshoot issues with their programs.

Enabling Analytic and Debug Logs

Typically, you enable Analytic and Debug logs for a specified period to gather troubleshooting data and then disable them again. To do this, you can use either a Windows interface or command-line commands.

To enable Analytic and Debug logs by using Event Viewer, right-click the Analytic or Debug log you want to enable, for example, the Debug log of the encrypting file system (EFS), and then select Properties. Select the Enable Logging check box in the Properties dialog box and click OK to clear the Event Viewer warning dialog box that tells you that Analytic and Debug logs are cleared when they are enabled. The Log Properties dialog box for a Debug log is shown in Figure 10-24. Click OK to close this dialog box.

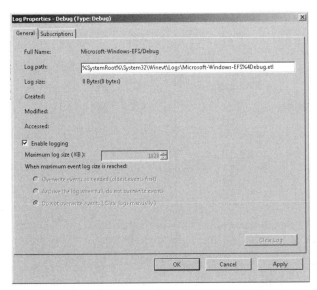

FIGURE 10-24 Enabling logging in the Debug log of the EFS.

You can also enable Analytic and Debug logs by using the command line. At an elevated command prompt, enter:

```
wevtutil sl <logname> /e:true
```

Here, *<logname>* is the name of the log. If this contains spaces, enclose it with quotation marks.

> **NOTE VIEWING ANALYTIC AND DEBUG LOGS**
>
> By default, Analytic and Debug logs are both disabled and hidden. To view them and work with them, start Event Viewer and click the View menu. Select Show Analytic And Debug Logs if it is not selected. If this option has already been selected, a tick will be beside it in the View menu.

Using the DNS Event Viewer

In Windows Server 2008, events compiled from Event Viewer can be immediately accessed through the DNS MMC snap-in, as shown in Figure 10-25. You can set up a filter for DNS events or look in the DNS logs in Windows Events or Applications and Services logs, but access from the DNS snap-in is more convenient.

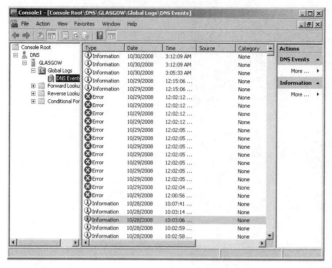

FIGURE 10-25 Viewing DNS events in the DNS MMC snap-in.

If you need more advanced DNS event log diagnosis, you can enable Debug Logging on a per-server basis. Enabling Debug Logging can affect server performance; you should not enable this feature, or keep it enabled, unless you need to. To enable Debug Logging, perform the following procedure:

1. If necessary, open Server Manager.

2. Expand Roles, expand DNS Server, expand DNS Nodes, and then click the name of the DNS server.

3. Right-click the server name and select Properties.

4. On the Debug Logging tab, select Log Packets For Debugging, as shown in Figure 10-26. Click OK.

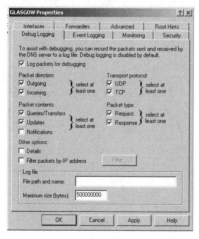

FIGURE 10-26 Enabling Debug Logging.

Adding Tasks to Events

You can configure a task to run when a specific event is logged. You do this by attaching the task to the event. In the Event Viewer console tree, navigate to the log that contains the event and right-click the event. Select Attach Task To This Event, as shown in Figure 10-27.

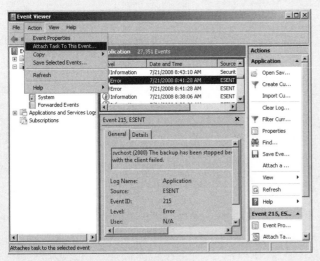

FIGURE 10-27 Attaching a task to an event.

You can then use the Create Basic Task Wizard to create or specify a task to attach to the event. This wizard enables you to schedule a basic task that will run when the specified event is logged. You can create more complex tasks and specify multiple task actions and triggers by clicking Create Task in the Event Viewer Actions pane.

The wizard gives you the option of running a program, sending an e-mail, or sending a message. If you choose to run a program, you can browse to an executable file such as an .exe or .bat file. Optionally, you can specify program arguments and specify a location where the program runs. If you need to configure the task properties, you can select the Open The Dialog Box For This Task When I Click Finish check box before you click Finish.

This is a straightforward procedure, but it has limitations. You cannot assign a task to an event in a saved log, nor can you assign a task to an event in an Analytic or Debug log. The task runs in the context of the user who created it and will not, by default, run if that user is not logged on when it is triggered. This is a severe limitation if you are a system administrator.

Fortunately, the Task Properties dialog box presents you with some powerful configuration tools. On the General tab, shown in Figure 10-28, you can specify Run Whether User Is Logged On Or Not. You can also specify a user or group to use when running the program. You can configure the task to run with highest privileges.

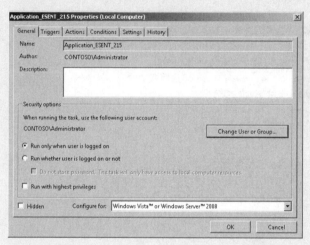

FIGURE 10-28 The General tab of the Task Properties dialog box.

On other tabs, you can add additional triggers and actions and set conditions; for example, the task will run only if the computer has been idle for a specified time or if the computer is running on AC power. You can wake the computer, if (for example) it is hibernating, to run the task, and you can specify that the task runs only if a particular network connection is available.

You can specify that the task runs on demand or, if scheduled, as soon as possible after a scheduled start is missed. You can specify restart conditions if the task fails and the maximum amount of time for which the task can run has expired. You can view a history that tells you when the task was created and when it ran.

You cannot delete an attached task through Event Viewer or the Task Properties dialog box, but, instead, you use the Task Scheduler MMC snap-in as shown in Figure 10-29.

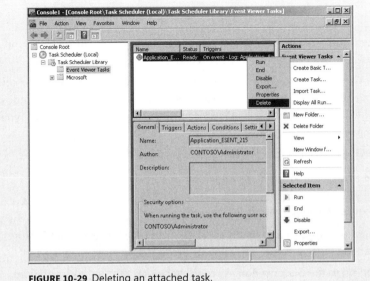

FIGURE 10-29 Deleting an attached task.

Forwarding Events and Creating a Custom View

In this practice, you configure the domain controller Glasgow to retrieve events from the Boston server. You also create a custom view. If you are using virtual servers, both the Glasgow and Boston computers need to be running before you carry out this practice.

EXERCISE 1   Configure a Computer to Collect Events

In this exercise, you configure the Glasgow domain controller to collect events.

1. If necessary, log on to the Glasgow domain controller, using the Kim_Akers account.

2. Open an elevated command prompt.

3. Enter the following command to configure the Windows Event Collector service:

   ```
   wecutil qc
   ```

4. When prompted to change the service startup mode to Delay-Start, type **Y** and press Enter.

EXERCISE 2   Configure a Source Computer

In this exercise, you configure the server Boston so that the collector computer Glasgow can retrieve events from it. You must complete Exercise 1 before carrying out this exercise.

1. Log on to the *contoso.internal* domain at Boston, using the Kim_Akers account.

2. Open an elevated command prompt.

3. Enter the following command to configure the Windows Remote Management service:

```
winrm quickconfig
```

4. When prompted to change the service startup mode, create the WinRM listener, and enable the firewall exception, type **Y**, and press Enter.

5. Verify that the Windows Remote Management service is configured to start automatically by opening Services in the Administrative Tools menu, checking that the Windows Remote Management (WS-Management) service is started, and that the Startup Type is set to Automatic (Delayed Start).

6. Enter the following command to grant Glasgow access to the event log on Boston:

```
net localgroup "Event Log Readers" Glasgow@contoso.internal /add
```

EXERCISE 3   Configure an Event Subscription

In this exercise, you create an event subscription on Glasgow to gather events from Boston. Complete Exercise 1 and Exercise 2 before carrying out this exercise.

1. If necessary, log on to the Glasgow domain controller, using the Kim_Akers account, and open Server Manager.

2. In Server Manager, expand Diagnostics, expand Event Viewer, right-click Subscriptions, and select Create Subscription.

3. If prompted, click Yes in the Event Viewer dialog box to configure the Windows Event Collector service.

   Note that you should not see this dialog box if you correctly configured Glasgow to receive events.

4. The Subscription Properties dialog box appears. In the Subscription Name box, type **MyNewSubscription**.

5. Click the Select Computers button. In the Computers dialog box, click Add Domain Computers. Type **Boston** and click OK.

6. In the Computers dialog box, click Test. Click OK when Event Viewer verifies connectivity. Click OK to close the Computers dialog box.

7. Click the Select Events button. In the Query Filter dialog box, select the Error, Critical, Warning, and Information check boxes. Select By Source. Click the Event Sources list and select Kernel-General.

   Your Query Filter dialog box should look similar to Figure 10-30.

8. Click OK.

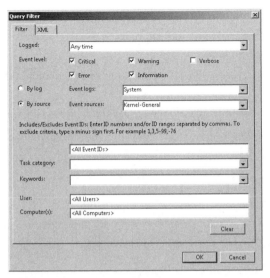

FIGURE 10-30 A configured Query Filter dialog box.

9. Click the Advanced button to open the Advanced Subscription Settings dialog box. Note that it is configured to use Machine Account by default.

This works because you have added the Glasgow computer's domain account to the Boston computer's Event Log Readers local group. Also note that the subscription is configured by default to use Normal Event Delivery Optimization, using the HTTP protocol. The dialog box should look similar to Figure 10-31.

10. Click OK.

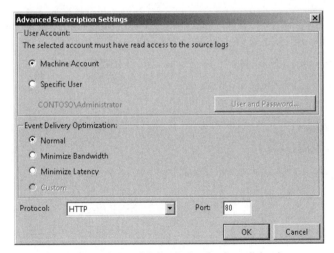

FIGURE 10-31 The Advanced Subscription Settings dialog box.

11. In the Subscription Properties dialog box, click OK.

12. To generate a Kernel event on Boston, log on to Boston, using the Kim_Akers account (if necessary) and change the system time.

13. Open Event Viewer and check the System log. You should see an Information event with a source of Kernel-General.

14. If necessary, log on to the Glasgow domain controller, using the Kim_Akers account.

15. Open Event Viewer and select the Forwarded Events log. The Kernel-General Information event should be stored in this log after, at most, 15 minutes.

EXERCISE 4   Create a Custom View

In this exercise, you specify filter conditions and save the filter as a custom view.

1. If necessary, log on to the Glasgow domain controller, using the Kim_Akers account.

2. Open Event Viewer.

3. On the Action menu, select Create Custom View.

   The Custom View dialog box appears.

4. To filter events based upon when they occurred, select the corresponding time period from the Logged drop-down list.

   You have the options of Last Hour, Last 24 Hours, Last 7 Days, Last 30 Days, or Custom Range. If you choose Custom Range, you can specify the earliest date and time from which you want to display events and the latest date and time from which you want to display events in the Custom Range dialog box.

5. Choose Last 24 Hours.

6. In Event Level, select the Critical and Error check boxes.

7. You can specify either the event logs or the event sources of the events that will appear in the custom view. Choose By Log and select Windows Logs.

8. In Event IDs, specify a range from 4624 through 4634 (type **4624-4634**).

   If you specify Event IDs, Task Category is grayed out.

9. In Keywords, specify All Keywords.

10. In User, enter **Kim_Akers**.

11. In Computer(s), enter **Glasgow**.

   Your configured Custom View dialog box should look similar to Figure 10-32.

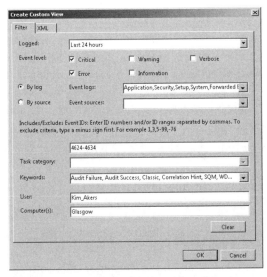

FIGURE 10-32 A configured Custom View dialog box.

12. Click OK.

13. In the Save Filter To Custom View dialog box, in Name, type **MyCustomView**.

14. In Description, type **Trial Custom View**. Click OK.

The Custom View you have created is now in Event Viewer, as shown in Figure 10-33. If you want to, you can export this and import it to other computers as described earlier in this lesson. Note that you can access preconfigured custom views by expanding Server Roles under Custom Views.

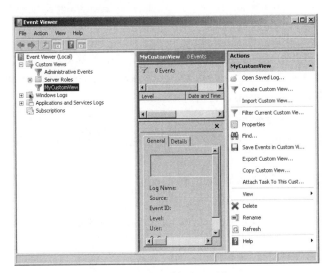

FIGURE 10-33 A Custom View listed in Event Viewer.

Lesson Summary

- Event forwarding transfers events that match a specified filter from one or more source computers to a collector computer. To use event forwarding, configure both the collector and source computers. Then you can configure the event subscription on the collector computer. In collector-initiated subscriptions, you configure the computers manually. In source-initiated subscriptions, you can use Group Policy to configure domain-based source computers.

- You can save an event filter as a custom view. This enables you to reuse it if you need to filter more events.

- Applications and Services logs are a new category of event logs in Windows Server 2008. They store events from a single application or component.

Lesson Review

You can use the following questions to test your knowledge of the information in Lesson 2, "Monitoring Event Logs." The questions are also available on the companion DVD if you prefer to review them in electronic form.

> **NOTE ANSWERS**
>
> Answers to these questions and explanations of why each answer choice is right or wrong are located in the "Answers" section at the end of the book.

1. You have configured a Windows Server 2008 server named Glasgow to collect events from a Windows Server 2008 server named Boston. Both computers are in the same domain. You configured the event subscriptions by selecting the default options for event delivery optimization and using the HTTP protocol. You are not collecting events from the Security Event log. You find that the subscriptions do not work. Which of the following actions would you carry out to ensure that events on Boston are collected by Glasgow? (Choose three. Each correct answer presents part of a complete solution.)

   A. Enter the *winrm quickconfig* command on Glasgow.

   B. Enter the *wecutil qc* command on Glasgow.

   C. Add the computer account for Glasgow to the local Event Log Readers group on Boston.

   D. Enter the *winrm quickconfig* command on Boston.

   E. Enter the *wecutil qc* command on Boston.

   F. Add the computer account for Boston to the local Event Log Readers group on Glasgow.

2. You are configuring a Windows Server 2008 server named Glasgow to retrieve events from a computer, running Microsoft Vista, named Melbourne. Both computers are in the *contoso.internal* domain. Which of the following commands would you run on the collector computer to configure the Event Collector service?

   A. *wecutil qc*

   B. *winrm quickconfig*

   C. *net localgroup "Event Log Readers" Glasgow$@contoso.internal /add*

   D. *%SYSTEMROOT%\System32\gpedit.msc*

3. You have created a subscription called Disk Problems. You need to configure this subscription to update every five minutes. Which commands should you enter? (Choose two. Each correct answer presents part of a complete solution.)

   A. *wecutil gs "Disk Problems" /hi:300*

   B. *wecutil gs "Disk Problems" /hi:300000*

   C. *wecutil gs "Disk Problems" /cm:custom*

   D. *wecutil ss "Disk Problems" /cm:custom*

   E. *wecutil ss "Application Failures" /hi:300*

   F. *wecutil ss "Application Failures" /hi:300000*

4. Your network is experiencing problems when you install or remove printers. You open Event Viewer and access the Applications and Services logs. You need to determine when printers were installed or removed and diagnose any problems that occurred. You also need to know whether applications failed to connect to printers. What event types should you search for? (Choose two. Each correct answer presents part of a complete solution.)

   A. Admin

   B. Operational

   C. Analytic

   D. Debug

Chapter Review

To further practice and reinforce the skills you learned in this chapter, you can perform the following tasks:

- Review the chapter summary.
- Complete the case scenarios. These scenarios set up real-world situations involving the topics of this chapter and ask you to create solutions.
- Complete the suggested practices.
- Take a practice test.

Chapter Summary

- Performance Monitor displays performance counters in real time or log files, created when you run a data collector set, that enable you to gather information about a computer's current state for later analysis. Reliability Monitor gives an indication of system stability and records application installations and failures.

- You can use Event Forwarding and event subscriptions to gather event information from a number of source computers and view this information on one collector computer. You can save event filters as custom views and access Applications and Services logs that store events from a single application or component.

Case Scenarios

In the following case scenarios, you apply what you've learned about monitoring performance and events. You can find answers to these questions in the "Answers" section at the end of this book.

Case Scenario 1: Troubleshooting a Performance Problem

You are a network administrator at Tailspin Toys. Recently, users have been experiencing intermittent performance problems when accessing a file server. You check resource usage on the file server by using Task Manager and Resource View, but you see no indication of excessive processor, memory, disk, or network resource usage. You need to monitor these resources over a period of time rather than look at a real-time snapshot. You need to monitor resources both when the performance problems are occurring and when they are not. Answer the following questions:

1. How can you generate performance logs that help you analyze disk, network, processor, and memory resource usage both when the problem is occurring and when performance is normal?

2. You suspect memory could be coming under stress due to a leaky application. What performance counters should you include in a data collector set to record memory usage specifically?

3. You know roughly when problems started to occur. How do you check what applications were installed or upgraded at that time?

Case Scenario 2: Monitoring Computers for Low Disk Space

You are a domain administrator employed by Northwind Traders. Recently, a number of your users have had problems downloading files and e-mail because the space on their local disks had reached a critical limit. You want to create a proactive method of identifying low disk space problems on client computers on your network so you can ask your desktop support technicians to free disk space on client computers before critical limits are reached. Answer the following questions:

1. How do you monitor client computers for low disk space events?

2. Which client operating systems can you monitor?

Case Scenario 3: Setting Up a Source-Initiated Subscription

You are an administrator at Blue Sky Airlines. Blue Sky has recently upgraded all its servers and domain controllers to Windows Server 2008. Blue Sky has made extensive use of virtual servers, Server Core installations, and RODCs whenever appropriate but has retained its single Active Directory domain structure.

You want to configure a server with Server Core installation to act as an event collector computer, but you still do not know exactly which computers will be event sources. You therefore need to set up a source-initiated subscription on that server. You log on at the server and open an elevated command prompt. Answer the following questions:

1. What command do you enter to configure Windows Remote Management?

2. What command do you enter to configure the Event Collector service?

3. What type of file do you need to create to hold the subscription configuration?

4. What command do you enter to create the source-initiated subscription?

Suggested Practices

To master the Monitoring and Managing a Network Infrastructure exam objective successfully, complete the following tasks.

Capture Performance Data

Complete all practices in this section.

- **Practice 1** A very large number of performance counters exist, and you are unlikely to be familiar with them all. However, you should investigate the more commonly used counters, and the best way of doing so is to use the Performance Monitor tool. A good starting point is the article at *http://technet.microsoft.com/en-us/magazine/cc718984 .aspx*.

- **Practice 2**   Run each standard data collector set and analyze the report each one generates.

- **Practice 3**   If you have access to any computers that have been running for some time (for example, more than a month), run Reliability Monitor on these computers and assess their stability indices. Try to identify the causes of any stability problems.

- **Practice 4**   Create a data collector set that logs counter values that can identify memory problems.

Monitor Event Logs

Complete Practices 1 and 2. Practice 3 is optional.

- **Practice 1**   Configure a source computer to transfer events to a collector computer. Practice using all three bandwidth optimization techniques. Use *wecutil* to customize the event forwarding configuration and reduce the time required to forward events.

- **Practice 2**   If you have access to a production network, examine the event logs on several client computers and identify events that could indicate problems. Configure the client computers to forward events to a central server and monitor the central event log. In this case, use a source-initiated subscription and configure the source computers by using Group Policy.

- **Practice 3**   Configure event filters and save them as custom views. Experiment with Applications and Services logs and look at the four types of events these can hold. Deliberately induce faults on your test network (for example, switch off a printer) and determine which events are recorded.

Take a Practice Test

The practice tests on this book's companion DVD offer many options. For example, you can test yourself on just one exam objective, or you can test yourself on all the upgrade examination content. You can set up the test so that it closely simulates the experience of taking a certification exam, or you can set it up in study mode so that you can look at the correct answers and explanations after you answer each question.

> **MORE INFO**   **PRACTICE TESTS**
>
> For details about all the practice test options available, see the "How to Use the Practice Tests" section in this book's Introduction.

CHAPTER 11

Server Deployment and Activation

There is a growing trend away from using physical media to install operating systems. Just over a decade ago, it was normal to install a server's operating system from diskette. Today, it is increasingly common for server operating system deployment to occur automatically over the network. This is possible because most network adapters support Preboot Execution Environment (PXE), a technology that enables a computer to receive a network address and retrieve a stripped-down operating system that it can load from a server located on the network. This stripped-down operating system environment, in turn, works as a platform to begin the installation of a more fully featured operating system such as Windows Server 2008. In this chapter, you learn how to set up Windows Server 2008 so that you can deploy future servers remotely over the network. You also learn how to use volume license keys to simplify the process of activating large numbers of computers.

Exam objectives in this chapter

- Deploy images by using Windows Deployment Services.
- Configure Microsoft Windows activation.

Lessons in this chapter:

Before You Begin

To complete the lessons in this chapter, you must have done the following:

- Installed and configured the evaluation edition of Windows Server 2008 Enterprise Edition in accordance with the instructions listed in the Introduction.

 REAL WORLD

Orin Thomas

The first class I took when I was learning to administer Microsoft Windows NT 4.0 involved a section on remotely deploying servers that my instructor, no matter how hard he tried, was completely unable to get working (which, as an aside, is why, when I talk at events such as Tech.ED, I like to use full screen recordings). Like many systems administrators, I was initially a little uncomfortable with remotely imaging servers. Client computers? Sure. A pack-'em and stack-'em approach seemed fine. However, servers are mission critical, and some part of me always felt that an administrator should be as hands-on as possible, not just performing the installation but crafting it, attempting to attain the best result possible. If a client goes down, it inconveniences one person. If a server goes down, it inconveniences everyone. The argument about crafting a server install today is a little harder to make, though, because even if you are sitting in front of the server console during the entire Windows Server 2008 installation routine, the amount of direct interaction required is minimal. Unattended installation files work a lot better and provide a consistent result. I am glad that I will never again have to swap driver diskettes for operating systems diskettes or try to get the driver for some unusual 10Base2 Ethernet card working from a boot disk.

Lesson 1: Deploying and Activating Windows Server 2008

Windows Deployment Services (WDS) enables you to deploy operating systems to client computers without performing a traditional install from media (IFM) such as from a DVD-ROM. With Windows Deployment Services, you can automate the installation process fully, so that all you need to do with the server hardware is switch it on. You can configure everything centrally, from the setup of a server's disk drives to the installation of custom hardware drivers. You can use volume activation keys to simplify the process of activating computers in your environment. Rather than using a unique key for each computer, you can use a single key to activate all computers. In this lesson, you learn how to configure both these technologies to simplify the deployment of Windows Server 2008 in your own organization's environment.

> **After this lesson, you will be able to:**
> - Configure WDS.
> - Capture WDS images.
> - Configure activation keys.
>
> **Estimated lesson time: 40 minutes**

Unattended Installations

Answer files are XML-based files that enable you to answer setup questions such as how to configure network adapters, how hard disk drives are to be partitioned, what product key to use, and the location of the Windows Server 2008 installation files. You can create answer files by using Windows System Image Manager (Windows SIM). Windows SIM is included with the Windows Automated Installation Kit (Windows AIK or WAIK), which you can download from the Microsoft Web site. Figure 11-1 shows how you can use Windows System Image Manager to add a section to the autounattend.xml answer file that automatically joins the computer to a domain with a specific set of credentials. Note that any credentials you provide for the answer file are not encrypted, so when deploying in a production environment, use an account that has been delegated only the necessary rights.

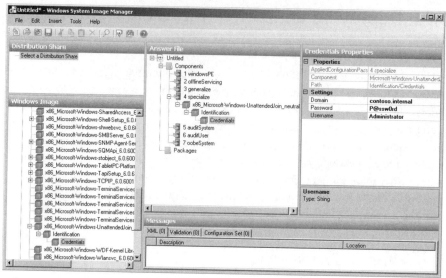

FIGURE 11-1 Configuring the answer file to join the computer to a domain.

MORE INFO   **DOWNLOAD WAIK**

You can download Windows Automated Installation Kit for Windows Vista SP1 and Windows Server 2008 from the following address on the Microsoft Web site: *http://go.microsoft.com/fwlink/?LinkId=79385*.

The Windows Server 2008 installation routine automatically checks all of a computer's local volumes, including any connected USB storage devices, for a file called autounattend. xml. If you want to use an autounattend.xml file that you have stored on a network share, you must boot into the Windows PE environment, make a connection to the network share, and then use the *setup.exe /unattend:z:\autounattend.xml* command (where *z:* is the path of the mapped network drive). Later in this lesson, you learn how to configure Windows Deployment Services to provide autounattend.xml automatically to computers installed over the network.

Windows Deployment Services

Windows Deployment Services (WDS) is a server role you can add to computers running Windows Server 2008 that enables you to perform network deployments of Windows Server 2008, and other operating systems such as Windows Vista, to computers that have PXE-compliant network cards. WDS is able to use multicast transmissions, which means that you can use WDS to deploy Windows Server 2008 to multiple computers at the same time. You can interact normally with the Windows Server 2008 installation or provide WDS with an autounattend.xml file so that the entire installation can occur over the network without requiring any intervention on your part.

NOTE COMPUTERS WITHOUT PXE-COMPLIANT NETWORK CARDS

You cannot use WDS directly with computers that do not have PXE-compliant network cards. You can get around this limitation by using discover images, which are covered later in this chapter.

There are two types of WDS servers, WDS deployment servers and WDS transport servers. You can install a WDS deployment server only on a computer that is a member of an Active Directory domain. WDS deployment servers require both Domain Name System (DNS) and Dynamic Host Configuration Protocol (DHCP) to be available on the network. After a WDS deployment server is installed, it must be authorized in Active Directory Domain Services (AD DS), similarly to how a DHCP server must also be authorized. You can authorize a WDS server from the Windows Deployment Services console or by using the *wdsutil.exe* utility.

MORE INFO WDSUTIL.EXE

To learn more about managing WDS from the command line, see the following TechNet document: *http://technet.microsoft.com/en-us/library/cc771206.aspx*.

WDS transport servers provide the core networking functionality of WDS, enabling administrators to create multicast namespaces and deploy operating system images from a server that is not a member of an Active Directory domain. Unlike WDS deployment servers, transport servers do not require AD DS, DHCP, or DNS to be present on the network. They are generally used to deploy images to clients in workgroup environments. When you install a WDS deployment server, the WDS transport server components are included automatically. Transport servers do not include the management tools that WDS deployment servers include and are managed using *wdsutil.exe*.

MORE INFO TRANSPORT SERVERS

To learn more about WDS transport servers, see the following TechNet document: *http://technet.microsoft.com/en-us/library/cc771645.aspx*.

NOTE SERVER CORE AND WDS

The WDS role cannot be deployed to a computer that uses the Server Core installation option.

If you deploy WDS on a computer that also functions as a DHCP server, you must perform additional configuration to ensure that the WDS PXE server does not conflict with the existing DHCP server. You can perform this configuration by editing the WDS server properties, as shown in Figure 11-2. The first step is to configure the WDS server not to listen for traffic on port 67. The second is to configure DHCP scope option 60. Although it is possible to configure

DHCP scope option 60 through the DHCP console, it is simpler to perform this task through the WDS console. You can also configure this option by issuing the *wdsutil.exe /Set-Server /UseDHCPPorts:no /DHCPoption60:yes* command.

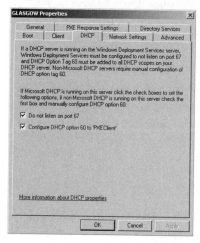

FIGURE 11-2 Configuring WDS and DHCP to coexist.

Importing and Creating Images

When configuring a WDS server, Microsoft recommends that you store images on volumes other than the system volume. WDS images are stored in image groups, which saves space when configuring WDS to deploy multiple versions of the operating system. For example, image groups enable you to store Windows Server 2008 Standard and Enterprise as well as the Server Core installation options in a single file. WDS uses four types of images. These are:

- **Boot images**   Boot images contain Windows PE and the WDS client. These images are transmitted across the network to the target client and allow the computer to boot into a minimal environment so that deployment of the operating system image can occur. A file named boot.wim is located in the \sources directory of the Windows Server 2008 installation media. This file can function as a boot image for WDS. You can also create custom boot images by using the WAIK tool, which was mentioned earlier in this chapter. You can add a boot image to WDS, using the WDS console or by using the *wdsutil.exe /Add-Image /ImageFile:Path_To_File\boot.wim /ImageType:Boot* command, where Path_To_File is the path to the boot.wim file.

- **Install images**   Install images are operating system images that WDS deploys to clients. In the practice at the end of the lesson, you load a Windows Server 2008 operating system image from the Windows Server 2008 installation media. You can add an install image to WDS, using the WDS console or the *wdsutil.exe /Add-Image /ImageFile:Path_To_File\install.wim /ImageType:install /ImageGroupName:Name* command. The install images for Windows Server 2008 are located in the install.wim file in the Sources directory on the Windows Server 2008 installation media. If you are attempting to import a spanned image in file.swm format, you must use ImageX to merge it into a .wim file.

- **Discover images** Discover images are loaded onto optical media or removable USB devices and enable non-PXE–compliant computers to boot so that operating systems can be deployed to them through WDS. You can create static discover images that are tied to a particular WDS server or dynamic images that will emulate the PXE process and locate any available WDS server.

- **Capture images** Capture images are bootable images that contain both Windows PE and the Windows Deployment Services Image Capture Wizard. This enables you to boot a computer that has been prepared with Sysprep so that you can capture an image of that computer and save it as a .wim file for use on a WDS server.

It is also possible to capture images by using other tools, such as ImageX, and to modify them with tools such as Windows System Image Manager. ImageX has some additional functionality that the image capture wizard does not have, although the image capture wizard enables you to upload captured images automatically on the WDS server, something that must be done manually when using ImageX.

If you want to limit which users can deploy specific install images, you can configure access control lists (ACLs) at both the image group level and the individual image level. You can do this using the WDS console or the *wdsutil.exe* utility.

> **MORE INFO** **WORKING WITH IMAGES**
>
> To learn more about creating, filtering, and using images, see the following page on Tech-Net: *http://technet.microsoft.com/en-us/library/cc731843.aspx*.

Configuring Deployment

You can configure WDS to use a multicast transmission to deploy a single install image to multiple computers. As Figure 11-3 shows, you can configure an auto-cast, which begins the transmission immediately, or configure a scheduled-cast in which you specify settings such as the number of clients that must connect prior to beginning the transmission, a time and date for the transmission to begin, or both. You can configure a multicast deployment to throttle the bandwidth it uses by selecting a network profile on the Network Settings tab of the WDS server's properties. The available profiles are 10 Mbps, 100 Mbps, 1 Gbps, and Custom. You can also throttle bandwidth by modifying the *HKLM\System\CurrentControlSet\Services \WDSServer\Providers\WDSMC\Profiles\Custom\TPMaxBandwidth* registry key and setting the value to the percent of available bandwidth that the server will use.

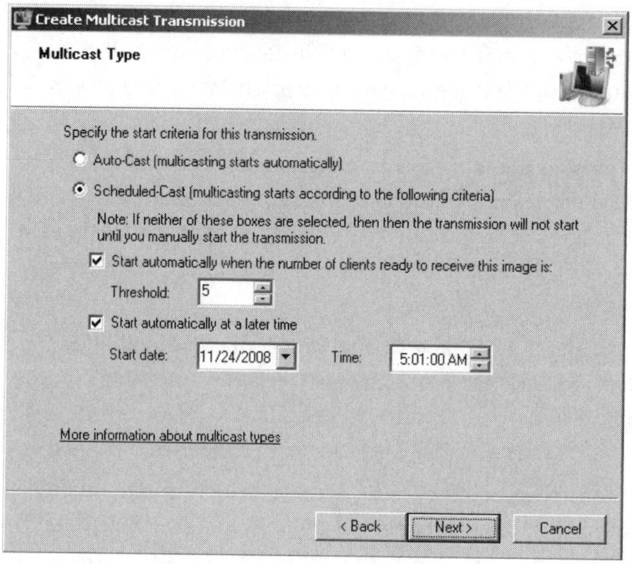

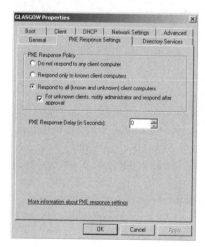

FIGURE 11-3 Configuring a multicast transmission.

You can configure how the WDS server responds to clients by configuring the PXE Response Settings tab of the server properties, as shown in Figure 11-4. The options are to disable WDS by having it not respond to any clients; to respond only to known client computers, where a known client has been pre-staged in AD DS; or to respond to all computers, with the option of notifying the administrator for approval. The PXE Response Delay setting enables you to configure certain PXE servers to respond after others in environments in which you have multiple servers.

FIGURE 11-4 The PXE Response Settings tab.

You can pre-stage client computers by using the *wdsutil.exe /Add-Device /Device: ComputerName /ID:<MAC Address>* command. You cannot pre-stage client computers by using the WDS console. You can use Active Directory Users and Computers to pre-stage client computers, if you know their GUID, by simply adding a new computer account and specifying the GUID. Alternatively, you can enable the auto-add policy so that when you approve the installation of an unknown client, a computer account will be created automatically within AD DS for the client. You can do this on the PXE Response Settings tab of the WDS server properties, as mentioned earlier in the lesson, or by issuing the *wdsutil.exe /Set-Server /AutoAddPolicy /Policy:AdminApproval* command.

You can use the Client tab of the WDS server properties to specify the location of answer files to be used for network deployment, as shown in Figure 11-5. Answer files are based on architecture, and you can specify an answer file for x86, ia64, and x64 processor architectures. If you do not specify an answer file, you must interact with the installation as you would if you were performing it in a traditional manner.

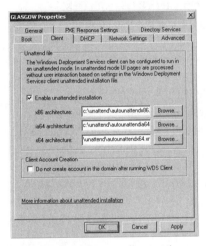

FIGURE 11-5 WDS server client settings.

MORE INFO   CONFIGURING DEPLOYMENT

To learn more about configuring deployments, see the following TechNet document: *http://technet.microsoft.com/en-us/library/cc732529.aspx.*

EXAM TIP

Remember which steps you must perform to configure the WDS role and DHCP roles when they are located on the same server.

✔ **Quick Check**

1. Which DHCP option must you configure if the WDS server and the DHCP role are collocated on the same server?

2. What is the name of the unattended installation file that you can use with Windows Server 2008?

Quick Check Answers

1. DHCP option 60

2. autounattend.xml

Activation of Windows Server 2008

Most IT professionals are familiar with two types of activation key, original equipment manager (OEM) keys and retail keys. OEM keys are tied to a computer's BIOS. With OEM keys, the vendor usually activates Windows prior to you deploying the computer in your environment, or activation occurs immediately after you first boot and configure the computer. Retail keys come with editions of Windows Server 2008 that you purchase. Retail keys must be manually configured and, in all but a few circumstances, apply only to a single computer. You must activate a retail key within a 30-day period after you perform initial installation.

If you did not enter a product key during the installation process, you can activate Windows Server 2008 by opening System in Control Panel and clicking Change Product Key. This opens the Windows Activation dialog box shown in Figure 11-6. You enter the product key and then either activate Windows over the Internet or, if your computer is not directly connected to the Internet, call a Microsoft clearinghouse operator by using a telephone.

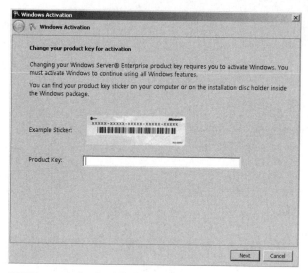

FIGURE 11-6 Activating Windows Server 2008.

You activate Server Core installations of Windows Server 2008 by using the *slmgr.vbs* command-line utility. You can also use this utility to activate a traditional installation of Windows Server 2008. You can use *slmgr.vbs* to manage license keys on remote computers running Windows Server 2008. *Slmgr.vbs* works in the following way:

- *Slmgr.vbs* with the *–ipk* option installs a new product key. This new product key will replace any existing product key configured for the server.
- *Slmgr.vbs* with the *–ato* option initiates the Activation process, which can be performed over the Internet or by telephoning a Microsoft clearinghouse operator.
- *Slmgr.vbs* with the *–skms* option specifies the name and port of the Key Management Service (KMS) computer the server will use for licensing. KMS is covered in more detail later in this lesson.

In enterprise environments, you can use volume activation keys, which enable you to activate a large number of computers with a single key. Volume activation keys are better suited to the needs of enterprises because you can use them with technologies such as WDS, which was covered earlier in this lesson. There are two types of volume activation keys, the Multiple Activation Key (MAK) and the Key Management Service key. You learn about the functionality of each type of key, and why you would choose one type of key over another, throughout the rest of this lesson.

> **MORE INFO** **VOLUME ACTIVATION OVERVIEW**
>
> To learn more about volume activation, see the following guide on TechNet: *http://technet .microsoft.com/en-us/library/cc303274.aspx.*

Key Management Service Keys

You can use KMS keys to activate computers automatically without requiring a direct or indirect connection to the Internet. When deploying KMS, you install a single key on a computer that is known as the KMS host (sometimes called the KMS server). A KMS client activates against a KMS host. You do need to activate the KMS host computer with Microsoft, although it is possible to do this either over the Internet or by calling a Microsoft clearinghouse operator. This means that you can deploy KMS as a volume activation solution on networks that are completely isolated from the Internet.

You can use KMS keys only in environments in which you have deployed five or more computers running Windows Server 2008 on physical hardware. KMS must receive activation requests from at least five physically deployed computers running Windows Server 2008 to remain functional. Virtual machines hosted under Hyper-V or another virtualization solution do not count toward this total, although virtual machines themselves can be KMS clients. The KMS host also does not count toward this total, although the KMS host can be a virtual machine. If your environment will not have the required number of physical servers, consider using MAKs as an alternative volume activation solution.

NOTE **CLIENT NUMBERS AND KMS KEYS**

Although the upgrade exam concentrates on Windows Server 2008, note that it is also possible to use KMS if you have deployed 25 physical client computers running Windows Vista. You can use a computer running Windows Server 2008 as a KMS host server and use Windows Server 2008 KMS keys to activate computers running Windows Vista client.

Unlike the activation of a retail key which, when activated, remains activated unless there is a substantial change in hardware configuration, KMS clients must reactivate against the KMS host at least once every 180 days. KMS clients that are unable to contact a KMS host after 210 days (180 days plus a 30-day grace period) will go into reduced functionality mode. This makes the availability of the KMS host critical to an organization's ability to use its computers.

To configure a KMS host, you must install the KMS key by using the *slmgr.vbs –ipk* command, which you learned about earlier in this lesson. Instead of specifying a retail key, you instead specify the KMS key that you have received from Microsoft as part of your organization's volume licensing agreement. You then perform the activation process, either by issuing the *slmgr.vbs –ato* command if connected to the Internet or, if attempting activation on an isolated network, using the *slui.exe* command to activate over the telephone.

Communication between KMS clients and the KMS host occurs over TCP port 1688. If you have deployed KMS clients on a perimeter network, you must ensure that they can communicate with a KMS server through any intervening firewalls. KMS clients can use two methods to locate a KMS host. When you configure a KMS host, it will automatically attempt to update DNS with a service (SRV) record named _vlmcs._TCP that points to the KMS host. Microsoft Windows 2000 Server, Microsoft Windows Server 2003, and Windows Server 2008 DNS servers support these SRV records. If the KMS client is unable to obtain the KMS host's location successfully through DNS, you can specify the location manually by running the *slmgr.vbs –skms kms.host.address* command on the KMS client. The address can be either the IP address or the DNS name of the KMS host computer.

Multiple Activation Key

MAKs are generally used in environments with fewer than 25 computers. When you purchase MAK keys, you purchase them for a specific number of activations. If you need to activate more computers than you have activations available, you must either purchase an additional MAK or contact Microsoft and purchase additional activations for your existing MAK. You can install MAKs manually in the same way that you install retail keys or, in larger deployments, you can use a tool such as the Volume Activation Management Tool (VAMT) to deploy a MAK remotely to computers. You can use a MAK in both a domain and a workgroup environment.

The advantage of using a MAK over KMS is that after you perform the activation process, Windows Server 2008 stays activated and does not need to contact a server on a regular basis. As is the case with retail keys, if the hardware configuration of a computer changes significantly, you must perform reactivation. Good record keeping is essential when using MAKs.

The VAMT can assist in this process, but record keeping is one reason many larger organizations choose KMS for volume activation.

NOTE DEPLOYING BOTH TYPES OF VOLUME LICENSE KEY

You can deploy both types of volume license key in a single environment. Many organizations use KMS at sites with large numbers of computers and MAK keys at branch office sites with small numbers of computers.

The VAMT, shown in Figure 11-7, enables you to configure and activate computers remotely, using MAKs. The VAMT can scan AD DS or a range of IP addresses to determine the activation state of computers on your network and which type of key (OEM, Retail, MAK, or KMS) computers are licensed with. You can use one of two methods with the VAMT to activate computers, Independent Activation and Proxy Activation. You must create a Windows Management Instrumentation (WMI) firewall exception so that computers that will have keys installed and which will be activated can be contacted by the computer with VAMT installed.

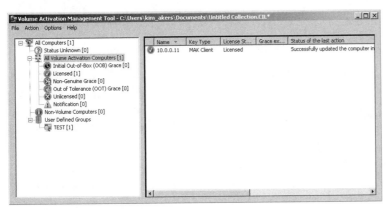

FIGURE 11-7 Volume Activation Management Tool.

MAK Independent Activation enables you to distribute a MAK to computers on the network. Independent Activation requires all computers to be members of the same Active Directory environment and able to connect to the Internet. You use the VAMT console to select the specific computers on which you want to perform the Independent Activation process. During Independent Activation, any existing activation key is overwritten with the MAK supplied to the VAMT. After the MAK is installed, activation over the Internet occurs. It is possible not to force activation during this process, but Windows will attempt automatic Internet activation when the grace period expires.

MAK Proxy Activation enables you to perform volume activation for computers that do not have a direct connection to the Internet. You can do this using two computers with VAMT installed or just one. One computer is present on the network isolated from the Internet, and another computer with VAMT installed is connected to the Internet. You export and import activation data, using removable media between the computers, allowing the computers to be activated. You can also do this with a single computer, removing it from the isolated network and connecting it to the Internet as required, and you can use the VAMT to perform reactivation on computers on which you have reinstalled the operating system after performing proxy activation. You can do this only if the reactivation is attempted from the same computer with VAMT installed that performed the original proxy activation.

You can also use VAMT to install and activate KMS client keys, configuring the KMS client to discover the KMS server automatically, using DNS or specifying the KMS server manually. In this scenario, none of the computers need to be able to contact the Internet, although the WMI exception still must exist for VAMT to configure the target computers.

> **MORE INFO** **VAMT**
>
> You can download the VAMT for free from the following address: *http://www*
> *.microsoft.com/downloads/details.aspx?familyid=12044DD8-1B2C-4DA4-A530*
> *-80F26F0F9A99&displaylang=en*.

EXAM TIP

Remember the reasons for which you would choose one type of activation key over another.

PRACTICE **Deploying Windows Deployment Services**

In this practice, you perform tasks similar to those you would perform when deploying and configuring a Windows Server 2008 WDS server in a production environment. In the first exercise, you install WDS. In the second exercise, you add images and configure a multicast deployment.

EXERCISE 1 Install WDS

In this exercise, you install the Windows Deployment Services role on server Glasgow and perform several preliminary configuration tasks.

1. Log on to server Glasgow with the Kim_Akers user account.
2. Open the Server Manager console and verify whether the DHCP server role has been installed. If the DHCP server role has not been installed, perform Exercise 1 in Lesson 2 of Chapter 1. After the DHCP role has been installed, proceed to step 3.
3. Open the DHCP console from the Administrative Tools menu.
4. Right-click the IPv4 node under the Glasgow.contoso.internal node, and then select New Scope.

   This opens the New Scope Wizard.

5. Click Next. On the Scope Name page, type **WDS Scope**, and then click Next.

6. Configure the IP Address range page as shown in Figure 11-8, and then click Next.

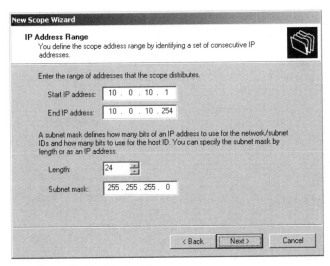

FIGURE 11-8 Configuring IP Address range.

7. Click Next on the Add Exclusions and Lease Duration pages. On the Configure DHCP Options page, ensure that No, I Will Configure These Options Later is selected, and then click Next. Click Finish to dismiss the wizard, and then close the DHCP console.

8. Open the Server Manager console from the Administrative Tools menu. Right-click the Roles node, and then select Add Roles to open the Add Roles Wizard. On the Before You Begin page, click Next.

9. On the Select Server Roles page, select the Windows Deployment Services check box, and then click Next. Review the Things To Note page, and then click Next.

10. On the Role Services page, ensure that both the Deployment Server and Transport Server check boxes are selected, as shown in Figure 11-9, click Next, and then click Install.

The Windows Deployment Services role is installed.

11. When the installation completes, close the Add Roles Wizard.

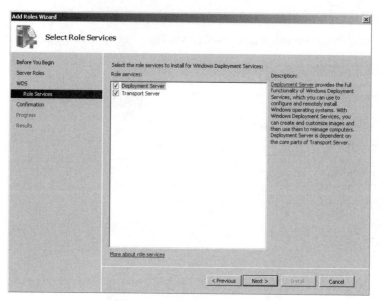

FIGURE 11-9 The Select Role Services page.

12. Open the Windows Deployment Services console from the Administrative Tools menu. Click Continue to dismiss the User Account Control dialog box.

13. In the Windows Deployment Services console, expand the Servers node. Right-click server Glasgow.contoso.internal, and then select Configure Server.

14. Click Next on the Welcome page of the Windows Deployment Services Configuration Wizard.

15. On the Remote Installation Folder Location page, verify that c:\RemoteInstall is selected, and then click Next. Review the System Volume Warning, and then click Yes.

16. On the DHCP Option 60 page, select both the Do Not Listen On Port 67 and Configure DHCP Option 60 to "PXEClient" check boxes, as shown in Figure 11-10, and then click Next.

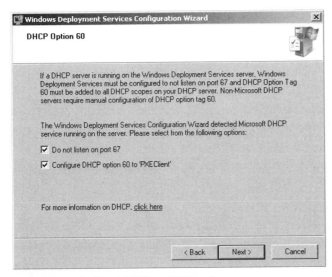

FIGURE 11-10 Configure DHCP and PXE options.

17. On the PXE Server Initial Settings page, select Respond To All (Known And Unknown) Client Computers. Also select the For Unknown Clients, Notify Administrator And Respond After Approval check box, and then click Finish.

The Windows Deployment Services Configuration Wizard will now configure WDS and complete.

18. On the Configuration Complete page, clear the Add Images To The Windows Deployment Server Now check box, and then click Finish.

19. Close the Windows Deployment Services console.

EXERCISE 2   Configure WDS

In this exercise, you add images to the WDS server, and then configure a multicast transmission.

1. Ensure that you are logged on to server Glasgow with the Kim_Akers user account.

2. Verify that the Windows Server 2008 installation media is accessible in your optical media drive and that you have at least 2 gigabytes of free storage space on volume C.

3. Open the Windows Deployment Services console from the Administrative Tools menu. Click Continue to dismiss the UAC prompt.

4. In the Windows Deployment Services console, right-click the Install Images node, located under Servers\glasgow.contoso.internal, and then select Add Install Image.

The Add Image Wizard starts.

5. On the Image Group page, select Create A New Image Group. Enter **Alpha** for the image group, and then click Next.

6. On the Image File page, browse to the sources directory on the Windows Server 2008 installation media. Select install.wim, and then click Open. Click Next when returned to the Image File page of the Windows Deployment Services – Add Image Wizard.

7. On the list of available images, ensure that only the first image is selected, and then click Next.

   The list of available images will vary depending on which installation media is used. You select only one image for this exercise.

8. Click Next on the Summary page.

   Windows Deployment Services will now add the image file to the remote installation directory.

9. Click Finish when the selected image is added to the server.

10. Right-click the Boot Images node, and then select Add Boot Image. On the Image File page of the Windows Deployment Services – Add Image Wizard, browse to the sources directory on the Windows Server 2008 installation media, select boot.wim, and then click Open. Click Next when returned to the Image File page of the Windows Deployment Services – Add Image Wizard.

11. Accept the default image name, such as the one shown in Figure 11-11, and then click Next.

    The image name will vary depending on which installation media is used.

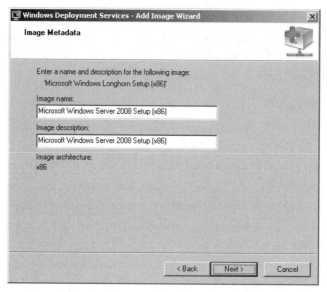

FIGURE 11-11 Boot image metadata.

12. On the Summary page, click Next.

    The image is transferred to the server.

13. When the image has been added, click Finish.

14. In the Windows Deployment Services console, right-click the Multicast Transmissions node, and then select Create Multicast Transmission.

    This launches the Create Multicast Transmission wizard.

15. On the Transmission Name page, enter **Server_Deployment**, and then click Next.

16. On the Select Image page, from the drop-down menu, select the Alpha image group, and then click Next.

17. On the Multicast Type page, select Scheduled-Cast. Select the Start Automatically When The Number of Clients Ready To Receive This Image Is check box and set the threshold value to 5, as shown in Figure 11-12. Click Next.

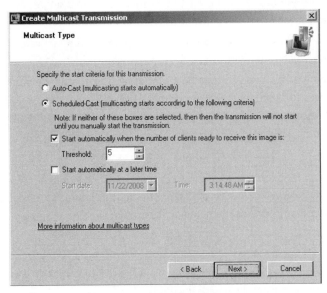

FIGURE 11-12 Multicast transmission properties.

18. On the Task Complete page, click Finish. Verify that the Server_Deployment multicast is configured as a Scheduled-Cast and that its status is set to Waiting.

19. Right-click and delete the Server_Deployment multicast before closing the Windows Deployment Services console and logging off.

    Performing this final step ensures that the multicast is removed from the server and will not interfere with later practices in this text.

Lesson Summary

- Windows Server 2008 uses an XML-based answer file named autounattend.xml that you can create using Windows System Image Manager.

- WDS enables the deployment of Windows Server 2008 to computers that have PXE-compliant network adapters.

- WDS uses four types of images. Boot images enable computers to boot over the network. Install images contain operating system images that you can deploy to client computers. Capture images enable administrators to create an image of an existing computer for later WDS deployment. Discover images enable you to boot non-PXE–compliant clients so they can use WDS.

- WDS can be collocated with DHCP if you configure WDS to listen to an alternate port and configure DHCP option 60.

- MAKs enable a specific number of computers to be activated using a single key. It is best used in small environments. MAK activation has to occur only once.

- The VAMT enables you to install MAKs remotely on computers and to activate computers with MAKs on isolated networks.

- KMS enables you to install a key on a single host that other hosts on the network contact every 180 days to retain their activation status. KMS does not need to be connected to the Internet, and a KMS host server's key can be activated over the phone.

Lesson Review

You can use the following questions to test your knowledge of the information in the chapter lesson, "Deploying and Activating Windows Server 2008." The questions are also available on the companion DVD if you prefer to review them in electronic form.

> **NOTE   ANSWERS**
>
> Answers to these questions and explanations of why each answer choice is right or wrong are located in the "Answers" section at the end of the book.

1. A domain controller, hosted at one of your organization's branch offices, hosts the DHCP and DNS server roles. You install the Windows Deployment Services role on this computer. When you start a computer that has a PXE network card in an attempt to deploy an operating system, you are unable to make a connection to the WDS PEX server. Which of the following configuration changes will resolve this problem?

   A. Alter Windows Deployment Services server settings.

   B. Alter DNS server settings.

   C. Alter DHCP server settings.

   D. Alter the default domain Group Policy object.

2. Yesterday, you deployed a new server with the Windows Deployment Services role in your organization's server room. You configured a multicast transmission to start when five clients are ready to receive the image. The five servers that will be the target of the WDS deployment are located in a special staging room, which is on the same subnet as the IT department's workstation computers. The server room is on a separate TCP/IP subnet from the staging room. You power on the five servers but find that the WDS deployment does not start. Which of the following strategies will resolve this problem?

   A. Create DNS records for the five servers.

   B. Create a separate IPv4 DHCP scope for PXE clients.

   C. Move the WDS server to the staging room.

   D. Deploy a Windows Internet Naming Service (WINS) server.

3. You want to use WDS to deploy Windows Server 2008 to ten computers that lack floppy disk and optical media drives. Which of the following configuration changes can you make to WDS to minimize the amount of direct intervention, such as having to boot into Windows PE, required during the deployment to these computers?

   A. Place the Unattended XML file on an accessible TFTP server.

   B. Configure an Unattended XML file using WDS server properties.

   C. Place an Unattended XML file on a file share.

   D. Place an Unattended XML file on an accessible web server.

4. You are helping set up the server infrastructure for a new company. The company currently has two computers running Windows Server 2008 Enterprise. One of these computers hosts a SQL Server 2008 instance. The other one functions as a domain controller but also has two Windows Server 2008 Enterprise virtual machines running under Hyper-V. You will be deploying more servers, both virtually and physically, in the future. What is the minimum number of extra servers you must deploy before you can use KMS for volume activation?

   A. One virtual server

   B. Three virtual servers

   C. Five virtual servers

   D. Three physical servers

5. Which of the following tools can you use to configure and activate recently deployed computers remotely, using a MAK?

   A. *Ntdsutil*

   B. *Dsquery*

   C. Windows Automated Installation Kit

   D. Volume Activation Management Tool

Chapter Review

To further practice and reinforce the skills you learned in this chapter, you can perform the following tasks:

- Review the chapter summary.
- Complete the case scenario. This scenario sets up a real-world situation involving the topics of this chapter and asks you to create a solution.
- Complete the suggested practices.
- Take a practice test.

Chapter Summary

- Windows Deployment Services is a Windows Server 2008 server role that enables you to deploy Windows Server 2008 and Windows Vista operating systems over the network to PXE-compliant computers.
- Volume activation keys enable you to manage more easily the activation of multiple computers running Windows Server 2008 by enabling you either to reuse a single key multiple times or to install a server, known as a KMS host, to manage all activations on your network.

Case Scenario

In the following case scenario, you apply what you've learned about server deployment and activation. You can find answers to the questions in the "Answers" section at the end of this book.

Case Scenario: Activation at Fabrikam, Inc.

You are planning the deployment of volume activation at Fabrikam, Inc. There are 20 Windows Server 2008 servers and 300 client computers running Windows Vista at the head office location. All will be located on a network that is connected to the Internet but protected by firewalls. Each branch office has four Windows Server 2008 servers located on a network that is completely isolated from the Internet. These servers manage industrial equipment. Branch offices have three Windows Server 2008 servers and 15 client computers running Windows Vista, located on networks that are connected to the Internet. Branch offices are connected to the head office over virtual private network (VPN) wide area network (WAN) connections. Activation traffic should not travel more than once across WAN links. As part of planning the deployment, your team must find answers to the following questions.

1. How can you deploy volume licensing for the four servers on isolated networks at each Fabrikam branch office?

2. Which volume licensing solution should you use for the branch office computers located on the networks connected to the Internet?

3. Which volume licensing solution should you use at the Fabrikam head office?

Suggested Practices

To help you successfully master the exam objectives presented in this chapter, complete the following tasks.

Configure Windows Deployment Services

To get a thorough understanding of Windows Deployment Services, complete both practices in this section.

- **Practice 1**   Download and install the Windows Automated Installation Kit (WAIK) from the Microsoft Web site. Use Windows System Image Manager, which is included within the Windows Automated Installation Kit, to create your own custom image based on the Windows Server 2008 installation media. You can use an evaluation version of Windows Server 2008 to create this custom image

- **Practice 2**   Use Windows System Image Manager, included within the WAIK, to create an answer file to assist in the automated deployment of Windows Server 2008.

Configure Microsoft Windows Activation

To get a thorough understanding of Microsoft Windows activation, complete both practices in this section.

- **Practice 1**   Download and install the Volume Activation Management Tool (VAMT) to server Glasgow.

- **Practice 2**   Use the VAMT to scan AD DS for the licensing status of the computers you use in your practices.

Take a Practice Test

The practice tests on this book's companion DVD offer many options. For example, you can test yourself on just one exam objective, or you can test yourself on all the upgrade exam content. You can set up the test so that it closely simulates the experience of taking a certification exam, or you can set it up in study mode so that you can look at the correct answers and explanations after you answer each question.

> **MORE INFO**   **PRACTICE TESTS**
>
> For details about all the practice test options available, see the "How to Use the Practice Tests" section in this book's Introduction.

CHAPTER 12

Terminal Services

As an experienced and certified IT professional, you are already familiar with the capability of Microsoft Windows Server 2003 Terminal Services. You understand the basics of Remote Desktop Protocol (RDP) and how Terminal Services is used, and you have most likely managed and supported the product on your own organization's network. Although you might be familiar with some of the configuration options discussed in this chapter, most of the chapter will focus on features new with Windows Server 2008 such as RemoteApp, Terminal Services gateway, and Terminal Services load balancing. Any upgrade exam is likely to test newer features more rigorously than features with which you have already demonstrated competence.

Exam objectives in this chapter

- Configure Windows Server 2008 Terminal Services RemoteApp (TS RemoteApp).
- Configure Terminal Services Gateway.
- Configure Terminal Services load balancing.
- Configure and monitor Terminal Services resources.
- Configure Terminal Services licensing.
- Configure Terminal Services client connections.
- Configure Terminal Services server options.

Lessons in this chapter:

Before You Begin

To complete the lessons in this chapter, you must have done the following:

- Installed and configured the evaluation edition of Windows Server 2008 Enterprise Edition in accordance with the instructions listed in the Introduction.

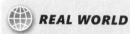 **REAL WORLD**

Orin Thomas

One day, back when I was the systems administrator for a large Australian industrial company, I got a few calls from users of the company Terminal Services server. The company had recently deployed the server as a way of saving money. It enabled users who had older workstations to run newer applications without the cost of having to upgrade their computers. The users were ringing me to complain that every afternoon after 2 P.M., the normally responsive server inherited the performance characteristics of a stunned wombat. When I had a spare five minutes, I logged on to check out their claims. I did some quick performance tests and found that even though all 25 users who could log on to the server had an active session, the server itself seemed to be experiencing a minimal to average processor load. Suspecting that something unusual was occurring, I set up Performance Monitor to take regular readings. During the early afternoon on the next day, I logged on and checked the records. The log indicated a recent and significant spike in CPU usage. Drilling down, I found that the spike was due to a single process, run by one user, that was hogging almost all the Terminal Services server's resources. The user had been running an accounting analysis application every afternoon starting at around 2 P.M. This application was so CPU intensive that it slowed all sessions running on the server. I had to find some way of ensuring that the 24 other users of the Terminal Services server were not inconvenienced when this one guy from the accounting department ran his business-critical application. Today, I could solve the problem by using Windows System Resource Manager and applying a resource policy that would distribute resources more equitably. If I'd been able to do this, the guy could have run his application but wouldn't be able to suck up all the server's resources in doing so. Back then, though, I didn't have access to such a tool. In the end, the only way we could solve the problem was to buy the guy a new workstation. This let him run the accounting analysis program locally without giving everyone else's Terminal Services sessions the responsiveness of the aforementioned stunned wombat.

Lesson 1: Configuring Terminal Services Servers

As an experienced systems administrator, you know that deployment is only the first step you need to manage in the life cycle of a server. Even with the most intensive planning prior to setting up initial options, you will find that when you deploy the server, you must modify its configuration to suit better the way actual people use it in your organization. In this lesson, you learn specific steps and configuration changes you can make that customize Terminal Services servers to meet your organization's specific needs.

After this lesson, you will be able to:

- Configure Terminal Server options, including remote control, RDP permissions, connection limits, and disconnection settings.
- Configure Terminal Services client connection settings, including single sign-on and home folders.
- Manage and maintain a Terminal Services licensing server.

Estimated lesson time: 40 minutes

Terminal Server Settings

As the administrator of your organization's Terminal Services servers, you will be responsible for maintaining their configuration after deployment. You will most likely need to monitor and tune these servers before you find the right balance between client experience and server capacity.

Four basic consoles are installed when you add the Terminal Services role service to a computer running Windows Server 2008. These are the Remote Desktops console, the Terminal Services Configuration console, Terminal Services Manager, and TS RemoteApp Manager. You learn about the Remote Desktops console later in this lesson and about TS RemoteApp in Lesson 2, "Supporting Terminal Services." The next few pages explain how you can configure Terminal Services, using the Terminal Services Configuration console and Terminal Services Manager.

The Terminal Services Configuration Console

The Terminal Services Configuration console is the main tool to use to configure and optimize a specific Terminal Services server. There are two areas of the console window, shown in Figure 12-1, to which you should pay special attention. The first is located under Edit Settings; the second is in the list of connections.

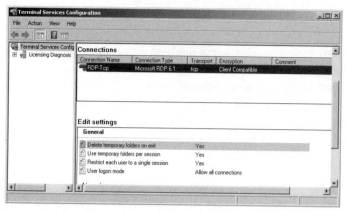

FIGURE 12-1 Terminal Services configuration console.

By changing the value of each item under Edit Settings, you can configure general Terminal Services settings that are independent of each connection. The settings you can configure in this manner include:

- **Use Temporary Folders Per Session**   By default, Terminal Services uses a temporary folder to store temporary files for each active session.

- **Delete Temporary Folders On Exit**   When you configure this setting, Terminal Services removes temporary folders when a session completes.

- **Restrict Each User To A Single Session**   Configuring this setting stops a single user account from logging on more than once to a specific Terminal Services server.

- **User Logon Mode**   You can configure this setting to allow all connections, allow reconnections but prevent new logons, or allow reconnections but prevent new logons until you restart the server. You are likely to use this final option when you are planning maintenance on a server and need to allow existing users to finish their work.

- **License Server Discovery Mode**   You can configure this setting to discover a license server or use a specific license server automatically.

- **Terminal Services Licensing Mode**   You can set the terminal server licensing mode to per user or per device. You learn more about licensing Terminal Services later in this lesson.

- **Member Of Farm In TS Session Broker**   You can configure membership of a TS Session broker farm by using this setting. You learn more about TS Session broker in Lesson 2.

The second area contains a list of connections. This lists the connection name, type, transport, and encryption level. The default connection name is RDP-Tcp, although it is possible to create different connection settings that use different levels of encryption and specific network adapters if the need arises.

Editing RDP-Tcp Connection Settings

Although the default connection name is RDP-Tcp, you can use any name for this connection. When you see the term RDP-Tcp connection properties in technical documents, it often means the properties of the default Terminal Services connection. The connection properties dialog box has the following tabs:

- **General** By editing the properties of this tab, you can configure the connection's encryption and authentication properties.

- **Log On Settings** Use this tab to configure information about accounts used for sessions.

- **Sessions** Use this tab to set session time limits and configure whether the server allows reconnection.

- **Environment** Use this tab to configure which applications launch when a user initiates a session.

- **Remote Control** Use this tab to specify whether administrators have remote control access to client sessions.

- **Client Settings** By editing the settings on this tab, you can limit the depth of colors displayed and the local resources clients can use in the Terminal Services session.

- **Network Adapter** Use this tab to specify the maximum number of sessions supported and which network adapter the connection uses. You can select either all network adapters or one specific adapter.

- **Security** By editing the properties on this tab, you can specify which users or groups can connect to Terminal Services sessions and have access to functions such as remote control.

In the next few pages, you learn how to configure specific settings that are relevant to the 70-649 upgrade exam.

You set the authentication and encryption of the session through the General tab shown in Figure 12-2. The security layer can be set to RDP, SSL (TLS 1.0), or Negotiate. Microsoft Windows XP clients prior to Service Pack 3 do not support RDP security. SSL provides stronger encryption than RDP, supports earlier clients, but requires an SSL certificate. You can create a self-signed certificate on the Terminal Services server, but unless you take further steps, clients will not trust this certificate. Consider deploying an enterprise certification authority (CA) in your environment and using it to issue the Terminal Services server with a Secure Sockets Layer (SSL) certificate. If Terminal Services is to be used by third parties, consider obtaining an SSL certificate from a commercial CA.

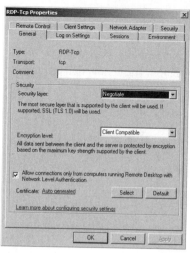

FIGURE 12-2 Connection security and encryption.

After Terminal Services authenticates a session, using RDP or SSL, the encryption level determines the encryption strength of the connection. The FIPS Compliant level uses Federal Information Process Standard (FIPS) 140-1 validated encryption methods. If you specify this level, clients that do not support these methods cannot connect. The High encryption level uses 128-bit encryption. Some older RDP clients do not support this level of encryption. The Client Compatible setting allows encryption at the maximum key length supported by the client. The Low encryption level uses 56-bit encryption. When Low encryption is used, the client encrypts data sent to the server, but the server does not encrypt data sent to the client.

If the Allow Connections Only From Computers Running Remote Desktop With Network Level Authentication Setting is enabled, user authentication occurs before the Terminal Services session is initiated. Although Windows XP with Service Pack 3 supports Network Level Authentication, not all RDP client software supports this feature. You cannot enable the Network Level Authentication option if the RDP Security Layer is in use.

The Log On Settings tab, shown in Figure 12-3, enables you to specify whether a client's account information or Terminal Services uses a specific general user account. General user accounts are useful in kiosk scenarios. You can also configure the Terminal Services server so that it prompts connecting users for passwords.

On the Sessions tab, you can configure how the Terminal Services server treats disconnected sessions as well as specify active and idle session limits. You can use an idle session limit to terminate a session when the user has been inactive within the session for a certain amount of time. This stops users from taking up resources on a Terminal Services server when they are not actually doing anything with their session. You use active session limits to specify the maximum length of time a user's session may stay connected. Use the End A Disconnected Session limit to allow users to reconnect for a certain amount of time if they are accidentally disconnected. If they do not reconnect within the specified time, Terminal Services ends their session. In Figure 12-4, you can see settings that will allow users to reconnect to disconnected sessions after 30 minutes, will terminate idle sessions after an hour, and will limit the length of any single session to eight hours.

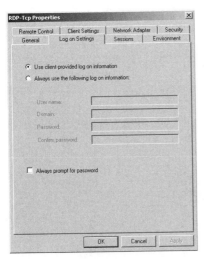

FIGURE 12-3 Log-on settings.

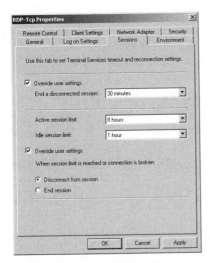

FIGURE 12-4 Session settings.

You can use the Remote Control tab of the RDP-Tcp Properties dialog box, shown in Figure 12-5, to set the level of assistance that support staff can provide to those connected to Terminal Services sessions. The default setting uses the settings configured on the Remote Control tab of the user's account Properties in Active Directory Users and Computers. The default settings for Remote Control in Active Directory are to allow remote control and interaction if the user grants permission. By configuring this setting, you can block the use of remote control, allow it with the user's permission, or allow it without prompting the user.

You can configure remote control so that a helper can interact with the session or simply view the session without interacting. When you configure the Do Not Allow Remote Control or Use Remote Control With the Following Settings options, you override the settings applied through the user's account properties.

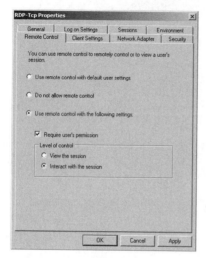

FIGURE 12-5 Remote control settings.

You can block client attempts to redirect resources through the Client Settings tab of a connection's properties in Terminal Services configuration, as shown in Figure 12-6. You can limit the maximum color depth displayed to 8, 15, 16, 24, or 32 bits per pixel, and you can disable the redirection of local volumes, printers, LPT and COM ports, Clipboard, Audio, and Plug and Play devices.

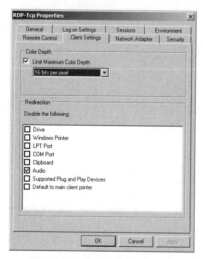

FIGURE 12-6 Limiting client resources.

On the Security tab, you can configure which groups and users have User Access, Guest Access, and Full Control over the Terminal Services service. User Access allows you to connect and log on locally. Guest Access allows logon but not connections to existing sessions. If Terminal Services has been deployed on a domain controller, it will be necessary also to modify the Allow Log On Through Terminal Services policy to allow remote desktop access. As you can see in Figure 12-7, the default settings allow members of the local Remote Desktop Users group User Access and Guest Access. The local Administrators group is assigned Full Control permission.

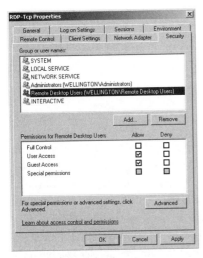

FIGURE 12-7 RDP-Tcp Security.

You can set specific permissions by clicking Advanced on the Security tab of the RDP-Tcp Properties dialog box. Rather than just setting Full Control, User Access, or Guest Access, the Advanced permissions enable you to set more granular rights. As Figure 12-8 shows, you can give security principals the right to use Remote Control to view an active session, forcibly disconnect a user from a session, configure connection properties, and obtain information about Terminal Services servers and sessions. You can use these permissions to allow Help Desk staff access to Remote Control functionality over user sessions without having to grant them local Administrator access on the Terminal Services server.

FIGURE 12-8 Advanced RDP-Tcp permissions.

Terminal Services Manager

Terminal Services Manager, shown in Figure 12-9, enables you to view currently connected users, sessions, and processes. You can use Terminal Services Manager to view this information across multiple Terminal Services servers in your organization. All you need to do to view information for multiple servers is, first, to add each Terminal Services server that you wish to view to a group. Terminal Services Manager groups have no purpose other than as collection points about Users, Sessions, and Processes related to Terminal Services within an organization. Administrators can use Terminal Services Manager to send messages to users and disconnect, log off, or reset sessions. The Users tab provides a list of users that are currently connected to Terminal Services. The Sessions tab within Terminal Services Manager tells you about current sessions and their states, including data about disconnected sessions and sessions during which remote control is in use. The Processes tab tells you about individual processes, which users are running them, and which Terminal Services server within a group is hosting that process.

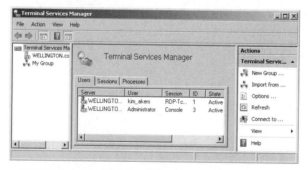

FIGURE 12-9 Terminal Services Manager console.

You access Remote Control through the Terminal Services Manager console. You can help a user out by using Remote Control only if you are connected to the Terminal Services server through an RDP session. You cannot use Remote Control when directly logged on to the Terminal Services server.

> **MORE INFO** **TERMINAL SERVICES MANAGER**
>
> For more information on Terminal Services Manager, consult the following Web page: *http://technet.microsoft.com/en-us/library/cc732985.aspx.*

Configuring Terminal Services Servers with Group Policy

If your organization has only a couple of Terminal Services servers, you will probably configure them manually on a per-server basis. When your organization has a substantial number of Terminal Services servers that you need to configure with similar settings, you should apply these settings through Group Policy. You will find policies relating to Terminal Services servers under the *Computer Configuration\Policies\Administrative Templates\Windows Components \Terminal Services\Terminal Server* node, as shown in Figure 12-10.

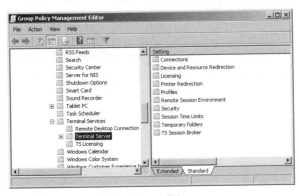

FIGURE 12-10 Terminal Services policies.

These nodes contain a large number of policies, and it is unlikely that you will be expected to recite all of them to pass the 70-649 upgrade exam. The following list should give you a good feel for the types of policies available under each node:

- **Connections** Under the *Connections* node are these policies: Automatic Reconnection, Allow Users To Connect Remotely Using Terminal Services, Deny Logoff Of An Administrator Logged In To The Console Session, Configure Keep-Alive Connection Interval, Limit Number Of Connections, Set Rules For Remote Control Of Terminal Services User Sessions, Allow Reconnection From Original Client Only, Restrict Terminal Services Users To A Single Remote Session, and Allow Remote Start Of Unlisted Programs.

- **Device and Resource Redirection** Under the *Device And Resource Redirection* node are these policies: Allow Audio Redirection, Do Not Allow Clipboard Redirection, Do Not Allow COM Port Redirection, Do Not Allow Drive Redirection, Do Not Allow LPT Port Redirection, Do Not Allow Supported Plug And Play Device Redirection, Do Not Allow Smart Card Device Redirection, and Allow Time Zone Redirection.

- **Licensing** Under the *Licensing* node are these policies: Use The Specified Terminal Services License Servers, Hide Notifications About TS Licensing Problems That Affect The Terminal Server, and Set The Terminal Services Licensing Mode.

- **Printer Redirection** Under the *Printer Redirection* node are these policies: Do Not Set Default Client Printer To Be Default Printer In A Session, Do Not Allow Client Printer Redirection, Specify Terminal Server Fallback Printer Driver Behavior, Use Terminal Services Easy Print Printer Driver First, and Redirect Only The Default Client Printer.

- **Profiles** Under the *Profiles* node are these policies: Set TS User Home Directory, Use Mandatory Profiles On The Terminal Server, and Set Path For TS Roaming User Profile.

- **Remote Session Environment** Under the *Remote Session Environment* node are these policies: Limit Maximum Color Depth, Enforce Removal Of Remote Desktop Wallpaper, Remove Disconnect Option From Shut Down Dialog Box, Remove Windows Security Item From Start Menu, Set Compression Algorithm For RDP Data, Start A Program On Connection, and Always Show Desktop On Connection.

- **Security** Under the *Security* node are these policies: Server Authentication Certificate Template, Set Client Connection Encryption Level, Always Prompt For Password Upon Connection, Require Secure RPC Communication, Require Use Of Specific Security Layer For Remote (RDP) Connections, Do Not Allow Local Administrators To Customize Permissions, and Require User Authentication For Remote Connections By Using Network Level Authentication.

- **Session Time Limits** Under the *Session Time Limits* node are these policies: Set Time Limit For Disconnected Sessions, Set Time Limit For Active But Idle Terminal Services Sessions, Set Time Limit for Active Terminal Services Sessions, Terminate Session When Time Limits Are Reached, and Set Time Limit For Logoff Of RemoteApp Sessions.

- **Temporary Folders** Under the *Temporary Folders* node are these policies: Do Not Delete Temp Folder Upon Exit and Do Not Use Temporary Folders Per Session.

- **TS Session Broker** Under the *TS Session Broker* node are these policies: Join TS Session Broker, Configure TS Session Broker Farm Name, Use IP Address Redirection, Configure TS Session Broker Server Name, and Use TS Session Broker Load Balancing.

Lesson 2 provides more detail about TS Session Broker–related policies.

As you can see, you can apply almost all the Terminal Services server settings you learned about in the section on manual configuration, automatically through Group Policy. When preparing for the exam, determine which settings you can apply to Terminal Services servers across the organization and which settings require configuration on a per-server basis. For example, you are unlikely to use the Limit Number Of Connections policy across all Terminal

Services servers in your organization if each has a different hardware configuration. One server might be able to support 50 connections and another server might be able to support only 20. In this type of situation, you would be reluctant to apply a general rule using Group Policy when the appropriate setting depends on each server's unique hardware configuration. Alternatively, it might make sense to apply the Restrict Terminal Services Users To A Single Remote Session policy across the organization even when each Terminal Services server's hardware has a unique configuration.

Tuning Terminal Services Servers

Although configuring the settings related to Terminal Services enables you to restrict the number of connections a server may host, there might be times when it is necessary to take a more proactive role in optimizing your user's Terminal Services experience.

Equitable resource allocation is a problem many Terminal Services administrators face. In a default Windows Server 2008 deployment of Terminal Services, it is possible for a minority of client connections to consume a majority of a server's hardware resources. Consider a Terminal Services server that hosts several applications, one of which relates to financial services. Although 20 clients might be connected, one user might be performing a CPU-intensive task that directly degrades everyone else's performance. As an administrator, you must find a way to ensure that everyone else's sessions are not adversely affected when Craig from Accounting needs to run a complex analysis. Put another way, you need to ensure that Terminal Services treats all client connections equally as opposed to the server allocating a disproportionate amount of resources to any single client. Windows System Resource Manager allows Terminal Services to be more equitable when it comes to allocating hardware resources.

You can install Windows System Resource Manager (WSRM) through the *Features* node of the Server Manager console. After it is installed, you can launch the WSRM console from the Administrative Tools menu. You can also use WSRM to manage Windows Server 2008 resources generally, but the coverage in this lesson concentrates on how to use it to optimize resource allocation for Terminal Services.

From the WRSM console, you can select and apply one of the four default policies shown in Figure 12-11. The Equal_Per_User and Equal_Per_Session policies are the most applicable to the management of Terminal Services. When you apply the Equal_Per_User policy, WSRM allocates resources on a per-user basis, even if a user account has more than one simultaneous connected session. For example, if Ian, Orin, and Rooslan all connect to the same Terminal Services server, but Rooslan has three open sessions to Orin's and Ian's single sessions, WSRM allocates resources equally to each person even though Rooslan has more connected sessions. If you apply the Equal_Per_Session policy and the same situation arose, WSRM would allocate each of Rooslan's sessions the same proportion of resources that it allocates to Orin's and Ian's sessions. It is a good idea to limit the number of active connections a single user can make when applying the Equal_Per_Session WSRM policy. You should also note that WSRM enforces policies only when there is contention for a resource. If you enforce the Equal_Per_User policy and there are three active sessions, but two of these sessions require minimal hardware resources, the third session will be able to use whatever resources are left.

It is only when sessions use all hardware resources that WSRM will redistribute them according to policy.

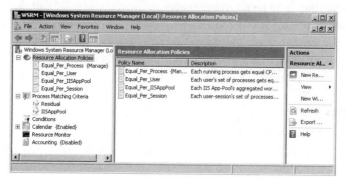

FIGURE 12-11 Windows System Resource Manager console.

You can use the accounting function in WSRM to track how processes running on Windows Server 2008 consume resources. You can configure WSRM to track resource usage on a per-user, per-application, or per-session basis. Using this information, you can make more-informed choices about how to tune a Terminal Services server to meet the needs of the users in your organization best. When you enable accounting, WSRM logs accounting data relevant to applications managed by the applied WSRM resource policy or any policy set to profiling. The advantage of using a policy set to profiling is that you can log application accounting data without the resource policy applying to current client sessions.

> **MORE INFO** **WINDOWS SYSTEM RESOURCE MANAGER**
>
> For more information on using Windows System Resource Manager with Terminal Services, consult the following TechNet article: *http://technet.microsoft.com/en-us/library /cc731377.aspx.*

Managing Terminal Services from the Command Line

Windows Server 2008 includes a large number of command-line utilities with which you can query and manage Terminal Services servers. Some of the more useful commands include:

- *Change.exe* Changes Terminal Services server settings for logons.
- *Logoff.exe* Logs a user session off from a Terminal Services server.
- *Qappsrv.exe* Displays a list of Terminal Services servers in the domain.
- *Query.exe* Displays a list of Terminal Services server processes, sessions, and Terminal Services servers.
- *Shadow.exe* Initiates a remote control session.

MORE INFO **TERMINAL SERVICES COMMAND-LINE UTILITIES**

For more information about command-line utilities related to Terminal Services, consult the following page on TechNet: *http://technet.microsoft.com/en-us/library/cc725766.aspx*.

 Quick Check

1. Where are remote control settings inherited from if you do not configure remote control settings on the Terminal Services server manually or through Group Policy?
2. Which of the default WSRM policies should you apply to ensure that no single user monopolizes hardware resources by creating multiple sessions?

Quick Check Answers

1. You can configure remote control settings in user account properties in Active Directory Users And Computers. If no settings are configured on the Terminal Services server, account settings will be used by default.
2. Apply the Equal_Per_User WSRM policy.

Terminal Services Client Connection Settings

Clients are able to use the Remote Desktop Connection application to configure a large number of options for a Terminal Services session. The basic Remote Desktop Connection dialog box enables a user to enter only the name of the Terminal Services server to which he or she wishes to connect. Clicking Options provides the user with six tabs through which he or she can enter specific settings. The tabs and their associated settings are as follows:

- **General**   You can specify a target Terminal Services server as well as the username you will use to connect to that server. You also have the option of saving credentials and saving the current connection settings to an RDP file for later use.

- **Display**   On the Display tab, you can specify the window size of the remote desktop connection and the color depth. Higher resolution and color depths require more Terminal Services and network resources. As you learned earlier, you can limit the maximum color depth transmitted by a Terminal Services server by editing the RDP-Tcp connection's properties.

- **Local Resources**   On this tab, you can specify which local resources, such as hard disk drives, printers, plug and play devices, and serial ports, are available in the Terminal Services session. You can also specify whether sound events in the Terminal Services session are transmitted back to the client computer and how Windows key combinations, such as ALT+TAB, function.

- **Programs**   Use the Programs tab to ensure that a specific application starts when a session is established.

- **Experience**   Use this tab to customize the remote desktop experience, selecting a connection speed to optimize the performance of a Terminal Services session. Available connection speeds include 28.8 and 56 Kbps Modem, Broadband, or LAN. As an alternative, you can enable the display of Desktop Backgrounds, Font Smoothing, Desktop Composition, Show Contents Of Windows While Dragging, Menu And Windows Animation, Themes, and Bitmap Caching. The more options you enable, the more bandwidth-intensive the connection becomes.

- **Advanced**   On the Advanced tab, you can select whether the identity of the Terminal Services server you are connecting to is verified. You can also configure TS Gateway connection settings. You will learn more about configuring TS Gateway in Lesson 2.

Although it is possible to configure the connection of printers by using the Local Resources tab of Remote Desktop Connection, the most comprehensive way to manage printer resources is through Group Policy. As Figure 12-12 shows, five printer redirection policies are available under the *Computer Configuration\Policies\Administrative Templates\Windows Components\Terminal Services\Terminal Server* node.

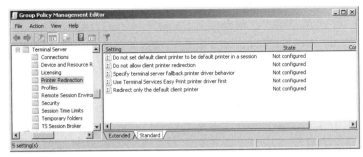

FIGURE 12-12 Printer Redirection policies.

You can use these policies in the following ways:

- **Do Not Set Default Client Printer To Be Default Printer In A Session** enables you to use the default printer specified on the Terminal Services server, rather than on the client printer, to be used as the default printer.

- **Do Not Allow Client Printer Redirection** disables printer redirection completely.

- **Specify Terminal Server Fallback Printer Driver Behavior** enables the Terminal Services server to choose an alternate printer if you have not installed a print driver for the client printer on the Terminal Services server.

- **Use Terminal Services Easy Printer Driver First** is the default behavior of Terminal Services. Set this policy to *Disabled* if you experience problems with the Easy Printer Driver.

- **Redirect Only The Default Client Printer** is useful when users have multiple printers installed on their local computers, but you want them to print only to their default printer.

Terminal Services Profiles

The default Terminal Services settings create user profiles whenever a new user connects for the first time. A problem that many administrators encounter is that when large numbers of users use a particular Terminal Services server, user profile data takes a large amount of disk space. There are two solutions to this problem. The first is to limit the size of users' Terminal Services profiles by implementing quotas. The most comprehensive way of implementing quotas is by using File System Resource Manager, a feature of Windows Server 2008. The second is to create Terminal Services–specific roaming user profiles by editing the Computer Configuration\Policies\Administrative Templates\Windows Components\Terminal Services\ Terminal Server\Profiles policies. Through these policies, you can specify a home directory— also known as a home folder—roaming profile path and whether mandatory profiles are used on the Terminal Services server. Microsoft recommends that organizations that already use roaming profiles configure the policies related to Terminal Services profiles. This is because using standard roaming profiles with Terminal Services can lead to data loss or corruption.

MORE INFO   **TERMINAL SERVICES USER PROFILES**

For more information on configuring Terminal Services user profiles, consult the following
article on TechNet: *http://technet.microsoft.com/en-us/library/cc742820.aspx*.

Installing Applications on Terminal Services Servers

There are a couple of tricks to installing applications on Terminal Services servers. The first is
that you must install applications after you have installed the Terminal Services role service.
Installing the Terminal Services role service enables the Terminal Services Install mode, a
special installation mode that ensures that applications can work with Terminal Services. This
includes verifying that appropriate registry and .ini files are created to support running the
application in a multiple-user environment.

You can enter Terminal Services Install mode by using the Install Application On Terminal
Server tool located in Control Panel. If you are installing an application from the command
prompt, you must use the *change user /install* command to put the server into TS Install
mode and then use the *change user /execute* command to place the server into Execution
mode. It is not necessary to force a Terminal Services server into Execution mode if you use
Control Panel. If you are installing a program that uses a Windows Installer package (MSI),
Terminal Services Install mode initiates automatically.

MORE INFO   **INSTALLING TERMINAL SERVICES APPLICATIONS**

For more information on installing applications in Terminal Services Install mode,
consult the following TechNet Web page: *http://technet.microsoft.com/en-us/library
/cc742815.aspx*.

Single Sign-On

Single Sign-On enables users in an Active Directory environment to connect directly to Terminal Services sessions without having to reenter their account credentials. Configuring Single
Sign-On can be especially useful if you have deployed a significant number of applications
using TS RemoteApp, a technology that you will learn more about in Lesson 2. To configure
Single Sign-On, enable the Allow Delegating Saved Credentials policy, located in Computer
Configuration\Policies\Administrative Templates\System\Credentials Delegation, and apply it
so that the Terminal Services server falls under the scope of the policy. Figure 12-13 shows the
properties of this policy. Use the Show button in the policy to add servers to the list. To add a
specific Terminal Server, use the TERMSRV/<*servername*> name. To allow Single Sign-On for
all Terminal Services servers, use the TERMSRV/* name.

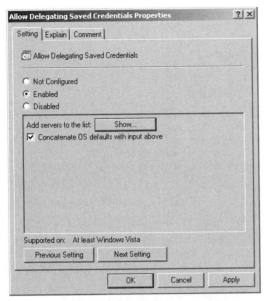

FIGURE 12-13 Allow Terminal Services Single Sign-On.

Remote Desktops Console

The Remote Desktops snap-in enables you to administer multiple computers at the same time through Remote Desktop. Rather than having multiple Remote Desktop windows open at the same time, the Remote Desktops console looks more like Microsoft Management Console (MMC), by which you can select a specific host to connect to from a list, as shown in Figure 12-14. You can configure the connections to log on automatically when the console starts, enabling you quickly to switch which connection has focus. Using the Remote Desktops console frees you from having to start multiple instances of the Remote Desktop Connection client when you have to perform your day-to-day systems administration tasks.

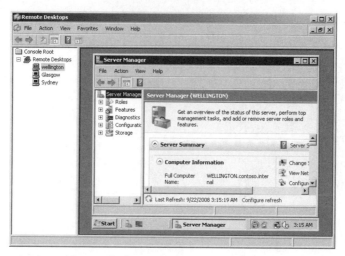

FIGURE 12-14 Remote Desktops console.

MORE INFO   **REMOTE DESKTOPS CONSOLE**

You can learn more about the Remote Desktops console by reading the following TechNet Web page: *http://technet.microsoft.com/en-us/library/cc770726.aspx.*

MSTSC

You can use the *MSTSC.exe* command-line utility to create Remote Desktop and Terminal Services connections, edit RDC configuration files, and migrate connection files created with Client Connection Manager to the .rdp format. For example, to edit an RDC connection file named example.rdp, issue the *mstsc.exe /edit example.rdp* command. To migrate Client Connection Manager files to .rdp format, use the */migrate* option.

You can use *mstsc.exe* with the */span* option to create a Remote Desktop session to span multiple monitors on the client, something that you cannot directly achieve using the Remote Desktop Connection dialog box. You can also use mstsc with the */w:* and */h:* options to specify the width and height of the Remote Desktop window. For example, the *mstsc. exe /v:Glasgow /w:640 /h:480* command will open a 640 x 480 pixel RDP session to server Glasgow.

MORE INFO   **MSTSC.EXE**

For more information on using mstsc.exe, consult the following TechNet article: *http://technet.microsoft.com/en-us/library/cc753907.aspx.*

Managing Terminal Services Licensing

Terminal Services requires access to a license server to operate. Without access to a license server, clients can connect for a 120-day grace period. This grace period expires either when the 120-day limit is reached or a permanent Terminal Services Client Access License (TS CAL) is issued by a license server to a client that establishes a session with the server. You can activate a Terminal Services license server by using one of three methods:

- **Automatic Connection** If the Terminal Services license server is able to make SSL connections to hosts on the Internet, you can use the Automatic Connection method. This works similarly to Windows Product Activation.

- **Web Browser** You can use the Web Browser activation method on the Terminal Services license server on any computer that has Internet connectivity. This enables you to activate a license server on an isolated network, using a computer on a network connected to the Internet.

- **Telephone** Just as it is possible to perform Windows Product Activation over the telephone, it is possible to place a telephone call to a Microsoft Clearinghouse operator to activate a Terminal Services license server. From most locations, this call is toll free.

The activation process installs a certificate on the Terminal Services license server. If the certificate expires or becomes corrupt, you may need to deactivate the license server. It is possible to deactivate a license server only by using the Automatic Connection and Telephone methods. Deactivated license servers can issue Per User CALs but only temporary Per Device CALs. You will learn more about Windows Server 2008 CAL types later in this lesson.

Understanding License Server Scope

When you install the Terminal Services License Server role, the wizard will ask you to what scope you want to set the discovery scope for the license server. Available scope options depend on whether the Terminal Services license server is a member of an Active Directory domain. The following license scopes are available:

- **Workgroup** The workgroup licensing scope is available only when installed on a standalone server that is not a member of an Active Directory domain. Terminal Services servers located in the same workgroup can detect this server automatically. If you join a licensing server to a domain, Windows updates this scope automatically to Domain.

- **Domain** This scope is available only when the server is a member of an Active Directory domain. If installed on a domain controller, Terminal Services servers in the domain will be able to detect this license server automatically. If installed on a member server, the license server is not automatically discoverable. You can change the scope of this license server to Forest. The account installing this role service must be a member of the Domain Admins group.

- **Forest**   In Windows Server 2003, this scope is called Enterprise scope. This scope is available only when the server is a member of an Active Directory domain. When installed on a member server, any Terminal Service server in the forest can automatically discover this license server because, unlike a license server configured to use the domain scope, when you configure a license server to use the forest scope, setup publishes the license server location to Active Directory Domain Services (AD DS).

Understanding TS CALs

TS CALs are separate from the other sorts of licenses with which you might be familiar. It is also important to note that unlike some previous versions of Terminal Services, no existing Windows client operating system includes a Terminal Services Client Access License. Clients connecting to Terminal Services sessions need a valid CAL. It is also important to note that you can install CALs only on an activated Terminal Services license server. A license server that is not yet activated can issue only temporary CALs that are valid for only 90 days. These temporary CALs cannot be renewed.

Windows Server 2008 TS license servers can issue two types of CAL: the Per User CAL and the Per Device CAL. Per User CALs are tied to a user account. They allow that user account to access any Terminal Services server within the scope of the license server, using any computer device. You can determine the number of TS Per User CALs that are in use, using the TS Licensing Manager console.

TS license servers issue Per Device CALs to specific computers or devices. Any user of licensed devices can connect to any Terminal Services server within the scope of the license server. TS Per Device CALs are automatically reclaimed after a period of 62 to 89 days. This has no impact on legitimate use because TS Per Device CALs are automatically reissued the next time the device reconnects. Automatic reclamation ensures that devices that are no longer used to access Terminal Services do not take up valuable TS Per Device CALs. It is also possible to revoke 20 percent of TS Per Device CALs on a per–operating system basis. For example, you can revoke 20 percent of TS Per Device CALs issued to Windows XP clients or 20 percent of TS Per Device CALS issued to Windows Vista clients. You can determine the number of TS Per Device CALs in use, using the TS Licensing Manager console.

> **MORE INFO   TS CLIENT ACCESS LICENSES**
>
> To learn more about TS CALs, consult the following TechNet Web page:
> *http://technet.microsoft.com/en-us/library/cc731629.aspx.*

Recovering TS License Servers

When you back up a TS license server, ensure that you include both the system state data and the directory in which you installed the *TS Licensing* database. You can use Review Configuration in the TS Licensing Manager tool, as shown in Figure 12-15, to verify the location of this database. It is important to note that if you restore the System State data and the *TS Licensing* database to the same computer, both issued and unissued licenses are restored correctly unless you have reinstalled the operating system. If you restore to a different computer or one on which you have installed a new instance of the operating system, unissued licenses will not be available. Existing issued licenses will still be available. To resolve this problem, you must contact the Microsoft Clearinghouse and get the licenses reissued. For this reason, try not to purchase licenses in excess of what you need.

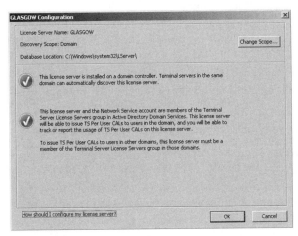

FIGURE 12-15 Review license server configuration.

> *MORE INFO* **RECOVERING TS LICENSE SERVERS**
>
> For more information on backing up and recovering TS license servers, consult the following article on TechNet: *http://technet.microsoft.com/en-us/library/cc753582.aspx*.

EXAM TIP

Upgrade exams focus on new features and new ways of doing things. In passing your MCSE, you have already demonstrated that you understand those features of Terminal Services present in Windows Server 2003. The key to passing the upgrade exam is demonstrating that you understand the features of Terminal Services that are new in Windows Server 2008.

In this practice, you install and tune Terminal Services on a computer running Windows Server 2008.

EXERCISE 1 Install Terminal Services

In this exercise, you install Terminal Services components and configure basic server settings, including client connection limits and disconnected session policies. To complete this practice, perform the following steps:

1. Log on to server Glasgow with the Kim_Akers user account.

2. If it does not start automatically, launch the Server Manager console. You might need to click Continue at a User Account Control prompt.

3. Right-click the *Roles* node, and then select Add Roles.

   This will start the Add Roles Wizard.

4. Click Next to bypass the Before You Begin page.

5. On the Select Server Roles page, select the Terminal Services check box, and then click Next twice.

6. On the Select Role Services page, select the Terminal Server check box and TS Licensing check box for role services. When prompted by a warning about installing Terminal Server on a domain controller, click Install Terminal Server Anyway (Not Recommended). Click Next twice.

7. On the Specify Authentication Method For Terminal Server page, select Require Network Level Authentication, and then click Next.

8. On the Specify Licensing Mode page, select Per User, and then click Next twice.

9. On the Configure Discovery Scope For TS Licensing page, ensure that the This Domain scope is selected, and then click Next. Click Install to complete the Add Roles Wizard. Reboot the server when prompted to complete the installation.

   Windows Server 2008 will warn you about Windows being unable to find a valid license server. This is because license servers are valid only after activation.

10. When the installation sequence completes and you have logged back on with the Kim_Akers user account, open the Terminal Services Configuration console from the Terminal Services folder located on the Administrative Tools menu. Click Continue to dismiss the User Account Control dialog box.

11. Right-click RDP-Tcp under Connections, and then select Properties.

    This will bring up the RDP-Tcp Properties dialog box.

12. Click the Sessions tab. In the top section, select the Override User Settings check box and use the drop-down list to end a disconnected session after 1 hour. Use the Active Session Limit drop-down list to set a limit of 12 hours. Use the Idle Session Limit

drop-down list to set a limit of 2 hours. In the bottom section, select the Override User Settings check box and verify that your settings match those displayed in Figure 12-16. Click Apply.

FIGURE 12-16 Configure Session settings.

13. Click the Network Adapter tab. Set the Maximum Connections setting to 30, and then click Apply.

14. Click the Remote Control tab. Select Use Remote Control With The Following Settings. Under Level Of Control, select Interact With The Session, and then click Apply.

15. Click OK to close the RDP-Tcp Properties dialog box, and then close the Terminal Services Configuration console.

EXERCISE 2 Configure Windows System Resource Manager

In this exercise, you install Windows System Resource Manager.

1. While logged on to server Glasgow with the Kim_Akers user account, open the Server Manager console. Right-click the *Features* node, and then select Add Features.

2. On the Select Features page, select the Windows System Resource Manager check box and click Next. If you are prompted by the Add Features Required For Windows System Resource Manager dialog box, click Add Required Features. Click Next, and then click Install. When the installation process completes, click Close.

3. Open the Windows System Resource Manager console from the Administrative Tools menu. Click Continue to dismiss the User Account Control dialog box.

4. When presented with the Connect To Computer dialog box, ensure that This Computer is selected, and then click Connect.

5. Expand the *Resource Allocation Policies* node. Right-click the Equal_Per_Session policy, and then select Set As Managing Policy. Click OK when presented with the warning about the calendar being disabled.

6. Close the Windows System Resource Manager console.

Lesson Summary

- You can configure Terminal Services servers to allow only a limited number of connections as a way of ensuring that they do not become overloaded. You can configure Terminal Services to close disconnected, idle, and active sessions after an appropriate period of time has elapsed.

- You can configure a TS licensing server's scope for the Workgroup, Domain, or Forest. Scope selection options depend on whether the licensing server is a member of a domain. TS Per User CALs are assigned to user accounts. TS Per Device CALs are assigned to devices.

- You can use Windows System Resource Manager to distribute Terminal Services server resources equally between users or sessions.

- Administrators can limit a user's access to his or her local computer's resources when connected to a Terminal Services session.

Lesson Review

You can use the following questions to test your knowledge of the information in Lesson 1, "Configuring Terminal Services Servers." The questions are also available on the companion DVD if you prefer to review them in electronic form.

> **NOTE ANSWERS**
>
> Answers to these questions and explanations of why each answer choice is right or wrong are located in the "Answers" section at the end of the book.

1. You want to allow users in your organization to reconnect to disconnected sessions for up to an hour after the initial connection. The Terminal Services server should terminate any session disconnected for more than an hour. Which of the following settings should you configure to meet this objective?

   A. Active Session Limit

   B. Idle Session Limit

   C. End A Disconnected Session

   D. Do Not Allow Remote Control

2. You want to enable help desk staff to assist with users' Terminal Services sessions. Help desk staff should be able to intervene directly in a session when granted permission by the user but should not have local Administrator access on the server that hosts Terminal Services. All members of the help desk staff are members of the Help_Desk_Staff group. Which of the following settings should you configure? (Choose two. Each correct answer presents part of a complete solution.)

   A. Enable the Require User's Permission setting with the View The Session option selected.

   B. Enable the Require User's Permission setting with the Interact With Session option selected.

   C. Change the permissions on RDP-Tcp Properties and grant the Help_Desk_Staff group Full Control.

   D. Change the permission on RDP-Tcp Properties and grant the Help_Desk_Staff group User Access.

   E. Change the permission on RDP-Tcp Properties and grant the Help_Desk_Staff group Guest Access.

3. Which Terminal Services licensing server scope should you select for a group of computers running Windows Vista at an office where there is no Active Directory domain?

   A. Tree

   B. *Domain*

   C. Zone

   D. Forest

   E. Workgroup

4. Which of the following license server activation methods can you use to activate a Terminal Services license server that is located on a network isolated from the Internet? (Choose two. Each correct answer presents a complete solution.)

   A. Automatic Connection

   B. E-mail

   C. Web Browser

   D. Telephone

   E. SMS messages

5. You need to convert a group of connection files created with Client Connection Manager to the .rdp format. Which of the following tools can you use to accomplish this goal?

   A. Qappsrv.exe

   B. Qwinsta.exe

C. Rdpsign.exe

D. Mstsc.exe

6. Which of the following settings can you NOT apply to the connection properties of a Windows Server 2008 Terminal Services server if you need to support clients connecting with default RDP software from both Windows XP with Service Pack 3 and Windows 2000 Professional with Service Pack 4? (Choose two. Each correct answer presents part of a complete solution.)

   A. RDP Security Layer

   B. SSL (TLS 1.0) Security Layer

   C. Allow Connections Only From Computers Running Remote Desktop With Network Level Authentication

   D. Client Compatible encryption level

   E. Low encryption level

7. Which Windows System Resource Manager policy should you apply when you need to ensure that no one session is allocated more resources than any other even when a single user has multiple active sessions?

   A. Equal_Per_User

   B. Equal_Per_Session

   C. Equal_Per_Process

   D. Equal_Per_IISAppPool

8. Which of the following tools could you use to log data relating to application resource usage during Terminal Services sessions?

   A. Reliability Monitor

   B. Task Manager

   C. File System Resource Manager

   D. Windows System Resource Manager

Lesson 2: Supporting Terminal Services

When you take the 70-649 upgrade exam, you are likely to be tested on three new Windows Server 2008 Terminal Services technologies. The first of these technologies load balances Terminal Services while ensuring that a client that disconnects from a session will be able to reconnect to the server hosting the original session. The second, RemoteApp, enables Terminal Services to stream the display of a specific application hosted on a server to a client rather than requiring the display of an entire desktop. The third, Terminal Services Gateway, enables you to configure access to Terminal Services for clients on remote networks, such as the Internet, without having to implement a full virtual private network (VPN) solution.

> **After this lesson, you will be able to:**
> - Configure Terminal Services load balancing, including setting up Session Broker redirection modes and DNS registration settings.
> - Configure Terminal Services RemoteApp settings, including Remote Desktop Web Connection.
> - Configure Terminal Services Gateway, including configuring resource authorization and connection authorization policies.
>
> **Estimated lesson time: 40 minutes**

Terminal Services Load Balancing

TS Session Broker solves an important problem with load balancing Terminal Services servers: How do you ensure that a client whose session disconnects is able to reconnect to the server hosting that session? TS Session Broker keeps track of session state data, including session IDs, user names, and the names of Terminal Services servers where sessions reside. When a client makes a new connection attempt, the Network Load Balancing service directs the client connection to the Terminal Services server that has the fewest sessions. The server then queries the session broker service to see whether the client has an existing session. If no prior session exists, the Terminal Server accepts the new session. If a prior session exists, TS Session Broker directs that client back to the Terminal Services server that was hosting the original session. The process is similar if you use DNS round robin, except that DNS directs the client randomly to one of the Terminal Services servers in the collection. The term for a collection of Terminal Services servers that participate in load balancing through TS Session Broker is *farm*. Only Windows Server 2008 Terminal Services servers can participate in a TS Session Broker farm.

If it is necessary to perform maintenance on one of the Terminal Services servers in a TS Session Broker farm, you can edit the RDP-Tcp connection properties of that server to stop the establishment of new connections. TS Session Broker monitors this setting and directs new connections to other servers within the farm.

You can add a Terminal Services server to a farm by using the Terminal Services Configuration console. You do this on the TS Session Broker tab in Terminal Services Properties as shown in Figure 12-17. (To access this tab, select Terminal Services Configuration in the console tree. Then, right-click Member Of Farm In TS Session Broker and choose Properties.) Through this properties dialog box, you can set the name of the TS Session Broker server, the farm name, and the weight you want to assign to the server in the farm. You can also specify whether to use IP address redirection. Disable IP address redirection only if the network load balancing method that you have employed supports TS Session Broker routing tokens. Additionally, you need to add the computer accounts of servers in the farm to the Session Directory Computers local group on the computer hosting the TS Session Broker role service.

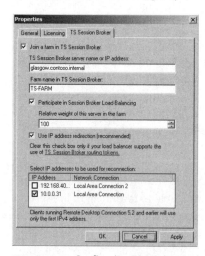

FIGURE 12-17 Configuring TS Session Broker settings.

You can configure all TS Session Broker settings, except the IP address used for reconnection and the server's relative weight, using Group Policy.

MORE INFO **TS SESSION BROKER**

To learn more about TS Session Broker load balancing, consult the following Step-by-Step guide available from the Microsoft Web site at *http://technet.microsoft.com/en-us/library /cc772418.aspx.*

Terminal Services RemoteApp

Most Terminal Services users connect to Terminal Services to use a single application. RemoteApp enables the user to run that application so that it appears as a window on the local desktop rather than within the window of a Terminal Services session. Technical documents often refer to this process as Presentation Virtualization because only the visual output of the application, not the application itself, is displayed on the client computer. In Figure 12-18, you can see WordPad running both locally and as a TS RemoteApp application. The RemoteApp application does not have the Windows Vista borders.

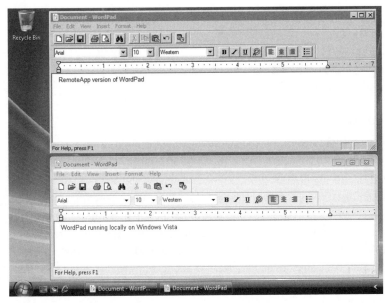

FIGURE 12-18 WordPad RemoteApp and running locally.

Terminal Services RemoteApp is a part of the Terminal Services role service. You use the TS RemoteApp Manager console to configure any application installed on the Terminal Services server to work through RemoteApp. To configure an installed application to run through RemoteApp, perform the following steps:

1. Open TS RemoteApp Manager.
2. In the Actions pane, click Add RemoteApp Programs.
   This starts the RemoteApp Wizard.
3. On the Welcome page, click Next.
4. Select the check boxes for the programs you want to add to the RemoteApp programs list, by using the RemoteApp Wizard dialog box shown in Figure 12-19.

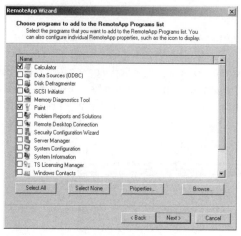

FIGURE 12-19 TS RemoteApp wizard.

5. Complete the wizard.

Terminal Services uses a single session to transmit multiple applications to the client. This means that if you have configured a Terminal Services server to limit sessions, a user who has three applications open is consuming only one of those available sessions.

You can deploy TS RemoteApp applications to clients in your organization, using one of three methods. You can create an RDP shortcut and distribute this file to computers through a shared folder or another method. You can create and distribute a Windows Installer package. You can also distribute this file through a shared folder or publish it to clients through AD DS. Finally, Terminal Services publishes all RemoteApp applications to the server's TS Web Access Web site if you have installed TS Web Access on the server. You will learn more about TS Web Access later in this lesson.

TS RemoteApp Manager gives you the option of digitally signing any RDP shortcuts you wish to distribute. This enables you to use Group Policy to restrict the use of digitally signed RDP files so that users in one organizational unit (OU) can use RDP files while denying use of the same RDP files to users in other OUs. Figure 12-20 shows the Digital Signature settings available for signing RDP files.

When you configure a Windows Installer package, you can determine where the shortcut icons will appear, as shown in Figure 12-21. You can also associate the RemoteApp application with specific file extensions. Be careful about doing this when the client computer has a local program associated with the same file extensions.

To use RemoteApp, a user must be a member of the Remote Desktop Users group or of another group that has the User Access permission on the Security tab of the RDP connection's properties. If you are in a branch office environment where you are deploying RemoteApp from a computer that also functions as a domain controller, you must modify the Allow Log On Through Terminal Services policy.

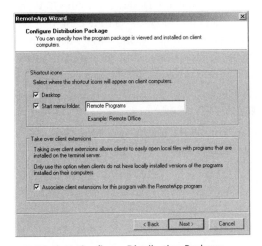

FIGURE 12-20 Digitally sign RDP files.

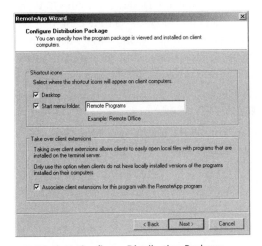

FIGURE 12-21 Configure Distribution Package.

> **MORE INFO**   **TS REMOTEAPP**
>
> To learn more about TS RemoteApp, consult the following TechNet Web page:
> *http://technet.microsoft.com/en-us/library/cc753844.aspx*.

Terminal Services Web Access

Terminal Services Web Access (TS Web Access) is a role service you can add to a Terminal Services server that enables clients to initiate sessions through their Web browsers rather than by opening an RDP shortcut or the Remote Desktop Connection client software. Remember that Windows Server 2008 TS Web Access uses the RDC client software, rather than a special

ActiveX control, for the Terminal Services session. You can establish sessions through TS Web Access only from computers that have Windows XP SP2, Windows Vista, Windows Server 2003 SP1, or Windows Server 2008. Installing TS Web Access requires the Web Server (IIS) role and the Windows Process Activation Service feature.

RemoteApp connections hosted on TS Web Access pages can target only a single Terminal Services server. The term for this Terminal Services server is *data source*. If the Terminal Services server hosting RemoteApp applications is not the server hosting TS Web Access, you can configure the Data Source setting by using the TS Web Access page. A shortcut for this page is accessible through the Administrative Tools menu. To configure an alternate data source, open the TS Web Access page, click the Configuration tab, and, in TS Web Access Properties under the editor zone, enter the name of the Terminal Services server that will function as the data source, and then click Apply. If the data source and the TS Web Access server are different computers, you will need to add the computer account of the TS Web Access server to the TS Web Access Computers security group on the Terminal Services server.

Also accessible through TS Web Access is Remote Desktop Web Connection. Remote Desktop Web Connection enables a user to connect using Remote Desktop from the TS Web Access Web site rather than initiating the connection directly, using the Remote Desktop Connection client software. The usual Terminal Services restrictions apply, and a user's account must be a member of the target computer's Remote Desktop Users group, or have equivalent permissions, before the user can establish a successful session.

> **MORE INFO   TERMINAL SERVICES WEB ACCESS**
>
> To learn more about Terminal Services Web Access, consult the following TechNet Web page: *http://technet.microsoft.com/en-us/library/cc731923.aspx*.

 Quick Check

1. Which user group must a user account belong to before it can access a Remote-App application?

2. Which configuration step do you need to perform on the Terminal Services server when the TS Web Access is located on a different server?

Quick Check Answers

1. Users must be members of the Remote Desktop Users group or another group that has been granted similar permissions.

2. Add the computer account of the TS Web Access server to the TS Web Access Computers security group on the Terminal Services server.

Terminal Services Gateway

Terminal Services Gateway enables you to access RDP servers on your protected network from clients on the Internet without implementing a full VPN solution. Although you will use this technology primarily to grant remote access to Terminal Services servers, it is also possible to allow Remote Desktop access to clients and servers through TS Gateway. Hence, a person can connect from his or her home computer over the Internet to his or her workstation or to a Terminal Services server in the office without having to make a successful VPN connection.

TS Gateway uses RDP over Secure Hypertext Transfer Protocol (HTTPS). As you learned in Chapter 3, "Network Access Configuration," using the SSL port (443) to carry connection data greatly simplifies client connectivity. As is the case with Secure Socket Tunneling Protocol (SSTP), clients can make Terminal Services Gateway connections from behind any firewall that allows HTTPS traffic. A client connects across the Internet to the TS Gateway server by using RDP over HTTPS. The TS Gateway server, which sits behind a perimeter firewall, then makes a standard RDP connection, using port 3389, to the RDP server on the internal network. Most TS Gateway servers will be located on an organization's perimeter network and will be directly addressable by hosts on the Internet.

ISA Server to Publish TS Gateway

You can use Internet Security and Acceleration (ISA) Server 2006 to publish TS Gateway access to clients on the Internet. When you do this, the client connects to ISA Server using RDP over HTTPS. ISA Server then creates an SSL-to-SSL bridge, forwarding traffic on to the TS Gateway server. The advantage of this configuration is that it allows application layer examination traffic as ISA Server decrypts and then re-encrypts the SSL stream as part of the SSL bridge. If ISA Server locates problematic traffic, the connection can be dropped before it reaches the TS Gateway server.

> **MORE INFO** **TS GATEWAY AND ISA SERVER**
>
> To learn more about publishing TS Gateway with ISA Server, consult the following TechNet article: *http://technet.microsoft.com/en-us/magazine/cc742827.aspx*.

Configuring Terminal Services Gateway

TS Gateway servers require an SSL certificate issued from a CA, which identifies clients that will use the server trust. In most cases, certificates issued from an internally managed CA will be sufficient because it is relatively simple to configure a client computer to trust an internal CA. If you are using TS Gateway to provide Terminal Services access to a wider audience, it might be simpler to obtain an SSL certificate from a trusted third-party CA. The name on the SSL certificate should match the fully qualified domain name (FQDN) clients will use for remote connections. This is especially important when issuing certificates from an internal CA that might use another name for the server hosting TS Gateway. Install the SSL certificate prior to adding the TS Gateway role service because the wizard will ask you to specify one during installation. Although it is possible to use a self-signed certificate, you should do this only during testing.

The TS Gateway role service relies upon the following roles, role services, and features:

- Web Server (IIS)
- RPC over HTTP Proxy
- Network Policy and Access Services

As Figure 12-22 shows, Windows Server 2008 will automatically install these components during the installation of the TS Gateway role service if they are not present on the server.

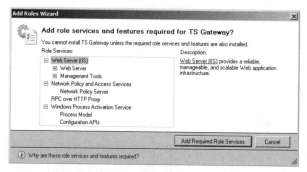

FIGURE 12-22 TS Gateway role services.

MORE INFO   TS GATEWAY

To learn more about TS Gateway, consult the following TechNet article: *http://technet*
.microsoft.com/en-us/library/cc731264.aspx.

After you have installed the TS Gateway role service, you must create a Connection Authorization Policy (TS CAP) and a Resource Authorization Policy (TS RAP). Without these policies, users will be unable to initiate Terminal Services or Remote Desktop sessions through the TS Gateway server.

Terminal Services Connection Authorization Policies (TS CAPs)

You use TS CAPs to specify users and computers that are able to make connections to the TS Gateway server. To create a TS CAP, perform the following steps:

1. Open the TS Gateway Manager console.

2. Locate and then right-click the *Connection Authorization Policies* node under the *TS Gateway Server \ Policies* node.

You can choose to create a new policy through a wizard or through the Custom method. When you choose the *Custom* method, the New TS CAP dialog box appears.

3. On the General tab, enter a policy name. On the Requirements tab, shown in Figure 12-23, enter the user group and, optionally, computer group to which the CAP applies.

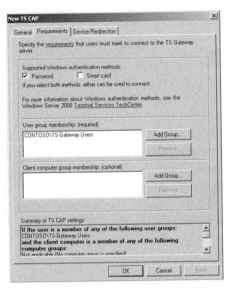

FIGURE 12-23 Create TS CAP.

4. On the Device Redirection tab, select whether you want to allow redirection of all, some, or no devices. Click OK to finalize policy creation.

Terminal Services Resource Authorization Policies

A TS CAP specifies which users can connect to the TS Gateway server. A TS RAP specifies the network resources that users can connect to through TS Gateway. You specify network resources through an Active Directory security group. For example, you could create a TS RAP that allows users in one security group, called Remote_TS_Users, to access a group of Terminal Services servers named Accessible_Remotely. It is then simply a matter of ensuring that you add the appropriate user and computer accounts to the appropriate groups. It is also important to remember that an incoming client connection must match both a TS CAP and a TS RAP.

TS Gateway and Network Access Protection

You can ensure that clients connecting to TS Gateway meet a benchmark standard of health by using Network Access Protection (NAP). By using NAP, you can ensure that clients connecting through the TS Gateway server have their antivirus and antispyware software up to date. NAP also enables you to ensure that the most recent software updates are present before allowing a connection. In most environments, people connect to TS Gateway from client computers that your organization has minimal control over. You learned about Network Access Protection in Chapter 4, "Network Access Security."

To implement TS Gateway NAP enforcement, you must configure NAP health policy to check on the TS Gateway server.

MORE INFO **TS GATEWAY AND NAP**

To learn more about integrating TS Gateway and NAP, consult the following TechNet article: *http://technet.microsoft.com/en-us/library/cc732172.aspx*.

In addition to configuring the TS Gateway server, it is necessary to configure the Remote Desktop Connection application on each client to channel traffic through the TS Gateway server. To do this, navigate to the Advanced tab of Remote Desktop Connection and click Settings under Connect From Anywhere. This displays the TS Gateway Server Settings dialog box, shown in Figure 12-24. The settings you can configure in this dialog box include automatically detecting TS Gateway server settings, using a specific TS Gateway server, whether TS Gateway should be bypassed for local addresses, blocking the use of a TS Gateway server, and whether TS Gateway credentials are used for the remote computer.

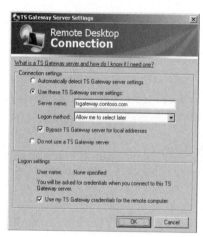

FIGURE 12-24 TS Gateway Server Settings dialog box.

It is also possible to configure TS Gateway settings through Group Policy. The appropriate policies are located under User Configuration \Policies \Administrative Templates\Windows Components \Terminal Services \TS Gateway. You should note that these policies are located under the *User Configuration* node and not under the *Computer Configuration* node like most of the policies that you learn about in this chapter. The three policies you can configure are:

- **Set TS Gateway Authentication Method** You can specify whether NTLM, Basic, locally logged on, or Smart Card credentials are required.
- **Enable Connection Through TS Gateway** When configured, you can allow or disallow connections through TS Gateway.
- **Set TS Gateway Server Address** You can specify the address of your organization's TS Gateway server.

All these policies give you the option of allowing users to alter the settings if required.

PRACTICE TS Web Access and RemoteApp

In this practice, you install TS Web Access and then publish several TS RemoteApp applications.

EXERCISE 1 Installing TS Web Access

In this exercise, you install TS Web Access on server Glasgow, enabling users to initiate Terminal Services sessions through their Web browser.

1. Log on to server Glasgow with the Kim_Akers user account. If the Server Manager console does not start automatically, open it manually. Click Continue to dismiss the User Account Control dialog box.

2. Expand the *Roles* node. Right-click Terminal Services, and then click Add Role Services.

3. On the Select Role Services page, select the TS Web Access check box. If prompted by the Add Role Services dialog box, click Add Required Role Services. Click Next three times and click Install. Click Close to complete the installation routine.

4. Verify that TS Web Access has installed correctly by navigating to *https://GLASGOW /ts*, using Microsoft Internet Explorer. Log on to the Web site, using the Kim_Akers user account credentials.

> **NOTE** **INTERNET EXPLORER ENHANCED SECURITY CONFIGURATION**
> You might need to disable Internet Explorer Enhanced Security Configuration to view this Web site.

5. Click Remote Desktop and verify that Internet Explorer matches Figure 12-25. Close Internet Explorer.

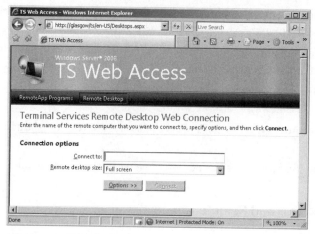

FIGURE 12-25 TS Web Access.

EXERCISE 2   Publishing TS RemoteApp Applications

In this exercise, you configure two applications to work with TS RemoteApp. You configure one application to be deployed as an RDP shortcut and another application to be deployed as a Windows Installer package.

1. Ensure that you are logged on to server Glasgow with the Kim_Akers user account. From the Terminal Services folder of Administrative Tools, select TS RemoteApp Manager. Click Continue to dismiss the User Account Control dialog box.

2. In the Actions pane, click Add RemoteApp Programs.

    This will start the RemoteApp wizard.

3. Click Next.

4. On the Choose Programs To Add To The RemoteApp Programs List page, select the Calculator and Paint check boxes, and then click Next. Click Finish.

5. In the TS RemoteApp Manager console, right-click Calculator in the list of RemoteApp programs, and then select Create .rdp File.

    The RemoteApp Wizard will launch.

6. Click Next.

7. Verify that the Specify Package Settings page matches Figure 12-26. Click Next, and then click Finish.

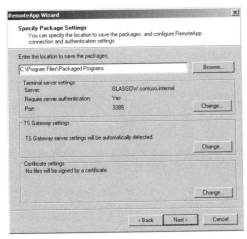

FIGURE 12-26 Package Settings.

8. In the TS RemoteApp Manager console, right-click Paint in the list of RemoteApp programs, and then click Create Windows Installer Package.

   The RemoteApp Wizard will launch.

9. Click Next.

10. On the Specify Package Settings page, click Next. Verify that the Configure Distribution Package settings match those in Figure 12-27, click Next, and then click Finish.

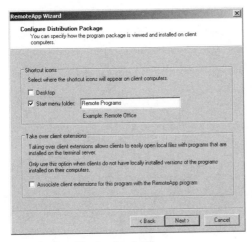

FIGURE 12-27 Distribution Settings.

Lesson Summary

- TS RemoteApp allows users to view only an application window of an application running on a Terminal Services server rather than having to view an entire Remote Desktop window.

- You can publish TS RemoteApp applications as RDP shortcuts and as Windows Installer packages and make them available through TS Web Access.

- TS Web Access allows users to access TS RemoteApp applications and to access Remote Desktop Web connection through their Web browsers rather than through traditional methods.

- TS Gateway allows users on the Internet to access Terminal Services servers on protected networks without needing a full VPN solution. TS Gateway uses the RDP over HTTPS protocol.

- TS CAPs define which users can connect to a TS Gateway. TS RAPs define which users can connect to specific computers on the internal network. An incoming session must match both a TS RAP and a TS CAP before a successful connection can be established.

- TS Session Broker can ensure that disconnected sessions are reconnected to the appropriate Terminal Services server when load balancing is implemented.

- A collection of Terminal Services servers participating in load balancing with Session Broker is known as a farm.

Lesson Review

You can use the following questions to test your knowledge of the information in Lesson 2, "Supporting Terminal Services." The questions are also available on the companion DVD if you prefer to review them in electronic form.

> **NOTE ANSWERS**
>
> Answers to these questions and explanations of why each answer choice is right or wrong are located in the "Answers" section at the end of the book.

1. You have installed the TS Session Directory role service on a computer named Copenhagen that is running Windows Server 2008 in the *fabrikam.internal* Active Directory domain. The TS Session Directory server will use network load balancing to distribute Terminal Services sessions equitably across six Windows Server 2008 Terminal Services servers. You have configured the farm name and set the address of the TS Session Broker server to Copenhagen on each Terminal Services server. You have set up and tested Network Load Balancing. Which of the following steps must you also perform?

A. Add the computer accounts of the six Terminal Services servers to the Remote Desktop Users group on Copenhagen.

B. Add the Copenhagen computer account to the Remote Desktop Users group on each Terminal Services server.

C. Add the computer accounts of the six Terminal Services servers to the Session Directory Computers local group on Copenhagen.

D. Add the Copenhagen computer account to the Session Directory Computers local group on each Terminal Services server.

2. Under which conditions should you disable the Use IP Address Redirection option when adding a Terminal Services server to a TS Session Broker farm?

A. Your network load balancing solution supports TS Session Broker routing tokens.

B. Your network load balancing solution does not support TS Session Broker routing tokens.

C. Your network environment supports only IPv6.

D. Your network environment supports only IPv4.

3. Which of the following methods can you use to distribute TS RemoteApp applications to users in your organization who do not have administrative privileges on their computers running Windows Vista? (Choose three. Each correct answer presents a complete solution.)

A. Place RDP shortcuts in a shared folder.

B. Publish RDP shortcuts, using Active Directory.

C. Publish Windows Installer files, using Active Directory.

D. Direct users to the Terminal Services Web Access page.

E. Place Windows Installer files in a shared folder.

4. You have just deployed an accounting application, using RemoteApp, by publishing a Windows Installer file through AD DS. Several users complain that they are unable to use the application. You check on your own computer and find that you are able to access the application without any problems. Which of the following will resolve this problem?

A. Decrease the connection limit on the Terminal Services server.

B. Add the user accounts of people who need to access the accounting application to the Remote Desktop Users group.

C. Disable device redirection on the Terminal Services server.

D. Reinstall the application on the Terminal Services server.

5. Clients' computers from outside your organization need to connect to your Terminal Services server through a TS Gateway server. Which of the following SSL certificates should you install on this server?

   A. Certificate issued from an internal enterprise root CA

   B. Certificate issued from an internal enterprise subordinate CA

   C. Certificate issued from an external third-party CA

   D. Certificate issued from an internal standalone root CA

6. On which TCP port are external connections to TS Gateway servers made?

   A. 80

   B. 443

   C. 3389

   D. 25

Chapter Review

To further practice and reinforce the skills you learned in this chapter, you can perform the following tasks:

- Review the chapter summary.
- Complete the case scenarios. These scenarios set up real-world situations involving the topics of this chapter and ask you to create solutions.
- Complete the suggested practices.
- Take a practice test.

Chapter Summary

- TS RemoteApp enables users' sessions to include only the presentation of the application rather than the presentation of an entire desktop.
- TS Gateway allows RDP connections from the Internet to internal Terminal Services servers without the necessity of a full VPN solution.
- TS Session Broker, also known as TS load balancing, load balances Terminal Services sessions while also ensuring that disconnected sessions are reconnected to the appropriate server.
- Windows System Resource Manager enables you to allocate the resources of a Terminal Services server on a per-user or per-session basis.
- License servers can operate on a workgroup, domain, or forest scope. Servers with a domain scope are discoverable only if installed on domain controllers. License servers can issue per-user and per-device CALs.
- You can configure Terminal Services servers to limit the maximum number of sessions, limit each user to a single session, and terminate disconnected sessions after a grace period has expired. You can also configure remote control settings so that administrators can interact with sessions only if users grant them permission.

Case Scenarios

In the following case scenarios, you apply what you've learned about Terminal Services. You can find answers to these questions in the "Answers" section at the end of this book.

Case Scenario 1: Wingtip Toys Terminal Services Deployment

You are in the process of deploying Windows Server 2008 to computers with the Terminal Services role service installed at Wingtip Toys. Wingtip Toys has a two-domain forest, *east. wingtiptoys.internal* and *west.wingtiptoys.internal*. After a series of trials to benchmark server performance, you have concluded that each server supports a maximum of 50 concurrent sessions. Approximately 220 users require access to Terminal Services. You will deploy only four servers during the initial rollout. You want to deploy only a single license server. With these facts in mind, you must find answers to the following questions:

1. Which licensing scope should you configure for the TS licensing server?

2. What steps can you take to ensure that a maximum number of users can connect to each Terminal Services server?

3. What steps can you take to ensure that no single user's session uses a disproportionate amount of each Terminal Services server's resources?

Case Scenario 2: Supporting Terminal Services at Fabrikam, Inc.

You are responsible for supporting an existing Windows Server 2003 and Windows Server 2008 Terminal Services deployment at Fabrikam, Inc. With that in mind, you must find answers to the following questions:

1. Which load balancing technology should you use to ensure that new sessions are distributed as equitably as possible?

2. What steps do you have to take with the Windows Server 2003 Terminal Services servers for them to participate in a TS Session Broker farm?

3. What steps do you need to take to ensure that the TS Web Access server can access RemoteApp applications on the RemoteApp server?

Suggested Practices

To help you successfully master the exam objectives presented in this chapter, complete the following tasks.

Configure Windows Server 2008 Terminal Services RemoteApp

Do both practices in this section.

- **Practice 1** Install and configure TS Web Access on one server. Configure the TS Web Access server to publish RemoteApp applications on a second server.

- **Practice 2** Publish a RemoteApp application as both an RDP file and a Windows Installer package.

Configure Terminal Services Gateway

Do both practices in this section.

- **Practice 1** Create a TS CAP that allows members of the Trusted_Users group access to TS Gateway.

- **Practice 2** Create a TS CAP that allows members of the Trusted_Users group access to Terminal Services servers in the Remote_Access_TS group.

Configure Terminal Services Load Balancing

Do both practices in this section.

- **Practice 1**   Install the TS Session Broker service on one computer running Windows Server 2008. Configure two other computers, running Windows Server 2008, as Terminal Services servers. Configure these servers as members of a Session Broker farm.

- **Practice 2**   Configure DNS round robin to support the TS Session Broker farm that you configured in Practice 1.

Configure and Monitor Terminal Services Resources

Do both practices in this section.

- **Practice 1**   Install the Windows System Resource Manager feature on a computer running Windows Server 2008 that has the Terminal Services role service installed.

- **Practice 2**   Apply the Equal_Per_Session policy to the computer running Windows Server 2008 that has the Terminal Services role service installed.

Configure Terminal Services Licensing

Do both practices in this section.

- **Practice 1**   Install Terminal Services licensing on a standalone computer running Windows Server 2008 that is not a member of an Active Directory domain.

- **Practice 2**   Verify the location of the license database by using the TS Licensing Manager console.

Configure Terminal Services Client Connections

Do both practices in this section.

- **Practice 1**   Configure quotas by using File System Resource Manager to ensure that Terminal Services user profiles do not exceed 100 megabytes (MB).

- **Practice 2**   Use the Remote Desktops console to manage two or more services, using RDP.

Configure Terminal Services Server Options

Do both practices in this section.

- **Practice 1**   Configure a limit of 10 simultaneous connections on a Windows Server 2008 Terminal Services server.

- **Practice 2**   Configure a maximum active session limit of two hours on a Windows Server 2008 Terminal Services server.

Take a Practice Test

The practice tests on this book's companion DVD offer many options. For example, you can test yourself on just one exam objective, or you can test yourself on all the upgrade exam content. You can set up the test so that it closely simulates the experience of taking a certification exam, or you can set it up in study mode so that you can look at the correct answers and explanations after you answer each question.

> **MORE INFO   PRACTICE TESTS**
>
> For details about all the practice test options available, see the "How to Use the Practice Tests" section in this book's Introduction.

CHAPTER 13

Configuring a Web Services Infrastructure

M odern Web sites allow users access through any standard browser and present users with functionality and a user experience that is equivalent to having a wide range of locally installed applications. Whatever their current operating systems (within limits) and their default browsers, users expect to access both external and internal databases and customize their environment.

Windows Server 2008 includes Internet Information Services version 7.0 (IIS7). This Web services platform supports a wide variety of Web content and applications. As a Windows professional, you are familiar with previous versions of IIS. IIS7 is significantly enhanced to provide improved reliability, scalability, and manageability to support the requirements of modern Web sites. It also provides backward compatibility to support the very large number of Web sites currently hosted by previous IIS versions.

This chapter discusses Web applications. It looks at how you use the Web Server (IIS) and Application Server server roles and various role services to support, implement, and manage Web sites. This chapter discusses Web site and Web application implementation and configuration and how to implement Web site security and authentication.

Exam objectives in this chapter:

- Configure web applications.
- Manage web sites.
- Manage Internet Information Services (IIS).
- Configure SSL security.
- Configure web site authentication and permissions.

Lessons in this chapter:

Before You Begin

To complete the lessons in this chapter, you must have done the following:

- Installed the Windows Server 2008 Enterprise server Glasgow configured as a domain controller in the *contoso.internal* domain as described in Chapter 1, "Configuring Internet Protocol Addressing."

- Optionally installed the Windows Server 2008 Enterprise server Boston in the *contoso.internal* domain as described in Chapter 2, "Configuring IP Services." You do not need to use this server for the practices, but it is required if you want to perform all the suggested practices.

 REAL WORLD

Ian McLean

A Web site is frequently an organization's window to the outside world and its public face. It needs to be active and dynamic but, at the same time, easy to navigate. If customers access services and purchase goods through a Web site, they should have an easy and pleasant experience when doing so but, at the same time, have confidence that their personal data, credit card numbers, or bank account details cannot be stolen by malicious third parties. Legitimate users should find the site accessible and easy to use. Attackers should be firmly and effectively blocked.

An organization's internal Web site should be considered as important as its external Web site. It presents a company's image to employees, and employees are as important as customers. An internal Web site should provide an easy method for employees to get information they need and to share information with colleagues. At the same time, confidential information such as salary details and Human Relations reports should be strongly protected. The malicious or careless insider can be as much of a threat to an organization as the external attacker, and the fact that an intranet is available only to staff does not mean you need be any less careful about security.

Security is always a balance. Users want easy access, your security specialist wants everything locked down as tightly as possible, and your Web application developer wants applications to run without permissions problems. So who, ultimately, takes responsibility when something goes wrong, when someone accesses something they should not, or when a key application fails to work?

If you are the one responsible for managing Web sites and servers, installing role services, and configuring application security, the answer is you.

Lesson 1: Configuring Web Applications

This lesson discusses how the Web Server and the Application Server server roles work together to enable you to implement Web applications. It covers the user experience and the various types of Web sites you can implement. The lesson covers the role services available in the Web Server server role and the facilities offered by the Application Server server role. It discusses the Default Web Site, adding Web sites and Web applications, the Microsoft .NET Framework, and how to create and configure application pools.

> **After this lesson, you will be able to:**
> - Install the Web Server server role and associated role services.
> - Explain the functions of the role services associated with the Web Server server role and decide which services to install.
> - Add and configure Web sites, Web applications, and application pools.
> - Discuss the .NET Framework.
>
> **Estimated lesson time: 50 minutes**

Using the Web Server Role

Users access Web-based content and applications from a wide range of client computers that run a variety of operating systems and browsers. Typically, there is no need to install or configure software on client computers. Because most operating systems support standards-based Web browsers, most users already have the basic client tools they need to access content, and software developers can use a range of technologies to present content and deploy applications.

Supporting Web Page Scenarios

When implementing Web applications, you must support a variety of scenarios, for example:

- Company intranets
- Public Web sites
- Enterprise Web sites
- Extranet scenarios
- Web hosting

As a Microsoft Windows Server 2003 professional, you should be familiar with these scenarios. Most organizations deploy several IIS role services to implement the various Web site scenarios they support. You need to know the features of the Web Server server role and understand how the Web services it offers can meet the specific needs of each deployment.

Web Server Role Features

When you install the Web Server server role in Windows Server 2008, the IIS platform installed is IIS7. You probably studied previous IIS platforms for your Windows Server 2003 examinations and might have worked with them as part of your job. For the Windows Server 2008 upgrade examinations, be aware of how IIS works in general and, in particular, the new features that IIS7 provides.

IIS7 includes new features that provide improved performance and functionality. You can take advantage of enhancements in the following areas:

- **Security** When you install the Web Server server role, IIS7 is enabled with only basic functionality. Even binary files for unused features are not available for access in standard operating system locations. As a systems administrator, you must explicitly enable additional services and features. This helps reduce the IIS attack surface. Functionality for automatically detecting common hacking attempts now ships with IIS7. This feature was typically enabled in previous versions by installing the *URLScan.exe* utility.

> **MORE INFO** URLSCAN
>
> For more information about *URLScan*, see *http://technet.microsoft.com/en-us/security /cc242650.aspx*. However, this is now an older utility and likely will not be tested in the upgrade examinations (except possibly as an incorrect answer).

- **Diagnostics and troubleshooting** Web services are a mission-critical component of most organizational infrastructures, and you must detect and resolve Web-based errors quickly. IIS7 makes it easier to pinpoint problems and obtain the details necessary to address them. For example, IIS7 offers a detailed errors facility and failed-request tracing. The Web Capacity Analysis Tool (WCAT) (an IIS6 tool that remains in use in IIS7) remains available for stress testing and you can orphan failed processes.

> **NOTE** DETAILED ERRORS
>
> IIS7 provides a verbose errors facility that gives much more information than was available in previous versions. This is implemented by the CustomErrorsIIS7 module and suggests corrective action or lines of inquiry. Details include the configuration section, the module in use, the current page, and so on. By default, verbose errors are delivered only to localhost.

> **MORE INFO** FAILED REQUEST TRACING
>
> To view a videocast about failed-request tracing and to obtain more information about failed-request tracing rules, see *www.microsoft.com/emea/spotlight/sessionh .aspx?videoid=569* and *http://technet.microsoft.com/en-us/library/cc742393.aspx*.

MORE INFO **WCAT**

For more information about WCAT and a link to a download page, see *http://msdn .microsoft.com/en-us/library/ms524518.aspx*.

- **Administration**   Previous versions of IIS presented you with a large number of property pages and dialog boxes. IIS7 offers new administration tools designed to manage the available options and settings effectively.

MORE INFO **WEB ADMINISTRATION TOOLS AND TECHNIQUES**

For more information about the Web administration tools and techniques provided by IIS7, see *http://technet.microsoft.com/en-us/library/cc268249.aspx*.

- **Centralized configuration management**   Large organizations typically support a considerable number of IIS installations. Sometimes you need to deploy a number of Web servers with the same configuration settings. In previous versions of IIS, you often needed to connect to each server and manage its configuration individually. IIS7 shares configuration information across server farms. IIS7 security accounts comprise a consistent set of user accounts, including globally unique identifiers (GUIDs). Administrators can use specific account names and settings when scripting and automating common processes. In addition, command-line support is considerably enhanced in IIS7.
- **Backward compatibility**   Typically, Web sites and applications created for previous versions of IIS are compatible with IIS. In addition, IIS6 management tools are provided for applications that depend on them.
- **Delegation**   IIS7 enables you to implement granular security configuration permissions to support Web-hosting environments and enterprise-level configurations.

MORE INFO **DELEGATING CONFIGURATION IN IIS7**

For more information about IIS7 configuration delegation, see *http://technet.microsoft .com/en-us/library/cc627314.aspx*.

In its simplest configuration, the IIS7 Web server component provides basic HTTP functionality. IIS7 is modular and includes components and features that support different types of content and applications. Most deployments require only a subset of these features, and administrators can enable only those components their Web applications require.

This modular approach requires you to enable explicitly the features you require. Also, modular architecture provides security advantages. Only the features required for your contents and applications are enabled, thus reducing the attack surface. This is especially important for public Web servers that might be targets for malicious attacks or unauthorized access attempts.

Another advantage of the modular approach is that it improves performance. Unnecessary components are not installed or enabled and therefore cannot use up system resources on the server running IIS7. By enabling only those features that are specifically required, you can retain server resources for use by other applications. This results in improved performance and scalability.

Organizations typically use IIS in various deployment scenarios whose security and functionality requirements vary significantly. A modular architecture enables you to customize each deployment based on its specific needs. For example, the authentication and security requirements of internal Web servers and Internet-accessible Web servers often differ. With IIS7, you can enable the required features for each Web site type independently.

> **MORE INFO**   **THE IIS WEB SITE**
>
> You will find a lot of information about IIS7 on the IIS Web site. This site was created by the IIS team at Microsoft and includes tutorials, technical articles, and other details about working with the IIS platform. The site includes links to downloads and information about products that work with (or on) the IIS platform. For more information, see *http://www.iis.net*.

Understanding IIS7 Role Services

IIS7 role services define which specific features and options of the IIS platform are available on the local Web server. When you have installed the Web Server server role (and hence IIS7) on a computer running Windows Server 2008, you can use Server Manager to add Role Services, as shown in Figure 13-1.

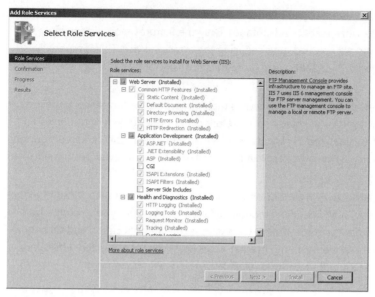

FIGURE 13-1 Adding Web Server role services in Server Manager.

Web Server role services are organized into the following areas:

- IIS Server Core features
- Common HTTP features
- Application development features
- Health and diagnostics
- Security features
- Performance features
- Web management tools

Installing the Web Server server role installs the core IIS services the optional components require. Each of the areas listed contains features and options related to that area, but several items depend on other role services. In general, if you select an IIS7 component to install without first installing its dependencies, you are prompted to add the required role services. For example, to install and use the ASP.NET role service, you must also install the ISAPI Extensions, ISAPI Filters, and .NET Extensibility role services.

Although adding a role service makes it available for use by Web sites and applications, you sometimes must perform additional configuration. For example, enabling selected authentication options will not automatically apply these options to all your Web sites, and you must configure Web site authentication separately.

In most IIS7 installations, you install additional features based on the specific requirements of the Web sites and Web applications the server is hosting. If you choose to install only the Web Server server role and accept the default configuration, your IIS functionality is limited.

This configuration is appropriate if your installation supports limited static content and does not need advanced security or development features. In many cases, you will want to enable additional options.

When you install the Web Server server role, some configuration features are automatically installed as part of the IIS Server Core (on both Server Core and Full Installation configurations). Other features are installed by default, while still others are optional and should be installed only if required. For example, most of the common HTTP features (with the exception of HTTP Redirection) are installed by default, whereas all the Application Development features are optional and available for installation if you require them.

Each of the areas listed contains features and options related to that area, but several items depend on other role services. In general, if you select an IIS7 component to install (for example, ASP.NET) without first selecting its dependencies, you are prompted automatically to add the required role services. You install the ASP.NET role service in the practice at the end of this chapter.

IIS Server Core Features

All IIS7 Server Core features are included in the Web Server server role. These features consist of the following:

- **Anonymous Authentication** This supports anonymous server access, which enables any user to access content without being required to provide credentials. Every IIS server needs to have at least one authentication mechanism configured, and anonymous authentication is the default mechanism.

- **Configuration Validation** This validates server and application configurations. If a server or application is incorrectly configured, IIS7 generates error messages that can help you detect and diagnose the problem.

- **HTTP Cache** This improves performance by loading a processed copy of a requested Web page from cache, resulting in reduced server overhead and faster response times. IIS7 supports output caching in both user and kernel mode. Kernel-mode caching boosts performance and increases the number of requests IIS can process.

- **Protocol Support** This supports common protocols that Web servers use, including HTTP keep-alives, custom headers, and redirect headers. HTTP keep-alives allow clients to maintain open connections with servers. This speeds up the request process after a client has established a connection with a server. Custom headers and redirect headers enable you to optimize IIS support for advanced features of the HTTP 1.1 specification.

MORE INFO **THE HTTP 1.1 SPECIFICATION**

You can access the HTTP 1.1 specification at *http://www.ietf.org/rfc/rfc2068.txt*. However, the upgrade examinations are unlikely to ask detailed questions based on the content of this document.

Common HTTP Features

HTTP features install the common services required for serving Web content. All these features install by default except for HTTP Redirection, which is optional. Common HTTP features include the following:

- **Default Document**   This supports the display of default documents. If a user enters a request with a trailing / character (for example, *http://www.tailspintoys.com/*), IIS7 redirects the request to the default document for the Web server or directory (for example, *default.html*).

- **Directory Browsing**   If Default Document is enabled but no default document exists for the URL specified, IIS uses Directory Browsing to generate a listing of the contents of the relevant directory. Directory Browsing sends information about the files and folders on a Web site to the client's Web browser. This is typically disabled for public Web sites.

- **HTTP Errors**   This supports custom error and detailed error notification. If you enable this feature and the server encounters an error, for example, if a page cannot be found or the server is busy, IIS7 returns an error message to all clients.

- **Static Content**   This supports static Web content, for example, HTML documents and GIF or JPEG images.

- **HTTP Redirection**   Unlike the other common HTTP features, HTTP Redirection is optional. It supports HTTP requests that redirect users from an old site to a new site. Requests for files in the old location are mapped to files in the new location. Redirection is the process of configuring the Web server to issue a redirect message that instructs the client to resubmit the request to the new location.

> **MORE INFO   HTTP REDIRECTION**
>
> For more information about HTTP redirection, see *http://technet.microsoft.com/en-us /library/cc732969.aspx* and follow the links.

 Quick Check

1. Which common HTTP feature supports custom error and detailed error notification?

2. Which common HTTP feature is optional?

Quick Check Answers

1. HTTP Errors

2. HTTP Redirection

Health and Diagnostics Features

Health and diagnostics features enable you to monitor and diagnose problems on your servers, sites, and applications. The HTTP Logging and Request Monitor role services are installed by default. The other health and diagnostics features are optional. Health and diagnostics features include the following:

- **HTTP Logging**   This enables support for logging Web site activity and permits IIS7 to store HTTP request information in text files on the server's file system, together with a set of default settings for logging requests. The default location for log files is %systemdrive%\inetpub\logs\logfiles.

- **Request Monitor**   This enables you to view details about currently executing requests within the Web server process, the run state of a Web site, or the currently executing application domains.

- **Custom Logging**   Installing this feature enables support for custom logging. Default HTTP logging provides a text-based format for storing Web request information, but you might prefer to use custom logging to create your own COM-based modules.

- **Logging Tools**   Installing this feature enables you to manage server activity logs and automate common logging tasks by using scripts. Typically, HTTP request logs are difficult to view and analyze manually. The Logging Tools feature helps you overcome this problem by providing utilities for accessing and analyzing log files.

- **ODBC Logging**   Installing this feature enables support for logging Web site activity to Open Database Connectivity (ODBC)–compliant databases. ODBC format can be read by, for example, Microsoft SQL Server and Microsoft Excel. Note, however, that ODBC logging can cause significant processing and storage overhead, especially on busy Web servers.

> **NOTE**   **USING LOG-ANALYZER APPLICATIONS**
>
> As an alternative to installing the Logging Tools and ODBC Logging role services, you can use log analyzer applications to process the text-based log files produced by HTTP Logging. These applications can isolate problems (such as erroneous links or missing content) as well as analyze traffic and the popularity of specific Web pages.

- **Tracing**   Installing this feature helps you trace failed requests. The feature retains information just long enough to determine whether execution was successful. If it was not, the results are stored on the Web server for later analysis.

> **NOTE**   **HTTP TRACING**
>
> If you choose not to install the Tracing role service, you can instead enable HTTP tracing to trace events and warnings through the IIS Server Core.

✔ **Quick Check**

■ Which role service (or feature) enables support for logging Web site activity to ODBC-compliant databases?

Quick Check Answer

■ ODBC Logging

Application Development Features

All the role services that support application development are optional. Typically, you would install some of or all of these features if you wanted to use dynamic Web services and Web application support. Some of these features require other role services to be installed in support. When you install a role service that requires other role services, the supporting services are listed automatically and you can install them with a single click. You can install the following application development features.

■ **.NET Extensibility**   This feature enables a Web server to host .NET Framework applications and provides for IIS integration with ASP.NET and .NET Framework. You can use the .NET Framework programming platform to make modifications to IIS Web server functionality, and the .NET Extensibility role service enables developers to access the IIS management namespaces and objects for building logic that interacts with Web server requests.

■ **ASP**   This feature enables a Web server to host classic Active Server Pages (ASP) applications. The ASP role service is the predecessor to the ASP.NET platform and provides a script-based method of developing Web-based applications. To use ASP, you must also use ISAPI Extensions.

■ **ASP.NET**   This feature enables a Web server to host ASP.NET applications. ASP.NET is the primary Microsoft Web server development platform and is based on the .NET Framework. To use ASP.NET, you must also use .NET Extensibility, ISAPI Extensions, and ISAPI Filters.

■ **CGI**   This feature enables a Web server to host Common Gateway Interface (CGI) executables. CGI is a standard that describes how executables specified in Web addresses, also known as gateway scripts, pass information to Web servers. By default, IIS handles all .exe files as CGI scripts.

■ **ISAPI Extensions**   This feature enables ISAPI Extensions to handle client requests. In the IIS Server Core, several components rely on handlers that are based on ISAPI Extensions, for example, ASP and ASP.NET. By default, IIS handles all .dll files as ISAPI extensions.

- **ISAPI Filters** This feature enables developers to add custom ISAPI filters that modify Web server behavior. ISAPI filters are custom code that developers can create to process specific Web server requests. This enables an application to receive Web request details and return the appropriate content based on server-side logic.

- **Server-Side Includes** This feature enables a Web server to parse files with Server-Side Includes (SSI). SSI is a technology that enables IIS7 to insert data into a document when a client requests it. This enables Web designers to embed common content, for example, site headers, navigation elements, and site footers on all their Web pages. If the SSI feature is disabled, IIS7 handles .stm, .shtm, and .shtml files as static content. The SSI feature is disabled by default.

Security Features

Security is an important concern for all Web sites, Web applications, and Web services. Role services that implement security features are optional, and you can enable a wide variety of security mechanisms, depending on your specific deployment and usage configuration. Lesson 4, "Configuring SSL Security," describes how you select and implement these security mechanisms. The following Security role services are available in IIS7.

- **Basic Authentication** This requires a user to provide a valid username and password to access content. All browsers support this authentication mechanism. However, the password is transmitted without encryption. If you want to specify Basic Authentication for a site or directory, disable Anonymous Authentication for the site or directory.

- **Client Certificate Mapping Authentication** This maps client certificates to Active Directory accounts for authentication. If you enable certificate mapping, this feature performs Active Directory certificate mapping to authenticate authorized clients.

- **Digest Authentication** This uses a Windows domain controller to authenticate user requests for content. You can use Digest Authentication through firewalls and proxies.

- **IIS Client Certificate Mapping Authentication** This maps Secure Sockets Layer (SSL) client certificates to Windows accounts for authentication. If you use this method of authentication, user credentials and mapping rules are stored within the IIS configuration store.

- **IP and Domain Restrictions** This enables you to grant or deny access to a server by IP address, network ID, or domain. Granting access permits a computer to make requests for resources but does not necessarily allow users to work with resources. Users still need to authenticate.

- **Request Filtering** This enables you to reject suspicious requests by scanning URLs sent to a server and filtering out unwanted requests (for example, requests from known spammers). By default, IIS blocks requests for file extensions that could be misused.

- **URL Authorization**   This supports authorization based on configuration rules. You can require logon and allow or deny access to specific URLs based on usernames, .NET roles, and the HTTP request method.

- **Windows Authentication**   This supports Windows-based authentication, using NTLM, Kerberos, or both. Windows Authentication is primarily used in internal networks.

Performance Features

IIS7 supports both static and dynamic compression. In addition to these features, IIS7 also offers optional enhanced Performance features. The following Performance features are available.

- **Static Content Compression**   This feature is enabled by default and works automatically, provided that users' Web browsers support HTTP compression. On modern servers, bandwidth is typically more limited than processing power. Microsoft therefore recommends that unless an organization has a specific reason to disable it, Static Content Compression should remain enabled.

- **Dynamic Content Compression**   This is disabled by default, but you can enable it to reduce bandwidth consumption for Web applications. Dynamic content typically displays different information to different users and often changes for each request that is made to the Web server.

- **File Cache**   This enhanced feature caches file handles for files opened by the server engine and related server modules.

- **Managed Engine**   This enhanced feature enables IIS7 to integrate with the ASP. NET run-time engine. If you do not configure this feature, ASP.NET integration is also disabled.

- **Token Cache**   This enhanced feature caches Windows security tokens for password-based authentication schemes, including Anonymous Authentication, Basic Authentication, and Digest Authentication.

- **HTTP Trace**   This enhanced feature supports request tracing whenever a client requests a traced URL.

- **URI Cache**   This enhanced feature caches the Uniform Resource Identifier (URI)–specific server state.

Web Management Tools

One of the primary IIS7 design goals is to provide support for IIS6-based Web applications. Although many applications can be moved directly to IIS7, several backward-compatibility features are included as role services. You can therefore use Web management tools for managing IIS7 or for backward compatibility with IIS6. Available Web Management Tools include the following:

- **IIS Management Console**   This is installed with the Web Server server role and in turn installs the Internet Information Services (IIS) Manager, which is the primary management tool for working with IIS7.

- **IIS Management Scripts and Tools**   This installs the IIS command-line administration tool and related features for managing Web servers from the command prompt. This tool is especially useful in Server Core installations.

- **IIS Management Service**   This installs the Web Management Service (WMSVC), which provides a Web core that acts as a standalone Web server for remote administration, using the IIS Management Console.

- **IIS Metabase Compatibility**   This implements backward compatibility with servers running IIS6 Web sites by installing a component that translates IIS6 metabase changes to the IIS7 configuration store.

- **IIS 6 WMI Compatibility**   This enables you to script servers running IIS6 Web sites by installing the IIS6 Windows Management Instrumentation (WMI) scripting interfaces.

- **IIS 6 Scripting Tools**   This enables you to script servers running IIS6 Web sites by installing the IIS6 Scripting Tools.

- **IIS 6 Management Console**   This installs the Internet Information Services (IIS) 6.0 Manager, which you use remotely to manage servers running IIS6 sites and to manage file transfer protocol (FTP) servers for IIS6.

Using the Application Server Server Role

Windows Server 2008 supports a range of application development technologies. Modern applications often rely on extensive communications features. Applications developers can save time and effort by taking advantage of features that are already available on their operating system platform, in particular, features associated with the Application Server server role.

> **NOTE**   **WINDOWS SERVER 2008 PLATFORMS**
>
> The Application Server server role is not available in Windows Server 2008 Web Server.

The Application Server server role is based on .NET Framework 3.0 technology and includes support for other communications and presentation features. It is an expanded Windows Server 2008 server role and provides an integrated environment for deploying and running server-based business applications that respond to requests that arrive over the network from remote client computers or from other applications. Typically, applications deployed and run on Application Server take advantage of one or more of the following technologies:

- IIS7
- .NET Framework v3.0 and v2.0
- ASP.NET
- COM+
- Message Queuing
- Built-in Web services associated with Windows Communication Foundation (WCF)

NOTE **APPLICATION SERVER AND WEB SERVER SERVER ROLES**

Although the Application Server server role is not specifically dependent on the Web Server server role, distributed applications that are built using ASP.NET or Windows Communication Foundation (WCF) will require both roles. You do not need to install the Application Server role unless a specific Web application or Web service requires it. Basic ASP.NET applications, for example, will run without the Application Server server role enabled on the server.

MORE INFO **.NET FRAMEWORK 3.5**

If you have applications that are built with .NET Framework 3.5, you can download and install .NET Framework 3.5 by accessing *http://www.microsoft.com/downloads/details .aspx?FamilyID=333325fd-ae52-4e35-b531-508d977d32a6&DisplayLang=en.*

Role Services Associated with the Application Server Server Role

As with all server roles, you install the Application Server server role by using the Add Roles Wizard in Server Manager. When you add the role, you optionally specify which additional role services you plan to enable. The associated role services include the following:

- **Application Server Foundation** This is a required feature of the Application Server role. It includes support for technology in the .NET Framework 3.0 platform. Primary technology components include Windows Presentation Foundation (WPF) and Windows Workflow Foundation (WF).

- **Web Server support** The Application Server role can be integrated with the Web Server server role to enable Web applications to access advanced features. If you select this option, the Add Roles Wizard automatically prompts you to install IIS7 if it is not already installed.

- **COM+ Network Access** The Component Object Model (COM) provides applications developers with a method for accessing different pieces of application code. Developers can access application code remotely across a network. You might need this feature if a Web site uses distributed applications that require multiple tiers of functionality.

- **TCP Port Sharing**   If you are working in distributed environments that support several server applications on a single computer, each application typically requires its own TCP port for responding to inbound requests. TCP Port Sharing enables multiple applications to share the same port. This simplifies server and firewall configuration.

- **Windows Process Activation Service support**   The Windows Process Activation Service (WAS) enables access application services over the network by using differing protocols and services. IIS7 can use WAS support for additional protocols and communications methods.

- **Distributed transactions**   If your applications use distributed transactions, they require coordination of multiple servers and applications before changes are made permanent. Distributed transactions enable incoming and outgoing remote transactions and support the WS-Atomic Transactions standard for Web Services. You must verify requirements with Web application developers to determine which Application Server components are required.

> *NOTE*   **SERVER CORE CONFIGURATION**
>
> The Application Server server role can be installed on a computer with Server Core configuration and is a good candidate for server virtualization. The Web Server server role can also run on a Server Core installation, although some functions, for example, creating IIS Manager (discussed later in this chapter), require a GUI and therefore must be done remotely. This should not be a problem because IIS Manager is typically used from a remote computer. However, remember that you cannot install the Application Server server role on a Windows Server 2008 Web Server installation.

 Quick Check

1. Which role service associated with the Application Server server role can be integrated with the Web Server server role to enable Web applications to access advanced features?

2. Which role service associated with the Application Server server role enables multiple applications to share the same port?

Quick Check Answers

1. Web Server support

2. TCP Port Sharing

Microsoft Recommendations

Typically, Microsoft recommends that you use the Application Server role service when you are deploying a business application that was developed for your organization and the developer indicates that specific role services are required. For example, your organization might have an application that accesses customer records stored in a database through a set of WCF Web services.

Not every server application benefits from the installation of the Application Server server role. For example, the Application Server server role on Windows Server 2008 is not required to support Exchange Server or SQL Server. Microsoft recommends that an organization's administrators work closely with application developers to understand the requirements of the application—for example, whether it uses .NET Framework 3.0 or COM+ components.

Application Server Functions

Application Server provides run-time support that implements effective deployment and management server-based business applications that in turn service requests from remote client systems. This includes Web applications on Web browsers that connect from the Internet or a corporate intranet.

The Application Server server role also supports .NET Framework 3.0, which provides developers with a simplified programming model for connected server applications. Developers can use the built-in .NET Framework libraries for many application functions, including Web services. The .NET Framework provides a secure and high-performance execution run time for server-based applications and a simplified application configuration and deployment environment.

You install the Application Server server role by using the Add Roles Wizard in Server Manager. The Add Roles Wizard guides you through the process of selecting the available role services or supporting features that are necessary to run specific applications.

Application Server Foundation

Application Server Foundation is the group of technologies installed by default when you install the Application Server server role. Application Server Foundation is, in effect,.NET Framework 3.0. By default, Windows Server 2008 includes .NET Framework 2.0, regardless of any server role you install, and .NET Framework 2.0 contains common language runtime (CLR), which provides a code-execution environment that promotes safe execution of code, simplified code deployment, and support for interoperability of multiple languages as well as extensive libraries for building applications. Application Server Foundation adds the .NET Framework 3.0 features to .NET Framework 2.0.

MORE INFO .NET FRAMEWORK 3.0

For more information about .NET Framework 3.0, see *http://msdn.microsoft.com/en-us /netframework/default.aspx*.

Using the Default Web Site and Adding Web Sites

When you install the Web Server server role, the installation includes a site called Default Web Site that is configured to respond to requests, using HTTP (port 80) and HTTPS (port 443). You can view the site bindings, shown in Figure 13-2, by right-clicking Default Web Site in IIS Manager and selecting Edit Bindings. You can also use the Bindings link in the Actions pane to open the same dialog box.

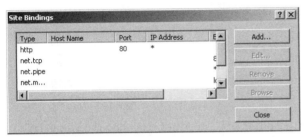

FIGURE 13-2 Viewing the site bindings for Default Web Site.

When you launch a Web browser and connect to a simple URL that does not specify directories or virtual directories, for example, *http://glasgow.contoso.internal*, you view the contents of Default Web Site. IIS7 receives the request on HTTP port 80 and returns the appropriate content from the Web site.

You can add a new site binding for the Default Web Site by clicking the Add button in the Site Bindings dialog box. You can specify the protocol type, IP address, port information, and (optionally) hostname. If you attempt to add a site binding that is already in use, you are reminded that you must configure a unique binding.

Adding Web Sites

You can add a new Web site by right-clicking the Sites container in IIS Manager and selecting Add Web Site. Figure 13-3 shows the Add Web Site dialog box.

In addition to specifying the default protocol binding for the site, you must provide the site name. This setting is a logical name that users do not see on the site. By default, IIS Manager creates a new application pool with the same name you provide for the Web site. You can also select an existing application pool by clicking the Select button. You learn more about application pools and their purpose later in this lesson.

FIGURE 13-3 The Add Web Site dialog box.

In the Content Directory section of the dialog box, you can specify the full physical path to the folder that is the root of the Web site. The default root location for IIS7 Web content is %SystemDrive%\Inetpub\wwwroot. The initial files for Default Web Site are located in this folder. You can create a new folder (either within this path or in another one) to store the content of the new Web site. You use the Connect As button to specify the security credentials that IIS7 requires to access the content. The default setting is Pass-Through Authentication, which means that the security context of the requesting Web user is used. You learn more about securing Web site content later in this chapter. Before you click OK to accept the Web site settings, you can specify whether you want the site to be started immediately.

If the Web site binding information is already in use, you are given a warning. Otherwise, the site is created and is displayed in the left pane of IIS Manager. You can start and stop Web sites individually by selecting them and using the commands in the IIS Manager Actions pane or by right-clicking and selecting the Manage Web Site menu. You can also use the *appcmd .exe* utility, which is discussed later in this lesson. Other settings, such as site bindings, can be modified at any time. This enables you to create, reconfigure, and stop sites individually without affecting other sites on the same server.

Configuring Web Site Limits

You can use Web Site Limits settings to specify maximum limitations on the amount of bandwidth and the number of connections that a Web site can support. You configure these settings to ensure that one or more sites on a server do not use excessive network bandwidth or consume too many resources. To configure Web site limits, you select the relevant Web site

and click Limits in the IIS Manager Actions pane. Figure 13-4 shows the default limit settings
for a new Web site.

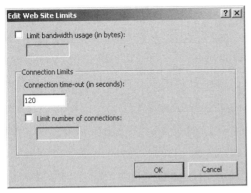

FIGURE 13-4 Default Web Site limits.

You can enable and use the Limit Bandwidth Usage option (which is initially disabled) to
configure the maximum number of bytes per second that the Web server supports. If this
limit is exceeded, the Web server throttles responses by adding a time delay.

Use the Limit Number of Connections setting to specify the maximum number of user
connections that can be active on the site. Each user connection times out automatically if
a new request is not received within the time you specify. (The default is 120 seconds.) You
can also configure the maximum number of connections allowed to the site. If this number is
exceeded, users who attempt to make a new connection will receive an error message stating
that the server is too busy to respond.

Configuring Site Logging

You configure site logging properties by selecting the relevant Web site in IIS Manager and
double-clicking Logging in Features View. Figure 13-5 shows the default logging options.

The options available depend on which role services are installed on the Web server.
By default, each new site is configured to store text-based log files in the %SystemDrive%\
Inetpub\Logs\LogFiles path on the local server. Each Web site is assigned its own folder that
contains one or more log files. The default log file format is W3C, which you can use to compare log information from different Web server platforms. You use the Select Fields button
to specify what information is stored in the log file. The default settings generally provide a
good balance between performance and useful information. If you add too many fields, this
can adversely affect performance, so log only the information you need.

Because log files are text-based, it can be difficult to manage and analyze large files. The
settings in the Log File Rollover section enable you to specify when IIS7 should create a new
log file. (The default is daily.) You can also specify the maximum size of each log file or use
only a single log file.

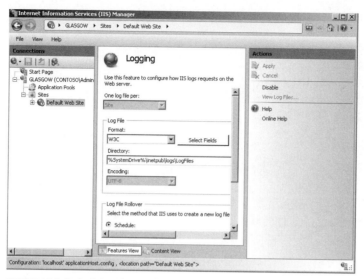

FIGURE 13-5 Default logging options.

Creating and Managing Web Applications

You can create Web applications within Web sites to point to the physical location of content files. For example, a site might include two Web applications, one for registered users and one for nonregistered users. Each Web application typically points to a separate physical folder on the computer so IIS7 can determine how to process requests. Web applications can also ensure that the common content is available to both sites.

Creating Web Applications

To create a new Web application, right-click the relevant Web site in IIS Manager and click Add Application. Figure 13-6 shows the Add Application dialog box. You can specify the alias to be used for the site. This is the name that users will type as part of their URL to connect to the content. For example, if you create a Web application with the alias Marketing on the Web server Glasgow in the *contoso.internal* domain, users will use *http://glasgow.contoso .internal/marketing* to access the content. You can also specify the application pool in which the application will be placed. You learn about application pools later in this lesson.

You configure the Physical Path option to specify the folder in which the Web application content is stored. This file system location should be unique and not shared with other Web applications. You can use the Connect As setting to specify a username and password or accept the default setting of Pass-Through Authentication. Use the Test Settings button to verify the connection details you have specified.

When you click OK to create a new Web application, the application is listed under the site object in IIS Manager. You can modify settings for the Web application by using the IIS Manager Features View.

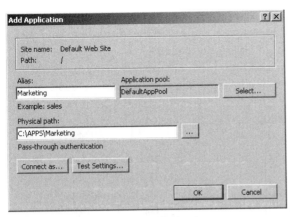

FIGURE 13-6 The Add Application dialog box.

Managing Web Applications

Many of the settings for a new Web application are inherited automatically by default from the Web site in which it was created. This enables you to use the same default settings easily for each new site. You can also (usually) override settings at the Web application level, based on specific application needs. To do this, double-click items in Features View and make the corresponding changes.

Using Application Pools

Application pools address one of the primary concerns involved in managing Web Servers—when one Web site or application affects operations of others on the same computer. Memory leaks and application bugs can cause a loss of service or reduced performance in apparently unrelated Web applications. Application pools isolate different sites from each other so that failures and other problems can be contained. Within each application pool, worker processes service Web requests. Each application pool contains its own set of worker processes, so problems in one pool do not affect processes in another. In addition, you can start and stop application pools independently of each other.

By default, IIS includes the Classic .NET AppPool and DefaultAppPool application pools along with an application pool that takes the same name as the application itself. Classic .NET AppPool supports applications that require .NET Framework 2.0, using Classic Managed Pipeline Mode. DefaultAppPool supports Default Web Site. It also supports .NET Framework 2.0, but it uses the new Integrated Managed Pipeline Mode.

By default, IIS Manager creates a new application pool when you create a new Web site. The application pool takes the same name as the site. This enables the processes within each Web site to run independently of each other. When you create a new Web application, you have the option of selecting from any of the available application pools.

For example, your network contains a Windows Server 2008 Web server that hosts multiple Web sites and you want to release memory for a single Web site. You want to configure the server to release memory automatically without affecting other Web sites hosted on the same server. To do this, you create a new application pool and associate the Web site with that application pool. If you add an application to a specific pool or associate a Web site with that pool, the application and Web site settings never affect applications in or Web sites associated with other pools. If the application process crashes or you reconfigure the Web site settings, only the new application pool is affected.

Creating Application Pools

You can use IIS Manager to create and manage application pools. As shown in Figure 13-7, you can view details of the application pools currently on the server.

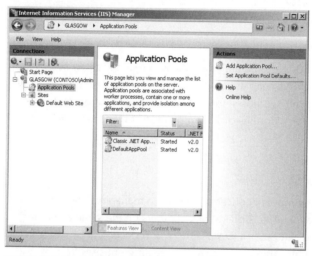

FIGURE 13-7 Application pools on the server.

To create a new application pool, right-click Application Pools and select Add Application Pool. Figure 13-8 shows the available options. You can use the Name option to identify the purpose of the application pool and, if relevant, the Web site it supports. The .NET Framework version options will be based on which versions are available on the local computer. By default, the .NET Framework 2.0 and No Managed Code options are available. If you select No Managed Code, .NET functionality will not be available for Web applications that are part of the pool.

Managed Pipeline Mode specifies the supported method for code that needs to intercept and modify Web request processing. The Classic option supports ASP.NET applications written for previous versions of IIS that depend on integrating with request pipeline events. The Integrated mode provides better performance, and Microsoft recommends it for those Web applications that do not depend on Classic Managed Pipeline Mode. Before clicking OK, you can choose whether you want to start the application pool immediately.

FIGURE 13-8 Available application pool options.

NOTE **USING THE *APPCMD ADD APPPOOL* COMMAND**

You can add an application pool to a server by using the *appcmd add apppool* command from an elevated command prompt, for example, *%systemroot%\system32\inetsrv \appcmd add apppool /name:Sales*. You can use the *appcmd* command to add an application pool that uses settings other than the default settings to a Web server. For example, to add an application pool named Marketing that does not run managed code and that uses classic mode, enter the *%systemroot%\system32\inetsrv\appcmd add apppool /name:Marketing /managedRuntimeVersion: /managedPipelineMode:Classic* command.

MORE INFO **ADDING APPLICATION POOLS**

For more information about adding application pools with both IIS Manager and command-line tools, see *http://technet.microsoft.com/en-us/library/cc731784.aspx*.

Stopping Application Pools

Each application pool on a Web server can be started and stopped without affecting any of the other pools. When you stop an application pool, this prevents any applications that are part of that pool from processing requests. Users that attempt to access content from these sites will receive an HTTP Error 503 message, "Service Unavailable." To verify which applications are using an application pool, right-click the application pool and select View Applications.

In addition to being stopped manually by an administrator, an application pool might stop automatically if application failures occur. After a certain number of failures, Rapid Fail Protection, a WAS feature, triggers. This feature is designed to stop application pools with a persistent failure condition and thus avoid an endless loop of failing to start worker processes. At this point, any requests to applications within the stopped application pool will result in the 503 error. The long-term solution is to repair or debug the failing application, but you can restart the application pool manually by running the *%systemroot%\system32\inetsrv\appcmd* *start apppool* command from an elevated command prompt on the Web Server. You must specify the name of the application pool in this command.

Recycling Application Pools

Rather than stopping an application pool, you can recycle it using the *Recycle* command in the Actions pane. This instructs IIS7 to retire any current worker process automatically after it has executed existing requests. Users do not see a service disruption, and the worker process is replaced by a new one as quickly as possible. Typically, you recycle application pools when you encounter memory leaks or when resource usage increases significantly over time and you suspect a defect in the application code. The long-term solution is to correct the code, but you can address the symptoms by recycling the application pool.

You can configure recycling options by selecting an application pool in IIS Manager and then clicking the Recycling link under Edit Application Pool in the IIS Manager Actions pane. Figure 13-9 shows the recycling options available.

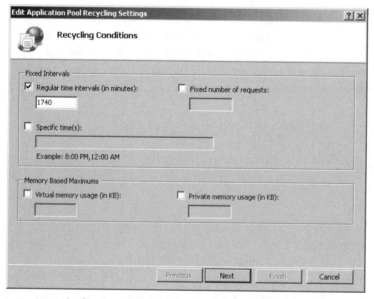

FIGURE 13-9 Configuring Application Pool recycling settings.

You can select either Fixed Intervals or Memory Based Maximums, depending upon the specific problems you are trying to troubleshoot. Recycling application pools too quickly can reduce performance, but if a Web application has serious problems, you should address them by recycling worker processes before users see slowdowns or errors on the Web site.

Keep track of application pool recycle events to ensure that your Web server and its applications are running as expected. For example, if you choose the Memory Based Maximums setting, you want to know how often the application pool has been recycled.

When the worker process terminates, a new one is started simultaneously. This type of recycling is called overlapped recycling and is the default for application pools. If an application cannot run in a multi-instance environment, configure only one worker process for an application pool, which is the default value. In this case, disable overlapped recycling by setting the Disable Overlapped Recycling option to True.

Advanced Application Pool Settings

You can configure additional application pool settings to control the behavior of worker processes. To do this, select an application pool in IIS Manager and click Advanced Settings in the Actions pane. In the Advanced Settings dialog box shown in Figure 13-10, configure the detailed parameters related to CPU and memory resource usage. In general, you should not change these parameters unless you are sure you need to. Some settings can result in reduced application processing speed, and others can reserve too many system resources for a particular pool.

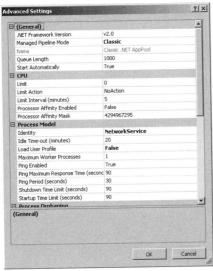

FIGURE 13-10 Application pool Advanced Settings dialog box.

Understanding .NET Framework

The .NET Framework is available with Windows Server 2008. It includes a library of pre-coded solutions to common programming problems and a virtual machine that manages the execution of programs written specifically for the framework. Most new applications created for the Windows Server 2008 platform use the .NET Framework.

Programs written for the .NET Framework execute in the CLR environment that manages the program's requirements. This run-time environment simulates an application virtual machine, so programmers need not consider the capabilities of the specific hardware that executes the program. CLR also provides services such as security, memory management, and exception handling.

Windows Server 2008 includes .NET Framework 3.0. Version 3.5 is available as a download at *http://www.microsoft.com/downloads/details.aspx?FamilyID=333325fd-ae52-4e35-b531-508d977d32a6&DisplayLang=en* and, at this time of writing, .NET Framework 4.0 for parallel computing has been recently announced. However, any examination questions are likely to be based on .NET Framework 3.0.

.NET Framework Components

.NET Framework 3.0 includes a set of application programming interfaces (APIs) integrated into Windows Server 2008 operating systems. It consists of the following components:

- **Windows Presentation Foundation (WPF)**   This is a user interface subsystem and API based on eXtended Markup Language (XML) that uses 3D computer graphics hardware and Direct3D technologies.

- **Windows Communication Foundation (WCF)**   This is a service-oriented messaging system that enables programs to interoperate locally or remotely.

- **Windows Workflow Foundation (WF)**   This enables you to build task automation and integrated transactions, using workflows. A workflow is a model that, for example, could describe a repeatable sequence of operations.

- **Windows CardSpace**   This is a software component that securely stores a user's digital identities and provides an interface for choosing an identity for a particular transaction, for example, logging on to a Web site.

ASP.NET is a Web application framework you can use to build dynamic Web sites, Web applications, and Web services. It is the successor to the Microsoft ASP technology. ASP.NET is built on CLR, enabling programmers to write ASP.NET code, using any supported .NET language. ASP.NET pages, known as Web forms, are used for application development. They are contained in files with an .aspx extension. They define server-side Web controls and user controls in which the developers place all the required static and dynamic content for the Web page.

.NET components are defined by the .NET initiative, which aims to make interoperable software services available over the Internet anywhere and on any device. The initiative is based on the .NET Framework, which combines a managed run-time environment with a comprehensive class library to facilitate building and deploying Web-enabled applications. .NET components support programming models embodied in the .NET Framework, including Windows Forms, Web Forms, and XML Web services.

.NET Framework Permissions

If you want a .NET Framework application to run without creating content or accessing system components, you might need to configure the .NET Framework Web site trust level to Full.

Suppose, for example, you have installed the Web Server server role on a Windows Server 2008 server, and you install and enable the .NET Framework on a Web site hosted on the server. You must ensure that all applications run on a minimum permission level as specified by company security policy. You want to configure the Web site application with permissions that execute without creating other content or accessing Windows Server 2008 system components.

In this case, the Web site application needs to have permissions to execute without creating other content or accessing Windows Server 2008 system components. You therefore configure the .NET Framework Web site trust level to Full. This configures the Web site application to have permission to execute without creating other content or accessing Windows Server 2008 system components.

PRACTICE   **Installing the Web Server Server Role and the ASP.NET Role Service**

In this practice, you install the Web Server server role on the Glasgow computer (if necessary). You then install the ASP.NET role service. The Web Server server role and the ASP.NET role service might already be installed on this computer, depending on the roles installed in previous chapters, so the exercises might only identify these settings.

EXERCISE 1   Install the Web Server Role (If Necessary)

In this exercise, you check whether the Web Server (IIS) server role is installed on the Glasgow server. (It likely is.) If it is not, you install it. You install the service with only the basic role services that are enabled by default.

1. Log on to glasgow.contoso.internal, using the Kim_Akers account.

2. If necessary, open Server Manager. Right-click Roles in the Tree pane and select Add Roles to open the Add Roles Wizard. Click Next on the Before You Begin page if it is displayed.

3. On the Select Server Roles page, determine whether the Web Server (IIS) server role is available or is selected and dimmed, as shown in Figure 13-11. If the Web Server

(IIS) server role is selected and dimmed, it is already installed. In this case, click Cancel, click Yes to confirm you want to cancel the wizard, and proceed to Exercise 2 in this practice.

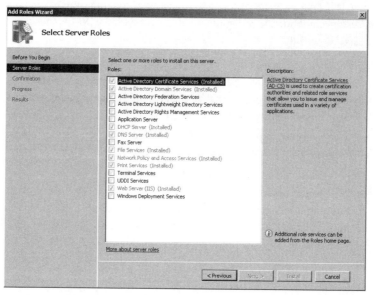

FIGURE 13-11 The Web Server (IIS) server role is already installed.

4. Otherwise, on the Web Server (IIS) page, read the basic introductory information about IIS and click Next.

5. On the Confirm Installation Selections page, verify the role service selections.

   Optionally, you can choose to print, e-mail, or save the information to record which components were installed.

6. When you are ready to begin the installation process, click Install.

7. When the installation process has completed, verify the installed roles and services on the Installation Results page. To complete the process, click Close.

EXERCISE 2   Install the ASP.NET Role Service

In this exercise, you install the ASP.NET role service and its dependencies. The Web Server server role must be installed before you can install this role service.

1. If necessary, log on to glasgow.contoso.internal, using the Kim_Akers account, and start Server Manager.

2. Expand Roles and select Web Server (IIS).

3. Click Add Role Services.

   The Select Role Services page appears, as shown in Figure 13-12. If the ASP.NET role service is selected and dimmed, the service is already installed.

4. If this is the case, click Cancel, and then click Yes to confirm that you want to cancel the wizard.

The practice session is now complete.

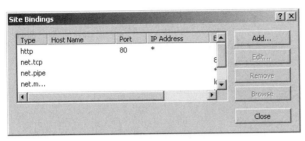

FIGURE 13-12 The Select Role Services page.

5. Otherwise, select the ASP.NET check box.

The Add Role Services Required For ASP.NET dialog box will likely appear, as shown in Figure 13-13. The role services you need to add (and whether this dialog box appears at all) depend on the services that are already installed on the Glasgow computer.

6. Click Add Required Role Services.

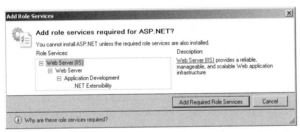

FIGURE 13-13 The Add Role Services Required For ASP.NET dialog box.

7. Click Next, and then click Install on the Confirm Installation Selections page.

Installation can take some time.

8. Click Close to close the Installation Results page when installation completes.

9. If required to do so, reboot the Glasgow computer.

Lesson Summary

- The Web Server server role provides access to Web site content, using the HTTP protocol. The Application Server server role provides support to applications that require features of .NET Framework 3.0, COM+, and Distributed Transactions. You can install role services associated with these server roles as you require them.

- You can use IIS Manager and the *appcmd.exe* command-line utility to configure Default Web Site, add and manage Web sites, and configure application pools.

■ .NET Framework 3.0 includes a set of APIs integrated into Windows Server 2008 operating systems.

Lesson Review

You can use the following questions to test your knowledge of the information in Lesson 1, "Configuring Web Applications." The questions are also available on the companion DVD if you prefer to review them in electronic form.

> **NOTE ANSWERS**
>
> Answers to these questions and explanations of why each answer choice is correct or incorrect are located in the "Answers" section at the end of the book.

1. All servers on the A. Datum Corporation network run Windows Server 2008. The Galveston Web Server hosts a Web application called StockControl that uses a custom application pool, which is set to recycle every 720 minutes. The StockControl application does not support multiple worker processes. Which of the following options should you choose to configure the application pool so that users can access Stock-Control after the application pool is recycled?

   A. Set the Disable Overlapped Recycling option to True.

   B. Configure Application Pool Recycling settings and select Fixed Intervals.

   C. Configure Application Pool Recycling settings and select Memory Based Maximums.

   D. Set the application pool to recycle every 1,440 minutes.

2. You are installing the ASP.NET role service on a Windows Server 2008 server that has the Web Server server role installed. What additional role services are you prompted to install (assuming they have not been previously installed) when you install ASP.NET? (Choose three. Each correct answer presents part of a complete solution.)

   A. ISAPI Extensions

   B. ASP

   C. ISAPI Filters

   D. .NET Extensibility

   E. CGI

3. Your organization provides Web hosting services. A Windows Server 2008 Web server on your network hosts multiple Web sites. You must configure a Web site for a new client on the Web server. While deploying the Web site, you discover that the Web site looks like an FTP download site instead of a normal HTTP page. You must configure the Web site to present the content through HTTP and ensure that the files are not downloaded by users. Which of the following actions must you perform? (Choose two. Each correct answer presents part of a complete solution.)

A. Configure a Domain Name System (DNS) zone for the domain that hosts the Web site and create a CNAME record.

B. From an elevated command prompt, enter the *%systemroot%\system32\inetsrv \appcmd set config/section:directoryBrowse/enabled: False* command.

C. Create a new application pool and configure the Web site to use it.

D. Configure the directory that hosts the Web site to grant Allow, Read, and Execute permission to Web site users.

E. Configure the default document setting to match the Web page file to the Web site.

Lesson 2: Managing Web Sites

In this lesson, you learn how to migrate sites and Web applications, publish IIS Web sites and FTP sites, and configure virtual directories. This lesson also discusses the command-line utilities available for Web site management.

> **After this lesson, you will be able to:**
>
> - Migrate Web sites to Windows Server 2008 and IIS7.
> - Publish Web sites and FTP sites.
> - Configure virtual directories.
>
> **Estimated lesson time: 30 minutes**

Migrating and Upgrading Web Sites and Applications

At the time of this writing, Windows Server 2008 does not support cross-machine migration of down-level IIS versions to IIS7; however, the IIS team expects to provide an IIS7 migration tool that enables you to move existing Web sites cross-machine to IIS7 on Windows Server 2008. You can keep track of this situation by accessing the Microsoft IIS team Web site mentioned earlier in this chapter and, in particular, *http://learn.iis.net/page.aspx/130 /understanding-setup-in-iis-70/*.

While this situation exists, a migration from, for example, an IIS6 Web site to IIS7 can be considered as an upgrade. IIS7 is backward compatible with IIS6 and generally supports IIS6 Web sites and Web applications with little or no modification. Upgrade considerations are discussed later in this section. To migrate an IIS7 Web site on one computer to another computer on which IIS7 is already installed involves moving content and settings manually and is typically accomplished by using the backup and restore process.

Migrating a UNIX Web Site

Migration is possible from non-Microsoft Web sites, for example, from a UNIX Web site on an Apache server to IIS7. In this case, you can use the IIS Migration Wizard.

First, download the IIS Migration Wizard Setup file from the Microsoft Download Center. The *iismigrationwizard_setup.exe* file is available for download at *http://download.microsoft .com/download/win2000platform/iismigwz/1.00.0.1/nt5/en-us/iismigrationwizard_setup.exe*. This file was originally written for Microsoft Windows 2000 Server and IIS5, but it works fine in Windows Server 2008 and IIS7.

Choose to save the installation program to disk and then run it from Windows Explorer. The *Iismigrationwizard_setup.exe* file is a self-extracting executable (.exe) file. If you run the file, it places installation packages and documentation on your computer. Each of these packages requires additional installation, as described in the tool's documentation.

Your next step is to prepare the source computer, which must have the Perl programming language installed. Note that this is not a Microsoft procedure, and you cannot test it on your test network. It is also unlikely that the upgrade examinations will test you on the procedure except to assess whether you know it exists.

To prepare the source computer, log on as root. Then open the folder on the destination computer onto which you extracted the IIS Migration Wizard files and use FTP to transfer the *IISv5MigrationUtility-ApacheSource.tar* file to a temporary folder on the source computer.

On the source computer command line (either locally or from telnet), enter the *tar -x < iisv5migrationutility-apachesource.tar* command. Then, in the temporary folder into which you copied the .tar file, enter the *perl install.pl* command. Follow the screen instructions to select the configuration file and turn on the source service.

When you have configured the source computer, install the target component from the source to the target computer running Windows Server 2008 and IIS7. You must be logged on to this computer as an administrator.

Open Microsoft Internet Explorer and connect to *http://<source>/iismu/welcome.htm*, where *<source>* is either the computer name or the IPv4 address of the source computer.

The IIS Migration Wizard starts. Click Next and then click the link to the target platform. Click Open to run the installer directly from the Web site. Alternatively, you can save the file and run it later. When the installation of the target component is complete, you can return to the IIS Migration Wizard in Internet Explorer and click Next to start a migration, or you can close the wizard and carry out the migration later. Before you start the migration process, Default Web Site must be configured and running.

After you install the source component and the target component, you can start the migration process (assuming you chose to close it and migrate later) by selecting Microsoft IIS v.5 Migration Wizard on the Programs menu. When the wizard starts, click Next. You will see a message telling you that the IIS Migration Wizard has already been installed on your computer. Click Next.

Click the option indicating that you have already installed the source software on your source host, type the IPv4 address of the source host in the Computer text box, and then click Next. You are prompted for the password you used to log on to the Apache server.

Open the root program folder for Apache and then type the name of the folder that contains the configuration files in the Server Mask text box. (Typically, the configuration files are in the Conf folder.) When you are prompted, select the server content, the settings, and the MIME information that you migrate for each virtual server, and then click Next to start the migration process.

The migration process takes from a few minutes to longer than an hour, depending on the size of the Web site you are migrating. When the migration is complete, the wizard displays a list of warnings and any additional steps necessary to complete the migration. To save the activity log or the migration archive file that contains migrated content and settings, click the appropriate link at the bottom of the wizard page. Click Finish.

EXAM TIP

The procedure for migrating a UNIX Web site is described for the benefit of readers who have Apache servers on their production network. The upgrade examinations are unlikely to test this in detail. It is probably sufficient for you to know that you can carry out such a migration and that the IIS Migration Wizard is the tool you use.

Upgrading an IIS6 Web Site

If you upgrade a Windows Server 2003 Web server with IIS6 installed to a Windows Server 2008 Web server with IIS7 installed, Web sites on the server are supported and upgraded, generally without user intervention. Any file system content not created or owned by Windows remains intact through the upgrade process, and all Web content on the original operating system remains present and supported after the upgrade. The process occurs in the following stages:

- **Detect and gather**   During an operating system upgrade to Windows Server 2008, IIS detection components run on the existing operating system before the operating system upgrade begins. If IIS is detected on the existing Windows operating system, all metabase and IIS state information is gathered.

- **Installation**   First the new operating system is installed and then server roles such as Web Server install, provided that equivalent functionality was detected on the original operating system. The choice of IIS updates to install is based on the IIS state information gathered from the original operating system.

- **Apply settings**   After the OS installation and optional feature installations such as IIS7 have completed, the state information gathered from the original operating system is applied. At this point, the metabase settings from the original IIS are translated and updated into the new IIS7 configuration store, *ApplicationHost.config*.

IIS 7.0 Components Installed During Upgrade

During the detect and gather phase, IIS upgrade checks for the presence of key IIS services and files and installs the following IIS7 updates:

W3SVC (installed as a service), IS-ASP, IIS-BasicAuthentication, IIS-CGI, IIS-ClientCertificate-MappingAuthentication, IIS-CustomLogging, IIS-DefaultDocument, IIS-DigestAuthentication, IIS-DirectoryBrowsing, IIS-HttpCompressionDynamic, IIS-HttpCompressionStatic, IIS-HttpErrors, IIS-HTTPLogging, IIS-HttpRedirect, IIS-HttpTracing, IIS-IISCertificateMappingAuthentication, IIS-IPSecurity, IIS-ISAPIExtensions, IIS-ISAPIFilter, IIS-LegacyScripts, IIS-LoggingLibraries, IIS-ManagementScriptingTools, IIS-ManagementService, IIS-ODBCLogging, IIS-Request-Filtering, IIS-RequestMonitor, IIS-ServerSideIncludes, IIS-StaticContent, IIS-URLAuthorization, IIS-WindowsAuthentication, IIS-WMICompatibility, WAS-ConfigurationAPI, WAS-NetFx-Environment, WAS-ProcessModel, MSFTPSVC (installed as a service), IIS-FTPServer, INETMGR. EXE, IIS-FTPManagement, IIS-LegacySnapIn, IIS-ManagementConsole, IISAdmin (installed as a service), IIS-Metabase.

Because the installation of updates during an upgrade is not as granular as is possible in an IIS7 clean installation, almost all Web Server features are installed during the upgrade. Microsoft advises revisiting your application dependencies on IIS functionality and uninstalling the IIS updates you do not need.

 Quick Check

- What tool should you download and use if you want to migrate a UNIX Web site on an Apache server to IIS7?

Quick Check Answer

- The IIS Migration Wizard

Using Virtual Directories

Often, a Web site needs to include content from folders that are located external to the Web site's primary folder structure. For example, multiple Web sites that share a set of images might need to access files from a single path. Virtual directories are designed to meet this requirement. You can create virtual directories at either the Web site level or within a specific Web application. A virtual directory includes an alias name (used in the requesting URL) and points to a physical file path.

You can create a virtual directory in IIS Manager by right-clicking the appropriate parent Web site or Web application and then selecting Add Virtual Directory. Provide security credentials, an alias for the virtual directory, and the physical path to the virtual directory. When a user request for this alias is received, IIS7 looks in the appropriate file system location for the requested content.

You can also create a virtual directory by using the *appcmd.exe* utility. For example, to create a virtual directory called Illustrations on the Default Web Site and specify a physical path D:\Illustrations on the Web server, enter the following command from the elevated command prompt:

```
%systemroot%\system32\inetsrv\appcmd add vdir /app.name:"Default Web Site/" /path:/
Illustrations /physicalPath:D:\Illustrations
```

When you move the location of a virtual directory's content in the file system, you must also update the physical path in IIS7 to ensure that users can access the content of the virtual directory. For example, the Windows Server 2008 Web Server Detroit hosts a Web application named DemoClips within the TechVideos Web site, which in turn uses the virtual directory with the physical path \\Detroit\MOV\Videos. Detroit is running out of hard disk space, and you install a new server named Denver on the network and move the contents of the virtual directory to the \\Denver\Movies\MOVData folder. You need to ensure that users can access the contents of the \\Denver\Movies\MOVData folder.

Because you must update the physical path in IIS7 to ensure users' access to the content of the virtual directory when you move the location of a virtual directory's content in the file system, you must change the path to the virtual directory's content. You therefore run the %systemroot%\system32\inetsrv\appcmd set vdir/ vdir.name:"TechVideos/MOV/Videos" /physical path:\\Denver\Movies\MOVData command.

> **NOTE   SETTING PERMISSION OPTIONS ON VIRTUAL DIRECTORIES**
>
> Because of the security settings in IIS7, generic ASP, ASP.NET, ISAPI, and CGI extensions cannot execute unless the extension is explicitly enabled. For example, you add a Web site to a Windows Server 2008 Web server that uses a virtual directory called MyVirtDir. The virtual directory holds an ISAPI application. You test the Web site and the ISAPI application fails. To configure the handler permission to enable the ISAPI application while fulfilling the policy permission requirements, you need to enable the Execute option on the MyVirtDir virtual directory.

Using the World Wide Web Publishing Service

FTP and World Wide Web (WWW) sites depend on the relevant publishing services, which present a number of functions and features that support IIS7 sites. The FTP Publishing Service is discussed in Chapter 14, "Configuring FTP and SMTP Services." This chapter discusses the IIS World Wide Web Publishing Service (W3SVC), sometimes known as the WWW Service. This service manages the HTTP protocol and HTTP performance counters. To work correctly, W3SVC must be free of any I/O errors involving file access, memory availability, and network connections. In addition, scripts must be accessible and running, and included files must be configured correctly.

W3SVC requires the WAS and the HTTP service to be working correctly; if the HTTP service is not available, W3SVC cannot process HTTP requests. You can configure W3SVC to collect performance data and to carry out HTTP compression, provided you specify a valid compression directory that resides on an NTFS volume.

W3SVC is a managed entity that includes the IIS Web site and ASP entities and contains the following aspects:

- **ISAPI functionality**   ISAPI extensions and filters extend and modify the request-processing capabilities of IIS. Although ISAPI filters can still be used in IIS7, it is easier for developers to add managed or native modules that integrate into the modular architecture of IIS7.

- **W3SVC logging**   You can configure an IIS7 Web Server for site, central binary, or central World Wide Web Consortium (W3C) logging. If you select central W3C logging, all client requests for all sites are logged to a single log file in W3C centralized format on the server. Central binary logging also logs all sites centrally to a single file but does so in centralized binary format. If you specify site logging, all client requests are logged at the site level rather than centrally at the server level.

- **W3SVC module configuration**   IIS7 enables developers to easily configure native and managed code modules that process requests made to the Web server. Module configuration requires you to specify a unique name and a valid type or path for the module. With managed modules, you can specify whether they should be invoked only for requests to ASP.NET applications or managed handlers. This setting can optimize performance.

- **W3SVC performance counters**   W3SVC enables HTTP-specific performance counters for Web sites. It initializes the counters and receives them from *HTTP.sys*, the protocol listener for HTTP. If W3SVC is not available, you cannot gather HTTP performance counter data.

Disabling Directory Browsing

A problem that sometimes occurs when you publish and deploy a new Web site is that it looks like an FTP download site. Instead of presenting their content, files such as default.htm are listed as hyperlinks for downloading. In this case, you must present the content through HTTP and disable directory browsing to ensure that users do not download files.

To do this, set up the Web site to present the content through HTTP. Then use the *appcmd.exe* command-line utility from an elevated command prompt to ensure that the files, for example, .jpg files that display illustrations, perform the functions they should perform rather than appearing as file names on a download list.

To carry out these tasks, first match the Web page file to the Web site by configuring the Default Document setting in IIS Manager. Enter the *%systemroot% \system32\inetsrv\appcmd set config/section: directoryBrowse/enabled: false* command from an elevated command prompt. This command disables directory browsing on the Web site.

You can obtain more information about the Default Document setting by accessing *http://learn.iis.net/page.aspx/203/default-documents/.* You can obtain more information about the *appcmd* utility by accessing *http://learn.iis.net/page.aspx/114 /getting-started-with-appcmdexe/.*

Using the Command Line

Rather than use a graphics tool such as IIS Manager, you can perform most Web site and Web application creation, deletion, and configuration operations from an elevated command prompt. This is especially useful in Server Core installations. The command-line utilities you use are the *servermanagercmd.exe* Server Manager command-line tool and the *appcmd.exe* utility.

Server Manager Commands

You can use the Server Manager command-line tool from the elevated command prompt to install or remove roles, role services, and features. The options associated with the *servermanagercmd.exe* utility enable users to view logs and run queries to display lists of roles, role services, and features that are both installed and available for installation on a computer.

> **MORE INFO**   **SERVERMANAGERCMD ANSWER FILE**
>
> You can use *Servermanagercmd.exe* with an XML answer file to expedite repetitive automated installations or removals of roles or features. For more information about the answer file that you can use with *servermanagercmd.exe*, see *http://technet.microsoft.com /en-us/library/cc766357.aspx*.

Servermanagercmd accepts parameters that install or remove a role, role service, or feature. When you want to install or remove more than one role, role service, or feature on a server by using a single command instance, you can use an XML answer file.

The command can take the *-query (-q)*, *-logpath*, *-inputpath (-p)*, *-install*, *-remove*, *-help*, and *-version* parameters. You can use role, role service, and feature command identifiers to specify entities you want to install or remove. For example, the following command installs Web Server (IIS) and all its role services; under the context of the administrator, it exports the results of the installation to an XML file called MyWebServer.xml, and it restarts the computer automatically when installation is complete.

```
servermanagercmd.exe -install web-server -allsubfeatures -resultpath C:\Admin\
MyWebServer.xml -restart
```

> **MORE INFO**   **SERVERMANAGERCMD.EXE**
>
> For more information about the *servermanagercmd.exe* utility, see *http://technet.microsoft .com/en-us/library/cc722408.aspx* and follow the links.

The *Appcmd.exe* Utility

Appmd.exe is the principal command-line tool for managing IIS7. It enables you to control a Web server without using graphical administration tools and to automate server management tasks without writing code. You can do the following with *appcmd*:

- Create and configure sites, Web applications, application pools, and virtual directories.
- Start and stop sites and recycle application pools.
- List running worker processes and examine currently executing requests.
- Search, manipulate, export, and import IIS7 and ASP.NET configuration.

The *appcmd.exe* utility uses a set of top-level server management objects such as Site and Application. You can use *appcmd* to perform actions on those objects and expose properties that can be inspected and manipulated.

For example, the Site object enables you to list, create, and delete site instances and stop and start sites. Each site instance contains properties, such as site name and site ID, that can be inspected, searched for, or set. The output of each command is always a list of object instances.

> **NOTE** **SPECIFY THE PATH TO *APPCMD.EXE***
>
> *Appcmd.exe* is located in the %systemroot%\system32\inetsrv\ directory. Because it is not part of the PATH automatically, you must use the full path to the executable when executing commands, for example, *%systemroot%\system32\inetsrv\appcmd.exe list sites*. Alternatively, you can add the inetsrv directory to the path on your machine so that you can access *appcmd.exe* directly from any location.

Appcmd executes a command on one of the supported management objects, with optional parameters used to further customize the behavior of the command. The command syntax is as follows:

```
appcmd (command) (object-type) <identifier> < /parameter1:value1 .. >
```

Most objects support the following basic set of commands:

- **List** Displays the objects on the machine. An optional object ID can specify a unique object, or one or more parameters can be matched against object properties.
- **Add** Creates a new object and sets the specified object properties during creation.
- **Delete** Deletes the specified object.
- **Set** Sets the specified parameters on an object.

An object often supports additional commands; for example, the Site object supports Start and Stop. Table 13-1 lists the management objects and the purpose for which each is used.

TABLE 13-1 Management Objects Used by *Appcmd*

OBJECT	PURPOSE
Site	Administration of virtual sites
App	Administration of applications
VDir	Administration of virtual directories
Apppool	Administration of application pools
Config	Administration of general configuration sections
Backup	Management of server configuration backups
WP	Administration of worker processes
Request	Display of active HTTP requests
Module	Administration of server modules
Trace	Management of server trace logs

For example, to list all the sites on a Web server, enter the following command:

```
%systemroot%\system32\inetsrv\appcmd list sites
```

To give a slightly more complex example, the Windows Server 2008 Web server Boston in the *tailspintoys.com* domain hosts the *www.tailspintoys.com* Web site. You want to create a virtual directory called Marketing with a physical path of C:\websites\marketing and access this through *http://www.tailspintoys.com/marketing*. To do this, use the following command:

```
%systemroot%\system32\inetsrv\appcmd add vdir /app.name:tailspintoys /path:/marketing
/physicalPath:c:\websites\marketing
```

More examples of the use of the *appcmd.exe* utility are given at the appropriate points in this chapter.

> **MORE INFO   APPCMD.EXE**
>
> For more information about the *appcmd.exe* utility, see *http://technet.microsoft.com/en-us /library/cc772200.aspx* and follow the links.

PRACTICE   Creating Virtual Directories

In this practice, you use IIS Manager and *appcmd.exe* to create virtual directories. If your Glasgow computer has more than one hard disk, consider placing the directories on the second hard disk. If so, amend the procedures accordingly. The practice assumes that IIS7 has default settings for Default Web Site.

EXERCISE 1   Set Up Virtual Directory Content

In this exercise, you create paths to two virtual directories, VirD1 and VirD2, and create default pages that identify the virtual directories.

1. Log on to the Glasgow domain controller with the Kim_Akers account.
2. Create a folder named **C:\Vdirs**.
3. Create folders named **C:\Vdirs\VirD1** and **C:\Vdirs\VirD2**.
4. Open Windows Notepad.
5. Type a message to identify VirD1 and save this as default.htm in C:\Vdirs\VirD1, as shown in Figure 13-14.

FIGURE 13-14 Message identifying VirD1.

6. Repeat the previous step but change the text to **This is the second virtual directory**. Save the file as **default.htm** in C:\Vdirs\VirD2.

EXERCISE 2 Create a Virtual Directory Using IIS Manager

In this exercise, you use IIS Manager create the VirD1 virtual directory on the Default Web Site. Complete Exercise 1 before carrying out this exercise.

1. If necessary, log on to the Glasgow domain controller, using the Kim_Akers account.

2. In the Administrative Tools menu, select Internet Information Server (IIS) Manager.

3. In IIS Manager, right-click Default Web Site and select Add Virtual Directory, as shown in Figure 13-15.

FIGURE 13-15 Adding a virtual directory.

4. Configure the Add Virtual Directory settings, as shown in Figure 13-16.

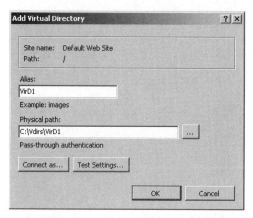

FIGURE 13-16 The Add Virtual Directory settings.

5. Click OK.

6. Open your browser and browse to *http://localhost/VirD1*.

   You should see the identifying message shown in Figure 13-17.

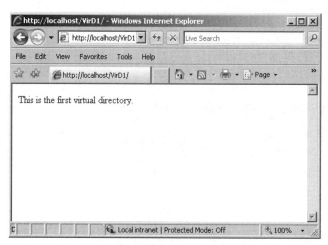

FIGURE 13-17 Accessing the VirD1 virtual directory.

EXERCISE 3   Create a Virtual Directory Using *Appcmd.exe*

In this exercise, you use *appcmd.exe* to create the VirD2 virtual directory on the Default Web Site. Complete Exercise 1 before carrying out this exercise.

1. If necessary, log on to the Glasgow domain controller, using the Kim_Akers account.

2. In the All Programs\Accessories menu, right-click Command Prompt and select Run As Administrator. If necessary, click Continue to close the UAC dialog box.

3. Enter the following command:

```
%systemroot%\system32\inetsrv\appcmd add vdir /app.name:"Default Web Site/"
/path:/VirD2 /physicalPath:c:\vdirs\VirD2
```

4. The virtual directory is added, as shown in Figure 13-18. Test this by browsing to *http:// localhost/VirD2*.

FIGURE 13-18 Adding a virtual directory with *appcmd.exe*.

Lesson Summary

- You can use the IIS Migration Wizard to migrate a site in a non-Windows operating system to Windows Server 2008 and IIS7.
- The WWW and FTP publishing services publish Web and FTP sites. An upgraded FTP publishing service that does not ship with Windows Server 2008 is available as a download.
- You can add virtual directories to Web sites and, optionally, store virtual directory content on a different hard disk or on a different computer.

Lesson Review

You can use the following questions to test your knowledge of the information in Lesson 2, "Managing Web Sites." The questions are also available on the companion DVD if you prefer to review them in electronic form.

NOTE ANSWERS

Answers to these questions and explanations of why each answer choice is right or wrong are located in the "Answers" section at the end of the book.

1. You want to create a virtual directory called Videos on Default Web Site and specify a physical path of E:\Videos on the Web server. You log on to the Web server interactively and open the Command Prompt console as an administrator. What command do you enter?

   A. *%Systemroot%\system32\inetsrv\appcmd set vdir /app.name:"Default Web Site/" /path:/Videos /physicalPath:E:\Videos*

   B. *%Systemroot%\system32\inetsrv\appcmd set vdir /app.name:"Default Web Site/" /path:/E:\Videos /physicalPath:Videos*

   C. *%Systemroot%\system32\inetsrv\appcmd add vdir /app.name:"Default Web Site/" /path:/Videos /physicalPath:E:\Videos*

   D. *%Systemroot%\system32\inetsrv\appcmd add vdir /app.name:"Default Web Site/" /path:/E:\Videos /physicalPath:Videos*

2. The *appcmd.exe* utility executes a command on a supported management object. Which of the following form the basic set of commands that are supported by most objects? (Choose four. Each correct answer presents part of a complete solution.)

   A. List

   B. Stop

   C. Start

   D. Add

   E. Delete

   F. Set

3. The Windows Server 2008 Web server Glasgow hosts a Web application named SalesApp within the HipHopVideos Web site, which in turn uses a virtual directory with the path \\Glasgow\Videos\Sales. You install a new server named Dundee on the network and move the contents of the virtual directory to the \\Dundee\MusicVideos\Sales folder. You need to ensure that users can access the contents of the \\Dundee \MusicVideos\Sales folder. Which command do you enter from an elevated command prompt to change the path to the virtual directory's content?

   A. *%Systemroot%\system32\inetsrv\appcmd set vdir/ vdir.name:"HipHopVideos /Videos/Sales" /physical path:\\Dundee\MusicVideos\Sales*

   B. *%Systemroot%\system32\inetsrv\appcmd set vdir/ vdir.name:"HipHopVideos /Videos/Sales" /physical path:\\Glasgow\Videos\Sales*

   C. *%Systemroot%\system32\inetsrv\appcmd set vdir/ vdir.name:"Glasgow/Videos /Sales" /physical path:\\Dundee\MusicVideos\Sales*

   D. *%Systemroot%\system32\inetsrv\appcmd set vdir/ vdir.name:" \\Dundee \MusicVideos\Sales " /physical path:/HipHopVideos/Videos/Sales*

Lesson 3: Managing IIS

To enable quick and graceful recovery if a Web server experiences a fault, you must not only back up the server and all its files as you would with any other server on your network; you must also back up your IIS7 configuration settings. You also need to capture logs and monitor IIS7 operations to identify and troubleshoot Web server performance problems. This can be a lot of work, and you should delegate tasks to more junior administrators. This lesson discusses Web site content backup and restore, IIS configuration backup, IIS monitoring and logging, and delegation of administrative rights.

> **After this lesson, you will be able to:**
> - Back up and restore IIS7 configuration settings.
> - Implement HTTP logging and IIS7 monitoring.
> - Delegate administration.
>
> **Estimated lesson time: 35 minutes**

Implementing IIS Backup and Restore

Backing up the files that implement a Web site, for example, default.htm, is part of Windows Server Backup, as described in Chapter 8, "Maintaining the Active Directory Environment." If a virtual directory has a physical path on the Web server, the directory is backed up by using the same process. If it is on another server, it is backed up at the same time as other directories on that server.

However, you also need to ensure that the configuration of the Web server is protected against data loss. Because IIS configuration settings are stored in the %SystemDrive%\Inetpub \History folder, ensure that this folder is included in file system backup policies in addition to backing up directories that hold Web sites and Web applications.

IIS Configuration Backup

You can use the *appcmd.exe* utility to create and restore IIS configuration backups. This enables you to recover from unwanted configuration changes and return to a known, good Web server state. Create a backup before making any significant configuration changes or installing components that might change the configuration. A configuration backup contains the current copy of the applicationhost.config root configuration file in addition to other, related server-wide state information such as FTP configuration and IIS Administration Tool configuration.

You use the *appcmd add* command of the backup object to create a configuration backup. This gives the backup a default name that includes the backup date and time but is otherwise less than user friendly. For example, you can enter the following command:

```
%systemroot%\system32\inetsrv\appcmd add backup
```

This results in a message similar to (but not the same as) the following:

```
BACKUP object "20081202T182530" added
```

You will likely choose instead to specify a name for the backup as in the following command:

```
%systemroot%\system32\inetsrv\appcmd add backup MyConfigBackup
```

This results in the following message:

```
BACKUP object "MyConfigBackup" added
```

You can display a list of available backups, using the *appcmd list* command of the backup object, as follows:

```
%systemroot%\system32\inetsrv\appcmd list backups
```

IIS Configuration Restore

You can restore a backup by using the *appcmd restore* command and specifying the name of the backup as follows:

```
%systemroot%\system32\inetsrv\appcmd restore backup "MyConfigBackup"
```

This results in the following message:

```
Restored configuration from backup "MyConfigBackup"
```

Appcmd also enables you to work with periodic configuration backups made by the configuration history service. These backups will be included in the list of backups generated by the *appcmd list* command and are available for restoration the same way as backups you made manually.

> **MORE INFO** **CONFIGURATION HISTORY**
>
> For more information about configuration history and the configuration history service, see *http://learn.iis.net/page.aspx/129/using-iis-7-configuration-history/*.

Monitoring and Logging Web Server Activity

HTTP Logging and Request Monitor role services are installed by default and enable you to monitor and diagnose problems on your servers, sites, and applications. You first enable the features, using the *appcmd.exe* utility, and then you configure them in IIS7. When you run the *appcmd.exe* tool, settings are updated in the %windir%\System32\Inetsrv\Config\Application-Host.config file.

NOTE LISTING ATTRIBUTES AND SETTINGS

To determine other IIS attributes and settings that you can change by using the *appcmd.exe* utility, you can view the full schema in the %windir%\System32\Inetsrv\Config\Schema \IIS_schema.xml file.

IIS7 enables you to monitor real-time state information about application pools, worker processes, sites, application domains, and running requests. You can also trace events that track a request throughout the request-and-response process. To enable the collection of these trace events, you can configure IIS7 to capture full trace logs, in XML format, automatically for any particular request, based on elapsed time or error response codes.

Failed Request Tracing

By tracing for failed requests, you can capture an XML formatted log of a problem when it occurs. This enables you to troubleshoot the problem without reproducing it. You can also define failure conditions for applications and configure which trace events to log on a per-URL basis.

You can configure tracing for failed requests at the following levels:

- **Site level**   At this level, you can enable or disable tracing and configure log file settings.
- **Application level**   At this level, you can specify the failure conditions for capturing trace events and configure which trace events are captured in the log file entries.

MORE INFO FAILED-REQUEST TRACING REQUIREMENTS

For more information about the levels at which you can perform failed-request tracing and the modules, handlers, and permissions that are required for these procedures, see *http://technet.microsoft.com/en-us/library/cc754017.aspx*.

To help you manage tracing rules for failed requests, you can view a list that contains all tracing rules for failed requests for a particular configuration level by path, associated trace providers, HTTP status codes, time taken for the request, or scope (local or inherited). You can also group rules by scope to see easily which rules apply at the current configuration level and which rules are inherited from a parent level.

You can use IIS Manager or the *appcmd.exe* utility to view a list of tracing rules for failed requests. To use IIS Manager, select a Web site in the console tree, and then double-click Failed Request Tracing Rules in Features View. You should see a pane similar to Figure 13-19.

This figure shows that Failed Request Tracing is not currently enabled. You can enable it by clicking Edit Site Tracing in the Actions pane and then selecting the Enable check box. In the Edit Web Site Failed Request Tracing Settings dialog box shown in Figure 13-20, you can specify the path to the directory in which the failed-request log files are stored and specify the maximum number of trace files. Click OK to save your settings.

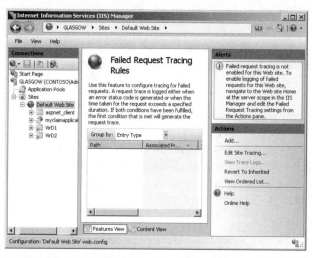

FIGURE 13-19 Failed-request tracing rules viewed through IIS Manager.

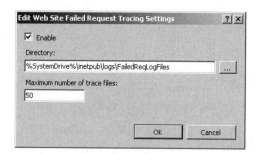

FIGURE 13-20 Enabling Failed Request Tracing.

You can also view a list of tracing rules for failed requests by entering the following command at an elevated command prompt:

```
%systemroot%\system32\inetsrv\appcmd configure trace "site"
```

The variable *site* is the name of the site for which you want to view a list of failed-request tracing rules.

Enable trace logging for failed requests when you want IIS7 to log information about a request that is failing to serve content from a site or an application. If trace logging for failed requests is enabled, IIS7 provides targeted logging. This means you no longer have to look through a list of irrelevant log entries to find a failed request, and you do not have to re-create an error to troubleshoot it.

To enable failed-request trace logging for a site from an elevated command prompt, enter a command with the following syntax:

```
%systemroot%\system32\inetsrv\appcmd configure trace "site" /enablesite
/directory:string /maxLogFiles:int
```

The *site* variable is the name of the site for which you want to enable trace logging for failed requests. The *string* variable specifies where you want to store the log files. The default is %SystemDrive%\inetpub\logs\FailedReqLogFiles. The *int* variable specifies the maximum number of trace log files you want to keep. The default value is 50.

You can also enable trace logging for failed requests at the URL level. To do so, enter a command with the following syntax:

```
%systemroot%\system32\inetsrv\appcmd configure trace "site" /enable /directory:string
/maxLogFiles:int
```

Disable site-level trace logging for failed requests when you no longer need to track failed requests for a site or for an application on the site. To disable site-level trace logging for failed requests by using IIS Manager, click Sites in the Connections pane. In Features View, click the site for which you want to enable trace logging and, in the Actions pane, under Configure, click Failed Request Tracing. In the Edit Web Site Failed Request Tracing Settings dialog box, clear the Enable check box, and then click OK.

You can also disable failed-request trace logging for a site by entering the following command at an elevated command prompt:

```
%systemroot%\system32\inetsrv\appcmd configure trace "site" /disablesite
```

The *site* variable specifies the site name.

You can define a failed-request tracing rule that captures and logs trace events if a request to a server fails or takes too long. Events are written to the trace log only if the request exceeds the time interval allocated for the request to complete processing or if the specified HTTP status and substatus code combination is generated for the response. As a result, the trace log contains only information specific to the failed request. You no longer need to search through large log files that contain information about every request to find a specific failed request.

You can create a failed-request tracing rule by using IIS Manager. This is a fairly complex procedure and is described in detail at *http://technet.microsoft.com/en-us/library/cc725948. aspx*. You can also use the *appcmd.exe* utility, although this requires a lengthy command. You get better at entering such commands with practice.

For example, to create a failed-request tracing rule that logs requests to an ASP.NET file called *pricelist.asp* on a site called Adatum when such a request takes 30 seconds or longer to respond, enter the following command at an extended command prompt:

```
%systemroot%\system32\inetsrv\appcmd configure trace "Adatum/pricelist.aspx" /enable /
path:*.aspx /timeTaken:00:00:30 /areas:ASPNET/Infrastructure,Module,Page,Appservices /
verbosity:Warning
```

EXAM TIP

The upgrade examinations might ask you to identify or interpret a command-line entry that defines a failed-request tracing rule. They are unlikely to ask you to generate one.

You can edit a tracing rule for failed requests and change the settings for failed-request tracing by using IIS Manager. You would do this when you want to change the failure definitions for a rule or when you want to collect different information about a failed request. For example, you might want to change the length of response time allowed for a request before it is considered to have failed. In IIS Manager Features View, double-click Failed Request Tracing Rules. On the Failed Request Tracing Rules pane, select the rule you want to change, and then click Edit in the Actions pane. You can then edit the rule properties.

You can remove a tracing rule for a failed request when it is no longer required. The procedure is the same as that for editing a rule except that you click Remove rather than Edit in the Actions pane and then click OK.

You can also use the *appcmd.exe* utility to remove a tracing rule for a failed request. For example, to remove a failed-request tracing rule that logs requests to an ASP.NET page for a site named Adatum, enter the following at an elevated command prompt:

```
%systemroot%\system32\inetsrv\appcmd configure trace "Adatum/ " /disable /path:*.aspx
```

HTTP Logging

To enable HTTP Logging, enter the following command from an elevated command prompt:

```
%systemroot%\system32\inetsrv\appcmd set config /section:httpLogging /dontLog:False
/selectiveLogging:LogAll
```

This command configures HTTP logging to use the default logging settings from the schema file for all Web sites configured on the Web server. The *selectiveLogging* attribute can also take one of the following values:

- **LogError**   All errors are logged.
- **LogSuccessful**   All successful requests are logged.
- **LogAll**   All requests are logged.

To disable HTTP logging requests, enter the following command from an elevated command prompt:

```
%systemroot%\system32\inetsrv\appcmd set config /section:httpLogging /dontLog:True
```

When you have enabled logging for HTTP requests, you can configure additional logging options. For example, you can specify specific information to log. The following command logs only HTTP substatus information for all Web sites:

```
%systemroot%\system32\inetsrv\appcmd set config /section:sites -siteDefaults.logFile.
logExtFileFlags:HttpSubStatus
```

> **MORE INFO**   **HTTP SUBSTATUS**
>
> For more information about status, substatus, and Win 32 status codes in HTTP logs, see *http://support.microsoft.com/kb/907273*. Although this article was written before Windows Server 2008 and IIS7 were released, it is relevant to these technologies.

Suppose, for example, you wanted to log HTTP substatus, host, time, and date information about a Web site with an ID of two. Enter the following command from an elevated command prompt:

```
%systemroot%\system32\inetsrv\appcmd set config /section:sites /[id='2'].logFile.
logExtFileFlags:HttpSubStatus,Host,Time,Date
```

> **MORE INFO** **CONFIGURING LOGGING**
>
> For more information about configuring logging in IIS7, see *http://technet.microsoft.com /en-us/library/cc732079.aspx* and follow the links.

Monitoring Worker Processes and Currently Executing Requests

With the IIS7 worker processes feature, you can monitor sites, application pools, server worker processes, application domains, and requests. You can view performance information about worker processes in application pools and about requests currently executing in a worker process. This can help you debug problems on your server such as hanging applications and memory leaks. It can also help you reduce the number of applications that cause problems on your Web server and help you decide how to fix issues.

For example, you might find that a particular application pool frequently shows a high level of CPU usage, and you can then determine which applications run in that application pool. It often assists your diagnosis if you isolate a suspect application by moving it to another application pool.

IIS7 lists worker processes with their associated application pool names. It provides the following information for each worker process:

- Application pool name
- Process ID
- State
- CPU percentage
- Private bytes
- Virtual bytes

To view a list of worker processes, open IIS Manager and, in the Connections pane, select the server node in the tree. In Features View, double-click Worker Processes. You can then view the list of worker processes in the grid, as shown in Figure 13-21. The figure shows that currently no worker processes are running on the server.

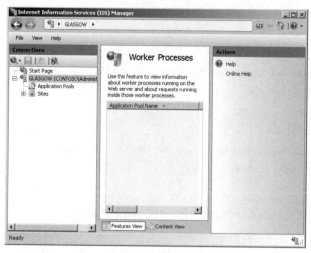

FIGURE 13-21 Viewing worker processes.

You can also perform this procedure by using the *appcmd.exe* utility. To view a list of worker processes, enter the following from an elevated command prompt:

```
%systemroot%\system32\inetsrv\appcmd list wps
```

If you consider that a worker process is using excessive resources on your Web server, or requests are taking an excessive time to process, you can view a list of current requests that are processing in a specific worker process. This helps you determine whether a problem occurs in a specific area of a site or application. If, for example, a request for a particular file is causing high memory usage, it might be necessary to optimize the code that implements the request (or ask an application developer to do so). If a worker process takes a long time to process requests, you can view which requests are currently being processed and identify the request that takes an excessive time to process.

IIS Manager returns the following information about requests in a worker process:

- Site ID
- URL
- Verb
- Client IP
- State
- Module Name
- Time Elapsed

To view currently executing requests in a worker process, open IIS Manager and, in the Connections pane, select the server node in the tree. In Features View, double-click Worker Processes and select the worker process from the grid. In the Actions pane, click View Current Requests. You can then view the list of requests in the grid.

You can also view a list of currently executing requests by entering the following command from an elevated command prompt:

```
%systemroot%\system32\inetsrv\appcmd list requests
```

> **MORE INFO** **MONITORING WORKER PROCESSES**
>
> For more information about monitoring worker processes in IIS7, see *http://technet .microsoft.com/en-us/library/cc725918.aspx* and follow the links.

Throttling Web Sites

One problem you might encounter during a monitoring process is excessive demand on network bandwidth, particularly during peak periods. This can be a serious problem for organizations such as Web hosting organizations, which manage a large number of public Web sites. A solution to this problem is to throttle each individual site so that no site can exceed a predefined bandwidth limit. You can do this through the Edit Web Site Limits option.

> **MORE INFO** **EDITING WEB SITE LIMITS**
>
> The settings in the Edit Web Site Limits dialog box are described at *http://technet .microsoft.com/en-us/library/cc731169.aspx*. To find out how to access this option, see *http://technet2.microsoft.com/WindowsServer2008/f/?en/Library/78c4e640-66ab-4ae2 -ab15-ecf0a2689a881033.mspx* and follow the links.

Delegating Site and Application Management

IIS7 enables you to delegate features in IIS Manager to nonadministrative users. Feature delegation enables you to configure which features of a site or application to delegate to IIS Manager users and Windows users or groups in IIS Manager. You can delegate control of specific features to site or application users without giving them full control of the Web server.

The IIS Manager Users feature enables you to create non-Windows user accounts known as IIS Manager accounts. These users can use their IIS Manager credentials to connect to a site or an application to which they have been granted permission through the IIS Manager Permissions feature. To create these accounts, you must be a member of the Administrators group on the Web server. Domain administrators are, by default, members of this group if the server is joined to a domain. You can grant permission to IIS Manager user accounts and to Windows users or groups on the computer to connect to a site or an application.

You can also configure the management service when delegating permissions. This service enables users to connect to IIS7 remotely, using IIS Manager. Additionally, it enables users to connect to sites and applications on the server locally.

Configuring User Accounts to Connect to Sites and Applications

You can create IIS Manager user accounts or Windows user accounts when you want to allow nonadministrators to configure delegated features in sites and applications on your Web server. To enable users to connect to the Web server through IIS Manager, add IIS Manager user accounts in IIS Manager or add new Windows users to your server and permit these accounts to connect to a specific site or application in IIS Manager. Finally, configure the management service to accept remote connections and specify whether the server accepts connections from Windows user accounts only or from both Windows user accounts and IIS Manager user accounts.

You create an IIS Manager user account when you want to allow a non-Windows user to configure delegated features in a site or an application in IIS Manager. IIS Manager user credentials consist of a username and password created and used exclusively in IIS Manager to access the IIS configuration files. When you have created an IIS Manager user account, you can allow the user to connect to sites and applications and configure delegated features in those sites and applications.

> **NOTE ACCESSING A WEB SERVER**
>
> It is most unlikely that nonadministrators, and especially not IIS Manager user accounts, will log on to a Web server interactively. Such users will access Web sites and applications remotely through IIS Manager.

To create such an account, open IIS Manager and select the node for your server in the Connections pane. Double-click IIS Manager Users in Features View and, on the IIS Manager Users page, click Add User in the Actions pane. Type a username in the User Name text box in the Add User dialog box and type a password in the Password and Confirm Password text boxes. Finally, click OK.

If you need to view a list of IIS Manager users, open IIS Manager and select your server in the Connections pane. Double-click IIS Manager Users in Features View. If you then (for example) want to change a user's password, select the user, and then click Change Password in the Actions pane. Figure 13-22 shows the creation of an IIS Manager user.

Users can configure delegated features in any sites or applications for which you grant them permission. These users can be IIS Manager users or Windows users and groups on the local computer or on the domain to which the computer belongs. Note that if you want IIS Manager users to connect to sites and applications, you must configure the management service to accept connections from users who have IIS Manager credentials. The procedure to do this is described later in this section.

To permit an IIS Manager user to connect to a site or an application, open IIS Manager. Expand the *Sites* node in the Connections pane and select the site for which you want to grant permission. Alternatively, expand the site and select the application for which you want to grant permission. In Features View, double-click IIS Manager Permissions and, on the IIS Manager Permissions page, click Allow User in the Actions pane. In the Allow User dialog box, select IIS Manager. This enables you to select a user account that is valid within IIS Manager but is not a Windows account. Click Select to open the Select User Or Group dialog box, select a user, and then click OK. Finally, click OK to close the Allow User dialog box.

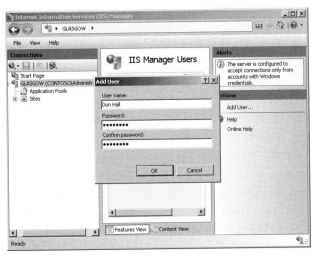

FIGURE 13-22 Creating an IIS Manager user.

The procedure to permit a Windows user or group to connect to a site or an application is very similar to that which permits an IIS Manager user to do the same. The difference is that, in the Allow User dialog box, you select Windows, which enables you to select a Windows user or group account.

Disable or remove an IIS Manager user account, Windows user account, or Windows group account when you no longer want the account to configure delegated features on a site or in an application. To do this, open IIS Manager, expand the *Sites* node in the Connections pane, and select the site for which you want to remove permission. Alternatively, expand the site and select the application for which you want to remove permission. Double-click IIS Manager Permissions in Features View and select a user or group from the list on the IIS Manager Permissions page. In the Actions pane, click Deny User, and then click Yes.

 Quick Check

- To what types of accounts can you grant permissions to configure delegated features in a site or an application?

Quick Check Answer

- IIS Manager user accounts, Windows user accounts, and Windows security group accounts.

Configuring Delegation for a Site or an Application

You can configure default delegation settings and custom delegation settings in IIS7 at site and application levels. When you configure default delegation settings at a parent level, you affect all children of that parent. For example, when you delegate a feature at the Web server level, you affect all sites on the server. Similarly, when you delegate a feature on a site, you affect all applications on that site. IIS Manager users and Windows users can then configure delegated features on the sites and in the applications to which you have granted them permission.

When you configure custom delegation settings, these affect only a specific site or application. For example, you can use the Feature Delegation page at the server level to delegate the Directory Browsing feature on all sites on the server. Then you can use the Custom Site Delegation page to remove delegation of the Directory Browsing feature from Default Web Site.

To configure default delegation settings for a site or an application, open IIS Manager. In the Connections pane, select the node for your server in the tree if you want to delegate features of all sites on your Web server. Alternatively, if you want to delegate features of all applications on a site, use the tools in the Connections pane to connect to the site that contains the applications. Select the site in the tree and then double-click Feature Delegation in Features View. Select a feature in the list on the Feature Delegation page and click the desired delegation state in the Actions pane. Figure 13-23 shows the Feature Delegation function in IIS Manager.

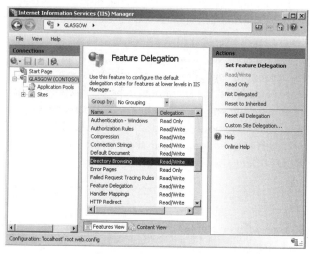

FIGURE 13-23 Feature delegation.

Configuring custom delegation settings for a site or an application involves a very similar procedure except that, in the Actions pane, you click Custom Site Delegation or Custom Application Delegation. On the Sites list or the Applications list, select the site or application for which you want to specify custom delegation settings, select a feature in the list, and then click the desired delegation state in the Actions pane.

Quick Check

- You have created an IIS Manager user called Don Hall. You have used the Feature Delegation page to delegate the Directory Browsing feature on all sites on the Web server Boston. However, Don cannot access the sites on Boston through IIS Manager. What do you still need to do?

Quick Check Answer

- You need to configure the management service on Boston to allow permitted users to manage delegated site features.

When setting the delegation state in the Actions pane, you can select Read to delegate the feature as Read Only. This is useful if you want users to know that the feature exists and to view its configuration, but you do not want to permit them to configure it. Alternatively, you can select Read/Write to delegate control of a feature on a site or in an application to a user so that you do not have to configure it yourself.

> **MORE INFO** **CONFIGURING DELEGATION**
>
> For more information about configuring delegation for a site or an application, see *http://technet.microsoft.com/en-us/library/cc770505.aspx* and follow the links.

Configuring the Management Service

The IIS7 management service enables you to manage a Web server remotely by using IIS Manager. The service also allows permitted users to manage delegated features of sites and applications on the Web server both locally and remotely by using the same tool. By default, remote connections are made over the HTTPS protocol on port 8172 and work through a firewall.

To enable remote management, open IIS Manager and select your server in the tree in the Connections pane. Double-click Management Service in Features View. In the Actions pane on the Management Service page, click Stop to stop the service. Select the Enable Remote Connections check box. This enables you to connect remotely to the server, sites, and applications. If you want to allow nonadministrators to connect to sites and applications by using IIS Manager, configure the following options under Identity Credentials:

- If you want to limit connections to users who have Windows credentials, select Windows Credentials Only.

- If you want to accept connections from users who have Windows credentials and from users who have IIS Manager credentials, select Windows Credentials Or IIS Manager Credentials.

In the Actions pane, click Apply, and then click Start.

To configure connection settings for the management service, open IIS Manager and select your server in the Connections pane. Double-click Management Service in Features View. Specify an IPv4 or IPv6 address that clients use to connect to the server under Connections on the Management Service page. If you do not want to use a specific IP address, accept the default of All Unassigned in the IP address box. Type the port number that clients use to connect to the server in the Port box or accept the default value. In SSL Certificate List, select the SSL certificate the service uses to encrypt data sent between the server and clients. If you want the server to log connection requests, select Log Requests To and type a physical path to the location of the log files. Finally, click Apply in the Actions pane, and then click Start.

> **NOTE** **ADDING AN SSL CERTIFICATE**
>
> Use the Server Certificates feature in IIS Manager if you want to add a new SSL certificate.

You can configure IPv4 address restrictions that specify whether a specific IPv4 address or address range is allowed or denied permission to connect remotely to sites or applications on the Web server. You would do this, for example, if you detect an unauthorized attempt to access the management service and you identify the IP address from which the attacks originate.

To configure an IPv4 address restriction for the management service, open IIS Manager and select your server in the Connections pane. Double-click Management Service in Features View and click Stop in the Actions pane on the Management Service page to stop the management service. Select the Enable Remote Connections check box and, under IPv4 Address Restrictions, click Allow or Deny to allow an IPv4 address or address range to connect to the management service or deny access to an IPv4 address or address range.

In the Add Allow Connection Rule dialog box or Add Deny Connection Rule dialog box, use one of the following procedures, and then click OK:

- To allow or deny a specific IP address, click Specific IPv4 address, and then type the IPv4 address in the box.
- To allow or deny a range of IP addresses, click IPv4 Address Range, type an IPv4 address in the box, and then type a subnet mask in the Subnet mask box.

You can delete an IPv4 address restriction by using the same procedure to access the Enable Remote Connections box. Then select a connection in the list under IPv4 Address Restrictions and click Delete. As previously, click Apply in the Actions pane, and then click Start.

Quick Check

■ You have created an IIS Manager user called Don Hall. You have used the Feature Delegation page to delegate the Directory Browsing feature on all sites on the Web server Boston. You have configured the management service on Boston to allow permitted users to manage delegated site features. However, Don reports that he can determine whether Directory Browsing is enabled on each site but cannot enable or disable the feature. What is the likely reason for this?

Quick Check Answer

■ When delegating the Directory Browsing feature, you probably specified Read rather than Read/Write permission.

PRACTICE   **Backing Up and Restoring IIS Configuration Settings**

In this practice, you back up IIS configuration settings. You then change a setting, restore IIS settings, and ensure that the setting is reconfigured to its original value.

EXERCISE 1   Back Up IIS Configuration Settings

1. If necessary, log on to the Glasgow domain controller with the Kim_Akers account and run the Command Prompt console as an administrator.

2. Enter the following command:

   %systemroot%\system32\inetsrv\appcmd add backup TestBackup

3. List the available IIS configuration backups, as shown in Figure 13-24, by entering the following elevated command:

   %systemroot%\system32\inetsrv\appcmd list backups

   Figure 13-24 shows the backups that are available.

FIGURE 13-24 Backing up IIS configuration and showing both manual and automatic backups.

EXERCISE 2   Change an IIS Configuration Setting

In this exercise, you change a setting. When you restore from backup, this setting should be reset to its original value. Complete the preceding exercise before carrying out this exercise.

1. If necessary, log on to the Glasgow domain controller with the Kim_Akers account and open IIS Manager.

2. In the Connections pane, select your server.

3. In Features View, double-click .NET Trust Levels. From the drop-down list, select the Minimal trust level, as shown in Figure 13-25.

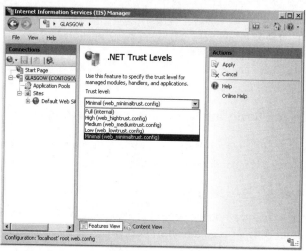

FIGURE 13-25 Selecting Minimal .NET trust level.

EXERCISE 3   Restore IIS Configuration Settings

In this exercise, you restore IIS configuration settings from backup. You must complete Exercises 1 and 2 in this lesson before carrying out this exercise.

1. If necessary, log on to the Glasgow domain controller with the Kim_Akers account and open an elevated command prompt.

2. Enter the following command:

    `%systemroot%\system32\inetsrv\appcmd restore backup "TestBackup"`

    You should see a confirmation of your restore, as shown in Figure 13-26.

FIGURE 13-26 Restoring IIS configuration backup.

3. To test the restoration, open IIS Manager (if necessary). If IIS Manager is already open, press F5 to refresh the view. In the Connections pane, select your server.

4. In Features View, double-click .NET Trust Levels.

5. Confirm that .NET Trust Levels has been reset to Full (Internal), as shown in Figure 13-27.

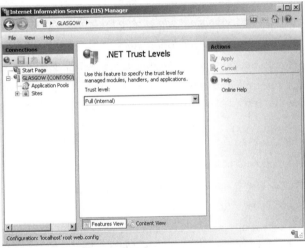

FIGURE 13-27 The IIS .NET Trust Levels configuration setting is restored to its original setting.

Lesson Summary

■ Use the *appcmd add backup* and *appcmd restore backup* commands to back up and restore IIS configuration.

■ IIS7 enables you to monitor real-time state information about application pools, worker processes, sites, application domains, and running requests. You can also trace events that track a request throughout the request-and-response process.

- IIS7 enables you to delegate features in IIS Manager to nonadministrative users. Feature delegation enables you to configure which features of a site or application to delegate to IIS Manager users and Windows users or groups in IIS Manager.

Lesson Review

You can use the following questions to test your knowledge of the information in Lesson 3, "Managing IIS." The questions are also available on the companion DVD if you prefer to review them in electronic form.

> **NOTE ANSWERS**
>
> Answers to these questions and explanations of why each answer choice is right or wrong are located in the "Answers" section at the end of the book.

1. You want to back up all the IIS7 configuration settings on your Web server. You want to call the backup PreTrialConfigDecNinth. You open an elevated command prompt. What command do you enter?

   A. *%Systemroot%\system32\inetsrv\appcmd add backup*

   B. *%Systemroot%\system32\inetsrv\appcmd add backup PreTrialConfigDecNinth*

   C. *%Systemroot%\system32\inetsrv\appcmd list backups*

   D. *%Systemroot%\system32\inetsrv\appcmd restore backup PreTrialConfigDecNinth*

2. You want to view a list of currently executing requests on a Web server. You log on to the server interactively and open an elevated command prompt. What command do you enter?

   A. *%Systemroot%\system32\inetsrv\appcmd get wps*

   B. *%Systemroot%\system32\inetsrv\appcmd get requests*

   C. *%Systemroot%\system32\inetsrv\appcmd list wps*

   D. *%Systemroot%\system32\inetsrv\appcmd list requests*

3. You work for a Web site hosting organization, configuring IIS7 on a Windows Server 2008 Web server that is not part of your domain. The Web server will host a large number of customer Web sites. Each Web site will have a unique administrator username and password. You want to ensure that remote administrators, who are not employed by your organization, can configure settings only on their own Web sites and cannot directly connect to the Web server. How do you configure security for the remote administrators?

A. Create individual Windows accounts and add them to the local Administrators group on the Web server.

B. Enable Anonymous Authentication for all the Web sites on the server.

C. Create an individual IIS Manager user account for each of the client Web sites.

D. Create a single IIS Manager user account for all client Web sites.

Lesson 4: Configuring SSL Security

As a Windows Server 2003 professional, you know that SSL encryption protects confidential or personal information sent between a client and a server. In this lesson, you learn about configuring certificates, requesting SSL certificates, configuring SSL settings, and exporting and importing certificates.

After this lesson, you will be able to:

- Obtain or generate an SSL certificate and configure HTTPS bindings.
- Configure SSL settings.
- Import and export certificates.

Estimated lesson time: 25 minutes

Configuring Server Certificates

One of your major security challenges is to protect communication between a Web client and a Web server. To help meet this challenge, you can use server certificates to provide added security for Web services. IIS7 provides built-in support for creating and managing server certificates and for enabling encrypted communications.

Server certificates provide a mechanism for a Web server to prove its identity to clients attempting to access it. Chapter 7, "Active Directory Certificate Services," describes the hierarchy of trust authorities and the various types of certificate authority (CA), including trusted third-party and internal certificates. The Web server itself can generate a self-signed SSL certificate, and you can obtain or generate certificates from the following types of CA:

- External trusted third-party CA
- Internal enterprise root CA
- Internal enterprise subordinate CA
- Internal standalone root CA
- Internal standalone subordinate CA

If, for example, you are setting up a sales application on a secure site that is accessed through the Internet by customers all over the world, you must obtain a certificate from an external trusted third-party CA.

You cannot create a secure HTTPS site until you have created an HTTPS site binding, and you cannot create such a binding until you have obtained an SSL certificate. The process for obtaining an SSL server certificate involves the following steps:

1. Generate a certificate request.

This request is created on a Web server, which produces a text file containing the information about the request in an encrypted format. The certificate request uniquely identifies the Web server.

2. Submit the certificate request to a CA.

In the case of an external intranet site, this is typically a trusted third-party CA, although you could use an enterprise subordinate CA for an intranet site. You submit the request by using a secure Web site or by sending an e-mail message. The CA verifies the information in the request and creates a trusted server certificate.

3. Obtain and install the certificate on the Web server.

The CA returns a certificate to the requester, usually as a text file. This file is then imported into the Web server to enable secure communications.

You can use IIS Manager to obtain an SSL certificate that you can use on an IIS Web server. On a Web server running Windows Server 2008, open IIS Manager and, in Features View, double-click Server Certificates. Certificate requests are for SSL server certificates at the Web server level, and you cannot generate them for other objects such as Web sites or Web applications.

Depending on the Web server configuration, some certificates might already be included in the default configuration. The IIS Manager Actions pane contains commands for creating new certificates.

To generate a certificate request, click Create Certificate Request, and then provide information about the requesting organization. The CA uses this information to determine whether to issue the certificate, and it must be exact. For example, the *Organization* field should include the complete legal name of the requesting company. The *Common Name* field generally defines the domain name to be used with the certificate.

Next, select the cryptographic method to be used to secure the certificate request. In the Cryptographic Service Provider setting, specify a method accepted by the certificate authority. Most third-party CAs accept the default, which is Microsoft RSA SChannel Cryptographic Provider. The Bit Length setting indicates the strength of the encryption. Larger values take more time to process but provide added security.

Next, provide a fully qualified path and file name in which the request will be stored. The request is stored in a text file that contains encrypted information. Submit the certificate request to a CA. Typically, the issuer's Web site requests you either to upload the certificate request or to copy and paste the contents into a secure Web site. The issuer also requires additional information such as details about your organization and payment information.

The amount of time a public third-party CA can take to process a request varies. When the request has been processed and approved, the CA sends a response by e-mail or through its Web site. You then store this response in a text file and export the file to IIS to complete the process.

To do this, select the appropriate request in the Server Certificates Feature View and click the *Complete Certificate Request* command in the Actions pane. You are asked to specify the path and file name of the response along with a friendly name for administration. Typically, you use a file name with a .cer extension for the response. If the certificate request matches the response, the certificate is imported into the IIS7 configuration.

Using CSR Files

In public key infrastructure (PKI) systems, a certificate signing request (CSR) is a message sent from an applicant to a CA to apply for a digital identity certificate. Before creating a CSR, you must generate a key pair. The CSR contains information identifying the applicant (such as a distinguished name in the case of an X.509 certificate) and the public key chosen by the applicant. The corresponding private key is not included in the CSR but is used to digitally sign the entire request. The CSR might be accompanied by other credentials or proofs of identity required by the certificate authority, and the certificate authority might contact the applicant for further information.

You can use CSR files to obtain a server certificate or to renew a certificate that has reached or is nearing its expiry date. If the request is successful, the certificate authority sends back an identity certificate that has been digitally signed with the private key of the certificate authority.

NOTE **THE CREATE DOMAIN CERTIFICATE OPTION**

The Create Domain Certificate option generates a request to an internal CA. You can use enterprise or standalone CAs to generate certificates in an organization that has its own certificate services infrastructure and uses internal certificates for intranet communication.

NOTE **CREATING A SELF-SIGNED CERTIFICATE**

In development and test environments, you can use self-signed certificates to test certificate functionality. You can create these certificates by using the *Create Self-Signed Certificate* command in the Actions pane. However, users who access the Web server using a secure connection will receive a warning that the certificate has not been issued by a third party. This contra-indicates the use of self-signed certificates on production Web servers.

Viewing Certificate Details

To view server certificate content, double-click an item in the Server Certificates list on a Web server. The Certificate dialog box provides information about the server certificate. The General tab, shown in Figure 13-28, displays details about the issuer of the certificate. For Internet-based certificates, this is the name of the trusted third party that issued the certificate.

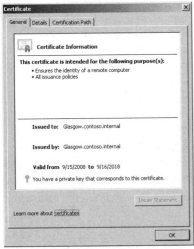

FIGURE 13-28 The General tab of the Certificate dialog box on the Glasgow Web server.

The Details tab displays additional certificate properties, including the encryption method. The Certification Path tab displays the entire trust hierarchy for the certificate. This is useful for tracking all the trust relationships in environments that have multiple levels of CAs.

In Internet Explorer, users can right-click a Web page and select Properties. The General tab shows a control for viewing the certificate's status and other details. This is useful for validating the identity of a Web server or organization.

Enabling SSL

When you add an SSL server certificate to an IIS Web server, you can enable connections by using the HTTPS protocol. HTTPS connections, by default, use TCP port 443. To modify details or to enable HTTPS for a Web site, you must configure the site bindings for the Web site.

You can also use IIS Manager to require SSL-enabled connections for specific Web sites. To do this, select a Web site, a Web application, or a folder, and then click SSL Settings in Features View. You can specify whether SSL is required to access the content. Optionally, you can specify whether client certificates are ignored, accepted, or required.

Certificate Policies and Practice Statements

A certificate policy is a set of rules produced by a CA that outlines the applicability or use of a certificate for a particular application. A certificate practice statement (CPS) is a detailed statement produced by a CA that describes how the certificate policy requirements are implemented and maintained. It enables users to determine the degree of trust they can place in the certificates issued by a CA.

A CPS is tailored to the organizational structure, operational procedures, facilities, and computer environment of the operating authority. A CPS identifies the certificate policies to which it conforms and the estimated size of the user community it intends to serve. It specifies the standards to which its internal interfaces conform, the form of name used in its certificates, and the namespace in which a CA issues certificates. It describes the mechanisms that identify principals, including Security Officer, Security Administrator, Directory Administrator, and User.

A CPS also specifies key management policies, local security practices, and operational practices. It explicitly identifies the legal statutes to which a PKI must conform and any cross-certification agreements that exist. The CPS includes a profile of the relevant certificates and certificate revocation lists (CRLs) it supports in addition to the directory schema and describes the procedures for development and maintenance of the CPS document. Chapter 7 discusses CPSs in more detail.

Importing Server Certificates

If you want to restore a lost or damaged server certificate from backup or install a server certificate sent to you by another user or CA, you must import the certificate. To do this, open IIS Manager and navigate to the appropriate level. In Features View, double-click Server Certificates, and then click Import in the Actions Pane. In the Import Certificate dialog box, specify a file name in the Certificate File text box or click the browse button (...) and navigate to the file in which the exported certificate is stored. If the certificate was exported with a password, type the password in the Password text box. If you want to be able to export the certificate, select Allow This Certificate To Be Exported. If you do not want to allow additional exports of the certificate, clear the Allow This Certificate To Be Exported check box. Finally, click OK.

Exporting Server Certificates

Typically, you export a certificate from a source server when you want to apply the same certificate to a target server or when you want to back up a certificate and its associated private key.

To export a certificate, open IIS Manager and navigate to the appropriate level. Double-click Server Certificates in Features View, select a certificate, and click Export in the Actions pane. In the Export Certificate dialog box, specify a file name in the Export To text box or click the browse button (...) to navigate to a file in which to store the certificate for export. If you want to associate a password with the exported certificate, type the password in the Password text box and retype the password in the Confirm Password text box. Finally, click OK.

Adding and Testing HTTPS Bindings

When you have obtained an SSL server certificate, you can use this certificate to add bindings for the HTTPS protocol to the Web site you want to secure with SSL. Open IIS Manager and, in the Tree view, select the site. Click Bindings in the Actions pane. This opens the Site Bindings dialog box that enables you to create, edit, and delete bindings for your Web site. Click the Add button to add a new SSL binding to the site.

New bindings default to HTTP on port 80. Select HTTPS in the Type drop-down list. Select the SSL certificate you obtained or created earlier from the SSL Certificate drop-down list and click OK. The new binding appears in the Site Bindings dialog box.

In addition to adding new bindings, you can edit existing bindings. In the Site Bindings dialog box, select the binding you want to change, and then click Edit. This enables you, for example, to select another SSL certificate to use with the Web site.

To test the new binding, open IIS Manager and select the site in the Tree view. In the Actions pane, under Browse Web Site, click Browse *:443 (HTTPS). This accesses the Web site, using the HTTPS protocol. Note that if you have used a self-signed certificate, you will see an error page telling you there is a problem with the site's security certificate. This is because the certificate is not trusted. In this case, click Continue To This Website (Not Recommended).

> **NOTE USING *APPCMD.EXE***
>
> You cannot use the *appcmd.exe* utility to request or create a certificate or to create an SSL binding.

Configuring SSL Settings

You can configure SSL settings if you want a site to require SSL, to require 128-bit SSL, or to interact in a specific way with client certificates. Open IIS Manager and select the site node in Tree view. On the site's home page, double-click SSL Settings in the middle pane. You then can select the Require SSL check box. If you require the site to use SSL, you can also select the Require 128-Bit SSL check box. In addition, you can choose whether to Ignore, Accept, or Require Client Certificates. Note that you cannot select Require Client Certificates unless you have selected Require SSL.

> **NOTE HOSTED WEB SITES**
>
> A special case occurs when a Web hosting company hosts a number of different Web sites. Although these Web sites are implemented on the same network and often on the same server, they cannot be treated in the same way as multiple company Web sites implemented by the same organization, usually in the same domain. These are different Web sites associated with different organizations and hosted on standalone Web servers. If they are to use HTTPS, they each require one (or more) separate SSL certificates.

A common error occurs when company policy states that users must use certificate authen-tication to access a secure site, but they can gain access with a username and password. Typically, this is because Require Client Certificates is not selected in SSL Settings.

PRACTICE   Configuring a Secure Site

In this practice, you generate a self-signed SSL certificate and use it to secure Default Web Site on the Glasgow computer. In a production environment, you would obtain a certificate from a trusted third-party CA and would not implement a secure site on a domain controller. The Glasgow domain controller must have the Web Server server role installed before you carry out this practice.

EXERCISE 1   Generate a Self-Signed Certificate

In this exercise, you generate a self-signed certificate that you use to configure an HTTPS binding for Default Web Site on Glasgow.

1. If necessary, log on to Glasgow with the Kim_Akers account and open IIS Manager.
2. Select the Glasgow server in the Tree view (under Connections).
3. Double-click Server Certificates in Features View.
4. Click Create Self-Signed Certificate in the Actions pane, as shown in Figure 13-29.

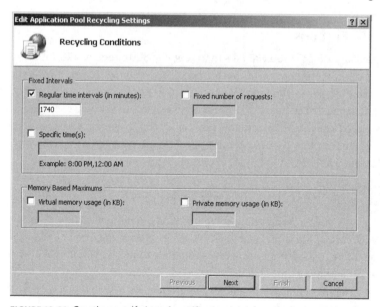

FIGURE 13-29 Creating a self-signed certificate.

5. Enter the friendly name **Test Certificate** for the new certificate and click OK.

EXERCISE 2   Create an HTTPS Binding

In the previous exercise, you created a self-signed certificate called Test Certificate that is marked for server authentication. In this exercise, you create an HTTPS binding for Default Web Site on Glasgow that uses this certificate as a server-side certificate for HTTP SSL encryption and for authenticating the identity of the server. You must complete the preceding exercise before attempting this exercise.

1. If necessary, log on to Glasgow with the Kim_Akers account and open IIS Manager.

2. Expand Sites and select Default Web Site in the Tree view.

3. Click Bindings in the Actions pane

4. Click Add in the Site Bindings dialog box.

5. In the Add Site Binding dialog box, shown in Figure 13-30, select HTTPS in the Type drop-down list. Select the Test Certificate self-signed certificate you created in the preceding exercise from the SSL Certificate drop-down list.

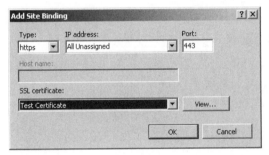

FIGURE 13-30 Selecting a site binding and a certificate.

6. Click OK. Click Close to close the Site Bindings dialog box.

EXERCISE 3   Testing the Site Binding

In the preceding two exercises, you generated a self-signed SSL certificate and configured an HTTPS site binding. You now test that you have secured Default Web Site. Complete the preceding exercises before attempting this exercise.

1. If necessary, log on to Glasgow with the Kim_Akers account and open IIS Manager.

2. Select the Default Web Site in the Tree view.

3. In the site's Actions pane, click Browse *:443 (HTTPS), as shown in Figure 13-31.

   Internet Explorer 7 shows the error page illustrated in Figure 13-32 because the self-signed certificate was issued by Glasgow, not by a trusted CA. Internet Explorer 7 will trust the certificate if you add it to the list of Trusted Root Certification Authorities in the certificates store on Glasgow or in Group Policy for the *contoso.internal* domain. However, external users will trust only a certificate obtained from a trusted third-party CA.

FIGURE 13-31 Testing an HTTPS binding.

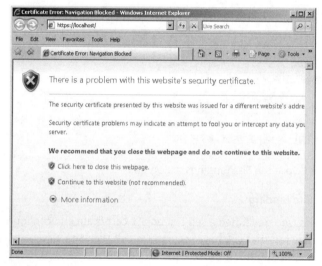

FIGURE 13-32 Error page generated when a certificate is not trusted.

4. Click Continue To This Website (Not Recommended) to access the Default Web Site.

Lesson Summary

- You must use a certificate issued by a trusted third-party CA to secure a Web site that is to be accessed by Internet users. Use self-signed certificates only in the test environments.

- To secure a Web site with SSL, you must obtain an SSL certificate and configure HTTPS bindings.

- You can configure SSL settings for a site and specify Require SSL and Require 128-bit SSL. You can choose between Ignore Client Certificates, Accept Client Certificates, and Require Client Certificates. You cannot choose Require Client Certificates unless you select Require SSL.

Lesson Review

You can use the following questions to test your knowledge of the information in Lesson 4, "Configuring SSL Security." The questions are also available on the companion DVD if you prefer to review them in electronic form.

> **NOTE ANSWERS**
>
> Answers to these questions and explanations of why each answer choice is right or wrong are located in the "Answers" section at the end of the book.

1. The Windows Server 2008 Web server Toronto hosts a restricted Web site that only members of the Management security group can access. Written company policy specifies that managers must user certificates to access the restricted Web site. While monitoring the server, you discover that managers are accessing the secure Web site by using usernames and passwords. How can you ensure that managers access the secure Web site only though user certificates?

   A. Configure SSL settings to require 128-bit SSL.

   B. Configure SSL settings to ignore client certificates.

   C. Configure SSL settings to require client certificates.

   D. Configure SSL settings to accept client certificates.

2. Don Hall, one of your junior network administrators, has used IIS Manager to configure an HTTPS binding for a Web site named Sales on the Detroit Windows Server 2008 Web server. While logged on to the server interactively, he opens IIS Manager and accesses the site in Tree view. In the Actions pane under Browse Web Site, he clicks Browse *:443 (HTTPS). Rather than accessing the site immediately, he receives an error message telling him there is a problem with the site's security certificate. Don clicks Continue To This Website (Not Recommended) and accesses the Sales Web site. However, this situation is not acceptable for a commercially available Web site. What does Don need to do to remedy it?

A. IIS Manager can configure only HTTP bindings. Don needs to use the *appcmd.exe* command-line utility.

B. It is not valid to test a site binding when logged on at the Web server that hosts the site. Don needs to access the site from another computer.

C. Don needs to configure SSL Settings and specify that the site requires SSL authentication.

D. Don must obtain an SSL certificate from a trusted third-party CA and edit the site binding to use this certificate rather than the one it is currently using.

3. An SSL certificate you are using to secure an HTTPS Web site has become corrupt. As an experienced administrator, you have been careful to back up the certificate and its private key. What is the first step you need to take to remedy the situation?

A. Import the certificate.

B. Export the certificate.

C. Reconfigure the Web site bindings to use the certificate you have as a backup.

D. Renew the certificate.

Lesson 5: Configuring Web Site Authentication and Permissions

Authentication is the process by which a user or computer proves its identity. On an IIS7 Web server, authentication settings and options determine how users provide credentials to access Web server content. IIS7 provides several methods for securing content. By default, content stored in new Web sites, Web applications, and virtual directories allows access to anonymous users who are not required to provide any authentication to retrieve data or use the application.

However, many Web sites and applications require stricter security, and users must provide authentication credentials. Users also must be sure that the site they are accessing is what it purports to be and not a spoofing Web site.

In this lesson, you learn about the authentication modes IIS7 supports, including client certificate mapping, and how you can configure them. The lesson also discusses authorization and permissions at site and application level and .NET trust levels.

> **After this lesson, you will be able to:**
> - Discuss the various authentication methods available and configure authentication to meet your organization's needs.
> - Configure client certificate mapping.
> - Configure authorization settings and select and configure the appropriate .NET trust level for an application.
>
> **Estimated lesson time: 30 minutes**

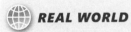

REAL WORLD
Ian McLean

In more innocent days, not all that long ago, security was mostly about ensuring that users you allowed to access your network were who they claimed to be. Users were authenticated by name and password, although even then it was considered bad practice to transmit passwords over a network in clear text. Encryption was used only in situations that were obviously risky such as using a private virtual network to send data through a potentially hostile environment such as the Internet. Secure HTTPS sites were simple. A purchaser sent name, address, and credit card information using SSL encryption, but almost everything else was done through HTTP.

Then came spoofing, man-in-the-middle attacks, and personal identity theft. It became important not only to protect networks against malicious users but to protect users against sites that pretended to be what they were not. Both sender and recipient needed to be authenticated. Decryption software became more sophisticated, so encryption became stronger. SSL has provided encryption over the Internet and intranets for some time, but in its modern incarnation of TLS/SSL, it is much more powerful than it was fifteen or even five years ago. HTTPS sites are more common, and much more sophisticated, than the simple sites that allowed you to input sensitive data a few years ago. Many organizations use HTTPS rather than HTTP for all external (and sometimes all internal) communication. Internet Protocol Security (IPsec) provides end-to-end security for all traffic, not just for Web traffic.

As a professional, you need to know more about security than the professional hacker and even than the programmer who wrote the software the hacker uses. You will never achieve total security—there will still be users who write their usernames and passwords on sticky notes stuck to their computer screens—but your job is to make the hacker's life as difficult as possible.

Good luck. You'll need it.

Implementing Authentication

The following methods of user authentication are available:

- Anonymous authentication
- Forms authentication
- Challenge-based authentication
- ASP.NET Impersonation
- Client certificates

Anonymous Authentication

Many Web sites and Web servers permit users to access at least a default page or some selected content without needing to provide authentication information. When you enable the Web Server role with default options, anonymous authentication is enabled for the Default Web Site and its associated Web content. Anonymous authentication provides access to content that is available to all users who can connect to the Web server.

When IIS7 receives a request for content, it automatically uses a specific identity to attempt to complete the request. By default, anonymous authentication uses the IUSR built-in account. This is the IIS 7 standard security account. By default, it has permission to access the content (based on NTFS permissions) and the request is processed automatically.

You can also use the *Set* command from the Command Prompt console to specify a username and password for an account other than IUSR. You should do this if you plan to use different NTFS permissions for different Web content. You can also use Application Pool Identity. This instructs IIS to use the credentials applied to the application pool used by the Web site or Web application. To use Application Pool Identity, enter the following command from an elevated command prompt:

```
%systemroot%\system32\inetsrv\appcmd set config -section:anonymousAuthentication
/username:"" --password
```

> **MORE INFO** **SPECIFYING APPLICATION POOL IDENTITY AS ANONYMOUS USER**
>
> For more information about specifying the Application Pool Identity as Anonymous User, see *http://learn.iis.net/page.aspx/202/application-pool-identity-as-anonymous-user/*.

If you want all the content on the Web server to be available to all users, then you do not need to configure any further authentication. However, you typically want to restrict access to some content on the Web server. For example, an intranet server might include a Web application or virtual directory that is intended for only members of the Sales department; you can use NTFS permissions to implement this. If credentials configured for anonymous authentication are not sufficient to access content, that content is not returned to the user automatically. In general, you must enable one of the other forms of user authentication in addition to anonymous authentication so that authorized users can access content.

Forms Authentication

Web developers often use standard HTTP forms to transmit logon information. Forms authentication uses an HTTP 302 (Login/Redirect) response to redirect users to a logon page. Typically, the logon page provides users with locations to type a logon name and password. This information is submitted back to the logon page, where it is validated. If the credentials are accepted, users are redirected to the content they requested. By default, form submissions send data in an unencrypted format. To secure the transmission of logon information, enable encryption through SSL or Transport Layer Security (TLS).

Forms authentication is frequently used on the Internet because it does not require a specific Web browser. Web developers build their own logon pages, and logons are typically validated against user account information stored in a relational database (for Internet sites) or against an Active Directory Domain Services (AD DS) domain. Default settings for forms authentication can be used by ASP.NET Web applications.

In forms authentication, the logon URL specifies the name of the Web page to which users are sent when they attempt to access protected content. When the user provides authentication information, the Web browser sends cookies to the Web server during each request. This enables the client to prove that it has authenticated with the Web server. The Cookie Settings section enables you to configure how cookies will be used by the site. The Mode options include:

- Do Not Use Cookies

- Use Cookies

- Auto Detect

- Use Device Profile

The option you choose should be based on Web browser requirements (for example, whether your Web site requires users to enable support for cookies) and the requirements of your Web application or Web content.

Challenge-Based Authentication

A challenge occurs when users who access Web sites on the Internet (or a company intranet) are required to provide a username and password to access secured content or to perform actions such as placing online orders. IIS7 supports three methods of presenting a security challenge to users who are attempting to access Web content that is secured through file system permissions. Each of these methods relies on sending an HTTP 401 challenge that prompts users to provide logon information. The authentication methods are as follows:

- **Basic authentication**   This method presents an authentication challenge to Web users through a standard method supported by all Web browsers. Users provide information that is encoded but not encrypted. If the information is intercepted, the logon and password details can be easily obtained. To transfer basic authentication information securely, ensure that your network connections are secure or enable encryption using SSL/TLS.

> **NOTE   BASIC AUTHENTICATION**
>
> Because it does not encrypt usernames and passwords by default, many security professionals consider basic authentication less secure than anonymous authentication.

- **Digest authentication**   This method uses the HTTP 1.1 protocol to provide a secure method of transmitting logon credentials. It uses a Windows Server 2008 domain controller to authenticate the user. This method requires clients' Web browsers to support HTTP 1.1. However, current versions of the most popular browsers support this method.

- **Windows authentication**   This method provides a secure and easy-to-administer authentication option. It relies on either NTLM or Kerberos authentication protocol to validate users' credentials against a Windows domain or local security database. Windows authentication is designed primarily for use in intranet environments, where clients and Web servers are members of the same domain. Administrators can use AD DS domain accounts to control access to content.

If you want to require users to provide logon information before accessing Web content, you must disable anonymous authentication and enable either forms or challenge-based authentication. If anonymous authentication remains enabled, content that is not protected by file system permissions is automatically available to unauthenticated users.

Note also that you cannot enable both forms authentication and challenge-based authentication for the same content.

ASP.NET Impersonation

Impersonation is a security method that processes an IIS Web request by using the security information provided by a specific user account or by the account of the user who is accessing the site.

ASP.NET Impersonation is disabled by default, and the security context for processing requests is based on the account used by the Web application. Enabling ASP.NET Impersonation is shown in Figure 13-33.

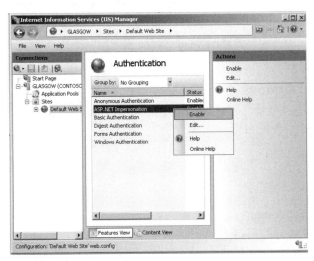

FIGURE 13-33 Enabling ASP.NET Impersonation.

Alternatively, you can configure ASP.NET Impersonation to the Authenticated User option. This specifies that the security permissions of a user who has been authenticated (using one of the other authentication options) provide access to content. This setting is useful when you want to use file system permissions that use specific users and groups to decide which content should be protected. The setting is appropriate for environments that support relatively small numbers of users, for example, department-level intranet Web servers.

Client Certificates

In addition to the other available types of authentication options, IIS7 supports client certificates to validate a Web user identity. This method requires users to have security certificates installed on their client computers. When a request is made for protected content, IIS7 automatically validates the identity of the client by querying this certificate information. The following are the three main modes by which client certificates are used:

- **One-to-one mapping** In this configuration, the Web server holds a copy of the client certificate every client computer uses that accesses restricted content. The server compares its copy of the certificate with the certificate the client presents to validate requests.

- **Many-to-one mapping** If it is impractical to manage certificates for all possible Web users on the Web server, you can use many-to-one mapping. This method is slightly less secure than one-to-one mapping. In many-to-one mapping, the Web server performs authentication by using information found in the client certificate. For example, the Web server could validate the organization information in the certificate to ensure that the user is coming from a trusted company.

- **Active Directory mapping** Active Directory Certificate Services (AD CS) can simplify the creation and management of client certificates. To use this method, an organization must set up its own certificate-based infrastructure. This method is typically used in environments in which systems administrators have control over end users' client computers. It is impractical to require certificates for publicly accessible Internet Web sites and applications.

Authentication Methods and Options

The authentication options available for a Web server are based on the Web Server role services that are installed. These include the following:

- Basic authentication
- Windows authentication
- Digest authentication
- Client certificate mapping authentication
- IIS client certificate mapping authentication

To add or remove a security-related role service, open Server Manager, expand the Roles section, right-click Web Server (IIS), and select either Add Role Services or Remove Role Services. Because role services affect the available authentication options for the entire Web server, you must determine the requirements of all the Web applications and Web content on your server.

In addition to role service settings, each of the authentication methods has specific module requirements, as shown in Table 13-2.

TABLE 13-2 IIS Authentication Methods and Their Requirements

AUTHENTICATION METHODS	REQUIRED MODULE(S)
Anonymous	AnonymousAuthModule
ASP.NET Impersonation	ManagedEngine
Basic	BasicAuthModule and TokenCacheModule

AUTHENTICATION METHODS	REQUIRED MODULE(S)
Client Certificates	iisClientCertificateMappingModule
Client Certificates (Active Directory Mapping)	CertificateMappingAuthenticationModule
Digest	DigestAuthModule
Forms	FormsAuthenticationModule
Windows	WindowsAuthenticationModule

Configuring Authentication Settings

IIS7 enables you to use the Web object hierarchy to define configuration settings. Authentication settings can be configured for objects at the following levels:

- Web server
- Web sites
- Web applications
- Virtual directories
- Physical folders and individual files

Authentication settings that are defined at parent levels (such as for a Web application) are automatically used for child objects. This makes it easier to manage settings for multiple Web sites, Web applications, and their related content.

To configure authentication settings, open IIS Manager, select the appropriate object in the left pane, and then double-click Authentication in Features View. Figure 13-34 shows the authentication options for the Default Web Site object.

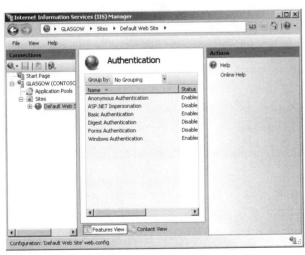

FIGURE 13-34 Authentication options for the Default Web Site.

The IIS Manager display shows a list of the available authentication options, grouped by the response type used. Each method can be enabled or disabled by selecting the item and using the *Enable* or *Disable* commands in the Actions pane. Some authentication options provide additional commands for managing settings. By default, when you enable or disable an authentication option, the setting applies to all lower-level objects and content in the IIS hierarchy. You can override this behavior by explicitly enabling or disabling authentication methods at lower levels.

To verify your authentication-related settings, always test access to content by using a Web browser. In some cases, it might be necessary to use a second computer to ensure that authentication is working properly. For example, if you are already connected to the Glasgow computer as a member of the administrators group and you want to test Windows Authentication, attempt to connect from another computer (for example, the Boston server on your test network). This prevents automatic authentication from affecting your test results. It is not essential that you do this on your test network, but it is one of the suggested practices at the end of this chapter.

Using the Command Line to Configure Authentication

You can also use the *appcmd.exe* utility from an elevated command prompt to configure authentication settings. For example, to enable or disable Anonymous authentication, enter a command that uses the following syntax:

```
%systemroot%\system32\inetsrv\appcmd set config /section:anonymousAuthentication
/enabled:true | false
```

You can also change the account used for anonymous access. For example, to use an account named Kim_Akers and a password of p@ssw0rd for anonymous access, enter the following command:

```
%systemroot%\system32\inetsrv\appcmd set config /section:anonymousAuthentication
/userName:Kim_Akers/password:P@ssw0rd
```

To enable or disable Basic authentication, enter a command that uses the following syntax:

```
%systemroot%\system32\inetsrv\appcmd set config /section:basicAuthentication
/enabled:true | false
```

For example, to use Basic authentication with a Default Domain named Contoso and a Realm of Contoso, enter the following command:

```
%systemroot%\system32\inetsrv\appcmd set config /section:basicAuthentication
/defaultLogonDomain:Contoso /realm:Public
```

Note that in general, you use the same value for the realm name as you used for the default domain, although this is not compulsory.

To enable or disable Digest authentication, enter a command that uses the following syntax:

```
%systemroot%\system32\inetsrv\appcmd set config /section:digestAuthentication
/enabled:true | false
```

You can specify the realm IIS7 uses for Digest authentication. For example, to use Digest authentication with a realm of Public, enter the following command:

```
%systemroot%\system32\inetsrv\appcmd set config /section:digestAuthentication
/realm:Public
```

To enable or disable Forms authentication, enter a command that uses the following syntax:

```
%systemroot%\system32\inetsrv\appcmd set config /commit:WEBROOT /section:system.web/
authentication /mode: None | Windows | Passport | Forms
```

> **NOTE** **THE *PASSPORT* MODE ATTRIBUTE**
>
> *Passport* is a supported value for the mode attribute. However, Passport authentication is not supported on Windows Server 2008.

By default, IIS7 sets the mode attribute to Windows, which disables Forms authentication. If you set the attribute to *Forms*, this enables Forms authentication. For example, to enable Forms authentication, enter the following command:

```
%systemroot%\system32\inetsrv\appcmd set config /commit:WEBROOT /section:system.web/
authentication /mode:Forms
```

To specify the logon URL for Forms authentication, enter a command that uses the following syntax:

```
%systemroot%\system32\inetsrv\appcmd set config /commit:WEBROOT /section:system.web/
authentication /forms.loginURL:string
```

The variable *string* is the name of the page on which clients log on. The default value is *Login.aspx*. For example, to specify the logon URL for Forms authentication, enter the following command:

```
%systemroot%\system32\inetsrv\appcmd set config /commit:WEBROOT /section:system.web/
authentication /forms.loginURL:login.aspx
```

To specify the authentication time-out for Forms authentication, enter a command that uses the following syntax:

```
%systemroot%\system32\inetsrv\appcmd set config /commit:WEBROOT /section:system.web/
authentication /forms.timeout:TimeSpan
```

The variable *TimeSpan* is the time in minutes after which the cookie used for authentication expires. The default value is 30 minutes. For example, to change the authentication time-out for Forms authentication to 20 minutes, enter the following command:

```
%systemroot%\system32\inetsrv\appcmd set config /commit:WEBROOT /section:system.web/
authentication /forms.timeout:20
```

> **NOTE CLIENT CERTIFICATE MAPPING AUTHENTICATION**
>
> You cannot use the *appcmd.exe* utility to configure Client Certificate Mapping authentication.

> **MORE INFO CONFIGURING AUTHENTICATION**
>
> For more information about configuring authentication, see *http://technet.microsoft.com /en-us/library/cc733010.aspx* and follow the links.

Managing Authorization and Permissions

Systems administrators use authorization to determine which resources and content are available to specific users. Authorization relies on authentication to validate the identity of a user or computer. When this identity has been proven, Allow and Deny permissions are implemented by authorization rules based on server, site, application, or file (where a file is specified by a URL). These rules determine which actions a user or computer can perform and what content a user or computer can access.

IIS7 secures various types of content, using URL-based authorization. Because Web content is generally requested using a URL that includes a full path to that content, you can configure authorization through IIS Manager or the *appcmd.exe* utility by creating and using URL authorization rules.

The necessary modules and handlers must be installed on the Web server and enabled at the level at which you perform this procedure. The procedures for configuring URL authorization rules can be performed at the following IIS7 levels:

- Web server
- Site
- Application
- File (URL)

Creating URL Authorization Rules

You must enable UrlAuthorizationModule to enable URL authorization. Authorization rules can be configured for specific Web sites, for specific Web applications, and for specific files (based on a complete URL path). URL authorization rules use inheritance so that lower-level objects inherit authorization settings from their parent objects (unless these settings are specifically overridden).

To configure authorization settings, open IIS Manager and select the appropriate object in the left pane. In Features View, double-click Authorization Rules. Figure 13-35 shows authorization rules configured for Default Web Site.

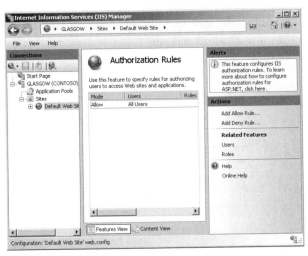

FIGURE 13-35 Default Web Site authorization rules.

There are two types of rules: Allow and Deny. To create a URL authorization rule, open IIS Manager and navigate to the appropriate level. In Features View, double-click Authorization Rules. In the Actions pane, choose Add Allow Rule or Add Deny Rule, depending on the type of rule you want to create.

In the Add Allow Authorization Rule dialog box or in the Add Deny Authorization Rule dialog box, select one of the following types of access:

- All Users
- All Anonymous Users
- Specific Roles Or User Groups (Type the role or user group in the text box.)
- Specified Users (Type the user ID in the text box.)

When you choose to specify users or groups to which the rule applies, you can type the appropriate names in a comma-separated list. The specific users and groups are defined using .NET role providers. This is a standard feature that is available to ASP.NET Web developers. Developers can create their own roles and user accounts and can define permissions within their applications. Generally, information about users and roles is stored in a relational database or is implemented by a directory service such as AD DS.

Optionally, select Apply This Rule To Specific Verbs if you want to stipulate further that the users, roles, or groups allowed to access the content can use only a specific list of HTTP verbs. Type those verbs in the text box. For example, if you want to apply a rule only for POST commands (which are typically used to send information from a Web browser to a Web server), add the POST verb to the rule. Finally, click OK.

For example, suppose you are configuring security for an internal IIS7 Web application. Clients access the site using *http://intranet.tailspintoys.internal*, and all clients that access the site have user accounts in the *tailspintoys.internal* domain. You want to limit access to a specific folder named Confidential located within the Web application's content structure so that only a small number of specified users have access to this folder. You want to avoid changing NTFS permissions. To accomplish this, create an authorization rule that restricts access to the folder content to the specified users. Authorization rules do not rely on NTFS permissions.

Using the Command Line

You can enter commands based on the *appcmd.exe* utility at an elevated command prompt to create URL authorization rules. To create an Allow rule for URL authorization, use the following syntax:

```
%systemroot%\system32\inetsrv\appcmd set config /section:system.webServer/security/
authorization /+"[accessType='Allow',roles='string',users='string',verbs='string']"
```

The variable *string* where it applies to users can contain a single user or a list of users, each separated by a comma. The variable *string* where it applies to roles can contain a single role or a list of roles, each separated by a comma. The variable *string* where it applies to verbs can contain a single verb or a list of verbs, each separated by a comma. For example, to create an Allow rule for all users, enter the following command:

```
%systemroot%\system32\inetsrv\appcmd set config /section:system.webServer/security/
authorization /+"[accessType='Allow',users='*']"
```

To create an Allow rule for anonymous users, enter the following command:

```
%systemroot%\system32\inetsrv\appcmd set config /section:system.webServer/security/
authorization /+"[accessType='Allow',users='?']"
```

To create an Allow rule for the Admin and Guest roles as well as for UserA and UserB and apply that rule to the GET and POST verbs, enter the following command:

```
%systemroot%\system32\inetsrv\appcmd set config /section:system.webServer/security/
authorization /+"[accessType='Allow',roles='Admin,Guest',users='UserA,UserB',verbs='GET,
POST']"
```

To create a Deny rule for URL authorization, use the following syntax:

```
%systemroot%\system32\inetsrv\appcmd set config /section:system.webServer/security/
authorization /+"[accessType='Deny',roles='string',users='string',verbs='string']"
```

The values you can set for the variables are the same as for Allow rules. For example, to create a Deny rule for the Admin and Guest roles as well as for UserA and UserB and apply that rule to the GET and POST verbs, enter the following command:

```
%systemroot%\system32\inetsrv\appcmd set config /section:system.webServer/security/
authorization /+"[accessType='Deny',roles='Admin,Guest',users='UserA,UserB',verbs='GET,
POST']"
```

The procedure for editing a rule through IIS Manager is very similar to creating the rule except that you edit the settings you previously specified. To edit a rule from the command line, modify the *accessType* parameter to specify the change. For example, to change a Deny rule for all users to an Allow rule for all users, enter following command:

```
%systemroot%\system32\inetsrv\appcmd set config /section:authorization
/[accessType='Deny',users='*'].accessType:Allow
```

To change a Deny rule for anonymous users to Deny only UserA and UserB, enter the following command:

```
%systemroot%\system32\inetsrv\appcmd set config /section:authorization
/[accessType='Deny',users='?'].users:User1,User2
```

> **MORE INFO**   **CONFIGURING AUTHORIZATION**
>
> For more information about configuring authorization, see *http://technet.microsoft.com/ en-us/library/cc772206.aspx* and follow the links.

Rule Inheritance

Authorization rules are inherited automatically by lower-level objects. This is useful when your Web site and Web content is organized hierarchically and based on intended users or groups. The Entry Type column shows whether a rule has been inherited from a higher level or has been defined locally. IIS Manager automatically prevents you from creating duplicate rules. You can remove rules at any level, including Inherited and Local entry types.

Securing Applications with ASP.NET

At the application level, Web security is mainly about securing pages so that they cannot be retrieved by unauthorized users. You might also want to know who requested the page so you can either take action if unauthorized access is attempted or personalize the page for an authorized user. In either case, you must identify the originator of each request and define rules that govern who can access which pages.

A Web server identifies callers using authentication. When a caller is identified, authorization determines which pages that particular caller is allowed to view. ASP.NET supports a variety of authentication and authorization models. When you select Windows authentication, ASP.NET uses IIS7 to authenticate the caller. IIS7 makes the caller's identity available to ASP.NET. For example, Windows authentication is enabled and Don Hall requests an .aspx file. IIS7 authenticates Don and forwards the request to ASP.NET along with Don Hall's access token. ASP.NET uses the token to make sure Don has permission to retrieve the page he requested. ASP.NET also makes the token available to the application that handles the request so that the application can impersonate Don—that is, temporarily assume the Don Hall identity—to prevent code executed within the request from accessing resources that Don lacks permission to access.

.NET Trust Levels

By default, applications that rely on ASP.NET run at the Full (Internal) .NET trust level, and the code can do anything the account running it can do. You can configure an application to run at a lower .NET trust level if, for example, the application should not be permitted to call unmanaged routines.

.NET applications can run at any of the following trust levels:

- **Full (Internal)** The application can do anything the account running it can do.
- **High** This is the same as Full trust except the application cannot call unmanaged code; call serviced components; write to the event log; access message queuing services; and access ODBC, OLEDB, and Oracle data sources. High trust level provides access to most configuration actions on the server and is designed for well-trusted and well-tested Web applications.
- **Medium** This is the same as High trust except the application cannot access files outside the application's directory, access the Registry, or make network or Web service calls. Medium trust level provides additional restrictions for Web applications that should not need to access the file system or Registry.
- **Low** This is the same as Medium trust except the application cannot write to the file system or call the Assert method, which tests application code and makes any out-of-process calls such as calls to a database or network. Low trust level further restricts application capabilities.
- **Minimal** This is the same as Low trust except the application is restricted from anything other than trivial processing (for example, calculating algorithms) and cannot perform actions that require permissions greater than Execute. Minimal trust level allows only execute permissions and prevents access to other resources on the computer.

Setting a .NET Trust Level

To set a .NET trust level, open IIS Manager and navigate to the application you want to manage. In Features View, double-click .NET Trust Levels and, on the .NET Trust Levels page, select a trust level from the Trust Level drop-down list. Click Apply in the Actions pane.

You can also set a .NET trust level from an elevated command prompt. To do so, enter a command with the following syntax:

```
%systemroot%\system32\inetsrv\appcmd set config /commit:WEBROOT /section:trust /level:
Full | High | Medium | Low | Minimal
```

For example, to set a trust level of High, enter the following command:

```
%systemroot%\system32\inetsrv\appcmd set config /commit:WEBROOT /section:trust
/level:High
```

PRACTICE   **Creating an Allow Rule for a Windows Account**

This practice contains only a single exercise. You create an Allow rule for the Don Hall Windows account. If this account does not exist in your domain, create an account with the username Don Hall and the password P@ssw0rd. Place this account in the Builtin Backup Operators security group on Glasgow.

EXERCISE   Create an Allow Rule for the Don Hall Windows Account

1. If necessary, log on to the Glasgow domain controller with the Kim_Akers account.

2. In All Programs/Accessories, right-click Command Prompt and select Run As Administrator.

3. Enter the following command:

   ```
   %systemroot%\system32\inetsrv\appcmd set config /section:system.webServer/
   security/authorization /+"[accessType='Allow',users='Don Hall']"
   ```

Lesson Summary

- The following methods of user authentication are available: anonymous authentication, forms authentication, challenge-based authentication, ASP.NET Impersonation, and client certificates.

- Authentication settings can be configured for objects at the following levels: Web server, Web sites, Web applications, virtual directories, and physical folders and individual files.

- A Web server identifies callers by using authentication. When a caller is identified, authorization determines which pages that particular caller is allowed to view.

Lesson Review

You can use the following questions to test your knowledge of the information in Lesson 5, "Configuring Web Site Authentication and Permissions." The questions are also available on the companion DVD if you prefer to review them in electronic form.

> **NOTE ANSWERS**
>
> Answers to these questions and explanations of why each answer choice is right or wrong are located in the "Answers" section at the end of the book.

1. You are a domain administrator at Tailspin Toys, configuring security for an internal IIS7 Web application. Users access the site at *http://intranet.tailspintoys.internal.* All users who access the site have accounts in the *tailspintoys.internal* domain. You want to limit access to a folder named NewDesigns located within the Web application's content structure so only members of the Designers global security group have access to this folder. How would you accomplish this without changing NTFS permissions?

   A. Create a new application pool specifically for the Web application and configure the application pool to restrict access to the application.

   B. Create an authorization rule that restricts access to the folder content to the specified users.

   C. Create a virtual directory called NewDesigns. Change the authentication settings to Specified User.

   D. Convert the NewDesigns folder to a Web application and assign Read/Write permission to the appropriate group account.

2. IIS7 supports the use of client certificates to validate a Web user identity. This method requires users to have security certificates installed on their client computers. When a request is made for protected content, IIS7 automatically validates the identity of the client by querying this certificate information. What are the main modes by which client certificates are used? (Choose three. Each correct answer presents a complete solution.)

   A. Many-to-one mapping

   B. One-to-many mapping

   C. One-to-one mapping

   D. Active Directory mapping

   E. Digest mapping

3. You want to create a URL authorization Allow rule for anonymous users. You log on to your Web server interactively and open an elevated command prompt. What command do you enter?

A. *%Systemroot%\system32\inetsrv\appcmd set config /section:system.webServer /security/authorization /+"[accessType='Allow',users='anon']"*

B. *%Systemroot%\system32\inetsrv\appcmd set config /section:system.webServer /security/authorization /+"[accessType='Allow',anon_users='True']"*

C. *%Systemroot%\system32\inetsrv\appcmd set config /section:system.webServer /security/authorization /+"[accessType='Allow',users='*']"*

D. *%Systemroot%\system32\inetsrv\appcmd set config /section:system.webServer /security/authorization /+"[accessType='Allow',users='?']"*

Chapter Review

To further practice and reinforce the skills you learned in this chapter, you can perform the following tasks:

- Review the chapter summary.
- Complete the case scenarios. These scenarios set up real-world situations involving the topics of this chapter and ask you to create solutions.
- Complete the suggested practices.
- Take a practice test.

Chapter Summary

- You can use IIS Manager and the *appcmd.exe* command-line utility to configure, add, and manage Web sites and add and configure application pools and virtual directories. You can also use the *appcmd.exe* to back up and restore IIS configuration. You can use the IIS Migration Wizard to migrate a site in a non-Windows operating system to Windows Server 2008 and IIS7.

- You can monitor and log information about application pools, worker processes, sites, application domains, and running requests. You can also track a request throughout the request-and-response process. You can delegate features in IIS Manager to IIS Manager and Windows nonadministrative users.

- To secure a Web site with SSL, you must obtain an SSL certificate and configure HTTPS bindings. You must use a certificate issued by a trusted third-party CA to secure a Web site that is to be accessed by Internet users.

- You can use IIS Manager and *appcmd.exe* to specify user authentication methods and authentication settings. A Web server identifies callers by authentication. When a caller is identified, authorization determines which pages that particular caller is allowed to view.

Case Scenarios

In the following case scenarios, you apply what you've learned about configuring a Web services infrastructure. You can find answers to the questions in these scenarios in the "Answers" section at the end of this book.

Case Scenario 1: Managing a Web Server

You are a senior administrator at Trey Research. One of the company's main remits is to develop Web applications on a test domain. Trey also has a production domain that hosts a large Internet Web site and an internal intranet site. Answer the following questions.

1. Web application developers require support for managing access to databases, security and authorization methods, and reliability and scalability features. They need to access the IIS management namespaces and objects so they can build logic that interacts with Web server requests. They need to use server-side components that can run on multiple Web server platforms, and they need to embed common content—for example, site headers, navigation elements, and site footers—on their Web pages. Which role services should you install on the development Web server?

2. Some of the Web applications are at an early stage of development, whereas others require nonstandard settings. How do you test these applications without affecting other applications on the development Web server?

3. On both the Internet and intranet Web sites, you want to implement Web pages but store the content files on a separate hard disk or even on a different computer from the content files for Default Web Site. How do you do this?

Case Scenario 2: Managing Web Server Security

You are a senior administrator with special responsibilities for Web site security at the A. Datum Corporation. A. Datum is a Web-hosting organization that hosts a large number of third-party Web sites. Answer the following questions.

1. One of your junior administrators has obtained an SSL certificate from a trusted third-party CA but is unsure how to use this certificate to secure a Web site. What do you advise her to do?

2. A secure site that should be accessed only by using client certificates is accepting username and password challenge authentication. What configuration changes are required?

3. You want to set a .NET trust level of High for a specific application. You log on to the Web server, open IIS Manager, and navigate to the application you want to manage. What do you do next?

Suggested Practices

To help you successfully master the exam objectives presented in this chapter, perform all of the following practices. Practices 4 and 5 are optional.

- **Practice 1** A large number of role services are associated with the Web Server server role. Find out more about these by accessing the relevant TechNet articles and by installing and experimenting with the role services.

- **Practice 2** Practice creating application pools and configuring their settings.

- **Practice 3** Configure the various authentication methods and experiment with each.

- **Practice 4** If you have the Boston server installed and running, configure Windows Authentication on Default Web Site on the Glasgow Web server and test this by accessing the Web site while logged on at the Boston server.

- **Practice 5** If you have the Boston server installed and running, create a virtual directory with a physical path that points to content files on that computer.

Take a Practice Test

The practice tests on this book's companion DVD offer many options. For example, you can test yourself on just one exam objective, or you can test yourself on all the upgrade examination content. You can set up the test so that it closely simulates the experience of taking a certification exam, or you can set it up in study mode so that you can look at the correct answers and explanations after you answer each question.

> **MORE INFO** **PRACTICE TESTS**
>
> For details about all the practice test options available, see the "How to Use the Practice Tests" section in this book's Introduction.

CHAPTER 14

Configuring FTP and SMTP Services

W indows Server 2008 ships with a version of the File Transfer Protocol (FTP) that can be described as FTP6. It is very similar to the FTP that shipped with Windows Server 2003. A version of FTP, which can be called FTP7, is designed for use with Windows Server 2008 but is provided as a separate download. FTP provides a standard method by which computers can transfer files and other types of data. It is used on both internal networks and on the Internet to upload and download content.

Simple Mail Transfer Protocol (SMTP) is a standard method for sending e-mail messages. Web applications use it to send notifications and communications to e-mail addresses. In this chapter, you learn how to configure FTP and SMTP in Windows Server 2008.

Exam objectives in this chapter:

- Configure a File Transfer Protocol (FTP) server.
- Configure Simple Mail Transfer Protocol Services (SMTP).

Lessons in this chapter:

Before You Begin

To complete the lessons in this chapter, you must have done the following:

- Installed a Windows Server 2008 Enterprise server configured as a domain controller in the *contoso.internal* domain as described in Chapter 1, "Configuring Internet Protocol Addressing." Have installed the Web Server server role on this computer, as described in Chapter 13, "Configuring a Web Services Infrastructure."

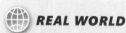

REAL WORLD

Ian McLean

FTP has been around for a very long time (in computing terms). It was used to transfer files across networks from the earliest days of the Arpanet and long before browsers were developed. Maybe these were more innocent days, or maybe nobody thought about security as much as they do now, but FTP takes an approach that can only be described as minimal.

I recall my first days of investigating network traffic with a protocol sniffer. The message sent in an ICMP ping command was of no great interest, but FTP traffic was an eye opener. Was it really that easy to access and read such interesting stuff and, more to the point, how did I stop anyone else doing it? I tried using Basic authentication. Surely that had to be more secure than anonymous access. No, the only effect was to put usernames and passwords as well as file contents in clear text on the network.

Pausing only to note my boss's bank account details (I'm joking), I warned colleagues not to put anything sensitive in files on an FTP site. I then went on to investigate various encryption scenarios and the use of virtual private networks (VPNs) in hostile environments. However, nothing changed the fact that FTP was (and, to an extent, still is) basically insecure.

Fortunately, things are improving. IPsec offers end-to-end encryption invisible to the user, and when we're all using IPv6 (as we eventually will be), IPsec is mandatory. FTP7, which will almost certainly ship with future Windows Server editions, supports Secure Sockets Layer (SSL) and enables you to configure FTP over SSL (FTPS) sites. I'm sure these developments will be welcomed by all.

Except for the sad old guy with the protocol sniffer—reading network traffic isn't fun anymore.

Lesson 1: Configuring FTP

Two FTP publishing services are available for IIS7. The first is installed by default with Windows Server 2008 and is a minor upgrade of the FTP service that was part of IIS6. FTP6 is little changed from the FTP service that shipped with Windows Server 2003 and that you studied for your Windows 2003 examinations.

The second is available as a download and is specifically designed to work with IIS7. FTP7 is available for Windows Server 2008 in 32-bit and 64-bit versions. Both FTP6 and FTP7 enable you to set up FTP sites so users can upload and download files easily. FTP7 also provides enhanced security and administration features.

In this lesson, you learn about how to use both versions of FTP on a computer running Windows Server 2008. The lesson concentrates mostly on FTP6 (as, at this time of writing, does the upgrade examinations). However, it also discusses the new features provided in FTP7.

After this lesson you will be able to:

- Install either the FTP6 or FTP7 publishing service.
- Configure the FTP6 publishing service.
- List and explain the enhancements that FTP7 offers.

Estimated lesson time: 50 minutes

Installing and Configuring the FTP Publishing Service

If you want to enable users to transfer files to or from a site, you must set up FTP on a Web server. The site can be on an intranet, an extranet, or the Internet, but the principles of providing a place to upload and download files using FTP are the same (although security considerations are different). You need to put files in directories on the FTP server and configure your site so that users can establish an FTP connection and transfer files by using an FTP client or FTP-enabled Web browser.

FTP is not installed on a Windows Server 2008 server by default. To set up an FTP site, first install the FTP service by using Server Manager in Windows Server 2008. Downloading and installing the new version of FTP that does not ship with Windows Server 2008 is discussed later in this lesson. This section discusses setting up FTP6.

When you install the FTP Publishing Service role service on a Web Server, this creates a default FTP site that you customize by using Internet Information Services (IIS) 6.0 Manager. You do this in the practice later in this lesson. When you install FTP, a default FTP directory is created at LocalDrive:\Inetpub\Ftproot.

MORE INFO   IIS 6.0 MANAGER

You can find the best sources of information about IIS 6.0 Manager on Windows Server 2003 Web sites. For example, see *http://www.microsoft.com/technet/prodtechnol /WindowsServer2003/Library/IIS/b0c14479-83e3-435d-a935-819fe396e7d2.mspx?mfr=true* and follow the links.

When you have installed the FTP Publishing Service role service, start it from either Server Manager or IIS 6.0 Manager. You can also start the service from an elevated command prompt by using the *net start* command or from the Services application programming interface (API) applet. If you decide later to install the new FTP7 Publishing Service, you must remove FTP6. Again, you can do this through Server Manager. You must be a member of the local Administrators group on the Web server to install or remove the FTP Publishing Service role service or to stop and start it.

Viewing FTP Site Configuration

Installing the FTP publishing service automatically installs IIS 6.0 Manager as a dependent role service. IIS 6.0 Manager can then be launched from the Administrative Tools program group. To view the configuration of the local server, expand the server object and the FTP Sites folder in IIS 6.0 Manager. By default, the FTP publishing service installs an FTP site called Default FTP Site.

To configure settings for Default FTP Site, or for any other site you subsequently create, first stop it (if it is running) by right-clicking the site object in IIS 6.0 Manager and clicking Stop. Then right-click the site object and select Properties. When you have configured the site properties as described in the remainder of this section, start the site to make the changes effective.

Configuring Ports and Connections

On the FTP Site tab, you can change the IP address and TCP port properties for the site. The FTP Site Connections section enables you to specify connection-related limits. The default settings allow up to 100,000 connections and inactive connections to time out after 120 seconds. You can reduce the allowed number of connections and the inactive connections timeout if you want to limit the amount of bandwidth and resources that a site uses.

Bear in mind that FTP servers are frequently targets for unauthorized usage. If an FTP site is insecure, unauthorized users can attempt to connect to it to upload their own content for various nefarious purposes. You can configure your security settings to prevent this, but it also helps to limit connections strictly to the number you anticipate will be used legitimately. Note that this is by no means a complete solution, but it can help counter a difficult situation.

In the Enable Logging section, click the Properties button to display the Logging Properties dialog box shown in Figure 14-1. This enables you to specify when new log files are created and where they are stored. On the Advanced tab of this dialog box, you can specify extended logging properties such as service name, server name, and server IP address.

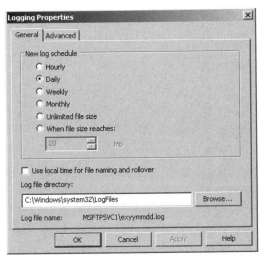

FIGURE 14-1 The Logging Properties dialog box.

Use the Current Sessions button on the FTP Site tab to view the users currently connected to the server. This information can be helpful for troubleshooting and for tracking site usage.

Configuring Security Accounts

As with Web sites (discussed in Chapter 13), the FTP publishing service uses the permissions assigned to a specific account to process upload and download requests when users connect to an FTP site by using anonymous credentials—by default, the IUSR_*computername* account (for example, IUSR_Glasgow). The Security Accounts tab (shown in Figure 14-2) enables you to specify a different username and password. Enabling Allow Only Anonymous Connections specifies that all users connecting to the site are restricted to the permissions granted to the security account you specify, regardless of whether they have provided valid Windows logon credentials.

> **NOTE ANONYMOUS CONNECTIONS**
>
> Because FTP has been around for a long time, some of the authentication methods it uses are insecure because they transmit usernames and passwords in clear text. Specifying that a site accepts anonymous connections and enabling Allow Only Anonymous Connections is one of the more secure methods of FTP site access.

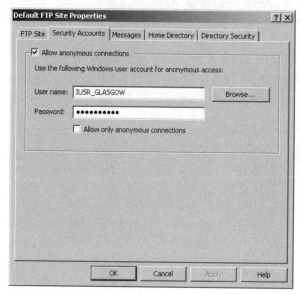

FIGURE 14-2 The Security Accounts tab.

FTP Server Messages

The Messages tab enables you to specify text displayed to the user. You can define a banner that displays before the user logs on to the FTP site. This can provide information about the site and contact information for site administrators. The Welcome message is sent after the user has successfully authenticated to the server. The Exit message is displayed when a user terminates a connection. The Maximum Connections message displays when the FTP server has reached the connection limit defined on the FTP Site tab.

Home Directory Options

Specify the file system location of the FTP site's root directory on the Home Directory tab. You access this tab in the practice later in this lesson. By default, you enter the path to a local folder. You can also choose whether you want to allow Read, Write, or Read and Write permissions and whether access to the folder should be logged. Directory Listing Style affects the format of file lists that are returned to the FTP client.

You can also use a home directory located on another computer. This, for example, enables multiple FTP servers to provide access to the same content. This functionality can also be implemented by a virtual directory, described later in this lesson. If you select A Directory Located On Another Computer, you can provide a Universal Naming Convention (UNC) network path to the content (for example, \\Glasgow\FTPData\).

The Connect As button enables you to specify the username and password credentials used to access the content. The default option is to use the authenticated user's credentials to validate access to the data. You can also designate a dedicated account for testing and validating permissions regardless of the user's credentials.

Directory Security Settings

You can configure settings on the Directory Security tab, shown in Figure 14-3, to restrict access to an FTP site based on IPv4 address information.

By default, all computers can access the site. You can add new entries for specific computers or groups of computers and change the default setting to either Granted Access or Denied Access.

For example, in an intranet scenario, you might want to limit access to a specific FTP site to clients that are coming from the network of a partner ISP. All permitted client connections come from a specific IP address range. In this case, you would allow access based on IP address and subnet mask settings.

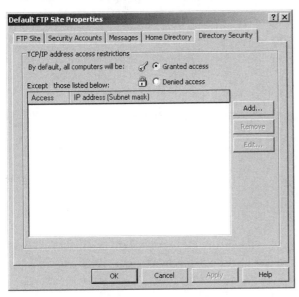

FIGURE 14-3 The Directory Security tab.

Creating a New FTP Site

Your Web server can host multiple FTP sites that respond on different ports and IP addresses. To create a new FTP site by using IIS 6.0 Manager, right-click the FTP Sites folder, click New, and then click FTP Site. This starts the FTP Site Creation Wizard. The first page of the wizard (after the Welcome page) asks you to provide a description value for the site. This is a descriptive name that helps you identify the site for administration purposes.

The IP Address And Port Settings page enables you to specify the IP address or addresses and the TCP port to which the server will respond. The default configuration is for the server to respond to requests on all unassigned IP addresses and use the default port of 21. Each FTP site on the server must have a unique combination of IP address and port assignments if sites are to run simultaneously.

On the FTP User Isolation page (shown in Figure 14-4), you can specify which content users are able to access.

The options are as follows:

- **Do Not Isolate Users**   All users can access all contents on the FTP site, including folders created by other users.

- **Isolate Users**   Each user is automatically placed in a folder that matches his or her logon name. This prevents users from accessing other folders or directories on the FTP server.

- **Isolate Users Using Active Directory**   Users can log on to the server if they have Active Directory domain accounts. Also, the path to a user's specified FTP home directory folder must exist.

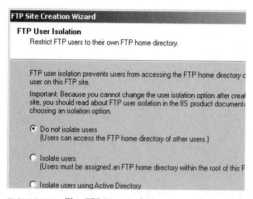

FIGURE 14-4 The FTP User Isolation page.

The FTP Site Home Directory page provides the root file system folder location for the FTP site. Typically, each new FTP site will have its own unique root folder. Default FTP Site is mapped to the %SystemDrive%\Inetpub\Ftproot folder.

On the FTP Site Access Permissions page of the FTP Site Creation Wizard, you can specify whether users are able to read, write, or both read and write files to the server. Read-only configurations are common for allowing users to download but not upload data. Write permissions are required to add files to the site. It is also possible to provide only Write permissions if the site is intended to allow users to upload files but not to view or download them. When you click Close on this page, the site is created. You then click Finish to close the FTP Site Creation Wizard.

When you have created a new FTP site, you can manage this site and its settings by using IIS 6.0 Manager. FTP sites that are configured using the FTP publishing service can be started, stopped, and paused independently. When an FTP site is stopped, it will not allow incoming connections.

NOTE MANAGING SITES AND SERVICES WITH *WMIC*

The Windows Management Instrumentation command-line utility (WMIC) provides a command-line interface for WMI and another method of administering FTP sites and services (and much more) from an elevated command prompt. A typical use of the *wmic* utility would be if you were administering a secure FTP site and wanted (for example) to ensure that the FTP service is not automatically available after restarting the server. In this case, you would use a *wmic /node* command to specify the computer on which the service is running, specify the FTP service, and call a routine that disables it.

MORE INFO WMIC

For more information about the *wmic* utility, see *http://msdn.microsoft.com/en-us/library /aa394531.aspx*.

EXAM TIP

WMI is not specified in the upgrade examination syllabus and will not be tested in detail. It is likely sufficient to know that the *wmic* utility exists and can be used for command-line administration.

NOTE IISFTP.VBS

The iisftp.vbs script used to manage FTP sites in IIS6 is not included in IIS7.

Adding a Virtual Directory

You can add a virtual directory to an FTP site so users can access files at a specified physical address that might be on a hard disk that does not usually reside under the FTP site's home directory or might be on another computer. A virtual directory is a friendly name, or alias, and the use of virtual directories enhances security because users do not know where files are physically located on the server relative to the FTP site's home directory; therefore, they cannot use that information to modify these files. Aliases also make it easier for you to move directories in your site. Rather than changing the URL for the directory, you need only change the mapping between the alias and the physical location of the directory.

Virtual directories enable you to publish content in multiple directories, and you can configure Read and Write permissions for each virtual directory separately. Even if User Isolation is enabled, you can share public content by creating a virtual directory with access permission for all users. To make a virtual directory accessible from multiple sites, you must add the virtual directory to each site. This enables each site to provide access to the same set of files at the same physical location.

If your FTP site contains files that are located in a directory other than the home directory, or on other computers, you must create virtual directories to include those files in your FTP site. To create a virtual directory that points to a physical directory on another computer, you specify the full UNC path to the directory and provide a username and password so you can specify user rights.

You can define nested virtual directories. For example, within a virtual directory called CompanyDocuments on an FTP site called Contoso, you could create a virtual directory called HR. The content in HR is then accessible using the *ftp://Contoso/CompanyDocuments/HR* URL.

Creating and Deleting a Virtual Directory with IIS 6.0 Manager

To create a virtual directory by using IIS 6.0 Manager, expand the local computer, expand the FTP Sites folder, expand the FTP site to which you want to add a virtual directory, right-click the site or folder within which you wish to create the virtual directory, point to New, and then click Virtual Directory to start the Virtual Directory Creation Wizard. On the Welcome page, click Next.

In the Alias text box, type a name for the virtual directory and then click Next. In the Path text box on the FTP Site Content Directory page, type the path for or browse to the physical directory in which the virtual directory resides, and then click Next.

Under Allow The Following Permissions, select the check boxes next to the appropriate access permissions, and then click Next. Finally, click Finish. You create a virtual directory in the practice later in this lesson.

If you want to delete a virtual directory from IIS 6.0 Manager, expand the FTP site, right-click the virtual directory, click Delete, and then click Yes. Deleting a virtual directory does not delete any folders or files in the physical path.

> **MORE INFO** **MANAGING VIRTUAL DIRECTORIES WITH IIS 6.0 MANAGER**
>
> For more information about managing virtual directories with IIS 6.0 Manager, see *http://www.microsoft.com/technet/prodtechnol/WindowsServer2003/Library/IIS/b0c14479-83e3-435d-a935-819fe396e7d2.mspx?mfr=true.*

> **NOTE** **IISFTPDR.VBS**
>
> The iisftpdr.vbs script used to create virtual directories in IIS6 is not included in IIS7.

Managing Authentication

You can configure an FTP6 server to allow anonymous access to FTP resources and (optionally) to allow only anonymous connections, or to require Basic authentication in the form of a username and password corresponding to a valid Windows user account. Note that Digest and Integrated Windows authentication cannot be used with FTP6 sites, and authentication settings must be set at the site level.

EXAM TIP

Windows authentication and IIS Manager authentication are available for FTP7. However, these authentication methods are not available for FTP6, which ships with Windows Server 2008.

Configuring Anonymous FTP Authentication

If you select Anonymous FTP authentication for a resource, all requests for that resource are accepted without prompting the user for credentials. IIS automatically creates the Windows IUSR_*computername* user account, and clients use the permissions associated with this account to access FTP sites and directories. If you do not want to use this account, you can specify another Windows user account for this purpose.

To enable Anonymous FTP authentication, open IIS 6.0 Manager and double-click the local computer. Right-click the FTP Sites folder, an individual FTP site folder, a virtual directory, or a file and then click Properties. Note that configuration settings made at the FTP Sites level are inherited by all the FTP sites on the server. You can override inheritance by configuring an individual site or site element.

Click the Security Accounts tab (shown previously in Figure 14-2) and select the Allow Anonymous Connections check box (selected by default), as was discussed earlier in this lesson. To allow users to gain access by anonymous authentication only, select the Allow Only Anonymous Connections check box.

If you do not want to access FTP resources in the context of the IUSR_*computername* account, type the anonymous logon username and password you want to use in the User Name and Password text boxes. You can then set the appropriate NTFS permissions for the anonymous account. Permissions and access control are discussed later in this section. Finally, click OK.

NOTE CHANGING SECURITY SETTINGS

If you change the security settings for an FTP site or virtual directory, the Web server prompts you for permission to reset the security settings for the child keys of that site or directory. If you choose to accept these settings, the child keys inherit the security settings from the parent site or directory.

Configuring Basic FTP Authentication

To establish an FTP connection with your Web server by using the Basic FTP authentication method, users log on with a username and password corresponding to a valid Windows user account. By default, this method sends username and password information, in addition to file content, across a network in clear text. Do not, therefore, use Basic authentication unless you have an encryption method such as IPsec in place.

EXAM TIP

You cannot create secure FTP sites if you are using the version of FTP (FTP6) that ships with Windows Server 2008. However, FTP7 supports SSL encryption; with it, you can configure sites to use the FTP over SSL (FTPS) protocol.

To configure the Basic FTP authentication method, first select or create a Windows user account you can use for this authentication method. If appropriate, add the account to a Windows user group. Take care if you are using the same accounts that users use to log on to a domain. Remember that unless you have configured end-to-end encryption, usernames and passwords are transmitted in clear text.

You can configure NTFS permissions (typically for all users) on the directory or file for which you want to control access. As part of the procedure, you also have the opportunity to configure NTFS permissions for each user account that will use Basic authentication. The most secure combination of permissions will apply.

The procedure for configuring Basic authentication in IIS 6.0 Manager is almost identical to that for configuring Anonymous authentication except that you clear rather than select the Allow Anonymous Connections check box. You specify the user account that uses Basic authentication and configure NTFS permissions as before.

MORE INFO **CONFIGURING FTP AUTHENTICATION**

For more information about configuring FTP authentication, see *http://www.microsoft .com/technet/prodtechnol/WindowsServer2003/Library/IIS/b0c14479-83e3-435d-a935 -819fe396e7d2.mspx?mfr=true* and follow the links.

Managing Permissions and Site Access

You can control which users and computers are allowed to access your Web server and its resources. You can use both NTFS and IIS security features, such as IP address restrictions, to specify access rights to FTP sites, directories, and files.

Securing Files and Folders with NTFS Permissions

As a Windows Server 2003 professional, you are familiar with NTFS permissions and how you can use them to control access to your Web server's files and directories and configure the access level granted to a particular user or group. Be aware, for example, that it is good practice to assign permissions to groups rather than to individual users, that you should never deny the Everyone group access to an object, and that explicit Deny permissions should be used very sparingly.

EXAM TIP

Always remember that inherited Deny permissions do not prevent access to an object if the object has an explicit Allow permission. Explicit permissions take precedence over inherited permissions, including inherited Deny permissions. You almost certainly know this, but, under examination conditions, it is easy to forget.

You can configure the security of an FTP site by configuring NTFS permissions for directories, virtual directories, or the site itself. You can use IIS 6.0 Manager or the *adsutil.vbs* Microsoft Visual Basic script utility in C:\Inetpub\AdminScripts.

In IIS 6.0 Manager, expand the local computer, right-click an FTP site or directory, and then click Permissions. You can then add a group or user that does not already appear in the Group Or User Names list box and change permissions for an existing group or user. Figure 14-5 shows the permissions for Default FTP Site.

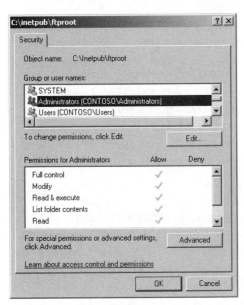

FIGURE 14-5 Viewing NTFS permissions for Default FTP Site.

Using NTFS Special Permissions

NTFS special permissions are permissions on a more detailed level. For better management, you typically assign broad-level permissions to users or groups. However, where it is applicable, special permissions allow more granular settings.

To secure an FTP site by using NTFS special permissions, expand the local computer in IIS 6.0 Manager; right-click an FTP site, directory, or virtual directory; and then click Permissions. Click Advanced to access the Advanced Security Settings dialog box shown in Figure 14-6. Select a user or group account, click Edit, select a permission, click Edit again, and then, in the Permission Entry dialog box, select or clear the appropriate Allow or Deny check boxes.

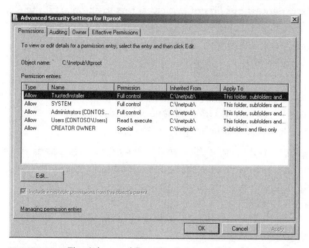

FIGURE 14-6 The Advanced Security Settings dialog box.

In the list box on the Permissions tab of the Advanced Security Settings dialog box, click the folders or subfolders to which you want these permissions to be applied. Typically, you assign permissions to folders at the highest possible level and then apply inheritance to propagate the settings to lower-level subfolders and files. If, however, you want to prevent child subfolders and files from inheriting these permissions, clear the Apply These Permissions To Objects And/Or Containers Within This Container Only check box.

Securing Sites with IIS Permissions

IIS permissions are sometimes known as Web site permissions, although they can apply to both FTP sites and Web sites. They are not intended to be used in place of NTFS permissions. Instead, they are used together with NTFS permissions to strengthen the security of site content. You can configure IIS access permissions for specific sites, directories, and files. Unlike NTFS permissions, IIS permissions affect everyone who tries to access a site.

If IIS permissions conflict with NTFS permissions for a directory or file, the more restrictive settings are applied. Disabling permissions restricts all users. For example, disabling the Read permission restricts all users from viewing a file, regardless of the NTFS permissions applied to those users' accounts. However, enabling the Read permission can allow all users to view that file unless NTFS permissions that restrict access have also been applied. If both IIS and NTFS permissions are set, the permissions that explicitly deny access take precedence over permissions that grant access.

To set IIS permissions in IIS 6.0 Manager, double-click the local computer; right-click the FTP Sites folder, an individual FTP site folder, a virtual directory, or a file; and then click Properties. In the Home Directory, Virtual Directory, Or File Properties dialog box, select or clear any of the following check boxes (if available):

- **Read**   Users can view directory or file content and properties.
- **Write**   Users can change directory or file content and properties.
- **Log Visits**   A log entry is created for each visit to the FTP site.

As stated previously, IIS permissions work in conjunction with NTFS permissions. For example, if you want to allow authenticated users to upload files to an FTP site, set the Write IIS permission on the site. However, unless you also set NTFS permissions for the Authenticated Users to allow Read/Write, users will receive warning messages when they try to upload files.

Note that this scenario does not permit authenticated users to download files from the FTP site even though they have NTFS Read/Write permission. If you want to allow this, set both Read and Write IIS permissions on the site.

Securing Sites with IP Address Restrictions

You can prevent or allow specific computers, groups of computers, or domains access to FTP sites, directories, or files. For example, if an FTP server on your domain contains internal files that should be accessed only by company employees, you can grant access only to Domain Users and prevent Internet users from connecting to the server.

Sometimes, however, the situation is more complex. An FTP server might be accessible both to internal users and through the Internet, but you want to block access to a specific IPv4 address or range of addresses that you have identified as the source of external attacks. You might want to block access to a particular ISP or to block all external access unless it is from one or more ISPs.

On an extranet, you might want to allow internal users and users from one or more partner organizations whose external IPv4 address ranges you know to access a site. In all these cases, you can allow or prevent access based on IPv4 address or address range, and you can use this method with other access methods. For example, on an extranet, you might want internal users to be able to both upload and download files but allow users in partner organizations only to upload. You can do this with IIS and NTFS permissions. You can block access to all other external users with IPv4 address restrictions.

NOTE   IP ADDRESS RESTRICTIONS

IP address restrictions apply only to IPv4 addresses.

To grant or deny access to a specific client computer, double-click the server object in IIS 6.0 Manager; right-click the FTP Sites folder, an individual FTP site, or a virtual directory; and then click Properties.

Click the Directory Security tab and select either Granted Access or Denied Access. If you select Denied Access, you deny access to all computers and domains except those to which you specifically grant access. Conversely, if you select Granted Access, you grant access to all computers and domains except those to which you specifically deny access. The Directory Security tab of a site's Properties dialog box was shown previously, in Figure 14-3.

Click Add, and then select Single Computer. If you prefer to search for computers or domains by name rather than by IP address, click DNS Lookup and enter the Domain Name System (DNS) name for the computer. Otherwise, type the computer's IPv4 address in the IP Address box. Finally, click OK to clear the various dialog boxes.

> **NOTE PROXY SERVER**
>
> A client accessing through a proxy server appears to have the IP address of the proxy server.

Similarly, for a range of addresses, click Add, and then select Group Of Computers. In the Network ID text box, type the IPv4 address of the first computer in the group and, in the Subnet Mask text box, type the subnet mask that identifies the group range. For example, to specify all computers with IPv4 addresses of 10.0.4.1 through 10.0.4.254, type **10.0.4.1** in the Network ID text box and **255.255.255.0** in the Subnet Mask text box.

Securing Virtual Directories

You can secure virtual directories mapped to sources on the Web server by using local user authentication. You configure virtual directory security when you create the virtual directory. You can also edit security settings on an existing virtual directory.

To create a secure virtual directory mapped to resources on the local Web server, expand the server object. In IIS 6.0 Manager, expand the FTP Sites folder, right-click the FTP site or folder within which you want to create the virtual directory, point to New, and then click Virtual Directory. In the Virtual Directory Creation Wizard, specify the alias and physical path for the new virtual directory, and then select the appropriate check boxes for the access permissions you want to allow and clear the check boxes for the permissions you want to deny.

To change the access permissions on an existing virtual directory mapped to resources on the local Web server, right-click the virtual directory in IIS 6.0 Manager and click Properties. On the Virtual Directory tab, under Local Path, select the check boxes for the access permissions you want to allow and clear the check boxes for the permissions you want to deny. This tab, shown in Figure 14-7, looks almost identical to the Home Directory tab for an FTP site, which you access in the practice later in this lesson.

MORE INFO **ACCESS CONTROL**

For more information about access control, see *http://www.microsoft.com/technet /prodtechnol/WindowsServer2003/Library/IIS/dcaf0a29-fac9-4ff4-a3d4-9cb38f659d23 .mspx?mfr=true* and follow the links.

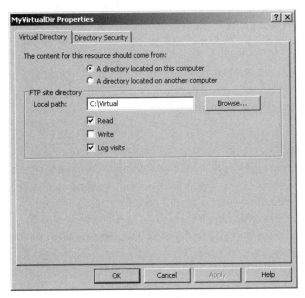

FIGURE 14-7 The Virtual Directory tab.

Using File Server Resource Manager

In Windows Server 2008, you install File Server Resource Manager as a role service associated with the File Services server role. However, you can use this tool with FTP6. For example, if you want to limit the kinds of files that can be uploaded through an FTP server, you can use file screening policies, which are available through File Server Resource Manager. You must be a member of the local Administrators group (or equivalent) to use File Server Resource Manager.

If the File Services server role is not already installed, install it and specify the File Server Resource Manager role service. If the server role is already installed, you can install the role service directly. You can then use the File Server Resource Manager Microsoft Management Console (MMC) snap-in from Administrative Tools. Alternatively, in Server Manager, expand Roles, expand File Services, expand Share and Storage Management, and then select File Server Resource Manager.

Storage Management Tasks

The following is a list of tasks that you can perform from the File Server Resource Manager snap-in.

- **Quota management** You can create, manage, and obtain information about quotas, which are used to set a space limit on a volume or folder. You can also create and manage quota templates to simplify quota management. By defining notification thresholds, you can send e-mail notifications, log an event, run a command or script, or generate reports when users approach or exceed a quota.

> **NOTE QUOTAS**
>
> You can also apply quotas using the Disk Management tool.

- **File screening management** You can create, manage, and obtain information about file screens, which block selected file types from a volume or folder. When users attempt to save unauthorized files, you can configure file screening to send an e-mail to (for example) members the local Administrators security group or to generate similar notifications. You can also create file screen exceptions to override certain file screening rules and create and manage file screen templates that simplify file screening management. Finally, you can create and manage file groups. You use file groups with file screens and file screen exceptions to determine which files are blocked and which allowed.
- **Storage reports management** You can schedule and configure storage reports. You can also generate storage reports on demand.

Configuring File Server Resource Manager

You can configure File Server Resource Manager options in the File Server Resource Manager Options dialog box. Options include default e-mail notification settings, default parameters for storage reports, and other settings that apply to multiple tasks. Some of these settings can be modified when you work with quotas or screen files or generate storage reports.

To configure File Server Resource Manager options, right-click File Server Resource Manager in the console tree, and then click Configure Options. In the File Server Resource Manager Options dialog box, click the appropriate tab (E-mail Notifications, Notification Limits, Storage Reports, Report Locations, or File Screen Audit) that holds the settings you want to alter. Configure your settings, and then click OK.

For example, if you want to send e-mail notifications to administrators or to users who exceed quotas or attempt to save unauthorized files, or to send storage reports over e-mail, you can specify the SMTP server to use and the default e-mail settings on the E-mail Notifications tab.

As another example, if you want to generate reports to help you monitor file screening, select Record File Screening Activity in the Auditing Database section of the File Screen Audit tab. This logs file screening activity in the auditing database, and you can use it later to generate File Screening Audit reports.

Managing Storage Resources on a Remote Computer

It is often useful to manage storage resources on a remote computer. This facility is particularly relevant if your FTP sites are on a Server Core installation that does not support GUIs.

You can connect to a remote computer through File Server Resource Manager, provided you access the tool from the Administrative Tools menu. You must be logged on to the local computer with an account that is a member of the local Administrators group (or equivalent) on the remote computer.

While you are connected, File Server Resource Manager displays the objects created on the remote computer, enabling you to manage them in the same way that you would manage resources on your local computer.

NOTE **SERVER CORE, WEB SERVER, AND VIRTUAL SERVERS**

You can install your FTP server on a computer with the Server Core installation, which augments security because the host has a smaller attack surface. You then administer the site remotely from another computer that has IIS 6.0 Manager and File Server Resource Manager installed. You can also configure FTP sites on a computer that has the Windows Server 2008 Web Server installation. Finally, FTP servers are good candidates for virtualization, enabling you to dedicate a server as an FTP server with no additional roles.

NOTE **FIREWALL EXCEPTION**

To enable remote connection through File Server Resource Manager, you need to enable the Remote File Server Resource Manager Management exception on the remote computer's firewall. Chapter 4, "Network Access Security," discusses Firewall configuration in detail.

Many administrators prefer to use command-line tools rather than the MMC snap-in. If your FTP server is running a Server Core installation and you log on interactively, you must use command-line tools. The following utilities are added to the system path when you install File Server Resource Manager; you must run them from an Administrator command prompt window:

- *Dirquota.exe*
- *Filescrn.exe*
- *Storrept.exe*

Each tool presents you with several options that perform actions similar to those available in the File Server Resource Manager MMC snap-in. To specify that a command performs an action on a remote computer instead of on the local computer, use the */remote:ComputerName* parameter.

For example, *dirquota.exe* includes a template export parameter to write quota template settings to an XML file and a template import parameter to import template settings from the XML file. Adding the */remote:ComputerName* parameter to the *dirquota template import* command imports the templates from the XML file on the local computer to the remote computer.

To manage remote resources with command-line tools, you must be logged on with a domain account that is a member of the local Administrators group on both the local computer and the remote computer.

DIRQUOTA

Use the *dirquota* command from an elevated command prompt to create and manage quotas, auto-apply quotas, and quota templates. For example, use *dirquota* with the *template export* option to export the settings for a custom quota template named 50 MB Limit to the *C:\test.xml* file on the local computer, as follows.

```
dirquota template export /file:C:\test.xml /template:"50 MB Limit"
```

> **MORE INFO   DIRQUOTA.EXE**
>
> For more information about the dirquota.exe utility, see *http://technet.microsoft.com /en-us/library/cc731290.aspx*. For more information about the use of the utility in template import and export scenarios, see *http://technet.microsoft.com/en-us/library/cc730873.aspx*.

FILESCRN

Use the *filescrn* command from an elevated command prompt. *Filescrn* includes subcommands for creating and managing file groups, file screens, file screen exceptions, and file screen templates and for configuring general administrative options for screening files.

For example, to list all file groups currently configured on the local computer, enter the following command:

```
filescrn filegroup list
```

To list the file name patterns included in and excluded from the Critical Files group, enter the following command:

```
filescrn filegroup list /filegroup:"Critical Files"
```

> **MORE INFO   FILESCRN.EXE**
>
> For more information about the filescrn.exe utility, see *http://technet.microsoft.com/en-us /library/cc730977.aspx*.

STORREPT

You use the *storrept* command from an elevated command prompt to configure report parameters and generate storage reports. You can also create report tasks and then use *schtasks.exe* to schedule the tasks.

For example, to list all storage reports configured on the local computer, enter the following command:

```
storrept reports list
```

To list storage reports that are currently running on the remote computer Boston, enter the following command:

```
storrept reports list /running /remote:Boston
```

> **MORE INFO   STORREPT.EXE**
>
> For more information about the *storrept.exe* utility, see *http://technet.microsoft.com/en-us/library/cc753567.aspx* and follow the links.

> **MORE INFO   SCHTASKS.EXE**
>
> *Schtasks.exe* is not specifically related to the File Server Resource Manager commands but is a general task scheduling utility. For more information about *schtasks.exe*, see *http://technet.microsoft.com/en-us/library/bb490996.aspx*.

Installing and Using FTP7

The new FTP publishing service includes a wide range of new features and improvements, for example:

- **Integration with IIS 7.0**   The new FTP service is tightly integrated with the IIS7 administration interface and configuration store.
- **Support for FTPS**   The service supports FTP over SSL, also known as FTP/SSL or FTPS, and uses a public key SSL/TLS certificate.
- **Support for standards and protocols**   The service supports the UTF8 Unicode encoding standard and the IPv6 protocol.
- **Shared hosting**   The service facilitates hosting FTP and Web content from the same site by adding an FTP binding to an existing Web site. It also supports virtual hostnames, which facilitates hosting multiple FTP sites on the same IP address. Improved user isolation facilitates isolating users through per-user virtual directories.
- **Extensibility**   The service supports developer (API) extensibility. This makes it easier for software vendors to write custom providers for FTP authentication.

- **Logging** The service improves FTP logging, which is enhanced to include all FTP traffic in the log files.
- **Improved troubleshooting** The service supports IIS7 troubleshooting features such as Event Tracing for Windows (ETW) and provides detailed error responses and messages for local users.

EXAM TIP

The Windows Server 2008 FTP7 service does not use metadata, and the new configuration store in IIS7 uses NET XML-based files to store configuration details.

MORE INFO DOWNLOADING THE FREE FTP PUBLISHING SERVICE

The new FTP publishing service is available as a free download at *http://www.iis.net /downloads/default.aspx?tabid=34&g=6&i=1619* (32-bit) or *http://www.iis.net/downloads /default.aspx?tabid=34&g=6&i=1620* (64-bit). An update for the 32-bit version is available at *http://www.microsoft.com/downloads/details.aspx?FamilyId=F23F366F-5D1C-4390 -934C-D5E9C3057661&displaylang=en&displaylang=en* and for the 64-bit version at *http://www.microsoft.com/downloads/details.aspx?FamilyId=1D4264C7-783A-4381-A65C -39EB148820DE&displaylang=en&displaylang=en*.

The service requires the Windows Server 2008 operating system and IIS7. If you want to manage the new FTP services by using the IIS7 interface, the Internet Information Services (IIS) Manager must be installed. However, many administrators find it more convenient to use command-line administration. The *appcmd.exe* command-line utility is described later in this chapter.

If you are using IIS7 shared configuration, you must disable it on each node in a Web farm scenario before you install the new FTP service. It can be re-enabled after the FTP service has been installed. The FTP service that ships with the Windows Server 2008 must be uninstalled before you install the new FTP service.

NOTE FTP7 INSTALLATION

You must uninstall FTP6 before installing FTP7.

When you download the appropriate file, you cannot specify that it should run automatically on download because User Account Control blocks access to the *applicationHost. config* file. Instead, run it from an elevated command prompt or use one of the following commands:

```
msiexec /i ftp7_x86_rtw.msi (for 32-bit)
msiexec /i ftp7_x64_rtw.msi (for 64-bit)
```

During installation, you can include some or all the following features:

- **Common Files** This provides common files for the Microsoft FTP Service for IIS, such as the FTP configuration schema file. Common files are required on all FTP servers using shared configuration mode.

- **FTP 7.0 Publishing Service** This is the core component that FTP needs to work. It requires the installation of the Process Model from the Windows Process Activation Service feature.

- **Managed Code Support** This is required when managed code features such as ASP. NET or IIS Manager are used with FTP. This feature is optional and does not work in Windows Server 2008 Server Core installations.

- **Administration Features** This supports administration through IIS Manager. It requires the installation of IIS Manager and Microsoft .NET 2.0 Framework.

You can confirm that the FTP Service is installed by verifying that the Microsoft FTP Service is running and (optionally) that the new IIS Manager FTP section displays management components for the FTP Service.

By default, the FTP server is locked down and does not accept any FTP requests. You use IIS Manager or the elevated command prompt to either publish a new FTP site or add FTP Publishing to an existing Web site.

The FTP service supports anonymous authentication, but Microsoft recommends that you not rely on this method. Recommended ways of authenticating your FTP users include the following:

- **Windows Authentication** In this method, users are located in the Active Directory Domain Services (AD DS) or local user store on the dedicated FTP server.

- **IIS Manager Authentication** This is a new feature. IIS Manager is used for user administration; all users are added using IIS Manager, and authentication is handled by the IISManagerAuth provider.

EXAM TIP

At this time of writing, the upgrade examinations are likely to test the version of FTP (FTP6) that ships with Windows Server 2008 rather than FTP7, which must be downloaded separately. You are likely to need to know only the significant differences between the two versions, such as that FTP7 supports Windows authentication, IIS Manager authentication, and SSL encryption, whereas FTP6 does not. You use IIS 6.0 Manager to manage FTP6 and IIS Manager to manage FTP7.

Installing the FTP Publishing Role Service and Creating a Virtual Directory

In this practice, you install the FTP Publishing role service. You place content directly on Default FTP Site. You then create a virtual directory that points to content elsewhere on the hard disk.

EXERCISE 1   Install the FTP Publishing Service

In this exercise, you install the FTP Publishing Service role service that ships with Windows Server 2008. This automatically installs the role service dependencies.

1. Log on to the domain controller Glasgow with the Kim_Akers account. If necessary, open Server Manager.

2. In Server Manager, expand the Roles section, right-click the Web Server (IIS) server role, and click Add Role Services.

3. On the Select Role Services page, select the FTP Publishing Service check box.

   As shown in Figure 14-8, this automatically installs the FTP Server and FTP Management Console role services.

4. Click Next.

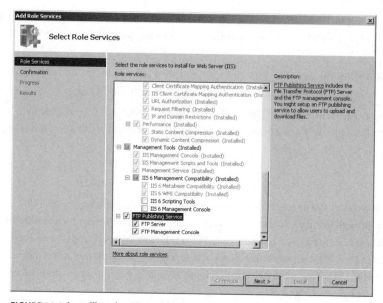

FIGURE 14-8 Installing the FTP publishing service and its dependencies.

5. On the Confirm Installation Selections page, verify that you have made the correct selections, and then click Install.

6. When the installation is complete, click Close.

EXERCISE 2 View the Default Web Site Configuration and Add Content

In this exercise, you view configuration settings for Default FTP Site on the Glasgow FTP server. You add and view site content.

1. If necessary, log on to the Glasgow domain controller with the Kim_Akers account.

2. Launch Internet Information Services (IIS) 6.0 Manager from the Administrative Tools program group.

3. Expand Glasgow, and then expand the FTP Sites folder.

   The Default FTP Site object exists but has not been started.

4. Right-click the Default FTP Site object and click Properties.

   As shown in Figure 14-9, the default settings are for the FTP site to respond on all unassigned IP addresses by using TCP port 21.

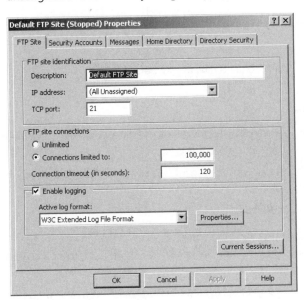

FIGURE 14-9 Default FTP Site settings.

5. Click the Home Directory tab to view the file system location for the FTP site's root directory.

   The default file system location is %SystemDrive%\Inetpub\Ftproot. The default permissions are only Read, for access to the contents of this folder, and Log Visits.

6. Click OK to close the Default FTP Site Properties dialog box.

7. Using Windows Explorer, open the root directory for the FTP site and create a new folder called MyFTPContents. Within this folder, create a new text file called **MyTestFile.txt**.

8. In IIS 6.0 Manager, right-click the Default FTP Site object and click Start. If prompted, click Yes to start the service and the site.

9. Open Internet Explorer. Navigate to ftp://Glasgow/MyFTPContents. View the contents of Default FTP Site, as shown in Figure 14-10.

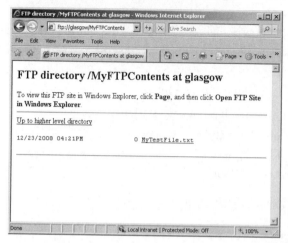

FIGURE 14-10 Accessing the MyFTPContents directory on Default FTP Site.

EXERCISE 3 Create a Virtual Directory

In this exercise, rather than put content directly on Default FTP Site, you create a virtual directory that points to a physical location on the hard disk.

1. If necessary, log on to the Glasgow domain controller with the Kim_Akers account and open Windows Explorer.

2. Create a directory named **C:\Virtual**.

3. In C:\Virtual, create text files named **Virtual1.txt** and **Virtual2.txt**.

4. If necessary, launch Internet Information Services (IIS) 6.0 Manager from the Administrative Tools program group.

5. Navigate to Default FTP Site. Right-click Default FTP Site, click New, and then click Virtual Directory.

6. Click Next.

7. In the Alias text box, type **MyVirtualDir**. Click Next.

8. In the Path text box, type **C:\Virtual**. Click Next.

9. Click Next to accept the default Directory Access permissions.

10. Click Finish.

11. If necessary, open Microsoft Internet Explorer. Browse to ftp://Glasgow/MyVirtualDir. You should see the files you created, as shown in Figure 14-11.

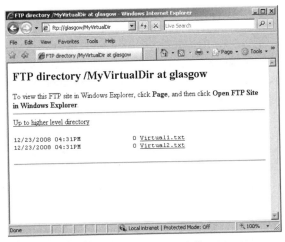

FIGURE 14-11 Accessing files in a virtual directory.

Lesson Summary

- You can configure general settings, security settings, home directory settings, messages settings, and directory security settings for FTP6 through the IIS 6.0 Server Manager GUI. You can also add and manage virtual directories by using the GUI.

- You can configure Anonymous or Basic authentication on an FTP6 site. You can use NTFS permissions, IIS permissions, and IP address restrictions to help secure the site. FTP6 offers no encryption facility; if you need encryption, configure IPsec. You can manage resources on both a local and a remote server by using File Server Resource Manager.

- FTP7 offers a number of enhancements, including SSL encryption and additional authentication methods.

Lesson Review

You can use the following questions to test your knowledge of the information in Lesson 1, "Configuring FTP." The questions are also available on the companion DVD if you prefer to review them in electronic form.

> **NOTE ANSWERS**
>
> Answers to these questions and explanations of why each answer choice is right or wrong are located in the "Answers" section at the end of the book.

1. You are an administrator for Litware, Inc. According to the Litware's written security policy, all confidential company data must be transmitted over the network in the most secure manner. However, a security check on the company's Windows Server 2008 Web Server FTP server, Boston, reveals that confidential information, including name and password information, is being transmitted to a partner organization in clear text. Your system is using Basic authentication and the version of the FTP publishing service that ships with Windows Server 2008. Your line manager has prohibited the download and installation of FTP7 until it has been piloted on your internal test network. How can you ensure that encryption is always used when the confidential files on the Litware Boston server are transmitted over a network?

   A. Use anonymous authentication on Boston and specify Use Only Anonymous Authentication.

   B. Configure the FTP sites on Boston to use SSL encryption. Publish the confidential files on Boston, using IIS, and then activate SSL on the IIS server.

   C. Use IPsec encryption between Boston and the partner network.

   D. Upgrade the operating system of Boston to Windows Server 2008 Enterprise.

2. You install the FTP Publishing role service on the Windows Server 2008 server, Perth. You configure Default FTP Site with Write IIS permission. Users complain that they receive warning messages when they upload files to the site. What should you do to allow authenticated users to access the FTP site and upload files without receiving warnings?

   A. Enter the *cscript iisftpdr /access Perth "Default FTP Site"* command at an elevated command prompt.

   B. Set NTFS permissions for the Authenticated Users security group to Allow Read/ Write Attributes.

   C. Specifically allow the authenticated users' client computers to access the site by allowing access based on IPv4 address.

   D. Configure Basic authentication.

3. You are configuring an FTP site on a Windows Server 2008 Web server in the *trey-research.internal* domain. The server uses the FTP publishing service that ships with Windows Server 2008.This facility enables researchers to submit a series of individual independent reports on a new product. Researchers should not be influenced by their colleagues' reports and should not be able to access content in their colleagues' directories. Directory location should be assigned through AD DS and only clients from a single designated company network should be able to access the FTP service. Which of the following settings should you configure on this FTP site? (Choose two. Each correct answer presents part of a complete solution.)

A. Configure access control to allow client computer access based on an IPv4 address range.

B. Configure access control to allow client computer access based on an IPv6 address range.

C. Configure SSL encryption.

D. Configure the site so that it does not isolate users.

E. Configure user isolation, using AD DS.

4. You are currently logged on interactively to the Glasgow Windows Server 2008 domain controller. You want to list all the storage reports currently running on the Windows Server 2008 member server, Boston, in the same domain. You open an elevated command prompt. Which command do you enter?

A. *storrept reports list*

B. *storrept reports list /running*

C. *storrept reports list /running /Boston*

D. *storrept reports list /running /remote:Boston*

Lesson 2: Configuring SMTP

You use Simple Mail Transfer Protocol (SMTP) in Windows Server 2008 to transport and deliver e-mail messages. SMTP enables servers to send messages through internal e-mail or across the Internet. Individuals and applications use SMTP to send notifications and other information. In this lesson, you learn how to enable and configure the SMTP Server feature in Windows Server 2008.

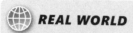 *REAL WORLD*

Ian McLean

I think it's all done to make me feel bad.

We have Simple Mail Transport Protocol, Simple Network Management Protocol, Lightweight Directory Application Protocol, and Trivial File Transfer Protocol. Who could possibly have problems with topics like that? I suppose my fifteen-month old granddaughter has it all worked out. She thinks "Silly-Grandpa" is all one word. So does her grandmother.

I once spoke to a gentleman on the Internet Engineering Task Force (IETF), and he told me that the simple standards were simpler than X509. That's a bit like calling the world's second largest sumo wrestler a lightweight. Also, of course, Trivial File Transfer handles only trivial files such as e-mail messages. I still have visions of my wife attaching all the digital photographs on a full 4 GB USB flash memory drive to an e-mail and sending the message to everyone she could think of. That was the day the world ran out of electrons.

So what (if anything) am I saying? Basically, if you don't understand something the first time, don't worry, not even if someone tells you it's simple or even trivial. Keep plugging away. It will all come clear eventually, and you'll wonder why you thought it difficult in the first place.

In the meantime, I'll be programming my new Sat-Nav. I'm told it's really simple—provided you don't mind going from Detroit to Windsor via Mexico City.

After this lesson you will be able to:
- Install the SMTP Server feature and create and configure a virtual SMTP site.
- Configure security, SMTP e-mail, and message delivery.
- Configure smart hosts, size limitations, authentication, and SMTP relay settings.

Estimated lesson time: 35 minutes

Installing the SMTP Server Feature

The Windows Server 2008 SMTP Server feature enables you to support applications and network connections that send messages across a network. For example, a Web application can use SMTP to send e-mail notifications to users. Messages can also be stored in a directory so they can be accessed by other applications. Users typically receive e-mail messages by connecting to their mailbox on the messaging server, using a protocol such as Post Office Protocol version 3 (POP3).

For example, if you want to configure a Web site on a Windows Server 2008 Web server to send e-mail to Internet users, configure the SMTP e-mail feature for the Web site on that server. The SMTP Server feature allows the e-mails to be sent to specified addresses.

EXAM TIP

SMTP sends messages. POP3 and IMAP4 retrieve them.

You can use Server Manager to install the SMTP Server feature on a Windows Server 2008 server. To do this, right-click Features and select Add Features. You can then add SMTP Server and its dependencies. You do this in the practice later in this lesson. You can also use Server Manager to remove the SMTP Server feature.

The SMTP server enables you to support applications and network connections that send e-mail messages. Messages can be stored in a file system location so they can be accessed by other applications. You can use IIS 6.0 Manager to configure SMTP settings by expanding the server object. You also configure SMTP settings in the practice later in this lesson.

Installing the SMTP server configures a default site called SMTP Virtual Server #1. You can also use the SMTP Virtual Server Wizard to create an SMTP virtual server. Each virtual server has a set of configuration settings and can be managed independently from other SMTP servers.

To create an SMTP virtual server by using IIS 6.0 Manager, right-click the server object, click New, and then click SMTP Virtual Server. Provide a name for the virtual server and select the network connections on which the SMTP server is to be available. If the server has multiple physical network adapters or multiple IP addresses, you can specify these settings from a drop-down list, which is useful when you want to limit access to the SMTP server for security reasons (for example, when blocking networks that are accessible from the Internet). The default IP address setting is All Unassigned, which specifies that the SMTP virtual server will respond on any IP address that is configured for the server.

Multiple SMTP virtual servers cannot run concurrently if they have the same IP address and port assignment. The default port for SMTP connections is port 25. If you attempt to create a new SMTP virtual server that has the same combination of IP address and port number, you will receive an error message. You can continue to create the server, but you must reconfigure its settings later before you can start it.

After you specify the virtual server name and network connection, the New SMTP Virtual Server Wizard Select Home Directory page enables you to specify the file system location for the root for the SMTP virtual server. Message files and other data are stored in this location. On the Default Domain page, specify the FQDN, for example, *SalesServer.contoso.internal*. When you click Finish in the New SMTP Virtual Server Wizard, the new server appears in IIS 6.0 Manager, and you can access its properties to make additional configuration changes.

Configuring SMTP Server Settings

To configure settings for an SMTP virtual server, you access it in IIS 6.0 Manager, right-click it, and then select Properties. On the General tab, you can specify the network connection settings for the SMTP server. Select an IP address or All Unassigned from the drop-down list. You can use the Advanced button to configure multiple bindings. The Advanced option, shown in Figure 14-12, also enables you to change the port number on which the SMTP server is accessed.

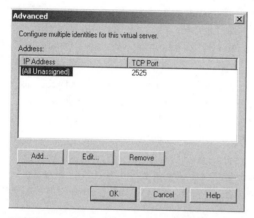

FIGURE 14-12 Configuring multiple identities on a virtual server.

Also on the General tab, you can limit the number of connections and set connection timeouts. This helps manage performance on busy SMTP servers. You can also use the Enable Logging option to store information about messages transmitted by the SMTP virtual server. The Properties button offers options for determining the storage location of the log files.

On the Advanced tab, you can specify which types of information are included in the log file. You can view Log files by using a standard text editor such as Windows Notepad. On busy SMTP servers, enabling logging can decrease performance and increase disk space usage.

Configuring Access Security on an SMTP Virtual Server

You can configure access rules for sending messages by SMTP to prevent unauthorized use of an SMTP virtual server. A large amount of spam is sent through unprotected SMTP relays, and if you fail to protect an SMTP site, you could have problems with other organizations, especially with ISPs identifying spam relayed through your site as being sent by you. You can manage rules for using the SMTP virtual server through the properties on the Access tab, shown in Figure 14-13.

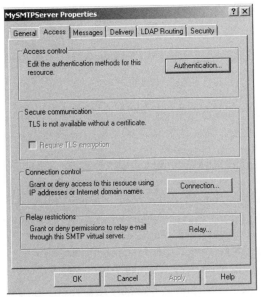

FIGURE 14-13 An SMTP virtual server Properties Access tab.

You can use the Authentication settings to determine how potential users of an SMTP virtual server pass their credentials to the service. The default setting is Anonymous Access, which specifies that no credentials are required to connect to the SMTP virtual server. Choose this option when you are using other methods (such as firewalls or trusted network connections) to prevent unauthorized access to the server.

The Basic Authentication option requires a username and password to be sent to the SMTP virtual server. By default, these logon credentials are transmitted using clear text and are, therefore, susceptible to interception. To prevent clear-text transmissions, you can configure Transport Layer Security (TLS). This enables encryption for sent messages. TLS uses a certificate-based approach to create the encrypted connection.

Integrated Windows Authentication relies on standard Windows accounts to verify credentials to access the system. This method is most appropriate for applications that use a single Windows account or when all potential users of the SMTP server have Active Directory domain accounts.

In addition to configuring authentication settings, you can also restrict access to an SMTP virtual server based on IP addresses or domain names. This helps ensure that only authorized network clients can use SMTP services. To add these restrictions, click the Connection button on the Access tab of the Properties dialog box for the SMTP virtual server. You can choose the default behavior for connection attempts, as shown in Figure 14-14.

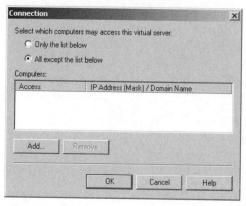

FIGURE 14-14 Connection settings for an SMTP virtual server.

The Only The List Below option means that only computers that match the entry rules you have configured will be able to use the server. This is most appropriate when all the expected client computers are part of one or a few networks. The All Except The List Below option means that the rules you add are for computers that are not allowed to use the SMTP virtual server. Click the Add button to create new configuration rules.

For reasons discussed earlier in this section, it is important to configure relay restrictions. SMTP relaying occurs when a message is sent with both to and from addresses that are not part of the virtual server's domain. Relaying is a common method by which spammers can use unprotected SMTP virtual servers to send unsolicited mail. The Relay Restrictions dialog box is shown in Figure 14-15.

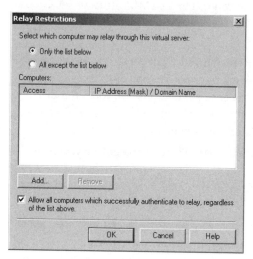

FIGURE 14-15 The Relay Restrictions dialog box.

The Relay Restrictions dialog box enables you to specify which computers can relay messages through the SMTP server. Relay restrictions enable you to control the destination IP addresses for which the SMTP server will accept mail. For example, if you want to ensure that an SMTP server on the *contoso.internal* network can transfer mail only internally, and if all internal e-mail addresses used the *contoso.internal* suffix, configure relay restrictions to exclude all other suffixes.

The default settings are for all users and computers to be allowed to relay messages, provided they are able to authenticate. Click Add to define which IP addresses, domain names, or both are allowed to relay messages. Click OK to save your changes.

When you want to ensure that sent messages are encrypted, you can enable TLS Encryption on the Access tab, but first you need to obtain and install the appropriate certificate. Except in internal test networks, this will be a certificate obtained from a trusted third-party certificate authority (CA). The process is the same as installing a certificate to create a secure Web site with SSL encryption, which was discussed in Chapter 13.

Managing Security Permissions

You can define which Windows users may manage SMTP Virtual Server settings by using the Security tab of your virtual SMTP server's Properties dialog box, shown in Figure 14-16. The list defines which users should be considered operators. Operators have permissions to change the configuration of the SMTP virtual server. By default, this includes the Administrators group and the Local Service and Network Service built-in accounts. You can click the Add button to include additional users or groups on the list of operators.

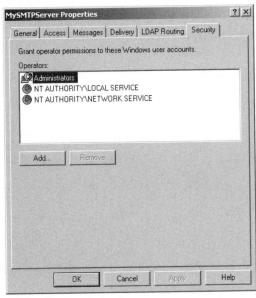

FIGURE 14-16 The Security tab of a virtual SMTP server's Properties dialog box.

Configuring SMTP E-Mail

You must configure SMTP e-mail when you want to deliver e-mail messages from your SMTP site. Mail can be delivered immediately or it can be stored in a file location on disk, from which it can be retrieved for delivery later.

You can configure SMTP e-mail for a Web application by using IIS Manager. You used IIS 6.0 Manager for virtual SMTP server configuration, but the more fully featured IIS Manager is used to configure e-mail settings. You can also use the *appcmd.exe* command-line utility from an elevated command prompt.

In IIS Manager, select the Server object and, in Features View, double-click SMTP E-mail. Type the e-mail address of the sender in the E-mail address text box on the SMTP E-mail page, as shown in Figure 14-17, and select one of the following delivery methods:

- **Deliver E-mail To SMTP Server**   This delivers e-mail messages immediately. An operational SMTP server for which the user has credentials must be available. Type the unique name of your SMTP server in the SMTP Server text box or select the Use Localhost check box. Enter a TCP port in the Port text box. Port 25 is the SMTP standard TCP port. More than one virtual server can use the same TCP port if all servers are configured by using different IP addresses. Under Authentication Settings, specify the authentication mode and supply credentials if required.

- **Store E-mail In Pickup Directory**   This stores e-mails in a file location on disk for later delivery by (for example) an ASP.NET application or by a user. Type the batch e-mail location in the Store E-mail In Pickup Directory text box.

Finally, click Apply in the Actions pane.

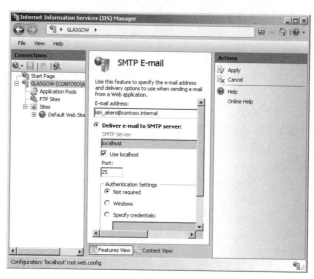

FIGURE 14-17 SMTP e-mail configuration.

To configure SMTP e-mail from the command-line to deliver e-mail messages immediately, enter a command with the following syntax:

```
%systemroot%\system32\inetsrv\appcmd set config /commit:WEBROOT
/section:smtp /from:string /deliveryMethod:network /network.port:int
/network.defaultCredentials:True|False /network.host:string
/network.userName:string /network.password:string
```

The variable *string* in the */from* parameter is the e-mail address of the sender. The variable *network* configures IIS to deliver e-mail messages immediately. The variable *int* specifies the TCP port IIS uses to deliver e-mail messages. The variable *string* in the */network.host* parameter specifies the host used for SMTP transactions. If *defaultCredentials* is set to *True*, Kerberos or NTLM is used, if the server supports these protocols. The *string* variables in the */network.userName* and */network.password* parameters specify a Basic authentication username and password.

To configure SMTP e-mail from the command-line to store e-mails in a file location for later delivery, enter a command with the following syntax:

```
%systemroot%\system32\inetsrv\appcmd set config /commit:WEBROOT /section:smtp
/from:string /deliveryMethod:PickupDirectoryFromIis|SpecifiedPickupDirectory
/SpecifiedPickupDirectory:string
```

The variable *string* in the */from* parameter is the e-mail address of the sender. The *string* variable in the */SpecifiedPickupDirectory* parameter specifies the file location in which the e-mail message is stored for later delivery.

The Message Delivery Process

Before SMTP delivers a message, that message is placed under the control of the SMTP Service. You can use the following methods of presenting a message to the SMTP Service for delivery:

- **Use an e-mail client** You can use an e-mail client such as Outlook Express. In the client application, specify the IIS server as the outgoing SMTP server for sending messages and then compose and send Internet e-mail in the normal way.

- **Place a properly formatted text file in the Mailroot\Pickup folder** Requests for Comment (RFCs) 821 and 822 define a properly formatted text file. Such a file, for example, includes the sender's and receiver's e-mail addresses in the header. All files copied to the Mailroot\Pickup folder are processed and delivered as regular mail. You can move a single file or many files into the Mailroot\Pickup folder for delivery, either manually or with a custom program or batch file. The file must also include your default local domain name. When you have placed the file in the Mailroot\Pickup folder, check the Mailroot\Drop folder for a new file with an .eml extension. If your message is not destined for a local domain, it should instead be sent to the Mailroot\

Queue folder. This option is useful if a user fills in a Web site form and the input information is placed in a text file that is sent as an e-mail to a support address.

> **MORE INFO** RFCS 821 AND 822
>
> For more information about properly formatted e-mail files, see *http://www.ietf.org/rfc/rfc821.txt* and *http://www.ietf.org/rfc/rfc822.txt*. These are old RFCs but are still in force. The upgrade examination, however, is unlikely to test you on the contents of these documents.

- **Use a remote SMTP server** The remote SMTP server connects to IIS, attaches to the SMTP Service on port 25 (the default), and transmits any messages destined for e-mail domains hosted on the IIS server. If the SMTP Service is configured to relay messages to domains hosted on other SMTP servers, the remote server transmits messages for routing to these other servers. In either case, the SMTP Service acquires the message and places it in the Mailroot\Queue folder. IIS attempts to send any new messages deposited in this folder immediately. If immediate delivery is not possible, IIS resends queued messages. When the destination of the message is an e-mail domain hosted on the IIS server itself, the message file is placed in the Mailroot\Drop folder.

Configuring Messages Options

The Messages tab of an SMTP virtual server Properties dialog box accessed through IIS 6.0 Manager, and shown in Figure 14-18, enables you to configure size limitations on messages sent through the server. The first two options specify the maximum size of a message (including attachments) as well as the maximum amount of data that can be sent through one connection to the server. You can also limit the number of messages sent per connection and the number of recipients to whom they can be sent. These methods all help reduce unwanted access to the server and preserve resources such as network bandwidth.

Incorrect addresses or domain names entered by the sending user frequently cause messaging failures. The Send Copy Of Non-Delivery Report To option enables you to specify an e-mail address to which undeliverable mail is forwarded. The Badmail Directory setting specifies the path to the folder into which these messages are sent. You can review these messages to detect undeliverable mail.

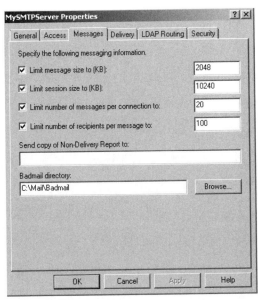

FIGURE 14-18 Enabling configuration of size limitations on messages that are sent through the server.

Defining Delivery Properties

Network routing issues and server failures on the Internet can cause service outages. SMTP servers automatically store copies of messages they are trying to send. If the destination server is unavailable, the SMTP server retries the operation. You can manage the details of this behavior through the properties of the Delivery tab. The Outbound rules define the intervals at which the server will attempt to retry the transmission of a message if a failure occurs.

You can also configure the Delay Notification and Expiration Timeout options for both the Outbound and Local settings to determine when the server should stop resending a message. Typically, SMTP servers send messages through other SMTP servers before they reach their final destination. You can configure SMTP servers to require authentication before they relay a message. The Outbound Security option on the Delivery tab, shown in Figure 14-19, enables you to specify the authentication information to be used when connecting to another SMTP server.

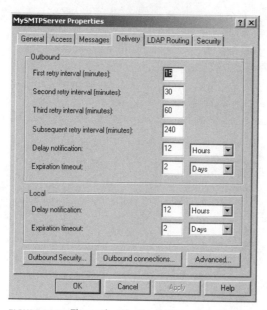

FIGURE 14-19 The authentication information to be used when connecting to another SMTP server.

The Outbound Connections settings specify limits on the number of connections to other SMTP servers and how long they will remain active. Clicking Advanced accesses additional options for managing how messages are processed by the SMTP virtual server. As shown in Figure 14-20, the options include the following:

- **Maximum Hop Count** When messages are forwarded to an SMTP server, the message itself includes a hop count to record the number of times it has been forwarded. When a message has exceeded the maximum hop count setting, it is considered undeliverable.

- **Masquerade Domain** A masquerade domain allows substitution of internal for external domain names when forwarding mail to external SMTP servers. The Masquerade Domain setting instructs the SMTP server automatically to rewrite the domain of the From address used for outbound messages. You can use this setting when you want to ensure that outgoing messages have a consistent domain name. For example, if you have an organizational network with multiple domains, you can use a masquerade domain so that all e-mail addresses use the same suffix.

- **Fully-Qualified Domain Name** The Fully-Qualified Domain Name setting enables you to specify the FQDN with which the SMTP server identifies itself when communicating with remote SMTP servers. This setting specifies the DNS address of the SMTP virtual server, based on Address (A) and Mail Exchanger (MX) records. In general, each SMTP server for a domain should have a unique FQDN that includes the server name (for example, *boston.mail.contoso.internal*).

- **Smart Host** Smart hosts enable you to forward all outgoing mail to a specific remote host. When a server name or IP address is defined for the Smart Host setting, all messages from this SMTP virtual server are routed through the specified server. This option is commonly used when multiple internal servers route their messages through a specific SMTP server that has access to the Internet (for example, a Web server at an ISP). Using a smart host configuration can save bandwidth and increase security because only specific servers require access to external networks. The Attempt Direct Delivery Before Sending To Smart Host option instructs the local SMTP server to attempt to connect directly to the destination SMTP server. If this operation fails, the message is forwarded to the designated smart host.

- **Perform Reverse DNS Lookup On Incoming Messages** This setting instructs the SMTP server to perform a DNS reverse lookup to verify that the user's domain matches the IP address in the message header. By enabling this option, you can reduce or prevent unauthorized usage of the SMTP server by messages that use inconsistent header information.

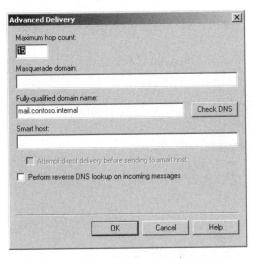

FIGURE 14-20 Advanced Delivery settings.

Enabling LDAP Routing

The Lightweight Directory Access Protocol (LDAP) is the primary standard by which directory services communicate with each other. AD DS and Exchange Server are examples of LDAP-compliant directory services. You can enable routing on the LDAP Routing tab of an SMTP virtual server's Properties dialog box to configure the server to use LDAP queries to resolve to and from addresses in mail messages. The configuration options specify to which type of LDAP system the SMTP server will be connecting and the address of the server. Other details include authentication information for connecting to and querying the LDAP server.

NOTE **BACKING UP AND RESTORING SMTP CONFIGURATION**

You back up and restore SMTP configuration settings when you back up and restore IIS7 settings by using the *appcmd.exe* command-line utility. Chapter 13 discusses configuration backup and restore in detail.

PRACTICE Creating an SMTP Virtual Server

In this practice, you install the SMTP Server and Telnet Client features. You then create an SMTP virtual server.

EXERCISE 1 Add the SMTP Server Feature

In this exercise, you add the SMTP Server feature. You also add the Telnet Client feature, which you can use to test SMTP virtual servers. This is one of the suggested practices at the end of this chapter.

1. Log on to the Glasgow domain controller with the Kim_Akers account. If necessary, open Server Manager.

2. In Server Manager, right-click Features, and then select Add Features.

3. Select the SMTP Server and Telnet Client check boxes.

4. In the Add Features Wizard dialog box, shown in Figure 14-21, click Add Required Features.

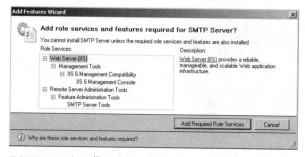

FIGURE 14-21 Installing dependent role services and features.

5. Click Next. Click Next again on the Web Server (IIS) page.

6. Click Next on the Select Role Services page.

7. On the Confirm Installation Selections page, click Install.

8. When the installation is complete, click Close.

EXERCISE 2 Create a New SMTP Virtual Server

In this exercise, you create a new SMTP virtual server by using IIS 6.0 Manager.

1. If necessary, log on to the Glasgow domain controller with the Kim_Akers account.

2. Open Windows Explorer and create a folder named **C:\Mail**.

3. Launch IIS 6.0 Manager from the Administrative Tools program group.

4. Expand the Glasgow (Local Computer) object and note that a default object, SMTP-Virtual Server #1, has already been created.

5. Right-click the Glasgow object, select New, and then select Virtual Server.

6. In the Name text box, type **MySMTPServer**. Click Next.

7. In the Select IP Address text box, do not change the default setting. Click Next.

8. Read the warning message, and then click Yes to continue. You resolve this conflict later by specifying a nondefault port number.

9. In the Home Directory text box, type **C:\Mail**. Click Next.

10. In the Domain step, type **mail.contoso.internal**.

11. Click Finish. Note that a new SMTP virtual server named MySMTPServer appears in the left pane of IIS 6.0 Manager, as shown in Figure 14-22.

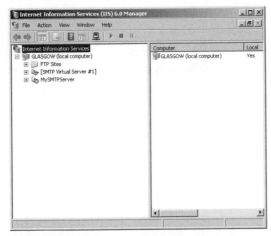

FIGURE 14-22 MySMTPServer has been created.

12. Right-click MySMTPServer and select Properties.

13. On the General tab, click Advanced to open the list of IP address and port number settings.

14. Select the (All Unassigned) entry in the list and click Edit.

15. Change the TCP Port setting to 2525 as shown in Figure 14-23. Click OK.
    This resolves the conflict with the default SMTP Virtual Server.

16. Click OK three times to close the dialog boxes and save the settings.

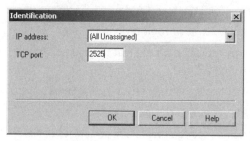

FIGURE 14-23 Specifying the SMTP port for an SMTP virtual server.

17. In IIS 6.0 Manager, right-click the MySMTPServer virtual server object, and then click Start.

Lesson Summary

- It is important to configure access security and, in particular, relay settings on an SMTP virtual server. If you allow third parties to relay spam through your SMTP servers, your site could be banned by ISPs and other organizations.

- You can configure Message options such as how to handle undeliverable and unreturnable mail. Other message option settings include Maximum Hop Count, Masquerade Domain, Fully-Qualified Domain Name, Smart Host, and Perform Reverse DNS Lookup On Incoming Messages.

Lesson Review

You can use the following questions to test your knowledge of the information in Lesson 2, "Configuring SMTP." The questions are also available on the companion DVD if you prefer to review them in electronic form.

> **NOTE ANSWERS**
>
> Answers to these questions and explanations of why each answer choice is right or wrong are located in the "Answers" section at the end of the book.

1. You are a network administrator for a Web-hosting organization. Each client Web site has a dedicated SMTP virtual server. You create a new SMTP virtual server on a Windows Server 2008 Web server on your domain and install it for a new client Web site. The Web server already hosts several SMTP virtual servers. The SMTP virtual server

fails to start. How do you configure the new SMTP server so it will start on the Web server? (Select two. Each correct answer presents a complete solution.)

- **A.** Install the SMTP Server feature on the Web server.
- **B.** Open an elevated command prompt and type **%systemroot%\system32 \inetsrv\appcmd add backup**.
- **C.** Open an elevated command prompt and type **%systemroot%\system32 \inetsrv\appcmd set config /commit:WEBROOT /section:smtp /from:*string*** where *string* is the e-mail address of the new client.
- **D.** Configure a different IP address for the new SMTP server.
- **E.** Configure a different port for the new SMTP server.

2. You administer an SMTP virtual server on a Windows Server 2008 Web server at Trey Research. A Web developer wants to create a set of Web pages that enable a user to type a message into a form and mail it to support@treyresearch.com. The form creates a properly formatted text file with the correct SMTP headers. Into which folder should the file be copied?

- **A.** Mailroot\Drop
- **B.** Mailroot\Queue
- **C.** Mailroot\Pickup
- **D.** Badmail

3. You create a new virtual SMTP server on a Windows Server 2008 Web server. You want to configure the new SMTP server to forward all e-mails to your ISP's mail server. How can you achieve this objective?

- **A.** Enter a command with the *%systemroot%\system32\inetsrv\appcmd set config /commit:WEBROOT /section:smtp /from:string /deliveryMethod:network /network .port:int /network.defaultCredentials:True* syntax from an elevated command prompt.
- **B.** Configure the SMTP server to use a masquerade domain.
- **C.** Configure a maximum hop count of two.
- **D.** Configure a smart host setting that specifies the ISP mail server.

4. You are configuring access security on the Access tab of an SMTP virtual server's properties box. You want to ensure that sent messages are encrypted. How do you configure your settings?

- **A.** Configure TLS encryption.
- **B.** Configure IPsec encryption.
- **C.** Configure Basic authentication.
- **D.** Configure Integrated Windows authentication.

Chapter Review

To further practice and reinforce the skills you learned in this chapter, you can perform the following tasks:

- Review the chapter summary.
- Complete the case scenarios. These scenarios set up real-world situations involving the topics of this chapter and ask you to create solutions.
- Complete the suggested practices.
- Take a practice test.

Chapter Summary

- The FTP6 publishing service ships with Windows Server 2008. Optionally, you can download and install the FTP7 publishing service. Both services enable you to create and configure FTP sites on a Web server. FTP7 offers a number of enhancements.

- Access security is particularly important on an SMTP server because attacks are common, especially when third parties attempt to relay spam e-mail. You can specify TLS encryption as part of access security, provided you first obtain and install the appropriate certificate.

- Configuring a smart host enables you to route e-mail through an external SMTP server. The masquerade domain replaces the local domain name used for the from e-mail address in outgoing messages. Maximum hop count limits how many SMTP servers a message can be routed through before a nondelivery report is returned to the sender. The Fully-Qualified Domain Name setting is the DNS name of the SMTP server.

Case Scenarios

In the following case scenarios, you apply what you've learned about configuring FTP and SMTP services. You can find answers to the questions in this scenario in the "Answers" section at the end of this book.

Case Scenario 1: Configuring User Isolation and IP Address Restriction Settings

You are the network administrator at an academic institution; you are configuring an FTP server hosted on a Windows Server 2008 Web server that is a member of your institution's domain. The server is to be used for the submission of student assignments. Only clients from designated academic networks should access the FTP service. Students should not access other students' directories. Student directory location should be assigned through Active Directory. Answer the following questions.

1. Which User Isolation setting (if any) should you configure?

2. How can you ensure that only clients from designated academic networks can access the FTP service?

Case Scenario 2: Configuring Message Size and SMTP Traffic Limitations

You have set up an SMTP virtual server on a Windows Server 2008 Web server. Performance on this server is deteriorating because of the volume of e-mail traffic. Answer the following questions.

1. How can you reduce the SMTP traffic caused by users sending very large attachments?

2. One particular user sends a very large number of e-mails, although very few of these have excessively large attachments. How can you limit this traffic?

3. Another user habitually clicks Send All when sending internal e-mail and typically sends external e-mails to everyone on a very large address list. How can you control this usage?

Suggested Practices

To help you successfully master the exam objectives presented in this chapter, perform all of the following practices.

Experiment with FTP Server Settings

- **Practice 1**   You can configure a large number of FTP settings. Configure these individually and in combination and observe the effect of each on your FTP operations.

- **Practice 2**   When you have finished experimenting with FTP6, uninstall it. Download and install FTP7. Discover the differences between the two packages. In particular, configure a secure FTP site.

Experiment with SMTP Virtual Server Settings

- **Practice 1**   Telnet to port 2525 and use the *ehlo* telnet command to test the SMTP virtual server you created in Exercise 2 in Lesson 2.

- **Practice 2**   Experiment with SMTP settings until you are familiar with what settings are available and where each can be found.

- **Practice 3**   Configure a masquerade domain and a smart host.

Take a Practice Test

The practice tests on this book's companion DVD offer many options. For example, you can test yourself on just one exam objective, or you can test yourself on all the upgrade examination content. You can set up the test so that it closely simulates the experience of taking a certification exam, or you can set it up in study mode so that you can look at the correct answers and explanations after you answer each question.

> **MORE INFO** **PRACTICE TESTS**
>
> For details about all the practice test options available, see the "How to Use the Practice Tests" section in this book's Introduction.

CHAPTER 15

Hyper-V and Virtualization

Virtualization enables you to make more efficient use of your organization's hardware resources by enabling you to host server operating systems in a virtual environment rather than always deploying them to expensive server hardware. In this lesson, you learn about the virtualization solution, called Hyper-V, available with Windows Server 2008. You learn the hardware requirements for Hyper-V and how to configure virtual networks, create and manage virtual hard disks, perform migrations of servers from traditional physical deployments to virtual ones, and back up virtual machines and Hyper-V.

Exam objectives in this chapter

- Configure Windows Server Hyper-V and virtual machines.

Lessons in this chapter:

Before You Begin

To complete the lessons in this chapter, you must have done the following:

- Installed and configured the evaluation edition of Windows Server 2008 Enterprise Edition in accordance with the instructions listed in the Introduction.

- Unlike other exercises in this book, the practices in this chapter cannot be completed in a virtual environment because you cannot install Windows Server 2008 with the Hyper-V Server role in a virtual machine. To perform these practices, you must have installed an x64 edition of Windows Server 2008 on physical computer hardware. Prior to performing the practice exercises, install the Hyper-V Server role.

 REAL WORLD

Orin Thomas

One of my favorite sayings is, "Wisdom is the result of experience, and experience is usually the result of a lack of wisdom." Part of being a good systems administrator is being able to learn from your mistakes. Although in the best of all worlds, none of us ever makes mistakes, trying out software updates, upgrades, and configuration changes on virtual machines enables us to make mistakes in a safe environment.

Lesson 1: Hyper-V

Hyper-V is a role service that can be added to x64 versions of Windows Server 2008 that enable the operating system to host virtual machines, similar to the way operating systems can be hosted under Virtual PC or Virtual Server 2005. Hyper-V uses a technology called a hypervisor, which, unlike Virtual PC or Virtual Server 2005, allows virtual machines greater access to a server's hardware resources.

> **After this lesson, you will be able to:**
> - Configure virtual networking.
> - Specify virtualization hardware requirements.
> - Manage Server Core as a virtual host.
> - Optimize Hyper-V.
>
> **Estimated lesson time: 40 minutes**

Hyper-V

Hyper-V is the name of the Windows Server 2008 hypervisor, which enables the operating system to function as a virtual machine server. A hypervisor is a software layer that runs under the host operating system. It grants both host and guest operating system equal access to hardware resources. The Hyper-V role service is available for x64 versions of Windows Server 2008 Standard, Enterprise, and Datacenter in both the standard and Server Core configurations. You cannot install the Hyper-V Server role on Windows Web Server 2008 or any x86 versions of Windows Server 2008. Hyper-V requires the computer it is installed on to support hardware-assisted virtualization and hardware data execution protection. AMD-V (with NX) and Intel VT (with XD) both support Hyper-V, although the hardware data execution protection functionality often has to be enabled within BIOS.

Virtual servers—also known as virtual machine hosts or virtual hosts—host virtual machines, also known as virtual guests. Virtual guests can run a variety of operating systems, although from the perspective of the 70-649 upgrade exam, you should assume that virtual guests are running a server operating system such as Microsoft Windows Server 2003 or Windows Server 2008.

Virtualizing servers, rather than deploying them physically, has the following benefits:

- **Improved availability** It is cheaper to virtualize existing servers and move them to a highly redundant virtual host, such as a Hyper-V failover cluster, than it is to provide a similar level of redundancy on all servers physically deployed throughout your organization. Put another way, it is cheaper to use one big server that hosts many virtual machines than it is to cluster a large number of small ones.

- **Role sandboxing** Sandboxing enables you to deploy separate servers for specific tasks. When hardware resources are tight, you often have to collocate server roles that should normally be separate. The problem with this is that one errant process can bring down an unrelated but important service. Running servers in virtualized sandboxes prevents this.

- **Better use of resources** Some servers, such as Dynamic Host Configuration Protocol (DHCP) and Domain Name System (DNS) servers, use only a minimal amount of a physical server's hardware. Virtualizing these servers frees up expensive hardware resources for servers that require greater use of processors, RAM, or disk resources.

- **Portability and capacity** If a guest requires more resources, you can deploy the guest to a virtual server with what is better provisioned. It is also cheaper to upgrade the hardware of a single virtual host than a large number of physical servers. By being able to move virtual guest servers across hardware, you can tailor your organization's hardware resource use more efficiently.

- **Intermittent services** Some servers on your network, such as root certificate servers or Windows Deployment servers, need to be available only on an irregular basis. Rather than tie up existing physical hardware, these servers can be virtualized and brought online as needed.

Hyper-V offers the following features:

- Support for 64-bit guest operating systems
- Ability to assign up to four processors to each virtual guest, as shown in Figure 15-1
- Ability to assign a maximum of 32 GB of RAM to each virtual guest
- Support for virtual machine snapshots

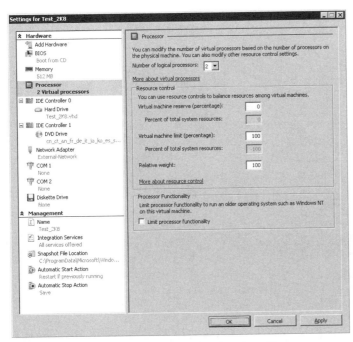

FIGURE 15-1 Assign multiple processors to a virtual machine.

Hyper-V and Server Core

You can add the Hyper-V Server role to a computer running the Server Core installation option of Windows Server 2008. Computers running Server Core make excellent Hyper-V hosts because the operating system has a smaller hardware footprint than a traditional Windows Server 2008 installation. To install the Hyper-V role on an x64 version of Windows Server 2008 Server Core, use the *ocsetup Microsoft-Hyper-V* command.

You manage Hyper-V on a computer running Windows Server 2008 Server Core by connecting from another computer with the Hyper-V Manager console. You can install the Hyper-V Manager console on a computer running Windows Server 2008, even one that uses an x86 version of the operating system, by adding the Hyper-V Tools category of the Remote Server Administration Tools feature, as shown in Figure 15-2. You can manage Hyper-V on a Server Core computer by installing the RSAT tools package, which can be downloaded from the Microsoft Web site.

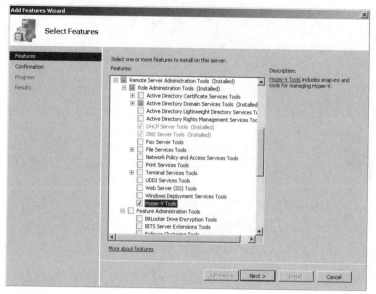

FIGURE 15-2 Installing RSAT Hyper-V Tools.

Virtual Machine Licensing

Like any physically deployed computer, you must ensure that each virtually deployed computer has the appropriate license. As an administrator, be aware that each edition of Windows Server 2008 includes a different number of extra virtual machine licenses. These licenses are as follows:

- Windows Server 2008 Standard includes a single license to run a Windows virtual guest.
- Windows Server 2008 Enterprise includes four licenses to run Windows Virtual guests.
- Windows Server 2008 Datacenter includes unlimited licenses to run Windows Virtual guests.

It is necessary to purchase additional licenses only after you exceed the limit of included licenses, except for Datacenter.

 Quick Check

1. What is a hypervisor?
2. How many licenses for Windows virtual machines are included in Windows Server 2008 Enterprise?

Quick Check Answers

1. A hypervisor is a software layer that runs under the host operating system. It grants both host and guest operating systems equal access to hardware resources.

2. Windows Server 2008 Enterprise includes four licenses to run Windows virtual hosts.

Configuring Virtual Networks

Microsoft recommends that you configure a Hyper-V server with at least two network adapters. Assign the first network adapter to the host server; the second and any additional adapters should be dedicated to the virtual machines.

By configuring virtual networks, you can limit which hosts can communicate with the Hyper-V guest. Using the Virtual Network Manager, shown in Figure 15-3, you can create three types of virtual networks. The selection of network type dictates how the virtual guests can communicate.

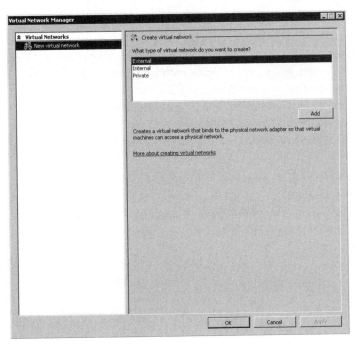

FIGURE 15-3 Virtual networks.

The three types of networks are as follows:

- **Private virtual network**   Private virtual networks allow communication only between virtual machines on the same Hyper-V host. The host server cannot communicate with the guest operating systems. Other external hosts cannot communicate with the guest operating systems.

- **External virtual network**   External virtual networks allow communication from hosts external to the Hyper-V server with guest operating systems. The host server can also communicate with the guest operating systems when an external virtual network is in place. Guest operating systems can also communicate with each other.

- **Internal virtual network**   Internal virtual networks allow communication between virtual machines on the same Hyper-V host. The host server can communicate with the guest operating systems. Other external hosts cannot communicate with the guest operating systems.

> **NOTE** **HYPER-V AND WIRELESS LOCAL AREA NETWORKS**
>
> Hyper-V does not support the use of wireless network adapters for connections to external virtual networks.

- Virtual machines connect to virtual networks, using virtual network adapters. Hyper-V has two types of virtual network adapters: a standard virtual network adapter and a legacy virtual network adapter. The standard virtual network adapter is available for all supported guest operating systems on which integration services can be installed. Guest operating systems that do not support integration services can use the legacy network adapter, which emulates an Intel 21140-based PCI Fast Ethernet Adapter. The legacy network adapter is also necessary if the virtual machine must boot from the network.

- It is possible to isolate virtual guest computers assigned to the same virtual network by assigning them to different virtual local area networks (VLANs). To assign a computer to a specific VLAN, edit the virtual machine's settings, select the network adapter, select the Enable Virtual LAN Identification check box, and enter a VLAN ID, as shown in Figure 15-4.

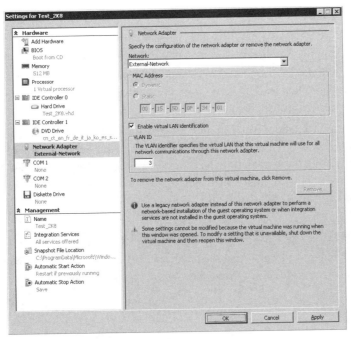

FIGURE 15-4 Configuring a VLAN ID.

MORE INFO **VIRTUAL NETWORKS**

To learn more about Hyper-V virtual networks, see the following TechNet Web page: *http://technet.microsoft.com/en-us/library/cc816585.aspx.*

Hyper-V Failover Clusters

To create a Hyper-V failover cluster, install Hyper-V and failover clustering on all nodes that will participate in the cluster. Creating failover clusters by using Windows Server 2008 is covered in more detail in Chapter 16, "High Availability and Storage." After you have configured failover clustering, ensure that all data related to the virtual guest is stored on a shared storage device. To make the virtual machine highly available, configure Services And Applications in the Failover Cluster Management tool by running the Configure A Service Or Application Wizard and selecting the virtual machine. When you make the virtual machine highly available, it is visible under the *Services And Applications* node in the Failover Cluster Management Tool.

MORE INFO **HYPER-V FAILOVER CLUSTERING**

To learn more about configuring a Hyper-V failover cluster, see the following TechNet document: *http://technet.microsoft.com/en-us/library/cc732181.aspx.*

Virtual Server 2005 R2 SP1

Virtual Server 2005 R2 SP1 enables you to host virtual machines on an x86 version of Windows Server 2008. Although Virtual Server 2005 R2 SP1 can host Windows NT 4 SP6a, Windows 2000 Server, Windows Server 2003, and Windows Server 2008 virtual machines, you cannot host virtual machines that use x64 versions of any of these operating systems. Virtual Server 2005 R2 SP1 also supports assigning only one processor per virtual guest.

With several important limitations, you can migrate Virtual Server 2005 R2 SP1 virtual machines to a Hyper-V host and Hyper-V virtual machines to a Virtual Server 2004 R2 SP1 virtual host. You can manage these migrations by using System Center Virtual Machine Manager (SCVMM) 2008. You cannot migrate a virtual machine that uses an x64 architecture from Hyper-V to Virtual Server 2005 R2 SP1.

> **MORE INFO** **MIGRATING FROM VIRTUAL SERVER TO HYPER-V**
>
> To learn more about migrating from Virtual Server 2005 R2 SP1 to Hyper-V, see the following TechNet document: *http://technet.microsoft.com/en-us/library/dd296684.aspx*.

> **EXAM TIP**
>
> Remember the differences between virtual network types.

PRACTICE Configuring Virtual Networks and Installing Virtual Guests

In this practice, you perform tasks similar to those you would perform when configuring Hyper-V on a computer running Windows Server 2008. The first exercise configures a virtual network; the second exercise involves installing a guest Windows Server 2008 virtual machine.

> **MORE INFO** **INSTALLING THE HYPER-V ROLE**
>
> It is possible to install the Hyper-V role only on an x64 version of Windows Server 2008 that has the Hyper-V update package installed. This package is available through Windows Update or from the following address on the Microsoft Web site: *http://technet.microsoft .com/en-us/library/cc794892.aspx*.

EXERCISE 1 Configure an Internal Virtual Network

In this exercise, you configure an internal virtual network. You use this internal virtual network when creating a virtual guest in Exercise 2, "Install a Windows Server 2008 Virtual Guest."

1. Log on to the computer running Windows Server 2008 on which you have installed the Hyper-V role with an account that is a member of the local Administrators group.

2. Open the Hyper-V Manager console from the Administrative Tools menu. Click Continue to dismiss the User Account Control dialog box.

3. In the Actions pane, select Virtual Network Manager.

4. In the Virtual Network Manager dialog box, select Internal, and then click Add.

5. Configure the new virtual network with the settings shown in Figure 15-5, and then click OK.

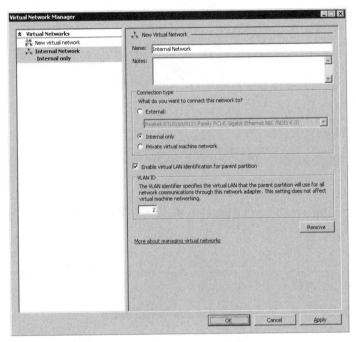

FIGURE 15-5 New virtual network.

EXERCISE 2   Install a Windows Server 2008 Virtual Guest

In this exercise, you install and configure a new Windows Server 2008 virtual machine under Hyper-V. You need access to the Windows Server 2008 installation media to complete this exercise.

1. If you have not already done so, log on to the server on which you installed the Hyper-V role and open the Hyper-V Manager console.

2. From the Actions menu, select New, and then click Virtual Machine.

3. On the first page of the New Virtual Machine Wizard, click Next.

4. On the Specify Name And Location page, enter **Test_Win2K8** and click Next.

5. On the Assign Memory page, leave the default value, and then click Next.

6. On the Configure Networking page, use the Connection drop-down list to select the internal network you created in Exercise 1, as shown in Figure 15-6, and then click Next.

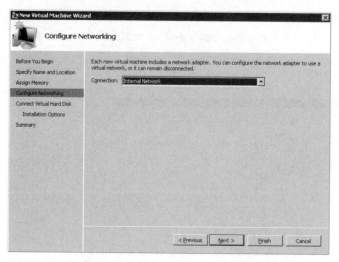

FIGURE 15-6 Configure virtual networking.

7. On the Connect Virtual Hard Disk page, select the Create A Virtual Hard Disk check box and set the hard disk size to 16 GB. Click Next.

8. On the Installation Options page, select Install An Operating System From A Boot CD/DVD-ROM, and then specify the location of the Windows Server 2008 installation media, as shown in Figure 15-7. Click Next.

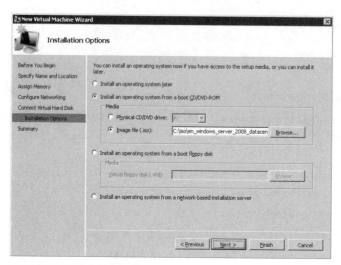

FIGURE 15-7 Installation options.

9. On the Completing The New Virtual Machine Wizard page, select Start The Virtual Machine After It Is Created, and then click Finish.

10. Proceed with the installation of Windows Server 2008. Use the default installation options.

11. After the installation has completed, shut down the virtual guest on the computer running Windows Server 2008.

Lesson Summary

- You can install Hyper-V only on x64 versions of Windows Server 2008 Standard, Enterprise, and Datacenter. The processor should support hardware-assisted virtualization and hardware data execution protection.

- You can install Hyper-V on the Server Core installation option of the x64 versions of Windows Server 2008 Standard, Enterprise, and Datacenter. You must install the Hyper-V Manager console on a separate computer and use it to manage the Server Core Hyper-V server remotely because you cannot perform management tasks locally.

- Windows Server 2008 Standard includes one virtual machine license. Windows Server 2008 Enterprise includes four virtual machine licenses. Windows Server 2008 Datacenter includes licenses to run an unlimited number of virtual machines.

- Private virtual networks allow communication between Hyper-V guests on the same host. Internal virtual networks allow communication between Hyper-V guests on the same host and between the host and the guests. External virtual networks allow communication between Hyper-V guests on the same Hyper-V server, between the Hyper-V server and the guests, and between hosts external to the Hyper-V server and the Hyper-V guests.

- When configuring Hyper-V failover clustering, you must install the virtual machine files on shared storage and configure the Hyper-V guest to be highly available using the Failover Cluster Management console.

Lesson Review

You can use the following questions to test your knowledge of the information in Lesson 1, "Hyper-V." The questions are also available on the companion DVD if you prefer to review them in electronic form.

> **NOTE ANSWERS**
>
> Answers to these questions and explanations of why each answer choice is right or wrong are located in the "Answers" section at the end of the book.

1. Which of the following editions of Windows Server 2008 support Hyper-V?

    A. Windows Web Server 2008 x86

    B. Windows Web Server 2008 x64

    C. Windows Server 2008 Standard x64 (Server Core)

    D. Windows Server 2008 Enterprise x86

2. Which edition of Windows Server 2008 includes a license to run an unlimited number of virtual instances under Hyper-V?

    A. Windows Web Server 2008

    B. Windows Server 2008 Standard

    C. Windows Server 2008 Enterprise

    D. Windows Server 2008 Datacenter

3. You work at an ISP. You are using Hyper-V on Windows Server 2008 to host Windows Web Server 2008 virtual guests. Customers use these virtual guests as Web site hosting platforms. Which type of virtual network should you configure for these guests?

    A. External virtual network

    B. Internal virtual network

    C. Private virtual network

    D. No virtual network

4. Which of the following tools can you use to make a virtual machine highly available when it is installed on a two-node Hyper-V failover cluster?

    A. Failover Cluster Management console

    B. Hyper-V Manager console

    C. Virtual Machine settings

    D. Network Load Balancing console

Lesson 2: Virtual Machine Migration and Backup

Physical-to-virtual migration is the process of redeploying a server from physical hardware to a virtual host. This process is not just a matter of backing up a physically deployed server, creating a new virtual server with similar characteristics, and performing a restoration. In this lesson, you learn about the tools you can use to transfer a physical server seamlessly to a virtual environment with a minimum of downtime to the server's clients. Just as it is important to back up physically deployed servers, it is necessary to back up virtual servers. An advantage you have as an administrator is that Hyper-V hosts are essentially a collection of files. It is far simpler to back up and restore a set of files than it is to back up and restore a physically deployed server.

> **After this lesson, you will be able to:**
> - Configure VM integration services.
> - Manage virtual hard disks.
> - Migrate servers from physical to virtual deployment.
> - Back up virtual machines.
>
> **Estimated lesson time: 40 minutes**

Physical-to-Virtual Migrations

A physical-to-virtual migration involves transferring a traditionally deployed server to a virtual environment. When performed properly, using the correct tools, it is possible for users of a server that is virtualized to be unaware that the server they are connected to has transitioned from a physical host to a virtual one. You can perform physical-to-virtual migration by using two tools, the Virtual Server Migration Toolkit and System Center Virtual Machine Manager 2008.

Computers that have relatively low resource usage, such as low CPU, RAM, and disk usage, are excellent candidates for virtualization. Computers that have consistently high CPU, RAM, and disk usage are less suitable for virtualization because this high resource use is likely to continue after the server is virtualized. One virtual guest that monopolizes a Hyper-V server's resources limits the resources available to all other virtual guests hosted on that server.

Virtual Server Migration Toolkit

The Virtual Server Migration Toolkit (VSMT) is an older tool that enables you to migrate physical computers running the Microsoft Windows NT 4 SP6a, Microsoft Windows 2000 SP4, and Windows Server 2003 operating systems so that they can be hosted under Virtual Server 2005 R2 SP1. Because you can migrate Virtual Server 2005 R2 SP1 virtual machines into Hyper-V, you can use the VSMT to perform physical-to-virtual migrations using Virtual

Server 2005 R2 SP1 as a bridge. The VSMT is a command line-based tool that uses Extensible Markup Language (XML) files to store system configuration data. It uses Automated Deployment services to capture an image of the virtualization candidate that is then deployed as a virtual machine on Virtual Server 2005 R2 SP1.

The drawback of using VSMT compared to the System Center Virtual Machine Manager 2008 tool, covered later in this lesson, is that there is downtime during the physical-to-virtual migration when the server to be virtualized is not available. Use the VSMT when you have a small number of virtual machines to migrate and your environment does not use enough virtual machines to make the deployment of System Center Virtual Machine Manager 2008 practical.

> **MORE INFO** **VSMT**
>
> To learn more about the VSMT, see the following Microsoft Web site: *http://technet .microsoft.com/en-us/virtualserver/bb676674.aspx.*

System Center Virtual Machine Manager 2008

SCVMM 2008 enables you to manage a large number of virtual machines in a single location. You can use SCVMM 2008 to:

- Monitor and manage up to 8,000 virtual machines.
- Monitor and manage up to 400 Hyper-V host computers.
- When connected to a Fibre Channel SAN environment, redeploy virtual machines between Hyper-V hosts as needed.
- Delegate permissions so that users who are not administrators can create and manage their own virtual machines.

You can use SCVMM 2008 also to perform a physical-to-virtual migration under the following conditions:

- The target computer has at least 512 MB of RAM.
- The target computer has an Advanced Configuration and Power Interface (ACPI) BIOS.
- There are no firewalls between the host computer and the SCVMM 2008 server.

SCVMM 2008 can perform online migrations of computers running Windows Server 2008, Windows Server 2003 SP1, Windows XP Professional SP2, and Windows Vista SP1. SCVMM 2008 can perform offline migrations of Windows 2000 Server SP4 but cannot migrate computers running Windows NT 4. To perform migrations of computers running Windows NT 4, use the Virtual Server Migration Toolkit.

During an online conversion, the following process occurs:

1. SCVMM 2008 installs the P2V (Physical to Virtual) agent on the source computer.
2. SCVMM 2008 gathers the computer's hardware and software configuration and determines whether the source computer can be virtualized.

3. A VSS image is captured for each volume; data is streamed, using Background Intelligent Transfer Service (BITS) to the destination Hyper-V server. Each physical volume on the source computer becomes a separate virtual hard disk.

4. SCVMM 2008 creates the virtual machine, attaching the hard disks, network adapters, and memory.

During an offline conversion, the following process occurs:

1. SCVMM 2008 installs the Virtual Machine Manager (VMM) agent on the source computer.

2. The agent installs a Windows Preinstallment Environment (PE) image on the source computer, alters the boot record, and then restarts in the PE environment.

3. SCVMM 2008 streams the physical disks to the host Hyper-V server.

4. SCVMM 2008 creates the virtual machine, attaching the hard disks, network adapters, and memory.

> **MORE INFO** **PHYSICAL-TO-VIRTUAL MIGRATIONS USING SCVMM 2008**
>
> To learn more about performing physical-to-virtual migrations using System Center Virtual Machine Manager 2008, see the following TechNet document: *http://technet.microsoft .com/en-us/library/cc764232.aspx*.

Virtual Machine Integration Services

Virtual Machine Integration services are a collection of tools and components you can add to a guest operating system. They include network adapter drivers, hard disk controller drivers, and drivers for other hardware devices that improve the performance of a virtual machine hosted under Hyper-V. They enable functionality such as the ability to use a mouse within a Virtual Machine Connection session when connected to the Hyper-V server, using remote desktop.

Integration services offer the following features, which can be selectively disabled through a virtual machine's settings dialog box:

- **Operating system shutdown from Hyper-V manager**   Enables you to perform a clean shutdown of the operating system from the Hyper-V manager without logging on to the virtual guest and performing a shutdown manually

- **Time synchronization**   Ensures that the virtual guest's clock synchronizes regularly with the Hyper-V host

- **Data exchange**   Allows data to be transferred between the Hyper-V host and the virtual guest

- **Heartbeat**   Enables Hyper-V to monitor the performance of the virtual guest

- **Backup**   Enables volume snapshots to be taken of the virtual guest

Integration services is not installed automatically on a virtual guest. You can install Integration services after the guest operating system is installed by logging on to the guest and then selecting Insert Integration Services Setup Disk from the Action menu in Virtual Machine Connection.

 Quick Check

1. What performance characteristics suggest that a physically deployed server would make a poor candidate for virtualization?

2. Which physical-to-virtual migration tool enables you to perform the migration with a minimum of downtime?

Quick Check Answers

1. Physically deployed servers that have consistently high CPU, hard disk, or RAM usage are poor candidates for virtualization because they would place a similar stress on the virtual host.

2. SCVMM 2008 enables you to perform a migration with a minimum of downtime.

Virtual Hard Disks

Virtual hard disks are stored as .vhd files. The contents of the virtual hard disk are stored within the .vhd file. When you create virtual hard disks, store them on a volume that has good read/write performance and, preferably, is fault tolerant, such as RAID 5 or RAID 10. You can use the following physical storage technologies to store virtual hard disk files:

- Direct Attached Storage such as SATA, eSATA, PATA, SAS, SCSI, USB, IDE, and Firewire drives.
- Storage area network devices such as iSCSI, Fibre Channel, and SAS.
- Network attached storage.

You can create virtual hard disks that emulate either IDE or SCSI disks. If you use IDE virtual disks, you are limited to two IDE controllers with two disks per controller. A virtual guest computer must always use an IDE controller for its startup hard disk, independent of whether the hard disk is virtual or physical.

You can install up to four virtual SCSI controllers in a single virtual guest. Each SCSI controller supports a maximum of 64 SCSI disks, meaning that it is possible to have 256 SCSI disks attached to a single virtual machine. You cannot use virtual SCSI hard disks as the virtual machine startup disk. When you install integration services in a virtual client, the performance of virtual SCSI and virtual IDE disks is essentially equal.

When you create a virtual hard disk using either the IDE or SCSI type, you have a choice of three types, as follows:

- **Dynamically expanding** When you configure a virtual hard disk as dynamically expanding, the .vhd file that hosts the hard disk data starts small and then grows, as data is added, to the maximum size you have specified for the disk. Although the disk expands as you add data, it does not shrink when data is removed. It will remain the same size until enough data is added to expand it beyond its current size. It is possible to perform a disk compaction using the Edit Virtual Hard Disk Wizard, but this process is not automatic.

- **Fixed**   When you configure a virtual hard disk as fixed, the .vhd file is created at the full size of the volume you created. Because the size of the .vhd file is fixed, it suffers significantly less disk fragmentation than disks of the dynamically expanding type. It is possible to extend the size of a .vhd file using the Edit Virtual Hard Disk Wizard, although this leads to an increase in the file's fragmentation.

- **Differencing**   When you configure a virtual hard disk to be of the differencing type, you specify a parent virtual hard disk that the differencing hard disk will record changes against. All changes made to the volume the parent and child represent are written to the child .vhd file. This enables changes to be made without alterations to the parent disk. You can manually merge changes made to the differencing disk.

To create a virtual disk from within Hyper-V Manager, perform the following steps:

1. In the Actions pane, click New, and then click Hard Disk.

    This launches the New Virtual Hard Disk Wizard.

2. Choose between a dynamically expanding, fixed size, or differencing disk.

    The default option is dynamically expanding.

3. Provide the disk with a name and specify the location in which the .vhd file will be stored.

4. Decide whether you want to create a new blank virtual disk or to copy the contents of an existing physical hard disk, as shown in Figure 15-8.

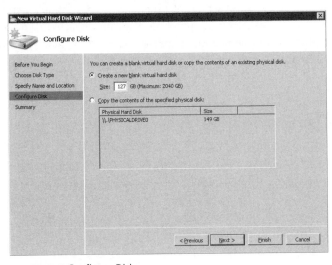

FIGURE 15-8 Configure Disk.

It is also possible to use a disk that is directly attached to the computer with a virtual machine. The drawbacks of this include inability to expand the disk dynamically and to take snapshots, and you cannot use differencing disks with directly attached disks. To configure physical disks to work directly with virtual machines, perform the following steps:

1. Add the storage device to the Hyper-V host.

   It will appear as a raw volume in an offline state when viewed using disk management.

2. Bring the disk online and initialize it using either the MBR or GPT partition stile. Return the disk to the offline state. If you do not return the disk to the offline state, it will be unavailable to Hyper-V.

3. Create a virtual machine and select the Attach A Virtual Hard Disk Later option.

4. Edit the virtual machine settings, select the controller you will attach the physical disk to, select Hard Drive, and then click Add.

5. In the Media section, select Physical Hard Disk and select the disk from the drop-down menu. Disks are available only in this menu if they are offline in Disk Management.

> **MORE INFO** **DISKS AND STORAGE**
>
> To learn more about implementing storage with Hyper-V, see the following TechNet Web page: *http://technet.microsoft.com/en-us/library/dd183729.aspx*.

Backup and Snapshots

Snapshots are point-in-time instances of a virtual machine that you can return to at any stage. You can create snapshots at any time, including when the guest operating system is active. Snapshots cause no disruption in service and write to disk in the background. This means that clients connected to a virtual machine guest server will experience no disruption in service when you take a snapshot. You can take up to 50 snapshots of an individual virtual machine. Figure 15-9 shows several snapshots taken of a virtual machine named Test_2K8. You take a snapshot and revert to that snapshot in the practice at the end of this lesson.

FIGURE 15-9 Snapshots of VM Test_2K8.

There are two methods for performing backups of virtual machines:

- **Perform a backup from the Hyper-V host**   You can perform a full server backup as long as the storage is compatible with Hyper-V and the Hyper-V Volume Shadow Copy Service (VSS) writer. This enables you to back up all data required to restore the Hyper-V host fully. Backup data will include the configuration of all virtual machines, virtual networks, snapshots, and virtual hard disks. You can perform this backup using Windows Server Backup only if you have added the registry key that registers the Hyper-V VSS writer.

- **Perform a backup from within the Hyper-V host**   Use this method when you need to back up data from storage devices not supported by the Hyper-V VSS writer, such as physical disks directly attached to the virtual machine or storage accessed through the virtual machine's iSCSI initiator.

You can perform an online backup on a running virtual machine, using a Hyper-V–aware backup application under the following conditions:

- Integration services is installed on the guest, and the backup integration service is active.

- All virtual machine disks are NTFS formatted.

- The virtual machine does not use dynamically expanding disks. You can back up dynamic .vhd disks only when they are offline.

- Volume Shadow Copy Service is enabled on all volumes that host the virtual machine, and VSS data must be stored on the disk it is enabled for.

You can perform an offline backup when you put the virtual machine into a paused state. Hyper-V–aware backup applications automatically pause virtual machines that are incompatible with online backup, performing an offline backup and returning them to service when the backup completes.

When you perform a restore of a currently active virtual machine, Hyper-V shuts down the active virtual machine and deletes it before allowing the restore. If you restore an online, rather than offline, backup, you might receive a warning that the operating system was not shut down properly. You can safely ignore this message.

> **MORE INFO**   **HYPER-V BACKUP**
>
> To learn more about backing up Hyper-V, see the following TechNet document: *http://technet.microsoft.com/en-us/library/dd252619.aspx.*

EXAM TIP

Remember the difference between the three virtual hard disk types.

PRACTICE   Snapshots, Restorations, and Integration Services

In this practice, you perform tasks similar to those you would perform when configuring a Windows Server 2008 Hyper-V server. In the first exercise, you take a snapshot and install integration services. In the second exercise, you modify the hardware configuration and restore it from the previous snapshot.

EXERCISE 1   Install Integration Services and Take Snapshot

In this exercise, you install Integration Services on a virtual machine and then take a snapshot of that virtual machine.

1. Log on to the server on which you installed Hyper-V and open the Hyper-V Manager console.

2. Under Virtual Machines, select the virtual machine that you installed during Exercise 2 at the end of Lesson 1, and then click Start under the Actions pane.

3. When the virtual machine has booted, click Connect in the Actions pane.

    This opens the Virtual Machine Connection window.

4. Log on to the virtual machine, using an account that is a member of the Administrators group. Use CTRL-ALT-DELETE in the Action menu rather than pressing those keys on the Hyper-V server.

5. After you have successfully logged on, click the Action menu, and then click Insert Integration Services Setup Disk.

6. When presented with the AutoPlay dialog box, click Install Hyper-V Integration Services. If presented with a warning about a previous version of Hyper-V integration services being detected, click OK.

7. When presented with the Installation Complete dialog box, click Yes to restart the virtual guest.

   The Windows Server 2008 virtual guest computer restarts.

8. When the virtual guest has restarted, log on, using an account that is a member of the Administrators group.

9. Click Snapshot in the Actions menu of the Virtual Machine Connection window. In the Snapshot Name dialog box, type **SnapshotOne**, as shown in Figure 15-10, and then click Yes.

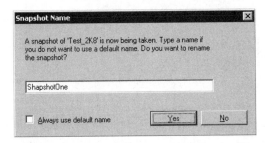

FIGURE 15-10 Taking a snapshot.

10. Shut the guest operating system down and close the Virtual Machine Connection window.

EXERCISE 2   Configure Virtual Machine Settings and Snapshot Restore

In this exercise, you make a significant configuration change to the guest virtual machine by adding a new SCSI hard disk drive. You then undo that change by rolling back to the snapshot you took at the end of the last exercise.

1. If you have not done so already, log on to the server on which you installed Hyper-V and open the Hyper-V Manager console.

2. In the Virtual Machines area, select the virtual machine that you created in Exercise 2 at the end of Lesson 1. In the Action menu, click Settings.

3. Select Add Hardware, and then select SCSI Controller, as shown in Figure 15-11. Click Add.

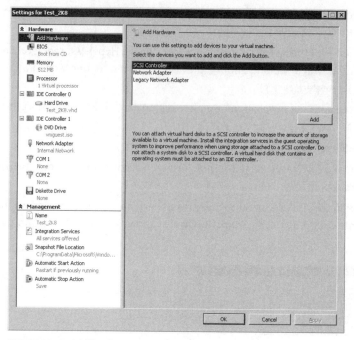

FIGURE 15-11 Add hardware.

4. When SCSI Controller is selected in the Hardware pane, select Hard Drive, and then click Add.

5. In the Hard Drive dialog box, select Virtual Hard Disk (.VHD) File, and then click New. On the first page of the New Virtual Hard Disk Wizard, click Next.

6. On the Choose Disk Type page, shown in Figure 15-12, select Dynamically Expanding, and then click Next.

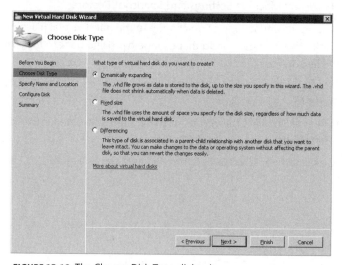

FIGURE 15-12 The Choose Disk Type dialog box.

7. Accept the default new virtual hard disk name, and then click Next.

8. Set the size of the new disk to 2 GB maximum, click Next, and then click Finish. Click OK in the Settings For Test_2K8 dialog box, shown in Figure 15-13.

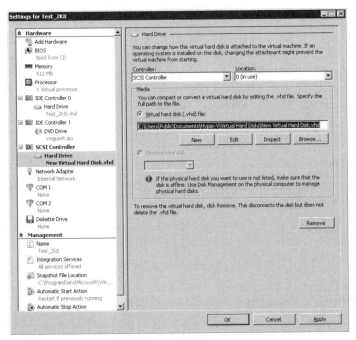

FIGURE 15-13 Add new disk.

9. Start the Test_2K8 virtual machine. Click Connect in the Actions menu. Log on with a user account that has local Administrator privileges.

10. If it does not start automatically, open the Server Manager console on the virtual guest and select the *Disk Management* node under the *Storage* node.

11. In Disk Management, right-click Disk 1 and set it to Online. Initialize Disk 1, using the MBR partition style, and then create a new simple volume, formatted using the NTFS file system.

12. From the Action menu in Virtual Machine Connection, click Revert. In the Revert Virtual Machine dialog box, click Revert.

13. When the virtual machine has finished restoring, open the Server Manager console and check under Disk Management to verify that the SCSI disk you added earlier in this practice is no longer present.

14. Shut down the guest virtual machine. When Test_2K8 is selected, click Settings under the Action menu. Verify that the SCSI adapter and the SCSI disk you configured are no longer present.

Lesson Summary

- Dynamically expanding virtual disks increase in size as data is added to the disk but do not shrink automatically when data is deleted. It is possible to compact a dynamic disk's .vhd file after data has been deleted from the volume it hosts.

- Fixed virtual hard disks use a .vhd file that is the same size as the disk. It is possible to extend the size of a fixed virtual hard disk.

- Differencing virtual hard disks are paired with a parent hard disk. The differencing disk records changes made to the parent disk without actually changing the parent disk. It is possible to merge parent and child disks.

- A virtual host can support a maximum of 256 SCSI disks and a maximum of 4 SCSI controllers. Virtual hard disks can be a maximum of 2,040 GB in size.

- Each virtual machine supports a maximum of 50 snapshots.

- You can use the Virtual Server Migration Toolkit to perform physical to virtual migrations on Windows NT 4, Windows 2000, and Windows Server 2003 servers.

- You can use System Center Virtual Machine Manager 2008 to perform physical-to-virtual migrations on Windows NT 4, Windows 2000, Windows Server 2003, and Windows Server 2008 servers.

Lesson Review

You can use the following questions to test your knowledge of the information in Lesson 2, "Virtual Machine Migration and Backup." The questions are also available on the companion DVD if you prefer to review them in electronic form.

> **NOTE ANSWERS**
>
> Answers to these questions and explanations of why each answer choice is right or wrong are located in the "Answers" section at the end of the book.

1. Which of the following tools can you use to virtualize two existing Windows Server 2003 servers so that they can be hosted as virtual machines on a Windows Server 2008 server with Hyper-V installed?

   A. Virtual Server Migration Toolkit

   B. Microsoft Application Virtualization

   C. Virtual Server 2005 R2

   D. Host Integration Server 2006

2. Assuming that you have adequate storage, what is the maximum number of snapshots you can take of a single guest virtual machine under Hyper-V?

   A. 10

   B. 25

   C. 50

   D. 100

3. What type of virtual disk should you create when you want to record changes made to an existing disk and only commit them to the original disk after you have reviewed the impact of those changes?

   A. Dynamically expanding

   B. Fixed

   C. Differencing

4. Several developers are about to upgrade an application that is running on a Windows Server 2008 virtual machine that you are responsible for managing through Hyper-V. You want to ensure that you can roll back to the configuration as it exists now if the application upgrade does not go as planned. Which of the following should you do?

   A. Configure an additional disk on the virtual machine and implement disk mirroring.

   B. Create a system restore point on the virtual machine.

   C. Pause the virtual machine by using Hyper-V Manager.

   D. Take a snapshot, using Hyper-V Manager.

Chapter Review

To further practice and reinforce the skills you learned in this chapter, you can perform the following tasks:

- Review the chapter summary.
- Complete the case scenario. This scenario sets up a real-world situation involving the topics of this chapter and asks you to create a solution.
- Complete the suggested practices.
- Take a practice test.

Chapter Summary

- Virtual networks enable you to limit which hosts can communicate with virtual machines.
- Hyper-V supports both virtual IDE and virtual SCSI hard disks.
- The Virtual Server Migration Toolkit and System Center Virtual Machine Manager 2008 can both be used to perform physical to virtual migrations.
- Snapshots can be used to roll back the configuration of a virtual machine to the state it was in when the snapshot was taken.

Case Scenarios

In the following case scenarios, you apply what you've learned about configuring Windows Server Hyper-V and virtual machines. You can find answers to these questions in the "Answers" section at the end of this book.

Case Scenario: Hyper-V at Contoso

You are the systems administrator at Contoso, Ltd., a New Zealand–based hovercraft manufacturer. You are consolidating and virtualizing existing servers under Hyper-V. Contoso has five branch offices located throughout the north and south islands. Each branch office has either two or three physically deployed Windows Server 2003 servers. The branch office servers use little in the way of hardware resources, and you would like to replace these with a single computer running Windows Server 2008, virtualizing and upgrading the existing Windows Server 2003 servers to Windows Server 2008 virtual guests. You also intend to virtualize six servers at the Contoso head office location in Auckland. These servers are mission-critical, so all the virtual machines hosted at the head office site must remain available even if the server hosting them fails. With this information in mind, answer the following questions.

1. Which tools can you use to perform a physical-to-virtual migration of the computers running Windows Server 2003 at each branch office?

2. Which edition of Windows Server 2008 should you deploy at each branch office to minimize the number of extra computer licenses required?

3. How can you ensure that the virtual machines at the head office remain available?

Suggested Practices

To help you successfully master the exam objectives presented in this chapter, complete the following tasks.

Configure Hyper-V Settings

To get a thorough understanding of configuring Windows Server Hyper-V and virtual machines, complete the practices in this section.

- **Practice 1**   Create a new external virtual network, using Virtual Network Manager.

- **Practice 2**   Edit the settings of the guest virtual machine that you created in the second exercise of Lesson 1. Add a new network adapter. Connect that network adapter to the new external virtual network.

Take a Practice Test

The practice tests on this book's companion DVD offer many options. For example, you can test yourself on just one exam objective, or you can test yourself on all the upgrade exam content. You can set up the test so that it closely simulates the experience of taking a certification exam, or you can set it up in study mode so that you can look at the correct answers and explanations after you answer each question.

> **MORE INFO**   **PRACTICE TESTS**
>
> For details about all the practice test options available, see the "How to Use the Practice Tests" section in this book's Introduction.

CHAPTER 16

High Availability and Storage

High availability technologies such as failover clusters and network load balancing help ensure that the servers you manage remain available to the network even when unforeseeable failures occur. In this chapter, you learn about the various high availability technologies you can use when deploying Windows Server 2008 to ensure that the servers you manage are almost always available to those who need them. The second part of this chapter looks at storage, concentrating on storage area networks (SANs). Increasingly common in medium and large network environments, SANs enable organizations to centralize storage. This facilitates storage provision because you can allocate storage from a central reservoir rather than adding yet another hard disk drive to a server when there is no alternative. When the storage reservoir starts to run out of space, you can add more storage centrally, storage that you can then redeploy throughout your organization as it is needed.

Exam objectives in this chapter

- Configure high availability.
- Configure storage.

Lessons in this chapter:

Before You Begin

To complete the lessons in this chapter, you must have done the following:

- Installed and configured the evaluation edition of Windows Server 2008 Enterprise Edition in accordance with the instructions listed in the Introduction.

- Installed two Windows Server 2008 Enterprise member servers, named Wellington and Wangaratta, in the *contoso.internal* domain. These computers should have IP addresses 10.0.0.25 and 10.0.0.35, respectively.

- Configured one of the servers, Wellington or Wangaratta, with five identical hard disks, one of which hosts the operating system. This is relatively simple to achieve if using virtual SCSI disks on a virtual machine.

 REAL WORLD

Orin Thomas

High availability solutions tend to be expensive. It is much easier to get a high availability budget item approved when it deals with a service an organization's executive uses than it is to get one approved for average staff members. The first high availability solution I ever had to manage was a clustered mail server. The head office site where I was working had two mail servers. One mail server, exclusively for the executives' use, hosted about 50 mailboxes. The second mail server, used by everyone else, hosted about 300 mailboxes. Guess which mail server was clustered. Unfortunately, clustering does not always ensure availability. Several months after we deployed the executives' clustered mail server, some workers digging up the road next door severed the underground power cable that provided power to the entire office park. Even though I was pretty sure that I had properly configured all the servers to shut down gracefully when on UPS power for more than a couple of minutes, Murphy's law dictates that unsupervised graceful shutdowns only ever work when they are supervised. So, being a bit paranoid, I went down to the server room to make sure that everything that should happen actually did. Unfortunately, no one had thought to ensure that the lighting for the windowless server room in the basement was highly available. I learned that it is a lot easier to supervise scripted server shutdowns when I don't have to stumble around a dark server room using someone's borrowed cigarette lighter for illumination.

Lesson 1: Configuring High Availability

Clusters ensure that the important services your servers provide to clients remain available. Clusters use multiple computers to provide the same service for sharing load, ensuring redundancy, or both. Although the failure of a server is something that keeps IT professionals up at night worrying, when you implement a high availability solution properly, using Windows Server 2008, and a failure does occur, your clients will not notice anything. In this lesson, you learn about the various Windows Server 2008 high availability strategies and the circumstances under which you can and should deploy them to ensure the reliable delivery of IT services to the people who depend on them.

> **After this lesson, you will be able to:**
> - Configure DNS round robin.
> - Deploy and manage network load balancing clusters.
> - Set up Windows Server 2008 failover clusters.
> - Explain the different failover cluster quorum models.
>
> **Estimated lesson time: 40 minutes**

DNS Round Robin

Domain Name System (DNS) round robin is the simplest method of distributing traffic across multiple hosts. DNS round robin works by having a DNS server return a different host IP address each time a client requests the round robin hostname. For example, you could configure DNS round robin by having IP addresses 192.168.15.10, 192.168.15.11, and 192.168.15.12 all mapped to the *www.contoso.internal* hostname. The DNS server would allocate each new client that asked about the *www.contoso.internal* hostname one of the three IP addresses on a round robin basis. This spreads new incoming client requests evenly across all three IP addresses.

All you need to do to configure DNS round robin is add successive host (A if using IPv4 or AAAA if using IPv6) records with the same name but with the IP address of each host. Figure 16-1 shows host records created to support DNS round robin for four hosts with the hostname *wangaratta.contoso.internal*. Multiple operating systems can participate in DNS round robin; unlike other solutions, you are not limited to running one processor architecture or edition of Windows Server 2008.

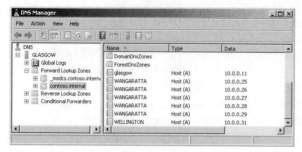

FIGURE 16-1 DNS round robin for Wangaratta.

As a load balancing solution, DNS round robin has several drawbacks. The first of these is that DNS round robin is not failure aware. A DNS server will still return the IP address of a server in a round robin group that has failed until an administrator manually removes the record relating to the failed server.

Another drawback is that although incoming client requests are balanced across the servers participating in DNS round robin, that does not mean that traffic is. Unlike network load balancing, which takes account of the actual load on a server, DNS round robin simply allocates traffic on a turn-based system irrespective of the target server's current workload. The existence of records within client DNS caches also impacts this balance, returning a client to the server it originally queried if an entry for that server still exists within its DNS cache.

DNS round robin is enabled by default on Windows Server 2008 DNS servers. The Enable Round Robin setting is located on the DNS server's Advanced tab, as shown in Figure 16-2. The Enable Netmask Ordering option, also enabled by default and visible in Figure 16-2, configures the DNS server to return an IP address on the requesting client's subnet if a host record with one exists.

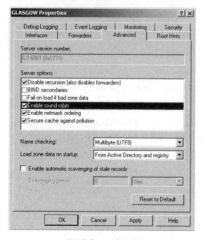

FIGURE 16-2 DNS Round Robin option.

Network Load Balancing

Network load balancing (NLB) distributes traffic between multiple hosts based on each host's current load. Each new client is directed to the host under the least load. It is also possible to configure NLB to send traffic proportionally to hosts within the cluster. For example, in a cluster with four hosts, you could configure an NLB cluster to send 40 percent of incoming traffic to one host and split the remaining 60 percent across the other three hosts. All editions of Windows Server 2008 support NLB.

You can add and remove nodes to NLB clusters easily by using the Network Load Balancing Manager console, shown in Figure 16-3. NLB clusters reconfigure themselves automatically when you add a new node or remove a node or a node in the cluster fails. Each node in an NLB cluster sends a message to all other nodes after a second, informing them of its status. The term for this message is *heartbeat*. When a node fails to transmit five consecutive heartbeat messages, the other nodes in the cluster alter the configuration of the cluster, excluding the failed node. The term for the reconfiguration process is *convergence*. Convergence also occurs when the heartbeat of a previously absent node is again detected by other nodes in the cluster. You can take an existing node in an NLB cluster offline for maintenance and then return it to service without having to reconfigure the cluster manually because the removal and addition process occurs automatically.

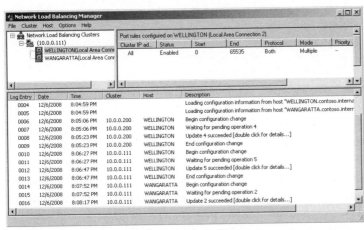

FIGURE 16-3 Network Load Balancing Manager console.

You must install the Network Load Balancing feature on each node before creating an NLB cluster in Windows Server 2008. You can load balance different editions of Windows Server 2008, and you can have x86 and x64 nodes in the same NLB cluster. Computers running Microsoft Windows Server 2003 and Windows Server 2008 can participate in the same NLB cluster. NLB detects server failure but not application failure, so clients can be directed to a node on which the application has failed. Failover clustering is the only solution that detects application failure. You create a network load balancing cluster in the practice at the end of the lesson.

Configuring NLB Cluster Operation Mode

The cluster operation mode determines how you configure the cluster's network address and how that address relates to the existing network adapter addresses. You can configure the operation mode of an NLB cluster by editing the cluster properties, as shown in Figure 16-4. All nodes within a cluster must use the same cluster operations mode. This tab also displays the virtual MAC address assigned to the cluster by using this dialog box.

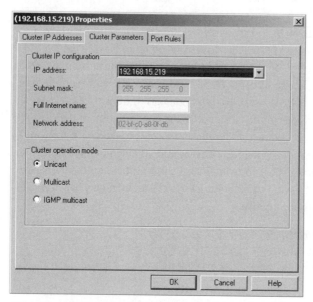

FIGURE 16-4 Unicast or multicast operation mode.

The cluster operations modes, and the differences between them, are as follows:

- **Unicast Mode** When an NLB cluster is configured to work in the unicast cluster operation mode, all nodes in the cluster use the MAC address assigned to the virtual network adapter. NLB substitutes the cluster MAC address for the physical MAC address of a network card. If your network adapter does not support this substitution, you must replace it. When nodes in a cluster have only a single network card, this limits communication between nodes but does not pose a problem for hosts outside the cluster. Unicast mode works better when each node in the NLB cluster has two network adapters. The network adapter assigned the virtual MAC address is used with the cluster; the second network adapter facilitates management and internode communication. Use two network adapters if you choose unicast mode and use one node to manage others.

- **Multicast Mode** Multicast mode is a suitable solution when each node in the cluster has a single network adapter. The cluster MAC address is a multicast address. The cluster IP address resolves to the multicast MAC address. Each node in the cluster can use its network adapter's MAC address for management and internode communication.

You can use multicast mode only if your network hardware supports multicast MAC addressing.

■ **IGMP Multicast Mode**   This version of multicast uses Internet Group Membership Protocol (IGMP) for communication, which improves network traffic because traffic for an NLB cluster passes only to those switch ports the cluster uses, not to all switch ports. The properties of IGMP multicast mode are otherwise identical to those of multicast mode.

Configuring NLB Port Rules

Port rules, shown in Figure 16-5, control, on a port-by-port basis, how network traffic is treated by an NLB cluster. By default, the cluster balances all traffic received on the cluster IP address across all nodes. You can modify this so that only specific traffic, designated by port, received on the cluster IP address is balanced. The cluster drops any traffic that does not match a port rule. You can also configure the cluster to forward traffic to a specific node rather than to all nodes, enabling the cluster to balance some traffic but not all traffic. You accomplish this by configuring the port rule's filtering mode. The options are multiple host or single host.

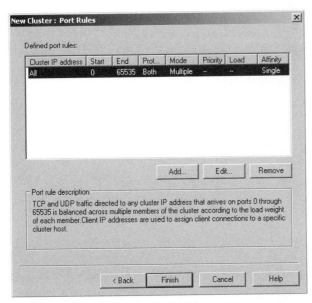

FIGURE 16-5 Cluster port rules.

For example, you might configure four hosts to be part of an NLB cluster for a Web site. One of these hosts might also function as an SMTP server. Although you want the cluster to balance incoming Web traffic, you want only one host to handle SMTP traffic. To support this configuration, you create two port rules. The first would direct Transmission Control Protocol (TCP) traffic on ports 80 and 443 to all hosts in the cluster. The second port rule would direct

SMTP traffic on port 25 to a single host, the one that has the SMTP service installed. The first port rule would use the multiple host filtering mode, and the second port rule would use the single host filtering mode.

When you configure a rule to use the multiple host filtering mode, you can also configure the rule's affinity property. The affinity property determines where the cluster will send subsequent client traffic after the initial client request. If you set the affinity property to Single, the cluster will tie all client traffic during a session to a single node. This is useful for applications such as e-commerce Web sites on which multiple client–server transactions occur over a session. The default port rule, shown in Figure 16-6, uses the Single affinity setting. When you set a rule's affinity property to None, the cluster will not bind a client session to any particular node. When you set a rule's affinity property to Network, a client session will be directed to cluster nodes located on a specific TCP/IP subnet. It is not necessary to configure the affinity for a single host rule because that rule already ties traffic to a single node in the cluster.

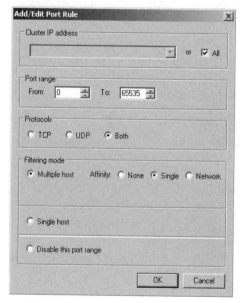

FIGURE 16-6 Default port rule.

You can edit the load placed on each node by editing port rules on each node of the cluster. Editing the load changes the load from balanced between all nodes to preferring one node or several nodes over other nodes. Do this when the hardware or one or more nodes have greater capacity than other nodes. You configure port rules in the practice at the end of this lesson.

When you need to perform maintenance on a node in an NLB cluster, you can use the Drain function to stop new connections to the node without disrupting existing connections. When all existing connections have finished, you can then take the cluster offline for maintenance. You can drain a node by right-clicking it from within Network Load Balancing Manager, clicking Control Ports, and then clicking Drain.

> **MORE INFO** **NETWORK LOAD BALANCING**
>
> To learn more about network load balancing, see the following TechNet article: *http://technet.microsoft.com/en-us/library/cc732855.aspx*.

 Quick Check

1. How many network adapters does an NLB cluster need if it is using the unicast operation mode and you want to manage the other nodes from the first node?
2. What type of records must you create in DNS to support DNS round robin when using IPv6?

Quick Check Answers

1. At least two. In unicast mode, nodes in a cluster cannot directly communicate with each other because they share a common MAC address. You can resolve this problem by adding a second network adapter to each node.
2. You must create host (AAAA) records to support IPv6 DNS round robin. Host (A) records support IPv4 DNS name mappings.

Failover Clustering

Failover clustering uses multiple servers in redundant configurations to ensure that the services they provide are highly available to clients on the network. In the unlikely event that one server fails, other servers can take on the failed server's load until you are able to return the failed server to operational status. Only Windows Server 2008 Itanium, Enterprise, and Datacenter support failover clustering. Windows Server 2008 Enterprise and Datacenter support up to 16 nodes in a failover cluster. Windows Server 2008 Itanium supports a maximum of eight nodes in a failover cluster.

Clusters run two general types of applications, single-instance applications and multiple instance applications. A single-instance application executes on one server at a time. When you deploy a single-instance application in a high availability configuration, you configure the single-instance application to function normally on one node and in standby mode on other cluster nodes. Multiple-instance applications run on multiple nodes in a cluster concurrently and share or partition data so that any node in the cluster can respond to a client query for that data. Microsoft SQL Server 2008 and Exchange Server 2007 are examples of multiple-instance applications.

Not all applications support deployment; check with your software vendor about whether clustering is supported. In general, an application that runs on a cluster requires the following properties.

- Client software must attempt to re-establish connectivity automatically when failure occurs. If client software times out, the application is not suited for failover clusters.

- The cluster application uses an IP-based protocol.

- It must be possible, on applications that require access to local databases, to configure where data can be stored. Data should be stored on a shared disk resource that will fail over with the Services and Applications group. The Services and Applications group is configured through the Failover Cluster Management tool.

All nodes within a Windows Server 2008 cluster must use the same processor architecture and should be members of the same Active Directory domain. You cannot mix Windows Server 2008 x64 nodes with x86 32-bit nodes, and you cannot create failover clusters using standalone servers. Microsoft recommends all nodes in a failover cluster to have the same hardware and software configuration.

Windows Server 2008 supports Fibre Channel, Internet Small Computer System Interface (iSCSI), serially attached SCSI (SAS), and shared storage. Windows Server 2008 clustering does not support direct SCSI connections to shared storage. You learn more about using Windows Server 2008 with Fibre Channel and iSCSI in Lesson 2, "Configuring Windows Server 2008 Storage."

Creating a Failover Cluster

The first step in creating a cluster involves installing the Failover Clustering feature on each computer running Windows Server 2008 that will be a node in the cluster. Installing this feature adds the Failover Cluster Management console to the Administrative Tools menu.

Prior to creating a cluster, run the Validate A Configuration Wizard, shown in Figure 16-7. The wizard will run the following tests on each prospective node in the cluster:

- **System Configuration Test**   Verifies that system settings are compatible with clustering

- **Network Test**   Ensures that network settings are compatible with clustering

- **Storage Test**   Checks that storage is compatible with clustering

- **Inventory Test**   Creates an inventory of all node settings and components

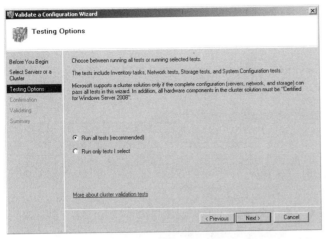

FIGURE 16-7 Validate A Configuration Wizard.

The validation wizard creates a report identifying any problems that need to be resolved prior to deploying a cluster. After you have resolved these problems, create a cluster from the Failover Cluster Management console by performing the following steps.

1. From the Action menu, select Create A Cluster.

   This launches the Create A Cluster Wizard.

2. Click Next on the Welcome page after reviewing the available information.

3. Enter the names of the servers you want to add to the cluster on the Select Servers page, shown in Figure 16-8, and then click Next.

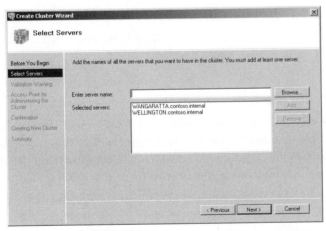

FIGURE 16-8 Add servers to cluster.

4. On the Validation Warning page, choose whether to run configuration validation tests. These are the same tests carried out when you run the Validate A Configuration Wizard.

5. On the Access Point for Administering The Cluster page, shown in Figure 16-9, enter a name for the cluster and an IP address the cluster will use, and then click Next.

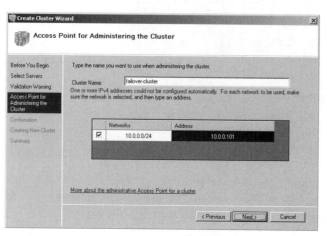

FIGURE 16-9 Access point for cluster.

6. The confirmation page will display a list of the settings you configure. When you click Next, the cluster will be created. Clicking Finish on the summary page will dismiss the Create Cluster Wizard.

> **MORE INFO   CREATING FAILOVER CLUSTERS**
>
> To learn more about creating failover clusters, see the following document on TechNet: *http://technet.microsoft.com/en-us/library/dd197584.aspx.*

Failover Cluster Quorum Models

A cluster quorum is the number of nodes in the cluster that must be active for the cluster to remain online. Different cluster quorum models have different benchmarks for when a cluster remains online, although the cluster quorum model you select also depends on the hardware you have available. There are four cluster quorum models, as follows:

- **Node Majority**   Each node's system disk stores the cluster configuration, and each node gets a vote. The cluster remains operational when half the nodes (rounded down) plus one remain operational. For example, in a nine-node cluster, five nodes must be available for the cluster to remain online. Use this cluster quorum mode when the cluster has an odd number of nodes and the minimum number of nodes where failure can occur and the cluster can remain operational is three. You can use this model when an application can run and store data only on the local system or boot drive, although you must have a separate mechanism for replicating data between cluster nodes.

- **Node and Disk Majority**   In this model, each node and a shared storage physical disk, known as the disk witness, can participate in the quorum. The shared storage physical disk essentially acts as an additional node without the cost of deploying another server. The cluster configuration is stored on each node's system disk and on the disk witness. The cluster remains operational as long as half the disks, rounded down, plus one, remain available. You can use this quorum model with a two-node cluster, and Microsoft recommends that you use it in clusters with even numbers of nodes.

- **Node and File Share Majority**   Node and File Share Majority is superficially similar to Node and Disk Majority except that rather than having a shared storage physical disk as a witness, a file share functions as a witness. The other difference is that the configuration is not stored on the file share, but the file share does keep track of which node has the most up-to-date copy of the configuration replica. Microsoft recommends Node and Disk Majority over Node and File Share Majority because failure of nodes that have an updated configuration, leaving only nodes with older configuration data, can stop the cluster from staying online even if enough nodes are present for quorum. For example, if you have a two-node cluster and the second node is switched off, the configuration on the first node is updated and the file share witness registers this update. If the first node is then switched off and the second node brought online, the file share witness will block the second node from forming the cluster because it will have registered the first node as having the only up-to-date version of the cluster configuration. This node is cheap to implement because it does not require a shared storage device or extra node. It works best when clusters have even numbers of nodes or are geographically dispersed, but it is not preferable to using the Node and Disk Majority model.

- **No Majority: Disk Only**   The No Majority: Disk Only quorum model keeps the most up-to-date version of the cluster configuration on the shared disk. Although copies of the cluster configuration are stored on each node, which allows the copy on the shared disk to be repaired if it is lost or corrupted, the shared disk itself presents a single point of failure. If the shared disk fails, the cluster fails. As long as one node and the shared disk remain operable, the cluster will remain online. Microsoft does not recommend the use of this cluster quorum model because the shared disk presents a single point of failure.

MORE INFO   **QUORUM MODES**

To learn more about failover cluster quorum modes, see the following document on TechNet: *http://technet.microsoft.com/en-us/library/cc770830.aspx.*

EXAM TIP

Try to remember the quorum modes and the clustering situations to which they are most appropriate.

Managing Failover Clusters

You can manage a failover cluster by using the Failover Cluster Management console. By right-clicking the *Services and Applications* node, you can start the High Availability Wizard, shown in Figure 16-10, to configure services or applications to run on the cluster. After configuration, this ensures that services and applications fail over to another node when there is a fault. To complete the wizard, specify a name and an IP address for that service and configure storage.

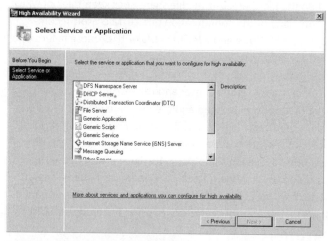

FIGURE 16-10 High Availability Wizard.

You can test the failover cluster by selecting a highly available service or application, listed under the *Services and Applications* node, and then clicking Move This Service Or Application To Another Node, as shown in Figure 16-11. If the service or application moves successfully, the cluster is functioning properly. Use this process to move services and applications from the active node if you need to take that node offline to perform maintenance. Transferring applications and services gracefully using the console is a lot better than just shutting down the server and waiting for failover to occur.

When you select an individual cluster node by using the Failover Cluster Management console, you can pause, resume, stop, and start the cluster service and evict the node from the cluster, using the Actions pane.

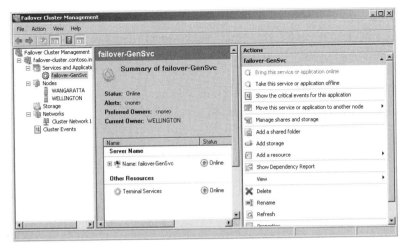

FIGURE 16-11 Moving a service or application.

You can back up a cluster only while it is active and within quorum. When backing up shared storage, you can back up only disks that are currently online for that node. Back up disks that other nodes have control of from those nodes. Similarly, you can restore data only to disks that are currently online for a node. If a disk was online when you backed it up, but another node now controls it, you must return control to the original node before performing a restoration. An authoritative cluster restore occurs when you restore a node, but choose the configuration stored with that node as authoritative over the configuration that might be stored on other nodes, the witness disk, or the file share. A nonauthoritative cluster restore occurs when you restore a node but let the current cluster configuration overwrite the one you restored from backup.

> *MORE INFO* **MANAGING AND BACKING UP CLUSTERS**
>
> To learn more about managing failover clusters, backing them up, and restoring them, see the following document on TechNet: *http://technet.microsoft.com/en-us/library /cc731618.aspx.*

PRACTICE Configuring Network Load Balancing

In this practice, you perform tasks similar to those you would perform when configuring a Windows Server 2008 NLB cluster. The first exercise configures network load balancing using multicast for cluster communication; the second exercise configures network load balancing port rules.

EXERCISE 1 Create an NLB Cluster

In this exercise, you configure two servers, Wellington and Wangaratta, as a network load balancing cluster. The instructions for setting up these servers are included in the "Before You Begin" section at the beginning of this chapter.

1. Log on to server Wellington with the Kim_Akers user account.

2. Use the Server Manager console to add the Network Load Balancing feature to the server.

3. Repeat steps 1 and 2 on server Wangaratta. Log off server Wangaratta when the Network Load Balancing feature is installed.

4. On server Wellington, open the Network Load Balancing Manager console from the Administrative Tools menu.

5. From the Cluster menu, select New.

   This opens the New Cluster: Connect dialog box.

6. In the Host textbox, type **10.0.0.25**, and then click Connect. Verify that the dialog box matches Figure 16-12, and then click Next.

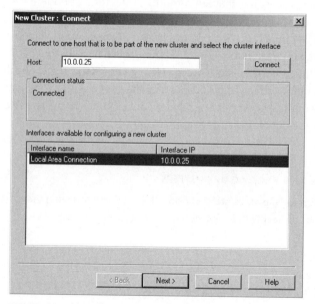

FIGURE 16-12 New Cluster: Connect dialog box.

7. On the New Cluster: Host Parameters page, ensure that Priority (Unique Host Identifier) is set to 1, and then click Next.

8. On the New Cluster: Cluster IP Addresses page, click Add. Enter the IP address and subnet mask information shown in Figure 16-13, and then click OK. Click Next.

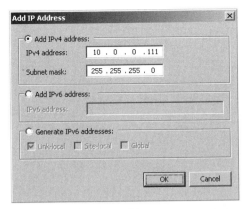

FIGURE 16-13 Cluster IP address.

9. On the New Cluster: Cluster Parameters page, set Cluster Operations Mode to Multicast, and then click Next.

10. On the New Cluster: Port Rules page, click Finish. Wait for the *Wellington* node of the cluster to reach the convergence state.

The node displays in green and the status is set to Enabled, as shown in Figure 16-14.

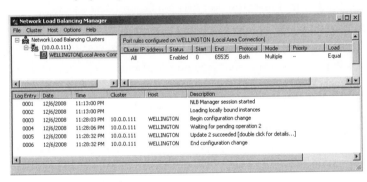

FIGURE 16-14 Single node convergence.

11. After the cluster has converged, right-click the 10.0.0.111 node, and then click Add Host To Cluster.

12. In the Add Host to Cluster: Connect dialog box, enter **10.0.0.35** and click Connect. When the IP 10.0.0.35 interface is listed in the Interfaces Available For Configuring The Cluster area, click Next twice, and then click Finish.

13. After a few moments, when the status of Wangaratta changes from Pending to Converged, as shown in Figure 16-15, close the Network Load Balancing Manager console.

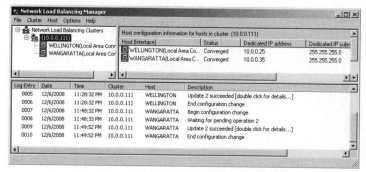

FIGURE 16-15 Dual node convergence.

EXERCISE 2   Configure NLB Port Rules

In this exercise, you alter the default port rule applied to the NLB cluster you created in the first exercise. You then create two new port rules, one to load balance a Web server and one for an SMTP service on the Wangaratta server.

1. Log on to server Wellington, using the Kim_Akers user account.

2. From the Administrative Tools menu, open the Network Load Balancing Manager console. Click Continue to dismiss the User Account Control dialog box.

3. Click OK when prompted by the warning. Right-click the 10.0.0.111 node, and then select Cluster Properties. In the Cluster Properties dialog box, click the Port Rules tab.

4. Select the default port rule (which applies to both TCP and UDP ports between 0 and 65535), and then click Remove.

5. Click Add.

   This opens the Add/Edit Port Rule dialog box.

6. Set the port range from 80 to 80, verify that the settings on the dialog box match those in Figure 16-16, and then click OK.

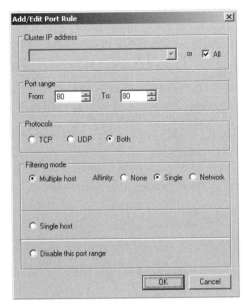

FIGURE 16-16 Create port 80 rule.

7. Click Add. Using the procedure from step 6, create a rule for port 443.

8. Click Add. Create a rule for port 25. Set the Filtering Mode to Single Host rather than Multiple Host, and then click OK twice.

9. After the cluster has converged, right-click Wellington, and then click Host Properties. Click the Port Rules tab, select the rule for Port 25, click Edit, and then change the Handling Priority setting to 3. Click OK twice.

10. After the cluster has converged, right-click Wangaratta, and then click Host Properties. Click the Port Rules tab, select the rule for Port 25, click Edit, and then change the Handling Priority setting to 1. Click OK twice.

11. After the cluster has converged, close the Network Load Balancing Manager console.

Lesson Summary

- DNS round robin provides a basic high availability solution by balancing requests across servers, but it is not failure aware.
- Network load balancing reconfigures itself if a failure occurs, but it is not a suitable high availability solution for all applications.
- Failover clustering provides high availability by allowing one node in the cluster to take on the duties of another node if that first node fails.
- The node majority cluster quorum model is suitable for an odd number of nodes and does not require shared storage. Node and disk majority requires shared storage and is suitable for clusters with even numbers of nodes.

Lesson Review

You can use the following questions to test your knowledge of the information in Lesson 1, "Configuring High Availability." The questions are also available on the companion DVD if you prefer to review them in electronic form.

> **NOTE ANSWERS**
>
> Answers to these questions and explanations of why each answer choice is right or wrong are located in the "Answers" section at the end of the book.

1. Which of the following quorum models does not require a file share witness or disk witness?

    A. Node Majority

    B. Node and Disk Majority

    C. Node and File Share Majority

    D. No majority: Disk Only

2. You have a seven-node Windows Server 2008 cluster that uses the Node Majority quorum model. What is the maximum number of node failures this cluster can tolerate while remaining operable?

    A. One

    B. Two

    C. Three

    D. Four

3. Which of the following cannot be used as a shared storage device for a Windows Server 2008 failover cluster?

    A. Serially attached SCSI (SAS)

    B. i-SCSI

    C. Fibre Channel

    D. USB 2.0 external hard disk drive

4. Your organization's public Web server is experiencing heavy load. You have configured two more identical Web servers and want to deploy them so that clients that interact with the public Web server experience better performance. The Web site is hosted locally on each computer, and a shared storage device is not used. If a Web server fails, you want to ensure that clients will be directed to the two other Web servers automatically. If necessary, you should be able to add more nodes in the future. Which of the following high availability strategies should you pursue?

A. Configure DNS round robin.

B. Configure a network load balancing cluster.

C. Configure a failover cluster that uses the Node and Disk Majority quorum model.

D. Configure a failover cluster that uses the No Majority: Disk Only quorum model.

5. You have a computer running Windows Web Server 2008 that is experiencing heavy load. The name of this computer is Alpha. You have two computers with the same software configuration and hardware. The names of these computers are Beta and Gamma. You want to distribute the load between these computers equitably. Each computer has a single network adapter. If one Web server fails, clients should be redirected automatically to another. You want to manage all three computers from Alpha. Which of the following should you do?

A. Configure DNS round robin. Use multicast mode.

B. Configure DNS round robin. Use unicast mode.

C. Configure network load balancing (NLB). Use multicast mode.

D. Configure network load balancing. Use unicast mode.

Lesson 2: Configuring Windows Server 2008 Storage

Data is the most important asset stored within your organization's IT infrastructure. Servers and software can be purchased and replaced if they are lost or destroyed, but data, if not stored correctly and backed up, is, if not always irreplaceable, often far more challenging to replace. SANs simplify the process of storing and accessing data in large network environments. SANs enable data storage to be centralized and simplify the process of provisioning more storage. Rather than haphazardly adding extra hard disk drive servers across your organization, you can add storage centrally to the SAN, which you can then distribute as needed across your organization.

> **After this lesson, you will be able to:**
> - Configure RAID.
> - Manage network attached storage.
> - Set up iSCSI and Fibre Channel.
>
> **Estimated lesson time: 40 minutes**

RAID

RAID uses multiple disks to provide performance and redundancy benefits to servers. Although disks do not have to be the same size, a RAID set uses the size of the smallest disk in the set as the basis for generating the RAID volume. For example, if you implement RAID 5 with a 30 GB, 40 GB, and 50 GB disk, the computer will use only 30 GB of the 40 GB and 50 GB disks when constructing the RAID 5 set. For this reason, it is better to use disks of identical sizes when constructing RAID sets.

Windows Server 2008 supports software RAID 0, RAID 1, and RAID 5, as shown in Figure 16-17. Windows Server 2008 also supports spanned volumes, which span multiple disks but do not provide any performance or redundancy benefit. When using software RAID, the operating system itself manages the disks and does not require any special hardware beyond the disk drives. Most administrators will be more familiar with hardware RAID solutions in which special hardware devices manage the disk drive arrays. Hardware RAID arrays offer more choices in the types of RAID that you can deploy. Hardware RAID is often faster than software RAID and is transparent from the operating system. For example, if you implement hardware RAID 10 and boot into Windows Server 2008, a single volume will be visible rather than a collection of disks that you must bind together into a RAID array.

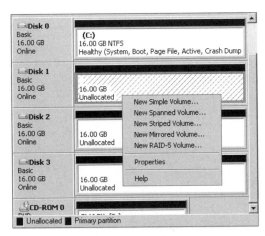

FIGURE 16-17 Windows RAID options.

- **RAID 0**   RAID 0 combines two or more disks into a larger volume. The benefit is that having multiple disks increases read and write speeds in a process known as disk striping. The drawback is that the failure of one disk in the set means that all data on the volume is lost. RAID 0 has no redundancy and requires a minimum of two disks.

- **RAID 1**   RAID 1 uses one disk to mirror another. If one disk fails, its mirror can be used as a replacement. RAID 1 provides no performance enhancement because data is not striped across disks but is instead written twice. RAID 1 is often used to provide redundancy to the drive that hosts the operating system.

- **RAID 5**   RAID 5 provides the performance benefit of disk striping but also includes parity information, allowing one disk in the set to fail while retaining data integrity. RAID 5 requires a minimum of three disks. The equivalent of one disk in a RAID 5 set is consumed with parity data.

- **RAID 10**   RAID 10 combines RAID 1, disk mirroring, with RAID 0, disk striping. This creates a large and fast fault-tolerant array of disks. RAID 10 requires a minimum of four disks, two disks that are striped in RAID 0 and the mirrors for those disks. RAID 10 is commonly used in enterprise environments and is supported by only hardware RAID.

You create a RAID 1 array and a RAID 5 array, using the Disk Management console, at the end of this lesson.

Managing LUNs with Storage Manager for SANs

A logical unit number (LUN) is a way of labeling a segment of a SAN storage subsystem. LUNs are superficially similar to volumes in that they can refer to part of a disk, an entire disk, or an array of disks. Access and control can be managed on a per-LUN basis. LUNs come in varieties that are similar to what is available in Windows Server 2008 disk options. Just as you can have simple, spanned, striped, mirrored, and striped with parity (RAID 5) volumes, you can have simple, spanned, striped, mirrored, and striped with parity LUNs.

Storage Manager for SANs, shown in Figure 16-18, enables you to manage Fibre Channel and iSCSI SANs. This console becomes available when you install the Storage Manager for SANs feature.

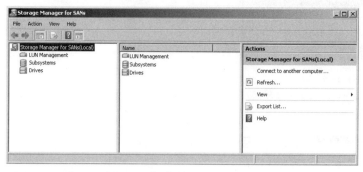

FIGURE 16-18 Storage Manager for SANs.

You can use Storage Manager for SANS to:

- View the properties of Fibre Channel and iSCSI storage subsystems.

- Create new LUNs, extend LUNs, and delete LUNs.

- Assign LUNs to SAN clients such as servers and clusters.

- Manage which host bus adaptor (HBA) ports, used by Fibre Channel, or iSCSI initiator adapters have access to LUNs.

- Manage iSCSI security settings through configuring the properties of iSCSI targets.

- Monitor LUN status and health.

You can extend an existing LUN if the storage subsystem that hosts the LUN has available storage space. You can extend the LUN by using Storage Manager for SANs; however, doing this does not extend the file system partition. To extend the file system partition on a LUN that you have extended, use a tool such as the Disk Management console.

Deleting a LUN is irreversible and, when you delete a LUN, you remove all data on all volumes associated with the LUN. You must shut down all applications that access a LUN prior to attempting deletion. You can delete a LUN by right-clicking it under the *LUN Management* node in Storage Manager for SANs and then clicking Delete LUN. If you simply want to remove a LUN from a server or cluster but retain the data it hosts, you can use the Unassign LUN function rather than deleting the LUN entirely. This enables you to reconnect the LUN later to another server.

Storage Manager for SANs can manage only disk drive storage subsystems that support the Virtual Disk Service (VDS) 1.1 specification. VDS is a set of application programming interfaces (APIs) that provide an interface through which you can manage storage subsystems. You must install the VDS hardware provider on the computer running Windows Server 2008 before you can manage LUNs, using Storage Manager for SANs. VDS providers are available from iSCSI and Fibre Channel subsystem vendors. You can use the *diskraid* command to determine which VDS providers are installed on a computer running Windows Server 2008.

MORE INFO   **STORAGE MANAGER FOR SANS**

To learn more about Storage Manager for SANs, see the following TechNet Web site: *http://technet.microsoft.com/en-us/library/cc755230.aspx.*

 Quick Check

1. How many 2 TB disks are required for a RAID 5 set if the array can store 10 TB of data?

2. How many 2 TB disks are required for a RAID 10 set if the array can store 10 TB of data?

Quick Check Answers

1. Six disks: five disks to store 10 TB of data and one disk to store parity information

2. Ten disks: five disks to store 10 TB of data in RAID 0 configuration and five disks to mirror those disks

Fibre Channel

Fibre Channel provides high-performance block I/O to storage devices located on the SAN. Based on serial SCSI, Fibre Channel is a widely deployed SAN technology. Fibre Channel devices differ from traditional parallel SCSI devices in that they do not need to contend for a shared bus. Fibre Channel uses specialized switches to relay data between servers and storage devices. Servers access Fibre Channel LUNs through HBA ports. You can use Storage Manager for SANs to specify which HBA ports will be used for LUN traffic, adding ports manually by World Wide Name (WWN). LUNs created on a Fibre Channel disk storage subsystem are assigned directly to a cluster or server. The drawback to Fibre Channel is that it requires specialized server HBAs, cabling, and switches. Hardware is specialized and often one vendor's Fibre Channel products do not fully interoperate with another.

iSCSI

Internet Small Computer System Interface (iSCSI) is a SAN protocol that uses TCP/IP to transmit SCSI commands from clients (called iSCSI initiators) to SCSI-based storage devices. Unlike Fibre Channel, by which LUNS are assigned to specific servers or clusters, iSCSI LUNs are assigned to iSCSI targets. An iSCSI target manages the connections between the iSCSI hardware and the servers that access it. iSCSI has an advantage over Fibre Channel in that it does not require specialized hardware such as cables or switches. There are even third-party products that enable you to convert a computer running a Windows-based operating system into a standalone iSCSI storage device.

The iSCSI protocol enables SAN connectivity over longer distances than Fibre Channel does, enabling you to connect hosts to SAN resources over wide area network (WAN) links. It is also possible to implement CHAP authentication and IPsec for encryption with iSCSI, something not possible with Fibre Channel. The drawback of iSCSI is the cost of deploying a 10-GB switch and cabling infrastructure, although this will lessen as local area network (LAN) speeds continue to develop in the future.

You can use the iSCSI initiator, also found within the administrative tools menu, to connect a computer running Windows Server 2008 to an existing iSCSI target. The iSCSI initiator does not modify the properties of the iSCSI fabric or LUNs but does connect to existing resources located on the iSCSI target. To use the iSCSI initiator to connect to an iSCSI target, perform these steps:

1. Open the iSCSI initiator from the Administrative tools menu.

   If you have not previously run the iSCSI initiator, you are prompted to configure the iSCSI service to start automatically and create a firewall exception to allow the service to communicate with an Internet Storage Name Service (iSNS) server through Windows Firewall.

2. On the Discovery tab of the iSCSI Initiator Properties dialog box, click Add Portal and enter the IP address or hostname of the iSCSI target.

3. On the Targets tab, click Refresh. The iSCSI target should now be visible. Click Log On to connect to the target.

   This brings up the Log On To Target dialog box. You can configure the iSCSI Initiator to restore the connection automatically each time the computer boots.

4. Click the Details button to open the Target Properties dialog box. On the Devices tab, shown in Figure 16-19, you can view the details of devices available on the iSCSI target.

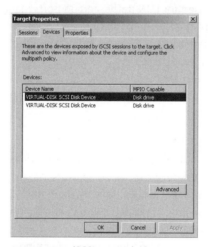

FIGURE 16-19 iSCSI target devices.

Managing Fabrics with Storage Explorer

Fabric is a term for a network topology in which one or more data paths connect storage devices. ISCSI fabrics include multiple iSNS servers. Fibre Channel fabrics include multiple Fibre Channel switches that connect servers and storage devices, using virtual point-to-point connections. The Storage Explorer console, available through the Administrative tools menu and shown in Figure 16-20, enables you to view and manage both iSCSI and Fibre Channel fabrics.

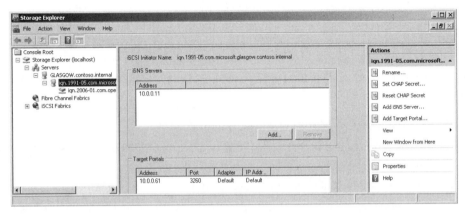

FIGURE 16-20 Storage Explorer.

Most of the iSCSI-specific management tasks you can accomplish using Storage Explorer can also be accomplished using the iSCSI initiator tool. You can use the Storage Explorer console to display information about servers connected to the SAN and inventory information about fabric components such as HBAs, Fibre Channel switches, iSCSI initiators, and iSCSI targets. You can also configure iSCSI security, add iSNS servers, and configure iSCSI target portals by using this tool.

> **MORE INFO** **STORAGE EXPLORER**
>
> To learn more about Storage Explorer, see *http://technet.microsoft.com/en-us/library/cc731884.aspx.*

> ## Configuring SAN Policies with *Diskpart*
>
> You can use the *Diskpart* command-line utility in the SAN context to configure the SAN policy for a computer running Windows Server 2008. The default policy is OfflineShared, which keeps the shared bus SAN disk offline disks and read-only but brings the boot and nonshared disks online. The OnlineAll policy brings all SAN disks online and makes them read/write. The OfflineAll policy keeps all disks, except the boot disk, offline and read-only.

EXAM TIP

Remember which tasks you can accomplish by using Storage Manager for SANs.

PRACTICE Configure Redundant Disks

In this practice, you perform tasks similar to those you would perform when configuring a Windows Server 2008 server for storage redundancy. The first exercise configures a mirror of the system volume; the second exercise configures a software RAID-5 array for data storage. The first exercise in this practice requires you to have two separate disks installed on your server. The second exercise requires three additional disks to be present besides the one that hosts the operating system.

EXERCISE 1 Configure Disk Mirroring on the System Volume

In this exercise, you protect the disk that hosts the Windows Server 2008 operating system by configuring it as a mirrored volume.

1. Log on to the server with the Kim_Akers user account.

2. If the Server Manager console does not open automatically, open it from the Administrative Tools menu.

3. Expand the *Storage* node and select Disk Management.

   This displays a list of disks connected to the server as shown in Figure 16-21.

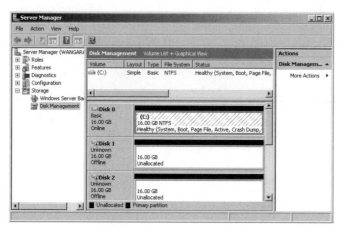

FIGURE 16-21 Disk Management.

4. Right-click Disk 1, and then select Online.

   This brings the disk online.

5. Right-click Disk 0, and then select Add Mirror. In the Add Mirror dialog box, select Disk 1, and then select Add Mirror.

6. Review the warning about the conversion of the selected disk from basic to dynamic, and then click Yes.

7. After the new mirror synchronizes, confirm that it has the status shown in Figure 16-22, and then proceed to Exercise 2.

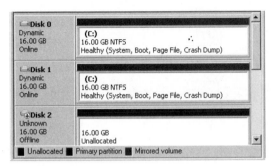

FIGURE 16-22 Mirrored disks.

EXERCISE 2   Configure Software RAID 5

In this exercise, you create a volume hosted on a RAID-5 set. RAID 5 is useful for storing data because it provides redundancy and performance benefits. You need three available disks to complete this exercise. If you have only two spare disks, you could break the mirror that you created in Exercise 1 to free up a spare disk for this exercise.

1. If you are not already connected, log on to the server, using the Kim_Akers user account; open the Server Manager console and select the *Disk Management* node under the *Storage* node.

2. Right-click each disk marked as Unknown and select Online.

3. Right-click the unallocated space area on the first Unknown disk, and then select New RAID-5 volume.

   This starts the New RAID-5 Volume Wizard.

4. Click Next.

5. On the Select Disks page, add all available disks, as shown in Figure 16-23, and then click Next.

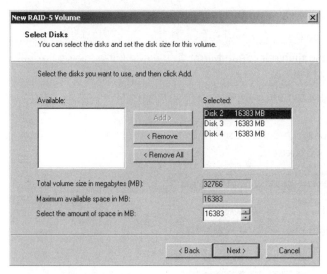

FIGURE 16-23 Add available disks.

6. On the Assign Drive Letter Or Path page, accept the default drive letter assignment, and then click Next.

7. On the Format Volume page, set the volume label to RAID-5, select the Perform A Quick Format check box, and then click Next. Click Finish to dismiss the New RAID-5 Volume Wizard.

8. Review the warning about the conversion of disks from basic to dynamic and click Yes.

9. After the disks have synchronized and formatted, verify that they appear in a manner similar to that shown in Figure 16-24.

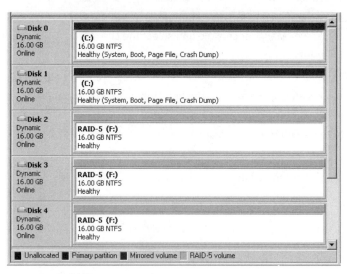

FIGURE 16-24 RAID array created.

Lesson Summary

- RAID 0 (disk striping without parity) requires a minimum of two disks, and all data is lost if a disk in the set fails. It provides better performance than a simple volume.

- RAID 1 (disk mirroring) uses two disks and provides no performance improvement, but no data is lost if one disk fails.

- RAID 5 (disk striping with parity), which requires a minimum of three disks, provides better performance than a simple volume, and data is not lost if one disk in the set fails.

- A logical unit number (LUN) is a logical reference to a portion of a storage subsystem. A LUN can represent a disk, a section of a disk, an entire disk array, or a section of a disk array in the storage subsystem.

- Servers and clusters connect to Fibre Channel arrays using host bus adapter (HBA) ports. Servers and clusters use iSCSI initiators to connect to iSCSI targets, which manage iSCSI arrays.

- Storage Manager for SANs creates and manages LUNs on iSCSI and Fibre Channel devices. Storage Explorer manages iSCSI and Fibre Channel fabrics.

Lesson Review

You can use the following questions to test your knowledge of the information in Lesson 2, "Configuring Windows Server 2008 Storage." The questions are also available on the companion DVD if you prefer to review them in electronic form.

> **NOTE** ANSWERS
>
> Answers to these questions and explanations of why each answer choice is right or wrong are located in the "Answers" section at the end of the book.

1. What is the minimum number of disks required to support software RAID-5 on a computer running Windows Server 2008?

    A. One

    B. Two

    C. Three

    D. Four

2. Which of the following tools can you use to manage the iSCSI fabric in your organization's storage area network?

    A. Storage Manager for SANs

    B. Device Manager

    C. Disk Management

    D. Storage Explorer

3. What is the minimum number of 5 TB disks required to create a RAID-5 volume that is 20 TB in size?

   A. Four

   B. Five

   C. Six

   D. Seven

4. You want to remove a LUN from a Windows Server 2008 server cluster but do not want to remove all data currently hosted on the LUN. Which of the following should you do?

   A. Create a new LUN.

   B. Extend the LUN.

   C. Delete the LUN.

   D. Unassign the LUN.

5. Which of the following tools can you use to unassign a LUN?

   A. Storage Manager for SANs

   B. Storage Explorer

   C. iSCSI Initiator

   D. Disk Management

Chapter Review

To further practice and reinforce the skills you learned in this chapter, you can perform the following tasks:

- Review the chapter summary.
- Complete the case scenarios. These scenarios set up real-world situations involving the topics of this chapter and ask you to create solutions.
- Complete the suggested practices.
- Take a practice test.

Chapter Summary

- High availability solutions that you can implement with Windows Server 2008 include DNS round robin, network load balancing, and failover clustering.
- Windows Server 2008 enables you to use software RAID 0, RAID 1, and RAID 5 on a server with the appropriate number of disks.
- Windows Server 2008 can use Fibre Channel or iSCSI SANs.

Case Scenarios

In the following case scenarios, you apply what you've learned about high availability and storage. You can find answers to these questions in the "Answers" section at the end of this book.

Case Scenario 1: Contoso, Ltd., Cluster Configuration

You are the senior systems administrator at Contoso, Ltd., a company with offices spread throughout Denmark and Sweden. You are planning the deployment of several clusters that will be used to ensure that important network applications remain available in the event of server failure. These clusters will be deployed in the Copenhagen, Billund, and Stockholm offices. The cluster that you intend to deploy in the Copenhagen office will consist of four servers and a shared storage device. The cluster that you intend to deploy in the Billund office consists of three servers only. Both the Copenhagen and Billund clusters will host multiple-instance applications. The Stockholm office has an existing Web server that you want to provide high availability to by adding a second Web server. With this information in mind, answer the following questions.

1. Which cluster quorum model should you choose to deploy in the Copenhagen office?
2. Which cluster quorum model should you choose to deploy in the Billund office?
3. What type of high availability solution should you deploy in Stockholm?

Case Scenario 2: Selecting LUNs Types

You have purchased several iSCSI devices that you will use to provide shared storage for several Windows Server 2008 deployments. You are planning the configuration of LUNs based on the shared storage needs of each server. The first server cluster will be hosting a SQL Server 2008 database, and it will be necessary to ensure that the LUN chosen supports both speed and redundancy. The second LUN will be used for the shared storage device that will function as the witness disk in an Exchange Server cluster that uses the Node and Disk Majority quorum model. This witness disk should be able to survive the loss of one of the disks hosting the LUN. The final LUN will host transaction logs where read/write performance is paramount. With this information, answer the following questions.

1. Which LUN type should you use for the database server cluster?

2. Which LUN type should you configure for the shared storage device that will host the transaction log data?

3. Which LUN type should you configure for the Exchange Server cluster's witness disk?

Suggested Practices

To help you successfully master the exam objectives presented in this chapter, complete the following tasks.

Configure High Availability

To get a thorough understanding of configuring high availability on Windows Server 2008, complete both practices in this section.

- **Practice 1**   Create a Windows Server 2008 cluster by using the Node Majority quorum model. Create this cluster, using the two servers, Wangaratta and Wellington, that you used for the practice at the end of Lesson 1, even though a minimum of three servers is recommended for this model. You will need to remove the network load balancing cluster prior to creating the failover cluster.

- **Practice 2**   After removing the cluster you created in the first practice, create a Windows Server 2008 cluster, using the Node and File Share Majority quorum model. Create a file share on server Glasgow to function as the file share witness for this failover cluster.

Configure Storage

To get a thorough understanding of configuring storage on Windows Server 2008, complete this practice.

- **Practice** Connect a Windows Server 2008 server to an iSCSI shared storage device. Although you might not have access to iSCSI hardware, several software-based iSCSI solutions that can run on virtual machines are available for free or on a trial basis from vendors on the Internet.

Take a Practice Test

The practice tests on this book's companion DVD offer many options. For example, you can test yourself on just one exam objective, or you can test yourself on all the upgrade exam content. You can set up the test so that it closely simulates the experience of taking a certification exam, or you can set it up in study mode so that you can look at the correct answers and explanations after you answer each question.

> **MORE INFO   PRACTICE TESTS**
>
> For details about all the practice test options available, see the "How to Use the Practice Tests" section in this book's Introduction.

Answers

Chapter 1: Lesson Review Answers

Lesson 1

1. Correct Answer: B

   A. **Incorrect:** A site-local unicast IPv6 address identifies a node in a site or intranet. It is the equivalent of an IPv6 private address, for example, 10.0.0.1.

   B. **Correct:** A global unicast address (or aggregatable global unicast address) is the IPv6 equivalent of an IPv4 public unicast address and is globally routable and reachable on the IPv6 portion of the Internet.

   C. **Incorrect:** A link-local unicast IPv6 address is autoconfigured on a local subnet. It is the equivalent of an IPv4 APIPA address, for example, 169.254.10.123.

   D. **Incorrect:** Two special IPv6 addresses exist. The :: unspecified address indicates the absence of an address and is equivalent to the IPv4 0.0.0.0 unspecified address. The ::1 loopback address identifies a loopback interface and is equivalent to the 127.0.0.1 IPv4 loopback address. Neither is the IPv6 equivalent of an IPv4 public unicast address.

2. Correct Answer: A

   A. **Correct:** The solicited node address consists of the ff02::1:ff (written ff02::1:ff00:0/104) 104-bit prefix followed by the last 24 bits of the link-local address, in this case, a7:d43a.

   B. **Incorrect:** Although the 104-bit prefix is written ff02::1:ff00:0/104, the /104 indicates that only the first 104 bits (ff02::1:ff) are used. Hence, the solicited mode address is ff02::1:ffa7:d43a.

   C. **Incorrect:** Addresses that start with fec0 are site-local, not solicited node.

   D. **Incorrect:** Addresses that start with fec0 are site-local, not solicited node.

3. Correct Answer: D

   A. **Incorrect:** ARP is a broadcast-based protocol used by IPv4 to resolve MAC addresses to IPv4 addresses. ND uses ICMPv6 messages to manage the interaction of neighboring nodes.

   B. **Incorrect:** EUI-64 is not a protocol. It is a standard for 64-bit hardware addresses.

   C. **Incorrect:** DHCPv6 assigns stateful IPv6 configurations. ND uses ICMPv6 messages to manage the interaction of neighboring nodes.

   D. **Correct:** ND uses ICMPv6 messages to manage the interaction of neighboring nodes.

4. Correct Answer: A

   A. **Correct:** A Teredo address consists of a 32-bit Teredo prefix. In Windows Server 2008 (and Windows Vista), this is 2001::/32. The prefix is followed by the IPv4 (32-bit) public address of the Teredo server that assisted in the configuration of the address. The next 16 bits are reserved for Teredo flags. The next 16 bits store an obscured version of the external UDP port that corresponds to all Teredo traffic for the Teredo client interface. The final 32 bits store an obscured version of the external IPv4 address that corresponds to all Teredo traffic for the Teredo client interface. The external address is obscured by XORing it with 0xffffffff.

   B. **Incorrect:** An ISATAP address starts with a 64-bit unicast link-local, site-local, global, or 6to4 global prefix. The next 32 bits are the 0:5efe ISATAP identifier. The final 32 bits hold the IPv4 address in either dotted decimal or hexadecimal notation. The IPv4 address is not obscured.

   C. **Incorrect:** The 0:0:0:0:0:0:w.x.y.z (or ::w.x.y.z) IPV4-compatible address is used by dual stack nodes that are communicating with IPv6 over an IPv4 infrastructure. The last four octets (w.x.y.z) represent the dotted decimal representation of an IPv4 address. The IPV4 address is not obscured.

   D. **Incorrect:** The 0:0:0:0:0:ffff:w.x.y.z (or ::ffff:w.x.y.z) IPv4-mapped address represents an IPv4-only node to an IPv6 node, hence, to map IPv4 devices that are not compatible with IPv6 into the IPv6 address space. The IPv4-mapped address is never used as the source or destination address of an IPv6 packet. The IPv4 address is not obscured.

5. Correct Answer: D

   A. **Incorrect:** The *netsh interface ipv6 show address* command displays the IPv6 configuration on all interfaces. It does not configure an IPv6 address.

   B. **Incorrect:** You can use the *netsh interface ipv6 add address* command to add the IPv6 address of, for example, a DNS server to an IPv6 configuration. You use *netsh interface ipv6 set address* to configure a static IPv6 address.

   C. **Incorrect:** With the *netsh interface ipv6 set interface* command, you change IPv6 interface properties but not an IPv6 address. You use *netsh interface ipv6 set address* to configure a static IPv6 address.

   D. **Correct:** You use *netsh interface ipv6 set address* to configure a static IPv6 address.

6. Correct Answer: A

   A. **Correct:** The *netsh interface ipv4 set address name="Local Area Connection" static 192.168.10.10 255.255.255.0 192.168.10.1* command configures the required settings.

   B. **Incorrect:** For IPv4 settings, you need to specify either the static or dhcp parameters. In this case, static is required.

C. Incorrect: The *netsh interface ipv4 set address name="Local Area Connection" static 192.168.10.1 255.255.255.0 192.168.10.10* command would set the IPv4 address to 192.168.10.1 and the default gateway to 192.168.10.10.

D. Incorrect: You must put spaces between the settings, not commas. This command would return an Invalid IP Address error.

Lesson 2

1. Correct Answer: B

   A. Incorrect: You use the *start /w ocsetup DHCPServerCore* command to install the DHCP server role on a Server Core installation of Windows Server 2008.

   B. Correct: The *sc config dhcpserver start= auto* command configures the DHCP Server service to start automatically on a Server Core installation of Windows Server 2008 when Windows starts.

   C. Incorrect: The *servermanagercmd -install dhcp* command installs the DHCP server role on a full installation of Windows Server 2008. You cannot use this command on a Server Core installation.

   D. Incorrect: The *net start DHCPServer* command starts the DHCP Server service after it is already installed.

2. Correct Answer: A

   A. Correct: This is 80 percent of the available addresses on VLAN1 plus 20 percent of the available addresses on VLAN2.

   B. Incorrect: This is 80 percent of the available addresses on VLAN2 plus 20 percent of the available addresses on VLAN1. These are the scopes that should be configured on VLAN2.

   C. Incorrect: This is 50 percent of the available addresses on VLAN1 plus 50 percent of the available addresses on VLAN2. This solution does not follow the 80:20 rule.

   D. Incorrect: These scopes overlap.

3. Correct Answer: C

   A. Incorrect: You can configure only one contiguous address range per scope.

   B. Incorrect: Configuring a scope option that assigns the DNS server address to clients does not prevent the scope from leasing out an address that is the same as the one statically configured on the DNS server.

   C. Correct: Creating an exclusion for the DNS server address is the simplest way to solve the problem. When you configure the exclusion, the DHCP server will not lease the 172.16.10.100 address, and the DNS server retains its static configuration.

   D. Incorrect: Microsoft recommends that you do not assign reservations to infrastructure servers such as DNS servers. DNS servers should be configured statically.

Chapter 1: Case Scenario Answers

Case Scenario 1: Implementing IPv6 Connectivity

1. Site-local IPv6 addresses are the direct equivalent of private IPv4 addresses and are routable between VLANs. However, you could also consider configuring every device on your network with an aggregatable global unicast IPv6 address. NAT and CIDR were introduced to address a lack of IPv4 address space, and this is not a problem in IPv6. You cannot use only link-local IPv6 addresses in this situation because they are not routable.

2. As with DHCP for IPv4, you should configure a dual-scope DHCPv6 server on each subnet. The scope for the local subnet on each server should include 80 percent of the full IPv6 address range for that subnet. The scope for the remote subnet on each server should include the remaining 20 percent of the full IPv6 address range for that subnet.

Case Scenario 2: Configuring DHCP

1. DHCPv6 is implemented by default in Windows Server 2008, and DHCPv6 scopes can be created on the existing DHCP servers. No additional hardware is required to implement DHCPv6. Most of the features of DHCPv4 are implemented in DHCPv6, and IPv6 configurations can be automatically assigned to client computers. It remains good practice to configure infrastructure servers statically.

2. Problems can occur if a virtual server in a Hyper-V cluster is also a DHCP server. If a virtual network is linked to a NIC, DHCP will not work on the LAN. The LAN NIC is effectively disabled in the parent partition, which is linked to the virtual network, not to the physical network. Microsoft recommends running nothing except the Hyper-V role in the parent partition. If you do not use DHCP to configure a Hyper-V virtual cluster, the Failover Cluster Management Wizard asks you to supply any IP address information manually.

Chapter 2: Lesson Review Answers

Lesson 1

1. Correct Answer: B
   A. **Incorrect:** This answer points to the router with the 10.0.0.11 address on the 10.0.0.0/24 subnet. This is currently the default router. To get to the 10.0.1.0/24 subnet, you must configure a route to the 10.0.0.21 router interface address.
   B. **Correct:** When using the *route add* command, you specify the destination network first— in this case, 10.0.1.0—and then the subnet mask. Finally, you specify the router interface address that will be used to access the remote network, in this case, 10.0.0.21.

C. **Incorrect:** The route is to 10.0.1.0/24, not to 10.0.0.0/24.

D. **Incorrect:** The destination network, not the router interface address, should be listed as the first parameter after *route add*.

2. Correct Answers: B, C, D, and E

A. **Incorrect:** Both Windows Server 2003 and Windows Server 2008 support RIPv2.

B. **Correct:** Windows Server 2008 does not support NWLink.

C. **Correct:** Windows Server 2008 does not support Services for Macintosh.

D. **Correct:** Windows Server 2008 replaces Basic Firewall with Windows Firewall.

E. **Correct:** Windows Server 2008 does not support OSPF.

F. **Incorrect:** Windows Server 2008 introduces SSTP.

3. Correct Answer: B

A. **Incorrect:** Network Address Translation (NAT) enables clients with private IP addresses to connect to computers on the public Internet. NAT does not automatically configure routing.

B. **Correct:** RIP is a routing protocol. It enables routers to broadcast or multicast a list of subnets to which each router provides access. If you enable RIP on a Windows Server 2008 server, it automatically identifies neighboring routers (assuming RIP is enabled on these routers) and forwards traffic to remote subnets.

C. **Incorrect:** OSPF is a routing protocol and would meet your requirements. However, Windows Server 2008 does not support OSPF.

D. **Incorrect:** You could use static routes to reach remote subnets. However, the question asks you to configure Windows Server 2008 to automatically identify remote networks. This requires a routing protocol.

4. Correct Answers: A and B

A. **Correct:** Routes with a 128-bit prefix length are host routes for a specific IPv6 destination.

B. **Correct:** Routes with a 128-bit prefix length are host routes for a specific IPv6 destination.

C. **Incorrect:** Routes with a 64-bit prefix length are subnet routes for locally attached subnets.

D. **Incorrect:** ff00::/8 routes are for multicast traffic.

5. Correct Answers: C and D

A. **Incorrect:** *Ping* tests connectivity to a single destination. You cannot easily use *ping* to identify the routers in a path.

B. **Incorrect:** Although you can use *ipconfig* to determine the default gateway, you cannot use it to determine all routers in a path.

C. **Correct:** *Pathping* uses ICMP to detect routers between a host and a specified destination.

D. **Correct:** *Tracert* uses ICMP to detect every router between a host and a specified destination. The main difference between *tracert* and *pathping* is that *pathping* computes accurate performance statistics over a period of time, whereas *tracert* sends only three packets to each router in the path and displays the latency for each of those three packets.

Lesson 2

1. Correct Answer: B

   A. **Incorrect:** The *netsh advfirewall* context does not support the *add rule* command. You must use the *netsh advfirewall consec* context.

   B. **Correct:** The *netsh advfirewall consec* context enables you to specify configurations that are specific to IPsec. In this context, the *add rule* command adds an IPsec rule.

   C. **Incorrect:** The *netsh firewall* context is provided for backward compatibility, and its use on a Windows Server 2008 server is not recommended. This context does not support the *add rule* command.

   D. **Incorrect:** The *netsh ipsec dynamic* context is provided for backward compatibility, and its use on a Windows Server 2008 server is not recommended. This context does support the *add rule* command, but you would not be able to specify any of the new features that Windows Server 2008 introduces.

2. Correct Answer: D

   A. **Incorrect:** AH provides data authentication but not data encryption.

   B. **Incorrect:** Tunnel mode provides interoperability with routers, gateways, or end systems that do not support L2TP/IPsec or PPTP connections. It does not require network communications to be encrypted.

   C. **Incorrect:** This would work but is not the best answer because AH does not encrypt data. Using AH with ESP increases the processing overhead unnecessarily.

   D. **Correct:** The ESP protocol provides encryption for IPsec.

3. Correct Answer: A

   A. **Correct:** You can use a certificate infrastructure, provided that both domains trust the certificates. Third-party certificates are often used for this purpose.

   B. **Incorrect:** The Kerberos protocol is built into Active Directory Domain Services to provide authentication for IPsec communication. However, Kerberos requires both domains to be in the same Active Directory forest.

C. **Incorrect:** A preshared key is the least secure authentication method, and you should use it only if no other method is available. Microsoft recommends that you do not use this method in a production environment. Using certificates is preferable in this scenario.

D. **Incorrect:** ESP provides encryption, not authentication.

Chapter 2: Case Scenario Answers

Case Scenario 1: Adding a Second Default Gateway

1. Because computers are configured with static IP addresses, you should use the Advanced TCP/IP Settings dialog box to configure multiple default gateways. Clients will automatically detect a failed default gateway and send traffic through the second gateway.

Case Scenario 2: Adding a New Subnet

1. You create a static route on the client computers specifying the router with IP address 10.0.1.2 as the path to the 10.0.2.0/24 network. Because 10.0.1.1 is the default gateway, all other communications will be sent to 10.0.1.1.

2. *route -p add 10.0.2.0 MASK 255.255.255.0 10.0.1.2*

Case Scenario 3: Implementing IPsec

1. You should use Kerberos because all IPsec communications are within the same Active Directory forest.

2. Assign the Client (Respond Only) IPsec policy to the computers used by the appropriate users. In this way, you can ensure that the IPsec policy does not affect communications with other computers and servers that do not require security.

Chapter 3: Lesson Review Answers

Lesson 1

1. Correct Answers: B and E

A. **Incorrect:** Many airport lounge and hotel firewalls block outbound traffic on all ports except common ones such as 80 and 443. SSTP was developed in part because many people found it impossible to establish VPN connections from airport lounges and their hotel rooms by using PPTP or L2TP/IPsec.

B. Correct: VPNs based on the SSTP protocol are likely to work from behind airport lounge and hotel firewalls because these firewalls are unlikely to block the port used for secure Web traffic, 443, which also carries SSTP VPN traffic.

C. Incorrect: Many airport lounge and hotel firewalls block outbound traffic on all ports except common ones such as 80 and 443. SSTP was developed in part because many people found it impossible to establish VPN connections from airport lounges and their hotel rooms by using PPTP or L2TP/IPsec.

D. Incorrect: Windows XP SP3 does not support SSTP VPNs.

E. Correct: Because Windows XP does not support SSTP VPNs, you must upgrade the laptop computers' operating systems to Windows Vista.

2. Correct Answer: B

A. Incorrect: All traffic passing through the external firewall will be directed to the IP address of the VPN server, not to the internal network, so creating a rule here would not work.

B. Correct: You can block VPN clients from accessing the sensitive subnet by creating a Routing and Remote Access filter on the VPN server.

C. Incorrect: Creating an inbound rule on the VPN server would not work because the inbound traffic is bound for the VPN server, not for the sensitive subnet.

D. Incorrect: An authentication exemption rule allows access where access might otherwise be blocked, which is not the problem in this case.

3. Correct Answer: A

A. Correct: Authentication between RADIUS clients and RADIUS servers occurs through a shared secret.

B. Incorrect: You cannot configure authentication between a RADIUS client and a RADIUS server by using a digital certificate.

C. Incorrect: You cannot configure authentication between a RADIUS client and a RADIUS server by using NTLMv2.

D. Incorrect: You cannot configure authentication between a RADIUS client and a RADIUS server by using EAP-TLS.

4. Correct Answers: A, B, and F

A. Correct: You must configure GAMMA as a RADIUS server that authenticates against AD DS so that clients connecting can authenticate using their domain credentials.

B. Correct: You must configure each dial-up access server appliance as a RADIUS client on GAMMA so that GAMMA responds to authentication traffic forwarded by the dial-up access servers.

C. Incorrect: The dial-up access servers must forward authentication traffic to GAMMA, not to domain controllers, which do not respond to RADIUS traffic.

D. **Incorrect:** GAMMA will function as the RADIUS server. The dial-up access servers must be configured as RADIUS clients.

E. **Incorrect:** Dial-up access servers function as RADIUS clients, not as RADIUS proxies. RADIUS proxies forward authentication traffic from RADIUS clients to RADIUS servers.

F. **Correct:** You must configure each dial-up access server to forward authentication requests to GAMMA, which functions as the RADIUS server.

5. Correct Answer: C

A. **Incorrect:** IMAP4 uses port 443; the command in question relates to the POP3 port, port 110.

B. **Incorrect:** HTTP uses port 80; the command in question relates to the POP3 port, port 110.

C. **Correct:** The *netsh routing IP NAT add portmapping name="Public" tcp 0.0.0.0 110 10.100.0.101 110* command forwards incoming POP3 traffic directed to the NAT server's public interface to the POP3 port on host 10.100.0.101. TCP port 110 is the POP3 port.

D. **Incorrect:** SSTP uses port 443; the command in question relates to the POP3 port, port 110.

Lesson 2

1. Correct Answer: A

A. **Correct:** When you have an NPS perform authentication for 802.1x-compliant switches, it is necessary to configure each 802.1x-compliant switch as a RADIUS client on the NPS.

B. **Incorrect:** 802.1x-compliant switches do not function as RADIUS servers because they forward authentication to an NPS.

C. **Incorrect:** 802.1x-compliant switches do not function as RADIUS servers because they do not forward authentication from other RADIUS clients to a RADIUS server.

D. **Incorrect:** Only the 802.1x-compliant switches need to be configured as RADIUS clients because it is they, not the computers, that will forward authentication traffic to the NPS.

2. Correct Answer: B

A. **Incorrect:** EAP-TLS requires the deployment of digital certificates to clients.

B. **Correct:** PEAP-MS-CHAPv2 is a password-based authentication mechanism you can deploy to authenticate 802.1x wired connections without having to deploy certificate services. Although you must install a certificate on the authenticating server, this can be a self-signed certificate or one obtained from a commercial CA.

C. **Incorrect:** PEAP-TLS requires the deployment of digital certificates to clients.

D. **Incorrect:** NTLMv2 cannot be used to authenticate 802.1x wired access.

3. Correct Answer: A

   A. **Correct:** PEAP-MS-CHAPv2 requires the NPS to have been issued a certificate that is trusted by all client computers. Certificates issued by enterprise root CAs in a domain are trusted by all client computers in the domain.

   B. **Incorrect:** Authenticating switches do not require certificates when deploying PEAP-MS-CHAPv2.

   C. **Incorrect:** Client computers do not require certificates when deploying PEAP-MS-CHAPv2.

   D. **Incorrect:** The NPS requires a certificate.

4. Correct Answer: D

   A. **Incorrect:** *Authmode=useronly* will not always work with *preLogon*, depending whether credentials have been cached.

   B. **Incorrect:** The *ssomode=postLogon* parameter indicates that 802.1x wired authentication occurs after the user has logged on to the computer.

   C. **Incorrect:** The *ssomode=postLogon* parameter indicates that 802.1x wired authentication occurs after the user has logged on to the computer.

   D. **Correct:** The *netsh lan set profileparameter authmode=machineonly ssomode=preLogon* command configures an 802.1x wired network profile so that authentication occurs using the computer's credentials prior to the user logging on.

5. Correct Answer: A

   A. **Correct:** Configuring Wired Network (IEEE 802.3) policies enables you to provide authentication data automatically to 802.1x-compatible switches. You can configure these switches to require a host to authenticate before the switch forwards any traffic to the network.

   B. **Incorrect:** Wireless Network (IEEE 802.11) policies are similar to Wired Network policies except that they automate authentication with wireless access points.

   C. **Incorrect:** IPsec policies can limit access to other hosts but cannot limit access to the network.

   D. **Incorrect:** Network Access Protection policies can deny or allow access to the network, based on the health status of a computer but do not require the host to authenticate itself to the switch prior to undergoing the NAP process.

6. Correct Answer: C

   A. **Incorrect:** You cannot create PSOs by using the Group Policy Management console.

   B. **Incorrect:** You cannot create PSOs by using *ntdsutil*.

   C. **Correct:** You can create Password Settings Objects (PSOs) by using ADSI Edit or *ldifde*.

   D. **Incorrect:** You cannot create PSOs by using Active Directory Users and Computers.

Chapter 3: Case Scenario Answers

Case Scenario 1: Configuring a VPN Solution at Fabrikam, Inc.

1. You must open TCP port 443 to support SSTP. You must open UDP ports 1701, 500, and 4500 to support L2TP/IPsec.

2. MS-CHAPv2 is the only password-based authentication protocol you can use with Windows XP that is supported by Windows Server 2008 VPN servers. EAP-MS-CHAPv2 and PEAP-MS-CHAPv2 are supported only by Windows Server 2008 and Windows Vista VPN clients and not by Windows XP.

3. You can configure filters on the VPN server to ensure that VPN clients are unable to access the accounting database server.

Case Scenario 2: Network Access at Contoso, Ltd.

1. PEAP-MS-CHAPv2 is the only authentication protocol that enables passwords to be used for 802.1x authentication.

2. Computer certificates must be deployed on the RADIUS servers when using PEAP-MS-CHAPv2.

3. You must configure the Windows Wired AutoConfig service to start automatically and then configure authentication settings through the Authentication tab of the network interface properties dialog box.

Chapter 4: Lesson Review Answers

Lesson 1

1. Correct Answer: A
   A. **Correct:** WPA2-Enterprise uses a RADIUS server for authentication. All other methods listed use a preshared key,
   B. **Incorrect:** WEP uses a preshared key to authenticate clients.
   C. **Incorrect:** WPA-PSK uses a preshared key to authenticate clients.
   D. **Incorrect:** WPA2-Personal (also known as WPA2-PSK) uses a preshared key to authenticate clients.

2. Correct Answer: C
   A. **Incorrect:** Although it is possible to use RADIUS proxies, you should configure wireless access points as RADIUS clients rather than as RADIUS servers.

B. **Incorrect:** You should configure the wireless access points, rather than the wireless clients, as RADIUS clients.

C. **Correct:** You should configure wireless access points as RADIUS clients because this will allow the Network Policy and Access Services server to authenticate traffic.

D. **Incorrect:** You should not configure wireless clients as RADIUS proxies.

3. Correct Answer: C

    A. **Incorrect:** For this method of authentication to work, the clients must trust the CA that issued the computer certificate to the NPS server.

    B. **Incorrect:** For this method of authentication to work, the clients must trust the CA that issued the computer certificate to the NPS server.

    C. **Correct:** The CA that issued the computer certificate to the NPS server must be trusted by the wireless clients.

    D. **Incorrect:** For this method of authentication to work, the clients must trust the CA that issued the computer certificate to the NPS server.

4. Correct Answer: D

    A. **Incorrect:** Allowing users to view denied networks will not allow connections to ad hoc networks created by Windows Meeting Space.

    B. **Incorrect:** Infrastructure networks require wireless access points. There are no wireless access points present in this scenario.

    C. **Incorrect:** Clients must be able to connect to ad hoc networks. The wireless policy to allow everyone to create wireless profiles allows users to create wireless profiles that apply to all users of the computer.

    D. **Correct:** Clients need to be able to connect to ad hoc networks for the executives to use Windows Meeting Space where there is no wireless access point.

5. Correct Answer: D

    A. **Incorrect:** WEP uses a preshared key, so no network authentication is required.

    B. **Incorrect:** WPA2-Personal uses a preshared key, so no network authentication is required.

    C. **Incorrect:** The Open authentication method does not use any authentication.

    D. **Correct:** The WPA2-Enterprise access point authentication method requires you to specify a network authentication method for when authentication occurs against the RADIUS server.

Lesson 2

1. Correct Answer: C

    A. **Incorrect:** Inbound firewall rules allow traffic based on program or port.

    B. **Incorrect:** Outbound firewall rules allow traffic based on program or port.

C. **Correct:** Isolation rules enable you to limit connections to a computer running Windows Server 2008, based on authentication criteria such as domain membership or health status.

D. **Incorrect:** Authentication exemptions enable you to exempt certain computers from existing connection security rules on the basis of computer address.

2. Correct Answer: A

A. **Correct:** Isolation rules restrict connections based on authentication criteria such as domain membership.

B. **Incorrect:** Server-to-server connection security rules authenticate connection between specific computers, not on the basis of authentication criteria such as domain membership.

C. **Incorrect:** Authentication exemption rules exempt computers from authentication criteria.

D. **Incorrect:** Tunnel rules authenticate connections between computers at the end of a tunnel, such as one across a public network. They do not restrict connections based on authentication criteria such as domain membership.

3. Correct Answer: D

A. **Incorrect:** Authentication exemptions exempt hosts from authentication.

B. **Incorrect:** Isolation rules restrict communications based on health status or domain membership. Nothing in the question setup indicates whether the computers discussed are members of the same Active Directory domain or forest.

C. **Incorrect:** Server-to-server rules authenticate groups of computers when no VPN tunnel separates them from each other.

D. **Correct:** Tunnel rules authenticate sets of computers in different locations that are connected by an encrypted tunnel such as an L2TP/IPsec VPN connection.

4. Correct Answers: B and E

A. **Incorrect:** The computers are not members of an Active Directory domain, so you cannot apply Group Policy to an OU containing their computer accounts.

B. **Correct:** You should configure all the necessary rules on a single computer running WFAS. You should then use the WFAS console to export these rules to a file. You can then import them on the other computers.

C. **Incorrect:** The computers are not members of an Active Directory domain, so you cannot apply Group Policy to an OU containing their computer accounts.

D. **Incorrect:** The *netsh firewall dump* command will export Windows Firewall rather than Windows Firewall with Advanced Security Rules.

E. **Correct:** After you have exported the WFAS configuration of a template computer, you can import that configuration to all other computers, giving them an identical WFAS configuration.

5. Correct Answers: A, D, and E

    A. **Correct:** DNS traffic uses port 53.

    B. **Incorrect:** POP3 traffic uses port 100.

    C. **Incorrect:** HTTP traffic uses port 80.

    D. **Correct:** SMTP traffic uses port 25.

    E. **Correct:** HTTPS traffic uses port 443.

Lesson 3

1. Correct Answer: B

    A. **Incorrect:** To resolve this problem, the SHV configuration on the Network Policy server must be updated rather than the SHA configuration on client computers.

    B. **Correct:** The SHV configuration enables you to set the benchmarks against which the report from the SHA on the client will be assessed. Although the SHA might report to the Network Policy server that the antivirus definitions are out of date, the client will be rendered noncompliant only if up-to-date definitions are compliance criteria.

    C. **Incorrect:** SHAs generate health reports, which are assessed against SHVs. The settings of the SHV need to be updated.

    D. **Incorrect:** SHVs are not installed on clients but are configured on Network Policy servers.

2. Correct Answer: B

    A. **Incorrect:** Users with local administrator access will be unable to bypass IPsec enforcement, so this would be a good solution.

    B. **Correct:** It is possible for users to circumvent DHCP enforcement by statically configuring their computer's IP address.

    C. **Incorrect:** Users with local administrator access will be unable to bypass 802.1X enforcement.

    D. **Incorrect:** VPN enforcement is a remote access NAP enforcement method. Having local administrator access does not allow a user to bypass NAP when this method is used.

    E. **Incorrect:** Although TS Gateway enforcement is usually used as a remote access NAP enforcement method, a user with local administrator access will not be able to bypass NAP when this method is used.

3. Correct Answer: D

    A. **Incorrect:** NAP with DHCP enforcement does not require the forest to be running at the Windows Server 2008 functional level.

    B. **Incorrect:** NAP with DHCP enforcement does not require domains to be running at the Windows Server 2008 functional level.

    C. Incorrect: NAP with DHCP enforcement does not require all domain controllers to be running Windows Server 2008.

    D. Correct: NAP with DHCP enforcement requires all DHCP servers servicing NAP clients to be running the Windows Server 2008 operating system.

4. Correct Answers: C and D

    A. Incorrect: You use IPsec certificates with the IPsec NAP enforcement method, not with the 802.1X NAP enforcement method.

    B. Incorrect: You use IP address leases with the DHCP NAP enforcement method, not with the 802.1X NAP enforcement method.

    C. Correct: You can use access point ACLs to implement the 802.1X enforcement method.

    D. Correct: You can use virtual local area networks (VLANs) to implement the 802.1X enforcement method.

    E. Incorrect: You cannot use subnet masks to implement the 802.1X enforcement method.

Chapter 4: Case Scenario Answers

Case Scenario 1: Contoso, Ltd., Wireless Access

1. Configure the wireless access points to use WPA2-Enterprise or WPA-Enterprise and configure a RADIUS server to authenticate wireless connections.

2. Microsoft: Protected EAP (PEAP) and Computer authentication. You deploy this method by installing computer certificates on both the client and the NPS/RADIUS server.

3. Configure two GPOs, one that allows access to all access point SSIDs and one that allows access to access point SSIDs below the fourth floor and denies access to access point SSIDs on the fourth floor and above. Apply these GPOs so that the former applies to the executives' computer accounts, the latter to all other wireless clients.

Case Scenario 2: Protecting Critical Infrastructure at Fabrikam, Inc.

1. Authentication should occur using client health certificates rather than just straight computer certificates.

2. Configure the isolation policy to require secure connections for incoming connections and request it for outbound connections. Another solution might be to create an exemption policy, although that would not directly answer the question asked.

3. Configure an authentication exemption rule that references the workstation located in the server room. Apply this rule to the servers in the server room by using Group Policy filtering so that it does not apply to file and print servers located elsewhere.

Chapter 5: Lesson Review Answers

Lesson 1

1. Correct Answers: B and D

   A. **Incorrect:** AD DS uses port 3268, which uses LDAP to access the global catalog.

   B. **Correct:** AD LDS (and AD DS) use port 636 as the default port for LDAP over SSL, or Secure LDAP. However, Microsoft recommends that you change this port for AD LDS to a port number in the 50,000 range (typically 50,001).

   C. **Incorrect:** If the Active Directory Lightweight Directory Services Setup Wizard detects that ports 389 and 636 are already in use, it proposes 50,000 and 50,001 for each port and then uses other ports in the 50,000 range for additional AD LDS instances. However, port 50,000 is not a default port.

   D. **Correct:** AD LDS (and AD DS) use port 636 as the default port for LDAP. However, Microsoft recommends that you change this port for AD LDS to a port number in the 50,000 range (typically 50,000).

   E. **Incorrect:** AD DS uses port 3269, which uses Secure LDAP to access the global catalog.

   F. **Incorrect:** If the Active Directory Lightweight Directory Services Setup Wizard detects that ports 389 and 636 are already in use, it proposes 50,000 and 50,001 for each port and then uses other ports in the 50,000 range for additional AD LDS instances. However, port 50,001 is not a default port.

2. Correct Answer: C

   A. **Incorrect:** *Oclist* will give you the name of all the roles and features to use with the *ocsetup* command. However, this is a full installation of Windows Server 2008, and *oclist* does not work on the full installation.

   B. **Incorrect:** Existing setup processes must complete before you can initiate another setup operation. Also, it is difficult to tell whether setup processes have completed when you use the command line unless you use the *start /w* command, which will return the command prompt only when an operation completes. After a reboot, you will find that there are no setup processes currently in operation, yet you still cannot uninstall AD LDS.

   C. **Correct:** You must remove all existing AD LDS instances before you can remove the role from the server. After all instances have been removed, you can remove the AD LDS role.

   D. **Incorrect:** Using Server Manager does not solve the problem because you must remove all AD LDS instances before you can remove the role.

3. Correct Answer: A

   A. **Correct**: This command, entered at an elevated command prompt, installs AD LDS on Server Core. Note that the command is case-sensitive, and the role name or service name for AD LDS must be typed in exactly as displayed. The *start /w* command ensures that the command prompt does not return until the role installation is complete.

   B. Incorrect: You use *oclist | more* to check that the AD LDS service is installed.

   C. Incorrect: The service name for AD LDS is DirectoryServices-ADAM-ServerCore, not DirectoryServices-ADLDS-ServerCore.

   D. Incorrect: You use the *ocsetup* command, not the *oclist* command, to install AD LDS on Server Core.

4. Correct Answer: D

   A. Incorrect: You can use the LDIF files and the *ldifde.exe* command to modify the instance, but schema modifications should be made through the Active Directory Schema snap-in.

   B. Incorrect: You can use the *ldp.exe* command to modify the instance, but schema modifications should be made through the Active Directory Schema snap-in.

   C. Incorrect: All AD LDS instances have a schema, and all instance schemas can be edited.

   D. Correct: When you use AD LDS Setup to create instances with default port numbers, the first port used on member servers is port 389. For example, to connect to the first instance, you must use Instance01:389. Because your AD DS schema also uses port 389, and your server is a member server in a domain, the Active Directory Schema snap-in will not connect to the instance.

Lesson 2

1. Correct Answer: A

   A. Correct: This report displays the list of user and computer credentials that have been referred to a writable domain controller for authentication or service ticket processing.

   B. Incorrect: This report displays the list of user and computer credentials currently cached on the RODC. This is not necessarily the same as the list of user and computer credentials that have been referred to a writable domain controller for authentication or service ticket processing.

   C. Incorrect: Membership of the Allowed RODC Password Replication Group enables the credentials of a user or computer to be cached on an RODC if these credentials are referred to a writable domain controller for authentication or service ticket processing. Group membership does not indicate that these credentials have been referred to a writable domain controller.

   D. Incorrect: Membership of the Denied RODC Password Replication Group prevents the credentials of a user or computer from being cached on an RODC if these credentials are referred to a writable domain controller for authentication or service ticket processing. Group membership does not indicate that these credentials have been referred to a writable domain controller.

2. **Correct Answers: A and C**

    A. **Correct:** The Password Replication Policy tab of the branch office RODC specifies the credentials that can be cached by the RODC.

    B. **Incorrect:** The Allowed RODC Password Replication Group specifies users whose credentials will be cached on all RODCs in the domain. The user needs to log on at only one branch office.

    C. **Correct:** By prepopulating the credentials of the user, you ensure that the RODC will be able to authenticate the user locally rather than over the WAN link.

    D. **Incorrect:** The user does not require the right to log on locally to any domain controller.

3. **Correct Answer: A**

    A. **Correct:** The Policy Usage tab of the Advanced Password Replication Policy dialog box enables you to evaluate the effective caching policy for an individual user or computer.

    B. **Incorrect:** When installing an RODC, you can use the Active Directory Domains and Trusts MMC snap-in to check and, if necessary, raise domain and forest functional levels. The snap-in does not indicate whether that user's or computer's credentials are cached on the RODC.

    C. **Incorrect:** The Resultant Policy tab of the Advanced Password Replication Policy dialog box enables you to evaluate the effective caching policy for an individual user or computer. It does not indicate whether that user's or computer's credentials are cached on the RODC.

    D. **Incorrect:** The Password Replication Policy tab of the RODC computer account Properties dialog box displays the current PRP settings and Add or Remove Users or Groups from the PRP. It does not indicate whether that user's or computer's credentials are cached on the RODC.

4. **Correct Answer: B**

    A. **Incorrect:** You use the *dsmgmt* command to configure administrator role separation on an RODC after that RODC has been installed.

    B. **Correct:** You must run *adprep /rodcprep* to configure the forest so that the RODC can replicate DNS application partitions.

    C. **Incorrect:** You use the *dcpromo* command to perform an installation of a domain controller, including an RODC.

    D. **Incorrect:** You use the *syskey* tool to configure the Windows Account database to enable additional encryption, further protecting account name and password information from compromise.

Chapter 5: Case Scenario Answers

Case Scenario 1: Create AD LDS Instances

1. Instance names identify the instance on the local computer as well as name the files that make up the instance and the service that supports it. You should therefore always use meaningful names to identify instances, for example, the name of the application that is tied to the instance. Names cannot include spaces or special characters.

2. Install a data drive on each server that hosts AD LDS instances. The servers will be hosting directory stores, and these stores should not be placed on a drive that holds the operating system. You should also place each store in a separate folder so it can be easily identified.

3. Each AD LDS instance should use an application partition even if no replication is required. Creating an application directory partition makes it easier to manage the instance.

4. You should use ports in the 50,000 range. Both AD LDS and AD DS use the same ports for communication. These ports are the default LDAP (389) and LDAP over SSL, or Secure LDAP, (636) ports. AD DS uses two additional ports, 3268, which uses LDAP to access the global catalog, and 3269, which uses Secure LDAP to access the global catalog. Because AD DS and AD LDS use the same ports, you should not use the default ports for your AD LDS instances. This will ensure that they are segregated from AD DS services, especially if the instance is installed within a domain.

5. You should use a service account for each instance. Although you can use the Network Service account, Microsoft recommends that you use a named service account for each instance. This way, you know exactly when the instance performs operations because you can view the logon operations of the service account in Event Viewer.

6. Install PKI certificates on each AD LDS instance and use Secure LDAP for communication and management. This should prevent an attacker from tampering with or detecting AD LDS data.

Case Scenario 2: Prepare to Install an RODC at a Branch Office

1. Ensure that all domains are at the Windows Server 2003 domain functional level and that the forest is at the Windows Server 2003 forest functional level. On the schema master, run *adprep /rodcprep*. Upgrade at least one Windows Server 2003 domain controller to Windows Server 2008.

2. You can delegate the installation of an RODC by pre-creating the computer accounts of the RODC in the Domain Controllers OU. When you do this, you can specify the credentials of the user who will attach the RODC to the account. That user (the technician) can then install the RODC without domain administrative privileges.

3. You use the *dsmgmt* command to give the technician local administrative privileges on the RODC.

4. You place the accounts of all the salespersons in the branch office (or a security group containing these accounts) in the Allowed list in the RODCs Properties dialog box that you access through the Active Directory Users and Computers tool on the writable Windows Server 2008 domain controller at the hub site.

5. You place the account of the branch office technician (or a security group containing this account) in the Denied list on the RODCs Properties dialog box that you access through the Active Directory Users and Computers tool on the writable Windows Server 2008 domain controller at the hub site.

6. You pre-position the CEO's account.

Chapter 6: Lesson Review Answers

Lesson 1

1. Correct Answer: B

   A. **Incorrect:** You cannot have more than one resource partner in an AD FS federation.

   B. **Correct:** This gives users in all the organizations access to the resources at Litware, Inc., and Woodgrove Bank and implements SSO.

   C. **Incorrect:** An AD FS federation can support several account partners, and the optimum solution is to create two federations.

   D. **Incorrect:** Forest trusts between multiple organizations are difficult to manage, and implementing SSO would require you to create VPNs or to open LDAP ports on firewalls. This is not the optimum solution.

2. Correct Answer: D

   A. **Incorrect:** You can (and typically do) add an account store on an AFS.

   B. **Incorrect:** You add an account store on a federation server, not on a proxy.

   C. **Incorrect**: Typically, you add an AD DS account store on a federation server.

   D. **Correct:** You can add only one AD DS account store to a federation server. If you cannot add an account store, it is likely that one already exists.

3. Correct Answers: A, C, E, F, and G

   A. **Correct:** Export the trust policy from the account partner (Litware) and import it into the resource partner (Northwind Traders).

   B. **Incorrect:** You should export the trust policy from the account partner and import into the resource partner. This answer proposes the opposite.

   C. **Correct:** Export the partner policy from the resource partner (Northwind Traders) and import it into the account partner (Litware).

   D. **Incorrect:** You should export the partner policy from the resource partner and import it into the account partner. This answer proposes the opposite.

E. Correct: Communicate with your counterpart to determine how you exchange policy files during the partnership setup.

F. Correct: Create and configure a claim mapping in the resource partner (Northwind Traders).

G. Correct: The Litware and Northwind Traders forests are independent, and their DNS servers do not know about each other. You, and your counterpart at Northwind Traders, must configure the DNS servers in each forest with cross-DNS references that refer to the servers in the other forest.

Lesson 2

1. Correct Answer: C

A. Incorrect: The account you use to install AD RMS is added to the AD RMS Template Administrators global security group. This enables this account to configure the new installation of AD RMS. Membership in this group is not necessary for a user to have full access to all content protected by an AD RMS implementation and to recover data generated by other users who have subsequently left the organization.

B. Incorrect: Membership in Enterprise Admins grants a user full administrative rights across the enterprise. Membership in this group is not necessary for a user to have full access to all content protected by an AD RMS implementation and to recover data generated by other users who have subsequently left the organization, and it would grant the user more permissions than necessary.

C. Correct: Members of the Super Users group have full access to all content protected by an AD RMS implementation and can recover data generated by other users who have subsequently left the organization.

D. Incorrect: Members of this group can manage logs and reports and have read-only access to AD RMS infrastructure information. Membership in the AD RMS Auditors global security group does not enable a user to have full access to all content protected by an AD RMS implementation and to recover data generated by other users who have subsequently left the organization.

2. Correct Answer: C

A. Incorrect: The server is running AD RMS because the AD RMS node is available in Server Manager. Also, AD RMS setup has completed without any errors.

B. Incorrect: If an AD RMS root cluster already existed in your AD DS forest, installation would not have proceeded without any errors.

C. Correct: During the installation, your account is added to the AD RMS Enterprise Administrators group on the local computer. However, you must log off and then log on again to ensure that your account has the required access rights to configure AD RMS.

D. Incorrect: To install AD RMS, your server must be a member of the domain. AD RMS uses the AD DS directory service to publish and issue certificates.

3. **Correct Answer: A**

   A. **Correct:** If the server certificate is not from a trusted CA, it will not be accepted when users try to access the URL. If you use a self-signed certificate, the URL works when you access it from the server because the server trusts its own certificate, but it will not work from user browsers because they do not trust the self-signed certificate.

   B. **Incorrect:** To access an HTTP over SSL URL, users need to use HTTPS.

   C. **Incorrect:** Users do not need an AD DS account to access AD RMS from outside the network.

   D. **Incorrect:** You know the URL is correct because you verified it from the server you used to set it up.

Chapter 6: Case Scenario Answers

Case Scenario 1: Using Active Directory Technologies

1. You can use AD DS to upgrade the internal directory service and update the central authentication and authorization store.

2. To support applications in the extranet, you implement identity federation with AD FS.

3. You should implement the AD FS federated Web SSO design in this scenario.

4. The applications are installed at Margie's Travel, which is therefore the resource partner.

5. To support the Windows-based applications in the extranet, you need access to a directory store. You should install the AD FS Windows token-based agent to support identity federation and AD FS-enable the Web-based applications by installing the AD FS claims-aware agent. To gain access to the applications, partner organizations and internal users will use AD FS, and the general public will use instances of AD LDS.

6. You should use AD CS to manage the certificates that provide communication security. You need to obtain a certificate from a third-party trusted CA to use as the root of your AD CS deployment so all certificates are trusted.

Case Scenario 2: Implementing an External AD RMS Cluster

1. You use cross-certificate publication based on trusted publishing domains. To do this, you export your SLC and its private key and then ask your counterpart at Contoso to import it into Contoso's AD RMS root. Your counterpart does the same. After the certificates are imported, both Litware and Contoso support the issue of publishing and use certificates for each other.

2. You need to download Windows RMS Client with SP2 and install this on your client computers running Windows XP.

3. When you remove an account, AD RMS disables the account but does not automatically remove the database entry. You need to remove the appropriate database entries by creating a stored procedure in SQL Server that will automatically remove the account entry when you remove the account or by creating a script that will do so on a regular basis.

Chapter 7: Lesson Review Answers

Lesson 1

1. Correct Answer: C
   A. **Incorrect:** You cannot take an enterprise root CA offline without causing significant problems in an enterprise CA hierarchy.
   B. **Incorrect:** To be able to take the root CA offline, you need a standalone root, not a subordinate CA.
   C. **Correct:** You should configure a standalone root CA because you can take this type of CA offline, and it can serve as the apex of a PKI hierarchy that includes enterprise subordinate CAs.
   D. **Incorrect:** To take the CA offline, you need a standalone root CA, not a subordinate CA.

2. Correct Answers: C and D
   A. **Incorrect:** You cannot install an enterprise subordinate CA on Windows Web Server 2008.
   B. **Incorrect:** You cannot install an enterprise subordinate CA on Windows Server 2008 Standard. Windows Server 2008 Standard supports only standalone CAs.
   C. **Correct:** You can install an enterprise subordinate CA on Windows Server 2008 Enterprise.
   D. **Correct:** You can install an enterprise subordinate CA on Windows Server 2008 Datacenter.

3. Correct Answer: A
   A. **Correct:** To be recognized as valid key recovery agents, the two users must be issued certificates that have the Key Recovery Agent OID.
   B. **Incorrect:** Certificates with the Enrollment Agent OID cannot be used for key recovery.
   C. **Incorrect:** Certificates with the Subordinate Certification Authority OID cannot be used for key recovery.
   D. **Incorrect:** Certificates with the EFS Recovery Agent OID cannot be used for key recovery.
   E. **Incorrect:** Certificates with the OCSP Response Signing OID cannot be used for key recovery.

4. Correct Answers: A, B, C, and E

   A. **Correct:** It is necessary to change the CRL distribution point URL to ensure that CRL checks execute against an active distribution point rather than against the offline root CA.

   B. **Correct:** It is necessary to change the AIA distribution point URL to ensure that CRL checks execute against an active distribution point rather than against the offline root CA.

   C. **Correct:** It is necessary to import the root CA certificate into the enterprise root store in AD DS so that the standalone CA is trusted by computers in the domain or forest.

   D. **Incorrect:** The CA must be online to issue signing certificates to the enterprise subordinate CAs.

   E. **Correct:** The AIA points must be published in AD DS; otherwise, the certificate chain verification will fail when enterprise subordinate certificates are published.

5. Correct Answer: C

   A. **Incorrect:** Adding this permission will not add the SSLCertManagers group to the list of certificate managers.

   B. **Incorrect:** Adding this permission will not add the SSLCertManagers group to the list of certificate managers.

   C. **Correct:** The SSLCertManagers group is not present in the list of Certificate Managers on the CA because it has not been assigned the Issue And Manage Certificates permission on the CA. After this permission is assigned, this group will be automatically added to the list of Certificate Managers.

   D. **Incorrect:** The permission to manage certificates is assigned through the CA properties rather than through the Certificate Template properties.

   E. **Incorrect:** The permission to manage certificates is assigned through the CA properties rather than through the Certificate Template properties.

Lesson 2

1. Correct Answers: C, D, and E

   A. **Incorrect:** Windows 2000 Advanced Server CAs do not support level 2 certificate templates.

   B. **Incorrect:** Customized certificate templates can be issued only by enterprise CAs. You cannot install an enterprise CA on Windows Server 2008 Standard.

   C. **Correct:** You can install an enterprise CA on Windows Server 2008 Enterprise that is able to issue customized level 2 certificate templates.

D. Correct: You can install an enterprise CA on Windows Server 2008 Enterprise that is able to issue customized level 2 certificate templates.

E. Correct: You can install an enterprise CA on Windows Server 2003 Enterprise that is able to issue customized level 2 certificate templates.

2. Correct Answer: D

A. Incorrect: Publishing the certificate in AD DS will not accomplish your goal.

B. Incorrect: This option would have the Basic EFS template supersede the Advanced EFS template when you want the opposite to happen.

C. Incorrect: Publishing the certificate in AD DS will not accomplish your goal.

D. Correct: When you specify the Basic EFS template as being superseded in the Advanced EFS template properties, when published, the Advanced EFS template will be used for future EFS certificate requests.

3. Correct Answer: B

A. Incorrect: You do not need to configure any certificate role for Rooslan's account; just issue Rooslan an enrollment agent certificate.

B. Correct: To function as an enrollment agent, a user account must be issued an enrollment agent certificate.

C. Incorrect: You do not need to configure any certificate role for Rooslan's account; just issue Rooslan an enrollment agent certificate.

D. Incorrect: You do not need to configure any certificate role for Rooslan's account; just issue Rooslan an enrollment agent certificate.

4. Correct Answer: E

A. Incorrect: Disabling this permission will not solve the problem because the problem is caused by the auto-enrollment Group Policy not being configured.

B. Incorrect: If you disable the Autoenroll permission, automatic enrollment will not be possible.

C. Incorrect: Enabling CA certificate manager approval will not allow auto-enrollment to occur if it is not already occurring. Enabling this option will slow down auto-enrollment because manual intervention will be required to issue the certificate.

D. Incorrect: Allowing the private key to be exported has no impact on auto-enrollment.

E. Correct: Auto-enrollment must be enabled in the Default Domain Policy GPO as well as in the appropriate permissions set in the certificate template.

5. Correct Answers: B and C

A. Incorrect: Publishing the CRL every 24 hours will increase network traffic rather than minimize it.

B. Correct: Publishing the CRL every two weeks will mean that clients need to download a new CRL only every 14 days.

C. **Correct:** Publishing a delta CRL every 48 hours meets the goal of informing clients in a timely manner about revoked certificates.

D. **Incorrect:** Although you could publish a delta CRL once a week, this does not meet the requirement of informing clients about revocations within 48 hours.

E. **Incorrect:** Although you could publish a delta CRL every two weeks, this does not meet the requirement of informing clients about revocations within 48 hours.

6. Correct Answer: A

A. **Correct:** Configuring Online Responder will mean that revocation checks for new certificates will be processed by Online Responder rather than at the CDP.

B. **Incorrect:** Increasing the frequency of CRL publication will put greater pressure on the CDP.

C. **Incorrect:** Increasing the frequency of delta CRL publication will put greater pressure on the CDP.

D. **Incorrect:** Decreasing the frequency of delta CRL publication will mean that clients are not informed in a timely manner about certificate revocations.

Chapter 7: Case Scenario Answers

Case Scenario 1: Tailspin Toys Certificate Services

1. You should use Windows Server 2008 Standard for the root CA. This minimizes the licensing costs for a server that will spend most of the time switched off.

2. You should use Windows Server 2008 Enterprise for the subordinate CA. This enables you to configure the subordinate CA as an enterprise CA, which enables the use of custom certificate templates.

3. Configure the CertApprove security group with the Certificate Manager role. Remove other security groups from this role.

Case Scenario 2: Contoso Online Responder

1. Install an OCSP response signing certificate on the computer hosting the Online Responder role service. Add the URL for Online Responder in the Authority Information Access (AIA) extension on the CA.

2. Previously issued certificates will not include information about Online Responder. Only certificates issued after Online Responder is deployed will have revocation checks against them serviced by Online Responder.

3. Configure an Online Responder array to load balance Online Responder traffic.

Chapter 8: Lesson Review Answers

Lesson 1

1. **Correct Answers: A and D**

   A. **Correct:** You need to run the script by using the local Administrator account because *wbadmin.exe* needs to be executed with elevated privileges. The script file will specify an account that has appropriate access permissions to the share, but the script does not run under this account.

   B. **Incorrect:** The permissions issue is that *wbadmin.exe* needs to be executed with elevated privileges, and you therefore need to run the script using the local Administrator account. The script file will specify an account that has appropriate access permissions to the share, but the script does not run under this account. Also, this answer specifies a weekly schedule, and you want to perform the backup daily.

   C. **Incorrect:** The question specifies that the task must run daily at 03:00 hours.

   D. **Correct:** The script runs under the local Administrator account credentials. You need to specify the credentials of an account that has appropriate access permissions to the remote share in the script.

   E. **Incorrect:** Local Administrator account credentials will not enable access to a remote shared folder because the remote computer does not use the same Administrator password. You therefore need to specify the credentials of an account that has appropriate access permissions to the remote share in the script.

2. **Correct Answer: C**

   A. **Incorrect:** Windows Server Backup can write scheduled backups to local external IEEE 1394 disks. DPM 2007, however, does not support IEEE 1394 devices.

   B. **Incorrect:** Windows Server Backup can write scheduled backups to local external USB 2.0 disks. DPM 2007, however, does not support USB devices.

   C. **Correct:** DPM 2007 can write scheduled backups to an iSCSI SAN. Windows Server Backup cannot. The same applies to Fibre Channel SAN, but this was not specified in the question.

   D. **Incorrect:** Both Windows Server Backup and DPM 2007 can write scheduled backups to a SCSI internal disk. In this scenario, the administrator cannot use Windows Server Backup to write scheduled backups and is therefore not backing up to an SCSI internal disk.

3. **Correct Answer: B**

   A. **Incorrect:** In Windows Server backup, critical volumes (volumes that contain operating systems) are selected by default and cannot be deselected. This procedure would back up system state data, which would include server role data, but it would also perform a critical volume backup.

B. Correct: This procedure backs up only the system state data and does not perform a critical volume backup. This is what the question requires.

C. Incorrect: This procedure marks an Active Directory object as authoritative. This is not what is required.

D. Incorrect: This causes the server to boot into DSRM. This is not what is required.

4. Correct Answer: C

  A. Incorrect: This command specifies the OU name instead of the computer account name and vice versa.

  B. Incorrect: You need to use the *Restore Object* command to restore an object such as a user or computer account. You cannot use *Restore Computer*.

  C. Correct: This command restores the Boston computer account to the Windows_Server_2008_Servers OU in the *contoso.internal* domain.

  D. Incorrect: You need use the *Restore Object* command to restore an object such as a user or computer account. You cannot use *Restore Computer*.

5. Correct Answer: D

  A. Incorrect: You cannot restore a deleted GPO by using an authoritative restore. You need to use the GPMC to restore GPOs.

  B. Incorrect: You cannot restore a deleted GPO by using the Restore Wizard. You need to use the GPMC to restore GPOs.

  C. Incorrect: You cannot restore a deleted GPO by using the Restore Wizard. You need to use the GPMC to restore GPOs.

  D. Correct: You use the GPMC to restore deleted GPOs by opening the GPMC, right-clicking the Group Policy Objects container, and then selecting Manage Backups. Browse to where backed up GPOs are stored and select the Vista Workstations GPO. Click Restore.

6. Correct Answer: D

  A. Incorrect: You cannot perform an authoritative restore, using an RODC.

  B. Incorrect: You have already performed a full server recovery on the RODC. This includes a nonauthoritative restore.

  C. Incorrect: If you perform a full server backup directly after a full server restore, the backup you take will be identical to the one you used to restore the RODC.

  D. Correct: Performing a full server recovery does not reapply BitLocker settings. You must reapply BitLocker settings after the full server recovery process is complete.

Lesson 2

1. Correct Answer: B

  A. Incorrect: After you enter **activate instance ntds**, you must enter **files** at the Ntdsutil prompt and then use the *compact to* command at the File Maintenance prompt.

B. Correct: The *compact to* command entered at the File Maintenance prompt both compacts and defragments the *Ntds.dit* database. You must first activate the ntds instance by entering **activate instance ntds** and then enter **files** to access the File Maintenance prompt.

C. Incorrect: The *compact to* command both compacts and defragments the *Ntds.dit* database.

D. Incorrect: The *compact to* command both compacts and defragments the *Ntds.dit* database.

2. Correct Answer: D

A. Incorrect: You can stop the AD DS service either through the command-line *net. exe* utility or through the Services console. There is no indication in the question that ChicagoDC2 is an RODC.

B. Incorrect: Unlike previous Windows Server operating systems, you don't need to boot into DSRM on a Windows Server 2008 domain controller to stop AD DS and perform database operations.

C. Incorrect: Windows Server 2008 introduces restartable AD DS.

D. Correct: If someone is working on the other domain controller in the forest root domain and has stopped the AD DS service (or taken the domain controller offline), you will not be able to stop the AD DS service on this server because at least one domain controller for each domain must be operational before the service will stop.

3. Correct Answer: A

A. Correct: This procedure carries out an authoritative restore of the Denver Computers OU.

B. Incorrect: You need to specify an authoritative restore by using *ntdsutil authoritative restore*.

C. Correct: You need to restore the OU and all its contents. You therefore need to use *restore subtree* rather than *restore object*.

D. Incorrect: You need to specify an authoritative restore by using *ntdsutil authoritative restore*. Also, you need to use *restore subtree* rather than *restore object*.

4. Correct Answer: C

A. Incorrect: You can use *wbadmin.exe* to configure backups. It does not recover tombstoned AD DS objects.

B. Incorrect: You can use *ntdsutil.exe* to mark restored AD DS objects as authoritative. It does not recover tombstoned AD DS objects.

C. Correct: You can use *ldp.exe* to recover tombstoned AD DS objects.

D. Incorrect: The *net.exe* utility has many uses. For example, you can use *net start* and *net stop* to start and stop a service. However, it does not recover tombstoned AD DS objects.

Lesson 3

1. **Correct Answer: A**

   A. **Correct:** *Repadmin /showrepl Chicago. northwindtraders.com* displays the replication partners for the Chicago domain controller in the *northwindtraders.com* domain. It also displays AD DS replication failures.

   B. **Incorrect:** *Dcdiag /test:replications* checks for AD DS replication errors. It does not, however, list the replication partners for a specific domain controller.

   C. **Incorrect:** *Rsop.msc /RsopNamespace:northwindtraders.com/RsopTargetComp:Chicago*, entered in the Search or Run box, opens RSoP as an MMC snap-in and displays RSoP logging mode for the *northwindtraders.com* namespace and the Chicago target computer.

   D. **Incorrect:** *Rsop.msc*, entered in the Search or Run box, opens RSoP as an MMC snap-in and displays RSoP logging mode for the currently logged-on user and computer.

2. **Correct Answers: D and E**

   A. **Incorrect:** By default, the collector set will run under the account that created it. It is not necessary to create a special account, although it is a good idea to do so. The lack of a special account will not cause the collector set to run continuously.

   B. **Incorrect:** The collector sets must be on a schedule; otherwise, they would stop when the user who created them logged off.

   C. **Incorrect:** An expiration date does not cause a collector set to stop. It stops new collections from starting after it has been reached.

   D. **Correct:** You must set a stop condition on each collector set to ensure that it stops.

   E. **Correct:** You must set a duration limit on the collector set when you schedule it to run; otherwise, it will not stop.

3. **Correct Answer: B**

   A. **Incorrect:** A data collector set based on the LAN Diagnostics template collects data from network interface cards, registry keys, and other system hardware. You can use it to identify issues related to network traffic on the local domain controller.

   B. **Correct:** A data collector set based on the Active Directory Diagnostics template collects data from registry keys, performance counters, and trace events related to AD DS performance on a local domain controller.

   C. **Incorrect:** A data collector set based on the System Performance template provides information about the status of hardware resources, system response times, and processes on the local domain controller.

   D. **Incorrect:** A data collector set based on the System Diagnostics template collects data from local hardware resources to generate data that helps streamline system performance on the local domain controller.

4. Correct Answers: A, C, E, and F

   A. Correct: Reliability Monitor helps you determine whether any recent changes to the domain controller could be causing performance bottlenecks.

   B. Incorrect: The *repadmin* command-line tool reports failures between replication partners. It does not, however, diagnose performance issues on a single domain controller.

   C. Correct: Event Viewer helps you determine whether error or warning messages about system performance have been generated. You should examine the System event log.

   D. Incorrect: Windows Server 2008 does not provide the SPA tool. WRPM provides that functionality.

   E. Correct: Task Manager displays a real-time view of resource usage that helps you identify potential bottlenecks.

   F. Correct: Performance Monitor helps you discover whether there are any performance issues with the current server configuration. You can compare current performance against benchmarks and use template-based data collector sets to gather your statistics.

Chapter 8: Case Scenario Answers

Case Scenario 1: Designing Backup and Restore Procedures

1. An internal SCSI or IDE hard disk must be installed or an external USB 2.0, SATA, or IEEE 1394 storage device must be attached to each domain controller so that scheduled backup data can be written.

2. You must use DPM 2007 because Windows Server Backup cannot write to Fibre Channel SAN.

3. You must create and schedule a batch file that backs up system state data on a regular basis. Although bare metal and critical volume backups also back up system state data, restoring AD DS from such backups can be difficult and is not recommended. If you need to perform an authoritative restore, you can first perform a nonauthoritative restore from system state backup in DSRM and then mark the deleted items you want to restore as authoritative by using the *ntdsutil.exe* utility.

Case Scenario 2: Compacting and Defragmenting the AD DS Database

1. You can stop the AD DS service either through the command-line *net.exe* utility or through the Services console. The *compact to* command in the *ntdsutil* utility both defragments and compacts the *Ntds.dit* database.

2. You cannot stop the AD DS service on a domain controller unless there is another domain controller in the domain. Because there are only two domain controllers in the Tailspin Toys root domain and another administrator is currently working with the other domain controller, it is likely that the AD DS service on that domain controller has been stopped or that the domain controller has been powered down.

Case Scenario 3: Monitoring AD DS

1. You need to create data collector sets based on the Active Directory Diagnostics and System Performance templates.

2. To create performance baselines, you run your data collector sets and sample and record counter values for 30 to 45 minutes each day for at least a week during periods of peak, normal, and low activity. If you make any significant changes to your network or to an individual domain controller, you must generate new baselines.

Chapter 9: Lesson Review Answers

Lesson 1

1. Correct Answers: A, C, and D
   A. **Correct:** Placing all computer accounts in a specific OU simplifies the process of applying Group Policy.
   B. **Incorrect:** Although Group Policy can be filtered by security group, the appropriate options to do this are not present in the available answers.
   C. **Correct:** To use client-side targeting, you must first create computer groups on the WSUS server.
   D. **Correct:** You should use the Client-Side Targeting Properties policy to configure computers to be members of the appropriate WSUS group.
   E. **Incorrect:** WSUS uses computer groups rather than user groups.

2. Correct Answers: B and C
   A. **Incorrect:** Configuring an automatic update rule for the all computer groups does not give you the chance to review updates for incompatibility before deploying them across the organization.
   B. **Correct:** An automatic approval rule for the test computers group allows updates to deploy automatically to these computers so that you can approve updates manually to the other computers in the organization.
   C. **Correct:** An automatic synchronization schedule means that updates will flow through to the WSUS server and on to the test group without direct intervention.

D. **Incorrect:** If you use the manual synchronization setting, updates will not deploy automatically to your group of test computers after those updates are published on the Microsoft update servers.

E. **Incorrect:** Replica mode moves approval settings to an upstream server. No upstream server is mentioned in this scenario.

3. Correct Answer: D

A. **Incorrect:** The Configure Automatic Updates policy specifies whether automatic updates are enabled, not which server the updates are retrieved from.

B. **Incorrect:** The Automatic Updates Detection Frequency policy determines how often the client checks the update server, not which server is checked for updates.

C. **Incorrect:** The Enable Client-Side Targeting policy enables you to separate computers into different WSUS groups.

D. **Correct:** You can specify the location of a local WSUS server by using the Specify Intranet Microsoft Update Service Location policy.

E. **Incorrect:** The Allow Automatic Updates Immediate Installation policy allows updates that do not interrupt the function of Windows to be installed automatically.

4. Correct Answer: A

A. **Correct:** Use WSUS to remove the update from the test computers. No further action is required until the vendor fix arrives.

B. **Incorrect:** Declining the update removes it from the WSUS database, making it difficult to approve when the vendor fix arrives.

C. **Incorrect:** Moving the computer accounts out of the Test_Group will not remove the update from those computers.

D. **Incorrect:** You should not set an approval date for 90 days away because this will not remove the update from the test computers, and the vendor fix might not arrive on schedule.

5. Correct Answers: C, D, and E

A. **Incorrect:** You must export updates from the connected WSUS server, not from the disconnected one.

B. **Incorrect:** You must export metadata from the connected WSUS server, not from the disconnected one.

C. **Correct:** The advanced options on the Internet-connected WSUS server must match the advanced options on the disconnected WSUS server.

D. **Correct:** Updates must be copied from the connected WSUS server to the disconnected WSUS server.

E. **Correct:** Metadata must be exported from the connected WSUS server, using *wsusutil. exe*, and then imported to the disconnected WSUS server by using the same utility.

Lesson 2

1. Correct Answer: C

    A. **Incorrect:** Use the MBSA tool to scan for vulnerabilities and missing updates; it cannot intercept network traffic.

    B. **Incorrect:** Telnet is a network communication protocol; you cannot use it to intercept network traffic.

    C. **Correct:** Network Monitor captures network traffic for later analysis.

    D. **Incorrect:** SNMP is a management protocol. It does not capture and analyze network traffic.

2. Correct Answer: C

    A. **Incorrect:** This filter will show all DNS traffic from the server. Because this filter uses the IP address of the DNS server, it will not limit the traffic captured to DNS traffic from the client only.

    B. **Incorrect:** This filter will display all DNS traffic and all traffic from the server.

    C. **Correct:** This filter displays DNS traffic from the client.

    D. **Incorrect:** This filter displays all client traffic and all DNS traffic.

3. Correct Answer: C

    A. **Incorrect:** Nmcap.exe is the Network Monitor command-line utility. You cannot use it to determine whether a computer is missing important updates.

    B. **Incorrect:** Ping is a network connectivity diagnosis utility; you cannot use it to determine whether a computer is missing important updates.

    C. **Correct:** The name of the Microsoft Baseline Security Analyzer command-line utility is *mbsacli.exe*. You can use this utility to scan a remote host to determine whether it is missing important security updates.

    D. **Incorrect:** Telnet is a communication protocol; you cannot use it directly to determine whether a client computer is missing important updates.

4. Correct Answers: A, B, and C

    A. **Correct:** You must enable the Server service on the remote computer for the MBSA tool to scan it successfully.

    B. **Correct:** You must enable the Remote Registry service on the remote computer for the MBSA tool to scan it successfully.

    C. **Correct:** You must enable the File and Print Sharing service on the remote computer for the MBSA tool to scan it successfully.

    D. **Incorrect:** You must enable the Workstation service on the scanning computer but not on the computer that is being scanned remotely.

    E. **Incorrect:** You must enable the Client for Microsoft Networks on the scanning computer but not on the computer that is being scanned remotely.

5. Correct Answers: B and D

    A. **Incorrect:** Dynamic Update is a DNS-related policy that enables clients to update their DNS records.

    B. **Correct:** The Communities policy defines the group of hosts the SNMP service can communicate with.

    C. **Incorrect:** The Traps For Public Community policy enables you to specify which hosts receive trap messages.

    D. **Correct:** The Permitted Managers policy defines which members of the SNMP community can query the SNMP agent for data.

    E. **Incorrect:** Update Security Level is a DNS-related policy and allows secure updates of DNS records.

Chapter 9: Case Scenario Answers

Case Scenario 1: Contoso, Ltd's WSUS Deployment

1. Configure separate WSUS server groups for the client computers and the servers. That way, you can approve updates for one group of computers without approving updates for the other.

2. Configure an automatic approval rule that deals with critical and security updates and has the WSUS group that you configured for the client computers as its scope.

3. Configure a disconnected WSUS server.

Case Scenario 2: Probing the Network at Fabrikam, Inc.

1. Perform a capture using Network Monitor to determine whether a communication problem exists between the client and the server.

2. Create a capture filter. A display filter will capture all data but only display a portion of this data. A capture filter limits the capture to what is specified by the filter.

3. Configure MBSA scans to run against the list of updates approved on the WSUS server rather than on the updates published on the Microsoft Update servers.

Chapter 10: Lesson Review Answers

Lesson 1

1. Correct Answer: B

    A. **Incorrect:** On the General tab, you can specify how frequently the graph updates and how much data is displayed in the graph before Performance Monitor begins overwriting the graph on the left portion of the chart. You can also specify whether Legend, Value Bar, and Toolbar are displayed and whether the Report and Histogram views show Default, Maximum, Minimum, Average, or Current values. You cannot choose whether to display current activity in real time or show log files saved using a data collector set.

B. **Correct:** On the Source tab, you can choose whether to display current activity in real time or log files saved using a data collector set. If you display a log file, you can use this tab to control the time range displayed in the Performance Monitor window.

C. **Incorrect:** You can use the Data tab to configure the display of specific counters. In the Counters list, you can select the counter you want to configure and adjust Color, Width, and Style. You can increase or decrease the Scale value. You cannot choose whether to display current activity in real time or log files saved using a data collector set.

D. **Incorrect:** You can use the Graph tab to select the scroll style and the type of graph to display. You cannot choose whether to display current activity in real time or log files saved using a data collector set.

E. **Incorrect:** If you keep multiple Performance Monitor windows open simultaneously, you can use the Appearance tab to change the color of the background or other elements. This makes it easier to distinguish between the windows. You cannot choose whether to display current activity in real time or log files saved using a data collector set.

2. Correct Answer: A

A. **Correct:** Reliability Monitor tracks application installations that use Windows Installer. It enables you to determine whether what applications have been installed and exactly when the installations occurred.

B. **Incorrect:** Network Monitor (discussed in Chapter 9, "Managing Software Updates and Monitoring Network Data") captures network traffic. It does not provide information about application installations.

C. **Incorrect:** Data collector sets capture current performance and configuration data. They cannot tell you when, in the past, an application was installed.

D. **Incorrect:** You can use Performance Monitor to view performance counters in real time or analyze performance data in a data collector set. However, Performance Monitor does not record when an application was installed.

3. Correct Answers: B, C, D, and F

A. **Incorrect:** Configuration errors that do not cause an application to fail are not recorded in Reliability Monitor.

B. **Correct:** Application failures are recorded in Reliability Monitor.

C. **Correct:** Windows errors are recorded in Reliability Monitor.

D. **Correct:** Application installs and uninstalls are recorded in Reliability Monitor.

E. Incorrect: a service starting or stopping is typically recorded in the event log but is not recorded by Reliability Monitor.

F. Correct: Device driver failures are recorded by Reliability Monitor.

4. Correct Answer: D

A. Incorrect: Creating a counter log to track processor usage does not help you identify which application is causing this high processor usage.

B. Incorrect: Creating an alert that triggers when the usage of the processor exceeds 80 percent for more than five minutes does not help you identify which application is causing this high processor usage.

C. Incorrect: The server's Application log displays Information, Warning, Error, and Critical events. It does not help you identify which application is causing high processor usage.

D. Correct: You can open Windows Reliability and Performance Monitor on the server and use Resource View to see the percentage of processor capacity used by each application. The Resource View screen in Windows Reliability and Performance Monitor provides a real-time graphical overview of CPU, disk, network, and memory usage.

Lesson 2

1. Correct Answers: B, C, and D

A. Incorrect: The *winrm quickconfig* command configures Windows Remote Management. In a collector-initiated subscription, you run it on the source computer, in this case, Boston. Although you can enter it on the collector computer if you are configuring a source-initiated subscription, this is not the scenario here because Glasgow is collecting events from Boston.

B. Correct: The *wecutil qc* command configures the Event Collector service on the collector computer.

C. Correct: You add the computer account for the collector computer (Glasgow) to the local Event Log Readers group on the source computer (Boston). You could instead put the Glasgow computer account in the local Administrators group on Boston, but this is not mentioned in the answers. You do not need to use the local Administrators group because you are not collecting Security Event log events.

D. Correct: In this scenario, the *winrm quickconfig* command on Boston configures Windows Remote Management.

E. Incorrect: You must enter this command on Glasgow, not on Boston.

F. Incorrect: You must put the computer account of the collector computer in the local Event Log Readers group on the source computer, not the other way round.

2. **Correct Answer: A**

   A. Correct: You can use the *wecutil* utility to configure the Event Collector service.

   B. Incorrect: The *winrm* command configures Windows Remote Management. Typically, you run it on the source computer. You can run it on the collector computer if you are configuring a source-initiated conscription, but this is not relevant to this scenario because Glasgow is retrieving events from Melbourne. In any case, this command does not configure the Event Collector service.

   C. Incorrect: You run this command on the source computer to add the computer account of the collector computer to the Event Log readers group.

   D. Incorrect: This command starts the Group Policy MMC snap-in. You can use Group Policy to add source computers to a source-initiated conscription, but this is not relevant to this scenario. In any case, the command does not configure the Event Collector service.

3. **Correct Answers: D and F**

   A. Incorrect: *Wecutil gs* displays the subscription interval. You cannot use this command to change the interval.

   B. Incorrect: *Wecutil gs* displays the subscription interval. You cannot use this command to change the interval.

   C. Incorrect: *Wecutil gs* displays the subscription interval. You cannot use this command to change the subscription to use custom settings.

   D. Correct: This command changes the subscription to use custom settings, which enables you to use a value other than the default for the interval.

   E. Incorrect: The subscription interval is in milliseconds. This command changes it to 300 milliseconds.

   F. Correct: This command changes the subscription interval to five minutes (300,000 milliseconds).

4. **Correct Answers: A and B**

   A. Correct: Admin events indicate a problem experienced by end users, administrators, and support personnel and provide a well-defined solution on which an administrator can act. For example, an Admin event might occur when an application fails to connect to a printer.

   B. Correct: You can use Operational events to analyze and diagnose a problem. They can trigger tools or tasks based on the problem or occurrence. For example, an Operational event occurs when a printer is added or removed from a system.

   C. Incorrect: Analytic events describe program operation and identify problems that cannot be handled by user intervention.

   D. Incorrect: Developers use Debug events to troubleshoot issues with their programs.

Chapter 10: Case Scenario Answers

Case Scenario 1: Troubleshooting a Performance Problem

1. You can use data collector sets to record a performance baseline when the server is performing normally. You can then run the same data collector sets manually when a performance problem occurs. If the performance problems occur at about a certain time of day, you can schedule the Performance data sets to record data at that time over an extended period. You can use Performance Monitor to analyze your results, compare them with your baseline, and identify the factors that could be causing the problems.

2. You could include some or all the following counters, which were described in Lesson 1.

   - Memory\Pages per Second
   - Memory\% Committed Bytes in Use
   - Memory\Available Mbytes
   - Memory\Free System Page Table Entries
   - Memory\Pool Paged Bytes
   - Memory\Pool Non-Paged Bytes

3. Reliability Monitor indicates the applications that were installed or updated at about the time that problems began to occur.

Case Scenario 2: Monitoring Computers for Low Disk Space

1. You can use Event Forwarding to transfer low disk space events to a central server. You can then monitor this event log to identify computers with low disk space. You can attach a task that informs you that a low disk space event has been logged.

2. Windows XP with Service Pack 2 and WS-Management 1.1 installed, Windows Server 2003 R2 with WS-Management 1.1.installed, Windows Server 2003 with Service Pack 1 or later and WS-Management 1.1installed, Windows Vista, and Windows Server 2008 all support Event Forwarding.

Case Scenario 3: Setting Up a Source-Initiated Subscription

1. *winrm qc -q*
2. *wecutil qc /q*
3. An event subscription XML file, for example, subscription.xml
4. *wecutil cs subscription.xml*

Chapter 11: Lesson Review Answers

1. Correct Answer: A

   A. Correct: To resolve this problem, you need to change the DHCP settings available through the Windows Deployment Services server settings. From here, you can configure WDS not to listen on port 67 and configure DHCP option 60. You can configure DHCP option 60 by modifying Windows Deployment Services server settings.

   B. Incorrect: This problem is related to the port WDS listens on, not to DNS server settings.

   C. Incorrect: This problem is related to the port WDS listens on. The configuration changes must be made within the Windows Deployment Services server settings.

   D. Incorrect: This problem is related to the port WDS listens on. You cannot resolve this problem by altering the default domain Group Policy object.

2. Correct Answer: C

   A. Incorrect: It is not necessary to create client records in DNS prior to attempting a WDS deployment.

   B. Incorrect: It is not necessary to create a separate IPv4 scope for PXE clients. The question suggests, by mentioning the IT department's computers being on the same subnet as the staging room, that DHCP works without a problem for this location.

   C. Correct: The information provided in the question and the possible answers suggest that the router that separates the server room from the staging room does not support multicast transmissions. There are two solutions to this problem: replacing the router with one that supports multicast or moving the WDS server so that multicast transmissions are not blocked because they are occurring on the same subnet.

   D. Incorrect: WINS does not need to be present on a network to use WDS.

3. Correct Answer: B

   A. Incorrect: You cannot use an Unattended XML file located on a Trivial File Transfer Protocol (TFTP) server for WDS deployments.

   B. Correct: You can configure a default unattended XML file on the WDS server by editing the server's properties.

   C. Incorrect: You can use an unattended XML file located on a file share only by booting into Windows PE because you must specify the location of a network file manually.

   D. Incorrect: You cannot use an unattended XML file located on a Web server for WDS deployments.

4. Correct Answer: D

   A. Incorrect: Virtual servers are not counted toward the minimum number of servers required to deploy KMS; only physical servers are counted.

   B. Incorrect: Virtual servers are not counted toward the minimum number of servers required to deploy KMS; only physical servers are counted.

C. **Incorrect:** Virtual servers are not counted toward the minimum number of servers required to deploy KMS; only physical servers are counted.

D. **Correct:** You must have a minimum of five physical servers before you can use KMS for volume activation.

5. Correct Answer: D

A. **Incorrect:** *Ntdsutil* is a utility you can use to manage the Active Directory database. You cannot use it to configure and activate computers with a MAK.

B. **Incorrect:** *Dsquery* is a utility you can use to query AD DS. You cannot use it to configure and activate computers with a MAK.

C. **Incorrect:** You cannot use the Windows Automated Installation Kit to configure and activate recently deployed computers remotely with a MAK.

D. **Correct:** You can use the Volume Activation Management Tool to configure and activate computers remotely with a MAK.

Chapter 11: Case Scenario Answers

Case Scenario: Activation at Fabrikam, Inc.

1. Use the VAMT and a MAK to activate the servers at each branch office. Install the VAMT on one of the servers and export activation data to a computer that is connected to the Internet and has a VAMT installed. Then, transfer the activation data back to the server on which you installed the VAMT on the isolated network. You cannot use KMS because only four servers are present on each isolated branch office network.

2. Use MAKs for the branch office computers located on networks connected to the Internet because there are only three physical Windows Server 2008 servers and 15 client computers running Windows Vista, which is not enough to use KMS.

3. Use KMS at the head office because it reduces the paperwork involved and more than enough computers are physically deployed.

Chapter 12: Lesson Review Answers

Lesson 1

1. Correct Answer: A and C

A. **Correct:** Active Session Limit enables you to restrict the length of time that any session may stay connected to a Terminal Services server.

B. **Incorrect:** Idle Session Limit enables you to terminate sessions that are still connected but in which there is no activity by the connected user.

C. **Correct:** The End A Disconnected Session setting enables you to terminate disconnected sessions after a specific amount of time. Until this time limit is reached, it is still possible for a client to reconnect.

D. **Incorrect:** The Do Not Allow Remote Control setting does not relate to the termination of disconnected sessions.

2. Correct Answers: B and C

A. **Incorrect:** The View The Session option does not allow for interaction with the user's session.

B. **Correct:** You must enable the Interact With Session option for staff to provide assistance.

C. **Correct:** You must grant the Full Control permission for a group of users to be able to use remote control.

D. **Incorrect:** The User Access permission does not enable users to provide remote control assistance.

E. **Incorrect:** The Guest Access permission does not enable users to provide remote control assistance.

3. Correct Answer: E

A. **Incorrect:** Terminal Services sessions cannot be licensed on the basis of a single tree in an Active Directory forest. You can configure license server scopes only for Workgroups, Domains, and Forests.

B. **Incorrect:** Because the client computers are not members of an Active Directory environment, you should not choose the Domain licensing scope.

C. **Incorrect:** Terminal Services sessions cannot be licensed solely on the basis of Domain Name System (DNS) Zone. They can be licensed only on the basis of Workgroup, Domain, and Forest.

D. **Incorrect:** Because the client computers are not members of an Active Directory environment, you should not choose the Forest licensing scope.

E. **Correct:** You should use the This Workgroup licensing scope when computers are not members of an Active Directory domain.

4. Correct Answers: C and D

A. **Incorrect:** You can use the Automatic Connection activation method only when the Terminal Services license server has a direct connection to the Internet.

B. **Incorrect:** Terminal Services license servers cannot be activated through e-mail.

C. **Correct:** You can use a Web browser on another computer to activate a Terminal Services license server located on an isolated network.

D. **Correct:** You can use a telephone to activate a Terminal Services license server located on an isolated network.

E. **Incorrect:** Terminal Services license servers cannot be activated by using SMS messages.

5. Correct Answer: D

    A. Incorrect: *Qappsrv.exe* displays a list of Terminal Services servers on the network.

    B. Incorrect: *Qwinsta.exe* displays information about sessions on a Terminal Services server.

    C. Incorrect: *Rdpsign.exe* signs .rdp files digitally.

    D. Correct: *Mstsc.exe* can convert previous connection files created with Client Connection Manager to the .rdp format.

6. Correct Answers: A and C

    A. Correct: Windows 2000 Professional with Service Pack 4 does not support RDP Security Layer encryption by default.

    B. Incorrect: Windows 2000 Professional with Service Pack 4 and Windows XP with Service Pack 3 support SSL (TLS 1.0) Security Layer.

    C. Correct: Windows 2000 Professional with Service Pack 4 does not support Network Level Authentication by default.

    D. Incorrect: Windows 2000 Professional with Service Pack 4 and Windows XP with Service Pack 3 support the Client Compatible encryption level.

    E. Incorrect: Windows 2000 Professional with Service Pack 4 and Windows XP with Service Pack 3 support the Low encryption level.

7. Correct Answer: B

    A. Incorrect: The Equal_Per_User WSRM policy allocates resources equally on a per-user, rather than on a per-session, basis.

    B. Correct: The Equal_Per_Session WSRM policy ensures that all sessions are allocated resources equally, even if one user account has multiple connected sessions.

    C. Incorrect: The Equal_Per_Process WSRM policy allocates resources on a per-process, rather than on a per-session basis.

    D. Incorrect: The Equal_Per_IISAppPool policy allocates resources on a per–Internet Information Services application pool basis, not on a per–Terminal Services Session basis.

8. Correct Answer: D

    A. Incorrect: You cannot use Reliability Monitor to log data about application resource usage during Terminal Services sessions.

    B. Incorrect: Although Task Manager can display point-in-time data about application resource usage, you cannot use Task Manager to log this data.

    C. Incorrect: File System Resource Manager manages files and quotas. FSRM cannot log application resource usage data during Terminal Services sessions.

    D. Correct: When configured in profiling mode, WSRM can log data about the resource usage of applications active in Terminal Services sessions.

Lesson 2

1. Correct Answer: C

   A. **Incorrect:** You do not add computer accounts to the Remote Desktop Users group when using TS Session Broker.

   B. **Incorrect:** You do not add computer accounts to the Remote Desktop Users group when using TS Session Broker.

   C. **Correct:** You need to add the computer accounts of Terminal Services servers that will participate in the farm to the Session Directory Computers local group on the computer hosting the TS Session Broker role.

   D. **Incorrect:** The Session Directory Computers local group is located on the computer hosting the TS Session Broker role, not on the Terminal Services servers.

2. Correct Answer: A

   A. **Correct:** You should disable the Use IP Address Redirection option only when your network load balancing solution supports TS Session Broker routing tokens.

   B. **Incorrect:** You should disable the Use IP Address Redirection option only when your network load balancing solution supports TS Session Broker routing tokens.

   C. **Incorrect:** Support of TS Session Broker routing tokens is independent of whether IPv6 or IPv4 is used.

   D. **Incorrect:** Support of TS Session Broker routing tokens is independent of whether IPv6 or IPv4 is used.

3. Correct Answers: A, C, and D

   A. **Correct:** You can distribute RemoteApp applications to users by placing RDP shortcuts on accessible shared folders.

   B. **Incorrect:** RDP shortcuts cannot be published using Active Directory.

   C. **Correct:** You can distribute RemoteApp applications by creating a Windows Installer File, using RemoteApp Manager, and publishing it through AD DS.

   D. **Correct:** Users can access RemoteApp applications by navigating to the Terminal Services Web Access Web page.

   E. **Incorrect:** Users without local administrator privileges cannot install software on their computers.

4. Correct Answer: B

   A. **Incorrect:** Reducing the connection limit is more likely to block users than to allow them access.

   B. **Correct:** Users must be members of the Remote Desktop Users group to access RemoteApp applications successfully.

   C. **Incorrect:** Disabling device redirection will not grant users access to RemoteApp applications.

D. Incorrect: The question states that you have successfully used the application, so reinstalling the application will not resolve the problem.

5. Correct Answer: C

   A. Incorrect: Client computers from outside your organization are unlikely to trust a certificate issued by an internal CA.

   B. Incorrect: Client computers from outside your organization are unlikely to trust a certificate issued by an internal CA.

   C. Correct: Client computers from outside your organization are more likely to trust a certificate issued by a third-party CA.

   D. Incorrect: Client computers from outside your organization are unlikely to trust a certificate issued by an internal CA.

6. Correct Answer: B

   A. Incorrect: TS Gateway does not accept connection on port 80.

   B. Correct: TS Gateway uses port 443, the HTTPS port, for external connections.

   C. Incorrect: Although port 3389 is the direct RDP port, clients connecting to TS Gateway servers use port 443.

   D. Incorrect: Port 25 is used for SMTP.

Chapter 12: Case Scenario Answers

Case Scenario 1: Wingtip Toys Terminal Services Deployment

1. Configure the TS licensing server to use the forest scope because it will service Terminal Services servers and clients in two domains.

2. Configure each Terminal Services server to allow only one connection per user. This way, a single user cannot consume multiple sessions.

3. Install Windows System Resource Manager on each Terminal Services server. Apply either an Equal_Per_User or Equal_Per_Session policy. Either policy will work because users are limited to a single session on each Terminal Services server.

Case Scenario 2: Case Scenario 2: Supporting Terminal Services at Fabrikam, Inc.

1. Network load balancing distributes sessions more equitably than DNS round robin.

2. Upgrade the servers to Windows Server 2008. Windows Server 2003 servers cannot participate in a TS Session Broker farm.

3. Configure the RemoteApp server as the data source in the TS Web Access server's settings. Add the TS Web Access server's computer account to the TS Web Access Computers security group on the RemoteApp server.

Chapter 13: Lesson Review Answers

Lesson 1

1. Correct Answer: A

   A. Correct: To configure the application pool to ensure that users can access StockControl after the application pool is recycled, set the Disable Overlapped Recycling option to True. If your application cannot run in a multi-instance environment, you must configure only one worker process for an application pool and disable the overlapped recycling feature if application pool recycling is being used.

   B. Incorrect: You can select either Fixed Intervals or Memory Based Maximums, depending upon the specific problems you are trying to troubleshoot. Recycling application pools too quickly can reduce performance, but if a Web application has serious problems, address them by recycling worker processes before users see slowdowns or errors on the Web site. However, neither of these settings will ensure that users can access Stock-Control after the application pool is recycled.

   C. Incorrect: You can select either Fixed Intervals or Memory Based Maximums, depending upon the specific problems you are trying to troubleshoot. Recycling application pools too quickly can reduce performance, but if a Web application has serious problems, address them by recycling worker processes before users see slowdowns or errors on the Web site. However, neither of these settings will ensure that users can access Stock-Control after the application pool is recycled.

   D. Incorrect: Changing the recycling interval will not affect whether users can access StockControl after the application pool is recycled. You must set the Disable Overlapped Recycling option to True.

2. Correct Answers: A, C, and D

   A. Correct: The ISAPI Extensions role service enables ISAPI Extensions to handle client requests. In the IIS Server Core, ASP.NET relies on handlers that are based on ISAPI Extensions.

   B. Incorrect: The ASP role service is the predecessor to the ASP.NET platform and provides a script-based method of developing Web-based applications. ASP enables a Web server to host classic Active Server Pages (ASP) applications. You are not prompted to install ASP when you install ASP.NET.

C. **Correct:** The ISAPI Filters role service enables developers to add custom ISAPI filters that modify Web server behavior. ISAPI filters are custom code that developers can create to process specific Web server requests. If you install the ASP.NET role service, IIS7 configures an ASP.NET ISAPI filter.

D. **Correct:** The .NET Extensibility role service enables a Web server to host .NET Framework applications and provides for IIS integration with ASP.NET and the .NET Framework.

E. **Incorrect:** The CGI role service enables a Web server to host CGI executables. CGI is a standard that describes how executables specified in Web addresses, also known as gateway scripts, pass information to Web servers. You are not prompted to install CGI when you install ASP.NET.

3. Correct Answers: B and E

A. **Incorrect:** You create a CNAME record when you do not want to include the name of the server in the URL, for example, *http://www.contoso.internal* rather than *http://glasgow. contoso.internal*. This does not solve the problem in this scenario.

B. **Correct:** When you have configured the Default Document setting to display the contents of the default Web page rather than the name of the file that holds this content, you then need to disable directory browsing with the *%systemroot%\system32\inetsrv\ appcmd set config/section:directoryBrowse/enabled: False* command.

C. **Incorrect:** You would put the Web site in its own application pool if you wanted to configure unique settings without affecting other Web sites. This is not the case in this scenario.

D. **Incorrect:** This gives Web site users excessive permissions and does not solve the problem of how the Web site displays its content.

E. **Correct:** You need to match the Web page file to the Web site by configuring the Default Document settings. This enables you to display the contents of the Web page rather than the file name. After that, you must disable directory browsing on the Web site.

Lesson 2

1. Correct Answer: C

A. **Incorrect:** The *appcmd set vdir* command configures an existing virtual directory. You must use the *appcmd add vdir* command to create a new virtual directory.

B. **Incorrect:** The *appcmd set vdir* command configures an existing virtual directory. You must use the *appcmd add vdir* command to create a new virtual directory. Also, the values for the *path* and *physicalPath* parameters have been transposed in this answer.

C. **Correct:** This creates the required virtual directory with the required physical path.

D. **Incorrect:** The values for the *path* and *physicalPath* parameters have been transposed in this answer.

2. **Correct Answers: A, D, E, and F**

   A. **Correct:** List is one of the basic set of *appcmd.exe* commands. It displays the objects on the machine.

   B. **Incorrect:** Stop is not one of the basic set of *appcmd.exe* commands, although it is supported by some objects, for example, Site.

   C. **Incorrect:** Start is not one of the basic set of *appcmd.exe* commands, although it is supported by some objects, for example, Site.

   D. **Correct:** Add is one of the basic set of *appcmd.exe* commands. It creates a new object and sets the specified object properties during creation.

   E. **Correct:** Delete is one of the basic set of *appcmd.exe* commands. It deletes the specified object.

   F. **Correct:** Set is one of the basic set of *appcmd.exe* commands. It configures the specified parameters on an object.

3. **Correct Answer: A**

   A. **Correct:** The *%Systemroot%\system32\inetsrv\appcmd set vdir/ vdir.name:"HipHopVideos/ Videos/Sales" /physical path:\\Dundee\MusicVideos\Sales* command moves the physical path of the virtual directory in the HipHopVideos Web site to the path on the new server.

   B. **Incorrect:** The *%Systemroot%\system32\inetsrv\appcmd set vdir/ vdir. name:"HipHopVideos/Videos/Sales" /physical path:\\Glasgow\Videos\Sales* command specifies the original physical path to the virtual directory. You must specify the new path on the new server.

   C. **Incorrect:** The virtual directory is *HipHopVideos/Videos/Sales*, not *Glasgow/Videos/Sales*.

   D. **Incorrect:** The *%Systemroot%\system32\inetsrv\appcmd set vdir/ vdir.name:" \\Dundee\ MusicVideos\Sales " /physical path:/HipHopVideos/Videos/Sales* command transposes the virtual directory name and the physical location.

Lesson 3

1. **Correct Answer: B**

   A. **Incorrect:** The *%Systemroot%\system32\inetsrv\appcmd add backup* command creates a backup with an autogenerated name that includes date and time information. The backup will not be called PreTrialConfigDecNinth.

   B. **Correct:** The *%Systemroot%\system32\inetsrv\appcmd add backup PreTrialConfigDec-Ninth* command generates a backup called PreTrialConfigDecNinth.

   C. **Incorrect:** The *%Systemroot%\system32\inetsrv\appcmd list backups* command lists all the IIS7 configuration settings backups on the Web server.

   D. **Incorrect:** The *%Systemroot%\system32\inetsrv\appcmd restore backup PreTrialConfig-DecNinth* command restores IIS7 configuration settings from PreTrialConfigDecNinth.

2. **Correct Answer: D**

   A. **Incorrect:** The *appcmd get wps* command gets configuration details for a specified object. It does not list all objects. Also, the object specified in this answer is worker process, not request.

   B. **Incorrect:** The *appcmd get requests* command gets configuration details for a specified object. It does not list all objects.

   C. **Incorrect:** The *%Systemroot%\system32\inetsrv\appcmd list wps* command lists the worker processes on the Web server, not the currently executing requests.

   D. **Correct:** The *%Systemroot%\system32\inetsrv\appcmd list requests* command displays a list of currently executing requests.

3. **Correct Answer: C**

   A. **Incorrect:** Making all the Web site administrators local administrators on the Web server gives them excessive rights, including the ability to change any server configuration, not merely Web site settings.

   B. **Incorrect:** Anonymous Authentication applies to anyone who accesses a Web site to view content and enables users to do so without supplying credentials. It is not relevant to access for administrative purposes as described in this scenario.

   C. **Correct:** IIS Manager user accounts provide access through IIS Manager for remotely administering a Web site without providing local access to the Web server itself. Creating an individual IIS Manager user account for each of the client Web sites ensures that Web site administrators can configure settings only on their own Web sites.

   D. **Incorrect:** Creating a single IIS Manager user account for all client Web sites would enable a Web site administrator to configure settings on any of the Web sites, which is not what is required.

Lesson 4

1. **Correct Answer: C**

   A. **Incorrect:** The Web site SSL settings are currently ignoring client certificates. In this scenario, it makes no difference whether 128-bit SSL is required.

   B. **Incorrect:** Currently, client certificates are ignored, which is the default. You ensure that managers access the secure Web site only through user certificates by requiring such certificates.

   C. **Correct:** By default, client certificates are ignored. If you want users to verify their identity by using a certificate before they access the content of a Web site, you must configure SSL to require client certificates.

   D. **Incorrect:** This setting allows access to be authenticated by user certificates or any other available method. If you want users to verify their identity only by using a certificate before they access the content of a Web site, you must configure SSL to require client certificates.

2. **Correct Answer: D**

    A. **Incorrect:** IIS Manager can create both HTTP and HTTPS bindings. You cannot create bindings using *appcmd.exe*.

    B. **Incorrect:** The problem is with the site's security certificate and will occur with whatever computer is used to access the site.

    C. **Incorrect:** The problem is with the site's security certificate. Requiring SSL will not address this problem.

    D. **Correct:** Don likely has used a self-signed certificate. He needs to replace this with a trusted certificate issued by a third-party CA.

3. **Correct Answer: A**

    A. **Correct:** You import a certificate when you want to restore a lost or damaged server certificate from backup.

    B. **Incorrect:** You export a certificate from a source server when you want to apply the same certificate to a target server or when you want to back up a certificate and its associated private key. It is pointless to export a corrupt certificate.

    C. **Incorrect:** You cannot specify a certificate backup when configuring a binding. You need to import the certificate first.

    D. **Incorrect:** You do not need to renew the certificate when you can import it from backup.

Lesson 5

1. **Correct Answer: B**

    A. **Incorrect:** Placing the application in its own application pool does not alter which users have access to the application.

    B. **Correct:** Authorization rule settings enable you to restrict access to specific content without altering NTFS permissions.

    C. **Incorrect:** Placing the application in a virtual directory does not automatically alter which users have access to the application. Changing the authentication settings to Specified User does not limit access to members of a specific security group.

    D. **Incorrect:** Converting the NewDesigns folder to a Web application does not automatically alter which users have access to the content without taking further action.

2. **Correct Answers: A, C, and D**

    A. **Correct:** In many-to-one mapping, the Web server performs authentication by using information found in the client certificate. For example, the Web server could validate the organization information in the certificate to ensure that the user is coming from a trusted company.

    B. **Incorrect:** One-to-many mapping implies that one client has many certificates. This is not a practical validation method.

    C. **Correct:** In one-to one mapping, the Web server holds a copy of the client certificate used by every client computer that accesses restricted content. The server compares its copy of the certificate with the certificate that the client presents to validate requests.

    D. **Correct:** Active Directory mapping can simplify the creation and management of client certificates. To use this method, an organization must set up its own certificate-based infrastructure.

    E. **Incorrect:** Digest is an authentication method. It cannot be used to validate clients through client certificates.

3. Correct Answer: D

    A. **Incorrect:** The *users='anon'* syntax is incorrect. It should be users='?'.

    B. **Incorrect:** The *anon_users='True'* syntax is incorrect. It should be users='?'.

    C. **Incorrect:** The *users='*'* syntax specifies all users. It should be users='?'.

    D. **Correct:** The *%Systemroot%\system32\inetsrv\appcmd set config /section:system.web-Server/security/authorization /+"[accessType='Allow',users='?']"* command creates an Allow rule for anonymous users.

Chapter 13: Case Scenario Answers

Case Scenario 1: Managing a Web Server

1. You must install ASP.NET, CGI, and Server-Side Includes role services. ASP.NET in turn requires the ISAPI Extensions, ISAPI Filters, and.NET Extensibility role services.

2. Create a separate application pool for each of the applications that could present problems. An application can run (or crash) in its own application pool without affecting other applications.

3. Create virtual directories and specify a physical path to the content files for each virtual directory.

Case Scenario 2: Managing Web Server Security

1. Advise the junior administrator to create an HTTPS binding for the Web site and configure the binding to use the certificate. It is also a good idea to back up the certificate by exporting it so it can be imported if it becomes corrupt.

2. You must configure SSL Settings to Require SSL and Require Client Certificates.

3. In Features View, double-click .NET Trust Levels and, on the .NET Trust Levels page, select High from the Trust level drop-down list. Click Apply in the Actions pane.

Chapter 14: Lesson Review Answers

Lesson 1

1. Correct Answer: C

   A. **Incorrect:** Using anonymous authentication would prevent usernames and passwords from being sent in clear text, but downloaded and uploaded files would be transmitted without encryption.

   B. **Incorrect:** FTP6, which ships with Windows Server 2008, does not support SSL encryption, and you are explicitly prohibited from using FTP7. Otherwise, if the question did not specify the FTP version or if you were not prevented from using FTP7, this would be a valid answer.

   C. **Correct:** You need to configure IPsec encryption between Boston and the client computers that need to access the confidential files.

   D. **Incorrect:** Windows Server 2008 Web Server can host FTP sites. Using Enterprise does not automatically make the sites more secure.

2. Correct Answer: B

   A. **Incorrect:** The *iisftpdr.vbs* script was used to create and manage virtual directories in IIS6, not to configure access control. You cannot use it in IIS7.

   B. **Correct:** IIS permissions allow authenticated users to upgrade files, but unless these users also have the required NTFS permissions, they will see warning messages when they attempt to do so.

   C. **Incorrect:** Authenticated users can already access the FTP site. You do not need to grant them access specifically, based on the IPv4 addresses of their client computers.

   D. **Incorrect:** The authentication method used does not affect the IIS and NTFS permissions.

3. Correct Answers: A and E

   A. **Correct:** You can specifically allow the designated network access, based on an IPv4 address range. This is much easier than specifically denying all other IPv4 addresses.

   B. **Incorrect:** You cannot configure FTP site access control based on IPv6 address ranges.

   C. **Incorrect:** It is unlikely that researchers will use a protocol analyzer to read their colleagues' reports, but if you do want to implement encryption, you must use IPsec. FTP6 does not support SSL.

   D. **Incorrect:** You must configure user isolation so researchers cannot access each other's directories.

   E. **Correct:** Because directory location is assigned through AD DS, you should configure user isolation, using AD DS.

4. Correct Answer: D

    A. Incorrect: This lists all storage reports on Glasgow, whether they are running or not.

    B. Incorrect: This lists all running storage reports on Glasgow.

    C. Incorrect: This is incorrect syntax. You need to use the */remote* switch to specify a remote computer.

    D. Correct: This command lists all the storage reports currently running on Boston.

Lesson 2

1. Correct Answers: D and E

    A. Incorrect: The Web server already hosts SMTP virtual servers. You do not need to install the SMTP Server feature.

    B. Incorrect: This command backs up IIS7 configuration. It will not start an SMTP virtual server.

    C. Incorrect: This command configures e-mail settings. It will not start an SMTP virtual server.

    D. Correct: Different SMTP virtual servers on a Web server must have different IP addresses or use different ports (or both).

    E. Correct: Different SMTP virtual servers on a Web server must have different IP addresses or use different ports (or both).

2. Correct Answer: C

    A. Incorrect: You copy the file into the Mailroot\Pickup folder. You can then check the Mailroot\Drop folder for a new file with an .eml extension.

    B. Incorrect: You copy the file into the Mailroot\Pickup folder. If your message is not destined for a local domain, it should be sent to the Mailroot\Queue folder.

    C. Correct: The file should be copied to the Mailroot\Pickup folder. Files copied to this folder are processed and delivered as regular mail.

    D. Incorrect: The Badmail folder stores mail that cannot be delivered or returned to sender.

3. Correct Answer: D

    A. Incorrect: You can use a command with this syntax to configure SMTP e-mail to deliver e-mail messages immediately. It will not forward all e-mails to the ISP mail server.

    B. Incorrect: A masquerade domain allows substitution of internal for external domain names when forwarding mail to external SMTP servers. Use a masquerade domain when you want to ensure that outgoing messages have a consistent domain name. You cannot use a masquerade domain to configure the new SMTP server to forward all e-mails to your ISP's mail server.

C.   **Incorrect:** The maximum hop count limits how many SMTP servers a message can be routed through before a nondelivery report is returned to the sender. You cannot use this setting to configure the new SMTP server to forward all e-mails to your ISP's mail server.

D.   **Correct:** To configure the new SMTP server to forward all e-mails to your ISP's e-mail server, set the smart host setting to use the ISP mail server. A smart host server helps deliver all your e-mail. It processes bounce-backs and retries.

4.   Correct Answer: A

A.   **Correct:** TLS enables encryption of sent messages by using a certificate-based approach.

B.   **Incorrect:** IPsec provides end-to-end encryption between two hosts. It encrypts all traffic and is not specific to SMTP. You cannot configure it on the Access tab.

C.   **Incorrect:** Basic authentication requires a username and password to be sent to the SMTP virtual server. It does not provide encryption.

D.   **Incorrect:** Integrated Windows authentication relies on standard Windows accounts to verify credentials to access the system. It does not provide encryption.

Chapter 14: Case Scenario Answers

Case Scenario 1: Configuring User Isolation and IP Address Restriction Settings

1.   You must configure User Isolation because students should not access other students' directories. Because student directory location is assigned through Active Directory, you must select Configure User Isolation Using Active Directory.

2.   You must configure IPv4 address restrictions so that all IPv4 addresses are blocked apart from the address ranges of the specified academic network. The allowed address ranges can be defined by start address and subnet mask.

Case Scenario 2: Configuring Message Size and SMTP Traffic Limitations

1.   On the Messages tab of the SMTP virtual server Properties dialog box, you can specify the maximum size of a message (including attachments).

2.   On the Messages tab of the SMTP virtual server Properties dialog box, you can specify the maximum amount of data that can be sent through one connection to the server. On the same tab, you can also limit the number of messages sent per connection.

3.   On the Messages tab of the SMTP virtual server Properties dialog box, you can limit the number of recipients to whom a message can be sent.

Chapter 15: Lesson Review Answers

Lesson 1

1. Correct Answer: C

   A. Incorrect: Windows Web Server 2008 does not support the Hyper-V role in either the x86 or x64 versions.

   B. Incorrect: Windows Web Server 2008 does not support the Hyper-V role in either the x86 or x64 versions.

   C. Correct: Only x64 versions of Windows Server 2008, not including Windows Web Server, support Hyper-V. The Hyper-V role can be installed on a computer configured with the Server Core installation option.

   D. Incorrect: X86 versions of Windows Server 2008 do not support the Hyper-V role.

2. Correct Answer: D

   A. Incorrect: You cannot install the Hyper-V role on Windows Web Server 2008.

   B. Incorrect: Windows Server 2008 Standard includes a license to run a single Windows virtual machine. Licenses for additional virtual machines must be purchased.

   C. Incorrect: Windows Server 2008 Enterprise includes licenses to run four Windows virtual machines.

   D. Correct: Windows Server 2008 Datacenter includes licenses to run an unlimited number of Windows virtual machines.

3. Correct Answer: A

   A. Correct: External virtual networks allow communication between hosts on an external network such as between the Internet and virtual guests hosted under Hyper-V.

   B. Incorrect: Internal virtual networks allow communication only between virtual machines hosted on the same Hyper-V server and the virtual machine management software.

   C. Incorrect: Private virtual networks allow communication between virtual machines hosted on the same Hyper-V server but do not allow communication between the Hyper-V server and the hosted virtual machines.

   D. Incorrect: Having no virtual network would block guest virtual machines from communicating with other hosts, both internal to the Hyper-V server and external, such as those on the Internet.

4. Correct Answer: A

   A. Correct: You use the Failover Cluster Management console to make a virtual machine installed on a two-node Hyper-V failover cluster highly available.

   B. Incorrect: You cannot make a virtual machine highly available using the Hyper-V Manager console.

C. Incorrect: You cannot make a virtual machine highly available by editing Virtual Machine settings.

D. Incorrect: The Network Load Balancing console is related to network load balancing, not to failover clustering.

Lesson 2

1. Correct Answer: A

    A. Correct: The Virtual Server Migration Toolkit, designed to virtualize existing servers for Microsoft Virtual Server 2005, is compatible with Hyper-V and can be used to virtualize physical deployments of Windows Server 2003, Windows 2000, and Windows NT 4. You can also use System Center Virtual Machine Manager 2008 to perform this task.

    B. Incorrect: Application virtualization enables you to virtualize applications, not physical server deployments.

    C. Incorrect: Virtual Server 2005 R2 enables you to host virtual machines from x86 editions of Windows Server 2008 but does not include tools to virtualize physical deployments of Windows Server 2003. You must use either Virtual Server Migration Toolkit or System Center Virtual Machine Manager 2008 to perform this task.

    D. Incorrect: Host Integration Server 2006 provides an application gateway between Windows networks and mainframe computers. It cannot be used to virtualize existing servers.

2. Correct Answer: C

    A. Incorrect: Hyper-V supports a maximum of 50, rather than 10, snapshots for an individual guest virtual machine.

    B. Incorrect: Hyper-V supports a maximum of 50, rather than 25, snapshots for an individual guest virtual machine.

    C. Correct: Hyper-V supports a maximum of 50 snapshots for an individual guest virtual machine.

    D. Incorrect: Hyper-V supports a maximum of 50, rather than 100, snapshots for an individual guest virtual machine.

3. Correct Answer: C

    A. Incorrect: Dynamically expanding disks use .vhd files that start small and grow as new data is written.

    B. Incorrect: Fixed disks use .vhd files that remain the same size.

    C. Correct: Differencing disks use .vhd files that record only the changes made to an original. It is possible to commit these changes manually after review.

4. Correct Answer: D

    A. Incorrect: Disk mirroring, also known as RAID 1, provides redundancy if a disk failure occurs; it does not enable you to roll back to a previous point in time.

B. Incorrect: System restore points are supported on client operating systems only. You cannot create a system restore point on a Windows Server 2008 virtual machine.

C. Incorrect: You should not pause the virtual machine by using Hyper-V Manager because this stops the virtual machine from functioning until it is resumed.

D. Correct: You should take a snapshot, using Hyper-V Manager. This enables you to roll back to the existing configuration if something goes wrong with the application installation.

Chapter 15: Case Scenario Answers

Case Scenario: Hyper-V at Contoso

1. You can use the Virtual Server Migration Toolkit or System Center Virtual Machine Manager 2008 to perform the physical-to-virtual migration at each branch office.

2. Deploy Windows Server 2008 Enterprise because it includes four licenses for Windows Server virtual guests. You should not purchase Windows Server 2008 Datacenter because a maximum of three virtual machines is required at each branch office.

3. Configure a Hyper-V failover cluster at the head office location. This enables virtual machines to fail over to another node if the hosting node fails.

Chapter 16: Lesson Review Questions

Lesson 1

1. Correct Answer: A

A. Correct: The Node Majority quorum model has no file-share witness or disk witness. Votes are assigned only to nodes.

B. Incorrect: The Node and Disk Majority quorum model uses a disk witness.

C. Incorrect: The Node and File Share Majority quorum model uses a file share witness.

D. Incorrect: The No majority: Disk Only quorum model uses a disk witness.

2. Correct Answer: C

A. Incorrect: A Node Majority quorum model cluster requires half the nodes (rounded down) plus one to remain operable. Four nodes must remain operable; hence, a maximum of three nodes may fail while the cluster remains operable.

B. Incorrect: A Node Majority quorum model cluster requires half the nodes (rounded down) plus one to remain operable. Four nodes must remain operable, hence, a maximum of three nodes may fail while the cluster remains operable.

C. **Correct:** A Node Majority quorum model cluster requires half the nodes (rounded down) plus one to remain operable. Four nodes must remain operable; hence, a maximum of three nodes may fail while the cluster remains operable.

D. **Incorrect:** A Node Majority quorum model cluster requires half the nodes (rounded down) plus one to remain operable. Four nodes must remain operable; hence, a maximum of three nodes may fail while the cluster remains operable.

3. Correct Answer: D

A. **Incorrect:** A serially attached SCSI (SAS) device can be used as a shared storage device for a Windows Server 2008 failover cluster.

B. **Incorrect:** An i-SCSI device can be used as a shared storage device for a Windows Server 2008 failover cluster.

C. **Incorrect:** A Fibre Channel device can be used as a shared storage device for a Windows Server 2008 failover cluster.

D. **Correct:** USB 2.0 external hard disk drives cannot be used as shared storage devices for Windows Server 2008 failover clusters.

4. Correct Answer: B

A. **Incorrect:** DNS round robin is not a failure aware solution. Clients will be redirected to a host in a DNS round robin configuration even if that host fails.

B. **Correct:** Network load balancing enables you to add nodes as necessary and is failure aware.

C. **Incorrect:** The Node and Disk Majority quorum mode uses a shared storage device.

D. **Incorrect:** The No Majority: Disk Only quorum model uses a shared storage device.

5. Correct Answer: C

A. **Incorrect:** DNS round robin does not reconfigure if a failure occurs.

B. **Incorrect:** DNS round robin does not reconfigure if a failure occurs.

C. **Correct:** NLB reconfigures the cluster if a failure occurs. You can use one node to manage others when each node has a single network adapter if multicast is in use.

D. **Incorrect:** Although NLB reconfigures the cluster if a failure occurs, you cannot use one node to manage others when each node has a single network adapter if unicast is in use.

Lesson 2

1. Correct Answer: C

A. **Incorrect:** RAID-5 cannot be implemented with one disk; it requires a minimum of three.

B. **Incorrect:** RAID-5 cannot be implemented with two disks; it requires a minimum of three.

C. **Correct:** RAID-5 requires a minimum of three disks.

D. **Incorrect:** Although you can implement RAID-5 with four disks, it requires a minimum of only three.

2. Correct Answer: D

A. **Incorrect:** Storage Manager for SANs cannot be used to manage iSCSI fabrics, although it can be used to manage LUNs for Fibre Channel and iSCSI disk storage subsystems that support VDS.

B. **Incorrect:** You cannot use Device Manager to manage iSCSI fabrics.

C. **Incorrect:** You cannot use Disk Management to manage iSCSI fabrics.

D. **Correct:** Storage Explorer can be used to manage iSCSI fabrics.

3. Correct Answer: B

A. **Incorrect:** The equivalent of one disk in a RAID-5 set is taken up with parity date; hence, five 5 TB disks are required to create a 20 TB RAID-5 volume.

B. **Correct:** The equivalent of one disk in a RAID-5 set is taken up with parity date; hence, five 5 TB disks are required to create a 20 TB RAID-5 volume.

C. **Incorrect:** The equivalent of one disk in a RAID-5 set is taken up with parity date; hence, five 5 TB disks are required to create a 20 TB RAID-5 volume.

D. **Incorrect:** The equivalent of one disk in a RAID-5 set is taken up with parity date; hence, five 5 TB disks are required to create a 20 TB RAID-5 volume.

4. Correct Answer: D

A. **Incorrect:** Creating a new LUN will not unassign an existing LUN.

B. **Incorrect:** Extending a LUN enables you to store more data on it, which does not address the question.

C. **Incorrect:** Deleting a LUN makes the LUN inaccessible and removes all data stored on the LUN.

D. **Correct:** Unassigning a LUN makes it inaccessible from a server but does not remove data stored on the LUN.

5. Correct Answer: A

A. **Correct:** Storage Manager for SANs enables you to manage LUNs.

B. **Incorrect:** Storage Explorer enables you to manage Fibre Channel and iSCSI fabrics but not to manage LUNs.

C. **Incorrect:** The iSCSI initiator enables you to connect to iSCSI subsystems but not to manage LUNs.

D. **Incorrect:** Disk Management enables you to manage disks but not to manage LUNs.

Chapter 16: Case Scenario Answers

Case Scenario 1: Contoso, Ltd., Cluster Configuration

1. The Node and Disk Majority quorum model is suitable for clusters with an even number of nodes and where a shared storage device is available.

2. The Node Majority quorum model is suitable for clusters with an odd number of nodes where no shared storage device exists.

3. You should deploy a network load balancing cluster in Stockholm, load balancing the existing Web server with a new one. There is no need to use a failover cluster in this instance because NLB ensures that clients are able to connect to the Web server if a node fails, and no mention is made of a shared storage device or shared folder, which is required for a two-node failover cluster to remain available in the event of a node failure.

Case Scenario 2: Selecting LUNs Types

1. The striped with parity LUN type maximizes performance while retaining fault tolerance.

2. Because performance is paramount for the transaction logs, you should use the striped LUN type.

3. The striped with parity LUN type ensures that the witness disk will survive the loss of one disk hosting the LUN.

Index

A

W

X

Z

About the Authors

IAN MCLEAN, MCSE, MCITP, MCT, has over 40 years' experience in industry, commerce, and education. He started his career as an electronics engineer before going into distance learning and then education as a university professor. Currently, he runs his own consultancy company. Ian has written over 20 books and many papers and technical articles. He has been working with Microsoft Server operating systems since 1997.

ORIN THOMAS, MCSE, MVP, is an author and systems administrator who has worked with Microsoft Server operating systems for more than a decade. He is the author of more than a dozen self-paced training kits for Microsoft Press, including *MCSA/MCSE Self-Paced Training Kit (Exam 70-290): Managing and Maintaining a Microsoft Windows Server® 2003 Environment*, second edition. He is also a contributing editor for *Windows® IT Pro* magazine.

System Requirements

We recommend that you use a test workstation, test server, or staging server to complete the exercises in each lab. The following are the minimum system requirements your computer must meet to complete the exercises in this book. For more information, see the introduction.

Hardware Requirements

You can complete almost all practices in this book other than those in Chapter 15, "Hyper-V and Virtualization," using virtual machines rather than real server hardware. The minimum and recommended hardware requirements are as follows:

- Personal computer with minimum 1 GHz (x86) or 1.4 GHz processor (2 GHz or faster recommended)

- 512 MB of RAM or more (2 GB recommended; 4 GB to host all the virtual machines specified for all the exercises in the book)

- 15 GB free hard disk space (40 GB recommended; 60 GB to host all the virtual machines specified for all the practice exercises in the book)

- DVD-ROM drive

- Super-VGA (1,024 x 786) or higher resolution video adapter and monitor

- Keyboard and Microsoft mouse or compatible pointing device

Software Requirements

The following software is required to complete the practices:

- Windows Server 2008 Enterprise. An evaluation version of both the x86 and x64 versions of Windows Server 2008 Enterprise are included with this textbook. You can also download an evaluation version of Windows Server 2008 from the Microsoft download center at *http://www.microsoft.com/Downloads/Search.aspx*.

- If you want to carry out the optional exercises in Chapter 16, "High Availability and Storage," you need two additional Windows Server 2008 member servers. These servers can be virtual machines. The practices in Chapter 15 require you to install an x64 evaluation version of Windows Server 2008 on physical hardware because Hyper-V cannot be deployed within a virtual machine.

- You must configure a workstation running Windows Vista Enterprise, Windows Vista Business, or Windows Vista Ultimate to complete the exercises in Chapter 1, "Configuring Internet Protocol Addressing." You can obtain evaluation software that enables you to implement a

Windows Vista Enterprise 30-day evaluation virtual hard disk (VHD) at *http://www.microsoft.com/downloads/details.aspx?FamilyID=c2c27337-d4d1-4b9b-926d-86493c7da1aa&DisplayLang=en*.

To minimize the time and expense of configuring physical computers, we recommend that you use virtual machines. To run computers as virtual machines within Windows, you can use Hyper-V, Virtual PC 2007, Virtual Server 2005 R2, or third-party virtual machine software.

- To download Virtual PC 2007, visit *http://www.microsoft.com/windows/downloads/virtualpc/default.mspx*.

- To download an evaluation of Virtual Server 2005 R2, visit *http://www.microsoft.com/technet/virtualserver/evaluation/default.mspx*. Some virtual machine software does not support x64 editions of Windows Server 2008.

What do you think of this book?

We want to hear from you!

Your feedback will help us continually improve our books and learning resources for you. To participate in a brief online survey, please visit:

microsoft.com/learning/booksurvey

...and enter this book's ISBN-10 or ISBN-13 number (appears above barcode on back cover). As a thank-you to survey participants in the U.S. and Canada, each month we'll randomly select five respondents to win one of five $100 gift certificates from a leading online merchant. At the conclusion of the survey, you can enter the drawing by providing your e-mail address, which will be used for prize notification only.*

Thank you in advance for your input!

Where to find the ISBN on back cover

Example only. Each book has unique ISBN.

* No purchase necessary. Void where prohibited. Open only to residents of the 50 United States (includes District of Columbia) and Canada (void in Quebec). For official rules and entry dates see: **microsoft.com/learning/booksurvey**

Stay in touch!

To subscribe to the *Microsoft Press*® *Book Connection Newsletter*—for news on upcoming books, events, and special offers—please visit:

microsoft.com/learning/books/newsletter